The Lorette Wilmot Library
Nazareth College of Rochester

For Reference

Not to be taken from this room

FILMS FOR,
BY AND ABOUT
WOMEN
Series II

by

Kaye Sullivan

The Scarecrow Press, Inc.
Metuchen, N.J., & London
1985

LORETTE WILMOT LIBRARY
NAZARETH COLLEGE
WITHDRAWN

The author gratefully acknowledges the Extension Media Center of the University of California, Berkeley, for granting permission to reprint annotations from the Center's film/video catalog and newsletters.

217115

Library of Congress Cataloging in Publication Data

Sullivan, Kaye, 1921–
    Films for, by, and about women, series II.

    Bibliography: p.
    Includes index.
    1. Feminist motion pictures--Dictionaries. I. Title.
PN1995.9.W6S95 1985   791.43'09'09352042   84–23522
ISBN 0-8108-1766-7

Copyright © 1985 by Kaye Sullivan
Manufactured in the United States of America

791.4309093
Sul

CONTENTS

FOREWORD

This compilation of approximately 3,200 film titles is a continuation of
the listing in FILMS FOR, BY AND ABOUT WOMEN (Scarecrow, 1980).
The two books are meant to be companion volumes. Films in this
publication are mostly current productions, exceptional in content
and in technical and artistic quality.

You will find films produced by such prolific and innovative
artists as Ray Eames and Doris Chase. There are many excellent
films on women's roles which will require and inspire studies in masculine roles. Therefore, you find such titles as Speaking of Men by
Christine Herbes and Ann-Carol Grossman and Between Men by Will
Roberts. There are many documentaries produced by women which
are political in nature and controversial as well as timely. All of
these films are for people and not for women only.

Since the publication of FILMS FOR, BY AND ABOUT WOMEN,
I have used my book on the job as film consultant at The Evergreen
State College, enabling me to evaluate and analyze the publication.
Based on this, the Subject Index of this edition now contains women's
names. This will expedite the search for film/films about a person.
For example, under Doris Humphrey you will find nine film titles.
Further, you will find new subject headings for topics which previ-
ously had little or no film coverage; for example, Child Custody,
Children's Rights, and Adoption. Also, under the subject heading
Women's Rights--Law and Legislation, you will find one title on "comparable worth": You've Come a Long Way, Maybe? This I wanted
to mention here since focus of the nation is on this matter and will
be for a long time to come. In 1983 the State of Washington finally
got the ball rolling on this inequity in women's rights which has ex-

existed for a long time. I don't think women will sit back and let it die now that the momentum is going.

Experience has taught me that for film users and those involved in film research, the information given in many synopses of the previous volume was inadequate. Therefore, I have tried in this work to include more information that is important to researchers. For example, in each synopsis, attention has been paid to the following: 1) including names of director, producer, choreographer, consultant, screenwriter, editor, etc.; 2) stating whether a script or handbook accompanies the film; 3) if adapted from a book, stating whether the film follows the text, etc.; 4) if the film is on sexuality, including information on whether "explicit sex" scenes are involved or not.

Even though obtaining funding is still a greater problem for women filmmakers than for men, I notice women are in the forefront of making documentaries that they feel are important. However insignificant their efforts may seem, I feel they will be felt and recognized with time. More and more, women are serving as the conscience of big government. Women all over the nation are organizing to get laws enacted or changed. They are not stopping there; they are seeing that lawmakers find funds so that these laws can be enforced. A recent example is the group Mothers Against Drunk Driving (MADD). The impact of legislation against driving while intoxicated sponsored by this group was felt nationwide in 1983. In the 1980's, it appears that focus also will be on "children," particularly in the area of child custody, missing children, adoption, parental rights, children's rights, as well as grandparent's rights, etc.

Economic conditions during the last few years have curtailed film purchases and rentals at all educational institutions. When money becomes scarce, it appears that most administrators cut films. Could it be that they still view films only as a medium of entertainment? Educational films have improved in all aspects and continue to get better. Of course, there are many old films of high quality that should never be overlooked. Some films are timeless. Films present information more vividly than print and should be used more than they are to implement and reinforce the learning process. Because films supplement and in some instances supplant books, I cannot stress enough that money allotted to film collections and film rental should be balanced to reflect this.

Film-oriented faculty and students are very disappointed when film budgets are cut. I have noticed that oftentimes it is the students who bring faculty attention to film/films that should be included in curriculum. It seems evident that many faculty members have never been trained to think "film." This suggests a strong need for film literacy education through workshops, seminars, etc.

Since there will always be the need to rent films, I would like to mention one thing about the "one-day-use" rental policy of most film distributors. To enhance viewer perception, films should be shown more than once. This cannot be accomplished, in most cases, in the allotted classroom time. I hope to see a "two-day-use" rental policy instituted, particularly for educational institutions.

Even though "comparable worth" legislation will come too late for a great many people, it is my fervent hope that the 1980's will mean the dawn of new hope for others. I dedicate this book to all feminists (male and female) who are working so diligently to accomplish this and to those documenting this important movement. It is almost unthinkable to have the twenty-first century come upon us without having accomplished this.

Kaye Sullivan
Summer 1984

USER'S GUIDE

If you know the title of the film, refer to the main section of this book, where film titles are arranged alphabetically word by word.

Abbreviations used are "m" (running time in minutes); "B" (black/white); "C" (color); "C/B" (Color/black and white); "p" (production date); "r" (release date); "si" (silent); "n.d." (no date); "ed." (edited version); and "c" (copyright). If you find any of the above omitted, it means the information was "not given."

Abbreviations used following the synopsis are "d" (director); "p" (producer); "d/p" (director/producer); "ex.p." (executive producer); "a.p." (associate producer); "a.d." (associate director); "p.s." (production supervisor); "s.w." (screenwriter); and "ed." (editor).

Directly following the film title in the main section, you will find indicated the running time, whether color or black and white (or both), production date, release date (if given), or no date (n.d.) if not given. Occasionally following this you'll find "scope," which indicates the film is in cinemascope. If the film is available in both regular and cinemascope, it will be indicated with "also scope." All films are in 16mm unless it is indicated otherwise following the date. The symbols used are S8, Video, Beta, VHS, SFS, slt (slidetape) or slc (slidecassette). Should "also" precede any of these format symbols, it means the film is available in both 16mm and the format indicated. Following this, if it is foreign language film, I have indicated the language used as well as whether English subtitles are included or whether the film is dubbed.

At the end of each synopsis, you will find symbols (separated by semicolons). If there's only one symbol, it means that the pro-

producer is also the sales and rental distributor. In this case, I have not located another source of distribution. Should there be more than one symbol, the first one is the sales or sales/rental distributor. All symbols following the last semicolon are symbols of rental distributor/distributors and are separated by commas.

To find the source, go to the List of Symbols (Appendix A) and locate the code(s) which you have found. They are listed alphabetically, followed by identification of each one. Next, go to the Directory (Appendix B) where you will find an address for the source. I have tried to list as many rental sources as possible located throughout the U.S. However, do not overlook checking your local libraries first if you are thinking about renting. Addresses are up-to-date at the time of publication. If there was any question regarding the most current address, you may find more than one address for a distributor.

The Directory section lists names and addresses of distributors in alphabetical order. However, in case of a corporate name, such as "William Greaves Productions, Inc.," you will find it listed under the surname as "Greaves, William, Productions, Inc."

If you do not know the title of a film, refer to the Subject Index. In cases where a category you have in mind cannot be located, think of others either broader or more specific.

Finally, for those of you interested in women filmmakers and titles of films made by each, I have included an Index of Women Filmmakers. It lists alphabetically the names of filmmakers followed by titles of their films listed alphabetically under each name. The main section of this book will tell you whether the filmmaker directed, produced, wrote, edited, or performed in these films.

FILMS FOR, BY AND
ABOUT WOMEN

AC-16 (4m C 1971)
A progressive metamorphosis of images, ranging from human forms
to mythical beasts. The turbulent, constantly moving animated paintings were created by the filmmaker in the medium of oil on canvas.
By repainting between single frame exposures, Gratz leads us on
a beautiful journey through constantly changing form, color and space.
p. Joan Gratz; NWMP.

A LA VOTRE see ANIMATED WOMEN

ABORTION: A WOMAN'S DECISION (22m C n.d.) (also Video)
Dr. Eugene F. Diamond clearly and calmly presents the facts
about abortion. Shows the dilemma of a pregnant high school girl
who must make her own decision among all the conflicting opinions
she receives from family, friends, and professionals. The three
most common methods of abortion are graphically shown. p. Cinema
Medica; CINMO.

ABORTION: LONDON'S DILEMMA (22m C 1969) First Tuesday Series
Presents the abortion controversy at the time when Britain was
one of the first countries in the western world to pass a law legal-
izing abortion, making London "The Abortion Capital of the World."
Women flocked to London from all over the world to receive abortions
in licensed clinics. Shows the many viewpoints and criticisms people
have about the abortion controversy. NBC-TV; FI; KENTSU.

ABORTION: THE DIVISIVE ISSUE (28m C 1979) (Video)
Documentary showing interviews with both pro-life and pro-
abortion factions present at two national abortion conferences (and
attendant demonstrations) held in San Francisco. Includes interviews
with women who have had abortions. p./d. Joanne Kelly; VFA.

ABORTION: THE SINGLE ISSUE (60m C 1979) (Video)
A documentary dealing with the anti-abortion movement and its
political strategies. p. NBC's Weekend; NARAL.

ABUELITAS DE OMBLIGO (GRANDMOTHERS OF THE BELLY BUTTON)
(30m C 1983) (Video, Beta, VHA)
Portrays the warmth and wisdom, the customs and spirit of the
peasant women who deliver most of the babies born in Nicaragua.

The camera follows a group of "pateras empiricas" or "granny mid-wives" through an innovative and unique program developed by the Nicaraguan Ministry of Health to train the women in basic hygiene, nutrition and maternal-child health care. As the women learn techniques of modern medicine, they are also sharing their folklore and wisdom with the medical practitioners. Also available in Spanish. p./d. Rachel Field, Jackie Reiter; WMM

ABUSIVE PARENTS (30m C 1977)
Presents, with a commentary, a panel of women incarcerated for child abuse who belong to a prison chapter of Parents Anonymous. Offers commentary from a social worker on the social context, personal, and family dynamics of child abuse. p. USNCCA; NAVC.

ACCEPT AND EXCEL! (28m C p1980, r1980) (also Video)
Motivational authority Marilyn Van Derbur presents stories of numerous people who faced seemingly insurmountable problems, overcame them and went on to live contributing and rewarding lives. Stressing that it is sometimes impossible for a person to change something in her/his life one does not like, Miss Van Derbur suggests that people acknowledge the problem, accept it and get on with their lives. People mentioned are Sammy Davis, Jr., Helen Keller, Eleanor Roosevelt, and a college student. p./d. Marilyn Van Derbur; VDBER.

ACCESS (23m C 1978)
Demonstrates that individuals with physical and emotional handicaps can re-enter society in a productive manner. Mildred, a dance instructor, contracted polio when she was 30. She explains how she raised her children, cooked, and did the household chores. She also tells why she returned to school to study filmmaking and found it rewarding. But, she admits, it took a long time to identify with other handicapped people. Roy developed a serious nervous disease. After two and a half years following hospitalization and physical therapy, he returned to work as an engineer. But he had to convince a company to hire him, without pay at first, to design computers. Artificial things concern employers, he explains, but most disabled people know their limitations and adjust to them. What they need is the opportunity to work. p. Peter Feinstein; d. Miriam Weinstein; POLYMR.

ACQUAINTANCE RAPE PREVENTION (28m C 1978)
This series of four films introduces to coed groups a delicate subject in a positive way. This program is for those who provide rape prevention education to teenagers, in an effort to reduce acquaintance rape among this high-risk population. Free loan. p. National Center for the Prevention and Control of Rape; MTPS.

ACQUIRING GREATNESS (28m C 1980)
Examines lives of successful people. Shows that hard work, discipline, dedication to excellence, and persistence play a greater

role than natural ability and luck. Marilyn Van Derbur, lecturer, stresses that people with natural ability or beauty may actually be handicapped because they are already appreciated and do not have to develop their skills and build up their confidence. She emphasizes that the choice belongs to everyone. Each person must decide what is right for her/his life and what the priorities will be toward achieving the goals. p./d./s.w. Marilyn Van Derbur; VDBER.

ACT OF BECOMING (28m C p1979, r1980)
A documentary film on Wendy Lehr, which explores her deep commitment to art. Ms. Lehr is a veteran actress and drama teacher at the Children's Theatre in Minneapolis. d. Mark Youngquist; p. Dan Satorius; KTCATV.

ACTION: THE OCTOBER CRISIS OF 1970 (87m C n.d.)
A look at those desperate days of October 1970 when Montreal awaited the outcome of FLQ terrorist acts. Compiled from news and film clips. Shows the independence movements past and present and their leaders; it reflects the mingled relief, dismay, defiance, when the Canadian army came to Montreal; and it shows how political leaders viewed the intervention. Awards. d. Robin Spry; p. R. Spry, Tom Daly, Norman Cloutier. NFBC.

ACTIVE PARTNERS (18m C 1979)
A powerful, yet sensitive, film showing a male quadriplegic and his able-bodied female partner of several years. He has no sensation below his shoulders and uses a permanent indwelling urethral catheter for bladder drainage. Depicts many sides of their relationship, including a strong, positive, mutually satisfying sexual side. The importance of good communication between partners and a sense of humor is apparent throughout the film. p. Dr. Marvin Silverman, Robert Lenz; MMRC.

ACTOR'S EYE, THE (28m B 1979)
An intimate cinema-verité study of a Berkeley (Calif.) theater group, the Berkeley Stage Company, as it goes through the month-long rehearsal process in the production of Baby by Drury Pifer. The film emphasizes the function of the director, Angela Paton, formerly a leading lady with the American Conservatory Theatre in San Francisco. She is shown working with the actors, discussing with them their motivation and actions, and asking them questions designed to deepen their feelings about their characters and to supply them with "memories." This presents a positive image of a woman and is an invaluable teaching instrument for actors as well as for veteran and neophyte stage directors. p. Lynn Hamrick; UCEMC.

ACTOR'S FACE AS A CANVAS (30m ea. C 1973) (Video)
In the theatre, the actor's face itself can be an expressive medium. Irene Corey, author of The Mask of Reality, An Approach to Design for Theatre, shows us the various techniques, from the

emphasizing of facial contours to the creation of fantasy in detail
in the creation of stage make-up in this three-lesson series: 1.
Modeling with Light and Shadows; 2. Stylized Realism; 3. Stylization
and Fantasy. NETCHE.

ACTUALIZATION THROUGH ASSERTION: A BEHAVIORAL APPROACH
TO PERSONAL EFFECTIVENESS (25m C 1976, c1978)
Demonstrates the principles and techniques of group assertion
training; interactions between clients and therapists as they pinpoint
areas of client need. Four clients work on developing an assertive
style by practicing appropriate eye contact, gestures, body movement, touch, facial expression, and voice tone and volume. p. Drs.
Larry King, Robert Paul Liberman and Barnett Addis w/the UCLA
Behavioral Science Media Lab. MEDIAG; UIL, PAS.

ADAPTATION AND AGING: LIFE IN A NURSING HOME (15m C 1979)
(also Video)
Investigates the adaptations and adjustments of one group of
elderly people to life in a nursing home. Scenes of a typical day
are intermixed with narrative comments by anthropologist Philip Stafford, a participant observer in the home. He describes events shown
in terms of the cultural adaptations of residents to life there. For
example, participation in organized activities or a contrasting reti-
cence by an individual can each be viewed as a desire to control
one's life. Stafford stresses the importance of observing significant
yet somewhat obscure details because "things are not always what
they seem." IU.

ADAPTATIONS FOR SURVIVAL: BIRDS (14m C 1969) (also Video)
Illustrates both structural and behavioral adaptations of birds to
their environments. The film is a laboratory observation at the ele-
mentary level as well as a stimulus to early discussion of evolution.
French version also available. p./d. Myrna I. Berlet, Walter H.
Berlet; IFB.

ADAPTATIONS FOR SURVIVAL: MAMMALS (17m C 1972) (also Video)
Explains the structural, physiological, and behavioral adaptations
of mammals in relation to their habits and environment. Examines
the place of humans, who make radical and sometimes harmful changes
in this environment. p./d. Myrna I. Berlet, Walter H. Berlet; IFB.

ADAPTING TO PARENTHOOD (20m C 1979)
A number of new parents talk about their initial problems--sleep-
lessness and crying babies, interfering grandparents, frustration
and guilt at not feeling the serenity they anticipated. This film
is particularly important to young people as it gives a sense of what
it is really like to be a parent. p./d. Alvin Fiering, POLYMR; UM.

ADOLESCENCE: A CASE STUDY (20m C 1978) Developmental Psychology: Infancy to Adolescence Series

Explores the psychosocial development of a 17-year-old, showing that she is so preoccupied with her image, her relationships, and her immediate future that performance of intellectual tasks often seems remote and inconsequential. Vignettes illustrate her social interactions and demonstrate her ability to use sophisticated cognitive processes. CRM; UM, UMO, USC.

ADOLESCENCE: THE WINDS OF CHANGE (30m C 1975)
Presents physical, sexual and cognitive changes in adolescents through interviews with them and with child development authorities John Conger, Jerome Kagan, and David Elkind. HAR; PAS, UMO.

ADOLESCENCE: THE WINDS OF CHANGE (20m C 1979)
The Alderian model holds that the difficulties with children as experienced by parents and other adults are primarily due to a lack of education. Dr. Oscar Christensen of the University of Arizona works with the Lohman family in front of an audience of parents and adults and discusses the impact of ordinal position. He hears the parents' concerns and validates these by checking with the children. He then summarizes the session and provides some encouragement and gives recommendations for the parents. EDMDC; IU, UNEV.

ADOLESCENT CRISES: PT. I (29m B 1973)
Simulated interview involving a potentially suicidal coed who calls a crisis center. Illustrates several possible responses by crisis center worker and the likely consequences. Includes information on how to open an interview, how to establish a relationship with client, how to gather facts, and how to approach client about further treatment. CPP; PAS.

ADOLESCENT CRISES, PT. II (31 m B 1973)
Based on the case history presented in Part I, factual information about suicide and the ways to handle such situations are discovered. CPP; PAS.

ADVOCATES: "SHOULD THE EQUAL RIGHTS AMENDMENT BE RATIFIED?", THE (59m C 1978) (Video)
Debating the question Should the Equal Rights Amendment be ratified? are pro advocate Laurence H. Tribe, Professor of Constitutional Law at Harvard University, and con advocate Jules Gerard, Professor of Constitutional Law at Washington University. Witnesses in favor of the ratification are Barbara Babcock, U.S. Ass't. Attorney General, Civil Division, and Eleanor Smeal, President of the National Organization for Women. Witnesses arguing against the proposition are Sam Ervin, former U.S. Senator from North Carolina, and Phyllis Schlafly, President of the STOP ERA Organization. Marilyn Berger, moderator, WGBH-TV, Boston; PBSV.

AFFIRMATIVE ACTION AND THE SUPERVISOR: IT'S NOT SIMPLY BLACK AND WHITE (20m C 1975)
Investigates the causes of conflict between white supervisors

and non-white employees and offers suggestions for reducing these conflicts. On the premise that cultural and social differences are more influential in producing failure than is a lack of skills and abilities, the film raises some provocative questions. Designed for use by supervisors and management personnel, the film presents a frank and candid discussion of reasons for dissatisfaction as given by supervisor and employee. p. Dibie-Dash Productions, Inc.; DIBIE; UMN.

AFGHAN WAYS (8m C p1980, r1980) (also Video)
Shows the customs, character and work of Afghan villagers in the last year of the monarchy. Made with a mixture of sepia tone and color. Much of this film was photographed and recorded in 1971. Scenes of the people, animals and industries of Afghanistan are shown as well as the traditional dress and habits of the people. One scene shows several women working together on a large carpet participating in Afghanistan's most developed industry. p. Carrie Aginsky, Yasah Aginsky; LAWRENP.

AFGHANISTAN: THREADS OF LIFE (29m C p1980, r1980)
Explores the natural landscape of Afghanistan. Shows the isolated villages of Tang-A-Bul-Hiyoti and the bazaar at Kabul, the capital city. Afghanistan is a country that has changed very little over the centuries. The country's arts and crafts illustrate the legends discussed and weave a rich heritage of the Afghans. The small self-sufficient nomadic Kashgai tribe at Tang-A-Bul-Hiyoti produce wheat, barley, figs and grapes. The women bake unleavened bread daily over open fires after they have walked for miles into the desert for water. The women, who no longer cover their faces in the village, weave carpets of traditional designs. The young boys often become silversmiths with their craft passed on from generation to generation. Twice a week a cattle market is held in the city of Kabul; the lengthy disputes and bargaining are shown. Life in the cities is centered around the bazaar and workshops, such as the salt shop, blacksmith, and bakery, with many people working 365 days a year. p./d. Irwin Dermer; EBEC.

AFRICA IS MY HOME (19m C p1979, r1979)
Explores the life of a Nigerian woman from birth through marriage, explaining through her eyes the basic issues of resurgent African nationalism. d./p. J. Michael Hagopian; ATLAP.

AFRICAN SCENE, THE (SERIES) see YOUTH BUILDS A NATION IN TANZANIA

AFRO-AMERICAN PERSPECTIVE SERIES see AFRO-AMERICAN PERSPECTIVES: A BLACK WOMAN'S PERSPECTIVE

AFRO-AMERICAN PERSPECTIVES: A BLACK WOMAN'S PERSPECTIVE (30m C 1976) (Video) Afro-American Perspective Series
Racism and sexism from the black woman's perspective. The

panel addresses specific issues, for example, the hiring practices
and policies of various institutions, such as colleges and universities,
school districts (public schools), and components of private industry.
Other issues addressed include the practice and process of sex stereotyping, as well as the need for positive female images and role
models for our various institutions. Washington State University/
KWSU-TV; WSU.

AFTER THE AXE (56m C 1981)
    A docudrama on the firing of business executives and the spe-
cialized way in which they reintegrate themselves into the job market.
An interesting look at the corporate jungle. d. Sturla Gunnarsson;
p. Steve Lucas; NFBC.

AFTER THE GAME (18m B p1979, r1979, r1980--U.S.)
    This is the story of two young women, close friends, as they
acknowledge and come to terms with their feelings of attraction for
each other. p. Women's Interart Center; d. Donna Gray; NFLC;
FOCUSI, IRISFC, MMRC.

AFTER THE "OUCH" (15m C p1978, r1978)
    After a series of small accidents, children apply first aid for
a cut, splinter, bruise, nosebleed, and minor burn. Animation shows
healing process. Includes correct response to a serious accident.
d. Jane Treiman; CF.

AFTER THE SUNSET AGAIN (45m ? 1974) (Video)
    The context is the stuff soap operas are made of: a relationship
between husband and wife that "kind of died on us a couple of years
ago"; a confusion of roles resulting from an internal struggle with
the women's movement and a new consciousness of the role of women.
Through poems and songs, the Mastens, as individuals and together,
offer a highly personal insight into their struggles with these questions.
Through their words, we begin to see how they put their relationship
back together. The center of the effort became "The Mastens' Annual Relationship Renewal," which "put the magic and the glue" back
into the marriage. p./d. Billie Barbara Masten, Ric Masten; NETCHE.

AFTERIMAGE (18m C 1979)
    Shows two people whose creative spirits were not deterred by
their visual handicaps. Articulate, award-winning sculptors describe
their individual experiences with blindness. p./d. Jan Krawitz,
Thomas Ott; DIRECT.

AFTERSCHOOL SPECIALS SERIES see FRANCESCA BABY

AGAINST WIND AND TIDE: A CUBAN ODYSSEY (55m C 1981) (also
    Video)
    Focuses on the Cuban refugees who came during the Mariel boat-
lift in 1980, though the message is clearly broader. There will always

be other groups looking for asylum here. How will this nation of
immigrants receive them? The film brings into focus an immigration
policy that is arbitrary, unclear, and often based on political exped-
iency. It shows an American public that is divided in its attitudes
towards newcomers. Academy Award nominee. d./p. Suzanne Bauman, Jim Burroughs, Paul Neshamkin; FILMLB.

AGE IS A WOMEN'S ISSUE (29m C 1977) (Video) Woman Series
    Tish Sommers, Co-coordinator of the National Organization for
Women's Task Force on Older Women, discusses how age discrimination affects older women. She describes the dilemma of the "displaced housewife," who finds herself without a place in society after
her children are grown, and talks about efforts to change societal
attitudes toward the older woman. Sandra Elkin is the moderator.
p. WNED-TV, Buffalo, NY; PBSV.

AGE IS BECOMING (29m C 1977) (Video) Woman Series
    Three women who are working to change the image of aging dis-
cuss the advantages of growing older and what to do about the disadvantages. The guests are Lydia Bragger, National Media Coordinator of the Gray Panthers; Marjory Collins, editor and founder of
Prime Time, a magazine for older women; and Tish Sommers, Co-
coordinator of the Task Force on Older Women for the National Organization for Women. Sandra Elkin is the moderator. WNED-TV,
Buffalo, NY; PBSV.

AGE IS MONEY BLUES (29m C 1977) (Video) Woman Series
    Laurie Shields and Tish Sommers describe the "Displaced Home-
makers Bill"--a proposed national self-help program for women who
have been homemakers and are being excluded from the job market
by age discrimination or a lack of marketable skills. Shields, National Coordinator of the Alliance of Displaced Homemakers, and Sommers, Co-coordinator of the Task Force on Older Women for the National Organization for Women, explain the provisions of the proposed
legislation. Sandra Elkin is the moderator. WNED-TV, Buffalo,
NY; PBSV.

AGES 4 and 5 (30m ? 1970) (Video)
    The camera visits the Ruth Staples Child Development Laboratory
at the University of Nebraska-Lincoln, where children are observed
at play and engaged in a variety of learning experiences. According
to Mrs. Petelle, the adequate nursery school should have a flexible
program, be a place for living and learning, and also offer an enjoyable experience to the children. Roberta Petelle, Instructor, Human
Development and the Family, University of Nebraska at Lincoln;
NETCHE.

AGING AND HEALTH IN A FIVE GENERATION AMERICAN FAMILY
    (49m C 1982) (Video)
    The purpose of the presentation is to listen and to share and

to try to synthesize the various portions of the human life span through a common experience. Participants: Mrs. Ruby Burshia, 87 years old; Mrs. Ada Potts, 69 years old (her daughter); Mrs. Andora Eichman, 51 years old (her daughter); Mrs. Debra Morud, 27 years old (her daughter); and Brittney Morud, 4 years old (her daughter). Presented by the Institute of Aging, University of Washington. Moderator: William R. Hazzard, M.D. p. University of Washington Press; UW.

AGING IN AMERICA SERIES see MOUNTAIN PEOPLE; RETIREMENT; SOUTH BEACH

AGING IN OUR TIMES SERIES see CROSSCURRENTS: A LOOK AT AGEISM; GERONTOLOGY: LEARNING ABOUT AGING; OLD IS ...

AGING IN THE FUTURE SERIES see WORK AND RETIREMENT; RETIREMENT INCOME SECURITY; HEALTH MAINTENANCE AND CARE; LIVING ARRANGEMENTS AND SERVICES; POLITICS OF AGING

AGNES De MILLE (30m C 1977) (Video)
Dick Cavett interviews Agnes De Mille, prime innovator in the field of dance and choreographer for ballet, Broadway and motion pictures since the early 1940's. p. WNET-TV; FI.

AGNES De MILLE'S CHERRY TREE CAROL (10m C 1971)
Through a simple, moving ballet choreographed on a bare stage, Agnes De Mille's Appalachian dance troupe translates the story of the Holy Family into a Southern mountain version of folksong. A black folksinger with a mellow voice sings the carol, which tells the legend of Joseph's anger at Mary when she asks for cherries, saying she is with child. p. Educational Broadcasting Corporation; PARACO; UIL.

AGONY OF JIMMY QUINLAN, THE (27m C n.d.)
Jimmy Quinlan is a derelict, one of some 5,000 men and women who have abandoned their jobs and families to live in the streets and alleys of Montreal. A powerful portrayal of life on skid row, this film tells of Jimmy's agonies--his attempt to get off the bottle. It's something he's tried before and will probably have to try again. d. Janice Brown, Robert Duncan, Andy Thomson; p. Peter Katadotis; NFBC.

AGUEDA MARTINEZ--OUR PEOPLE, OUR COUNTRY (16m C 1977)
Agueda Martinez, a native New Mexican, is a remarkable, self-sufficient woman. Like generations before her, a deep-rooted relationship with the land nourishes and supports her life-style as a farmer and weaver. In this picture of her daily life, her close-to-the-earth philosophy is shown to be direct and simple, and we

have a rare glimpse of tradition and proven values. She says, "Land is a blessed thing because it is what produces our food. It produces the clothes I have.... It supports the cow that is meat and milk. How can the land not be blessed? I shall never sell my ranch in my lifetime." EDMDC; PAS, UFL, UIL, UM, UNEV, KENTSU.

AHA (3m C 1979) (Video)
Abstract patterns of brilliant colors make up this tape of electronically manipulated source material. d./p. Mimi Martin; MARTIN.

AIR FOR THE G STRING (6m B 1934)
The only sound film on Doris Humphrey available for distribution. As an example of Miss Humphrey's early choreography, the dance shown is an important part of the history of modern dance. Choreographed in 1928. Dancers: Doris Humphrey, Cleo Athenof, Ernestine Hennoch Stodell, Dorothy Lathrop, Hyla Rubin; Choreographer: Doris Humphrey. DAN/UR; UIL, WAYSU.

ALASKA NATIVE HERITAGE FILM SERIES, THE see AT THE TIME OF WHALING; FROM THE FIRST PEOPLE (see Films for ...); ON THE SPRING ICE; TUNUNEREMIUT, THE PEOPLE OF TUN-UNAK

ALBANIAN WOMEN'S SONG AND FOLKDANCES FROM ZUR (7m C 1971)
Folk dances and songs for women, from Zur, southeast Europe. p. H. Kaleshi, S. Pilana, H. J. Kibling; Institut für den Wissen-Schaftlichen Film, Göttingen; PAS.

ALBERTA HUNTER: BLUES AT THE COOKERY (45m C 1982) (also Video)
At 87, Alberta Hunter sings the blues like nobody else. She has played with Louis Armstrong, Fats Waller and Sidney Bechet. She has triumphed over adversity and brings to her listeners an irresistibly affirmative message. Between her renditions of "I Got Rhythm," "Sweet Georgia Brown," and the other numbers she performs at New York's The Cookery, we learn about the fascinating life of this remarkable black woman--who gave up music for 20 years to work as a hospital nurse and began to sing again professionally at age 82. Today, her career is stronger than ever. p. Teleculture Inc.; TELCULT.

ALCOHOL AND THE WORKING WOMAN (24m C n.d.)
Dr. Dale Masi, Director, Office of Employee Counseling Services, Department of Health and Human Resources and worldwide authority on alcoholism in the work place, deals with the specific problems of alcholism and the working woman. Dr. Masi used examples of her experience as the director of many employee assistance programs to point out the problems and solutions for working women with alcohol problems. Representatives of leading EAP and occupational

alcoholism programs also share their experience and insights. p. Motivational Media; MTVTM.

ALCOHOLIC WITHIN US, THE (25m C 1973)
An allegorical film in which the mind is represented as a house inhabited by six emotions that stop the mind from coping with life: Loneliness, Fear, Insecurity, Inadequacy, Resentment and Guilt. Maturity calls a meeting when the house becomes troubled, but Immaturity leads the feelings away to a part of the house where they find an effortless solution--alcohol. Written and narrated by a young alcoholic, this open-ended film provides a valuable discussion starter for groups concerned with alcohol or other forms of chemical dependence. p. Noel Nosseck; PF.

ALCOHOLISM AND THE FAMILY: THE SUMMER WE MOVED TO ELM STREET (28m C 1968)
The plight of an alcoholic beginning his descent into the maelstrom of progressive disintegration is tragically portrayed in this film. The relationships between members of the family as seen through the eyes of a nine-year-old child provide the audience with an understanding of the nature of the drinking problem, its symptoms and effects. d. Patricia Watson; p. Guy Glover; NFBC: CRM.

ALEATORY (7½m B 1974)
The final film of a series experimenting with increased layers of dance movement syncopated and superimposed at sporadic intervals. The improvisations of a single dancer and pianist, reflected in a mirror, are used throughout. d./p. Christie Ann Piper; PIPER.

ALEXANDRA DANILOVA (30m C 1978) (Video)
Dick Cavett interviews Alexandra Danilova, supreme ballerina, who teaches at the American Ballet School and has a featured role in the theatrical film The Turning Point. WNET-TV: FI.

ALGERIA: THE IMPOSSIBLE INDEPENDENCE (43m C 1976)
This controversial film is a direct critique of the concepts presented in FROM THE EARTH TO THE MOON. The filmmaker claims that nationalization is not in itself an answer to the problems of the underdeveloped countries. This only leads to greater dependence on the West--for capital, for knowledge, for equipment and for technicians. The results are frightening--growing unemployment, the destruction of agriculture, the emergence of a new "class" of technocrats, and eventually the export of cheap labor to the already developed countries. p. Marie Claude Deffarge, Gordian Troeller; ICARF.

ALICE ELLIOTT (11m C 1977)
Brief but insightful look at the life and work of one of the few remaining Pomo Indian basketmakers. Stills showing Indian life in earlier days are accompanied by gentle music of flutes. Beautifully

handcrafted baskets are shown. Alice, born in 1896, tells of her
childhood and how she learned her art from the older women in her
village. She discusses the traditional designs and how she was taught
never to change them. There is a poignancy in her words, for she
represents a way of life and a belief in traditions that are rapidly
disappearing. She sings a basketmaking song and smiles as the film
dissolves to a concluding series of E. S. Curtis prints that capture
the Pomo life of another time. UCEMC.

ALICE NEEL: COLLECTOR OF SOULS (30m C 1978) The Originals:
   Women in Art Series
   Presents a portrait of the forthright artist and her many works.
Highlights include a reception at New York's Graham Gallery where
people are seen next to their portraits and her induction into the
American Academy and Institute of Arts and Letters. But the heart
of the film is the actual process of painting a portrait, an exhilarat-
ing event. p. Nancy Baer, Cine 16; FI; PAS.

ALL FOR ONE (29m C 1977) (Video)
   The Lamaze method of childbirth is documented in this program
which follows a young couple through training classes and into the
delivery room. Donna and Ed Musselman allowed cameras to record
their instruction in Lamaze techniques and the actual birth of their
first child. Lamaze instructor Maureen Tyrell explains the theory
behind this method of childbirth and points out that it does not guarantee a perfect labor and delivery. When complications occur near
the end of the delivery and the obstetrician steps in to assist, the
viewer witnesses how Lamaze-trained parents cope with the situation.
p. WLVT-TV; PBSV.

ALL MY TOMORROWS (17m C 1979)
   A dramatized story shot in slow motion about the tragic consequences that can result from mixing alcoholic beverages and barbiturates. Film begins with 18-year-old Peggy feeling the stresses
of trying to cope with pressures many young people experience
in today's society: parental authority, a dead-end job, feeling unfulfilled. Too many drinks at one particular party, combined with
barbiturates, cause Peggy to lapse into a coma. Paramedics are called
and she is rushed to the hospital. Remainder of the film centers
around Peggy's thoughts and reflections on her life as she lies in
a comatose state, suffering permanent brain damage. Shows the
effects of her plight on family and friends, as well as herself. p.
Gordon-Kercknoff Productions; CENTEF; UIL, WSU.

ALL-ROUND REDUCED PERSONALITY, THE (98m B 1979) (German/
   subtitled)
   A sensitive yet wryly humorous portrait of the challenges facing
a young single mother in West Berlin who has decided to run her own
life as she copes with the conflicting demands of her home (and daughter) and her career as a photographer. In a sardonic reversal of the

phrase "the all-round realized Socialist personality" heard repeatedly on East Berlin radio broadcasts, the film's heroine considers herself an "all-round reduced personality," devoted to a number of causes but only half-good at any of them. d. Helke Sander (one of Germany's leading feminist filmmakers); UNIFILM

ALL SUCCESSFUL PEOPLE HAVE IT (28m C p.1980, r1980) You Can Do It ... If Series
Features people who knew what they wanted to accomplish, decided how to do it, and then did it. Marilyn Van Derbur, motivational specialist, speaks about those people as well as those who drift through life without any specific goals. The film ends with the quotes, "Beware of what you want for you may get it" and "If you can think of nothing, that may be what you will get." p./s.w. Marilyn Van Derbur; VDBER.

ALL YOU HAVE TO DO (54m C 1981)
Shows how one young woman goes about living with cancer. Explores how the life of Pat Logan has changed radically with the disease, its treatment, and the reality of death. Through interviews, Pat discusses how her illness has affected her sense of herself and her relationships with others; her husband, three children and several friends articulate how the experience has changed their own lives. d. Chris Shynot/Bronwen Wallace; MOBIUS.

ALL YOUR PARTS DON'T WEAR OUT AT THE SAME TIME (28m C n.d.)
Susan Rowland is a dramatic dynamo who decides to try theatre to fight the sense of obsolescence which burdens many over 65 years of age. The members of the drama group, known as the "Senior Players" and sponsored by Actors Theatre in Louisville, Kentucky, were chosen for openness to new experiences. They begin with short, humorous skits, taken from their lives, on the theme "we were young once." The thoughtful camera helps us to know each as a person. The rewards of their risks can be seen in their own lives and in the faces of their appreciative audiences. This is a moving message of hope for later years, and a demonstration that all your parts do not wear out at the same time. p. Alfred Shands Production, WAVE-TV; MMM.

ALMOST HOME (27m C 1982)
One of a series of original short dramas dealing with the problems and conflicts in dual-career marriages. When Rick and Sarah, a young professional couple, welcome into their home their nine-year-old niece, Dee, whose parents have died in a car accident, they find their careers and their marriage disrupted in unexpected ways. Comprehensive instructor's guide available. d. Marilyn Weiner/Hal Weiner; p. Barbara Wolfinger; UCEMC.

ALPHA (1m C 1972)
A bravura about algebraic construction, presenting the

architecture of algebra with exuberance. p. Ray and Charles Eames; PF.

ALTERNATIVE CHILDBIRTH (65m C 1979) (also Video, S8)
Depicts all the choices in childbirth available to couples today. Hospitals, birth center, and home births (attended and unattended) are shown. An excellent overview of the childbirth scene in America today. CINMD.

ALTERNATIVES TO ESTROGEN (29m C 1970) (Video) Woman Series
Medical writer Barbara Seaman and psychiatrist Dr. Gideon Seaman discuss alternatives to the use of synthetic estrogens for birth control and menopause. They also comment on the DES (diethylstilbestrol) controversy. Sandra Elkin is the moderator. WNED-TV; PBSV.

ALWAYS IN FASHION (19m C 1979) (also Video)
Examines the modern sweatshops of metropolitan New York. Unmarked and tucked away in garages and basements are numerous small factories where mostly undocumented aliens work long hours for well below the minimum wage. Some factories are union shops, but the unions, as well as government manufacturers, look the other way as wage-hour, fire, child labor, and tax laws are flagrantly ignored. Workers are caught in the middle, terrified to complain. They could lose their jobs or they might be deported. These intolerable conditions exist, but government representatives and union officials say they don't know where they exist; they blame cultural and language differences and claim more competition leads to more exploitation. p. Stephanie Meagher; FI; UIL, UMN.

AM I NORMAL? (24m C 1979)
A situation comedy about the experiences boys go through during puberty. Using three fictional characters, it presents the facts about male sexual development, while raising important issues about masculinity, identity and peer pressure. A good discussion film for young people--boys and girls. d./p./s.w. Debra Franco, David Shepard; p. Copperfield Films; NEWDAY.

AMAHUACA: A TROPICAL FOREST SOCIETY IN SOUTHEASTERN PERU (24m C 1973)
An anthropologist-made film useful for study purposes, this work documents the daily activities and festivals of the Amahuaca. Living in isolated family groups, they subsist by hunting wild game and growing corn through slash-and-burn agriculture. Detailed sequences include making bows and arrows and, later, using arrows to catch fish. A harvest festival takes place and preparations for it include scenes of facial painting and making men's headdresses. p. Dr. Gertrude Dole; PAS.

AMAZING BOW WOW, THE (32m C 1977) (Video)
The story is about a hermaphroditic dog and its masters. The

male owner calls the dog "He" and the woman calls it "She." When
the man becomes convinced that the dog can talk and is flirting with
his wife, he cuts out the animal's tongue. The couple finally resell
the dog to the circus man from whom they bought it. p. Lynda
Benglis; p. The Kitchen Center; CASTSON.

AMAZING NEWBORN, THE (25m C 1979)
    Portrays the remarkable degree of behavioral development already
present in infants. Presents three normal babies, one to seven days
of age, who are shown reacting to visual, tactile and auditory stim-
uli. Demonstrates states of awareness common to all infants. By
paying attention to their child's behavior, parents can learn to recognize not only when their child is alert but recognize their individuality. p. Maureen Halk, M.D.; POLYMR; KENTSU.

AMBASSADOR (25m C 1978)
    Traces the career of Frank Devine from his service in the United
States Army during World War II, through diplomatic assignments
in seven foreign countries, to the appointment as United States Ambassador to El Salvador. Discusses the government of El Salvador
and explores the role of a U.S. Ambassador in a foreign country.
SCRESC.

AMERICA: FROM HITLER TO MX (90m C 1982)
    An urgent statement against the U.S. escalation of the arms race,
clarifying the long-standing first strike posture, and the increasing
danger of nuclear annihilation. It includes interviews, historical
footage, news headlines, and articles verifying events kept secret
since the U.S. support of the rise of Hitler to wipe out socialism,
and the more often documented secrecy around the use of the A-
bomb. d. Joan Harvey; p. Albee Gordon/Ralph Klein/Saul Newton;
ed. Joan Harvey/Trudy Bagdon/Ken Eluto; PARFD.

AMERICAN BALLET THEATRE: A CLOSE-UP IN TIME (90m C 1973)
    Complete performance of Pillar of Fire. Also, the Black Swan
pas de deux from Swan Lake and excerpts from Les Sylphides, Rodeo,
The River, and Etudes. Interviews with Agnes De Mille, Lucia Chase,
and Antony Tudor are featured. d. Jerome Schnur; CANTOR.

AMERICAN FAMILY: AN ENDANGERED SPECIES?, THE (Series)
    see PEGGY COLLINS (Single Mother); under FAMILY PORTRAIT:
    ... SEAN'S STORY (Divided Custody); ... SHARE-A-HOME
    (Group Home for the Elderly); ... THE EDHOLMS (Blended Fam-
    ily); ... THE GLEGHORNS (Unemployed Father); ... THE HART-
    MANS (Mother Returns to Work); ... THE KREINIK AND BOS-
    WORTH FAMILIES (Single Adoptive Parents); ... THE MARINOS
    (Divorcing Parents); ... THE SCHUSTER-ISSACSON FAMILY
    (Lesbian Mothers); ... THE SORIANOS (Extended Family)

AMERICAN FASHION: RAGS AND RICHES (52m C 1980)
    An inside look at how fashions are dreamed up by famous design-

ers and skillfully promoted to influence American consumers. In the garment center along New York's Seventh Avenue, a young designer, Michaele Vollbracht, shows how he works to create new ideas for American women. The enormous impact of the media on the garment industry is explored. Publications such as Vogue, Harper's Bazaar, and Glamour tell upper-class women what they are supposed to wear. The "bible" of the fashion trade, Women's Wear Daily, is read assiduously by retailers who make the decisions on what will finally go on sale. In another area of the big business of fashion is the manufacturer who "knocks off" (copies) the latest big-name designs and gets them into retail outlets for a fraction of the original brand-name asking price. Besides Vollbracht, designers Bill Blass, Halston, and Calvin Klein also appear in the film. p. Adrienne Cowles; reported by Robin Young for NBC News. FI; UMN.

AMERICAN FIRST LADIES (25m C/B 1966) The Smithsonian (Series)
A guided tour of the Hall of First Ladies at the Smithsonian Institution and interior scenes of the White House provide for an anecdotal history of the women who have served as hostess for the President of the U.S. Black and white film footage and photographs record the Christmas celebration of the more recent families--the Theodore Roosevelts, Franklin Roosevelts, Trumans, Eisenhowers, Kennedys and Johnsons. NBC-TV; CRM; UIL, KENTSU.

AMERICAN FOLK ART (25m C 1967) The Smithsonian (Series)
Presents the Smithsonian Institution's collection of eighteenth- and nineteenth-century American folk art. Traces the development of the folk art from the American Revolution to the Civil War and discusses themes and techniques characteristic of folk art. NBC-TV; CRM; UIL.

AMERICAN INDIAN: A QUIET REVOLUTION, THE (29 m C 1976) (Video)
An examination of the Native American fight for the right of self-determination and a look at existing government policies. The program cites the 1974 Boldt Decision. Includes essay on Chief Seattle as well as statements by various Indian representatives and excerpts from the 32nd Annual Council of American Indians. Among the guests is Lucy Covington, a Colville Indian. p. KWSU-TV; PBSV.

AMERICAN INDIAN ARTISTS: HELEN HARDIN (29m C 1975) (Video, Beta, VHS)
A profile of American Indian artist, Helen Hardin. She is seen at work in her Tesuque, New Mexico studio and relaxing among the Puye Cliff ruins of her ancestors. The film explores her attempts to integrate her Indian and artist selves. She uses her Indian heritage as a point of departure for contemporary images. Host is Rod McKuen. p. KAET-TV; PBSV.

AMERICAN INDIAN ARTISTS: MEDICINE FLOWER AND LONEWOLF (29m C 1975) (Video, Beta, VHS)

A profile of American Indian artists Grace Medicine Flower and her brother Joseph Lonewolf, both potters from Santa Clara Pueblo, New Mexico. They have revived and extended the traditional forms and techniques of their pre-Columbian ancestors, the Mimbres people, in their work. Host is Rod McKuen. p. KAET-TV, PHOENIX; PBSV.

AMERICAN LIFESTYLE--CULTURAL LEADERS SERIES see FRANK LLOYD WRIGHT'S FALLINGWATER; JOHN RINGLING'S CA D'ZAN; MARK TWAIN'S HARTFORD HOME; WILL ROGERS' CALIFORNIA RANCH

AMERICAN LIFESTYLE SERIES--INDUSTRIALISTS AND INVENTORS see CORNELIUS VANDERBILT II's THE BREAKERS; WILLIAM RANDOLPH HEARST'S SAN SIMEON

AMERICAN NAISSANCE: JOURNEY WITH A FRIEND (26m C 1971) Woman and husband train for birth of first child. Highlights principles of psychoprophylaxis in childbirth and the doubts and expectations of the couple training by the method. Shows actual labor and birth (perineal view) in a modern American obstetrical situation. p. Pomes and Popcorn; PAS.

AMERICAN PICTURE PALACES (23m C p1982, r1983) The heyday, decline and rebirth of an American treasure: the Picture Palace. Explores the achievement of visionary architects and showmen. Its live footage and stills of palaces across the country demonstrate how these extravagances of the Jazz Age have become practical solutions to the performing arts' needs of today and how they help revitalize our cities. d. Lee Bobker; p. Karen Loveland; SMITHS.

AMERICAN REVOLUTION, THE (SERIES) see MARY KATE'S WAR

AMERICAN SHORT STORY SERIES see JILTING OF GRANNY WEATHERALL, THE

AMERICAN WOMAN, THE: A SOCIAL CHRONICLE (C 6/SFS n.d.) A survey of the social and economic history of women in the U.S. EDENM.

AMERICANA SERIES see CLARA BARTON: ANGEL OF THE BATTLEFIELD

AMERICANA SERIES, ART IN AMERICA see ART IN AMERICA: ART CAREERS; PHOTOGRAPHY: MASTERS OF THE 20TH CENTURY

AMERICA'S WETLANDS (28m C 1981) From the Atchafalaya River Swamp in lower Louisiana to Alaska's arctic tundra, reveals the hidden values of wetlands. Swamps, marshes, prairie potholes and other water-saturated lands have been traditionally viewed as worthless and dispensable. The film conveys a national perspective of wetlands, their natural benefits to people and wildlife, and the potential impact of their loss. d. Tom Ramsay; ex. p. Cecilia Ramsay. Sponsored by U.S. Fish and Wildlife Service /U.S. Environmental Protection Agency. NAVC.

AMISH: A PEOPLE OF PRESERVATION, THE (31m C 1976)
Illustrates the life-style of an Amish community in Lancaster County, Pennsylvania. Examines the courtship customs, education, clothing, religion, and closeness to nature that characterize the Amish. Provides historical background and shows how the Amish have maintained the way of life and language they used in the old country. Presents the views of Dr. John Hostetler, foremost authority on Amish culture, and of an Amish man who left the community to attend a university. p. Heritage Productions; EBEC; IU, UCEMC, UMO, UW, PAS.

AMNIOCENTESIS (15½m C 1983)
Shows in animation how an accident in the cells of one parent can cause Down's syndrome. The amniocentesis procedure, along with its medical and legal risks, is explained. Patient undergoes sonography prior to procedure. Discusses recuperation, lab procedures and final report. MIFE.

AMPHIBIANS: WHAT, WHEN AND WHERE? (15m C 1976) (also Video)
Each spring amphibians wake from their winter hibernation and gather at ponds to sing and mate. The film examines three species of amphibians--frogs, toads, and salamanders--comparing and contrasting their habits, mating behavior, and life cycles. p. Myrna I. Berlet, Walter H. Berlet; IFB.

ANATOMY OF YOUTH--WITH DR. MARGARET MEAD (22m C 1970)
Dr. Margaret Mead, anthropologist, writer, and educator, is interviewed in an informal setting against a carnival-like background of young people "doing their thing" on a Sunday in New York City's Central Park. Stating that these post-World War II babies are pioneers in a new world, she comments on their reactions to war, violence, the establishment, authority, dropouts, fashions, and especially the generation gap. Dr. Mead recommends that parents listen to what the youngsters have to say and try to understand what they are all about. p. ABC-TV; MEDIAG; UIL.

ANCIENT ART OF BELLY DANCING, THE (30m C 1977)
Traces the ancient art of belly dancing as far back as ancient Mesopotamia and Egypt. A dancer offers her interpretations of how those historic styles of belly dancing might have been performed. French painters of the nineteenth century incorporated harem girls into their works. This dance form was introduced in America at the Chicago World's Fair of 1893. Since then belly dancing became a popular art form in America. Concludes with interviews in which

members of a modern belly dancing class speak of the art as a means of self-expression and an outlet for acting out personal fantasies. d. Stewart Lippe; s.w. Ann Lippe; PHOENIX; UCEMC.

AND A TIME TO DANCE (18m C n.d.)
A dramatic improvisation showing present-day use of commedia dell'arte with preparatory exercises revolving around the theme of an incident in the westward trek of American pioneers. Performers: Perry-Mansfield staff and students; d. Charlotte Perry; p. Rainbow Pictures; MANSPR.

AND BABY MAKES TWO (27m C 1978) (also Video)
Every year teenage pregnancies push more than a million children into instant adulthood. At a school for pregnant teenagers, girls talk openly about their problems. Most say they never thought of birth control--sex was unplanned and spontaneous. Some are bitter, some philosophical, but all agree their lives have changed radically, and not for the better. Both boys and girls express frustration at the lack of information and their inability to communicate. They feel that ignorance and misconceptions are primary factors in pregnancy. The film provides no answers and does not moralize, but it makes a strong statement about a burgeoning problem. Hosted by Valerie Bertinelli. d. Nancy Littlefield; p. John Korbelak, NBC-TV; FI.

... AND JUSTICE FOR ALL (25m C 1977)
Portrays the functions and responsibilities of a jury, and to show the importance of the jury system and the safeguards it provides. Shows jurors meeting for the first time. A jury clerk explains the responsibilities of jury members, and how a jury is selected. Also, she clarifies the difference between civil and criminal cases and between federal and statecourts, and defines some of the legal terminology they will need to know. p. Shana Corporation under a grant from the Law Enforcement Assistance Administration; p./d./s.w. Shelby Newhouse; POSTSC.

AND THE EARTH QUAKES (13½m C p1979, r1979)
In California, because a disastrous earthquake can strike any day without warning, critical steps have been taken to insure that telephone service will survive or be quickly restored for emergency use by public service agencies. This film gives insight into these preparations and reveals metropolitan and suburban areas that sit precariously on or near major fault lines not only in California, but throughout the U.S. d. Dan E. Weisburd; p. Elaine Simone, Dan E. Weisburd; ELDAN.

AND THE WALLS CAME TUMBLING DOWN (26m B r1975)
An intense documentary of an improvisational drama workshop conducted by actress Marketa Kimbrell (The Pawnbroker) with inmates of the Queens House of Detention for Men in New York City. A play

that eventually will be performed for the entire prison is planned, written, and rehearsed through improvisation sessions. The film captures many short but remarkably effective glimpses of Ms. Kimbrell's compelling teaching technique and of the genuine emotion experienced and conveyed by the inmate actors as they transform their prison experience into drama. Between sessions, the prisoners discuss their effectiveness and the value of their dramatic training. The film provides keen insights into prison life and the emotions it generates as well as the mechanics of theatrical training. Contains unedited street language. UCEMC.

AND THEN ... (21m C r1978)
Valerie and Michael, a young married filmmaking couple, run into trouble when their feature film script is accepted by a big Hollywood producer. This stroke of good luck almost finishes their collaboration when they try to rewrite the screenplay according to the producer's requirements. But just in time, they realize how much they need each other, "and then ..." they continue to argue happily ever after. p. Caroline Ahlfours Mouris, Michael Pulitzer, Jr.; d. Frank Mouris; PHOENIX.

AND THEY ALL FALL DOWN (6m B 1976)
Portrait of a young hobbyist's absorption in the creation of elaborate designs with dominoes. The careful planning involved in arranging the structures is juxtaposed with his delight in their chain reaction destruction. Dominoes are seen toppling from various perspectives, including a worm's eye view. p./d. Bonnie Cutler, Sheri Herman; TEMPLU.

AND WHEN YOU GROW OLD (26m C 1976) (Video)
Five profiles of elderly people who share their feelings about growing old. Positive role models. AOTA.

ANGEL THAT STANDS BY ME: MINNIE EVANS' PAINTINGS, THE
    (29m C 1983)
Minnie Evans is the embodiment of the visionary artist. She is an 88-year-old Afro-American painter who lives in Wilmington, North Carolina. The film captures, with striking clarity, the connection between her visions, her religious fervor, and her art. It traces her slave ancestry, her life as an impoverished gate keeper at the Airlie Gardens where we see her painting. It contains scenes from her African-Methodist church, with her 101-year-old mother, and the Evans' family reunion of six generations. Minnie Evans has had a number of solo shows, among them one at the Whitney Museum in New York. p. Light-Saraf Films, LISARF.

ANGELA AND DAVID (28m C 1974)
Depicts a contemporary wedding for which the bride and groom have written their own ceremony. Reception provides opportunity to observe interaction between generations, as well as between people

of differing life-styles. Unexpected visit from members of a nearby commune adds to the festive atmosphere. p. Hornbein-Wood Films; PAS.

ANIMAL BEHAVIOR SERIES (11m ea. C 1973) (also Video)
Four films on the behavior of animals during seasonal changes in North America. Titles in the series are Animal Behavior: Fall; Animal Behavior: Winter; Animal Behavior: Spring; Animal Behavior: Summer. p. Myrna I. Berlet, Walter H. Berlet; IFB.

ANIMALS AND THE SUN (14m C 1975)
Uses wildlife footage of over 20 creatures to explain how animals have adapted to regions that are influenced by the relationship between the earth and the sun. p. Myrna I. Berlet, Walter H. Berlet; IFB.

ANIMATED WOMEN (15m C 1977)
Provocative comments on today's female of the species in animation by young animators--three women and a man. The animation techniques are every bit as fresh, arresting and contemporary as the themes they portray. p. Deborah Healey; TEXFM.

ANIMATION FOR LIVE ACTION (25m C 1979)
Using both live action and animation--cut-out, line drawings, pixilation--Neubauer has created a revealing, rapid-fire film on the perplexities facing women today. d. Vera Neubauer; p. British Film Institute; MMA.

ANITA ELLIS: FOR THE RECORD (30m C p1980, r1980)
Documents a recording session of the legendary singer Anita Ellis, with the equally renowned pianist Ellis Larkins. It includes rehearsal and performance of a number of classic popular songs, together with brief interview segments in which Ms. Ellis reminisces about her work in radio and Hollywood. She talks as well about her childhood and some of the sources of her uniquely poetic song interpretations. We also see Ms. Ellis in an intense practice session with her vocal coach. d. Tony Silver; p. T. Silver, James Szalapski; SILVT.

ANN BOLEYN (92m C 1976) The Six Wives of Henry VIII (Series)
Focuses on Henry VIII's desire to produce a male heir, portraying his growing dissatisfaction with Ann Boleyn when her son was born dead. Relates Henry's and Thomas Cromwell's plot to accuse Ann and find her guilty of treason, adultery, and incest. Depicts the trial and beheading of Ann Boleyn as well as the methods used to extract confessions from the accused parties. Reveals Henry's wishes to banish Ann's daughter Elizabeth. p. BBC-TV, TIMLIF; CWU, IU.

ANNA KARENINA (81m C [Scope] 1974)
Based on Leo Tolstoy's famous novel and choreographed by Maya

Plisetskaya to music by Rodion Shchedrin. This film is a vehicle for the extraordinary talents of Mme. Plisetskaya. Co-starring the spectacular Alexander Godunov as Vronsky, Anna Karenina is a completely cinematic rendering of this acclaimed production. Dealing primarily with the psychological elements of the character Anna, the ballet is a genuinely remarkable work, beautiful and penetrating. p. B. Boguslavsky, B. Geller; CORINTH.

ANNAPURNA: A WOMAN'S PLACE (45m C p1980, r1981)
Documents the American Women's '78 Expedition to Annapurna I, 26,540 feet up in the Himalayas, Nepal. The expedition successfully placed the first women/Americans on the summit of Annapurna; two other team members were tragically lost. Explores the women, their process and struggles. It was an all women expedition and film crew as well. d./p. Marie Ashton, Dyanna Taylor; SERBC.

ANNE (40m C 1976)
Are institutionalized mental patients still individuals? This film presents Anne in her mid-fifties who has spent most of her past 20 years in mental hospitals. It deals with her perception of her own situation and the world around her in and out of hospitals. This is a cinema-verté study useful as a base for discussion. Showings are restricted. p. Ben Levin, Eastern Pennsylvania Psychiatric Institute; PSU-TV; PAS.

ANNE MEYERS: BEYOND THE GIFT OF MUSIC (9m C p1981, r1982)
Takes us into the life and feelings of an eleven-year-old violin virtuoso. d./p. Tony De Nonno; DENOP.

ANNE OF CLEVES (94m C 1976) The Six Wives of Henry VIII (Series)
Dramatizes Henry VIII's political marriage to Anne of Cleves, a German princess, to cement England's alliance with Germany against France. Depicts the developing conflict between the Duke of Norfolk and Thomas Cromwell, who suggested the alliance with Anne of Cleves and Germany. Relates Anne's clever maneuver to persuade Henry to agree to an annulment when the political alliance fails. Mentions the eventual dismissal and condemnation of Thomas Cromwell. BBC-TV, TIMLIF; CWU, IU.

ANNIE AND THE OLD ONE (15m C 1976)
A dramatized film for young people, with nonprofessional Navajo actors, about the relationship between a ten-year-old girl and her grandmother. The death of the grandmother is a future event that Annie tries to prevent and, through various plans that children will recognize, she attempts to stop time. By finally accepting the grandmother's understanding of the values of natural cycles--such as birth, growth and death--Annie matures, indicated in the film as becoming ready to learn weaving, the skilled art of the women of her family. The entire film, including the dialogue and thoughts of the characters, is narrated. p. Greenhouse Films, Miska Miles; BFA; UAZ, IU.

ANNIE MAE--BRAVEHEARTED WOMEN (84m C p1980, r1981)
Current Native American history, including Wounded Knee occupation and the killing of two FBI agents on the Pine Ridge Reservation, is traced through the personal perspective of Annie Mae Aquash, a young Indian woman whose commitment to social change resulted in her death. d./p. Lan Brookes Ritz; BROBIP: UMN.

ANNUCIATION (16m C p1976, r1977)
Interweaves moments from a woman's life, revealing many levels of consciousness, traversing past, present, and future. This collaboration between a filmmaker, Marcelo Epstein, and a choreographer, Sandra Adominas, extends the definitions of both media through the sharing of an artistic vision. p./d. Marcelo Epstein. PHOENIX.

ANONYMOUS WAS A WOMAN (30m C p1977, r1978) The Originals: Women in Art Series
Explores the origins of American folk-art traditions in the everyday creative activities of women in the eighteenth and nineteenth centuries. Focuses on samplers, paintings, quilts, rugs and needlework pictures, and describes the lives of the unknown women who created them. Provides a broad aspect of how women and their roles were viewed by men and by themselves. d. Mirra Bank; p. WNET-TV; FI; PAS, UCEMC, UM, UMO, UMN, RARIG.

ANOTHER CHANCE (24m C 1982)
Portrayal of an alternative to prison. Prison fellowship, an international group founded by former Nixon-aide Chuck Colson, began a program of community service projects as restitution for nonviolent offenders. This film documents the first project as six Federal prisoners lived for two weeks with suburban Atlanta families while they insulated and repaired the modest homes of two older women in the inner city. The experiences of the six prisoners and their host families demonstrate the challenging hope that offenders can be involved in active programs of benefit to the community. d. Fran Burst-Terranella; p. Fran Burst-Terranella, Cheryl Gosa; IDEAIM.

ANOTHER KIND OF MUSIC (24m C 1978) (U.S.)
Tells how a young drummer meets a young Jamaican and through their common interest in music became good friends. Can be stimulating in exploring the advantages of a multi-cultural society. For use in elementary and intermediate levels. p. Rebecca Yates, Glen Saltzman, for Frutis and Roots Productions. PHOENIX.

ANTEUS (20m C 1982) (also Video)
Based on a short story by Borden Deal. Designed to inspire students in creative writing classes. p. Elaine Halpert Sperber, Highgate Pictures; d. Mark Cullingham; s.w. Bruce Harmon; LCA.

ANTHONY'S BIRTH AT HOME (17m C n.d.)
When the woman in this film was expecting her first child she

could not find a medical attendant who would come to her home for her labor and delivery. She and her husband decided to have the baby at home without medical supervision with the husband attending. This film tells the story of Anthony, their fifth child, born at home, delivered by his father. p. Jay Hathaway Production; CINMED.

ANTON RASMUSSEN, PAINTER: ABSTRACTIONS FROM NATURE
    (10m C p1977, r1977) Four Artists, Live Series
    Records the creation of an abstract painting from the stage of canvas preparation to the completed work. Anton Rasmussen is observed at work on a large painting as he discusses his method of working, his theories on art and the influence which helped to develop his style. p. Claudia Sizemore; SIZEMF.

ANYONE CAN DANCE (30m C n.d.)
    Stephanie Roberts, a young teacher of experimental dance and movement, demonstrates with a mixed, nonprofessional group of students some of the preliminary exercises and the improvisatory routines which allow ordinary people without formal training to express themselves through movement. p. Open University, Great Britain; AF.

APPETITE OF A BIRD (14m C 1972)
    Animated view of the confusion of man-woman relationships. As man changes into lion form, woman takes on bird form and is crushed beneath the lion's paw. The bird experiences rebirth by crawling through the lion's toes, and rising up to completely devour the lion. SERV; FI; KENTSU.

APPLAUSE (26m C n.d.)
    Dr. Georgette McGregor presents seven steps that will take you from self-consciousness to self-confidence when you are called upon to speak ... whether to an audience of one, 100 or 1,000. This fast-moving film features Dr. McGregor and Fred Holliday; CALLYC.

ARCHERY TECHNIQUES (30m C 1971) (Video)
    Darlene Wells, Advisor, Bear Archery Company, demonstrates the basic techniques of archery. NETCHE.

ARE YOU DOING THIS FOR ME, DOCTOR, OR AM I DOING IT FOR YOU? (52m C 1975) Nova Series
    It is becoming increasingly important that medical experiments be accompanied by high ethical standards. Research projects in some major hospitals reveal such scenes as a relatively dangerous diagnostic procedure which does the sick patient no good at all physically. Present ethical codes rely on the concept of the subject's fully-informed consent. BBC; WSU.

ARE YOU LISTENING SERIES see AT THE HOUSTON WOMEN'S
    CONFERENCE; CHILDREN OF WORKING MOTHERS; COUPLES

WHO ARE SHARING RESPONSIBILITIES; HOUSEHOLD TECHNI-
CIANS; JOURNALISTS AT INTERNATIONAL WOMEN'S YEAR;
KEY WOMEN AT INTERNATIONAL WOMEN'S YEAR; MEN WHO
ARE WORKING WITH WOMEN IN MANAGEMENT; MOTHERS WHO
ARE PART OF SUPPORTIVE DAY CARE; OLDER PEOPLE; PAR-
ENTS AND CHILDREN WHO HAVE ADOPTED EACH OTHER; PEO-
PLE WHO HAVE EPILEPSY; SINGLE PARENTS; VILLAGE WOMEN
IN EGYPT; WIDOWS; WOMEN BUSINESS OWNERS; WOMEN WHO
DIDN'T HAVE AN ABORTION;WOMEN WHO HAVE HAD AN ABOR-
TION; WORLD FEMINISTS

ARSHILE GORKY (29m C 1982) (Video)
The creative growth of the American artist Arshile Gorky is
traced through a detailed look at his art. Extensive interviews with
his wife, sister, and close associates are combined with archival footage to form an intimate portrait. p. Cort Productions Inc.; d. Charlotte Zwerin; DIRECT.

ART CAREERS see ART IN AMERICA, PART V: ART CAREERS

ART IN AMERICA (PT. V): ART CAREERS (30m C 1978) Americana
    Series, Art in America No. 24
    Explains that from the earliest times the artist has played a vital
role in our society. Today the artist collaborates with engineers
and scientists, and helps to shape our future by envisioning what
it might be. At work in their studios, contemporary artists talk
about their work, the beginning of an art career, special demands
of various art disciplines, and how their work is marketed. Professions covered include painting, sculpture, graphic design, industrial
design, illustration, interior design, architecture, photography, teaching museum work, costume design, and crafts. d./p./s.w. Irene
Zmurkevych; HANDEL; PAS, UIL.

ART OF BEING HUMAN, THE (SERIES) see ART OF LIVING--WHAT
    IS LOVE?

ART OF CHINESE COOKING, THE (60m C 1983) (Video)
    This step-by-step video cooking lesson by Madame Wong and
Sylvia Schulman, authors of the million-copy selling Long Life Chinese
Cookbook, shows how to prepare a complete Chinese meal. p./d.
Gary Youngman; DIRECT.

ART OF DANCING: AN INTRODUCTION TO BAROQUE DANCE, THE
    (21m B 1979) (Video)
    The program is based on Kellom Tomlinson's dance manual, "The
Art of Dancing," first published in London in 1720. The focus is
on the minuet, which is presented as a dancing lesson by Mr. Tom-
linson, Dancing Master, who narrates the program. Choreographer:
Catherine Turocy; d. Catherine Turocy/Celia Ipiotis; p. C. Turocy,
C. Ipiotis, Jeff Bush; ARCVD.

ART OF FILM SERIES, THE see ROLE OF WOMEN IN MOVIES, THE

ART OF LIVING: WHAT IS LOVE?, THE (60m C 1978) (Video)
An author engages in writing a history of love. Through his thought and fantasies, choreographed and danced by a ballet troupe, new insights are developed on the multiple meanings of one of humanity's most elusive ideas. The focus is on sexist attitudes and stereotyped roles. By following the lives and thoughts of five people before, during, and after a 20th high school reunion, the film dramatizes the difference between what people actually are and what they pretend to be for society's sake. p. Miami-Dade Community College; FI.

ART ON THE OUTSIDE (17m C p1980, r1980)
A college program in which students are trained to conduct art workshops for the aged, the mentally ill, urban ghetto youth and prison inmates. The film shows how this program, by offering people in community institutions an informal "artistic" experience, helps them to develop a sense of personal worth and potential. d. Professor Judith Peck; p. Jay Kaufman; RAMAPO.

ART SCENE: NEWTON ELEMENTARY SCHOOLS (13m C 1976)
Shows variety of elementary art teaching techniques in Newton, Maine: open classrooms, art appreciation, instruction, multimedia teaching, teaching art through nature perception, learning by doing. d./p. Judith Grunbaum; GREENBJ; PAS.

ART STUDIO TOO (30m ea. B n.d.) (Video, Beta, VHS)
Hostess Linda Schmid, a grade-school teacher, shows how to use common and inexpensive household items to create art objects and uses examples of visual art--from every period of time--to inspire easy-to-do family projects. p. KQED-TV; KQEDTV.
These are films in the program: YOU; MORE THAN YOU; FACE IN THE MIRROR; PORTRAITS; THE EYES HAVE IT; LOOK OUT; THE COLLECTOR; WRAP IT UP; PEACE; U'S AND I'S; PRINT; HEAR AND NOW; SNIP SNAPSHOT; WATCH OUT; PETS AND PALS; THE ELEPHANT IS AN ODD ANIMAL; JUST IMAGINE; TREES, PLEASE; MOODS IN LANDSCAPES; CITY IMPRESSIONS; CITY RHYTHMS; THE CITY IS A PLACE FOR PEOPLE?; ON THE WATERFRONT; THE LOWER DEPTHS; FLYING CREATURE; OUTER SPACE; GET MOVING; URBAN SUBURBAN

ARTISAN, THE (13m C p1977, r1978)
Shows a young man walking through the town's industries to the solitude of his own studio. Here, the film chronicles this person's journey through the painstaking process of creating a musical instrument--a guitar. From the solitude of swirling wood shavings and the warm timbre of tools, accompanied by a personal commitment to expression, a thing of lasting artistry emerges. d. Steve Marts; p. Ruth Marts; ESSENTIA.

ARTIST AND THE COMPUTER (10M C 1976)
Shows Lillian Schwartz at work on her computer animation films.
Gives a fascinating background on her painting and sculpture. p.
Larry Keating Productions, Inc. for AT&T; LILYANP.

ARTIST WAS A WOMAN, THE (58m C p1980, r1980) (also Video)
A social history of women artists from 1550 to 1950. Features
a representative survey of the achievements of women in art beginning with Renaissance painter Artemesia Gentileschi and ending with
a final interview with French decorative artist Sonia Delaunay prior
to her death in 1980. Includes interviews with Germaine Greer, Linda
Nochlin and Ann Harris. Jane Alexander narrates. d. Suzanne
Bauman; p. S. Bauman, Mary Bell; ABCWWL; UIL, UMN.

ARTISTIC GYMNASTIC EVENTS CIA U SERIES see WOMEN'S
FLOOR EXERCISES

ARTISTS AT WORK: A FILM ON THE NEW DEAL ART PROJECTS
(35m C 1981)
A documentary on the New Deal art projects by Mary Lance.
Focuses on the federal programs for the support of artists during
the Depression. Includes interviews with Alice Neel, Chaim Gross,
Lee Krasner, Jacob Lawrence, and several other artists. d./p.
Mary Lance; NEWDAY.

ARTISTS IN THE LAB (57m C 1982) (Video) Nova Series
A look at twentieth-century pioneers who are using computers
and lasers to produce an array of new artistic expressions. Among
the new art forms studied are video and the three-dimensional "photos" called holograms. p. WGBH-TV/Barbara Holecek; s.w. Barbara
Holecek; TIMLIF.

ARTS AND CRAFTS (28m C p1979, r1979)
An explanation distinguishing arts from crafts opens this film
which shows craftmaking today. The film covers making of pottery,
baskets, quilts, textiles, tapestries, furniture, glass, silver objects,
jewelry, blacksmithing materials, decorated eggs, paper designs, and
musical instruments. In each case, a brief history of the craft in
the U.S. precedes the demonstration by an artist. A good introductory film for those beginning in the study of arts and crafts. d./p.
Irene Zmurkevych; HANDEL.

ARVILLA (29m C 1977) (Video, Beta, VHS)
A portrait of Arvilla Groesbeck, a 63-year-old woman dairy farmer
struggling to survive in an occupation where male dominance is still
unchallenged. After several years of working her upstate New York
farm alone, she was unable to keep up payments and lost the farm.
She now keeps her 22 cows in rented barns and sells their milk,
which is her only source of income. The program shows Arvilla working in the barns and fields as she talks about her life, politics and
economic problems. p. WMHT-TV; PBSV.

AS IF BY MAGIC (11m ? 1981)
This documentary follows puppeteer Louie Gizyn as she designs and performs the opera Carmen with a large and decorative cast of handcrafted puppets. Music performed by the Portland Opera Association with effects by Billy Scream. p./d. Jan Baross; MEDIAP.

AS IF IT WERE YESTERDAY (86m B p1979, r1980)
Documents the little known heroism of the Belgian people who, during the Nazi occupation, hid, placed or helped over 4,000 Jewish children escape deportation and extermination, often doing so at the risk of their own lives. This film is made by two women--one American (Myriam Abramowicz) and one French (Esther Hoffenberg)-- whose parents both spent the war in hiding. Through interviews with grown-up survivors and with Belgians who hid Jewish children, a deeply moving story unfolds that will never obliterate the cruel, heinous and destructive aspects of recent history, but that allows us "to not lose sight of a great number of generous examples given by people of good will." p./d. Myriam Abramowicz, Esther Hoffenberg; ALMI.

AS IT HAPPENED SERIES see SHE ALSO RAN

AS LONG AS THERE IS LIFE (40m C p1980, r1980)
A cinema-verité record of the last six weeks of life of Pat Forest, a young woman with two children, who is dying of cancer. It shows the role of the Hospice home care team in helping the family cope with the crises. d. Bill Jersey; p. Alberta Jacoby; HOSPICE.

ASANTE MARKET WOMAN (52m C 1982) (Video) Disappearing World
  Series
In the Asante tribe of Ghana, men are polygamous and women are subordinate in all domestic matters. But surprisingly, there is one arena where women reign supreme--the market place. These tough, assertive women have evolved their own power structure. A head woman--the queenmother--arbitrates all disputes over price and quality. Amidst the noise and color of the Kumasi Central Market we perceive the intricacies of this matrilineal society. d. Claudia Milne; p. Andre Singer for Granada Television International; FILMLB.

ASIAN NEIGHBORS--INDONESIA SERIES, THE see MASTRI--A
  BALINESE WOMAN

ASPARAGUS (19m C 1978)
The artist describes this film as "an erotic allegory of the creative process in which a woman views and performs the passages of sensual and artistic discovery." It is also the masterwork of contemporary American animation, integrating a variety of techniques with spectacular artistry. p. Susan Pitts; BELVFF, UMN.

ASSERTIVENESS ISSUES (15m C 1981) (also Video) Trigger Films
  on Human Interaction Series

This open-ended film is designed to help people who are learning how to assert their rights or points of view. The 12 vignettes will give participants opportunities to develop their own style of self-assertion through practicing a range of situations. A guide is included. p. Family Information Systems and Resource Communication; MTITI.

ASTRONAUT SALLY RIDE (15m C 1979) Women in Science Series, Pt. IV
An interdisciplinary panel of women scientists, featured at the Washington State University "Futures in Science for Women" Conference, discuss their work and their lives in Parts I and II. The Panel answers questions from the audience of undergraduate women science majors in Part III. Conference keynote speaker Sally Ride, NASA astronaut, is interviewed in Part IV. p. Kelly Frederickson, KWSU-TV; WSU.

AT MY AGE (26m B 1966)
Generates interest in the unique employment, personal problems, and work potential of older people looking for new jobs before and after retirement age. Includes tips on how to help older workers interpret, understand, and adapt prior work habits to new work environment. NAVC; UIO.

AT THE HOUSTON WOMEN'S CONFERENCE (29m C 1977) (Video)
Are You Listening Series
This program, made at the first national women's conference in Houston, Texas in 1977, was originally broadcast as a one-hour live special on KPRC-TV. There are two parts to the program: the first, three short selections from earlier "Are You Listening" programs (Household Technicians, Key Women at International Women's Year, Women Business Owners); the second, a studio discussion among leading women from the conference about the issues raised in these segments and by the conference itself. The participants, all active in women's issues, talked particularly about the media and its impact not only on this conference but on the entire process of defining issues in the women's movement. This is a high-powered group discussing issues crucial to the continued development of the woman's movement and will be of interest to anyone who shares these concerns. p./d. Martha Stuart; STUARTM.

AT THE TIME OF WHALING (45m C n.d.) The Alaska Native Heritage Film Series
Examines the economic and cultural transition and the conflicts and dilemmas that face people in Shungnak. Nostalgic for the stability of traditional life yet seeking freedom from the dangers of the past, Alaskan Eskimos juggle old with new, confronted and encompassed by cultural change. p. Sarah Elder, Leonard Kamerling; DER.

ATHENS see MELINA MERCOURI'S ATHENS

ATOMIC CAFE, THE (88m C/B 1982)
    Radioactive rock 'n' roll, blues, country, and gospel music punc-
tuate this compilation film of government, schoolroom and early TV
reportage extolling the glories of the bomb, and warning Americans
to "duck and cover" in the event of an attack. Jackie Doll and His
Pickled Peppers and Little Caesar join Harry S Truman and Nikita
Khrushchev in a journey of chilling nostalgia. p./d. Kevin Rafferty,
Jane Loader, Pierce Rafferty; The Archives Project, Inc.; NYF.

ATTIC SONGS (15m C 1975)
    Multiple images of dancing figure and body parts. Dancer/Chor-
eographer: Susie Bauer; p. E. J. Clark; CLARKEJ.

AUDITION (9m C 1981)
    In this animated film, a young woman prepares herself for a the-
atrical audition. While worrying about the try-out, the aspiring
actress/singer grapples with her conflicting desires for a career and
a family. Her dilemma is universal. p. Candy Kugel; DIRECT.

AUGUST 1978 (6m C 1978)
    A young woman holding an umbrella walks, head down, along
a beach. The subject of her reverie is a man whose image approaches
and recedes again and again, with the rhythm of a painful memory.
The third shot, of trees sliding past to the roar of a passing train
underscores the increasing time and distance separating the woman
from the man. p. Susan Rubin; RUBINS.

AUGUSTA (17m C r1978)
    Daughter of a Shuswap chief, Augusta was separated from her
parents at age four. She was sent to a Catholic mission school where
only English was allowed. She married a white man in 1903, thus
losing her status as an Indian. The film knits together pieces of
Augusta's past and present life. Today, at 88, Augusta lives alone
in a log cabin without running water or electricity in the Caribou
country of British Columbia. This is her home, and she wouldn't
live anywhere else. d. Ann Wheeler; p. John Taylor; ex. p. J.
Taylor, Peter Jones; NFBC; PHOENIX.

AUTHOR SERIES, THE see AUTHORS: EMILY DICKINSON, THE

AUTHORS: EMILY DICKINSON, THE (22m C p1977, r1978)
    A professional actress, Susan Kay Monts, recreates the person-
ality of the famous poet in a garden monologue scene. She recounts
some of her attitudes regarding significant events and people in her
lifetime. p. Gilbert Altschul Productions and Producers Group; JOU;
UIL.

AUTOBIOGRAPHY OF A PRINCESS (57m C 1975)
    Interweaves rare archive footage shot in India in the 1920's,
1930's, and 1940's of life at the courts of the maharajahs with a

fictional story of two of the survivors of that way of life. These survivors, a Rajput princess living in self-imposed exile from the modern India she can no longer face, and an old Englishman who was tutor to her father, meet to reminisce about a way of life that is now completely vanished. d. James Ivory; p. Ismail Merchant, Merchant Ivory Production; s.w. Ruth Prawer Jhabvala; ALMI, CORINTH.

AUTUMN AFTERNOON, AN (112m C 1962) (Japanese/Subtitled)
Presents the tale of a widower's decision to marry off his only daughter. Includes a look at ultra-modern Japan where golf on the rooftops is the "in" thing, but where women are still bartered in marriage. d. Yasujiro Ozu; NYF.

AUTUMN PASSAGE (26m C p1980, r1980)
Traces the subtle changes that occur on the prairies and farmlands of the Midwest as fall gives way to winter. This is a poetically beautiful film. p. Christine Olsenius, d. Richard Olsenius; BLUEST.

AWAKE FROM MOURNING (50m C p1981, r1982) (also Video)
Focuses on three women who struggle against the indignities of South Africa's racial policies in Soweto, a black community near Johannesburg. All three have suffered imprisonment and still suffer feelings of terror, but resolutely try to help their people, especially the women who are isolated in that place. This is a distressing but thought-provoking film well visualized with historic motion pictures and in-depth interviews with the principal figures involved in the improvements taking place in Soweto, South Africa. p. Chris Austin, Betty Wolpert, London; VILLON.

AYAKO AND JOE (40m C p1982, r1983) (Video)
A portrait of an American family from different racial and cultural backgrounds. Joe, the husband and father of the family, is American. Ayako, the wife and mother, is Japanese. This tape examines the mismatch of cultural expectations and the pressures on such a marriage in America. p./d. Daw-Ming Lee; TEMPLU.

AYN RAND--INTERVIEW (25m C n.d.) (Video)
Ayn Rand's novels Atlas Shrugged and The Fountainhead and her unique philosophy of objectivism have gained her a worldwide audience. In this interview program, Ms. Rand describes her point of view and the background and influences that helped form her philosophy. NORTONJ.

-B-

BABBAGE'S CALCULATING MACHINE OR DIFFERENCE ENGINE (4m C 1968)
A brief visual essay on Babbage's calculating machine--the forerunner of today's electronic computer. Opens with a view of the

mechanical apparatus of the calculating machine (difference engine) actually operating, with a narrator reading the inventor's original directions for how to use the machine. Excellent for visualizing a complex machine that is relatively simple compared to today's modern computers. d./p. Ray Eames, Charles Eames; PF.

BABIES MAKING BABIES (25m C 1980) (also Video)
A dramatization on the sexual morals of two black teenagers. Through the eyes of a pregnant 13-year-old girl named Yonda, insight is gained into the problem of black girls having babies at lower and lower ages. As Yonda recounts the events that led to her own pregnancy, she reveals the frustrations and dilemmas of a young black woman in today's society. This film is geared to elicit discussions following its screening. p. Black Spectrum Theater; BLACKFL.

BABY CLOCK (54m C 1982) (Video)
A sensitive look into the lives of five articulate career women in their thirties who make their own choices about having children, dealing with many of the concerns faced by all women under the pressure of the biological countdown. d./p. Elvira Lount; ed. Barbara Evans; original music: Ann Mortifee; MELKIM.

BABY MAKERS, THE (43m C p1979, r1980) (also Video)
Birth without sex, frozen embryos and selective breeding are concepts once confined to science fiction; now they are becoming reality. The birth of Baby Louise, the world's first "test-tube baby," received worldwide attention, yet the art of artificial reproduction is often practiced in an atmosphere of secrecy. Explores the many controversies, as well as the moral and ethical questions, surrounding artificial insemination, egg-embryo manipulations (babies created outside the body), and the use of surrogate mothers. Offers never-before-seen footage, such as the actual freezing of embryos. p. Jay L. McMullen; CBS-TV; CRM; USFL, USC, UIL, IU, KENTSU.

BABY STORY (11m C 1979)
This animated cartoon by Bruno Bozzetto interprets the processes going on in the womb during intercourse, fertilization, pregnancy, and birth. The ovule is personified by a frumpy queen reigning from a cracked eggshell, the sperm become Keystone Cop figures battling their way to the queen's chamber. Once fertilized, the ovum turns into a baby which comically reflects the activities of the mother. Ends with the baby being coaxed from his home in the womb into the bright lights of the delivery room. p./d. Bruno Bozzetto; FI; UIL.

BABYDANCE (15m C 1978)
Features a woman who has been a dancer for ten years. Then she danced for eight months during her pregnancy and started a class in dance and exercise for expectant mothers. Some of the feelings of pregnancy are discussed including the need for daily naps,

how activities have helped stabilize her shifting moods, and the good feeling of being with growing things. p. Elysa Markowitz, Dan Bessie, Babydance Productions; STANFH.

BABYSITTER SERIES see HANDLING BABYSITTING EMERGENCIES; PLANNING BABYSITTING; UNDERSTANDING BABYSITTING

BABYSITTERS' GUIDE (10m C 1975)
    A fire? A poisoning? A stranger at the door? Situations like these can confront any babysitter. From the first meeting with the parents to the trip home after a job well done, the film discusses all the steps necessary for a safe and happy experience for both sitter and child. p. Sid Davis Productions; AIMS.

BABYSITTING (27m C 1973) Community Protection Series
    Stresses the responsibility involved in babysitting and that babysitters should be qualified for the job, especially in the face of emergencies. Covers many aspects of dos and don'ts and relates babysitting to both young people and parents. Summerhill Productions; PARACO; AIMS.

BABYSITTING BASICS (12m C 1975)
    After exploring the great variety of duties performed by the babysitter, the film follows a young sitter through a typical experience, illustrating the advantage of meeting the family and children before the actual time of the job, the wisdom of prompt arrival, how to determine a fair pay scale, and the essential information the sitter must know. The film covers specifically what to do about emergencies, opening the door to strangers, bedtime and discipline, personal safety, and much more. p. Charles Cahill and Associates, Inc.; AIMS.

BABYSWIM (13m C p1979, r1980)
    An impressionistic look at a swim class for babies in the Bahamas. Aged 6 to 18 months, the babies are shown in swimming pools and in the ocean, by day and by night, on diving boards and on the coral reef. Shot mostly underwater, and set to an original musical score, it shows that infants have little fear of the element they knew so well before birth. d. Harriet Lynch, John Hoskyns-Abrahall; p. H. Lynch; BULFRG; PAS, UIL.

BACKTRACK (14m C 1977)
    This is a nightmare for the "freed" exponents of casual sex. A man finds out from the family lawyer, when he attempts to collect his mother's inheritance, that his mother had been supporting the man's daughter. The man has no knowledge of a daughter, but remembers a liaison 16 years before that has apparently resulted in a 15-year-old daughter. He traces the friend's whereabouts because he wants to see his daughter. He finally meets his daughter, a victim of Down's syndrome. A good discussion film on sexual responsibility,

and whether one can be really "sexually" free.   p. Ron Ellis; PHOE-
NIX, VIEWFI.

BAD BOYS (120m B p1978 [ed.], r1979) (also Video)
    Examines in cinema verité the treatment of troubled youth at three
institutions: Bryant High School, Spofford Juvenile Center, and
Brookwood Center (a maximum security prison for boys under 16
years of age who have committed designated felonies).   p. Susan
Raymond, Alan Raymond; p. Video Verité Production; DIRECT.

BALI: THE MASK OF RANGDA (30m C 1975)
    In Bali, the link between humanity and God, conscious and un-
conscious, is acted out frequently in elaborate ceremonies and dramatic performances, such as the self-stabbing trance of Barong-
Rangda and the Ketjak trance. Filmed recently in remote villages
of Bali far away from presentations of similar rites performed for
tourists, this film is an authentic picture of a culture, as yet un-
touched by the West, which has developed this extraordinary means
of exorcising violence to preserve "The Spirit of Cooperation."   p.
Elda Hartley; HARTLEY.

BALINESE TRANCE SEANCE, A (30m C n.d.)
    Jero Tapakan, a spirit medium in a small, central Balinese village,
consults with a group of clients in her household shrine. An introduction precedes the main séance, providing a visual impression of
a séance and background information on the medium and her profession. The clients wish to contact the spirit of their dead son, to
discover the cause of his death and his wishes for his cremation
ceremony. Jero is possessed several times in the course of the séance: first by a protective house-yard deity who demands propitiatory
offerings that had previously been overlooked; then by the spirit
of the petitioner's deceased father, who requests further offerings
to ease his path in the other world; and finally by the spirit of the
son. In an emotional scene the son's spirit reveals the cause of
his premature death (vengeful magic) and instructions for his forth-
coming cremation. Between each trance the medium converses with
her clients, clarifying vague points in the often ambiguous trance
speech. p. Linda Connor, Timothy Asch; DER.

BALLAD OF LUCY JORDAN, by Ian Moo Young see ANIMATED
    WOMEN

BALLAD OF THE LITTLE SQUARE (7m C 1953)
    Dance drama suggested by a poem by Federico García Lorca.
The dancer is Harriette Ann Gray. p. Portia Mansfield; MANSPR.

BALLERINA (28m B 1963)
    This film is about ballet dancer Margaret Mercier, Prima Ballerina
of Les Grands Ballets Canadiens, graduate of Sadler's Wells Ballet
and student of the Bolshoi Ballet. The film follows her through

rehearsal and a scene from Prokofiev's Cinderella. Choreographers:
Ludmilla Chiriaeff, George Kaczender; d. George Kaczender; p. Nicholas Balla; NFBC.

BALLET FOR ALL--1: HOW BALLET BEGAN (26m B 1972)
First of a series of seven films performed by Ballet for All, an
offshoot of the Royal Ballet. The series was first presented on
Thames Television. Each program combines narration and dance excerpts. The first traces ballet from the mid-seventeenth-century
royal European courts through the early nineteenth-century. Excerpts are from Ballet de la Nuit (1653), Jon Weaver's Loves of Mars
and Venus (1716), Jean Georges Noverre's Petits Riens (1778), Bournonville's Konservatoriet (1849). Leading off the film are the last
part of the adagio of the Sleeping Beauty pas de deux and part of
the duet from Kenneth MacMillan's Concerto. Dance Company: Ballet for All. Choreographer: Mary Skeaping. d. Nicholas Ferguson;
p. Thames Television; HERVSL; UIL.

BALLET FOR ALL--2: BALLET ENTERS THE WORLD STAGE (28m
B 1972)
Excerpts from Giselle in a version for four dancers, one piano,
and one viola. The accompanying narration touches on stylistic,
thematic, and costume developments and mime language. Also in
the film is the Sylph's opening dance from Bournonville's La Sylphide.
Dance Company: Ballet for All. d. Nicholas Ferguson. p. Thames
Television; HERVSL; UIL.

BALLET FOR ALL--3: HOW BALLET WAS SAVED (29m B 1972)
Excerpts from the modern and the original versions of Coppelia.
The 1870 version, in which a woman was used in the role of Franz,
is based on the memories of Paulette Dynalix. The narrator contrasts modern and original style and ballet training and talks about
the male role in ballet of the 1870's. Dance Company: Ballet for
All. d. Nicholas Ferguson; p. Thames Television; HERVSL; UIL.

BALLET FOR ALL--4: TCHAIKOVSKY AND THE RUSSIANS (27m
B 1972)
Compares Marius Petipa and Lev Ivanov, particularly discussing
Ivanov's portions of Swan Lake. The complete adagio from Act II
is danced in costume. Other excerpts are the adagio from the Sleeping Beauty pas de deux and the coda of the Bluebird pas de deux.
Also, there are film clips of the Bolshoi corps dancing in Swan Lake,
Act IV. Dance Company: Ballet for All, Bolshoi Ballet (briefly).
Choreographers: Marius Petipa, Lev Ivanov. d. Nicholas Ferguson;
p. Thames Television; HERVSL; UIL.

BALLET FOR ALL--5: THE BEGINNINGS OF TODAY (27m B 1972)
Focuses on these excerpts with narration: the waltz pas de deux
from Les Sylphides; parts of the Swan Lake and Sleeping Beauty
duets; the male solo from Les Sylphides; two parts from Petrouchka;

Pavlova in parts of two solos, "La Nuit" and "Dying Swan." Dance Company: Ballet for All. Choreographers: Michel Fokine, Marius Petipa. d. Nicholas Ferguson; p. Thames Television; HERVSL; UIL.

BALLET FOR ALL--6: BALLET COMES TO BRITAIN (26m B 1972)
Most of these excerpts are from English versions of Diaghilev ballets: the Ballet Rambert version of Nijinsky's Afternoon of a Faun; the cancan duet from Massine's La Botique Fantasque (1919); the hostess' solo from Nijinska's Les Biches (1924). Also, there are excerpts from Ninette de Balois' The Rake's Progress. Dance Companies: British Royal Ballet, Ballet Rambert. Choreographers: Vaslav Nijinsky, Leonide Massine, Bronislava Nijinska, Ninette de Valois. d. Nicholas Ferguson; p. Thames Television; HERVSL; UIL.

BALLET FOR ALL--7: BRITISH BALLET TODAY (26m B 1972)
Prefaced by the duet from Kenneth MacMillan's Concerto, most of this film presents portions of Frederick Ashton's La Fille Mal Gardée (1960). Dance Company: Ballet for All. Choreographers: Kenneth MacMillan, Frederick Ashton. d. Nicholas Ferguson; p. Thames Television; HERVSL; UIL.

BALLOON SAFARI (55m C p1978, r1981) (also Video)
Presents Alan Root with his wife, Joan, exploring the intricacies of hot air ballooning over the African Plains. The beauty and wonder of the Masai people, the Tsavo Game Preserve, the Amboseli National Park, and the Lake Naivsha region near Nairobi are captured by the filmmakers. Narrated by David Niven. p. Joan Root/Alan Root; BENCHMF.

BARABAIG, THE (39m C p1978, r1979)
Explains the ecological adaptations and socioeconomic system of an East African herding society. This film documents the field work of anthropologist George J. Klima. The Barabaig are cattle herders who live high in the rolling plains of northern Tanzania in North Africa. Women are seen as they prepare the skin of a dead animal to be used for clothing and sew glass beads, acquired from traders, onto garments to be used for special celebrations. A wedding is filmed showing the bride anointed from head to foot with ocher and butter; the groom does not attend his own wedding. A circumcision ceremony is held for young boys. Women punish two men by beating one of their bulls to death because they infringed on women's rights by watching a woman in childbirth. The scientist Klima proves to what extent their lives revolve around their cattle, with social customs passed from one generation to the next. p. George J. Klima; PAS.

BARB: BREAKING THE CYCLE OF ABUSE (28m C 1978)
Shows the role of the social worker in providing long-term guidance and support with sensitivity and realism. Shows scenes from actual counseling workshops, intercut with re-enactments to tell the

story of a young woman, Barb, and her struggle in dealing with the
frustrations and tensions that caused her to beat her child. In her
therapy sessions Barb learns there are others who abuse their children and admit they had. Finally Barb was able to face up to the
fact that she had indeed abused her child, and with the therapist's
help, begins exploration of some of the deeply rooted fears and problems that caused her abusive behavior. p. Cavalcade Productions,
Inc.; d./s.w. Dale McCulley; MTITI.

BARBARA ROQUEMORE (PARACHUTING) (22m C n.d.) Women in
Sports--A Series
Accuracy and style make a winner in parachuting competition,
a sport where judges have repeatedly found Barbara Roquemore a
champion. After watching Barbara fall 2,500 feet to land within one
foot of a four-inch target, it is astonishing to learn that she is afraid
of heights. She says, "I have a desire to learn in spite of fear."
p. Tele-Sports; PARACO.

BAROQUE DANCE, 1675-1725 (23m C 1979) (also Video) The Movement Style and Culture (Series)
The film with its expository method treats the many facets of
baroque dance as it travels from ballroom to theater. A highlight
and culminating dance, "Suite for Diana and Mars," choreographed
for John Dryden's Secular Masque, was first performed in London
in 1700. Although the original choreography and music were lost,
other dances of the period offer a fair degree of authenticity. The
background research in dance, music and costume is lucid, comprehensive, and adds significant depth to the visual images. However,
the film itself would be more effective with a stereo sound track.
d. Allegra Fuller Snyder, Shirley Wynne; UCEMC.

BARREL: A DANCE MIME, THE (11m C n.d.)
This short film presents a dance mime adapted from Edna St.
Vincent Millay's poem about Diogenes in search of an honest man,
and finding a woman in a barrel. Choreographer: Harriette Ann
Gray; d. Barney Brown; Portia Mansfield Motion Pictures; MANSPR.

BASIC NUTRITION: LET'S MAKE A MEAL (17m C 1981)
In a fast-paced, lively game show, an emcee and nutritionist
help contestants learn facts and fallacies of nutrition, including how
the body uses nutrients, calories and weight, diet and disease, and
helpful meal planning. p. Professional Research, Inc.; FLMFR.

BATHING YOUR BABY ... A TOUCH OF LOVE (20 m C n.d.)
Demonstrates, step by step, the proper way to bathe a baby.
Emphasizes the importance of touch in the physical and emotional
development of an infant. Replaces the film Baths and Babies. Free
loan. Johnson and Johnson Baby Products Company; MTPS; WSU.

BATTERED (98m C 1979)
This unflinching drama deals with a widespread but largely

concealed social problem--wife-beating--and tells of the agencies now available to help these women. Starring Karen Grassle. For edited version, see BATTERED WIVES. LCA.

BATTERED CHILD (58m B 1977)
    A documentary study of child abuse based on the book The Battered Child by Drs. C. Henry Kempe and Roy E. Helfer. These doctors have created a team consisting of psychiatrists, pediatricians, and social workers to study the causes of physical child abuse and to treat children affected mentally. The team is shown at the University of Colorado Medical Center working with actual cases. It is argued that the mental illness evidenced by parents who abuse children is as real as the consequent suffering of the children and, therefore, these parents may need psychiatric therapy rather than penal action. NET; IU; UMN, UM.

BATTERED TEENS (11m C p1980, r1982) (also Video)
    History has shown that the abused child often becomes the abused teenager and, eventually, an abusive parent. This film tells the story of Lisa Hutchinson, age 16, and her parents, who are attempting to break the tragic chain of abuse. Lisa's parents attend a group called Parents Anonymous to talk through their problems, and Lisa helped organize a teen group where abused teens can help each other. CBS News; FI.

BATTERED WIVES (29m C 1979) (Video) Woman Series
    Lisa Leghorn, co-author of Houseworkers' Handbook, and Del Martin, author of Battered Wives and coordinator of the National Organization for Women's Task Force on Battered Women and Household Violence, discuss wife-beating and the problems faced by victims and law enforcement agencies in dealing with it. Sandra Elkin, moderator. p. WNED-TV, Buffalo, NY; PBSV.

BATTERED WIVES (45m C p1977, r1979)
    Examines the problem of woman abuse and tells what community resources are available and ways of dealing with family violence. Two marriages in which husbands beat their wives are dramatized in this film, which can be a springboard for discussions on family crisis. d. Peter Werner; p. Henry Jaffe Enterprises; LCA; CWU, UCEMC, KENTSU, IU.

BATTERED WIVES: A LEGACY OF VIOLENCE (29m C 1980)
    Explores the historical, social, psychological and legal complications of the problem of wife abuse. Discussion guide available. p. Transition House; WOMEYE.

BATTERED WOMEN: VIOLENCE BEHIND CLOSED DOORS (24m C 1977)
    In group discussions and individual interviews, victims and aggressors offer insights into the causes and consequences of wife-

beating. Also explores some support systems available to battered women and their children. Awards. MTITI; UCEMC, IU, PAS, UM.

BATTLE FOR THE VOTE, THE (29m C 1975) (Video) Woman Series
Part I
Midge MacKenzie, the British film director and writer who created and produced the television series "Shoulder to Shoulder," explains her interest in the suffragists. She describes the lives of militant suffragist movement leaders Emmeline and Christabel Pankhurst, and talks about some of the confrontation tactics used by movement participants. She also describes the hunger strikes staged by women in prison and the violence suffered by women who publicly demonstrated for suffrage. Sandra Elkin is the moderator. p. WNED-TV, Buffalo, NY; PBSV.

BATTLE FOR THE VOTE, THE (29m C 1975) (Video) Woman Series
Part II
Midge MacKenzie, the British film director and writer who created and produced the television series "Shoulder to Shoulder," discusses what she calls the "hidden history" of the fight for women's suffrage. She tells of the great personal hardships endured by British suffragettes and of their determination to win the vote in spite of beatings and violence. Sandra Elkin is the moderator. p. WNED-TV, Buffalo, NY; PBSV.

BATTLE OF BEECH HALL (28m C 1981)
Documents an eight-month struggle by senior citizens to save their homes. Politicians in Toronto's Borough of York had decided to "phase out" the subsidized apartment complex of Beech Hall to make way for a new development. The residents--all senior citizens-- were asked to vacate the premises. However, with help from a young alderman and a tenant organizer the seniors launched a determined campaign to save their homes, their self-respect and their independence. d./p. Christopher Wilson; p. Cinemagic Productions; UIL, UM.

BATTLE OF THE WESTLANDS, THE (59m C 1980) (Video, Beta, VHS)
Discusses the conflict between agribusiness corporations and small farmers. At issue is control of 600,000 acres of California's vast Central Valley, the Westlands District, one of the richest farmlands in the world. The irrigation project was part of a federal land reclamation project designed to populate previously arid lands of the western states with thousands of new farmers who would live on the land they worked. Twenty years after the project was inaugurated, only a little over 200 farming operations exist, basically owned by ten companies. Now the federal government has decided to enforce laws limiting the size of farms that benefit from federal water projects. At the heart of the issue is who shall control America's food supply and its price. There are a dozen bills before Congress now to resolve this "classic American struggle." d./p. Sandra Nichols, Carol Mon Pere; KTEH-TV, San Jose; MMA.

BAXTERS: SUSAN'S NEW JOB, THE (22m C 1978) The Baxters
(Series)
Susan is offered a promotion which will cause her salary to exceed Stan's. He does not want to diminish her job, but his feelings
of insecurity are too great. They are expressed in Stan's troubled
sleep in a male chauvinist's nightmare of role reversals--a hilarious
"sitcom" with serious implications, later brought out by members
of the audience. p. WCVB-TV, British Broadcasting Institute; ABC-
TV; UIL.

BAXTERS, THE (SERIES) see BAXTERS: SUSAN'S NEW JOB,
THE

BAYADERKA: A CLASSICAL BALLET (9m B 1943)
Presents scenes from the Bayaderka Ballet performed by the
Ensemble of the Leningrad State Academy Theatre of Opera and Bal-
let, featuring Natalia Dudinskaya and Vachtang Tchabukiani. Choreo-
grapher: Marius Petipa; composer: Leon Minkus. p. Leningrad
Film Studios, Artkino; MACMFL; IU, UU, SYRACU.

BAYADERKA BALLET see BAYADERKA: A CLASSICAL BALLET

BE FAIR TO YOUR FOOD (17m C p1980, r1980)
Shows that many foods contain important nutrients which may
be easily destroyed if we do not know the proper ways of shopping
for, storing and cooking them, and how to protect foods from heat,
light, air and water. d. Stephen Wallen; p. Alfred Higgins Productions; HIGGIN.

BEAN PLANET (2m C 1979)
An exercise in metamorphoses: the seeds are sown, the plant
grows. p. Joanne Corso; SERBC.

BEAT PLUS ONE (3m C 1982) (Video)
A work concerned with form, color, rhythm and movement. Com-
puter-generated imagery is intertwined with a percussive audio track.
There are rhythmic permutations in time encompassing chroma phase
shifts, movements within animated modules, sequencing of these modules, and rapid-fire editing. Video is two media in one. Neither
the aural nor the visual axis should dominate the other. In this
tape, the music and the imagery in unison synthesize a confluent
form. d. Maureen Nappi; s.w./ed./camera: Maureen Nappi; original music: Liquid Liquid; NAPPIM.

BEATRIX POTTER: A PRIVATE WORLD (42m C 1979)
Examines the life of Beatrix Potter, author of many of the best-
known children's books. Filmed largely in England's Lake District
which was so much a part of her life and books. Drawing on the
diaries which she wrote--in code--as a young girl, her books and

the memories of those who knew her, this film provides a fascinating
insight into the private world of Beatrix Potter. CANTOR.

BEAUTIFUL LENNARD ISLAND (23m C n.d.)
   Lennard Island is a beautiful bit of land in the rough seas of
Canada's west coast. Only four people live there: Stephen Holland,
his parents, and his brother, David. Stephen narrates this film.
To Stephen and others of his family, life of a lighthouse keeper is
not one of boredom or loneliness. Stephen remains an ordinary boy,
joyful at being able to have an extraordinary childhood. d. Beverly
Shaffer; p. Yuki Yoshida, Kathleen Shannon; NFBC; MEDIAG;
KENTSU.

BEAUTY AND THE BEAST; PTS I AND II (50m C n.d.)
   This unusual and entertaining production of the delightful fairy
tale combines the dramatic narrative of Miss Hayley Mills with the
lavish staging of the San Francisco Ballet and the music of Tchaikovsky, performed by the San Francisco Ballet Orchestra under the
baton of Gerhard Samuel. The San Francisco Ballet, founded in
1938, is America's oldest classical ballet company. p. Gordon Waldear;
ABC Films; MACMFL.

BEAUTY IN THE BRICKS (29m C p1981, r1981)
   "BEAUTY IN THE BRICKS goes beyond cultural stereotypes and
reveals with sensitivity and candor the black teenage girl growing
up in urban America. It is truly exciting to watch this film portray
Baba as she dreams her version of the American dream."--Dr. Joan Weston, Sociologist, Dallas County Community College District. p. Cynthia Salzman Mondell, Allen Mondell; Media Projects, Inc.; NEWDAY.

BECAUSE SOMEBODY CARES (27m C p1979, r1980)
   Realistically depicts the problems of the elderly who have long
been mysterious, unseen and seldom talked about or to, but as the
mean age of Americans rises, the elderly have entered the public eye.
BECAUSE SOMEBODY CARES inspires the viewers to get involved.
The film is consciousness-raising. d. James Vanden Bosch; p. Terra
Nova Films and LU Productions; FILMLB; UIL, UM.

BECAUSE THEY LOVE ME (33m C p1980, r1981) (also Video)
   Provides deep insight into how parents can emotionally abuse
children. Points out how mental abuse can be just as damaging as
physical abuse. Also shows how parents can be overburdened, especially the mother in a situation where the father is often absent.
Fine demonstration of the cumulative effects of abuse on a child.
d. Jackie Rivett-River; p. Lois Hausslman; p. Lifestyle Productions
for Springfield Area Parents Anonymous; CORONET; IU, UIL, WSU.

BECKY: THE VALUE OF A LIFE (24m C 1980)
   In this medical ethics film, the roles are played by those most
deeply involved in the actual event. Becky Braznell was born a

hydrocephalic and doctors gave her no chance for a normal life. The parents, who already had one child born deaf and mentally retarded, were grief stricken. Then the parents learned of a young child who needed a kidney. They felt Becky should donate one of her kidneys to save a life otherwise doomed. The tissue match was acceptable. In a discussion with their physician and clergyman, doubts were expressed that the donation of Becky's kidney could be approved by the parents without the consent of Becky herself. And, of course, Becky could not give that consent. Recreating the events leading up to this crucial decision, they discuss the major ethical, legal and medical issues involved. KENJP; RARIG.

BECOMING A DANCE THERAPIST (18m B 1979)
Documents the progress of a graduate dance therapy student-- her motivation for a new career, her dance background, her progress and work with patients in a mental hospital. d./p. Robert Sasson; HUNTERC.

BECOMING AMERICAN (58m C 1982) (also Video)
After living for six years amidst the hardships of a refugee camp in northern Thailand, a Hmong family, informed of their acceptance as immigrants to the U.S., begin preparations for a long and arduous journey to an alien world. The film follows that family on their odyssey to a new home in America and records their intense culture shock as they resettle. Within nine months, members of a preliterate tribe are in the process of becoming American. p./d. Ken Levine, Ivory Waterworth Levine; NEWDAY.

BECOMING AWARE (30m C 1981) Stress Management: A Positive
Strategy Series
In this program, viewers learn what stress is and how to identify their own personal "stress triggers." They are taught how to reach a reasonable "comfort zone" in managing anxiety and that the sooner they become aware of stress symptoms, the less likely that stress-related illness will result. The "flight/fight" response to stress is explained, along with other effective and ineffective coping styles. Leader's manual and participants' handbooks included. TIMLIF.

BEGIN WITH GOODBYE SERIES see CHANGES; DEATH OF IVAN
IIYCH; EXITS AND ENTRANCES; MIRROR, MIRROR ON THE
WALL; TIME TO CRY, A; TURNED LOOSE;

BEGINNING OF LIFE, THE (30m C 1970)
Acclaimed photographer Lennart Nilsson catches the ever-growing, self-transforming evolution of a single cell into a human baby--the immemorial story of life, repeating itself without end. BENCHMF, VIEWFI; UMN, WSU.

BEGINNING OF PREGNANCY, THE (29m B 1956) Months Before
Birth--A Series
Describes what happens to the mother and baby during the early

months of pregnancy. Also explains how characteristics are inherited and how twins are produced. p. WQED-TV; AF.

BEGINNING OF TOTAL GROUP (16m C r1974)
Illustrates the educational philosophy of Lenore Wilson, a leading specialist in early childhood education, by showing her teaching a classroom of five-year-olds at the Nueva Day School and Learning Center, an alternative school in Hillsborough, California. She explains that she believes kindergarten-age children want to play out adult life, and she therefore introduces learning materials such as building blocks in a way that emphasizes their similarity to the kinds of tools used by adults. She stresses the need for teachers to work out a year-long curriculum so that daily activities may be blended into a general pattern, and she discusses the importance of teaching the relationships between objects and ideas and listening attentively to what the children say. Candid classroom scenes demonstrate the warm rapport between Ms. Wilson and her students and show children engaged in building projects, in group discussions, and carrying out scientific experiments. UCEMC.

BEGINNINGS (26m C 1977)
A detailed visual study of the School of American Ballet. Students and faculty outline their aims and attitudes briefly in their own words, but it is the camera that elucidates the growth of the vocabulary of movement and documents the exceptional teachers in action. A New York City Ballet performance of Coppelia gives students a taste of the stage and provides a colorful climax. d./p. Maren Erskine, Reed Erskine; LITWKS.

BEGINNINGS (9m C p1980, r1980)
Describes the highly personal universe of the animator. Spawned by an eclectic imagination, this universe draws on historical literary and classical sources to illustrate man's close ties with nature. Delves into the unconscious, from which it conjures up visions of surrealistic beauty. The images flow into one another in a glorious celebration of love and life. p./d. Clorinda Warny for NFBC; NFBC.

BEHAVIORAL INTERVIEWING WITH COUPLES: AN APPROACH TO EFFECTIVE MARITAL COUNSELING (14m C p1976, c1978)
Demonstrates one method of behavioral interviewing of couples during the initial counseling sessions. Six stages--beginning treatment, establishing goals, identifying issues, interacting, play-by-play analysis, and contracting--are designed to assist in the design of individualized clinical intervention for couples. RESPRC; CRM; IU, KENTSU, PAS, UM.

BEING PART OF IT ALL (24m C 1981) (also Video)
It is easy to see that Gary and Barbara, both moderately mentally handicapped, have a strong affection for one another and enjoy their married life. Gary, 27, and Barbara, 33, spent most of their

lives in the institution where they met. Six years ago they were
given the opportunity to live in a supervised group home. Eventually they decided to get married and set up a life of their own.
Their transition to independent living was accomplished with the help
of the strong support system in their Canadian community. A visiting social worker, a speech therapist, sheltered workshops and government subsidies continue to help the couple manage their affairs.
These services sound expensive, but the cost is actually less than
institutional living. Personal ties with in-laws play an important
role in their lives. This spontaneous portrait shows the viability
of marriage between the mentally handicapped, given the right circumstances. p. Richard Burman; d./s.w. Suzanne Donahue, Dwight
Little; p. NFBC; FILMLB.

BELFAST REEL, THE (26m C 1976)
    Presents the similarities, subtle and human, between the two
warring factions in Belfast, Ireland. This documentary is a call
for the people to start listening to and cooperating with one another.
p. Cecropia Company; d. Kathleen Dowdy. PHOENIX.

BELLE OF AMHERST, THE (120m C 1979)
    Using just a desk, a tea trolley, a sofa, a bed, a parasol, a
quilt and a box containing Emily Dickinson's poems and letters, Julie
Harris clearly dramatizes the life of poet-recluse Emily Dickinson
in this marvelous one-woman show. Harris' performance is a tour
de force that encompasses Emily's entire physical and fantasy worlds,
including three-dimensional characterizations of her family and portraits of her mentor Thomas Higginson and of Charles Wadsworth,
the man she supposedly loved. Through it, we understand how her
isolation became a focal point for her marvelous creative force. d.
Charles Nelson Reilly; s.w. William Luce; p. Sunrise Entertainment;
TWY.

BELLY DANCING: A HISTORY AND AN ART (24m C 1979) (also
    Video)
    A comprehensive film on classical belly dancing. Traces the
origin of the dance to the Neolithic age in the Sahara. Also presents historical data on the instruments, costumes, and basic methodology of the dance. Choreographer/d./p. Alicia Dhanifu; DHANIFU.

BELLY DANCING: IMAGES FROM VANCOUVER (60m/30m C 1979)
    (Video, Beta)
    Presents a great variety of dances and dancers of different lev-
els of expertise. Fourteen dancers are featured in 20 dance segments that include solo as well as group performances, ethnic as well
as cabaret styles. Some examples of the dances are a dance to the
Moon Goddess Artemis, an ancient Egyptian Ritual Dance, a Sword
Dance, a Bedouin Dance, a Fan Dance, a Guedra and a Candle Dance.
The half-hour version was edited for television and is intended for
general audiences. Eight dancers are featured in ten dance segments

of ethnic and cabaret styles. The main emphasis, however, is on solo performances. p. Melkim Productions; MELKIM.

BENEFACTOR, THE (60m B 1966)
The pros and cons of abortion presented in dramatic form in an episode from "The Defenders" television series. p. CBS-TV; CAROUF; PAS.

BEN WATTENBERG'S 1980 (SERIES) see INTERVIEW WITH BARBARA JORDAN

BENT TREE, THE (14m C p1980, r1981) (also Video)
Using sand animation accompanied by an old Yiddish folk song, a poem by Itsik Manger, the viewer is beguiled by the music and the motion of the smooth changing visuals. d./p. Sally Heckel; TEXFM.

BERIMBAU (12m C 1974)
The well-known Brazilian black musician Nana uses a berimbau, a one-stringed musical bow, to play traditional melodies for "capoeira," a dance in which the performers fight each other. Included in the film, along with the capoeira music, is a capoeira dance. Also, there are Rugendas' nineteenth-century engravings of colonial Brazil. p. Toby Talbot; NYF.

BERLIN see HILDEGARD KNEF'S BERLIN

BERNICE BOBS HER HAIR (48m C 1978)
The problems of "fitting in" and coping experienced by a young lady of the pre-flapper generation appear as modern as those of to-day's young women. Bernice is a phototypical "drag" of that older generation and under the tutelage of her know-it-all cousin becomes all too adept at attracting men. The source of this story is a letter of advice from F. Scott Fitzgerald to his sister on how to be popular. d./s.w. Joan Micklin Silver. CORNET; PAS, SILU, UMO.

BERTHA (35m C 1980)
Society has labeled Bertha mentally retarded. One of ten chil-dren of a poor family, she has lived in foster homes, been a chronic truant, and left school after the seventh grade still unable to read. For help in the analysis and evaluation of Bertha's case, she is sent at 15 to a leading diagnostic institution. There the professionals decide to implant an intrauterine device in Bertha to protect her from pregnancy when she returns home. Because she is ward of the state, her parents were not consulted. Later, after having the intrauterine device removed, she returns to the institution to ask the crucial questions, "What right did you have to do this to me?" Why am I called retarded?" "Why didn't you trust me?" Bertha herself and the professional who cared for her appear in this film and reappraise the decisions they made which have influenced her

life. Panel participants are professionals who discuss these key questions of labeling, the nature of retardation, the morality of curtailing another's reproductive rights even temporarily, and the issues of contraception, sterilization and sexual permissiveness. p. Joseph P. Kennedy Foundation; KENJP; PAS.

BEST HORSE (28m C p1979, r1979)
Presents a story in which a mother and her teenage daughter both learn not to impose their values on others, and things do not always go as planned. Based on the book The Best Horse by Elizabeth Van Steenwyk. d./s.w. Stephen Gyllenhaal; p. Chapman and Olsen Film Company in association with Scholastic Magazine. LCA.

BEST OF THE NEW YORK FESTIVAL OF WOMEN'S FILMS, THE (90m) (Video)
Write to New Line Cinema for details. p. New Line Cinema; NLC.

BETTER ANSWER, A (35m C 1973)
Designed to be an informal authoritative training film for officials, managers and supervisors, this film focuses on the prevention of equal employment legal problems and the provision of equal opportunity for females and minority members. Interspersed with practical, professional panel discussions are four employment scenes with real workers depicting common supervisory pitfalls which can lead to serious Title VIII problems. A professional narrator emphasizes critical points, such as the law, supervisory pitfalls, and affirmative action. MTPS; UMN.

BETTER HEALTH (SERIES) see CANCER TREATMENT; GENETICS AND RECOMBINANT DNA; HEART ATTACKS; OBESITY; PEPTIC ULCERS

BETTER PLACE, A (34m C p1981, r1982)
A bittersweet drama about selling the family house. In AS YOU LIKE IT, Touchstone remarks: "Ay now am I in Arden, the more fool I. When I was at home I was in a better place, but travelers must be content." The selling of the family home serves to dramatize the paradox we all face in growing up, in becoming independent, in becoming "travelers." Where then is the "better place?" d./p. Deborah Reinisch; DBRF.

BETTER SAFE THAN SORRY (30m C 1978)
Presents various situations in which children encounter strangers under potentially dangerous circumstances. Film is designed to stop at several points to allow children viewing the film to discuss each situation for themselves. FLMFR; CWU, UMN.

BETTER SAFE THAN SORRY, II (15m C p1982, r1983) (also Video)
Presents three simple rules to follow which can prevent and/or deal with potential sexual abuse. Host/narrator Stephanie Edwards

meets with a group of children aged five to nine to discuss how to avoid situations of potential sexual abuse and what to do if abuse does occur. The children take turns dramatizing situations and are asked to make decisions based on the circumstances they encounter. The children are made aware that sexual abuse is always the adult's fault, and adults who do it need help which can only be received if someone is told about the incident. The three rules "SAY NO. GET AWAY. TELL SOMEONE are repeated by all the children as the film ends. p. Vitascope Film; d. Bethany Kim; FLMFR.

BETTER WAY--LEARNING TO CARE, THE (26½m C 1972)
A documentary about the Las Palmas California School for Girls. Dance teacher tells of rewarding signs of rehabilitation and growing self-awareness of troubled girls. p. Charles Cahill and Associates, Inc.; AIMS.

BETWEEN MEN (57m C 1979)
Explores how society molds male behavior and looks at the assumptions, biases and penalties in going against its set pattern. Includes interviews with career soldiers, several generations of war veterans. Reveals military attitude to be a microcosm of American societal attitudes that attempt to exclude all that is considered "feminine" from acceptable male behavior. A provocative investigation into the influence of the American military on prevailing concepts of male identity. p. Will Roberts, United Documentary Films; TRNSIT.

BETWEEN THE MOTION AND THE ACT FALLS THE SHADOW (6m C 1981) (Video)
Depicts choreographer/dancer Vicki Stern dancing a trio with her images reproduced electronically. A variety of forms, color schemes, and both analog and digital image processing are arranged to evoke a muted, shadowy, but intense kinetic energy. The music, which frequently controls the image motion and color changes, was drawn largely from recorded footfalls of a bharatanatyam dancer. d./p. Reynold Weidenaar; WEIDNR.

BEWARE: THE GAPS IN MEDICAL CARE FOR OLDER PEOPLE (20m C 1982)
A family's concern for Beatrice, a 78-year-old depressed woman who is hospitalized after a fall and again after a severe emotional episode. Following medical and laboratory testing, Beatrice's condition is diagnosed as "reversible organic brain syndrome." With reduced medication and home health service, she returns to her own home and resumes an independent life. Explores over-medication, stereotypes, and the need for special knowledge in treating older people. d./p. Maria Oliva; ADELPHIP.

BEYOND GOOD AND EVIL (126m C 1980) (Italian/Subtitled)
Director Cavani synthesizes fact and fiction in her portrayal of a turn-of-the-century ménage à trois involving a young poet,

Friedrich Nietzsche, and an early champion of women's liberation.
With Dominique Sanda, Robert Powell, Erland Josephson, Virna Lisi.
d. Lilliana Cavani; FI.

BEYOND SAND DUNES (29m C 1976) (Video)
     Public Television's horticulturalist Thalassa Cruso narrates a
visual essay about the dunes and forests of Cape Cod, along the
Atlantic coastline in Massachusetts. She recalls her first impression
of the natural world as she walks along the dunes and describes
the desolate landscape and the slow transition from beach sand to
plants and from shrubs to forest. At the Atlantic White Cedar Swamp,
she points out evidence of an ancient forest engulfed by the dunes
and explains the disastrous ecological mistakes of the Cape's earliest
settlers who destroyed forests and overgrazed the land. p. WGBH-
TV, Boston; PBSV.

BEYOND SHELTER (25m C 1979)
     Examines and appraises the limited choices of shelter available
to old people in North America. For many years Denmark has provided services that make it possible for people to grow old with dignity. They no longer build large-scale homes for the aged; the emphasis is on integrating the old people into the community. Shows
discussions with urban planners, builders, and old people themselves.
Presents a variety of approaches to housing providing different degrees of care. d. Ron Blumer; p. Gilbert Rosenberg, M.D.; POLYMR.

BEYOND THE STARS: A SPACE STORY (12m C 1981)
     A small boy looks out of his bedroom window at the stars and
asks, "Do people live on them?" In answer to the question, BEYOND
THE STARS: A SPACE STORY is both a factual introduction to the
sun and the planets and a science fiction film. Based on a book
by Karla Kuskin entitled A Space Story, the film takes young viewers
on a trip from the boy's window out through our solar system and
beyond. A Polestar production for LCA by Ireland Don Duga; LCA.

BIBA (60m C p1978, r1980--U.S.)
     Shows how an Israeli woman, Biba, and her family, living in
a small farming village, are affected by the wars fought by Israel.
Usi, Biba's husband, was killed in the Yom Kippur War. Biba was
left with her father-in-law and three children to operate the farm
and carry on with life. The filmmaker's visit with Biba is highlighted
by conversations with family members, comments from neighbors and
friends, and scenes of war, and on the farm. A powerful film comment on Biba and her family's attempt to live life fully from day to
day, amidst an almost intolerable situation where war takes the lives
of those they love most early. p. Israel Film Service, d. David
Perlov; ALDEN.

BIG APPLE MINUTE: (NEW YORK AQUARIUM) (1m C p1980, r1980)
     (Video)
     One of the continuing series of mini-programs saluting the New

York metropolitan area's cultural and recreational and historic resources. This example is a visit to the New York Aquarium at Coney
Island. p. Susan Butler; ex. p. Paul Noble; METROT.

BIG BANG AND OTHER CREATION MYTHS, THE (11m C p1981,
r1981) (also Video)
Presents in animation the various myths regarding the creation
of the world from the point of view of different cultures. d./p.
Faith Hubley; p. Hubley Studios; Animation by William Littlejohn,
Constance d'Antuono, Emily Hubley; music composed and directed
by Elizabeth Swados; PF.

BIG BOYS DON'T CRY: THE CHANGING AMERICAN MAN (28m C
p1982, r1983) (also Video)
Explores how men's traditional roles and values are changing.
Explaining that while male roles used to be clear and everyone understood that men were strong, decision-makers, providers, aggressive
sexually and on the job and did not show emotions, this film shows
that those roles are in the midst of a major reevaluation. Editors
of Esquire, Playboy, Ms Magazine and Gentlemen's Quarterly discuss
the changing role of men. Michael Castleman, author of Sexual Solutions speaks about the changes in how men judge themselves sexually. A good discussion film for groups concerned with this problem. p. Francine Achbar, Group W. Productions; d. Chuck O'Neill/
Bill Huggins; s.w. Francine Achbar/Ken Tucci; MTITI.

BILL--A LONE PARENT (15m C p1980, r1980)
Bill is an English migrant living in Australia with his two young
children, Mandy (18 months) and Janie (3 years), whose mother left
them twelve months earlier. This film shows the problems of a lone
father caring for his children in a society geared for two-parent
families and also the effects of the separation on the children themselves. d./p. Barbara Chobocky; AFC.

BILL AND SUZI: NEW PARENTS (13m B n.d.)
Bill and Suzi discuss their feelings about Becky with Dr. Brazelton during Becky's checkup. They talk about the pleasures she
brings, coping with her when she's difficult, and the adjustments
they have had to make in their own lives. Bill also mentions the
jealousy he felt both before and after the birth of their daughter.
EDC.

BILL OF RIGHTS IN ACTION, THE (SERIES) see EQUAL OPPOR-
TUNITY; WOMEN'S RIGHTS

BILLIE JEAN KING (TENNIS) (22m C 1972) Women in Sports--A Series
Billie Jean King is one of the most dominating forces in women's
tennis today. Although Ms. King wins far more competitions than
she loses, included in this profile is a match in which she is overwhelmingly defeated by sensational young Chris Evert. p. Tele-
Sports; PARACO; SILU.

BIMBO (17m C p1978, r1978)
Kenny is 30 when he meets his two best friends from high school
for a private reunion. They have changed. Seeing them forces
Kenny to reevaluate his career choice. As a result, he changes
his life. p. Martha Coolidge, Carlos Davis; FI.

BIOFEEDBACK: LISTENING TO YOUR HEAD (19m C 1976)
Neurophysiologist Dr. Barbara Brown and biomusician David Ro-
senbloom explore the impact of biofeedback, the use of brainwaves
to control diseases and emotional problems and to open up new avenues of communication. p. Hobel-Leiterman Productions; MACMFL;
PAS.

BIOFEEDBACK: THE YOGA OF THE WEST (40m C 1974, r1975)
"If we can make ourselves sick, then perhaps we can learn to
make ourselves well." Based on that assumption, Dr. Elmer Green
and his wife, Alyce, daughter Judy, and colleagues at the Menninger
Foundation research the ability of the mind to control the body ...
they test Indian yogis who can stop their hearts at will or remain
in an airtight box for over seven hours ... they study a Dutchman
who can skewer his arm with a rusty needle and prevent pain, bleeding and infection ... they use biofeedback training to help patients
overcome disease, to give prisoners a sense of self-mastery, and
to give ordinary people deeper insight into their subconscious. p.
Elda Hartley, Hartley Productions; SERBC; UIL, UMN.

BIOGRAPHY OF ELEANOR ROOSEVELT (25m B n.d.)
This documentary highlights the public and private lives of the
former American "First Lady," who, in her role as a United Nations
delegate and as an ardent humanitarian, became known in later years
as the "First Lady of the World." Set against the panorama of world
history, the film offers an exciting kaleidoscope of American politics
in the 40-year period from the time Franklin Roosevelt ran as the
unsuccessful vice-presidential candidate in 1920 through the election
of John Kennedy in 1960. WESTCF.

BIRDS AND THEIR YOUNG (10m C 1979)
Using music, natural sound effects, a minimum of narration, and
shots of more than 35 different species, this film shows that many
different types of birds have similar habits of courting, mating, and
nesting. It also shows how parents care for the young until the
offspring are ready to leave the nest. p. Myrna I. Berlet, Walter
H. Berlet; IFB.

BIRDS OF PASSAGE (36m C n.d.)
This is a composite portrait of three West Coast Japanese Ameri-
cans--a gardener, a tuna fisherman, and the widow of a farmer--who
came to the U.S. in the decade before World War I. We learn about
their values as they talk about their lives. Adapting to an alien and
often hostile country while hoping one day to return to Japan, they

drew strength from their own traditions and culture. The World War II round-up and internment of Japanese Americans remains a searing memory for each of them. Thirty years after the war, they now understand that their place is here with their children and grandchildren, helping them keep the traditions and culture alive. ADL.

BIRTH (57m C r1977) (also Video)
This documentary takes a critical look at childbirth practices in Western society. Eminent psychiatrist Dr. R. D. Laing raises questions as to the immediate and long-term effects of many of the detached, often inhumane procedures that overlook the feelings of mothers and babies at the time of their greatest vulnerability. It is hoped that this film will act as a catalyst towards humanitarian change and a reappraisal of birth techniques. d. Sam Pillsbury; FI; PAS, UMN.

BIRTH: HOW LIFE BEGINS (23m C p1978, r1981) (also Video)
Provides basic information about the conception and prenatal development of the human fetus. Allan and Barbara Klass attend childbirth classes together and prepare for the birth of their fourth child. Animation is used to illustrate menstruation and fertilization and to describe how a single cell becomes billions of cells by the time the baby is born nine months later. It is emphasized that food, smoking, drugs, noise and even emotional attitudes of the mother can be passed on to the baby. The birth of the Klass' new baby girl is shown, and the immediate closeness between mother and child is stressed. p. Charles Sutton, Avatar for EBEC; s.w. Paula Levenback; EBEC; UIL.

BIRTH AT HOME (14m C p1978, r1980)
Many people fear that in a birth at home, things could go wrong. In this film we see Sister Edith Gosling, an experienced midwife, gently and skillfully resuscitate a child born with the cord wrapped three times around its throat. Edith also demonstrates the value of Zonal therapy and massage before and after the birth. Does not advocate home over hospital births, but it does show a mother and her baby's needs being met in a relaxed and supportive environment. d./p. Barbara Chobocky; AFC; FILMLB.

BIRTH CENTERS (24m C 1979) (also Video, S8)
To combat the trend toward more home births and to avoid the dehumanization of the labor and delivery room technology, birth centers have opened in and out of hospitals around the country. In this film, you will see and hear parents and professionals give their views on birth centers, and you will see couples giving birth in them. CINMD; UMN.

BIRTH EXPERIENCES (29m C 1976) (Video) Woman Series
Lolly Hirsch, a leader in the women's health movement questions so-called improvements in the birth procedure and whether sophisticated medical technology has had negative effects on women. She

217115

discusses mechanical and surgical procedures such as fetal monitoring
and episiotomy and the emotional abuse some women have felt as a
result of typical maternity ward practices. Sandra Elkin is the moderator. p. WNED-TV, Buffalo, NY; PBSV.

BIRTH OF A BABY, THE (17m C 1975)
Shows delivery of a child by means of natural childbirth at Char-
lotten Lund Clinic in Copenhagen, in a specially designed delivery
room with the mother in street clothing, her husband in attendance,
and a trained midwife in charge of the entire procedure. The narrator explains what is happening as the labor progresses. A doctor
stands by in case of complication. p. Columbine Films, Ltd., Denmark; RAYMBA.

BIRTH OF A FAMILY (24m C 1975)
Designed for couples or single women to demonstrate preparation
for childbirth. We see one couple attending a class on childbirth
preparation in order to secure accurate information and to make themselves physically as well as psychologically ready for the event. The
scenes of class instruction are juxtaposed with scenes of the actual
birth, recording early labor, transition and the full emergence of
the baby and the placenta. The film clearly demonstrates the relationship between careful preparation and actual delivery. p. Catfish
Productions; PEREN; UMN.

BIRTH OF AMANDA (25m C n.d.)
Delivered by natural childbirth, Amanda enters the world surrounded by family and friends. As she is laid on her mother's breast;
her father cries and all hands embrace her in one of life's most intense moments. This fond and intimate portrait includes sequences
of the pregnancy, and of the birth of a new human being. p./d.
Laird Sutton; National Sex Forum; MMRC.

BIRTH OF THE BABY, THE (29m B 1956) Months Before Birth--
    A Series
Discusses the process of birth from the onset of labor pains,
through the stages of labor, to the actual birth itself. Follows an
expectant mother from admittance to hospital until delivery of baby.
p. WQED-TV; AF.

BIRTHDAY (28m C n.d.) Something Personal Series
Portrait of a unique woman, a dedicated and caring doctor. Dr.
Lonny Higgins is a Boston obstetrician/gynecologist who is working
to introduce the LeBoyer birth method at her hospital. She is also
a wife and mother of a two-year-old son. The film traces her professional development, shows her attempt to balance the demands of
career and family, and describes how her personal and professional
concerns have given her a unique motivation and approach to her
career. The major goal of her career is the improvement of medical
care for women having babies in hospitals. Though she is opposed

to home deliveries because of the danger of complications, Dr. Higgins is dedicated to bringing the emotional fulfillment and warmth associated with home births to the hospitals. Shows Dr. Higgins counseling a young couple in the LeBoyer method and delivering their child. This film should be of particular interest to those interested in career options for women, to medical, paramedical and nursing students, and to staff and participants in prenatal classes. p. Nancy Porter; WGBH-TV; EDC.

BISHOP HILL (27m C p1979, r1979)
   Traces the Jansenist religious dissidents from their rual Swedish homes to their farming and manufacturing commune in Illinois, Bishop Hill Colony, from 1846 to 1961. Thirteen surviving Colony buildings and a remarkable collection of folk paintings of the colonists make an impressive backdrop for family reminiscences by communalists' descendants who live in Bishop Hill today. d. Yvonne Hannemann; p. Anna Wadsworth Murray; HILLB.

A BIT WITH KNIT II (SERIES) (29m ea. C 1975) (Video)
   A series for the home seamstress that deals exclusively with women's clothing made from easy-care knit fabrics. Instructor Rita Barker, a teacher and home economist, uses modern prints and patterns appropriate for teenagers and young women. Some advanced sewing techniques and complicated variations are included in the programs, which cover a jiffy skirt and sweater, several types of slacks, a jacket and informal outfits for summer wear. WSWP-TV, Berkley WV; PBSV.
   These are the individual program titles: INTRODUCTION, JIFFY SWEATER; JIFFY, SKIRT; SHIRTWAIST BLOUSE; SHIRTWAIST BLOUSE (continued); SHIRTWAIST BLOUSE (continued); SCARF, SLACKS VARIATIONS; SLACKS VARIATIONS (continued); SLACKS VARIATIONS (continued); JACKET VIEW A AND C; JACKET (continued); JACKET (continued); JACKET (continued); SHAWL COLLAR JACKET; RAGLAN WRAP-AROUND DRESS, HALTER TOP; SCOOTER SKIRT, EVENING DRESS.

BITTER TEARS OF PETRA VON KANT (124m C 1972) (German/Subtitled)
   Deals with the shifting power relationships among three lesbians: a successful liberated fashion designer, her contented slave girl, and a sultry slug of a model who makes the master a slave. Accompanied by the music of Verdi and The Platters, dressed in an incredible melange of glitter and C. B. DeMille, imprisoned in a florid set dominated by fleshy nudes and ghastly white mannequins, these three women act out a supercharged melodrama of sadomasochistic passion. d. Rainer Werner Fassbinder; NYF.

BITTERSWEET MOONLIGHT DANCING SONG (12m C 1977) (Video)
   "By colorizing and synthesizing a body in motion, the tapemakers create an image that is both concrete and abstract. A woman's voice

LORETTE WILMOT LIBRARY
NAZARETH COLLEGE

tells a story relating to the dancer."--Village Voice, October 28,
1978. p./d. Luna Pettebone, Elaine Velasquez; CREOUT.

BIX PIECES, THE (30m B 1973) (Video)
    A set of dances-with-lecture, in which Twyla Tharp demonstrates
dance construction, dance relation to the music, and her personal
conceptions about interrelationships among dance styles. Choreographer: Twyla Tharp; Narrator: Marion Hailey; d. Merrill Brockway; PACT.

BLACK COAL, RED POWER (41m C 1974)
    A competent, thoughtful exploration of the problems that have
been caused by strip mines on the Hopi and Navajo lands in Arizona.
On the one hand, the mines have provided sorely needed jobs for
the Native American people here. On the other hand, strip mining
has caused severe erosion of their land, and damaged the ecology
of the desert. Raises one very important question: how can we increase or exploit the supplies of remaining fossil fuels without doing
permanent damage to both the land and the people on it? p. Shelly
Grossman; IU.

BLACK DAWN (20m C p1978, r1980) (also Video)
    With music, history, folklore, and animation of paintings by 13
of Haiti's foremost artists, this film tells the story of how the people
came to live on that Caribbean island and their long battle for independence from the France of Napoleon Bonaparte. p. Robin Lloyd,
Doreen Kraft, Meri Furnari; p. Green Valley Film and Art Center;
ICARF.

BLACK GIRL (30m C 1982) (also Video) The Planning Ahead Series
    Billie Jean is an impulsive but talented young black teenager
who has dropped out of high school and secretly taken a job as a
dancer and waitress at a local nightclub. She dreams of becoming
a ballet dancer but doesn't know how to pursue her goal in the face
of strong opposition from her mother and two scheming stepsisters.
Billie Jean has an ally in Netta, an older "foster sister" now in law
school. But will the envious stepsisters succeed in sabotaging Netta's
efforts to encourage Billie Jean to plan for a dance career...? A
study guide is included with the film. Also, a workbook for students
is available. p. Barbara Wolfinger, Berkeley Productions; UCEMC.

BLACK HILLS ARE NOT FOR SALE, THE (28m C 1980) (Video)
    In this videotape, shot at the 1980 International Survival Gather-
ing in South Dakota, Sioux people tell why "the Black Hills are not
for sale." The film gives historical background on the Laramie Treaty
of 1868 which guaranteed the Sioux ownership of their lands. The
treaty was violated as early as 1874 by General Custer who led an
expedition in to search for gold. Conflicts led to the Battle of the
Little Big Horn, and the following year Congress took the lands from
the Sioux. As a result of the Sioux land claims pursued in the courts

over the past 60 years, a cash settlement for the seized 7.3 million acres was awarded by the U.S. Court of Claims in 1978. However, the Oglala Sioux have not agreed to accept money; it is the land itself which is of value. Because of the rich mineral resources, the U.S. government is unwilling to honor the 1868 treaty by returning the lands. The International Survival Gathering brought together members of the Black Hills Alliance with other groups concerned with energy and environmental issues. A member of WARN (Women of All Red Nations) describes the group's study of serious health problems on the Pine Ridge Reservation related to radioactive tailings polluting the reservation's water source. In the final scene, Medicine Man Wallace Black Elk movingly sums up the thoughts expressed throughout--that protecting their lands is the only way for Indian people to survive, not only in the present generation, but as the legacy for those yet to come. p. Sandra Osawa (Native Visions); AMERITC.

BLACK ISLAND (58m C p1978, r1980--U.S.)
An entertaining children's adventure story set in the coastal countryside of England. d. Ben Bolt; p. Carole Smith, Children's Film Foundation, England; LUCERNE.

BLACK MALE-FEMALE RELATIONS: PROBLEMS/SOLUTIONS (58m C 1980) (Video)
Examines two programs aimed at solving the problems black men and women have developing and maintaining healthy, supportive and harmonious relationships. Dr. Robert Tucker, Associate Professor of Psychiatry at Yale University Medical School conducts a "Black Love Workshop" in which he employs a psychological approach to solving problems of black male-female interaction. R. A. Straughn, author and lecturer, teaches a course of study called "Spiritual Culture" which advocates a return to African ancestral traditions as a means of promoting more spiritually sound relationships. This video tape is excellent for secondary, college, and graduate level courses in human relations, psychology and Afro-American studies or public library, church and community group programs on marriage and the family. p./d. Melvin R. McCray, p. Media Genesis Production; BLACKFL.

BLACK PERSPECTIVE ON THE NEWS, SERIES 1 (29m C 1975-76) (Video)
Dr. Dorothy Height (President, National Council of Negro Women) discusses sexism, racism and the priorities of her organization. WHYY-TV, Philadelphia; PBSV.

BLACK PERSPECTIVE ON THE NEWS, SERIES 8 (29m C 1975-76) (Video)
Margaret Bush Wilson (Chairwoman of the Board of Directors for the National Association for the Advancement of Colored People) discusses the status of blacks in the areas of housing, health care, economics, education and politics. WHYY-TV, Philadelphia; PBSV.

BLACK PERSPECTIVE ON THE NEWS, SERIES 11 (29m C 1975-76)
(Video)
Rep. Bella Abzug (D-NY) discusses congressional, presidential
and party politics, the Equal Rights Amendment, the Republican Administration's attitude toward New York City's economic troubles and
the role of minorities and women in the political structure. WHYY-
TV, Philadelphia; PBSV.

BLACK PERSPECTIVE ON THE NEWS, SERIES 17 (29m C 1975-76)
(Video)
"A look at 1975," with journalists Delores Barclay (Associated
Press), Vern Odom (WXIA-TV, Atlanta), Maurice Lewis (WANC-TV,
Boston) and Roger Wilking (The New York Times). WHYY-TV, Phila-
delphia; PBSV.

BLACK PERSPECTIVE ON THE NEWS, SERIES 35 (29m C 1975-76)
(Video)
Rep. Yvonne Burke (D-CA) and Basil Peterson (Vice-Chairman
of the Democratic National Committee) discuss Black political strategy
in the 1976 elections, full employment and the Humphrey-Hawkins
Bill, energy, crime, rural development and revenue sharing. WHYY-
TV, Philadelphia; PBSV.

BLACK PERSPECTIVE ON THE NEWS, SERIES 41 (29m C 1975-76)
(Video)
Eleanor Holmes Norton (Commissioner on Human Rights for New
York City) discusses New York's economic problems, the Equal Rights
Amendment, abortion and the 1976 elections. WHYY-TV; PBSV.

BLACK PERSPECTIVE ON THE NEWS, SERIES 50 (29m C 1975-76)
(Video)
Rep. Yvonne Burke (D-CA) discusses 1976 national political is-
sues as they affect blacks, redistribution of wealth, the Humphrey-
Hawkins full employment bill, black voter registration and her predic-
tions about the results of the Republican National Convention. WHYY-
TV; PBSV.

BLACK SHIPS, THE (8m C 1970)
Commodore Perry's 1853 "opening of Asia," seen through the
Japanese documents of the times and showing the special situation
that occurs when two highly diverse cultures come together for the
first time. p. Ray and Charles Eames; PF.

BLACK WEST, THE (30m C 1979)
A collection of anecdotes about blacks who helped settle the West.
p. Carol Mundy Lawrence; d. Robert Zagone; SABAN.

BLOOD AND SAND--WAR IN THE SAHARA (58m C 1982)
A report on U.S. involvement in the Western Sahara War. Presents revealing interviews with key policymakers in the Carter and

Reagan administrations. In addition, the filmmakers travelled hundreds of miles of barren desert on both sides of the battlefront. Offers an analysis of U.S. foreign policy and detailed account of U.S. arms sales. d./p. Sharon I. Sopher; s.w. Sharon Sopher/ Peter Kinoy; ed. Peter Kinoy; FIRRNF.

BLOOD OF THE CONDOR: PARTS I AND II (71m B 1969)
Reenactment of an actual incident involving sterilization of Quechuan Indian women as part of a U.S.-imposed birth control program. Depicts the various levels of contemporary Bolivian society, from the impoverished Indian communities in the Andes highlands to the privileged white and working class Mestizo (half-caste) populace in La Paz. Quechua and Spanish dialogue with English subtitles. d. Jorge Sanjines; UNIFILM; PAS.

BLOOMERS (27m C r1980)
This love story of a daughter for a mother is wrapped in the complexities of a child-parent, woman-woman, life-surging/life-ebbing relationship. Hildy Brook, filmmaker, plays the daughter and Pearl Shear the mother. The daughter, a painter in her thirties, is facing success in her work and problems in her marriage. She seeks advice from her mother, who lives in an old-world Jewish environment of Miami, only to find her mother has just returned from the hospital following a heart attack. The old and new relationships of daughter-mother revolve around the metaphor of allowing the young woman to wash the older's bloomers. d./p./s.w. Hildy Brooks; CORONET.

BLOSSOM IN VIRGO (13m C p1977, r1979)
The opening scene reveals a woman and a man in a farm house as the evening shadows deepen and they wait for the birth of a child. There is no narration but the sound track records the labored breathing exercises and an occasional moan or cry of pain. Throughout the night, the man attends to the needs of the pregnant woman. The vigil continues until the next night. Then, through natural childbirth, the baby arrives, lustily proclaiming its presence. p./d. Michael Day; PHOENIX.

BLUE SQUAWK (3m C 1980-81) (Video)
Eva Maier choreographs her dances for one camera propped on the ground, proving that one does not need an elaborate, multicamera recording setup to make video dance. She dances here with an unusual corps de ballet--a flock of chickens pecking in the foreground. Seen far down the road, Maier slowly approaches, making marvelous cryptic gestures with her arms and legs, movements suggested by her "feathered" dance company. Comes with WRIST BRAKES, 5 minutes. d./p. Eva Maier; MAIER.

BOARD AND CARE (27m C p Dec. 1979, r1980)
Photographed in California's Central Valley, this Academy Award winning short film features a Down's syndrome girl and a boy who

reveal the deep need of human beings for closeness with each other. Ricky and Lila meet at a country picnic, eating and talking. They each long for the opportunity to get together again. Lila is taken away to school and is broken-hearted to leave without seeing Ricky again. The last scenes show Ricky searching the town in vain for Lila. A poignant message for everyone about the needs of the retarded. p. Sarah Pillsbury, Ron Ellis; d. Ron Ellis; PF; UM.

BODY DEFENSES AGAINST THE OUTSIDE WORLD (13m C p.1979 r1979)
Using live action and animation, this film introduces the protective devices built into the human body which defend it from dangers present in the environment. d. Susan Shippey; ed. Robert Churchill; CF.

BODY FIGHTS DISEASE, THE (13m C 1980)
Shows how skin and mucous membranes impede germs. In sections on bacteria and viruses, illustrates action of white cells, macrophages, and the lymphocyte role in producing antibodies and as killer cells. Discusses immunization and antibiotics. Extensive animation. d. Diane Franklin, Bob Churchill; CF.

BODY HUMAN: FACTS FOR GIRLS, THE (30m C 1980) (also Video)
Actress Marlo Thomas leads preadolescent and adolescent girls in an informal discussion about their changing bodies and some of the myths surrounding reproduction and menstruation. Illustrations of the female biological functions are interspersed with live-action discussions at an all-girl "slumber party," on a jogging track, and during other typical teenage activities. p. Tomorrow Entertainment Medcom; TIMLIF; UIL.

BODY, MIND AND SPIRIT (40m C 1981)
The holistic health movement is growing, and centers calling themselves holistic are springing up all over the country. What are the ingredients of an ideal holistic health center? This film seeks to put them all together--western medical technology combined with many of the techniques of psychotherapy developed in recent years plus nutrition, biofeedback, structural alignment, massage, aerobic exercise, music and color therapy--techniques that bring the patient in touch with his/her deeper self and help one to take responsibility for one's own health. Filmed primarily at the A.R.E. Clinic in Phoenix, one of the oldest and most prestigious centers in the country. p. Elda Hartley; HARTLEY.

BODY TALK: EIGHT MOVEMENT THERAPIES (58m B 1975) (Video)
A documentary of eight experiential sessions at a northern California dance therapy conference. Commentary explains the therapy goals of the various approaches shown. Made with financial assistance and support from the Northern California Chapter of the American Dance Therapy Association. d./p. Sybil Meyer; MEYERS.

BON APPETIT (10m C p1981, r1982) (also Video)
Presents a language and cultural awareness film designed for
use in French classes. p. Mary Joan Barrett, Joseph Koenig; d.
Martin Duckworth; BEACON.

BOND OF BREASTFEEDING (20m C 1978)
Based on the experiences of breastfeeding mothers, this documentary imparts facts to expectant mothers so they can decide for
themselves whether to breastfeed or not to breastfeed. The viewer
sees how antibodies are formed to protect the baby from germs and
infection; how the baby controls the volume and flow of milk, how
to avoid physical problems the mother may have and the advantages
and convenience of the method. Yet, the key concept of the film
is that breastfeeding mothers supply to their newborns not only food
but emotional warmth, love and comfort which creates an inextricable
bond between mother and baby. p. Julian Aston; PEREN.

BONES (29m C p1979, r1982) (also Video)
Portrait of John Henry "Bones" Nobles, a resident of Beaumont,
one of the few remaining practitioners of the art of creating rhythms
with dried beef bones. Noble plays the bones with blues singer
Taj Mahal and philosophizes about his life and times. p./d. Carol
Mundy Lawrence; Nguzo Saba Films, Inc.; BEACON.

BONNE BELL MINI-MARATHON, THE (25m C p1977, r1978)
Shows the mini-marathon for women in New York's Central Park.
This film account of that annual race is intercut with comments and
interviews with students, grandmothers, teenagers, housewives, a
five-year-old and many others. Winning obviously is not the goal
for all of the 2,500 women in this race. More and more women are
running for fun and health. p./d. Yvonne Hannemann; WOMBAT.

BONNIE RAITT (40m C 1979)
Shows Bonnie Raitt, Los Angeles-born country blues singer,
daughter of Broadway star John Raitt. Bonnie began in the late
sixties on the college and folk festival circuits. An accomplished
guitarist and a rockin' performer, Bonnie has grown to the position
of internationally popular concert headliner. BBC; TIMLIF.

BOOMSVILLE (11m C 1969)
In animation, the film makes a timely statement about the limits
of the earth's resources and humankind's relentless pursuit of bigger
and better. d. Yvonne Mallett; p. Robert Verrall; NFBC; LCA.

BORN DRUNK: THE FETAL ALCOHOL SYNDROME (10m C p1979,
r1980) (also Video)
Even moderate drinking during pregnancy can cause tragic birth
defects known as the fetal alcohol syndrome (FAS). Doctors and
parents of FAS children tell what alcohol can do to the fetus, and
how to avoid America's leading preventable birth defect. p. David
Meyer for ABC News' 20/20; ABCWWL; UIL.

BORN TO RUN (24m C p1979, r1980--U.S.) (also Video)
Using animation, focuses on the global arms race. Traces the
history of man's aggression, progressing from cavemen with clubs
and knights with swords to the atomic missile age. d. Peter Shatalow;
p. Llana Frank, Martin Harbury; p. Window Films, Ltd., Toronto,
Canada; WOMBAT.

BORN WITH A HABIT (30m C 1977)
Documentary on the complex medical, social and ethical problems
related to pregnant, narcotic-addicted women. Addicts discuss their
backgrounds, experiences with medical and social professionals, and
their guilt and fears for their babies. Authorities argue about a
mother's right to keep her baby versus the state's responsibility
to protect the child. Pediatrician demonstrates withdrawal syndrome
in newborns. p. Edward A. Mason, M.D.; MHTRFP; PAS.

BOROM SARRETT (20m B 1964) French/Subtitled
A story of a young man's struggle for survival in Dakar. The
film gives tremendous insight into the reasons why two cultures--
the African and European--even today, remain worlds apart. d.
Ousmane Sembene; NYF.

BORROWED FACES (29m C p1980, r1980) (also Video)
Explores the audition and casting process from the viewpoint
of both performer and director. It examines the real world of theatre, following the individual actors from pre-audition warmups,
through casting, to rehearsal and performance. Depicts the intense
pressure, personal discipline, and emotional rewards and disappointments inherent in the profession, and explores through the director's
eyes the criteria, priorities and artistic concepts used to select the
cast. d./p. Linda Moulton Howe, KMGH-TV, Denver; CRM.

BOTTLE UP AND GO (18m C p1980, r1980)
Captures the simple, deliberate life-style of a rural black couple
in southern Mississippi as they go about their daily chores. Traces
of distant African ancestry emerge from Louis Dotson's one-strand
guitar and haunting bottle yodeling. d./p. Bill Ferris, Judy Peiser;
SOFOLK.

BOTTOM LINE, THE (31m C 1981) (Video)
Examines the dilemma of the working people of this country.
Open-ended. p. Lori Cohen/Sally Kingsbury; ASAP.

BOY AND A BOA (13m C r1975)
A story about Martin and his pet boa. Informative and entertaining. It will help children to better understand and appreciate the
nature of snakes. p. Lora Hays; d. Renata Stoia. PHOENIX.

BOY AND THE CAT, THE (10m C p1977, r1980) (also Video)
Tells a story about friendship and responsibility using animation

with very little dialog. p. Sheila Graber; music by Brenda Orwin;
TEXFM.

BOY OR GIRL: SHOULD THE CHOICE BE OURS? (60m C 1980)
    (Video) Hard Choices Series
    Because of a procedure devised to check for serious genetic ab-
normality in a fetus, it is possible to know the sex of a baby well
in advance of birth; early enough, in fact, to choose to abort it.
Experimental procedures are moving toward the possibility of sex
choice at the time of conception. Yet, should this choice be ours?
Dr. Willard Gaylin hosts this inquiry into another of society's hard
choices. PBSV.

BOYS BEWARE (3rd ed.) (14m C 1980)
    Boys, as well as girls, could be the target of sexual attack.
Three dramatized vignettes show typical approaches used by molesters of young teenage boys and point out that molesters are often
people known and trusted by the victim. Shows common sense precautions, and emphasizes the importance of reporting incidents.
AIMS; UMN.

BREAD AND ROSES: THE STRUGGLE OF CANADIAN WORKING WOMEN
    (35m C n.d.) (Video)
    Using rare Canadian photographs and film footage, this film pre-
sents the experience of working women ranging from domestic servants
and pioneer wives to the first women doctors and lawyers, and traces
the changing focus of the women's movement in seeking workplace
reforms. Surveys the period from 1850 to the present. p. University of Toronto; s.w. Sylvia Van Kirk; University of Toronto; MEDIAC.

BREAKFAST TABLE, THE (14m C 1979) (Video)
    Thacher's comic-tragic approach emphasizes the distance inherent
in intimacy, and shows how fantasy can be used to transcend the
drudgery of domestic life. As the businesslike husband tries to
solve his crossword puzzle while ordering his wife to bring him food,
she escapes from her menial tasks into amusing flights of fantasy.
p. Anita Thacher; ELARTI.

BREAKING THROUGH (27m C 1981)
    The psychological and physical process women experience in train-
ing for jobs in the skilled trades and technology. Profiles pre-trades
training programs for women, with intimate portraits of women 18
to 60 years old whose self-confidence and competence grow with new
skills. Dispels myths about "men's work" and "women's work." d.
Janine Manatis; p. Kem Murch; WOMWK.

BREAKING UP (90m C 1979) (Video)
    Story of a woman struggling to survive the break-up of her long-
time marriage and lead an independent life. Stars Lee Remick.
TIMLIF.

BREAKOUT (28m C 1979) (Video)
Presents women in nontraditional jobs: as pipefitter, mechanic, electrician, firefighter, and heavy equipment operator. Young and middle-aged, black and white, the women interviewed exude confidence and a strong sense of accomplishment and self-sufficiency. Frank, articulate, and spontaneous, they discuss their experiences and attitudes about work and working with men, providing a credible, informative, often exhilarating introduction to women in non-sex-stereotyped jobs. d. Jeffrey Hurst, James S. Elliot; EDUATX.

BREAKUP (15m C 1973) The Inside-Out Series
Presents Becky whose feelings of guilt, loneliness, anger and fear are stirred up as she anticipates a visit by her father who is separated from her mother. Follows her emotions as she imagines the frightening consequences of divorce. KETC-TV; NITC; IU.

BREAST CANCER CONTROVERSIES (29m C 1976) (Video) Woman
    Series
Medical journalist Rose Kushner (Breast Cancer: A Personal History and an Investigative Report) discusses breast cancer and treatment. She expresses belief that the American women have not been given accurate information. She criticizes routine medical procedures and faults federal and private agencies for the fact that breast cancer research is a low priority. Sandra Elkin, Moderator. WNED-TV, Buffalo; PBSV.

BREAST CANCER UPDATE (29m C n.d.) (Video, Beta, VHS) Woman
    Series
Medical writer, author and breast cancer patient Rose Kushner explores the controversy over the use of mammography (breast X-ray) in cancer detection, the risk factors for breast cancer and the development of a "phantom breast" for the testing of X-ray equipment. Kushner, who wrote Breast Cancer: A Personal History and an Investigative Report, is the founder of the Breast Cancer Advisory Center in Kensington, Maryland. Sandra Elkin is the moderator. WNED-TV, Buffalo; PBSV.

BREAST FEEDING (14m C n.d.)
Presents a detailed explanation on how to be a nursing mother. Discusses preparing ahead, the first weeks of nursing, how to involve the other children, the father, and time away from the baby. The bonding experience is also covered. Also available in Spanish. MIFE.

BREAST SELF-EXAMINATION (11½m C n.d.)
Follows a typical woman through a routine physical checkup where she is instructed how to examine her own breasts. Demonstrates home self-examination, what to check for and when to consult your physician. Stresses routine checkups. Also available in Spanish. MIFE.

BREAST SELF-EXAMINATION (28m C 1978) The Inner Woman (Series)
Provides specific instructions for monthly breast self-examination.
Explains different types of malignant and nonmalignant growths that
can occur in the breast. Stresses importance of early diagnosis.
Marilyn Poland, R.N., moderator. CRM; PAS.

BREAST SURGERY, PARTS I AND II (13m, 9½m C n.d.)
Part One deals with a pre-menopausal woman who detects a lump
in her breast. Describes the final diagnosis, the various surgical
procedures available for removal plus other therapies available. Part
Two deals with a post-menopausal woman's lump and her greater cancer risk. Also explains available surgical options and other therapies
for removal. MIFE.

BREASTFEEDING (8m C p1978, r1980)
Demonstrates and explains the benefits and techniques of breastfeeding and answers common questions relating to it. A well-
documented film. p./d. Myles Breen; MCFI.

BREASTFEEDING (8m C n.d.) (also Video)
In a park-like setting a pregnant woman asks a group of nursing
mothers questions about breastfeeding. Many misconceptions and
"old wives tales" are dispelled as these mothers and their babies
demonstrate and explain the benefits and techniques of breastfeeding. CINMD.

BREASTFEEDING: A SPECIAL CLOSENESS (23m C 1977)
Speaking simply and effectively, this warm supportive film addresses common questions people have about breastfeeding. People
from different lifestyles, backgrounds and economic levels tell how
they have successfully adjusted to a nursing infant. The benefits
of breastfeeding, both nutritionally and psychologically, are pointed
out in a very low key manner by parents, pediatric and nutrition
authorities. MOTINC.

BREASTFEEDING: PRENATAL AND POSTPARTAL PREPARATION
(26m C 1979)
Designed to guide health professionals in instructing expectant
and new mothers in the preparation and care of their breasts for
breastfeeding. Covers the following: breast support, breast cleans-
ing, nipple conditioning, nipple rolling, breast massage, manual expression, as well as awakening the baby, positioning the baby, initiating feeding, removing the baby from the breast, burping, and air
drying the nipple. p. Case Western Reserve University; POLYMR.

BREASTFEEDING EXPERIENCE, THE (23m C p1978, r1978)
Explores feelings, offers basic hints and shares the experiences
of 21 mothers nursing 22 babies (one set of twins). Includes breastfeeding from moments after delivery through postpartum in hospital,
to the first year of life in a variety of cross-cultural situations.
p./d. Gay Courter; PARPIC; UIL.

BREASTFEEDING FOR THE JOY OF IT (24m C n.d.)
Presents the facts of why it is important to breastfeed. Shows
emotions of breastfeeding mothers from all walks of life. Dr. Robert
S. Mendelsohn lends his expertise on the subject. CINMD; CWU.

BREATH/LIGHT/BIRTH (6m B p1975, r1978) (U.S.)
Presents a poetic evocation of the mystery of birth. In this black
and white film collage of abstracted images and natural sounds of a
woman in labor, motion picture techniques record that event in symbolism as she writhes in pain, struggles to move the fetus in position,
breathes in rhythm, screams, and finally from that agony, produces
a baby. p. Bruce Elder, Lightworks Production, Canada; PHOENIX.

BREATH ONE (3½m C 1975)
Explores dance movement based on sound. During a performance,
the natural movements of the dancer are amplified and repeated seven
times. The intended result is to perceive what a dancer hears with
a visual accompaniment. Dancer: Diane Hartwig; d. Agamemnon Andrianos; p. Kathleen Schreck; ANDRINOS.

BREWS AND POTIONS see ANIMATED WOMEN

BRIDEGROOM, THE COMEDIENNE, AND THE PIMP, THE (23m B
1968) German/Subtitled
Experimental mix of Munich Street hustling, a wedding benedic-
tion, three poems of St. John of the Cross, and the killing of a pimp.
Interspersed is a theatre piece by Ferdinand Bruckner. d. Jean-
Marie Straub; NYF.

BRIDES ARE NOT FOR BURNING (24m C 1981)
Though officially banned, the custom of dowry in India is thriving. In recent years, the demands for greater and larger dowries
on the families of the brides have driven many young women to suicide. This report looks at the families of the brides and grooms, the
government's reaction to this custom and the plight of these women.
JOURVI.

BRIDGET RILEY (28m C 1979)
Bridget Riley's perceptual art--from the black-and-white paintings
of the early 1960's, which first established her international reputation, to her recent concern with the self-generating luminosity of
pure color--has always involved the effects and processes of what
she calls "the great privilege of sight." This film explores the in-
spirations she draws from visual experiences in nature and follows her
into her studio where she organizes and activates her paintings. Excellent art film. Not much biographical data. d. David Thompson;
AFA.

BRIEF MOMENT (70m B 1933)
A nightclub blues singer marries and attempts to reform her

spendthrift alcoholic husband while her well-heeled new in-laws, who strongly disapprove of her as having no poise and no class, keep close watch. Since hubby receives $4,000 monthly allowance (for doing nothing), he proves difficult to reform. When, ultimately, "Woman's Tenacity" prevails and he does amount to something, however trivial, the family looks upon her with a bit more benevolence. This typical class-distinction 1930's comic-tragedy is played with all stops out! d. David Burton; Columbia; KPF.

BRIEF VACATION (106m C 1975) Italian/subtitled
Acclaimed for its incredible "sensitivity to women's feelings" by The New York Times, this film is a moving lyrical portrait of a Milanese factory worker who is sent to an elegant Alpine Sanitarium when the responsibilities of supporting her extended family begin to break down her health. In the idyllic mountain setting, she experiences the first pangs of self-awareness and becomes romantically involved with a tender young man. d. Vittorio De Sica. FI.

BRING BACK MY BONNIE (51m C 1982)
Patricia Neal, the actress who successfully fought back against the debilitating attack of a stroke, narrates this documentary explaining how strokes occur, the damaging effect they have and how people can be helped to recover. We meet several patients who have made great strides toward recovery. d./p. Heather Cook; FILMLB.

BRITTLE BONES (21½m C 1982)
Shows a number of people who are afflicted with brittle bones disease. Their struggle to cope with the disease, as well as their families' involvement, is documented. The film also contains some medical explanations about the disease, its treatment and what research is being done to find a cure. d./p. Elizabeth MacCallum; s.w. Katherine Gilday; ed. Elizabeth McCracken; AMBBS; FILMLB.

BROKEN PROMISE (28m C 1980) (Video)
A documentary on the tragedy of hundreds of thousands of old people starving in America. This program examines the fear, frustration and anger of being old, lonely and without enough to eat. Interviews with national experts are combined with the personal stories of Wayne County, Michigan seniors to create a factually documented program that conveys the human impact of hunger. d. Carl Bidleman; p. C. Bidleman/David M. Gregorich; FOCUSH.

BRONX BAPTISM (24m C p1979, r1980)
An experimental view of a service of baptism in a large Pentecostal congregation in the South Bronx, this film shows religious ritual as drama, performance, emotion, community, poetry, art and survival. d. Dee Dee Halleck; p. Dee Dee Halleck, Carlota Schoolman; HALLECK.

BRUGES--THE STORY OF A MEDIEVAL CITY (59m C p1977, r1978) (2 pts) (Video)

Illuminations from medieval manuscripts, paintings by Memling and Van Eyck, and live footage of Bruges and its reconstructed festivals capture the essence of the city when it was a flourishing center of European trade. Part I explores the foundations of Bruges, the formation of guilds, the charter that gave the citizens of Bruges their first liberties, the battles with the French, and most important, the flooding of the North Sea that gave Bruges' port to the world. Part II begins with the conflict between Ghent and Bruges and the war with France which cost the Flemish burghers their freedom. The reigns of the Valois Dukes of Burgundy--Philip the Bold, John the Fearless, Philip the Good, and Charles the Bold--are examined with emphasis on the court of Philip the Good. When Charles died, his daughter married Maximilian of Austria. Soon Bruges would succumb to Austrian rule, plague, and poverty. p./s.w. Mary Norman; p. Unicorn Productions, Inc.; IFB.

BRUJO (SHAMAN) (55m C p1975-6, r1978)
Study of the cults and shamanism of Mayan Indians in southern Mexico and Guatemala. Through three distinct healing ceremonies, the film illustrates the Indians' uses of their native medicine. Also available in French. p. Claudine Viallon, Georges Payrastre; Okexnon Films; DER.

BRUSH AND BARRE: THE LIFE AND WORK OF TOULOUSE-LAUTREC (59m C 1979) (also Video)
Documents the development of "Treclau," a UCLA master's thesis in dance theatre choreographed by Linda Fowler. Study of the preparation and thought required to create a new dance work. Concludes with a performance of "Treclau," a dramatic piece in seven tableaux, peopled by Henri de Toulouse-Lautrec's "characters," performed to original music and danced in costumes patterned after those seen in the artist's works. Choreographer: Linda Fowler; UCEMC.

BRUSHSTROKES (3m C 1982)
A simple artist is taken aback when characters step out of a door he has just drawn and inform him that his drawing-style is just not up to par. They then seize him, pull him into the world of the easel, and place him in an insane asylum for artists. Eventually, he manages to escape and returns to his own reality, where he resumes drawing the way he has always loved to draw. d./p./ed. Sylvie Fefer; CANFDC.

BUCKDANCER (6m B r1980) (also Video)
Recorded on the Sea Islands of Georgia. Black musicians dance on a front porch accompanied by voices, clapping, and broomstick. A craftsman shows how he made his fife and how he plays it. p. Bess Lomax Hawes; UCEMC.

BUDDHISM: THE PATH TO ENLIGHTENMENT (30m C 1978)
Traces the life of the Buddha from his birth as a prince through

time spent as a wandering mendicant in search of a solution for life's sorrow, to his later years when he trudged the dusty paths of India preaching his ego-shattering, life-redeeming message. That message is threaded throughout the film as we visit monasteries and families in two different craft communities and see how Buddhism has influenced the lives of these gentle people in southeast Asia. p. Elda Hartley; HARTLEY.

BUFFALO CREEK FLOOD: AN ACT OF MAN (39m C 1975)
Sometimes the by-product of the industrial processes by which we seek to produce energy is destruction of land and people. A very dramatic instance of this was the Buffalo Creek Valley disaster in Kentucky. A dam built of coal waste burst, flooding the entire valley. Many were left homeless, some killed. Includes interviews with survivors and company officials, all giving their version of what happened and why. d. Mimi Pickering; APPAL.

BUILDING A DREAM (24m C 1981)
Fourteen families pioneer a cooperative owner-built housing program, and during the year-long construction process discover not only the struggle and pride in building one's own home but also the excitement of creating a community. d. Julie Roman; p. Cindy Chostner/Maria Taylor/Julie Roman; FOCPRO; LAWRENP.

BUILDING CHILDREN'S PERSONALITIES WITH CREATIVE DANCING (30m B/C 1963)
Demonstrates the skillful personal guidance of children in dance experiences toward confidence in their own personalities and individual styles. The children are aged five to ten. The teacher encourages free expression of the children's feelings by suggesting word pictures to them and by praising their efforts. Dance teacher: Gertrude Copley Knight; p. Lawrence P. Frank, Jr., Gary Goldsmith; DIMENF; BU, IU, KENTSU, NILLU, PAS, SYRACU, UCEMC, UCLA, UIL, UMO, USC.

BUILDING FAMILY RELATIONSHIPS (30m C 1980) (also Video) Look at Me Series
Highlights: Building trust; building confidence; building a sense of belonging and security. Family relationships are fundamental in shaping the adult the child will become. Inclusion in family projects depicted in the film give children positive images of themselves. The trip to the beach and dramatization of a day at the zoo emphasize the need for patience and flexibility on the part of parents. p./s.w. Jane Kaplan, Wendy Roth; p. WTTW-TV: FI.

BUILDING MAINTENANCE: PLUMBING (26m C 1981) (Video)
Kevin McLean demonstrates plumbing skills to a targeted audience of building superintendents. His concise presentation affords immediate comprehension, and the discussion of plumbing problems and tools answers commonly asked questions. The tape offers instruction about

copper welding to repair broken water pipes, a toilet auger to clear
toilet stoppage, and an electric sewer cleaner for stoppages in sinks,
bathtubs, and washing machine lines. d. Debbie Viar; p. Richard
Derman; TEMANC.

BURGHERS OF CALAIS, THE (9m C p1980, r1981) (also Video)
    Tells fourteenth-century historian Jean Froissart's story of the
takeover of the French port city of Calais by Edward III, King of
England. The camera moves revealingly over the figures of Auguste
Rodin's monumental sculpture of the Burghers of Calais. After the
takeover, King Edward III gave orders that all citizens of the city
be killed. However, when soldiers begged for leniency, he commanded
instead the sacrifice of six citizens so the others could be saved.
Each figure in Rodin's sculpture is described in close-up detail, each
man is named and his background and reasons for volunteering to
die are considered. p. Leonora Pirret Hudson; MMM.

BURKS OF GEORGIA, THE (56m C 1976) Six American Families (Se-
    ries)
    The Burks of Georgia are a poor but proud family for whom sur-
vival is everything. Arlo and Grace live on five acres beyond the
Dalton city dump. Ten of their 13 children are alive and living with
wives, husbands and children in a collection of small houses and
trailers in the vicinity. Theirs is a solid, loving clan, but the lack
education and their menial jobs keep them chronically poor. p. Elinor Bunin Productions; p. Westinghouse Broadcasting Co.; d. WBCPRO,
CAROUF; KENTSU, PAS, UIL, USFL, UM.

BURNOUT (25m C 1980)
    A humorous look at a very serious vocational problem. Defines
"burnout"--the symptoms and types. Explains coping strategies, support systems, detached concern, compartmentalizing, and being aware
of vulnerabilities. Recommended for those in the helping professions,
both staff and managers. d./p. Mitchell/McDonald; MTITI; IU, PAS,
UCEMC, UM, UMN, UW.

BUSINESS OF AGING, THE (27m C 1982) (also Video)
    Examines the economics of nursing home operation and the reasons
why these institutions are often less than adequate. In privately-
owned facilities, owners want to maximize profits. Publicly-funded
homes operate on a tight budget. Both require cost-cutting, often
accomplished at the expense of services offered to the elderly. We
hear the frustrations of dedicated staff members who must neglect
the needs of the residents for lack of time. They deplore the over-
use of restraints and medication that keep patients docile. Citizen
action groups have been formed by relatives of patients to try to
improve conditions. The film seriously questions whether there is a
fundamental conflict between operating at a profit and providing good
care. It looks at the problems of both residents and staff caught in
this economic bind. d. Laszlo Barna; s.w. Laura Alper; p. National

Film Board of Canada in association with Canadian Union of Public employees; FILMLB.

BUSINESS OF NEWSPAPERS, THE (43m C p1978, r1979)
A comprehensive examination of the past, present and future of the newspaper business. Hugh Rudd interviews newspaper publishers, writers, and others concerned with news gathering to bring together a picture of the current status of newspapers in America. The film ends with Congressman Maurice Udall proposing that congress study newspaper conglomerates to determine if the public is best served by such massive chains. p. CBS News; p./s.w. Irina Posner; CAROUF.

BUT, DOCTOR, YOU SAID ... (29m C 1982) (also Video)
This film is designed to increase awareness of the role that communication plays in the health care process and to help health professionals and patients improve their own skills in communicating with each other. Part One consists of three scenes--"The Prescription," "The Hospital," and "The Surgeon and the Mother"--which show what can happen when barriers are erected and communication breaks down. In Part Two, health care professionals discuss the issues raised in Part One, giving examples from their own experience. p. Metropolitan Life Insurance Company; MTPS.

BUT I'LL NEVER BE A DANCER (5m B si 1976)
The artist's ambition to be a dancer is realized in her choreographic manipulation of filmic images. By using multiple exposure and repetition of rephotographed self-portraits, she creates dance movements in syncopated rhythms. p. Marcelle Pecot; WMM.

BUTTERFLY AND MOTH FIELD STUDIES (18m C 1966) (also Video)
Uses close-up photography to illustrate the life cycles of the butterfly and moth. p. Myrna I. Berlet, Walter H. Berlet; IFB.

BY DAYLIGHT AND IN DREAM (15m C p1978, r1979)
John Hall Wheelock (1886-1978) was one of America's most distinguished poets with a long and honored career in American letters. In this film, produced shortly before his death at 91, the poet reads from his work, including "Night Thoughts in Age" and "The Divine Insect." Shows scenes of his boyhood home in East Hampton, the very scenes that inspired and sustained him. p. Carolyn Tyson, Robert Blaisdell for Guild Hall of East Hampton, Inc.; d. Robert Blaisdell; Black Lions Productions, Ltd.; FILMLB.

-C-

CHD AND YOU (30m ea. ? 1976) (Video) (3 Pts.)
In three lessons, Sandra Stork (Assistant Director of Dietetics, Coordinator of Clinical Services and Associate Director of Division

of Medical Nutrition, University of Nebraska Medical Center) and
Debbie Luthy (Pediatric Dietition) will help the viewer to understand
the causes of coronary heart disease (CHD) and provide concrete
methods of personally controlling coronary heart disease. NETCHE.

CACHUCHA, THE (14m C 1980)
Shown is the famous ballet solo "The Cachucha" as reconstructed
from Zorn notation by Dr. Ann Hutchinson Guest. Performed twice
by Margaret Barbieri of the Sadlers' Wells Royal Ballet. DAN/UR.

CADDIE (102m C 1981)
A depression-era true story of a young housewife who runs away
from a violent and unfaithful husband, taking her children. Although
in 1925 women were told they couldn't make it on their own, Caddie
wasn't listening. A study in feminist perspectives. Starring Helen
Morris. p. Anthony Buckley; d. Donald Crombie; s.w. Joan Long;
Film Australia; IVY.

CAMERA THREE: DIRECTOR IN EXILE (29m c p1980, r1980) (Video)
Jonas Jurasas, successful Lithuanian theatre director, left the
U.S.S.R. because his work was censored and he was forced to compromise his artistic integrity. We see Jonas at a critical moment in
his career in America, when after years of struggle to find work
here, he has his directorial debut with "The Suicide" at the Trinity
Square Repertory Company in Rhode Island. The outcome of this production could shape his future. d./p. Nancy Porter; NOVACOM;
KINGF.

CAMERA THREE SERIES see COLORED GIRL, A: NTOZAKE SHANGE

CAN ANYBODY HEAR ME? (58m C 1982)
The vital need to communicate and to be understood is explored
through the achievements of people profoundly deaf since infancy.
Presented in three separate segments. The first introduces "a first"
--The American Deaf Dance Company filmed in rehearsal and intimate
performance. In the second segment, scenes from the busy life of
Emily, five years old and deaf since birth, are interwoven with her
parents' comments. Finally, world-renowned actor Bernard Bragg,
in interview and performance, reflects upon his life as a deaf child
of the 1930's and as an actor of the 1980's. p. Terese Finitzo-Hieber
/Valentine Gentile; d. V. Gentile; FUTMED.

CAN I HAVE IT ALL? (29m C 1977) (Video, Beta, VHS)
An investigation of whether women can successfully combine
marriage, children and career. Taped primarily at a women's conference on careers in science at the University of Wisconsin, Milwaukee.
Among the guests exploring th question from a variety of angles are
two working couples: Ted and Diane Johnson of Madison, and Sid and
Ethel Sloane of Milwaukee. The couples discuss individually and together how dual careers affect a marriage, relocation, children,

housework, and finances. Other guests are Elizabeth Janeway, author of A Man's World, Woman's Place; Sheila Tobias, Associate Pro-
vost of Wesleyan University; and Betty Vetter, Executive Director
of Scientific Manpower Commission. p. WMVS-TV, Milwaukee; PBSV.

CAN YOU HAVE IT ALL? DO YOU WANT IT ALL? PT. I: WHAT
    WOMEN SAY; PT. II: WHAT MEN SAY (60m C 1980) (Video)
    In Part I, four young women who have each made different career
and family choices discuss career, marriage, and family. They cover
such questions as, Can I combine career and marriage? How do children fit into my plans? If I choose all three--career, marriage, and
children--what options do I have to make it all work? In Part II,
four young men who have similarly made different career and family
decisions discuss the new roles they are finding themselves in as
women choose more frequently to pursue careers. d. Jerry Chamberlain; CATALYST.

CANADIANS IN CONFLICT: A HISTORIAN'S VIEW see BREAD AND
    ROSES: THE STRUGGLE OF CANADIAN WORKING WOMEN

CANCER TREATMENT (60m C 1980) (Video) Better Health (Series)
    Dr. Vincent DeVita, Director of the Division of Cancer Treat-
ment, National Cancer Institute, reviews various approaches to cancer treatment--surgery, radiation, and chemotherapy. Cancer is explained by comparing normal cell growth with the disordered growth
typical of tumors. Free loan. p. National Institute of Health, MTPS.

CAN'T STOP THE MUSIC (118m C 1980) (also in Scope)
    Former fashion model Valerie Perrine lives in Greenwich Village
with aspiring young composer Steve Guttenberg. To help him get
his music heard, she puts together a demo tape and the search begins for musicians that eventually become the Village People. With
Valerie Perrine, Bruce Jenner. d. Nancy Walker; AFD; SWANK.

CAN'T TAKE NO MORE (28m C p1980, r1981)
    The first film to trace the history of the occupational health and
safety movement in the U.S. from the Industrial Revolution to the
present. Examines the interplay among industry, government, and
labor in the formulation of American health and safety policy for the
workplace. Use of rare archival footage and photos links the past
to the present with modern documentary segments. Narrated by
Studs Terkel. d. Ginny Durrin; p./s.w. Janet Hayman. Music
score by Oscar Brand. Produced for OSHA by Durrin Films; DUR-
RIN.

CANTICO (40m C 1982)
    This collaboration between a composer and a filmmaker has re-
sulted in a sensuous work on the life of St. Francis of Assisi, the
eighth centenary of whose birth was celebrated in 1982. Shot in
Assisi, the film lyrically evokes the evolution of the saint from a

dissolute young man to an ascetic visionary. Through re-photography, the images are fragmented into a dreamlike experience. The composer uses electronically processed Renaissance music to provide an aural counterpoint to the imagery. d. James Herbert; p. Barbara Kolb; music: Barbara Kolb; ed./s.w. James Herbert; HERBERTJ.

CARE AND MAINTENANCE OF A GOOD MARRIAGE, THE (28m ea. C 1982)
In each of the films, Dr. O. Dean Martin shares the results of his observations and experiences gained through his extensive counseling during the past 20 years. Dr. Martin is Pastor of the Trinity United Methodist Church in Gainesville, Florida. He is also acclaimed as a lecturer and visiting professor in the field of marriage counseling. The films are designed for group use and discussion. The series provides the basic resource for a six-session program or course on marriage preparation or enrichment. A guide is included. p. UMCom Production; MMM.

These are the films included: I: WHY GOOD MARRIAGES OFTEN FAIL; II: IDENTIFYING AND RAISING THE LITTLE YOU; III: SCRATCHING WHERE IT ITCHES; IV: SEX: RESETTING THE THERMOSTAT; V: CLEARING STATIC ON THE LINE; VI: KEYS TO KEEPING A GOOD THING GOING

CARE OF THE NEWBORN BABY (12m C n.d.)
Stresses the attitudinal changes and physical adjustments required of a young couple on the arrival of their new infant. Includes deciding to nurse or bottle-feed, burping, changing diapers, use of rectal thermometer and bathing the baby. Stresses being relaxed and loving to truly enjoy a new baby. Also available in Spanish. MIFE.

CAREER DEVELOPMENT: A PLAN FOR ALL SEASONS (26m C 1978)
Management Training Series
Career development programs offer one of the best means of analyzing an employee's work goals and coordinating them with an organization's plan for positive, directed results--a total human resource development system. This film describes the philosophy behind implementation and the very positive results of such a program at Collins Food International, including interviews with Dr. Beverly Kaye, a career development consultant, and a variety of enthusiastic employees ranging from hourly workers to upper management. Skyline Career Development Center in Dallas is featured as an example of pre-career planning, a training facility that allows experimentation and education in a variety of jobs as a testing ground for young adults. p. CRM/McGraw-Hill Films; CRM; CWU, PAS, UMO.

CAREER DEVELOPMENT OF WOMEN SERIES see LIFE CAREER PATTERNS OF WOMEN; MALE PERSPECTIVES ON WOMEN'S CHANGING ROLES

CAREER IN THE 70's SERIES see WOMEN IN CAREERS

CARNIVAL OF RHYTHM (20m B 1939)
This Brazilian dance-story features songs and dances from Brazil, a South American Indian courtship dance and a dance from Africa. The dance numbers included are "Ciudade Maravillosa," "Los Indios," "Batucada," and "Adeus Terras." Dance Company: Katherine Dunham Dance Company; Choreographer: Katherine Dunham; p. Warner Bros. Pictures; d. Jean Negulesco; DANCFA.

CARNIVORE (59m C 1976) (Video)
This is a documentary about meat-eating habits in the United States which examines the anthropological aspects of meat eating and the different species of red meat and poultry. The economic structure of the livestock industry and the increased interest in vegetarianism due to new claims of health hazards associated with meat are also examined. Interviews with chefs, beef producers, agricultural economists are included. p. Iowa P.T. Network; PBSV.

CAROLE MORISSEAU AND THE DETROIT CITY DANCE COMPANY (14m C 1981)
A young, energetic dance company is put through its paces as choreographer and artistic director Carole Morisseau rehearses her company in preparation for opening night. Morisseau's thoughts on dance and performance combine with views of rehearsal and opening night performance to produce an intimate backstage look at the world of dance. p. Sue Marx/Robert Handley; LREDF.

CASE OF BARBARA PARSONS, THE (52m C p1978, r1980--U.S.) (also Video)
Dramatizes a situation that could happen in any unionized company--a violation of a contract between management and labor--and illustrates the four main steps to be followed in the grievance procedure. p. Parker Film Associates, Montreal for Labour Canada; d./s.w. Morton Parker; MOKINA; PHS, UW.

CASE OF WORKING SMARTER--NOT HARDER, A (15m C p1981, r1982)
Shows one tremendous manager's unique system of management and the positive effects his system has on his subordinates, his superiors, himself, and the productivity of the entire organization. d. Ron Underwood; p. Dixie J. Capp/R. Underwood; CRM; IU.

CASTLE MAN (13m C p1978, r1979) (also Video)
Documents the life work of a "20th century Knight," Mr. Harry Andrews, and provides the viewer with some insight into what it is that makes him eternally young. p. Mary Uible Nebergall; JOURVI; WSU.

CASTLES OF CLAY (55m C p1978, r1979)
Presents a film study of the life cycle and ecology of the African termite. p. Joan Root, Alan Root, Survival Anglia Ltd.; BENCHMF.

CAT: A WOMAN WHO FOUGHT BACK (27m C p1978, r1978) (also Video)

Cat tells the story behind the headlines. Undefeated with 14 K.O.'s, the 24-year-old female boxer takes on the New York State Athletic Commission, Joe Frazier and Muhammad Ali, who all insist that the ring is no place for a lady. She fights with conviction and courage both in the ring and the legislative arena to strike down laws that have prevented women from boxing professionally. p./d. Jane Warrenbrand, Champion Films, Ltd.; FI, VIEWFI, UIL.

CATHERINE HOWARD (93m C 1976) The Six Wives of Henry VIII (Series)
Focuses on the Duke of Norfolk's attempts to promote his family by convincing Henry VIII to marry his niece, Catherine Howard, a young, beautiful woman who is disenchanted with the aging Henry. Reveals Catherine, unable to bear Henry a son, seducing Master Culpepper at the suggestion of Norfolk. Concludes with the beheading of Catherine, the execution of her lovers, and the banishment of Norfolk. p. BBC-TV; TIMLIF; IU, CWU.

CATHERINE OF ARAGON (94m C 1976) The Six Wives of Henry VIII (Series)
Portrays Catherine of Aragon, a Spanish princess living in England and a widow of Henry VIII's brother. Depicts the youthful Henry marrying Catherine, who bears his daughter Mary and lives happily with him for 18 years. Dramatizes Henry's decision to leave Catherine for Anne Boleyn in the hopes of producing a male heir. Includes the controversy of the Church's position on the divorce as well as the opinions of such persons as Cardinal Wolsey, John Fisher and Thomas More. Shows Catherine in her final days as Queen, refusing to deny her position as Queen and her daughter's right to the throne. p. BBC-TV; TIMLIF; CWU, IU.

CATHERINE PARR (91m C 1976) The Six Wives of Henry VIII (Series)
Portrays Catherine Parr, a plain but intelligent woman who brings new life to the aged and sickly Henry VIII. Depicts the controversy among Bishop Winchester, Bishop Cranmore, and the Seymours over the successor to the throne. Highlights Catherine's concern for Henry's children and her courage in opposing Winchester on the issue of religious persecution. Concludes with Henry's death and Catherine's acceptance of Thomas Seymour's marriage proposal for the sake of the heir's protection. p. BBC-TV; TIMLIF; CWU, IU.

CATHERINE THE GREAT: A PROFILE IN POWER (26m C 1974) Profiles in Power Series
Explores through the use of an imaginary historical interview the life and role of Catherine the Great of Russia. Discusses the use of feminine wiles and her genius for public relations which helped her ascend from insignificance to the Russian throne. Records Catherine's life as a ruler, noting numerous instances of her abuses of power. Features Zoe Caldwell as Catherine. LCA; IU.

CATHY (14m C p1982, r1983)
A funny and inspiring story about courage, determination and
the pursuit of a dream. Geri Jewell of NBC's "Facts of Life" stars
as Cathy, a teenager with cerebral palsy, who decides to try out for
cheerleader. Cathy is willing to risk being laughed at as she seeks
her goal. Her friends and family try to persuade her not to try out,
but she decides to go ahead anyway. The film is open-ended. p.
Fran Burst-Terranella, Cheryl Gosa; IDEAIM.

CATS, THE (93m B 1964) Swedish Dialogue/Subtitled
Whenever they have a chance, the women in this depressing, in-
dustrial environment lighten their long days by talking about sex.
Depicts with candid realism the emotions and expressions in a group
of women in an atmosphere of oppression that leads to frustration
and anger. Based on a play by Sigyn Sahlin with Eva Dahlbeck,
Gio Petre, Isa Quensel. d. Henning Carlsen; s.w. Sigyn Sahlin.
ABF.

CAUTION: WOMEN WORKING (29m C 1980) (2' HB Tape)
In this musical portrayal of the role of American women in society
and as members of the work force, folksinger-composer Sheila Ritter
weaves a story through rich, comic and serious songs. Host: Professor Gayle D. Ness, Department of Sociology, University of Michigan. UMMRC; UM.

CE SIECLE A 50 ANS see DAYS OF OUR YEARS

CEDDO (120m C p1977, r1978) Wolof/Subtitled
Deals with Senegal's convoluted past. Focuses on the revolt by
the "ceddo" (the villagers or peasants) against a converted Muslim
king and his councilors. Involved also is the kidnapping of a princess and the attempts to rescue her. Set in a Senegalese village and
accompanied by dynamic music, the film has an ethnicity of an anthropological document and the epic quality of a Greek morality drama.
It raises important issues: Islamic colonialism, African involvement
in providing slaves for the Western hemisphere, the status of women
in Africa. d. Ousmane Sembene; p. Higher Ground Cinema; NYF.

CELEBRATION (4m C 1982)
An impressionistic documentary on California watercolorist Katherine Myers as she sets out one rainy day to create from scratch a
particularly large painting. Interwoven into the fabric of the film
is a mini-retrospective of the artist's past work, punctuated by the
musical flourishes of a Bach concerto and culminating in a study of
the newly finished piece. p./d./s.w. Erik Friedl; FRIEDL.

CELTIC TRILOGY, A (96m C 1981)
An ambitious and impressionistic blend of dramatic folklore and
documentary about the Celtic people. Combines rich and textured
imagery from locations in Brittany, Ireland and Wales with an evocative

collection of tales from Celtic mythology and history as told by Siobhan McKenna, critically acclaimed Irish stage actress. Ms. Dowdy
has chosen to structure the film within an episodic, rather than narrative, framework in which a series of vignettes are linked together
to form an entirety. There are also interviews with contemporary
Celts. p. Kathleen Dowdy; FIRRNF.

CESAREAN CHILDBIRTH (18m C n.d.)
    Shows that even in a surgical delivery many of the principles of
family-centered maternity care can still be followed. The woman in
this film is having a repeat cesarean section. She is administered
spinal anesthesia and as a result is aware and able to converse with
her husband and medical attendants throughout the delivery of her
child. CINMD.

CHAIN TO BE BROKEN (26m C 1978)
    Deals with individual and community solutions and alternatives
to the child abuse problem. Highlights Parents Anonymous, a working solution for parents with abuse problems. FMSP; CWU.

CHALLENGE TO CHANGE, THE (23m C 1977)
    Dramatized story about the fear a woman executive must overcome
when she learns she is being promoted to an overseas position. Excellent resource for organizational programs designed to help people
cope with change. RTBL; UCEMC.

CHAMPIONS, THE (113m C n.d.)
    Renê Levesque and Pierre Elliott Trudeau, Canada's chief polit-
ical protagonists, are the focus of this documentary. Part I covers
their early years up to 1967; Part II continues to 1977. Using rare
photos, newsreel footage and interviews with close political colleagues,
the film provides the background to the struggle between the two
men and their ideologies. p. NFBC in cooperation with the Canadian
Broadcasting Corporation; d. Donald Brittain; p. Janet Leissner, D.
Brittain. NFBC.

CHANGES (28m C 1979) Begin with Goodbye Series
    CHANGES introduces the theme of the series--that all of life is
beginnings and endings, "Each involving saying goodbye to yesterday
so we can get on with tomorrow." Guide included. MMM.

CHANGING AMERICAN FAMILY, THE (25m C c1980) (slt)
    Compares preindustrial, industrial and postindustrial families and
charts the connections between family type and broad changes in the
larger society.
    Using current photographs and research, this program examines
prevailing notions about the "ideal" family and considers what family means in today's terms. It looks at alternative life-styles and
how changing social values affect families, describes advances in reproductive technology, and points to issues raised by "the new bi-

ology." Analyzes census data, survey material and recent trends, and speculates on the future of the family in an information-based society and within the emerging solar economy. CHRSTA.

CHANGING COURSE: A SECOND CHANCE (28½m C p1980, r1981)
A recently divorced and a widowed woman who had been home-bound each learn about new educational and job opportunities at the Displaced Homemakers Center in Oakland, California. Other women in similar circumstances develop electronics skills in a special program for women in Boston. All lead new and different life-styles because of their changed roles in society. d./p. Pat Naggier, P. Powell; ex. p. Robert Richter; PTVP.

CHANGING COURSE IN THE SPIRIT OF TITLE IX (28½m C p1980, r1981)
Title IX, prohibiting sex discrimination in all federally assisted education programs, is interpreted by a Black Sex Equity Supervisor with examples: a young girl challenges her male auto shop teacher's attitudes; girls participate in the "boys only" Project Adventure; high school girls discuss strategies to change sex discrimination; Karen Logan, pro-basketball player, describes her career struggles without Title IX. d./p. Pat Powell; ex. p. Robert Richter; PTVP.

CHANGING COURSE: SEE WHAT WE CAN BE (28½m C p1980, r1981)
Methods of counteracting early onset of sex stereotyping are shown (new toys, books). Boys opt to be ballet dancers in a nursery school circus. Girls are encouraged to do carpentry. Older Hispanic children learn about community leaders. Children visit an engineer and ferry boat pilot, both women. All illustrate the value of non-sexist education from the earliest age of a child through career exploration by junior high students. Sponsor: U.S. Office of Education. d./p. Pat Naggiar; ex. p. Robert Richter; PTVP.

CHANGING ROLE FOR MEN (29m C 1980) (Video) One on One Series
The changing role of men in American Society is discussed by Dr. Ansel Woldt, Associate Professor of Counseling Psychology at Kent State University. Interviewed by Sandy Halem. p. KSU-TV; KSU-AV; KENTSU.

CHAPARRAL PRINCE, THE (20m C 1982)
A dramatization of an O. Henry story. Designed to inspire students of creative writing classes. d. Mark Cullingham; p. Elaine Halpert Sperber, Highgate Picture; LCA.

CHAPTER IN HER LIFE, A (87m B 1923)
Lois Weber was one of the pioneering women directors, and this is one of the rarest examples of her work still extant. Shows the relationships between a child and the adults in her life. d. Lois Weber; EMGEE.

CHARLEEN (58m C p1979, r1980)
Portrait of Charlotte, North Carolina native Charleen Swansea
Whisnant, protégée of Ezra Pound, a highly innovative, widely acclaimed teacher in the Poetry-in-the-Schools Program. Shows a month
in her eccentric life, including classroom teaching scenes, poetry
performance, and one emotional breakdown. d./p. Ross McElwee;
MCELWD.

CHARLESTON HOME MOVIE (5m C p1980, r1980)
An animated "home movie": images and memories of living in
Charleston, South Carolina. Music by Keith Jarrett. d./p. Deanna
Morse; PICTS.

CHEROKEE (26m C 1976)
While presenting a clear, though brief, history of the Cherokee
and the removal of the Western Cherokee to Oklahoma, this television
program illustrates a significant feature of contemporary Indian life--
the pressures for an Indian community to be self-supporting in a
money economy and the difficulties to find the means to do it. For
the Eastern Cherokee leadership, encouraged by the Bureau of the
Indian Affairs, the answer has been to develop tourism, which they
are trying to do. The film reflects the variety of opinions about this
kind of development among community people. Some stress the advantages of increasing affluence and others their anxieties over the
weakening of Cherokee culture and sense of community. p. Brenda
Horsefield; ex. p. Philip Hobel; p. Document Associates/BBC; DOCUA.

CHERRY TREE CAROL (10m C 1975)
A ballet based on a traditional Christmas carol. The story of the
Holy Family (and of Mary's wish for cherries when she is with child)
is translated into a Southern mountain version. Dance Company:
Appalachian Dance Troupe; Choreographer: Agnes De Mille; p. Ed-
ucational Broadcasting Corporation; Paramount; BUDGET; UIL, SYRA-
CU, UMN, PSU.

CHIANG CHING: A DANCE JOURNEY (30m C 1982)
Sensitive biographical portrait of a talented and innovative young
Chinese American dancer and choreographer. Traces her childhood
in China, where she trained at the exacting Peking Dance Academy,
as well as her emigration to Hong Kong, where she became a teenage movie star. In the early 1970's she moved to America and founded
her own dance company. Excerpts from several performances, filmed
in New York City and during a triumphant return visit to China in
1980, show that she is creating a new dance idiom that integrates
the rigorous principles and techniques of traditional Chinese dance
with the free expression of modern Western styles. Visually beautiful production. p. Lana Pih Jokel; UCEMC.

CHICANA (22m C 1979)
Traces the traditional and the emerging roles of Chicanos from

pre-Columbian times to the 1970's. Shows how women have made important contributions as workers, mothers, activists, educators, and leaders despite their generally oppressed status in the Latino culture. p./d. Sylvia Morales; RUIZP; USC.

CHICKEN (28m C p1980, r1981) (ed.) (also Video)
Explores reasons behind alienation of teenagers from school peers, formation of gangs, vandalism. Based upon a strong faith of Mr. Fisher, a high school teacher, that there are better ways to deal with a very serious crime wave within the school and among the students, than calling in the police. This story reflects real situations handled in a realistic way. p. Judy Conway Greening, Mike Rhodes; s.w. Richard Fielder; PAULST.

CHICKEN IN EVERY POT, A (30m B n.d.)
Focuses on several merchants who work in the Italian Market of South Philadelphia. Loosely interrelated sequences depict the routine of their workday and establish the ambience of this European-style street market. In discussions and interviews the merchants recall the past of the community, argue about prices and politics, and ponder their plans and hopes for the future. The film stresses both the role of tradition and the influence of American culture as forces that shape the hopes and ambitions expressed by the main characters. p. Jan Krawitz, Thomas Ott; TEMPLEU.

CHILD ABUSE (29m C 1978)
Three common types of child abuse--battered child, father-daughter incest, and wanton neglect--are dramatized to explain legal aspects law enforcement personnel should know, including key indicators in battered child cases and the right in these cases to warrantless search and seizure in an emergency. Defines felony child endangering. p. Attorney Generals Office/State of California; WSU.

CHILD ABUSE (PART I) (29m C 1980) Feelings Series
Do parents really have to use physical means to punish children or to show them who's boss? In this two-part special, 8-year-old Cheri and 12-year-old Dennis--both child-abuse victims whose parents sought help--tell Dr. Lee Salk about parents who hurt. In both programs, clips of their mothers talking about their abusive behavior form a striking counterpoint to the children's reactions when they first hear how their mothers feel. p. PBS Video; PBSV.

CHILD ABUSE: A PERSPECTIVE ON BEING A PARENT (29m C 1977)
(also Video)
A series of excerpts from interviews with six abusive or potentially abusive parents. The parents' stories indicate what leads to abuse: isolation, absence of love as a child, and economic stress. Also emphasized is the function of positive treatment programs in effecting a change in abusive parents' lives. CORNELL.

CHILD ABUSE: A PERSPECTIVE ON PARENT AIDES (28m C 1977)
     (also Video)
     Parent aides act as caregivers to abusive parents by getting to
know them more intimately than most professionals and by providing
the friendship and role modeling these parents lacked as children.
Aides are a vital part of the rehabilitative services of a coordinated
team approach (as described in CHILD ABUSE: A TOTAL TREAT-
MENT PERSPECTIVE below). Six parent aides candidly share their
experiences and provide insight into the nature of abusive parents
and the role of the parent aide. CORNELL.

CHILD ABUSE: A TOTAL TREATMENT PERSPECTIVE (30m C 1976)
     (also Video)
     The team approach illustrates the importance of a coordinated
program for child-abuse treatment. Professionals are selected from
public and private organizations in the community to meet the specific needs of a family. The focus is on the abusive parents, who
are committed to participate in most meetings. Intended for use with
case workers, child protection personnel, public health nurses, therapists, lawyers, parent aides, and community task forces on child
abuse and neglect. Discussion guide included. CORNELL.

CHILD ABUSE AND THE LAW (27m C r1977)
     Familiarizes viewers with federal and state laws concerning child
abuse. Tells what teachers can do to help abused or neglected children. d. Dan Q. Lundmark; p. The Motion Picture Co. Inc.; s.w.
Richard Singerman; PEREN.

CHILD ABUSE: CRADLE OF VIOLENCE (20m C 1976)
     Intimate interviews with abusive parents in the areas of child be-
havior and discipline create an understanding of child abuse and the
need to break the cycle. Alternatives to corporal punishment and
potential stress situations are presented. p. Motorola Teleprograms,
Inc.; MTITI; CORNELL, PAS, IU, UCEMC, UIL, UMN, UM.

CHILD ABUSE: DON'T HIDE THE HURT (13m C 1980)
     Children learn the importance of reporting incidents of real abuse
to a responsible adult while gaining understanding that guilty parents
need and really want help in controlling their violence. The story
of Greg dramatizes aspects of a typical case, from the sense of guilt
of the child to the legal protection available and the help available
to the guilty parent. At the end, Greg's concern for a neglected
neighborhood child indicates the value of successful counseling. p.
Aims Media; AIMS.

CHILD ABUSE: THE BATTERED CHILDREN (60m C n.d.) (Video)
     In 1977, in New York City alone, 22,000 children were either
hurled through windows, branded, starved or otherwise abused;
and at least 200 were beaten into the obituary columns. In candid
interviews with parents who have allegedly abused their children,

as well as with psychiatrists, clergymen, social workers and the victims themselves, the program traces the social epidemic that has become the leading cause of infant death in the United States. p. Jeffrey Norton Publishers, Inc.; NORTONJ.

CHILD ABUSE; THE PEOPLE NEXT DOOR (20m C p1980, r1980)
(also Video)
Abandoned by her husband and alone with her two small children, Mary is isolated and without emotional support. Her mounting frustration has led her to physically and emotionally abuse her children. Fortunately, Mary's neighbor Angie is sensitive to Mary's problems and helps her confront them honestly. Together, Mary and Angie visit a parents' counseling center where they both learn about the individual and group counseling, crisis hotline, parenting classes and other support available to parents. Mary learns that she is not a monster, but a person in need of support and more effective methods of parenting. p. Shire Films Production; BARRF; UIL.

CHILD CUSTODY (29m C 1975) (Video) Woman Series
Dan Molinoff, a New York father who recently won joint custody of his children in a precedent-setting legal decision, and Doris L. Sassower, the women's rights attorney who represented him, discuss the case and its meaning in the area of women's rights as well as equal rights for fathers. Sandra Elkin, Moderator. p. WNED-TV, New York; PBSV.

CHILD IS BORN, A (22m C 1971)
Traces the intimate and beautiful relationship between a young wife and her husband from the moment they decide to have children to the birth and homecoming of their first baby. Illustrates the development of the embryo and fetus through delivery. Also emphasizes pre- and post-natal care of the infant and mother. Adapted from the Swedish film, The Child. p. Ealing Films; CORNELL.

CHILD MOLESTATION: A CRIME AGAINST CHILDREN (11m C n.d.)
How's a youngster to know what is molestation and what isn't? Who are the offenders? What should kids do if they are molested-- or think they're going to be? Interviews with youngsters who have been through it--and have been helped by counselling--provide clear and helpful answers to these questions. Kids tell viewers things that are difficult for many adults to articulate. AIMS.

CHILD MOLESTATION: WHEN TO SAY NO (14m C 1980)
Without sensation or scare tactics, this straightforward film tells the truth in a way the child can understand and gives young viewers the confidence they need if they should ever be approached themselves. Four vignettes dramatize typical encounters. In each case, the attempt proved futile because the children have learned how to "say no," plus the importance of reporting such incidents to a responsible adult immediately. AIMS; WSU.

CHILD MOLESTERS: FACTS AND FICTION (30m C 1974) Community
Protection Series
A film to increase understanding of pedophilia (abnormal child-
adult sexual relationships) and to prevent or decrease incidents of
it in the community. Parents and children discuss the problem; myths
about it are contrasted with the facts. A dramatization of an incident includes parents' reactions, both negative and positive, and a
psychiatrist gives guidance on handling the child's experience. Discusses the probable results for offenders and the role of police and
the courts. p. Summerhill Productions; PARACD; UNEV, IU.

CHILD OF THE ANDES (24m C p1978, r1978)
High in the Andes Mountains of Peru is a small village where the
ancient skill of carving stories and folklore on dried gourds is still
flourishing. Twelve-year-old Julia learns this art from her uncle, a
carver, whose gourds are intricately crafted. Shows Julia completing
a fine gourd and taking it to sell at a huge Sunday market in the
city. d. Paul Salzman; p. Deepa and P. Salzman; SUNRIF.

CHILD/PARENT RELATIONSHIPS; SELECTED SEGMENTS (29m C 1978)
This film is a composite of selected segments from the first five
films. Infant stimulation; supermarket and shoe store scenes; grand-
mother/child relationships; home math activities; story-time and puppetry; helping a working mom with cooking; self-help ideas. p.
WTTW-TV; PEREN; KENTSU.

CHILDBIRTH BLUES (20m C 1979)
About natural childbirth and an unwed mother. Explores the
circumstances surrounding the birth, the actual birth, and follow-up
one year later. d./p. Mary Halawani; HALWAM.

CHILDBIRTH FOR THE JOY OF IT, PT. I (23m C n.d.)
Shows five couples involved in childbirth. Husbands are in the
delivery room, and women are delivering with minimal intervention.
As the focus is on the delivery itself from the patients' point of view,
very little first-stage labor is shown. p. Cinema Medica; CINMD.

CHILDBIRTH FOR THE JOY OF IT, PT. II (24m C n.d.)
Shows many of the advances made in family-centered maternity
care. There is less medical intervention. This film shows first-stage
labor, actual births from the doctor's side of the table and more
mother-child bonding than was shown in Part I (see above). All
the couples toast their newborns with orange juice and walk out of
the delivery room with their children in their arms. This sequel was
made five years after Part I. Cinema Medica; CINMD.

CHILDHOOD SEXUAL ABUSE: FOUR CASE STUDIES (45m C 1977)
Juvenile Justice Series
Documentary of the trauma experienced by women who were sex-
ually abused during their childhood. Although shown in a peer-

counseling workshop, the emphasis is on the women's experience and problems, rather than on methods of clinical treatment. Study guide by Dr. Nahman Greenberg is included. p. Motorola Teleprograms, MTITI; IU, PAS.

CHILDHOOD'S END (28m C 1981) (also Video)
Troubling statistics reveal that 6,000 to 8,000 adolescents take their own lives each year. For every one who commits suicide there are 50 more who attempt it. Suicide is the second leading cause of death in this age group. This documentary portrait of three suicidal youngsters will help counselors, parents and young people begin a constructive and possibly preventive dialogue on this emotionally charged subject. The film does not try to simplify a very complicated phenomenon. It leaves a lasting impression of the tragedy and waste of this irreversible action and the importance of using all resources to help troubled youngsters. p./d. Robert Lang; p. Kensington Communications; FILMLB; UM.

CHILDREN: A CASE OF NEGLECT (56m C 1974)
A documentary about the plight of children in America who do not receive adequate, if any, health care. These number at twelve million. Shows the insufficiency of Medicaid and examines correctable health problems in rural and urban areas of both the very poor and the middle income groups. p. D. Pamela Hill; p. ABC-TV; MACMFL.

CHILDREN AND SEAT BELTS (½m C p1980, r1980) (Video)
Urges parents to use seat belts for their children. d. Phil Schulman; p. Wendy Mayer; MTPS.

CHILDREN AT BIRTH (24m C 1979) (also Video, S8)
From the hatching of chickens to the birth of a baby and the delivery of the placenta, this very gentle film prepares children of any age for the miracle of birth. Children are present at their siblings' births which occur both in and out of the hospital setting. p. Cinema Medica; CINMD; UMN.

CHILDREN DANCE (14m B 1970)
Boys and girls from kindergarten through third grade in suburban and inner city classrooms in Washington, D.C., are filmed during their dance sessions. The children express feelings, moods, and ideas through rhythmic patterns and produce dance improvisations. The film suggests ways that teachers who don't specialize in dance can awaken children's creativity in movement. d. Geraldine Dimondstein, Naima Prevots; p. G. Dimondstein; p. UCEMC; UCEMC, UIL.

CHILDREN, ENFANTS, NIÑOS (23m C p1979, r1981)
This nonnarrated film illustrates the joys and the difficulties of childhood. It looks at the everyday life of children around the world: fetching water in Thailand, herding cattle in Africa, swinging in hammocks in the Amazon jungle or playing hockey in Canada. d. Tina Viljoen; p. Barrie Howells; CRM.

CHILDREN OF DIVORCE (37m C 1976) (also Video)
This study of the impact of divorce on children points up the
necessity for parents to bury their own hostilities, to communicate
without anger, and to provide the children with free access to both
parents. Children are the real victims of divorce since they do not
understand the situation. Touches on child-support laws and describes the public and private agencies which help children and single
parents to adjust. Custody is no longer automatically given to the
mother. The courts are finally considering the child's rights and
welfare above the "rights" of either parent. d. Mike Gavin; FI;
KENTSU, UIL, UMN.

CHILDREN OF OUR TIME (58m C 1974)
Portrays the horrors faced by today's children, including parental divorce. p. Larry Gosnell; CBC.

CHILDREN OF THE LONG-BEAKED BIRD (29m C 1976)
A portrait of a modern Native American family that erases the
stereotype made infamous by Westerns. Dominic Old Elk is a 12-year-
old Crow Indian. He lives next to Custer Battlefield, Montana. His
great great grandfather was one of the scouts who warned General
Custer not to attack the large force of Sioux and Cheyenne camped
by the banks of the Little Big Horn. Today Dominic is proud of his
heritage, but he's part of young America too. He likes rock music
and riding horses. He's equally at home in a coke shop or a teepee.
He knows everything about Muhammad Ali and Old Man Coyote. Starting with a concise review of Native American life and history, children learn to accept and appreciate another American culture. p.
Peter Davis and Swedish Television/Amanda and Burton Fox, John
Hoskyns-Abrahall, Winifred Scherrer; BULFRG.

CHILDREN OF THEATRE STREET, THE (90m C 1977--U.S.) (English)
For over a century, the Vaganova Choreographic Institute (the
Kirov School) in Leningrad has been acknowledged as one of the
world's great ballet schools. From it have come such legendary performers as Nureyev, Pavlova, Nijinsky and Baryshnikov. This behind-the-scenes documentary shows the training of their successors.
Focusing on three students at different stages of their careers, the
film examines the intense competition for entry into the school and the
eight years of grueling training which follow. The students' intense
commitment culminates in the Kirov's extraordinary commencement performance, in which the professional futures of the young dancers are
determined. p. Earle Mack; d. Robert Dornhelm, E. Mack; s.w. Beth
Gutcheon; a.p. Jean Dalryple; ed. Tina Frese; p. Mack-Vaganova
Production; CORINTH.

CHILDREN OF WORKING MOTHERS (29m C 1979) (also Video) Are
You Listening Series
Producer Martha Stuart has gathered together a group of chil-
dren to discuss their experiences growing up in homes with working

mothers. These children, ranging in age from 10 to 18 and from rural, suburban, and urban environments, talk about the things that are important to them: how it feels to come home after school to an empty house and the ways they have developed to cope with this; the greater sense of independence they have gained from being more on their own; their pride in their mother's work; and their feelings about being (married to) working mothers someday. p. Martha Stuart; STUARTM.

CHILDREN'S ART CARNIVAL--LEARNING THROUGH THE ARTS (17m C 1979)
The Children's Art Carnival has been cited by the National Endowment for the Arts as a model for the nation for its innovative approach to learning. Founded by the Museum of Modern Art, this educational institution is now independent and housed in a brownstone in Hamilton Heights in Harlem. The film traces the various activities of the Art Carnival both on its site and around New York City. "Learning through the arts" clearly illustrates why the Children's Art Carnival has been successful in its creative approach to learning for the past decade. p./d. Monica J. Freeman; p. The Black Filmmaker Foundation; TRNSIT.

CHILDREN'S AUTHOR: JUDY BLUME (17m C p1979, r1980) (also Video)
An author of best-selling books for juveniles, Judy Blume might be called a surrogate parent. She writes about a subject parents are reluctant to discuss--sex. Blume has sold some seven million books, mainly to youngsters in the 10- to 13-year-old bracket. Her rapport with her readers is evident in the film when she talks with a group of youngsters at an elementary school in Aurora, Colorado, and in the long lines of young people at a bookstore autograph session. Other scenes were filmed at her home in Sante Fe, New Mexico, and in a northern California school where her book for young adults, Forever, is used as a text in a sex education course. Among parents, Blume is controversial; but the kids are unanimous in feeling that Blume fills a need which their parents and teachers either cannot or will not. Reported by Jack Perkins for "Prime Time Sunday." p. George Paul, NBC News; FI.

CHILDREN'S GROWING TV SPOTS: THE CHAIR, RABBIT (1m C p1979, r1979)
Provides young viewers with direct examples of ways that they can resolve conflict situations without using violence. THE CHAIR looks at alternatives to violence when two children want to sit in the same chair. RABBIT looks at what children can do to resolve conflict when two of them want to feed the rabbit at the same time. d. Ellen Hovde, Muffie Meyer; p. Jeff Weber; UMETHC.

CHILD'S EYE VIEW, A (29m C r1979)
Presents children from selected schools on five continents. They

were taught by the United Nations how to use Super 8 cameras and
animation techniques to make films about things important to them.
Written, directed, photographed, acted and animated by children,
this film reveals that the children's concerns are same around the
world. p. Elspeth MacDougall for United Nations; BARRF.

CHILD'S PLAY (2½m C 1979)
  All kinds of child's play in rapid and delightful succession. p.
Carole Trepanier; SERBC.

CHILD'S PLAY (29m C p1982, r1983)
  Demonstrates the path to excellence in the performing arts, with
students and faculty of the Community School of Performing Arts in
Los Angeles. Narrated by 12-year-old pianist Grace Huang, the film
shows both the frustration and the fun of making music and doing
dance as both the earliest beginning, intermediate and accomplished
students of various ethnic groups go through their daily paces. At
the end, the glamour of a formal recital rewards and refuels the dedication of these kids and their families. d./s.w. Susan Rogers; p.
Susan Rogers/Jonathan Wacks; Sponsor: Community School of Performing Arts; COMSPA.

CHILD'S QUARREL WITH THE WORLD, A (22m C 1977)
  Case studies of three autistic children at the Manhattan School
for Mentally Ill Children illustrate the symptoms and treatment of a
problem marked by withdrawal from reality. Shown are three children, the treatments given them, and their progress. p. Nancy
Bergerman, Alicia Weber; FI.

CHILE PEQUIN (30m C 1982) (also Video) The Planning Ahead (Series)
  Irma, a young and spirited Chicana who choses to leave home to
obtain a university education and pursue her ambitions, is summoned
back for her father's funeral. Her visit revives painful memories of
her adolescent clashes with her parents over the constraints of her
small town, her father's traditional Hispanic values, and her closely
knit family. The film highlights the problems facing many young
people who wish to break away from the expectations of their family.
p. Barbara Wolfinger, Berkeley Productions; UCEMC.

CHILLYSMITH FARM (55m C 1981) (also Video)
  An unforgettable film on intergenerational caring. The film, ten
years in the making, is about four generations of a remarkable family
presenting an eloquent example of how to live and how to die.
p./d. Mark Jury, Dan Jury; FILMLB; IU, PAS, UIL, UM.

CHINA: LAND OF MY FATHER (28½m C p1979, r1980)
  Takes an unusual and intimate look at China through the eyes of
an American-born Chinese as she meets her grandmother for the first
time, learns about a country "that used to seem strange and faraway,"

and compares her life with that of a working mother in China. Shows a commonality of experience of all people whose ancestors came from a foreign land. d./p. Felicia Lowe; p. KQED-TV; NEWDAY.

CHINATOWN: IMMIGRANTS IN AMERICA (60m C p1976, r1977)
Examines the plight of some 20,000 Chinese immigrants who arrive in New York from Taiwan and Hong Kong each year. They cannot speak English but all know one word--"Chinatown"--the most crowded neighborhood in New York City. This is the story of their struggle against language and cultural barriers, and how they are exploited by both the system and their fellow Chinese. A revealing and startling documentary. p. Keiko Tsuno, Jon Alpert Co-prod. with WNET-TV; DOWCTC.

CHINESE FOLK DANCES (10m C 1955)
Having learned traditional dances from natives in China, Tai Ailien choreographed and performs the "Yao Ceremonial Prelude," a marriage and funeral drum dance of the Yao tribe living in southwest China, and "Mute and the Cripple," an adaptation of a dance from a drama, also from southwest China. Chinese song has English subtitles. Dancer/Choreographer: Miss Tai Ai-lien; p. Wan-go-Weng; PICTURA.

CHLOE IN THE AFTERNOON (97m C 1972) (French/Subtitled)
Commuting from his suburban home and family, Frederic fantasizes another way of life with Chloe, a woman he meets in the city. As their relationship becomes more complex, and Frederic's fantasy life becomes another set of real-life responsibilities, he discovers that he must measure the nature of his life with Chloe against the suburban life he has tried to escape. d. Eric Rohmer; p. Barbet Schroeder, Pierre Cottrell; CORINTH.

CHOICE 1976 SERIES see HOUSING: A PLACE TO LIVE

CHOOSING SUICIDE (58m C 1980) (Video)
When New York artist Jo Roman learned she had terminal cancer, she decided to end her life, opting for "rational suicide." This film documents her decision, opening with her announcing this to her friends and family, and following her as she plans her death and the completion of a sculpture. Jo's death takes place off camera. The tape was made for, with, and by Jo Roman: her need to control the events of her life and death also control and limit the insights of the tape. The film never seems to go beyond Jo to explore the complex issues and emotions of her family and friends. Although it raises questions about death and "rational" suicide, the tape fails to disclose the inner realities, leaving some viewers feeling angry rather than sympathetic. d. Richard Ellison; VIDTM.

CHOREOGRAPHY (5m C p1980, r1980)
In this abstract animated film, geometric forms seem to dance in subtle movements and transitions. d./p. Margaret Criag; PICTS.

CHOSEN CHILD, THE (54m B 1963)
Follows a young, childless couple through the process of adopting a child, describing the application process, the various phases of investigation and explains why some children are considered unadoptable, discusses the private placement of children by doctors and lawyers, and presents differing views about various adoption processes. NBC News; CRM; KENTSU, UMN.

CHRIS AND THE MAGICAL DRIP (24m C p1977, r1978)
A dramatization that will help children to become more aware of common sounds which we hear but do not think about. Shows a brief sequence of animals that depend on sound such as the bats, dolphins, and whales. Music by Neil Diamond. p./d. Joan Marks; PHOENIX.

CHRISTMAS LACE (24m C p1978, r1978)
Set in Quebec in the 1880's, this is the tender story of a young girl's unselfish act which illustrates that anyone can be affected by the Christmas spirit. d. George Mendeluk; p. Linda Sorensen, G. Mendeluk; VECT.

CHRISTMAS ROUND THE WORLD (3m C p1979, r1980) (also Video)
This animated film without narration shows an ever-changing Santa Claus delivering Christmas presents all around the world, changing appearance as he arrives in different countries. p. Sheila Graber; TEXFM.

CHRISTMAS TREE (9m C 1976) (also Video)
Animated wooden puppets star in this allegorical tale of cooperation and helping one another. d. Hermina Tyrlova; p. Whitehill Films; FI.

CHRONICLES OF AMERICA SERIES see FRONTIER WOMAN, THE

CHRONICLES OF ANNA MAGDALENA BACH (93m C 1967) (German/ Subtitled)
A portrait of composer Johann Sebastian Bach which is now considered a monument of structural cinema. The serene visuals of the film, suggestive of Dutch painting, are juxtaposed with a spoken text, drawn from the letters and manuscripts of the composer, revealing a life of poverty and frustration: Bach, a Protestant, wrote most of his music for Catholic patrons, and he and his second wife, Anna Magdalena, performed at the harpsichord to support their 13 children. Choral and instrumental selections include Brandenburg Concerto No. 5 and the Art of the Fugue, performed by Gustav Leonhardt and other musicians on period instruments. d. Jean-Marie Straub; NYF.

CIRCLE CIRCUS (7m C 1979) (also Video)
Suggests properties of a circle by demonstrating several ways to construct circles: by end points of radii, diameters, and sets of line

segments; by a rotating angle of constant measure interior or exterior to the circle; and by other means. All are dynamically presented. p. Katharine Cornwell, Bruce Cornwell; IFB.

CIRCLE SERIES see CIRCLE CIRCUS; HOW FAR IS ROUND

CIRCUS RIDERS (20m C n.d.)
The story involves three characters: a deaf-mute, a ventriloquist, and a mime. Actually they are less "characters" than the characterizations, since each is in reality only a composite of distinguishing gestures, attributive objects, and typified ways of moving. As these three provide narration, it becomes quite clear that the story deals with the art of storytelling itself, the needs that give rise to it, and the deceptions and mysteries it perpetuates. Its rules are those of a circus, and its inhabitants are riders of the three rings, the three stars of the big top. p. Martha Haslanger; CCC.

CITIZEN SEAT (16m C 1981) (also Video)
Animated characters convey valuable information about seat belt safety while involved in a series of amusing incidents. p. Sondra Zuckerman, Ontario Ministry of Transportation and Communications (Canada); s.w. Ken Sobel; d. Bob Fortier; FI.

CIVILIZED TRIBES (26m C 1976)
In the southeast U.S., the five "civilized tribes"--Seminoles, Choctaw, Creek, Chickasaw and Cherokee--made their homes. They were successful agriculturalists, building small towns and centers of government. In 1830 the Indian Removal Act was passed by which they lost their farmlands and towns and were marched to Indian Territory west of the Mississippi. Some remained on reservations in the southeast. This television program briefly shows us aspects of the contemporary life of two tribes, surveying their history and discussing important issues with tribal leaders and tribe members. One of the three Seminole reservations (Hollywood, Florida) is featured here. People discuss their living conditions, tourism as a source of income, and competition with white developers for the small amount of land remaining to them. For the Choctaw, living in Philadelphia, Mississippi, there is massive unemployment reflecting the near impossibility of getting industry onto the reservation. Provides an overview of the conditions facing Indians on reservations in the southeast U.S. and, in its focus on economic needs, surveys a spectrum of possible reactions to the development of tourism and dependence on Federal agencies. p. Brenda Horsefield; ex. p. Philip Hobel; p. Document Associates/BBC; DOCUA; IU.

CLAIRE DE LUNE (MOONLIGHT) (5m C 1963)
A ballet, choreographed and performed by Diana Budaska, from Spain, to Debussy's "Claire de Lune." It takes place in a formal garden in Santa Cruz de Tenerife, Canary Islands. Dancer/Choreographer: Diana Budaska; p. Robert Davis Productions; DAVISR; UMN.

CLAIRE FALKENSTEIN, SCULPTOR (29m C p1977, r1979)
Presenting the scope of Claire Falkenstein's work, from sculpture on giant scale to jewelry and printmaking, this film reveals the myriad of activities which make up Claire's life. Insight into her world, into the development of her aesthetic philosophy and her particular mode of working, is provided through commentary by the artist herself, as well as by her friends and colleagues in the artistic community. Among those interviewed are Peggy Guggenheim, art historian Allan Temko, and museum directors Henry Hopkins of the San Francisco Museum of Modern Art and George Neubert of th Oakland Museum. p./d. Jae Carmichael; a.p. Joan L. Carter, PHOENIX; UIL, PAS.

CLARA BARTON: ANGEL OF THE BATTLEFIELD (25m C 1978)
Americana Series
Story of a dedicated New England teacher who pioneered women's role in federal government, then risked her life to feed and nurse both Union and Confederate soldiers wounded in battle during the Civil War. She directed an office that identified 22,000 war dead and spoke out strongly for women's rights and the welfare of the newly freed slaves. She was the founder and the first president of the American Red Cross, and for nearly quarter of a century she personally supervised disaster relief operations all over the world, remaining in the thick of operations until she was in her eighties. Photographed at many authentic sites where Clara Barton worked and lived. HANDEL; KENTSU, UIL.

CLASSICAL BALLET (29m B 1960) A Time to Dance (Series)
Presents a brief history of classical ballet and demonstrates the essential positions and steps every student must learn. Maria Tallchief and Andre Eglevsky perform the pas de deux from Swan Lake and Sylvia. Illustrates with drawings, prints, and photographs. NET; IU.

CLAMATION (18m C p1978, r1978)
Will Vinton and other animators discuss and demonstrate the principles and processes of clay animation technique. Shows the mixing of colors, creation of characters who move, production and editing of the live-action film which serves as an animation guide, music scoring, and the slow, demanding process of working with the clay itself. Many awards. p./d. Susan Shadburne, Will Vinton, music and special effects by Billy Scream, Paul Jameson; s.w. Susan Shadburne; PF.

CLAYSONG (12m B 1977)
Shows a young female potter as she lays out the clay, rolling, cutting, and kneading it to attain the desired texture. The clay is then placed on the wheel, where close-ups of the ceramist's hands involve the viewer in the feel of her work as the wet clay is shaped and molded. When the vase is the desired size and shape, a design

is worked into its sides. The finished product--etched, adorned and painted--is viewed at the film's conclusion. No narration. p. Harry Dawson, Jr.; DAWSONH.

CLERICAL SHOW, THE (? ? 1979) (slt)
A historical look at the issues which concern women office workers: lack of respect, low pay, lack of advancement, racism, etc. Also examines what women are doing about it. p. Community Media Workshop; COMMDW.

CLIMATES/CLIMATS (10m C 1976) (also Video)
Presents animation of textures rather than designs. The climates here are of the mind--of atmosphere and mood. Water color designs, often no more than washes, suggesting landscape through which faces and figures constantly emerge, produce a dream-like effect. p. Suzanne Gervais, NFBC; IFB.

CLIMBERS (29m C p1980, r1981)
A dance-drama based on the Japanese women's climb of Mount Everest in 1975. It explores in mythology and legend the acts of climbing while at the same time it is meant to parallel the wider, more universal tale of women's struggle for liberation. d./p. Rosalind Gillespie; AFC.

CLOSE FEELINGS (12m C 1973) Living Vignette Series
A sensitive and honest confrontation with a basic concern of most adolescents. How do you define love? How does what you are willing to give to an intimate relationship compare with what you expect to receive? How do you feel about premarital sex? Do you know how your parents feel? A good discussion film. p. Paulist Productions; MEDIAG.

CLOSE-TO-NATURE GARDEN, THE (24m C 1981) (Video)
A study of the natural, do-nothing farming methods of Japanese farmer-philosopher Masanobu Fukuoka, author of The One-Straw Revolution. Fukuoka's ecologically perfect techniques and his spiritual way of life are contrasted with modern-day Japanese farming, which depends heavily on chemicals and modern technology for the same yields. p. Margie Kamine; p. NHK-Japan; RODALE.

CLOTHING AND FASHION: A HISTORY (26m C n.d.)
The evolution of fashions in clothing from Egyptian times until today is perceived in amusing yet meticulously authentic animation. Most people do not have a clear concept of the constant changes, the squeezing in and pushing out of the body parts, the exposures and covering of different areas that has gone on throughout recorded history. This film brings it all together and makes one wonder why. BENCHMF; VIEWFI.

CLOWN FACE (16m C 1976)
Made for Ringling Bros. and Barnum and Bailey Circus as a

training film for their Clown College in Florida, this is a close look
at the precise and classical art of putting on clown makeup. p. Ray
and Charles Eames; PF; UIL.

CLUBFIGHTER (47½m C p1980, r1980) (Video)
Depicts the story of Mike "Nino" Gonzales, 21-year-old New Jersey welterweight champion. It is a story of his struggle to fight
his way out of the poverty of Bayonne to the prize money and power
attainable in the ring ... someday. p. Amanda Kissin; METROT.

CLYTEMNESTRA (90m C 1979) (Video)
Martha Graham choreographed and reconceived her 1958 Clytemnestra especially for this television program: "May We Dance" Series
of "Great Performances" on WNET/13. Dance Company: Martha Graham Dance Company; Choreographer: Martha Graham; d. Merrill
Brockway; p. Emile Ardolino, Judy Kinberg, ex. p. Jac Venza; p.
WNET-TV; WNETTV.

COAL MINING WOMEN (40m C p1981, r1982)
Experiences of women as they enter this traditionally male-
dominated field and the problems they encounter in their fight to
end sex discrimination in the coalfields are related through interviews
at home and at work in and around mines in Kentucky, Virginia, Tennessee, West Virginia and Colorado. Explores the historical place of
women in the United States and European coal mines and the present
employment situation in Appalachia and the western coalfields where
the economy is dominated by the coal industry. The collective story
of women coal miners captures their feelings about the advantages
and disadvantages of their chosen occupation--the compromise they
face between their health and safety and the benefits of high wages.
d./p. Elizabeth Barret; APPAL.

COCKTAIL MOLOTOV (100m C n.d.) (French/Subtitled)
The story takes up with Anne, the heroine in the film PEPPER-
MINT SODA, five years later at age 18. After a fight with her
mother, Anne runs away from Paris with two boys to Venice, where
they intend to hop on an Israel-bound freighter. Over the radio,
they learn that a revolution has broken out in Paris. Their money
and car stolen, these three rolling stones spend most of the film
hitchhiking across strike-paralyzed France in an attempt to reach the
revolution before it ends without them. One critic called the film
"the most accurate portrait to date of growing up, and out, of that
tumultuous decade." d. Diane Kurys; NYF.

COLETTE (13m C 1979) (also Video)
A portrait of Gabrielle Claudine Colette, an amazing literary artist, so suffused with creative dynamism that in her 81 years she gave
the broadest scope to her talents--as mime, dramatist, music hall entertainer, critic, novelist, short story writer, actress, journalist,
dancer, and film scenarist. More than anything, she was a writer.

Reflected in this poetic evocation of Colette are all the warmth and charm that are synonymous with her very name. An excellent intro- duction to the author and her works. American version written by Israel M. Berman; d./s.w. Edouard Berne; p. Janus Films; CORO- NET; UIL, PAS.

COLETTE (1873-1954) see COLETTE

COLLEGE OF MEDICINE PRESENTS (SERIES) see MANAGEMENT OF SEXUALLY ASSAULTED WOMEN

COLORED GIRL: NTOZAKE SHANGE, A (30m C 1979) (Video) Cam- era Three Series
A documentary on poet, playwright, and director Ntozake Shange, author of For Colored Girls Who Have Considered Suicide.... Shange is seen at readings of her work, interviewed on her views of grow- ing up black and female in America and being an artist, and in con- versation with Joseph Papp. Staged segments of works from her plays also included. p. WGBH-TV; NOVACOM; UMN.

COLTER'S HELL (14m C 1973)
An interpretative study of the hot springs and bubbling mud pools of Yellowstone National Park which makes imaginative contra- puntal use of sound and image. p./d. Robin Lehman; PHOENIX.

COME CLOSER (23m C p1979, r1979)
Shot in five museums throughout the country that provide exem- plary programs for disabled and general audiences, this film gives concrete examples of solutions for accessibility to visitors. The film focuses on some of the best programs in the arts for disabled persons, particularly in museums. p. Ellen Bynum; d. Mark Centkowski; SKYEP.

COMEDIENNE (82m C p1982, r1983)
Covers three years in the lives of two women in New York who are struggling to express themselves through the art of stand-up comedy. The two women profiled are Cheryl Klein and Zora Rasmus- sen. d./p. Katherine Matheson; s.w. Matheson/Rasmussen/Klein; ed. Donna Marino; STRAIF.

COMING HOME (33m C 1979)
A documentary that examines America's "post-Vietnam syndrome" and the plight of the Vietnam veteran. Focuses on two veterans-- Richard Linder, a 28-year-old black from Brooklyn, and Donald Sproehnle, a 25-year-old white youth from Philadelphia. They dis- cuss why they joined the army in their teens and movingly recount their wartime experiences. Linder, morally sickened by the wanton killings, turned to drugs; he returned to the United States as a junkie and eventually went to jail for bank robbery. Sproehnle step- ped on a land mine and nearly lost his leg; today, years later, he

experiences recurring nightmares about the death and destruction he saw there. In separate and group interviews with other veterans, they talk about their feelings of hurt and anger towards a society which has used them and now disregards them. p. Sarah Oakes, Stu Bird; UNIFILM.

COMING OF AGE (60m C 1982) (also Video)
    A large group of racially and sexually mixed teenagers gather at a summer camp to directly confront important issues in their lives: male-female relations, racial identity, and family dynamics. The film unfolds a completely original and emotionally moving portrait of to-day's young people by revealing their "unspoken thoughts." An excellent discussion starter for students, educators, counselors or any group interested in human relations. Study guide included. d. Josh Hanig; p. Dennis Hicks, J. Hanig; NEWDAY.

COMMON FEMALE SEXUAL DYSFUNCTIONS (17m C n.d.)
    This sexual counseling film discusses the three most common types of female sexual dysfunction--vaginismus, dyspareunia and anorgasmia. It deals in depth with the secondary anorgasmia of a married woman. The film also features documentary interviews with real women describing their own sexual experiences and orgasms. MIFE.

COMMON GROUND: CHANGING VALUES AND THE NATIONAL FOR-
    ESTS (29m C p1977, r1978)
    Examines complex forest policy issues--harvesting of old growth timber, wilderness designation, recreation development, and protection of local life styles and values--through the eyes of backpackers, loggers, foresters, and residents of forest communities. All explain what the forest means to them. Filmed on the Umpqua National Forest in Oregon and the Jefferson National Forest in Virginia. d./p. Janet Mendelsohn; CONSF.

COMMON SENSE SELF-DEFENSE (27m C 1978)
    This film is narrated and defense techniques are deomonstrated by Dr. Mary Conroy, one of the nation's leading authorities on self-defense, and features Gene Rayburn, host of the television series "Match Game," as guest assailant. Three strategies in self-defense are shown: how to eliminate danger from our daily lives, how to recognize and avoid danger, and how to fight when necessary. A Superior Court judge discusses the legalities of using self-defense; a convicted murderer explains what people should and should not do if attacked; a rape victim reveals her six-hour ordeal and tells how self-defense will instill confidence; and a 73-year-old woman defends herself against a 230-pound rapist. A complete course outline and a 20-lesson curriculum (study guide) are included with the film. p. Dr. Mary Conroy; FLMFR; PAS.

COMMUNICATING WITH THE APHASIC PATIENT (22m C 1982) (Video)
    Designed to help nurses, as well as all allied health personnel,

deal with the sensitive subject of communicating with people who have lost the ability to use or comprehend words. The viewer is given many tools with which to help the patient and the family manage this painful, awkward affliction. d./p. Maria Keckan; FAIRVW.

COMMUNICATIONS PRIMER, A (22m C 1953)
Illustrates recent theories on communications. Intended to reveal a broader concept of what communications is and how it operates in many areas of our lives. p. Ray and Charles Eames; PF; UIL.

COMMUNISTS FOR 1000 YEARS (43m C 1973) (also Video)
Today South Yemen is the only country of the Arab world which dares to claim kinship with scientific Marxism. For the past 1,000 years there have been communists in South Yemen. A millennium ago the Carmathians were believers in the full equality of women, atheists who owned and worked their land communally, a people who had abolished inheritance and who did not have any decision-making body other than the entire group. In the year 930, the Carmathians captured Mecca and took away the Black Stone which they kept for more than 30 years. The ensuing repression was terrible; the survivors fled to the mountains of Yafa in South Yeman. There they continued an underground movement, though dissolved into small tribes. p. Marie Claude Deffarge, Gordian Troeller; ICARF.

COMMUNITY FIGHTS RAPE, A (12m C p1978, r1979)
Shows one community's approach to improving response to the rape problem. An estimated 90 percent of the half million rape victims chose not to report assaults to the police due to fear, embarrassment, shame or anticipated scorn. Shown are scenes of how concerned people of San Jose, California worked with police to develop an anti-rape movement by instituting a decoy squad, a rape crises center, and training and awareness programs. A CBS crew riding with the police and using a special viewing device illustrates how the decoy program operates. The police and women activists are seen giving advice to high school students and community organizations. Special attention is given to rape victims entering the hospital, and staff provides privacy and a thorough examination and explanation to the victim. CBS News; MTITI.

COMMUNITY PROTECTION SERIES see BABYSITTING; CHILD MO-
LESTERS: FACTS AND FICTION; FRAUD? YOU LOSE!; HITCH-
HIKING; HOME AND PROPERTY PROTECTION; WATCHWORD:
CAUTION

COMPANIONS (11m C 1982)
A Canadian humane society initiates a program of taking small animals on visits to nursing homes for the elderly. d./p. Paulle Clark/Wendy Campbell; FILMLB.

COMPANY TOWN (36m C 1979) (also Video)
What happens to a community when its economy is dependent on

one industry and that industry shuts down? The film takes a look at such a situation in Westfir, Oregon, shortly after the lumber mill closed in June of 1977. Mill workers organized to buy the mill and run it as a cooperative, but the mill owners refused to sell. This film explores the intricacies of relationships and responsibilities among community residents, industry and state, as it studies a situation which is more and more common in the Northwest. p. Sharon Genasci, Kris Jensen; p. Rainbow Films; MEDIAP; PAS.

COMPLICATIONS OF PREGNANCY (29m C 1978) (Video) Daniel Foster, M.D. Series
Host Daniel Foster and his guest Dr. Norman F. Gant, Jr., Professor and Chairman of the Department of Obstetrics and Gynecology at the University of Texas Health Science Center, discuss the major complications of pregnancy. Dr. Gant explains that hemorrhage, infection and toxemia may be detected in advance of delivery by a number of simple tests. The program includes a film of Dr. Gant and a team of physicians delivering a baby by caesarean section. p. KERA-TV, Dallas, Texas; PBSV.

COMPREHENSIVE SKILLS SERIES see GETTING THE FACTS

COMPUTER PERSPECTIVE (8m C 1972)
A collection of artifacts, ideas, events and memorabilia belonging to the six decades that led up to 1950 and the electronic computer. p. Ray and Charles Eames; PF.

CONCEPT SERIES see ELECTRA TRIES TO SPEAK; GLASS CURTAIN; LIES; MASK; SKYFISH; THREE STORY SUITE; TRAVELS IN THE COMBAT ZONE; WINDOW

CONCEPTION AND PREGNANCY (28m C 1978) The Inner Woman Series
Physiology of conception, early indications, causes of common difficulties and the importance of prenatal care are examined. The necessity of open communication between men and women is stressed; guidance for family planning is provided in an interview with medical professionals. Marilyn Poland, R.N., moderator. CRM.

CONCERNS OF AMERICAN INDIAN WOMEN (29m C 1977) (Video) Woman Series
Dr. Connie Redbird Uri, a physician and member of the Choctaw Cherokee Tribe, and Marie Sanchez, Chief Judge of the Northern Cheyenne Tribe, discuss the problems of American Indian women. They cite poor health care, forced sterilization and lack of control over their own affairs as serious threats to their existence. They also talk about the proposed installation of more coal gasification plants around Indian reservations. Sandra Elkin is the moderator. p. WNED-TV, Buffalo, New York; PBSV.

CONCERT OF THE STARS (86m B 1952)
Depicts a Russian concert. Galina Ulanova and Vladimir Preobraz-
hensky perform a pas de deux from Les Sylphides. Natalia Dudinskaya and Konstantin Sergeyev are in scenes from Raymonda. Scenes
from Gayane, including the "Sabre Dance," are performed. The State
Folk Dance Ensemble directed by Igo Moiseyev performs Moiseyev's
"The Strollers." Also, there are opera excerpts from The Queen of
Spades, Ivan Susanin, and Song of the Forests, an oratorio. Opera
sequences are sung in Russian, with English subtitles. Dance companies: soloists of the Bolshoi Theatre; Corps de Ballet of the Kirov
Opera House; State Folk Dance Ensemble; d. Igor Moiseyev; Choreographers: Michel Fokine, Marius Petipa, Igor Moiseyev, Nina Aniso-
mova; d. A. Ivanovsky, G. Rappoport; p. Lenfilm Studios, Russia;
MACMFL.

CONEY (5m C r1975)
CONEY is a quick jaunt through New York's infamous Coney Island area. The island is seen at all times of the day and night, and
during all seasons of the year. The harsh reality of Coney Island
today is viewed through the sweet, emotional/visual filter of pink cotton candy. p./d. Caroline Ahlfours Mouris, Frank Mouris; PHOENIX,
VIEWFI, KPF.

CONFESSIONS OF A STARDREAMER (9m C r1979)
A young actress (Diane Gardner) talks about her struggles in
the world of show business, while Canemaker's colorful animated images
comment on, mirror, and probe hidden meanings in her words. p./d.
John Canemaker; PHOENIX.

CONFLICT AND AWARENESS SERIES see JOB INTERVIEW: I GUESS
I GOT THE JOB

CONGENITAL BRONCHO-OESOPHAGEAL FISTULA IN AN ADULT (10m
C n.d.)
Filmed record of a surgical operation performed in a Montreal hos-
pital in December 1968 to correct a rare congenital anomaly in a 66-
year-old male--a case in which there was a bronchial segment. A
report of this case was published in the Canadian Medical Association
Journal, May 9, 1970, Vol. 102. d. Claudia Overing, Jean Roy; p.
François Seguillon; NFBC.

CONGRUENT TRIANGLES (7m C 1978) (also Video)
Using animation, various relationships of angles and sides to con-
gruency are demonstrated. Key concepts are presented in captions
and the tempo of the series of examples is keyed to music. p. Katharine Cornwell, Bruce Cornwell; IFB.

CONSUMER ECONOMICS WITH NETTIE MOOSELOCK: BANKING (23m
C 1977)
Uses dramatization to show the advantages of checking and savings

accounts. April has been hiding her paychecks in a potted palm. Nettie Mooselock, who collects rent and dispenses gratuitous information, takes April in hand, leaving her (and the viewers) much wiser on matters of banks, savings and loans, checking and savings accounts, statements and balances, interest and miscellaneous services. CF; UIL.

CONSUMER ECONOMICS WITH NETTIE MOOSELOCK: CREDIT CARDS (22m C 1977)

Landlady Nettie Mooselock describes the three basic kinds of credit cards: bank cards, company cards, travel and entertainment cards. Her tenant, Sheldon Prufrock, wants to be the owner of a credit card but doesn't know how to obtain one. He takes his problem to Nettie, who provides a wealth of information about credit cards, their uses and misuses, risks and limitations, obligations, and finance charges. Sheldon listens and learns and, with Nettie's help, finally gets his credit card. CF; UIL.

CONSUMER ECONOMICS WITH NETTIE MOOSELOCK: TAXES (22m C 1977)

Focuses on the personal responsibility each American worker has in reporting personal income and paying income taxes. Ersatz Flambe, outraged by the recurrent indignities of the System, is restrained repeatedly by his landlady and mine of information, Nettie Mooselock. She leads him through the mysteries of a Social Security card, W-2 form, withholding taxes, and even helps him fill out his income tax return. Nettie's only real failing for Ersatz is her penchant for illustrating percentage with real apple pies. CF; UIL.

CONSUMER FRAUD, THE (SERIES) (C 1976)

A series of five films designed to increase consumer awareness through a comical dramatization of some of the most common frauds perpetrated on the public. p. PF.

Series titles are these: BAIT, BITE AND SWITCH (10m); HOME SWEET HOME IMPROVEMENTS (10m); I'LL ONLY CHARGE YOU FOR THE PARTS (10m); THOSE MAIL ORDER MILLIONS (10m); YOUR CREDIT IS GOOD, UNFORTUNATELY (10m); CONSUMER CON CAPERS (23m); CONSUMER GAME, THE (17m)

CONSUMER OFFENSIVE, THE (26m C n.d.)

American consumers, cynical about government and industry's indifference to their needs, are discovering how to get better products for less money, protect their environment, and improve the quality of their lives--by joining local and national consumer organizations. Over the past 75 years, the Consumer Movement has lobbied for the passage of consumer protection laws, boycotted and demonstrated, tested and rated brand products, and organized consumer groups that do everything from run food co-ops to vote for legislation against unsafe nuclear plants. Since the 1960's Ralph

Nader, assisted by his young volunteers, has shown how much one person can do to improve life for all consumers. BENCHMF.

CONSUMERISM IN MEDICINE: WHOSE BODY IS IT ANYWAY? (26m C r1976)
Importance of comparing cost versus quality of different drugs on the market. Benefits versus risks of taking any medication. People must make informed decisions about treatment of their own minds and bodies. MACMFL; DOCUA; PAS, WSU.

CONSUMERS (20m C p1977, r1978)
Shows how individuals and groups can take action against faulty products and services. Presented are types of actions that can be taken concerning a product or service, and organizations available to aid consumers. Emphasis is placed on the fact that only through organization and unity can consumers bring economic and political force to bear in their own behalf. p. Cine Manifest Productions, Whitney Green, Robert Dalva; RAMFLM.

CONSUMING INTEREST, A (26m C 1980) Think Nutrition Series
This last film in the series combines the principles of good nutrition with the principles of smart shopping. Judy Dean, a noted dietician and host of the series, takes the viewer on a tour of the typical American grocery store. As we stroll down the aisles she points out those foods that offer us the best buys for our money and our health. Students are shown the different food categories available and how the food budget can best be fit into these categories. It is certain to increase the viewer's awareness of the importance of good eating habits and will prove once and for all that, no matter how you look at it, eating right is a bargain. p. National Film and Video Center; NATFVC.

CONTACT (22m B p1980, r1980)
Introduces dancers and non-dancers to the elements of an increasingly popular dance form. The black and white images serve to re-create the sensual rhythms and patterns which are inherent to the Contact Improvisation dance experience. d. Ann Tegnell, Susan Warner; p. John Gamble; p. Cinema Associates; CINAS.

CONTEMPORARY DANCE SERIES see DANCE AND THE NEW MEDIA; DANCEMAKING; DANCERS ON THE MOVE; SEEING DANCE; SOUND FOR DANCE; SPACE FOR DANCE; WHAT NEXT?; WHERE THE DANCE IS

CONTEMPORARY WOMEN POETS (29m C 1976) (Video) Woman Series
Poet Audre Lord From a Land Where Other People Live and poet/novelist Marge Piercy (Women on the Edge of Time, Living in the Open) read and discuss their works and share their views on contemporary poetry. Sandra Elkin is the moderator. p. WNED-TV, Buffalo, New York; PBSV.

temporary poetry. Sandra Elkin is the moderator. p. WNED-TV, Buffalo, New York; PBSV.

CONTRACEPTION: ARTIFICIAL METHODS (12½ C n.d.)
Gives detailed information on various artificial methods including condoms, foams, jellies, the diaphragm, the I.U.D., the pill, male and female sterilization techniques. The pros and cons of each are discussed. Also available in Spanish. MIFE.

CONTRAST (8½m C 1977) (Video)
A portion of VIDEO DANCES (see that entry). Dance Company: Dancer's World of Springfield, Massachusetts. Choreographer: Trish Midei; p. Harry Weisburd; WEISBURD.

CONTROLLING INTEREST: THE WORLD OF THE MULTINATIONAL
CORPORATION (45m C 1978)
An account of the growing power of the multinational conglomerates and their influence over global affairs and international policies. Raises many of the basic questions about the conflict between the profit motive and expansion needs of the corporation and the human needs of the people of the world. What will happen when the world begins to move to a more simple global economy in the face of waning industrial possibilities? d. Janet Roach; p. California Newsreel; CALNWS.

CONTROVERSIES WITHIN THE WOMEN'S MOVEMENT, PART I (29m
C 1976) (Video) Woman Series
Karen DeCrow, president of the National Organization for Women, discusses the background, new directions and implications of the organization's efforts to include political action by more groups. She explains the tactics that will be used to accomplish these goals, such as endorsement of political candidates who favor feminist legislation. Sandra Elkin is the moderator. p. WNED-TV; PBSV.

CONTROVERSIES WITHIN THE WOMEN'S MOVEMENT, PART II (29m
C 1976) (Video Woman Series
Feminist author Betty Friedan, founder of the National Organization for Women, discusses charges that the organization is being infiltrated for divisive purposes. She presents her view that these charges are true and that the real problem is how to face and deal with infiltration in a way that will preserve the structure of the organization. She also talks about the nationwide growth of the women's movement and increasing identification with it by women of all ages and life-styles. Sandra Elkin is the moderator. p. WNED-TV; PBSV.

CONVERSATION (5½m B 1981)
Multiple images combine with still-frame, in digital mode, of a Puerto Rican filmmaker's telephone conversation with a repairman. Performed by Ruth Maleczeck; music by Bob Telson, s.w. Lee Breuer; d./p. Doris Chase; CHASED.

CONVERSATION WITH ELIZABETH JANEWAY, A; PART I (29m C
 1975) (Video) Woman Series
 Author Elizabeth Janeway (<u>Daisy Kenyon</u>, <u>Man's World, Women's
 Place</u>) talks about discrimination against older women, the future of
 the women's movement and what the absence of women from history
 means to culture. She also explains her philosophy of "selective insensitivity" and how it applies to attitudes toward men. Sandra Elkin is the moderator. p. WNED-TV; PBSV.

CONVERSATION WITH ELIZABETH JANEWAY, A; PART II (29m C
 1975) (Video) Woman Series
 Author Elizabeth Janeway (<u>Daisy Kenyon</u>, <u>Man's World, Women's
 Place</u>) explains why she disagrees with the theory that if women ever
 achieved power they would use it as badly as men have. She states
 her belief that women must go very deeply into themselves and their
 feelings before they can have the courage to accept power. Sandra
 Elkin is the moderator. p. WNED-TV; PBSV.

CONVERSATION WITH EUDORA WELTY (30m ? 1973) (Video)
 Eudora Welty uses her perception of the distinct southern character to explore the universal duality in human nature. As one of
 her characters puts it, humanity is involved in, and normally losing
 a continuous battle between "our desires for love, safety, blind acceptance, communion, and our equally strong desires for separateness, danger, clear knowledge and individual and primal joy." In
 this conversation, Miss Welty talks about her commitment to the region and the way in which she draws on it. She says she approaches
 writing as though she were sitting on the front porch on a hot night
 telling the tallest tales she could think of. NETCHE.

CONVERSATION WITH FLORYNCE KENNEDY, A (29m C 1975) (Video)
 Woman Series
 Attorney and feminist Florynce Kennedy, who has acquired a national reputation as the resident wit of the women's movement, discusses her views on what she terms the "pathology of oppression."
 Kennedy, a black, also shares her ideas about the problems that have
 arisen when white women attempted to recruit black women into feminism by talking about the sexism of all men. Sandra Elkin is the
 moderator. p. WNED-TV; PBSV.

CONVERSATION WITH HELEN, A (30m C p1978, r1979) (also Video)
 Presents Helen, a teenage single mother reflecting on her experimentation with drugs, fear that she might harm her daughter, contemplation of suicide and uncertainty about her future. Helen gives
 a candid account of a sick and troubled single mother. She recalls
 being heavily into drugs, drinking, and smoking dope, and finally
 asking for help. Her daughter was placed in a foster home for six
 months while she tried, with the help of counseling and a parent
 aide, to pull her life together. The therapy visits helped her to sort
 things out and to see things from a new point of view. Comparing

her feelings and attitudes of two years ago with the present, Helen realizes with some pride how far she has come and speaks of her goals for the future. d./p. Bruce E. Harding; CORNELL.

CONVERSATION WITH JEANNE MOREAU, A; PART I (29m C 1976) (Video) Woman Series
Film actress Jeanne Moreau (The Bride Wore Black) shares her observations on men, women and directors. She also discusses her experiences directing her own film Lumière, which describes the close relationships that can develop between women friends. Sandra Elkin is the moderator. p. WNED-TV; PBSV.

CONVERSATION WITH JEANNE MOREAU, A; PART II (29m C 1976) (Video) Woman Series
Film actress Jeanne Moreau (The Bride Wore Black) talks about her career and the difficulties she has encountered reconciling her domestic and professional roles--a conflict that she says destroyed her first marriage. She also comments on the lack of female parts in American films. Sandra Elkin is the moderator. p. WNED-TV; PBSV.

CONVERSATION WITH LOTTE JACOBI, A (29m C 1977) (Video) Woman Series
Portrait photographer Lotte Jacobi discusses her life, politics and photographs. Jacobi, who was the oldest working journalist at the 1976 Democratic National Convention, has photographed the famous during her outstanding career. Credits include Eleanor Roosevelt, Robert Frost, Marc Chagall, Lotte Lenya, Albert Einstein and many others. She comments on the trend toward gadgetry in photography, reminisces about pre-World War II New York City, tells about some of her subjects, explains her "camera-less" pictures and shares her reactions to politicians from Hitler to Carter. p. WNED-TV; PBSV.

CONVERSATION WITH ROBIN MORGAN, A (29m C 1977) (Video) Woman Series
Author, feminist and former leftist militant Robin Morgan discusses her personal philosophy and assesses the progress of the women's movement. Morgan, who edited Sisterhood Is Powerful and wrote Going Too Far, the Personal Chronicle of a Feminist as well as two books of poetry, describes how her roles as wife and mother have affected her politics and how they have, in turn, been influenced by her activism. Sandra Elkin is the moderator. p. WNED-TV; PBSV.

CONVERSATION WITH SIMONE de BEAUVOIR, A (60m C 1977) (Video) Woman Series
Author and feminist Simone de Beauvoir discusses her work and philosophy during an interview with her old friend Dorothy Tennov, Professor of Psychology at the University of Bridgeport. From her Paris apartment, de Beauvoir talks about the abortion issue, which

led her to assume an active role in the women's movement. She also describes her feelings about monogamy and marriage, her celebrated relationship with philosopher Jean-Paul Sartre and the reactions of her male friends to her book The Second Sex. Following the interview, journalist Gloria Steinem and author Elizabeth Janeway discuss the impact de Beauvoir has had on the women's movement. p. WNED-TV; PBSV.

CONVERSATIONS WITH WILLARD VAN DYKE (59m C p1980, r1981) (also Video)

In 1936, photographer Willard Van Dyke became a filmmaker because he believed films could "change the world." This candid portrait traces the outspoken Van Dyke's career from film, to his directorship of the Department of Film at the Museum of Modern Art in New York, to his recent return to photography. Included are conversations with colleagues Ralph Steiner, Joris Ivens, and Donald Richie, and clips from THE RIVER, THE CITY, VALLEY TOWN, and other films. d. Amalie R. Rothschild; p. A. Rothschild, Austin Lamont; Anomaly Films; s.w. A. Rothschild, Julie Sloan; NEWDAY.

CONWAY THOMPSON: SCULPTOR FROM DRY BRIDGE (20m C 1977)

Presents work and philosophy of Conway Thompson, artist and sculptor. Ms. Thompson studied art in New York and continued her studies in Italy and Mexico. These skills and influences Ms. Conway brought back to Virginia where she now strives to capture her own Southern agrarian heritage in assemblage sculpture that is often done by incorporating a tool commonly used on farms. p. Charlotte Schrader; SCHRADR.

COOKIE GOES TO THE HOSPITAL (25m C p1980, r1981--U.S.) (also Video)

Designed to comfort, educate, and help children overcome their fear of hospitals. p./d. Linda Schuyler, Kit Hood; p. Playing With Time, Inc., Canada; s.w. Amy Jo Cooper; LCA.

COOKING IN FRANCE: AN ALPINE MENU (25m C p1978, r1978)

All humanity shares in common the need to eat. But in France, specifically Alpine France, eating is more than a necessity. Explores the genius of the great French Chef André Revest and, in so doing, introduces the viewer to the culture and people of the country of France. d. Hal Weiner; p. Marilyn Weiner, H. Weiner; SCRESC.

COOL HANDS, WARM HEART (16m B si 1979)

A film in which private acts become public spectacles: on stage, on a crowded street, women perform familiar rituals. The stage recalls a slave block, while the attentive audience that gathers around (unrehearsed) makes one aware of one's own voyeurism as film audience. A story of sorts develops, due to the increased interaction between a woman from the crowd and those on stage. Her role as agent provocateur is ambiguous; intertitles which appear both in the form of her introspective musings and a narrator's warnings contribute to the emotional and physical struggle. The action shifts to a game parlour, but circles back inevitably to the source of the dilemma: the stage. Both through confrontation and through escape, the woman in question learns the value of a steady hand and an angry heart. "In defiance of the dominant cultures' definition of violent acts, I want to expose some of the more subtle, internalized, 'trivial' forms of violence. I see a dense web of unacknowledged violence, inflicted both from within and without, that permeates our lives much more profoundly than the less frequent and more dramatic violence of wars and disasters."--Su Friedrich. International Awards. p. Su Friedrich; WMM.

CO-OPS: AN ECONOMIC UTOPIA (29m C 1979) (2" HB Tape)
Co-ops, member-owned and operated businesses based on a certain set of principles, are discussed with Stewart Kohl, Executive Director of the North American Students of Cooperation. Also included are sequences of Maggie Kuhn and Ralph Nader discussing consumerism. p. Michigan Media, University of Michigan; UMMRC; UM.

COPERNICUS (10m C 1973)
Presents the background against which Copernicus came to understand a new structure of the universe. It examines the surroundings in which the astronomer lived and worked, and the artifacts and documents of his life. p. Ray and Charles Eames; PF; UCLA.

COPING WITH CHANGE (28m C n.d.) Prime Time (Series)
A look at people who have discovered that change is a part of growing, not just growing older. And how you cope with change determines the rest of your life--no matter how old you are. Narrated by Don McNeill. p. Sears-Roebuck Foundation. Free loan. MTPS.

COPING WITH CHANGE (30m C 1981) Professional Skills for Secretaries Series
An overview of the office of the future is given, focusing on increased use of automation and new technology and the opportunity it affords today's secretary. The age of technology offers major areas of career advancement for secretaries, particularly in such fields as word processing, which didn't even exist a few years ago. The point is made clear, however, that the new technology also enhances the career of the secretary who decides not to specialize. Once relieved of mechanical tasks, the general secretary is free to do more administrative work and to utilize the skills learned earlier in this course. Leader's manual and participants' handbooks included. TIMLIF.

COPING WITH HERPES, VIRUS OF LOVE (30m C 1978) (Video)
About herpes virus, a venereal disease which is spreading at an epidemic rate. The tape aims to help people cope with the disease

and to explain the basic, known facts about it. Two women and two men candidly discuss how they felt when they first contracted the disease and how they learned to handle it. (Global Village, December 1, 1978) d. Karen Mooney; SYLOGY.

COPING WITH SERIOUS ILLNESS SERIES see DOCTORS AND PA-
TIENTS; FACING DEATH; FINANCES; PAIN; RELATIONSHIPS
AND STRESS; SEXUALITY

COPING WITH STRESS (72m C 1980) (slc)
Covers symptoms and causes of stress, the type A personality, monitoring our stress level, maintaining ourselves in the face of stress, maneuvering to reduce stress, relaxation and meditation, discovering our own stress level. By recognizing the causes and learning how to combat the effects, every individual can cope better with stress. UCEMC; CORNELL.

COPING WITH THE MINOR DISCOMFORTS OF PREGNANCY (8m C n.d.)
Describes the many minor complaints by pregnant women. Discusses the causes and relief of nausea, dizziness, fatigue, frequent urination, constipation, swelling, headaches, backaches, indigestion, varicose veins, hemorrhoids, uterine contractions and muscle spasms. Also available in Spanish. MIFE.

COPING WITH TOMORROW SERIES see FOOD: SURVIVING THE
CHEMICAL FEAST

COPPELIA--ACT II (28m B 1970)
Act II of the famous ballet about a lifelike mechanical doll, based on E.T.A. Hoffman's Der Sandmann. Dance Company: Illinois Ballet; Choreographer: Lev Ivanov, Enrico Cecchetti; d. Richard Ellis, Christine DuBoulay; ORION.

CORLETTO AND DON (27m C 1982) (also Video)
"Mike Corletto wants nothing more than to labor 'up top' with his ironworker father, who sees instead a college education and profession for his son. This conflict ... is credibly developed. A plausible discussion starter for high school guidance classes and for library and community organization teen groups."--Booklist. p. Cineflics Production; LCA.

CORNELIUS VANDERBILT II'S THE BREAKERS (24m C 1977) American Lifestyle Series
Presents a tour of two mansions of the Vanderbilt family, especially The Breakers in Newport, Rhode Island. E. G. Marshall provides a brief history of the Vanderbilt family as he conducts this tour of The Breakers and Marble House. A most fascinating view of the life-style of a period in our history when sons and grandsons of farmers and immigrants built monuments to the success of their families. p. Ann Lane Shanks; PARACO.

CORONA--A DANCE DOCUMENTARY (28m B 1977)
The development process of a group dance piece, from choreography through performance. Focus is partly on a young choreographer, Gail Chodera, stepping from the role of dancer to choreographer. Performed at Ohio University School of Dance. Dancer/Choreographer: Gail Chodera; d. Michael B. Fleishman; FLEISHMAN.

CORRECTIONAL JUSTICE SYSTEM see WOMEN AND THE LAW, THE (SERIES)

COTTON CANDY AND ELEPHANT STUFF (29m C p1978, r1979)
Focuses on the arduous, yet romantic, life of a small family traveling circus troupe. Offers insight into why people choose careers and how the fantasy of a job differs from its day-to-day reality. d./p. Jan Krawitz, Thomas Ott; DIRECT.

COUNSELING CHANGES (29m C 1980) (Video, VHS, VH) One on One Series
Nancy Gabalac, a rehabilitation counselor and consultant, discusses the changes in the types of problems brought to counseling during the 1970's. Emphasis is given to the concerns of women. Interviewed by Sandy Halem. p. KSU-TV; KSU-AV; KENTSU.

COUPLES (50m B 1975)
In separate vignettes, three young couples attempt to analyze their relationships with emphasis on roles, goals, and actual or potential areas of conflict. Two of the couples are married and have children; the third is living together. Verbal and bodily responses to the filming process vary considerably. p. Thomas Benson; The Pennsylvania State University; PAS, IU.

COUPLES COMMUNICATION (23m C 1981) (also Video) Trigger Films on Human Interaction Series
The vignettes in this film consist of typical arguments which illustrate many of the ways that couples manage to block rather than facilitate communication and understanding. The film is designed to be used by couples in analyzing the numerous places the arguments get "off the track," and in developing better approaches to communication. Some of the communication problems illustrated are bringing up the past; generalizing from one or two incidents; implied insults and actual name-calling; taking something too literally and missing the real point; guessing at and criticizing the other person's motivation. Guide included. p. Family Information Systems and Resource Communications, Inc.; MTITI.

COUPLES COMMUNICATION SKILLS (30m ea. C [4 parts] 1980) (Video)
Marriages are often destroyed because couples simply don't know how to communicate effectively with one another. Larry and Sue Frahm, Instructors of the Couples Communication Program offered through the Extension Division, University of Nebraska-Lincoln,

outlines in this four-part series some of the techniques which have been used to help couples communicate better. The segments are 1) Self-Awareness, 2) Shared Meaning, 3) Communication Styles, and 4) Esteem Building. NETCHE.

COUPLES WHO ARE SHARING RESPONSIBILITIES (29m C 1974)
   (Video) Are You Listening Series
   Focuses on couples who are in the process of restructuring their marriages through "mutual respect" contractual agreements because of the breakdown of traditional roles and patterns. Discussion centers upon structure and lack of it, mutuality of options, the social isolation of women with children, self-interest as opposed to self-sacrifice, the economics of "bread winning," and the differences of each partner's life-style. It is easy to understand why people do not attempt to make the changes with which these couples are experimenting: change is rough. It is pointed out several times that women traditionally carry the emotional burdens and insights of the family: to turn this around is to risk the male image and thus influence the marriage. Although "professional help" is played down in this presentation, one important concept offered is that of supplemental people--child care support or a group of friends to be brought in to widen perspectives on the couples' problems. Since most of the participants are very articulate, the topics of conversation evolve into some really important insights on sharing responsibilities and, particularly, on the involvement of the male in the emotional life of the family. p. Martha Stuart; STUARTM.

COURAGE TO SUCCEED (28m C p1977, r1978)
   At 25, Diana Nyad is the world's first-ranked marathon swimmer. The film follows Diana into the Hudson River on her first attempt to swim around New York's Manhattan Island--an attempt which fails. Her second try was a record-breaking triumph. Next, Diana is seen in Dover, England, as she prepares to swim the freezing, perilous waters of the English Channel. Throughout, Diana articulates with exceptional force and clarity the two basic factors in an athletes performance: physical fitness and stamina, the courage to succeed. p. Bernard (Barney) Edmons, Alan Halperin, Saxton Communications Group, Ltd.; TEXFM.

COWHAND'S SONG: CRISES ON THE RANGE, A (28½m C 1981)
   Presents the life of family ranchers in northern California and Nevada who graze their cattle on public rangelands. It's a hard life, a constant struggle against the elements, both environmental and social. Over the past few decades, the ranchers' traditional use of the public lands has been challenged by environmentalists, recreationists, developers, and federal agencies. The film examines the conflicting viewpoints. d./p. Gwen Clancy/Nancy Kelly; p. Cattle Kate Communications; NEWFRF.

CRAMPS (25m C 1982)
   Primary dysmenorrhea affects millions of women and accounts for

140 million hours of absenteeism each year. Insight and understanding about this major women's health issue is explored through discussion, drama and animation. Dr. Penny Budoff, author of No More Menstrual Cramps and Other Good News explains how prostaglandins work and how anti-prostaglandins act to relieve menstrual pain. d./p. Marilyn A. Belec; MOBIUS.

CRANE AND THE HERON (10m C n.d.) (also Video)
An animated Russian folktale of a gawky, awkward crane and a dainty, graceful heron and their courtship. d./p. Yuri Norshtein; FI.

CRAZY JANE ON GOD (3m C si n.d.)
Choreography of a poem by W. B. Yeats. Multiple high-contrast color imagery and movement. Dancer: Lynn Juba-Jones; p. Geoffrey De Valois; CCC.

CREATING A LEARNING ENVIRONMENT (30m ea. [3 parts] C 1975) (Video)
A learning environment is "joyous, productive, reflective and sharing, as opposed to those that create anxiety and division among students and teachers." This three-lesson sequence presents methods of reaching that environment, illustrated with classroom segments with junior high students. The segments are 1) Using Discovery Techniques; 2) Value Clarification and Decision-making; 3) Role-Play, Simulations and Evaluating Classroom Environment. p./d. Mrs. Ruth Weatherl, Educational Service Unit Bicentennial Project Director; NETCHE.

CREATION (9m ? 1981)
A visually turbulent rendition of a creation poem read by James Earl Jones. Animator Joan Gratz pioneers a new animation technique --clay painting--to create a stunning metamorphosis of colors and images set to an original sound track by jazz bassist David Friesen. 1981 Academy Award Nominee. p. Will Vinton Studios, Joan Gratz; MEDIAP.

CREATIVE DANCE FOR CHILDREN SERIES see CREATIVE MOVEMENT EXPRESSION; TENSION AND RELAXATION; CREATIVE SOUND AND MOVEMENT; STUDIES IN MOVEMENT DESIGN

CREATIVE ELIZABETH: CHILDREN'S FESTIVAL OF THE ARTS (11m C 1976)
Pennsylvania State's Festival of the Arts for children is the culminating activity of ten weeks of learning for young art students and their teachers. Shows glimpses of the preplanning that produces such a festival and some of the typical activities. p./d. Dr. Alice M. Schwartz; p. The Pennsylvania State University; PAS.

CREATIVE MOVEMENT EXPRESSION (22m B 1977) Creative Dance for Children Series I

Boys and girls at the Tucson Creative Dance Center under the direction of Barbara Mettler, work on "Creative Movement Expression." p. Will Carbo; METTLER.

CREATIVE SOUND AND MOVEMENT (18m B 1977) Creative Dance for Children Series III
Boys and girls at the Tucson Creative Dance Center, under the direction of Barbara Mettler, working on "Creative Sound and Movement." Dance accompaniments are sounds of hands, feet and percussion instruments. p. Will Carbo; METTLER.

CREATIVE STORYTELLING TECHNIQUES: MIXING THE MEDIA WITH DR. CAROLINE FELLER BAUER (30m C 1979) (Video, Beta, VHS)
Dr. Caroline Feller Bauer, author of Handbook for Storytellers, demonstrates the use of variety of media--including puppets, toys, craft items and other simple props--to bring stories alive to audiences of all ages. She tells more than a dozen stories during the course of the program and also explains how to create and effectively use a variety of props. p. American Library Association; PBSV.

CREATIVITY SERIES see PORTRAIT OF MAYA ANGELOU, A

CREDIT DISCRIMINATION see WOMEN AND THE LAW, THE (SERIES)

CRIME OF VIOLENCE, A (17m C 1976) (slt)
This slide-tape program seeks to dispel the myths surrounding sexual assault, a crime which has been shrouded in misconception. It also seeks to promote attitudes which will lead to increased reporting of crimes and the prosecution of assailants. There are many kinds of sexual assault besides rape. Forcible rape is not a crime of passion; it is a crime of violence. The ugliest myths are those which question the integrity and morality of sexual abuse victims. The program advises viewers how to protect themselves and what to do if they are sexually assaulted. It also covers provisions of the Minnesota Criminal Sexual Conduct Law which has provided the foundation for change, making prosecution less difficult for the victim. p. Russell-Manning Productions; RUSMAN; UMN.

CRIME; SENIOR ALERT (18m C 1978)
Dramatizes, using senior citizens as actors, several vignettes to describe ways senior citizens can avoid becoming crime victims in their homes, cars, or in high-risk areas. Details how to prevent a purse snatcher from taking anything of value. Demonstrates proper behavior (complete cooperation) when threatened with a weapon. Stresses the avoidance of such high-risk areas as halls, laundromats, and parking lots. AIMS; IU, PAS.

CRIME TO FIT THE PUNISHMENT, A (46m C p1982, r1983)
The story of how U.S. government officials and the Hollywood

film industry conspired to stop the production and distribution of the 1953 labor film SALT OF THE EARTH. It reconstructs the unfolding events in the country and the struggles of the blacklisted filmmakers on location under the threat of violence. It addresses the rights of the filmmakers and the ultimate survival of the film and its craftspeople. d./p. Barbara Moss/Steve Mack; FIRRNF.

CRIMES AGAINST WOMEN (55m B 1979) (Video)
A documentary about four women arrested for taking direct action against violent pornography; synthesizes personal statement and feminist ideology and practice which directly confronts male power. p. Martha Gever; GEVERM.

CRIS WILLIAMSON ON WOMEN'S MUSIC (29m C 1976) (Video) Woman Series
Singer-songwriter Cris Williamson discusses her experiences in the music industry and why she moved to a recording company completely staffed by women. She describes her feeling for women's music and performs two of her compositions: "Sister," which was written for the proposed musical on the life of evangelist Sister Aimee McPherson; and "The Ballad of Calamity Jane." Sandra Elkin is the moderator. p. WNED-TV; PBSV.

CRITTER THE RACCOON (11m C p1982, r1982) (also Video)
This charming live action film acquaints children with the habits of a young raccoon that became a summertime pet and was eventually returned to its natural habitat. p./d. Myrna I. Berlet, Walter H. Berlet; IFB.

CROSS-CULTURAL APPROACH TO THE ACQUISITION OF SEX ROLES AND SOCIAL STANDARDS (25m C 1975) Development of The Child Series
An intriguing and informative approach to the study of the basic mechanisms by which social standards and, in particular, sex role orientations are acquired. Three different cultural settings--Guatemala, Kenya and Japan--illustrate the similarities and/or differences in social standards which are the result of modernization, economic status, and degree of isolation. Children are shown learning by the mechanisms of observation, imitation, praise, and punishment. In-depth analysis is made of identification with an "ego ideal." Of special interest are the differences in sex role standards acquired by children. p. Jerome Kagen; UMO, PAS.

CROSSCURRENTS: A LOOK AT AGEISM (13m C n.d.) Aging in Our Times Series
Examines how negative attitudes about the elderly have been perpetuated. Explores the phenomenon of stereotyping which has caused many of the elderly to be considered second-class citizens. Points out that such discrimination is robbing America of needed talent and skills. A trip up a trout stream with a carpenter and his granddaughter becomes a journey toward self-awareness, STEREF.

CROSSROADS: SOUTH AFRICA (50m C 1981)
Every day throughout South Africa in communities like Crossroads --an illegal squatters' town--a tense drama unfolds as blacks confront the labor controls and forced resettlement programs of apartheid which often split workers from their families who have been forcibly relocated to the remote bantustans. The families of Crossroads, however, have refused to be separated. Instead, they built this squatters' community of 20,000 complete with their own schools, active community organizations, and a sense of pride, community, and common purpose. In South Africa, this constituted an illegal act of brazen defiance of the apartheid regime which attempted to bulldoze the shanty town. Three women emerge as the leading figures in Crossroads' confrontation with the authorities. They are angry but surprisingly confident with an almost palpable belief in the ultimate victory of both their community and the black majority. p./d. Jonathan Wacks; CALNWS.

CRUZ BROTHERS AND MISS MALLOY, THE (54m C p1979, r1980)
The picaresque adventures of three Puerto Rican brothers' struggle to survive in a small town, and their poignant encounter with an elderly Irish lady, Miss Malloy, who hires them to renovate her mansion before she dies. Featuring Randy Ruiz, Lionel Pina, Jose Machado, and Sylvia Field. d./p. Kathleen Collins; COEF.

CUNA, THE (30m C 1975)
The Cuna Indians living on the San Blas Islands off the east coast of Panama are widely known for their distinctive woman's blouse, the mola, appreciated for its inventive appliquéd designs. Developing from the older custom of body painting, the blouses depict geometric patterns, plants and animals, scenes of village life, legends and myths, and more recently, objects from the outside world. Through narration the film provides a broad sketch of the Cuna-- tribal history, religion, customs, social and economic life, and the art of the mola. With only a few exceptions, the film is entirely narrated and would have gained a sense of immediacy through the use of natural sound and commentary by Cuna people. p. Marianne Huber /Robert Huber; LOSTNF.

CYCLE (5m C n.d.)
Free-line animation, in which the movement as much as the designs reflect the artist's thoughts on humankind and the universe. What evolves is a stream of ideas about the elemental situation of people, poised midway between the primary dust and the measureless universe yet unplumbed. Titles in French. No narration. d. Suzanne Gervais; p. Pierre Hebert; NFBC.

CYCLES IN NATURE (14¼m C p1980, r1980)
Explores the effects of cycles outside our bodies, such as the seasons and day and night as well as the cycles that occur inside us every day. p. Marjorie Bean, Norman Bean; BFA; PHOENIX.

-D-

D IS DAFFODIL YELLOW (29m C 1973) (Video)
Jazz singer-pianist Marian McPartland spends a delightful half-hour with a group of children from the Huntington (Long Island, New York) Public Schools, explaining jazz and encouraging the children's musical expression through singing, dancing and playing rhythm instruments. The youngsters also help compose an original piece by calling out notes around which Miss McPartland improvises. She explains to them that "different keys are different colors ... I think of A as pink, B as blue and D is daffodil yellow." p. WLIW-TV; PBSV.

DADI'S FAMILY (58m C p1980, r1981)
An intimate portrait of the women of a village family in India, and of a family in crisis. The women of Dadi's family break many of our stereotypes about women in the Third World as they reflect on their lives, the roles they play in the family, and their perceptions of change. d. Rina Gill/Michael Carmerini; p. James MacDonald, M. Camerini; DER.

DAGUERREOTYPES (74m C 1975)
In homage to early photographer Jacques Louis Mande Daguerre, Agnes Varda presents a witty view of days in the lives of her neighborhood shopkeepers and artisans on the rue Daguerre located in a working-class quarter of Paris. The unobtrusive moments spent observing the daily activities of the residents of the rue Daguerre and their interactions with clients are interspersed with interviews in which the shopkeepers tell us about themselves. Surprisingly, each and every person interviewed grew up in provincial villages, most moved to Paris in the fifties. An interesting ethnographic study in which we observe closely the daily functions of the shopkeepers as well as their social and cultural origins and the values of their society. d. Agnes Varda; FI.

DAME EDITH EVANS: I CAUGHT ACTING LIKE THE MEASLES (56m C 1977)
Dame Edith Evans was one of the greatest actresses of her generation, a generation that spanned some of the grandest years of the English theatre and cinema. Bryan Forbes, who guided Miss Evans to an Academy Award nomination in The Whispers and a close personal friend, filmed this relaxed conversation with her at her lovely Tudor home in Kent during the last months of her life. Describing this, his first film for television, as a "labor of love," Forbes convinced Miss Evans to talk revealingly and engagingly about her remarkable life. d. Bryan Forbes; CANTOR.

DAME JUDITH ANDERSON ACTRESS (30m ? 1969) (Video)
Dame Judith admits that the theatre is the one love of her life. From the age of eight she has wanted to do nothing else. She has

succeeded. She has won two Emmies for her performances as Lady Macbeth and has been awarded the Order of the Crown by Queen Elizabeth II. Dame Judith talks about her start in theatre and her uncertainty about recent works. She ends the lesson by performing two readings--a collection of thoughts and feelings by Robinson Jeffers and a contemporary poem, "The Noble Flower." NETCHE.

DANCE, THE (26m C 1977)
Shows four episodes: "The Dance, a Festival" (ballroom and popular); "The Dance: An Expression" (about Carolyn Carlson, choreographer, who directs the Theatrical Research Group of the Paris Opera); "The Dance: An Art" (about study in the Paris Opera dancing school directed by Prima Ballerina Claude Bessy); "Dancing Is Living" (showing Wilfrid Piollet and Jean Guizerix, stars of the Paris Opera Ballet Troupe). Choreographer: Carolyn Carlson. FACSEA.

DANCE AND THE NEW MEDIA (29m B 1970) Contemporary Dance Series VIII
Alwin Nikolais discusses and demonstrates dance and mixed media with host Robert Luscombe. "Check-in Time," a mixed media work for television by Sylvia and Richard Turner, is shown. It consists of slides, films, and various sound and video devices. An excerpt of "Totem" is shown. Dancers: Sylvia and Richard Turner; Choreographers: Alwin Nikolais, Sylvia and Richard Turner; d. Marshall Franke; p. University of Michigan Television Center; UM.

DANCE CHROMATIC (7m C 1959)
Abstract animated paintings combine with the dancing of 15-year-old Nancy Fenster. p. Ed Emshwiller; GROVE, FILMC.

DANCE COMPOSITION AS TAUGHT IN THREE CALIFORNIA COLLEGES (18m C n.d.)
Discussion and demonstrations by three teachers and their students. Eleanor Lauer directs "Studies in Rhythm," Mills College; Dr. Lois Ellfeldt directs "Studies in Space," University of Southern California; Barbara Lydanne Neel directs "Studies in Content," University of Redlands. p. Portia Mansfield Pictures; MANSPR.

DANCE: DANCE HISTORY/ETHNIC/FOLK/MODERN/BALLET/MIME/ SOCIAL, THE (74m B n.d.)
A history of dance, produced in Germany, with English narration. It begins with cultures of prehistory and the still-known primitive dance forms. Katherine Dunham is shown performing a dance based on native dances of Africa. The second part shows folk dance performances of more than 15 nations. This culminates in the social dances of the present including waltz, fox-trot and mambo. In contrast are shown the more formal types of dance with photography of the programs of study at many outstanding dance schools. Scenes of German ballet and modern dance classes are shown including a sequence of Mary Wigman teaching her students. Excerpts of classical

ballets are shown performed by Ludmilla Tcherina, Melissa Hayden, John Kriza and others. Harold Kreutzberg performs an excerpt from his Job and Kurt Jooss' The Green Table is shown in part performed by his company. The film ends with an examination of modern dance. Choreographers: Katherine Dunham, Alan Carter, Harold Kreutzberg, Kurt Jooss, Uore Hoyer; Mime: Marcel Marceau; Dance teachers: Mary Wigman, Lola Roget; p. Dr. Heinz Weris. MACMFL.

DANCE DESIGN: EXPLORATIONS IN MOVEMENT (19m C 1975)
Explores turns, descent and ascent, kinetic problem-solving exercises for individuals and groups, characteristics of body parts. d. Robert Cooley; technical advisors: Nancy W. Smith, Greta Weatherill, Jeanne Beaman, Willia Grissom; p. Athletic Institute; AAHPER.

DANCE DESIGN: SHAPING (16m C 1975)
The motion picture camera used in filming the dancers is placed below a transparent floor allows the viewer to see clearly the movements of dancers relative to shape, space, and time. Dance demonstrators: Lynda Davis, Susan Kennedy, Mary Ann Kellogg, Clay Taliaferro; Technical Advisors: Nancy W. Smith, Greta Weatherill, Jeanne Beaman, Willie Grissom; d. Robert Cooley; Athletic Institute; AAHPER.

DANCE DESIGN: SPACE (18m C 1975)
Dancers are shown moving in space in various ways. Dance demonstrators: Lynda Davis, Susan Kennedy, Mary Ann Kellogg, Clay Taliaferro; Technical Advisors: Nancy W. Smith, Greta Weatherill, Jeanne Beaman, Willie Grissom; d. Robert Cooley; Athletic Institute; AAHPER.

DANCE FILM (4m B si)
"She builds up a rhythm slowly, alternating the gesturing hands with blackness until a face of a woman appears, then the face of a bearded man and some things like shadows which change, and then it really does seem like a dance although no feet are seen dancing."-- Carmen Vigil, Cinemanews. p. Margaret White; CCC.

DANCE FOUR (6½m C 1977)
Choreographer Kei Takei dances to the music of George Kleinsinger, Eric Eigen and Mike Mahaffey. The film captures the essence of dance and brings a vivid kinesthetic awareness of movement. p. Doris Chase, WNYC-TV, New York; CHASED.

DANCE FRAME (7m C 1978)
The sensation of a hall of mirrors with its repetitive, dizzying, larger-than-life effect is aptly achieved in this dance tape in which Doris Chase intermixes images created by a video synthesizer, strobe lights, musical rhythms, and whirling dancers in an imaginatively sinuous fashion. The fluid motion of the dancers is circumscribed by frames of every shape and color. The tension resulting from

conflict between fluidity and stability provides an underlying dynamism. p. Doris Chase; CHASED.

DANCE IN AMERICA SERIES see TRAILBLAZERS OF MODERN
    DANCE; MARTHA GRAHAM DANCE COMPANY, THE; SUE'S
    LEG: REMEMBERING THE THIRTIES/TWYLA THARP AND
    DANCERS

DANCE IN AMERICA TV SERIES see MAKING TV DANCE

DANCE IN DARK AND LIGHT (8m B 1970)
    A camera study in light and dark, black and white, of ballet
dancers as they move to music of a flute solo written for this dance.
The dancers' forms create silhouettes, filling the screen with movement, form and imagery. Choreographer: Ben Johnson; d./p. Kiku
Adatto; Dance Company: Joffrey Ballet; SYRACU.

DANCE IN PROGRESS (29m B 1965) (also Video)
    A discussion of the creation and performance of modern dance.
Demonstrations by a dance instructor, Elizabeth Weil, and two dance
students. UM.

DANCE INSTRUMENT: ALIGNMENT, THE (17m C 1975)
    The movement possibilities for various parts of the body are explored and cultivated as an aid in creating a usable technique and a
vocabulary of communication for the dancer. Dance demonstrators:
Lynda Davis, Susan Kennedy, Mary Ann Kellogg, Clay Taliaferro;
Technical Advisors: Nancy W. Smith, Greta Weatherill, Jeanne Beaman, Willie Grissom; d. Robert Cooley; p. Athletic Institute; AAHPER.

DANCE INSTRUMENT: HOW TO MOVE BETTER, THE (19m C 1975)
    Shows elements contributing to a better performance--plié, elevé,
jumping movement of back and spine, and abdominal flexibility. Dance
demonstrators: Lynda Davis, Susan Kennedy, Mary Ann Kellogg,
Clay Taliaferro; Technical Advisors: Nancy W. Smith, Greta Weatherill, Jeanne Beaman, Willie Grissom; d. Robert Cooley; p. Athletic Institute; AAHPER.

DANCE OUTLINE (4m C 1978)
    A film from a videotape produced in cooperation with WNYC-TV,
New York City. Dancer/Choreographer: Sara Rudner; p. Doris
Chase; CHASED.

DANCE TEN (8m C 1977)
    A duet of Jonathan Hollander, choreographer/dancer, and a video-synthesized image of one of the "Chase Kinetic Sculptures for Dance."
"A striking combination of human and sculptural form constantly
changing color and shape."--Andy Bobrow, Filmmakers Newsletter.
p. Doris Chase; CHASED.

DANCE THREE (8½m C 1977)
   Dance on a theme from "Light Part Nine" choreographed by Kei
Takei. Music by George Kleinsinger. p. Doris Chase; CHASED.

DANCE WITH JOY (13m C 1971)
   Stressing that children are natural dancers when given the opportunity, this film shows the freedom of movement which develops
in an atmosphere in which no standards of achievement are set. Music and rhythm stimulate the children's responses. Each child is
encouraged to express his/her own way of moving. Dance teacher:
Gertrude Copley Knight; d./p. M. T. Hollingsworth; p. Documentary
Films; DOCF.

DANCE YOUR OWN WAY (10m C 1961)
   A group of boys and girls create their own dances to phonograph
music. The children moving freely and confidently, while mastering
the skills of dancing by interpreting rhythms. Dance teacher: Gertrude Copley Knight; p. Lawrence P. Frank, Gary Goldsmith; KENTSU,
PAS, SYRAU, UIL, UAZ, PSU, UMN.

DANCEMAKING (29m B 1970) (also Video) Contemporary Dance Series
   Presents characteristics of contemporary dance as they appear in
the two dances recorded in the films SONG (Elizabeth Bergmann) and
EVERSTAR (Sylvia Turner). The focus of the discussion is on the
differences between the two styles presented and their characteristics. Dancers/Choreographers: Elizabeth Bergmann, Sylvia Turner;
d. Marshall Franke; p. Selma Odom; p. University of Michigan Television Center; UM.

DANCEPROBE (28m C 1978)
   Shows performances of Native American spiritual dances, ballet,
modern dance and creative movement. p. Peggy Mundt; MUNDTP.

DANCER'S CLASS, A (20m B 1978)
   Advanced technique of Lester Horton with additional choreography
by Joan Kerr as performed by six dancers of her company. Choreographers: Joan Kerr, Lester Horton; p. Joan Kerr Dance Company;
KERRJ.

DANCER'S GRAMMAR, A (18m C 1977)
   The rigorous training routines practiced by ballet dancers are captured in this film as female and male dancers demonstrate the exercises in their daily training sessions. The camera catches close-up
views of their hands, feet, faces, and well-formed muscles straining
to develop the illusion of effortlessness. Captions identify the exercises performed. No narration. p./d. Nina Feinberg; PHOENIX;
UCEMC, UMN.

DANCERS IN SCHOOL (28m C 1971)
   Filmed in Troy, Alabama and Glendale, California school systems,

a pilot project of the artists-in-schools program. The dancers and their companies performed in the schools, taught classes, held classes for teachers and rehearsed in the school gyms. Virginia Tanner and her students introduce school children to fundamentals of dance. Commissioned by the National Endowment for the Arts and the Office of Education. Dance Teacher: Virginia Tanner; d./p. D. A. Pennebaker; PAS, UIL.

DANCERS ON THE MOVE (29m B 1970) (also Video) Contemporary
    Dance Series
    The members of the José Limón Dance Company, in residence at the University of Michigan, discuss the professional gap in dance between New York and the rest of the United States, with host Robert Luscombe and other university staff members. A film of two master lessons taught by Betty Jones and Daniel Lewis is shown. Essence of the Humphrey-Limón technique and style is explained by Luscombe while the classes are in session. d. Marshall Franke; p. Selma Odom, University of Michigan Television Center; UM.

DANCES OF SCOTLAND, THE; PT. I, THE HIGHLAND FLING (20m
    C 1965-67)
    Each of the six steps of the Highland Fling are explained and demonstrated in slow motion and normal speed followed by a performance to bagpipe accompaniment by Herbert Crowe of a traditional tune, "The Devil in the Kitchen." The demonstration and performance is prescribed and approved by the Scottish Official Board of Highland Dancing. Narration: James Jamieson; Project Director: Nadia Chilkovsky Nahumck; p. Calvin De Frenes Corporation; FRANDA.

DANCES OF SCOTLAND, THE; PT. II, SWORD DANCE AND GHILLIE
    CALLUM (20m C 1965-67)
    A dance dating from 1054 when Malcolm Canmore, symbolizing his victory over one of Macbeth's chiefs, placed his sword across that of his defeated opponent and danced triumphantly over the blades. The dance, approved by the Scottish Official Board of Highland Dancing, is performed to bagpipe music performed by Philip Townsend. Dance Teacher: Marguerite Reed; Narrator: McLain McLeod; Project Director: Nadia Chilkovsky Nahumck; p. Calvin De Frenes Corporation; FRANDA.

DANCES OF SCOTLAND, THE; PT. III, SEAN TRIUBHAS, STRATH-
    SPEY, AND HALF REEL OF TULLOCH (12m C 1965-67)
    "Sean Triubhas" (Dance of the Trousers), a dance cemmorating the lifting of restrictions against wearing kilts as a national costume; "Strathspey"; and "Half Reel of Tulloch," originally performed only by men, are performed to bagpipe music played by Philip Townsend. Dance Director: Marguerite Reed; Project Director: Nadia Chilkovsky Nahumck; Narrator: McLain McLeod; p. Calvin De Frenes Corporation; FRANDA.

DANCES OF SOUTHERN AFRICA (55m C 1973)
Recreational dances performed by various tribal groups in South Africa and Rhodesia (now Zimbabwe), including the Xhosa shaking dance, high-kicking Ndlamu dance of the Zingili Zulo, and tumbling dance of the Ndau. Each dance is completely recorded. Ethnochoreologist: Nadia Chilkovsky Nahumck; p./d. Alfred Gei Zantzinger; PAS.

DANCING IN BERLIN (12m B n.d.)
Shows Tatjana Gsovsky's dancing school in Berlin and excerpts of her students' work. p. unknown; UCLA.

DANGER! RADIOACTIVE WASTE (50m C 1976) (also Video)
Although the debate over the safety of nuclear energy continues, the major stumbling block in the development of this kind of energy is the problem of disposing of radioactive waste. In 1950, hundreds of barrels of radioactive waste were sunk into the oceans. In 1975, the Environmental Protection Agency discovered that these barrels of waste had leaked into the sea, causing what scientists believed genetic mutations in marine sponges brought about by excessive radiation. Now, radioactive waste is buried in the ground. However, no box, bin or other containers invented will last forever; radioactivity continues for hundreds of millions of years. This is one of the major problems scientists must solve if nuclear power is to become a generally acceptable, practical source of energy. d. Joan Konner; FI.

DANGEROUS STRANGER (3rd ed.) (10m C 1972)
Children themselves, properly informed, are their own best defense against the child molester. A series of vignettes dramatize the methods that molesters use to win a youngster's confidence--gifts, friendly conversation, the offer of a ride. How to act when approached by a stranger--perhaps just how to say "No, thank you"--is the film's most valuable lesson. p. Sid Davis Productions; AIMS.

DANIEL FOSTER, M.D. SERIES see COMPLICATIONS OF PREGNANCY; ESTROGEN AND THE MENOPAUSE; NUTRITION AND FAD DIETS

DARK CIRCLE (82m C 1982)
A human portrait of America in the nuclear age, told through the lives of those directly affected by it. Shot on location at the Rocky Flats Nuclear Weapons Facility near Denver, the Diablo Canyon Nuclear Power Plant in central California, and in Japan, the film interweaves personal stories with rare footage of the secret world of nuclear weapons production. An in-depth look at the human costs of a nuclear economy--even in the absence of a nuclear war. p. Judy Irving, Ruth Landy, Chris Beaver; NYF.

DATE, THE (7m C 1980) Rape Prevention Series
Confronts the myth that a girl owes a boy some sexual favor if

he spends a lot of money on a date. Observes a girl inviting the
boy in after a special night out, even though her parents are not at
home. Open-ended. p. ODN Production; MTITI; IU.

DATE, THE (20m C 1977)
    Exploration through dramatization about what boys want from
girls and girls want from boys, and how peers influence expectations.
p. Larry Klingman; d. Donald MacDonald; LREDF.

DAUGHTER RITE (53m C p1978, r1979)
    Explores the mother/daughter and sibling sister relationships as
seen from the perspective of the daughters of two different families,
dealing with the themes of anger, love, grief, betrayal, manipulation,
and patterning. p./d. Michelle Citron; IRISFC; UMN.

DAUGHTERS OF TIME (29m C p1980, r1981)
    This compelling film sensitively conveys the current trends in
midwifery. Thousands of women are right now seeking nurse-midwives
to be their primary care-givers during pregnancy and birth. Shown
are many women certified nurse-midwives who still must struggle to
practice their time-honored profession. p. Durrin Films, Inc.; NEW-
DAY; UIL, UM.

DAUMIER: PARIS AND THE SPECTATOR (18m C 1978)
    Nineteenth-century Paris as seen by its illustrators and carica-
turists, particularly Daumier. The spectator, a typical theme of the
time informs us of the city and its inhabitants, their preoccupations
and diversions. p. Ray Eames, Charles Eames; d./s.w. Judith Wech-
sler; PF.

DAVID CHAMBERLAIN: A SEARCH FOR PERFECTION (12m C 1981)
(Video)
    Sculptor David Chamberlain derives inspiration from the natural
forms of the sea shell. This program watches the stages of the creative process as these themes develop and the forms evolve into finished works. The viewer is exposed along the way to the sculptor's
sense of when things work, when they don't, and why. d. Marilyn
Felt/Henry Felt; p. Family Information System and Resource Communications; PUCSAFR.

DAWN RIDERS: NATIVE AMERICAN ARTISTS, THE (27m C 1969)
    Modern Indian painting is based on a long figurative tradition--
pictographs. Plains hide paintings of tribal history and nineteenth-
century drawing in ledger books and on muslin. The modern style,
using color and line in a similar way, is said to have begun in 1918
with students in Anadarko, Oklahoma, known as the Five Kiowa.
The 1920's saw the first flowering of modern Indian painting throughout the nation and in Europe. There are now numerous Indian artists using both traditional and modern forms of expression. Shown
are three prominent Indian painters: Woody Crumbo (Potowatomi),

Blackbear Bosin (Kiowa-Comanche) and Dick West (Cheyenne) who talk about their work and the influences on their art. p. Dona De-Weese, Robert DeWeese; LODESTAR.

DAY OF THE DEAD (14m C 1977)
Dealing with special objects and events surrounding the annual Mexican celebration of "All Souls Day," this film is not only a rich flood of folk art, but a view of the structured way that Mexicans come to terms with death. p. Ray and Charles Eames; PF.

DAY ON EARTH (20m C 1972)
A work of choreographer/dancer Doris Humphrey, set to Aaron Copland's "Piano Sonata." The performance, in 1972 at the Juilliard School, features dancers Peter Sparling, Janet Eilber, Ann de Gange, and Elizabeth Haight. Tells of humankind's brief, but self-perpetuating, passage on earth. p. Juilliard School, University of Rochester/Dance Archives; DAN/UR; UIL, UCLA.

DAY WITH DARLENE (59m B 1976)
Another visit with Darlene provides an informational resource and supplement to the earlier film VISITING WITH DARLENE, further exploring the life-style of an Appalachian woman who knows only poverty and hopelessness for herself and her children whom she loves. Restricted in Pennsylvania, unrestricted elsewhere. p. Pennsylvania State University Television, p./d. Lisa J. Marshall, P. J. O'Connell; PAS.

DAY WITHOUT SUNSHINE, A (60m C 1976) (Video from PBSV)
This documentary, narrated by James Earl Jones, examines the living conditions of Florida farmworkers--presenting an update of the information contained in Edward R. Murrow's film HARVEST OF SHAME. These interviews with three farm workers--one black, one white, and one Chicano--as well as with citrus and agribusiness leaders, union organizers, government officials and growers, attempt to explain why in 20 years conditions have not improved and how the politically powerful citrus industry maintains near total control over their work force. The camera follows the workers into the fields, homes or camps. p. Robert Thurber, Florida Public Broadcasting, National Council of Churches; UM, UMN, PBSV.

DAYDREAMING (30 sec C 1980) (Video)
Designed to alert the public that young children who persistently daydream may be experiencing absence seizures. These types of seizures are frequently missed because they are so brief and subtle and are usually mistaken for daydreaming or lack of attention. They are most common in children. d. Phil May; p. Ann Scherer; sponsored by Epilepsy Foundation of America; EFA.

DAYS OF OUR YEARS (81m B 1951)
Here is France, with its alliances and dalliances, its fads and

fancies, its world wars, pre-war isolationism, post-war fashions, its backfiring colonializations, its noble moments, its foolish times, its brilliance, its art, its stupidity, its Dada period, its nihilism, its hero worship, its riots, its space shots. Beginning in 1900 and ending in 1950, the film's brilliant editing and extensive use of fresh archive material sets it apart from a straight documentary and makes it an entertainment to be savored. d./ed. Denise Tual, Roland Tual. France. English narration, slightly abridged. KPF.

DEAD ARE NOT SILENT, THE (80m C/B p. 1978, r1978)
Isabel Letelier and Moy de Toha were the wives of two Defense Ministers of the Chilean Unidad Popular. They became widows as a belated result of the fascist coup because their husbands knew too much. These two women tell their story with dignity and without haste, and their personal fate becomes ever closer entwined with their nation's. d. Heynowski and Sheumann; p. Studio H and S; NEWTF.

DEAD END (92m B 1937)
Features the Dead End Kids in their film debut, Humphrey Bogart in a crucial transitional role and Gregg Toland behind the camera in Sidney Kingsley's socially conscious story of New York gangster activities. d. William Wyler; s.w. Lillian Hellman. Based on the play by Sidney Kingsley. ABF.

DEAD SEQUENCE (5m B 1960)
Stills of famous people who died in the 1950's. p. Ray and Charles Eames; PF.

DEALING WITH THE AGGRESSIVE CHILD (14m C p1980, r1980)
(Video)
The use of time out, or brief social isolation, as a consequence for such child behaviors as fighting, verbal abuse and hitting, is explained and modeled. Special attention is given to common problems parents encounter in using the procedure. The importance of noticing and reinforcing cooperative child behaviors is emphasized. d. Elaine Velazquez, s.w. Janet Farrell; NWMP.

DEAR DIARY (25m C 1981) (also Video)
Presented in a situation comedy format, the film raises and answers the key questions teenagers have as they enter puberty. Information about body changes and maturation is presented tastefully, with humor and reassurance. The important issues of self-image, peer pressure and pressure to date are dealt with in a way girls can identify with and understand. p. Debra Franco; d. Debra Franco, David Shepard with the Boston Family Planning Project; p. Copperfield Films; NEWDAY.

DEAR MR. AND MRS. BERTHOLF (8m B n.d.)
Arthur and Helen Bertholf are 80 and 85, respectively. They

have been married for 17 years and have seven children and 26 grandchildren. Having traveled extensively throughout the world, they now travel with their slide presentations to neighborhood schools sharing their experiences with children. d./p. Helen Abrahms; TEMPLU.

DEARLY BELOVED (15m C 1981)
In a remote region of Utah, Alex Johnson, a Mormon, lives with his eleven wives and two fiancées. This program examines his attitudes toward family, monogamy, and morality. Interviews with his wives provide insight to this unusual life-style. p. Journal Video, Inc.; JOURVI.

DEATH: A TIME TO REMEMBER (28m C n.d.)
Chronicles the history of funeral rites, beliefs and burial customs around the world from prehistoric times to the present. The film shows how many religions have approached the inevitability of death, and describes some of the fears and superstitions sometimes associated with death. Encourages viewers to deal with the subject of death from both a historical and a personal approach, and to ponder the inevitability of death as a rite of passage that deserves our attention, care and preparation. p. H. Roy Thompson, Mort Layton; p. MPS Productions; MMM.

DEATH AND DYING: A CONVERSATION WITH ELISABETH KUBLER-ROSS, M.D. (29m C 1974)
Psychiatrist Elisabeth Kubler-Ross, M.D. discusses her work and philosophy during an interview with Bill Varney. Kubler-Ross, an international consultant in the care of dying patients and their families and author of the best-selling book On Death and Dying, explains how she handles death in her own family and shares her views on euthanasia and death with dignity. She also expresses her belief that "beyond a shadow of a doubt" there is life after death. p. WITF-TV; Hershey, Pennsylvania; PBSV.

DEATH AND DYING: A TEENAGE CLASS (10m C 1981) (also Video)
The mere mention of death can arouse discomfort, anxiety, concern and a natural curiosity. In a Washington, D.C. high school course, teenagers have the opportunity to learn the facts of death. DEATH AND DYING takes students into a funeral home, cemeteries and embalming rooms as part of course work. It records results of a variety of assignments such as personal interpretations of death, how one's parents wish their bodies disposed of, and the writing of one's own imaginary obituary. CBS News; CRM; UIL.

DEATH AND DYING: THE PHYSICIAN'S PERSPECTIVE (29m C 1981) (also Video)
Nine doctors candidly discuss their feelings, both personal and professional, on the sensitive subject of death and dying. Their discussion covers many aspects of terminal illness, including how long

to sustain someone who is nearly dead, how to tell a patient he or she is dying, what to say to the family, predicting death, and encounters with dying patients in medical school. p./d. Elizabeth Bradbury; SERBC.

DEATH BY REQUEST (25m C n.d.)

Meg Murphy, 78, argues for her right to receive help to end her life when it is no longer meaningful to her. Mrs. Murray, a widow, is concerned that the multiple sclerosis she has had for 40 years may disable her so that she will be unable to end her life when the time comes that she wishes to do so. Her goal is to repeal the English law which makes assisting someone to end his/her own life a criminal act. A nurse psychotherapist, Ms. McNulty, expresses her concern to Mrs. Murray that if all dying patients were allowed this privilege-- other elderly and chronically ill persons would feel obligated to end their lives, thus releasing their families from emotional, physical and financial problems created by their case. p. Granada TV International; CONCFD.

DEATH IS AFRAID OF US (26m C 1980--U.S.)

In the mountains of Soviet Georgia there is a large population of men and women who live to be over 100 years old, leading active, vigorous lives. One woman, who still works every day--and smokes heavily--claims to be 140. Another centenarian hunts with a musket handed down in his family since the eighteenth century. Someone remembers the Crimean War. This is a life where adolescence stretches into what we consider middle age. p. Dr. Alex Comfort; Granada Novosti Productions, London; FILMLB.

DEATH OF A NEWBORN, THE (33m C 1979)

The death of a newborn is a tragedy for any family, followed by a prolonged period of grief. The couple in this film is interviewed by Dr. Marshall Klaus, three-and-a-half months after the death of their two-pound normal daughter who died of septicemia after 28 days. Portrays each parent's grieving process. This film is intended to assist health professionals in providing support to bereaved parents. p. Case Western Reserve University; POLYMR.

DEATH OF IVAN ILYCH, THE (28m C 1979) Begin with Goodbye Series

The DEATH OF IVAN ILYCH introduces the most profound change any of us can imagine--our own death. A dramatization of Tolstoy's moving short story. "The Death of Ivan Ilych" is performed for a group of seriously ill hospital patients who afterward share their responses, each person recognizing some aspect of his/her condition in the Tolstoy story. With guide. MMM.

DEATH ROW (59m C p1979, r1980)

Shows how men get by on death row in Texas, how they fill their time, fight their sentences and manage to stay sane. Includes interviews with many of the inmates. p. Diane Christian, Bruce Jackson. p. Documentary Research, Inc.; DOCRES.

DEBBIE (15m B p1980, r1980)
A personal, self-revealing profile of a 21-year-old mentally handicapped woman, her struggle with loneliness and her will to survive. d./p. Bohdan Montasewych; CANFDC.

DECISION: ENERGY FOR THE FUTURE (12m C p1978, r1980) (also Video)
This animated film uses graphs and manipulates screen time to demonstrate that our dependence on fossil fuel is an extremely recent phenomenon. If continued, it will lead to disastrous consequences. But there is a clear choice--to switch to renewable energy sources. Study guide and games for the amateur trustee included. d./s.w. Deborah Cohen; p. Grania Gurievitch, Howard Brown/Earth Metabolic Design and Togg Film; BULFRG.

DECK THE HALLS (18m C 1981) Time Out Series, I
A dramatic portrait of domestic violence from the man's point of view. Al Greensboro thinks he's losing ground at the office, losing his youthful charm and losing sway over his family. He releases his anger in violent attacks on his wife. Depicts the "cycle of violence" that shatters the family's Christmas celebration and leaves Al spent, remorseful and scared. d. Christina Crowley; p. Nancy Graham; ODNPRO.

DECLINE OF WESTERN CIVILIZATION, THE (100m C/B 1981)
This mind-blowing documentary is an uncompromising, dispassionate look at life and values among Los Angeles' punk rockers. Club owners acknowledge the violence of "speed rock," as do punk writers and editors who analyze the music. Los Angeles bands such as Catholic Discipline, Germs, X, Circle Jerks and Fear perform in local night spots (with lyrics often subtitled). At home, musicians candidly discuss their lives and art, fleshing out a portrait of an alienated, reactionary subculture in which violence is almost routine. Critics of music and film unanimously agree, THE DECLINE ... has set the standard of excellence in contemporary music films. p./d. Penelope Spheeris; CORINTH.

DEER FAMILY OF NORTH AMERICA (18m C 1965) (also Video)
Examines origins, ranges, habitats, characteristics, and life histories of the North American members of the deer family. Uses animation, wildlife photography, and maps to show the evolution, adaption, and migration patterns of the moose, elk, caribou, and deer. p. Myrna I. Berlet, Walter H. Berlet; IFB.

DEGAS IN THE METROPOLITAN (10m C 1980)
This comprehensive study of French artist Edgar Degas takes us on a tour through the Metropolitan Museum of Art's extraordinary collection of his works. p. Ray Eames, Charles Eames; PF.

DE GAULLE SKETCH (2m B 1959)
The photos and cartoons that appeared in the press during the de Gaulle crisis in a highly condensed résumé. p. Ray and Charles Eames; PF.

DE KOONING ON DE KOONING (58m C p1981, r1982)
An intimate, lively and informative portrait of the life and art of Willem de Kooning. In a rare collaboration with his family, friends and the filmmakers, de Kooning tells his own story in relaxed conversation in his home and studio. d. Charlotte Zwerin; p. Courtney Sale; DIRECT.

DELIVERY MAN (7½m C 1982)
An animated personal narrative film in which a young woman discusses her feelings towards surgery. She relates five true dreams and experience involving the doctor who delivered her, her mother who survived surgery and her father who did not. D. Emily Hubley; PICTS.

DEMETRI ALEXANDROS' DIVE (9m C 1977)
Depicts the importance of the Holy Cross Service in the life of a Greek-American community. d. Jackie Rivett-River; p. Myrna Ravitz, p. Lifestyle Productions, Inc.; EBEC.

DEMONS AND DANCERS OF CEYLON (30m B 1971)
Students of the Government School of Dance in Colombo, Sri Lanka, demonstrate the various dance forms of the Singhalese people of Sri Lanka. Student classes as well as expert dancers and musicians, in both solo and group performances, are filmed. The masked dance-drama at the Kolam Theatre in Ambalangoda is described and shown in part. The famous Kandyan dancers are shown. Concludes with the annual Esala Perahera, a procession of canopied elephants, acrobats, dancers and musicians from all parts of Sri Lanka. Music taped on location. d./p. Margaret Fairlie Kennedy; p. Instructional Resources Center, Ithaca, New York; KENMF.

DENISE: THE TRAGEDY OF CHILD ABUSE (58m C p1980, r1980)
(also Video)
Denise Gallison, convicted of child abuse and the murder of her three-year-old daughter, tells the tragic story of her own shattered life. Casts new light on the tangled social and psychological forces that lead to the neglect and abuse of more than one million American children. p. Boston Broadcasters, Inc.; ABCWWL.

DENISHAWN (10m B 1915, 1930)
The first half of the film was made in 1915 and shows scenes around the Denishawn School in Los Angeles. Ruth St. Denis and Ted Shawn are seen teaching class and administering the school. The second half was made in 1930, with sound. In it, Miss St. Denis dances excerpts intended to demonstrate characteristic racial gestures

of dances from Siam, Java, and India (Nautch). Dance Company:
Denishawn; Dancer: Ruth St. Denis; DAN/UR.

DES: THE TIMEBOMB DRUG (27m C p1982, r1983)
    The history of diethylstilbestrol, its past and present uses, and
the medical consequences of exposure to this known carcinogen. Five
case histories are intercut with medical authorities, a pharmaceutical
representative, and consumer advocates, to illustrate the importance
of maintaining stringent drug laws in this country. Narrated by
Linda Kelsey. d./p. Stephanie Palewski; ed. Joanne Burke; LILGHT.

DES DAUGHTERS AND SONS, PART I (29m C 1977) (Video) Woman
    Series
    Medical researcher Kay Weiss describes the current incidence of
cancer and vaginal tissue abnormalities in the daughters of women
who took prescribed DES and other female hormones during their
pregnancies. Given to an estimated six million women between 1940
and 1971 to combat infertility, miscarriage and other difficulties of
pregnancy, DES and other estrogens have since been found to cause
deformation in the vagina and cervix of developing female fetuses.
Weiss identifies procedures necessary to detect a problem and tells
women who suspect they may be "DES daughters" what they can do.
Sandra Elkin is the moderator. p. WNED-TV; PBSV.

DES DAUGHTERS AND SONS, PART II (29m C 1977) (Video) Woman
    Series
    Medical researcher Kay Weiss discusses the current use of diethyl-
stilbestrol and other estrogens to treat a variety of symptoms, in
spite of a 1971 warning by the Food and Drug Administration not to
prescribe female hormones during pregnancy. She also describes the
effects of the "morning after" pill, the possible consequences of taking birth control pills while pregnant, the risk of stimulating a latent
cancer with estrogens and the effects of estrogen received "in utero"
on DES sons. Sandra Elkin is the moderator. p. WNED-TV; PBSV.

DES ENSEMBLES (3m C n.d.)
    A play on color, form and movement of two simple figures--a
flower and a star. The effect is gay and lively, a constant surprise,
but the movement has a mathematical precision as multiples of figures
form sets of ensembles, forming and reforming on the screen in absorbing, piquant harmony. Titles in French. No narration. d. Suzanne Olivier; p. Pierre Herbert; NFBC.

DESERT ECOLOGY (14m C 1970) (also Video)
    Introduces plants and animals living in a hot desert climate. Em-
phasizes adaptations to heat and long dry periods. Plants examined
include creosote bushes, the saguaro cactus, the ocotillo, and the
palo verde. Animals include the kangaroo rat, gila woodpecker, the
roadrunner, the desert coyote, the spadefoot toad, lizards, tortoises,
and rattlesnakes. p. Myrna I. Berlet, Walter H. Berlet; IFB.

DESIGN IN DANCE (29m B 1967) (also Video)
A discussion of the relationship of painting and sculpture to the art of choreography. Choreographer: Barbara Berofsky; UM.

DESIGN Q & A (5m C 1973)
Charles Eames answers questions about design. p. Ray and Charles Eames; PF.

DESIGN WITH THE SUN: PASSIVE SOLAR ARCHITECTURE (28m C 1982)
Internationally recognized authority on solar energy, Bill Yanda, takes you on a tour of selected passive solar homes and buildings across the country. With leading solar experts--David Wright in California, Sara Balcomb and Bill Mingenbach in Northern New Mexico, Douglas Taff in Vermont--he describes innovative designs and building techniques that utilize passive solar principles. Included are such basic concepts as direct gain, built-in greenhouse and Trombe wall systems. Also covers climatic and site considerations, orientation to the sun and wind, thermal mass and insulation, construction materials and techniques, R factors, air circulation, overhangs, window placement, and other design details. p. Danamar Film Production in association with Susan and Bill Yanda. A film by Mario and Dana Balibrera; BULFRG.

DESIRE PIE (4½m C 1977 (SFS)
DESIRE PIE "is an animated celebration of universal lovemaking as demonstrated by a pair of contented couples to the beat of a funky clarinet. As their ecstasy increases, the lovers metamorphose into a spectrum of ages, races and possibilities." --Ron Epple, Filmmakers Newsletter. p. Lisa Crafts; SERBC.

DESPERATE HEART, THE (11m B 1951)
Valerie Bettis performs a work to the words of a poem by John Brinnin about a woman's anguished memory of lost love. Dancer/ Choreographer: Valerie Bettis; d. Walter V. Strate; MACMFL; UMN.

DESPERATE HEART, THE (12m C 1974)
Valerie Bettis' famous dance solo performed by Margaret Beals under Ms. Bettis' personal direction, with an introduction by Ms. Beals, Ms. Bettis and dance critic Walter Terry about the transference of a dance role from one artist to another. Choreographer: Valerie Bettis; Narrators: Margaret Beals, Valerie Bettis, Walter Terry; BROOKSV.

DETACHED AMERICANS, THE (33m B 1964)
Study of the psychology of people who "don't want to get involved." The theory of conditioned family relationships is explored as one of the possible causes of the apathy, which reaches epidemic proportions at times. p. WCAU-TV, Philadelphia, for Philadelphia Gas Works; CAROUF.

DETECTION AND DIAGNOSIS OF CERVICAL CANCER (28m C p1979, r1979)
Primary purpose of the film is to communicate the need and benefits of early cervical cancer detection. Includes current statistical information and the proper procedures for pelvic exam along with pap screening. The current grading system for the stages of cervical cancer are discussed in detail with clinical examples. Further diagnostic steps such as Schiller's stain and colposcopy are also presented. A real life conization surgical procedure is demonstrated. d. Richard Milner; p. David Milner; AMCS.

DETOUR, THE (13m C 1977)
Presents Catherine Hamilton, an 83-year-old woman, who is dying in a hospital. The story unfolds through Catherine's eyes, and her unspoken thoughts are heard by viewers but not by anyone in the film. Although her only wish is to die with peace and dignity, the doctors and staff are making every effort to keep her alive which Catherine fiercely resents. p. Caroline Ahlfours Mouris, Shelby Leverington; d./s.w. S. Leverington; KPF, PHOENIX, VIEWFI, IU, UM.

DETOUR: A CHALLENGE (28m C p1980, r1980)
A filmed lecture by Marilyn Van Derbur, intended to inspire people to reach their ultimate levels of personal achievement. Several actual situations are cited as evidence, often involving highly successful and famous individuals. The fact that Mozart learned from Bach, and Henry Ford learned from Thomas Edison reinforces the concept that most successful women and men draw wisdom from many sources. p./d. Marilyn Van Derbur; VDBER.

DEVELOPING AESTHETIC CONCEPTS THROUGH MOVEMENT (29m B 1966)
Third-grade children demonstrate aesthetic response through exploration, discussion, interpretation of poetry and art under the guidance of their teacher, Betty Rowan. She describes concepts of rhythm, sound quality, and structural form as they relate to aesthetics and various modes of expression. Produced under a United States Office of Education grant. Dance Teacher/Writer/Narrator: Betty Rowan; d. Paul Williams; p. Teacher's College, Columbia University; National Archives and Records Service; DANFA.

DEVELOPMENT OF THE ADULT (29m C 1978)
An introduction to the field of life-span developmental psychology, which focuses on the psychological and behavioral changes that take place during the period of young adulthood (18-29) to old age (beyond 75). Uses candid sequences, dramatizations, and interviews with leading authorities to examine the nature of common adult-life events and "crises," and the various ways in which individuals cope with them. p. Harper and Row Publishers, Inc.; HAR; PAS.

DEVELOPMENT OF THE CHILD SERIES see CROSS-CULTURAL

APPROACH TO THE ACQUISITION OF SEX ROLES AND SOCIAL STANDARDS

DEVELOPMENTAL PSYCHOLOGY: INFANCY TO ADOLESCENCE SERIES see ADOLESCENCE: A CASE STUDY

DEVELOPMENTAL PSYCHOLOGY SERIES see GROWING OLD: SOMETHING TO LIVE FOR

DIAL A-L-C-O-H-O-L SERIES see LEGEND OF PAULIE GREEN, THE

DIALOGUES IN MEDICINE, PT. I (25m C n.d.) (also Video, S8)
An interview with Dr. Beatrice Tucker. She shares some of her thoughts on home obstetrics and the state of medical practice in general. Dr. Tucker has been the director of the Chicago Maternity Center for 50 years where she supervised 100,000 home births qualifying her as one of the world's foremost experts on the subject of childbirth at home. CINMD.

DIALOGUES IN MEDICINE, PT. II: NUTRITION IN PREGNANCY see NUTRITION IN PREGNANCY

DIANA (40m C 1978) People You'd Like to Know Series
Diana talks about her feelings and those of her family and friends regarding the amputation of her leg because of cancer. She is exceedingly cheerful eight days after her operation, the therapists had her up and walking with crutches and an artificial leg. She participates in sports such as horseback riding and skiing, and generates a positive philosophy about her handicap. She has definite goals for her future and looks forward to life. p. WGBH-TV, Boston; EBEC.

DICK AND JANE AS VICTIMS: SEX STEREOTYPING IN CHILDREN'S READERS (30m C 1982) (s/t)
Examines sexism in elementary readers. The sample included 150 children's books from 16 major publishers. Only a quarter of the books featured females, who were rarely treated as capable, intelligent beings. Activeness and bravery in boys are constrasted with passivity and frailty in girls. Based on the book of the same title published by Women on Words and Images, a feminist consulting firm. Script included. p. Women on Words and Images; UMN.

DIET FOR A SMALL PLANET (28m C 1973)
Shows how to get good quality protein from non-meat sources. Encourages us to take individual responsibility for ending world hunger. Based on best-selling book of the same name. Features the author, Frances Moore Lappe, and Ellen Buchman Ewald, author of Recipes for a Small Planet. With nutritionist/biochemist Dr. Kendall King, they explore three main topics: The Nutrition of Protein, The Ecological Cost of Meat Protein, and Cooking with Complementary Protein. p. Bullfrog Films/Amanda and Burton Fox, John Hoskyns-Abrahall, Winifred Scherrer; BULFRG; UM.

DIET INTERVIEW: A GUIDE FOR THE PARAPROFESSIONAL (30m C 1980)
Emphasizes the need for accurate diet information; identifies common interview problems; and introduces, illustrates, and reviews elements of good diet interview technique through two interviews which take place in a WIC office between a Community Nutrition Worker and an expectant mother. A packet of instructional materials, handouts and evaluation forms is available. UM.

DIET UNTO DEATH: ANOREXIA NERVOSA (13m C p1980, r1980) (also Video)
Explores the emotional illness anorexia nervosa which takes the lives of thousands of young women. Four young women tell of being afraid to swallow food, refusing to eat more than a spoonful of ice cream a day, exercising to lose more weight and going without any food as a punishment to themselves. A family therapy session is filmed in which the doctor hopes to make one girl realize she is ready to grow up. Another twenty-year-old is taken to the hospital near death. She weighs 53 pounds and is attached to intravenous feedings to give her nourishment. Victims of anorexia nervosa are seen to be overachievers who set high standards for themselves and strive for an impossible level of perfection. ABCWWL; PAS.

DIETING: THE DANGER POINT (20m C 1979) (also Video)
Examines the physical and psychological dangers of a current upsurge in the disease known as anorexia nervosa. An epidemic number of today's bright, healthy young girls are willfully starving and overexercising themselves in the pursuit of a slender figure. Shows the effects such behavior has on the girls and their families. d./ p./s.w. Brad White, Elizabeth Anderson; CRM; CWU, UCEMC, WSU.

DIETS FOR ALL REASONS (21m C 1981)
Explores in an amusing fashion the foolishness and fallacies as well as the advantages of certain alternatives to the "standard" American diet. Some far-out fad diets being eaten by various young people are shown to be dangerously deficient in nutrients. Crash weight loss diets are seen to be not only nutritionally bad, boring and physiologically draining, but ultimately useless. A vegetarian diet is experienced by the misfortunes and victories of a young person who learns to cook well-balanced vegetarian meals. The special problems of the vegan diet are shown. The film covers the importance of the four food groups and the need for balanced meals in any eating pattern chosen. CF; UW, UCEMC.

DIFFERENT APPROACH, A (22m C 1978)
Uses broad comedy strokes to deal with the traditionally serious subject of employment of the handicapped. Attempts to break down barriers to employment and correct misconceptions and prejudices by using cameo appearance by celebrities to introduce short skits. The skits are satirical take-offs from advertising approaches. d. Fern

Field; p. F. Field, Jim Belcher; South Bay Mayors' Commission;
SBMAYC.

DIFFERENT FOLKS (SEX ROLE IDENTIFICATION) (15m C 1975)
Deals with nontraditional sex roles in the home. The father is
an illustrator of children's books, works at home and does most of
the housework. The mother is a veterinarian and provides most of
the family income. Matt and his sister, Judy, are assigned household
tasks. Matt's friends chide him about his family being "weird," but
the problem is resolved when Matt's friends learn that apparent sex-
roles can be deceiving. p. Northern Virginia Educational TV Association; NITC; KENTSU, UMO.

DIGNIFIED EXIT, A (28m C p1979, r1981) (also Video)
Under British law, suicide is no longer illegal, but the abetting
of it is an offense. This is a paradox that confronts hundreds of
terminally ill or elderly and infirm men and women--and those who
must watch them suffer. This film looks at three such cases and
also at the efforts of Exit--a society for those who want the right to
choose to end their own lives. Presents various views on this disturbing and painful problem. Brian Blake for Granada TV; FILMLB;
UW.

DIGNITY OF DEATH (30m C 1973)
Explains the concept, purposes and methods of the hospice as
first conceived in Britain by Dr. Cicely Saunders, and carried out at
St. Christopher's. "Hospice," a medieval designation of travelers'
way stations, was chosen as an appropriate way to characterize those
sources of help for the terminally ill, as opposed to meanings already
associated with "hospital." Care of the patient is deemed to be mental and spiritual as well as physical, and is extended to those "significant others" touched by his or her suffering. Includes careful
philosophical distinctions between hospice care and euthanasia. p.
National Council of Churches, ABC-TV; ABCWWL; MMM, UIL.

DIONNE QUINTUPLETS see DIONNE YEARS, THE

DIONNE YEARS, THE (87m C 1978)
Back in 1934, Elzire Dionne delivered five identical girls; Cecile,
Emilie, Marie, Yvonne and Annette. The film follows 21 years of
their strange upbringing. When the girls were just infants, the
Premier of Ontario issued a court order removing them from parental
care. Cut off from the world and their family, over-publicized, viewed
twice daily in a special viewing compound, they grew up as prize exhibits. Director Donald Brittain uses old newsreel footage, home-
movie sequences and interviews to depict a historic event that became a tragic exploitation of a family. d./p. Donald Brittain; NFBC.

DIRECTION CENTER (30sec C 1981) (Video)
A typical day at the Direction Center. Alerts the community to

the value of early identification and remediation of handicapped children. Also being used as a "child find" vehicle, it conveys the Direction Center message: If you are worried about the way a young
child is growing, walking, talking, behaving or learning, call for
help. d./p. Loni Ding; CHIFAA.

DISABLED WOMEN'S THEATRE PROJECT, THE (60m C 1982) (Video,
    Beta, VHA)
A series of skits and performances by the Disabled Women's Theatre Project. In exploring and communicating the experience of disability through theatre, the Company conveys the outrageous, absurd,
funny, painful and dramatic moments of their lives. By presenting
these often humorous situations, the Company increases public awareness of both the creative abilities and the needs of the disabled community. Performances are by women with a variety of physical disabilities, strong artistic capability, and an awareness of challenge
facing disabled women in this society. Members of this group are
available for speaking engagements and personal appearances. p.
Women Make Movies; WMM.

DISAPPEARANCE OF AIMEE, THE (103m C p1976, r1979 ed.)
Presents the story of the disappearance of Aimee Semple McPherson in 1926 and the court trial that followed her disappearance one
month later. Focuses on the hearing and the later trial resulting
from charges that with her lover, radio engineer Kenneth Ormiston,
and with her mother, Minnie Kennedy, they committed acts injurious
to public morals in a kidnapping hoax. Flashbacks depict the events
and the people testifying at the hearing and trial revealing, among
other things, the character, personality, and complex relationship
between Aimee and her mother ... upon which this film conjecture
is based. Stars Faye Dunaway as Aimee, Bette Davis as Minnie Kennedy. p. Tomorrow Entertainment, Inc., Paul Leaf; d. Anthony Harvey; s.w. John McGreevey; LCA.

DISAPPEARING WORLD SERIES see ASANTE MARKET WOMEN;
    MASAI WOMEN; WITCHCRAFT AMONG THE AZANDE

DISCIPLINE (30m C 1980) (also Video) Look at Me Series
Highlights: Defining the goal of discipline; understanding the
processes involved in achieving the goal. The goal in establishing
discipline is to reach the point at which a child's behavior is governed
by self-discipline. Disciplined children learn to follow rules--first
their parents', then society's, and finally their own. The problems
of temper tantrums, toilet training, and teaching children right from
wrong are discussed. p./s.w. Jane Kaplan, Wendy Roth; WTTW-TV;
FI.

DISCOVERING THE ART OF KOREA (58m C p1979, r1979)
Based on recent excavations, this film reveals the glittering,
golden heritage that comprises 5,000 years of Korean art. Shot on

location in Korea and the United States, the film covers a spectrum from early bronzes to royal gold crowns and ornaments, Buddhist sculptures, celadon ceramics to delicate landscape paintings. p. Paula L. Haller; d. Paul Asselin; FFHUM.

DISCUSSION WITH PARENTS OF A MALFORMED BABY, A (37m C 1979)
Illustrates how parents learn about and adapt to the special needs of their malformed child and learn to cope with their feelings of grief, guilt, anger and blame. The parents of a six-week-old infant with Down's syndrome is interviewed by Dr. John Kennell. Both negative and positive aspects of the care the parents received at the hospital are presented. Useful for promoting sensitivity among hospital and nursing staff and evaluating hospital policies. p. Case Western Reserve University; POLYMR.

DISCUSSIONS WITH PARENTS OF PREMATURE INFANTS (32m C 1979)
Parents of premature infants are interviewed regarding their experiences and how they coped with the situation at the hospital and at home. This film would be helpful to other parents in similar situations. It also could be used as a focus for discussion groups. Interview by Marshall Kalus, M.D. p. Case Western Reserve University; POLYMR.

DISEASE CONCEPT OF ALCOHOLISM, THE (43m C 1982) (also Video)
Dr. David Ohlms reviews the medical and biochemical evidence that alcoholism is a disease. p. Gary Whiteaker Company, WHITG.

DISTANT ISLANDS (7m C p1981, r1982)
Recalls a young girl's visit to the Gulf Islands near Vancouver, British Columbia during a vacation. The unique animation uses stitchery and appliqué. d. Bettina Maylone; p. Jack Long, NFBC; EBEC.

DISTINGUISHED CONTRIBUTORS TO COUNSELING SERIES see ON BEING AN EFFECTIVE PARENT

DIVIDED TRAIL: A NATIVE AMERICAN ODYSSEY (33m C r1978)
Provides an important perspective on the complex dilemmas faced by Native Americans today, and conveys their determination to maintain their cultural integrity as they work to gain equal rights within American society. Filmed over an eight-year period, this documentary follows the lives of two Chippewa Indians, Michael Chosa and his sister, Betty Chosa Jack, who along with their friend Carol Warrington migrated from their Northern Wisconsin reservations to the slums of Chicago. This is the story of their struggle to overcome the near disintegration of their individual and tribal identities under the enormous pressures of contemporary urban living. p./d. Jerry Aronson; PHOENIX.

DIVINE HORSEMEN: THE LIVING GODS OF HAITI (54m B 1947-51/ 1977)

Although Maya Deren's work as an avant-garde filmmaker is well known, film students may be less familiar with her ethnographic studies. This footage, which deals with the Vodun religion of Haiti, was shot by Ms. Deren during 1947-51 and edited after her death by Teiji Ito and Cherel Ito. Deren had been initiated as a priestess of the Vodun religion in Haiti, and so was able to capture with her camera intimate details of ceremonial rituals and dances. The title refers to the phenomenon of spirit possession; "man is like a horse being mounted by a divine spirit." d. Maya Deren; ITOC.

DIVINE MADNESS, A (28m C p1979, r1981) (also Video)

"The mad ladies who dance in the woods" was how the neighbors referred to Portia Mansfield and Charlotte Perry in 1914 when they established a dance school in the Colorado wilderness. This is both a history of the Perry-Mansfield Camp, which grew from tottering beginnings to an influential force in modern dance, and a tribute to the courage and dedication of two strong-willed women in challenging the frontier and giving life to a dream. Old photographs and early motion pictures enhance the contemporary footage, capturing the personalities of the subjects and their passion for creative interpretation of life. Narrated by Julie Harris. p. Leonard Aitken, Candice Carpenter; p. Oak Creek Films; FI.

DIVORCE see WOMEN AND THE LAW, THE (SERIES)

DIVORCE (29m C 1980) (Video, Beta, VHS) Feelings (Series)

An estimated two out of every five children born in the last decade will live in a single-parent home for some part of their childhood, and statistics show a higher incidence of emotional disturbance among youngsters from divorced families. But where does the real harm lie--in the divorce itself, or in the way children are dealt with during the breakup? Dr. Lee Salk explores the subject through the personal experiences of three children of divorce, 11-year-old Laurie and 13-year-old Pam and Danny. PBSV.

DIVORCE: A CHILD'S RIGHTS, PT. 1, #4 (29m C 1975) (Video)
   Dynamics of Divorce Series

Paul Casperson, Marriage and Divorce Counselor, discusses how parents should deal with the child's questions and his or her feelings. p. University of Minnesota; UMN.

DIVORCE: A CHILD'S RIGHTS, PT. 2, #5 (29m C 1975) (Video) Dynamics of Divorce Series

This program deals with the subject of visitation and custody of the child. Experts in setting up viable visitation programs discuss some of the common difficulties. p. University of Minnesota; UMN.

DIVORCE: A LEGAL PERSPECTIVE, PT. 2, #6 (29m C 1975) (Video)
   Dynamics of Divorce Series

A discussion of the philosophical and legal distinctions between the fault and no-fault legislation regarding divorce. Guest is Judge Suzanne Sedgwick of Hennepin County, Minnesota. p. University of Minnesota; UMN.

DIVORCE ... AND OTHER MONSTERS (21½m C p1980, r1980) (also Video)
Sandy's parents have recently divorced, and she is experiencing the anger, fear, guilt and rejection that many children feel after a divorce. After talking with her friends, her teacher, and her mother and father, Sandy realizes that the divorce wasn't her fault and that no matter how hard she tries, her parents won't love each other more. Sandy also learns that by talking about the monsters in her life, she can more easily cope with them. d./p. Ron Underwood, s.w. Nancy Bond, Phyllis Wapner, BARRF; UCEMC.

DIVORCE AND YOUNG PEOPLE (18m C 1980) (also Video)
The traumatic effects of divorce are explored, along with how children sometimes respond to the breakup of their parents' marriage, and what adults can do to ease the pain, confusion and insecurity the child may be experiencing. The main focus is on the child's needs, feelings, fears, and concerns that he/she may be responsible for the divorce. It is pointed out that youngsters need to understand that communication is essential to the healing process and that seeking help is a strength, not a weakness. p. Golden Coast Film Productions; PEREN.

DIVORCE AND YOUR FAMILY (20m C 1981) (also Video)
Trends in divorce show that three out of ten children will live with only one parent by age 18. Shows a group of teenagers of divorced families discussing their problems and concerns. The need to be realistic, to express emotions, not blame themselves for the divorce or feel they can change the state of affairs, and to communicate with their parents are all emphasized. The three stages of divorce discussed are the psychological stage, the social stage, and the legal stage. The narration suggests that seeking outside help may be a real strength and asks teens to remember that divorce is not the end of a family but only a reorganization of it. p. Golden Coast Film Productions; PEREN.

DIVORCE: GRIEF OR RELIEF, PT. 1, #2 (29m C 1975) (Video) Dynamics of Divorce Series
Marriage and Divorce Counselors Judi Savage and Chris Santella discuss whether or not divorce can be a healthy choice enabling people to be free of unhealthy conflict. p. University of Minnesota; UMN.

DIVORCE: GRIEF OR RELIEF, PT. 2, #3 (29m C 1975) (Video) Dynamics of Divorce Series
Marriage and Divorce Counselors Judi Savage and Chris Santella

discuss the common feelings of divorcing men and women: ambivalence, guilt, failure, confusion and anxiety. p. University of Minnesota. UMN.

DOC: THE OLDEST MAN IN THE SEA (29m C p1980, r1980)
At 58 "Doc" Counsilman, Indiana University swimming coach and two-time Olympic coach, became the oldest individual to swim the English Channel. Highlights of his record-breaking swim are interwoven with flashbacks showing Doc in training for the event and at work coaching his university swimming team. Providing most of the narration, Doc reflects upon prior attempts by others to swim the Channel, his belief in the health and recreational value of swimming for older people, and his life as coach and researcher. d. Kathryn Larson; p. William Kroll for WTIU-TV; IU.

DR. WAYNE DYER, THE SKY'S THE LIMIT (55m C p1981, r1982)
(also Video)
Shows Dr. Wayne Dyer, psychologist, counselor, therapist, teacher, and author of the books Your Erroneous Zones, Pulling Your Own Strings, and The Sky's the Limit, speaking to a group of business and civic leaders in a two-part seminar. Dr. Dyer introduces his audience to his philosophy of "no-limits living." He describes the steps required to achieve mastery and belief in one's self. Clearly, much of his messages' value lies in personal evaluation. p. Patti Kaplan, R. G. Kaplan; p. Intergroup Productions for Learning Corporation of America; d. Rudolf Gartzman; LCA.

DOCTOR WOMAN (22m C p1978, r1981)
Tells about the life and times of Dr. Elizabeth Bagshaw. Elizabeth Bagshaw was determined to become a doctor, despite the discriminatory practices and male prejudices of the early 1900's. One of Canada's earliest woman pioneers in medicine and birth control, she retired in 1975 at the age of 94 with the distinction of being Canada's oldest practicing doctor. In filmed interviews her prescription for a long and happy life is seen to center around being useful and following the golden rule. Delivered by her mother and a neighbor, Elizabeth was born October 19, 1881, in Victoria County, Ontario. In medical school, she found men indignant at the idea of women in their classrooms. She practiced in Hamilton County during the days of quarantine, blood-letting, diphtheria and typhoid. Her opening of a birth-control clinic brought accusations from the church that she was teaching immorality, but an eventual court case settled the matter in her favor, enforcing the legality of birth control in Canada. Elizabeth Bagshaw spent 30 years with the clinic and 70 years as a doctor. d. Mark McCurdy; p. Beryl Fox; p. Lockwood Films, London, for National Film Board of Canada. NFBC.

DOCTORS AND PATIENTS (30m C 1980) Coping with Serious Illness Series
Documentary on the last years of Joan Robinson, a woman who

was dying of cancer. Examines the ongoing relationship among Joan and her doctor and other medical personnel. Shows the problems in dealing with doctors and the criteria for choosing a doctor. Clergy and nurses also discuss their special bonds with patients. TIMLIF; PAS, UIL.

DOCUMENTARY (135m B/C 1979)
An international history of the documentary as social statement, political education and art form, compiled from sequences of major films from NANOOK OF THE NORTH through HARLAN COUNTY, U.S.A. p./d./s.w. Sonya Friedman, Herman J. Engel; TEXFM.

DODOTH MORNING (16m C r1976)
An ethnographic study of a tribe in northern Uganda. Although they are a pastoral people, the Dodoth grow a variety of crops, of which millet is a staple. Using a slice-of-life style with sparse narration, the film focuses on a series of family interactions one morning during harvest time, illustrating a great many aspects of Dodoth life, including social roles and the division of labor between the sexes, marital customs, relationships between parents and children, village organization, and religious and mythological beliefs. Though simple in story line, the film is richly detailed and well observed; each scene is filled with valuable and spontaneous data on a people's daily life. By Timothy Asch, noted for his films dealing with the Yanomamo Indians of Southern Venezuela. The book Warrior Herdsmen by Elizabeth Marshall Thomas can be used to enhance understanding of the film and the culture. UCEMC.

DOGS DREAM (9m C r1974)
A colorful example of "felt-cut" animation telling the poignant story of a young dog's desire for a family. Saddened because he is alone when all the other animals enjoy the warmth and happiness of family life, the little dog dreams of finding the perfect mate. When, at last, he does find her, many obstacles must be overcome before his dream can come true. d. Hermina Tyrlova; p. Short Film Prague--Gottwaldov Film Studio; PHOENIX.

DOIN' WHAT THE CROWD DOES (? C 1982) (also Video)
A unique presentation in which teenagers encourage their peers to not always follow the crowd. An effective way of delivering this important message to adolescents who are certain to be affected by this imaginative production. d. Peter Wallach; p. Jane Warrenbrand for the Scott Newman Foundation; CF.

DOING IT RIGHT (6m C 1980)
This humorous film chronicles the adventures of a teenage girl as she decides for better or worse to "loose her virginity" and sets out to do it. The film addresses important general issues such as peer pressure and sexual activity, love and sex vs. sex. It also touches on birth control and venereal disease. Sexually non-explicit. d./p. Maria Gargiulo; MMRC.

DOLLEY AND THE GREAT LITTLE MADISON (28m C n.d.)
Television and stage actress Lois Nettleton portrays Dolley Madison, wife of President James Madison, through a historical chronicle that covers the 42 years of their happy marriage. Nettleton's narration is illustrated with art treasures, architecture and artifacts of the period. Free loan. p. Philip Morris, Inc.; MTPS.

DOLL'S HOUSE: THE OPPRESSION AND EMANCIPATION OF WOMEN (31m C 1977)
Edited from the film version of Hillard Elkins' 1973 production of Henrick Ibsen's classic. A Doll's House has been called the first women's liberation statement--the compelling analysis of a woman trapped into being a mechanical toy to be played with at the whim of her husband. Claire Bloom portrays Nora in the modern version of Ibsen's play. p. Paramount; AIMS; UM.

DOLLY (10m C 1976)
Relates in animation the attempt of one woman getting close to another woman and its inevitable failure. A good discussion film on human relations. p./d. Jennifer Mead. PHOENIX.

DONA MARIA (20m C 1981) (Video)
A glimpse into the active life of a 100-year-old Mexican curandera (healer) living in Oakland, California. Explores Dona Maria's personal philosophy for long life and happiness, while observing her use of massage and herbal remedies in the dying art of traditional healing. d. David L. Marton; p. D. L. Marton/Dorothy Edwards; ALAMEC.

DON'T BOTHER ME, I'M LEARNING--COMPUTER IN THE COMMUNITY (22m C 1983) (also Video)
Provides a survey of the many uses of microcomputers. Shows people of all ages working with computers. A resident of "Computertown U.S.A.," Menlo Park, California, describes that community's goal of giving everyone in town a chance to use computers. Computers are placed in different areas where people congregate. After a review of the many uses of computers, the narrator claims it is only a question of what people will use their computer for, not whether they will have one. d. Karen J. Carlson; p. David Shepardson; p. One Pass Film and Video, Inc.; s.w. Jane Heath Donohue; CRM.

DOROTHY SERIES, THE
An animated series for children about a bold and curious little girl and her clever and resourceful pet parrot. d. Bozena Mozisova; p. Short Film Prague; PHOENIX.
The films in the series are these: DOROTHY AND THE FLAME (9m C r1978); DOROTHY AND THE NECKLACE (8m C r1976); DOROTHY AND THE PARROT (6m C r1976); DOROTHY AND THE POP SINGER (9m C r1974); DOROTHY AND THE STAR (8m C r1978); DOROTHY AND THE WITCH (7m C r1976).

DOSE OF REALITY, A (16m C 1978)

Nurse Joy Ufema of Harrisburg, Pennsylvania has a special job: to make the last days of the terminally ill warm, involved and dignified. She helps families recognize that a dying relative should not be excluded from everyday decision-making and restores to her patients an autonomy that doctors often ignore. Excerpt from the CBS "Sixty Minutes" program. d. Suzanne St. Pierre; CAROUF; PAS, UIL, UMN.

DOUBLE CONCERTO (53m C 1982)

Roger Woodward is Australia's "most prestigious cultural export" --patron of Solidarity in Australia. Wanda Wilkomirska, world-renowned Polish violinist, is ex-wife of Poland's Deputy Prime Minister Rakowski. They tour Australia together, playing magnificent music by Chopin, Tchaikovsky, Beethoven and Bach. This film explores their art and their politics. d. Hugh Piper; p. Angela Catterns; AFC.

DOUBLE JEOPARDY (41m C 1978)

Uses case histories to examine the often traumatic and demeaning treatment a child victim of sexual abuse receives in judicial proceedings. Seeks to sensitize child-advocate professionals to these problems. Emphasizes the importance of understanding child development, the dynamics of sexual abuse, the role of the child advocate, interviewing techniques, and prosecutor courtroom techniques. Produced for the University of Washington Sexual Assault Center. p. MTI Teleprograms, Inc.; MTITI; PAS.

DOUBLE STRENGTH (17m C 1978)

A portrait of the stages of a lesbian relationship between the filmmaker and a trapeze artist, a study of stillness and motion in relationship and film. The film begins with the dreams of two new lovers and goes on to delicately explore monogamy, friendship, rage, and the ending of the relationship. The visual magic of trapeze art and experimental re-photography combine to make this the finest of Barbara Hammer's films to date. p. Barbara Hammer; WMM; IRISFC.

DOUCHING AND FEMININE HYGIENE: WHY, WHEN AND HOW (15m C n.d.)

Designed to take the mystery out of douching. It begins with a simple explanation of how a woman's body works--her reproductive system, menstrual cycle, vaginal secretions. It then moves on to explain douching--what it is, what it will and will not do. Available to senior high school girls and other interested women audiences. Not for mixed audiences. Free loan. p. Beecham Products; MTPS.

DOWNHILL (36m C 1974)

About a man's second youth, the time in his middle years when he overstrains his passion for life and love. While on a ski trip with a young woman, the man suffers a heart attack. The wife is deceived but not beyond understanding, and the son hurt but protective of parental folly. Life is the test imposed on strength and

will by the downhill swoop of the snow and the unreckoning nights
in the snug chalet. A reckoning there is, but when it comes it, too,
is invested with the pride and promise of those hills. d. Robin Spry,
NFBC; FI, VIEWFI; KENTSU.

DOZENS, THE (78m C p1980, r1981)
  Until this production there had been no single film that explored
women's various social roles in relation to current criminal justice issues, though there had been an evident need for one. Boston filmmakers, Christine Dall and Randall Conrad produced and directed this
intriguing fictional account of one young woman's efforts to make a
successful transition from prison to life on the outside. Based on
documentary research, THE DOZENS defies many current stereotypes
and offers a wide perspective on the social status of women as well
as today's rising crime statistics. Presents these issues in all their
complexity without offering simple solutions. Guide available. d./p.
Christine Dall, Randall Conrad; CALLIFR.

DRAGGERMAN'S HAUL (18m C r1975)
  A natural resource, personal independence, and a sense of pride
in one's work--all threatened by "progress" in the form of bigness,
pollution, and short-sighted conservation policies. Shows a small
fishing fleet of independent operators on the United States' East
Coast. Over-fishing by modern factory ships is seen not only as a
threat to a basic food resource but dehumanizing influence. Increasing ocean pollution is blamed for confusing patterns of fish migration.
Visuals follow the fishermen through their daily chores as two of the
operators talk about a life they enjoy and the problems they face.
p. Wendy Wood; FLMFR.

DRAGON FOLD ... AND OTHER WAYS TO FILL SPACE (8m C 1979)
  (also Video)
  Using animation, the concept of a single closed curve which is the
the focus of a point that touches every point in a unit area is shown
in the Dragon Fold Curve and in the Sierpinski Curve. Each succeeding generation moves without limit toward the inclusion of every point
in the unit area. p. Katharine Cornwell, Bruce Cornwell; IFB.

DREAM AGE (12m C 1979)
  A 70-year-old lesbian feminist, seeing little change in the society
after years of work, sends out her 40-year-old self on a journey
which takes her around the perimeters of the San Francisco Bay.
During her quest, she encounters aspects of her personality: the
guardian angel who has all that she needs; the seductress who leads
her astray; the wise woman of goddess secrets whom she meets underground. The film culminates in a visual crescendo ascending the
tower as the heroine's hair is painted white by her counterparts. A
dream vision film telling us that the quest must go on. p. Barbara
Hammer; IRISFC.

DREAM DANCES OF THE POMO (30m C 1964)
   Southwestern, or Kashia, Pomo women dance the Bole Maru of today nearly a century after it first evolved, blending the native Kuksu cult with the Maru, or dream religion. The five dances--Hand Power Dance, Star Hoop Dance, Feast Dance, Marriage Dance and War Flag Dance--reflect recent influences including Christianity and World War II. Each is danced in elaborate costume around a fire within a brush enclosure. The shaman, who controls the forms and details of the dancing, expresses her religious beliefs and explains the significance of the dances. Ceremonial activities and the termination feast are interwoven between the dances. p. UCEMC.

DREAM OF AN ALCHEMIST, THE (12m C n.d.)
   Poetic fantasy based on the Greek legend of Jason and the Golden Fleece. Dance Company: Hanya Holm Dance Company; Choreographer: Hanya Holm; d./p. Thomas Bouchard; BOUCHT.

DREAM YOUR OWN DREAMS (20m C 1978) Woman of Purpose Series
   Features author, publisher, artist and ecologist Gwen Frostic. Discusses her humor, her philosophy of life, and her love for people and nature. p. Lizabeth Camp Communications/Dick Arnold Productions; FLMFR; KENTSU, UIL.

DREAMER THAT REMAINS: A PORTRAIT OF HARRY PARTCH, THE (27m C 1973)
   Harry Partch, now 73 and at last accepted by institutions which once rejected his musical artistry, puts on multimedia performances in this film, using a gallery of his exotic instruments and playing his nonconventional new scales and modes. He shares his comments on life and youth, and on music revealing himself to be prophet, eccentric and philosopher. d. Stephen Pouliot; p. Betty Freeman; ex. p. Saul Rubin, Elaine Attias; MACMFL.

DREW ARCHIVE
   The films gathered together in the Drew Archive represent a major force in the development of cinema verité. Collectively the Archive provides a truthful kaleidoscope of the political, cultural, and social events of the last two decades. Contact the distributor for titles in this collection as more are being added. Betsy A. McLane, Director, Drew Archive; DIRECT.

DRUG ABUSE CASE STUDY--SUSAN: APRIL TO JUNE (23m C n.d.) (Video)
   Susan is a 23-year-old Santa Monica prostitute who works the streets to support her heroin habit. In staccato color vignettes, the filmmaker shows Susan to be a woman struggling to overcome the burden of her addiction. p. Linda Jassim; NORTONJ.

DRUGS, SMOKING AND ALCOHOL DURING PREGNANCY (11½m C 1983)
   Discusses the confusion many pregnant women face about what

may be harmful to their fetus. The film then gives the facts that are known about smoking, alcohol and drugs during pregnancy. Also covers over-the-counter drugs such as cold and headache remedies. p. Milner Fenwick, Inc.; MIFE.

DRUM IS MADE--A STUDY IN YORUBA DRUM CARVING, A (24m C p1976, r1978)
Shows how the famous "talking" drum is made and played by a drummaker in Western Nigeria. p. Mary S. Thieme, Darius L. Thieme; d. Francis Speed; IFB.

DU COTE DE MEMPHIS (58m C 1980) (also Video)
Originally a documentary made for French television, this film opens with the folk art of the Southern black radio disc jockey, moves on to the "passing parade" of Beale Street in Memphis, and becomes a kind of paean to the Center for Southern Folklore and its work, making a record of the past and the present. Emphasis is on the film work of the Center and the collaboration of Bill Ferris and Judy Peiser in painting a "portrait of the world overlooked in Hollywood and and television." That world centers on the folk and life along the Mississippi. d. Rene Booyer; p. Pathe Cinema/Bella Beeson; SOFOLK.

DUBOWITZ ASSESSMENT OF NEWBORN GESTATIONAL AGE (44m C 1979)
Shows an inexpensive and reliable method of assessing gestational age developed by Dr. Lilly Dubowitz and husband, Dr. Victor Dubowitz. Demonstrates the examination and the criteria for scoring plotted on graphic charts and a scoring graph. p. Case Western Reserve University; POLYMR.

DUCKY (2m C 1980)
A zappy soundtrack sets the pace for a pastiche of madcap images. p. Sally Cruikshank; SERBC.

DUNE DANCE (40m C 1980)
Dancers (led by Sara Rudner) cavort through sand dunes as the camera artfully explores how the sand affects their movement. p. Carolyn Brown; DAN/UR.

DYING (98m C 1975) (avail. in Video from PBSV)
Explores the lives of people with terminal cancer. Three individuals and their families, living with the awareness of death, cope with it in styles that are uniquely theirs. p. Michael Roemer; p. WGBH-TV; PAS, UMN, UM.

DYING SWAN (3m B 1973)
A set of still photographs of Vera Fokina precisely synchronized with the music according to the published requirements of the choreographer. DAN/UR.

DYNAMICS OF DIVORCE SERIES   see   SOCIAL CONTEXT OF DIVORCE,
#1; DIVORCE: GRIEF OR RELIEF, Pt. 1, #2; DIVORCE: GRIEF
OR RELIEF, Pt. 2, #3; DIVORCE: A CHILD'S RIGHTS, Pt. 1,
#4; DIVORCE: A CHILD'S RIGHTS, Pt. 2, #5; DIVORCE: A
LEGAL PERSPECTIVE, Pt. 2, #6; STANDING ALONE, Pt. 2, #7

-E-

EAMES CELEBRATION: SEVERAL WORLDS OF CHARLES AND RAY
   EAMES (90m C 1975)
   A profile of Charles and Ray Eames, a creative couple renowned
for their design work in architecture, filmmaking, science, communications, painting and furniture. Includes excerpts from a number of
their films, views of exhibits, a visit to their unique California home,
and comments by colleagues on their remarkable achievements. p.
WNET-TV; FI; IU, UM.

EAMES LOUNGE CHAIR (2m B 1956)
   A stylized, speeded-up scene of the assembling of the Eames
leather lounge chair and ottoman, with music by Elmer Bernstein.
p. Ray and Charles Eames; PF.

EARLY ABORTION (8m C 1978)
   Shows a simple and accurate description of atraumatic aspiration
(vacuum) abortion procedures. Designed for use by doctors, clinics,
hospitals, medical centers and health centers with the woman who is
about to terminate an early pregnancy. Adrienne Barbeau, TV actress, narrates an animated step-by-step explanation. p. Ramsgate
Films; PEREN; IU.

EARLY DANCE FILMS (12m B si n.d.)
   Eleven short dance films, 1894-1912, as restored from the Library
of Congress paper print collection: "Chrissie Sheridan," "Ameta,"
and "Annabella," this last one in color; a skirt dance; "Flag Dance,"
by Annabelle Whitford Morre; two dances by variety dancer Ella Lola;
a French acrobatic dance; and others. Dance Film Archive; DAN/UR.

EARLY GOLD SEEKERS, THE (15m C 1982)
   Dramatizes the rush to California in 1848-49 by gold seekers from
all over the globe. The various techniques and tools used are demonstrated and explained, as is their camp life and social organization.
Emphasizes the importance of the migration to the subsequent development and industrialization of the American West. d. Phyllis A. Stanton; p. Thomas J. Stanton; STANF.

EARRINGS OF MADAME DE, THE (105m B 1953) (French/Subtitled)
   A remarkable portrait of the vanity and frivolity of the upper
classes in the nineteenth century. Earrings that were once given to
Madame De by her husband (and sold by her to pay off debts) are

later given to her by her lover. Only now do they have special
meaning to her. But she is trapped by the earrings into revealing
her infidelity to her husband. Because of that she loses her lover
and dies of a broken heart. Cast: Danielle Darrieux, Charles Boxer,
Vittorio deSica, Jean Debucourt, d./s.w. Max Ophuls; CORINTH.

EARS TO HEAR (28m C p1975, r1978) (also Video)
Shows how profoundly deaf children can be taught to speak normally and to hear the sounds of ordinary speech. Dr. Daniel Ling
of McGill University explains the advantages of his auditory method
of therapy, and the film depicts it in practice. Recommended for
everyone concerned with hearing problems in children. d. Heather
Cook; CBC; FILMLB.

EARTH (9m C p1975, r1976)
Through hundreds of images of people, places and things, "Earth"
traces the course of man's inventiveness from the ax to the rocket,
the creation of cities, and the new view, from the moon, of our planet
as a unity in balance. Premiered at the celebration of the United
Nation's thirtieth birthday before world leaders, both political and
religious, and acclaimed as a strong and moving statement for a world
unity. Narrated by John Houseman. p. Elda Hartley; HARTLEY.

EARTH IS OUR HOME, THE (28m C 1980)
The filmmaker is trying to reconstruct a Paiute material lifeway
from the memories of the older women of the tribe, with whose passing
will go many of the tribal survival skills. Agnes Phillips, who since
the making of this film, has passed away, demonstrates making of
baskets and rabbit fur blanket. By showing examples of the Paiute
ingenuity in dealing with survival, the filmmaker hopes to preserve
a reasonably accurate picture of a rapidly disappearing culture. p.
Elizabeth Patapoff, p. KOAP-TV; MEDIAP.

EARTHBREAD (20m C n.d.)
A step-by-step demonstration of how to make a loaf of whole
grain bread intercut with an explanation as to how and why the staff
of life became the squeezable wonder loaf. Breadmaking is a tactile
art, one that is hard for a book to convey. But on film, Reza Kuner
is both informal and inspiring. While the dough is rising, the film
traces the history of bread, illustrating its nutritional, economic, and
spiritual importance through the ages. A guide with a dozen recipes
is included. p. Rodale Press/Amanda and Burton Fox, John Hoskyns-
Abrahall, Winifred Scherrer; BULFRG.

EASE ON DOWN THE ROAD (20m C 1979)
Documentary about the needs of the aging and the ways in which
some church and synagogue congregations have responded to these
needs. Through programs started by churches or synagogues, the
elderly are shown participating in group activities, classes, trips,
one-to-one counseling and home visiting services. Most of these

programs began with one person realizing a need and taking a step to get it started. Useful film for those concerned with aging problems. p. Karl Holtsnider; d. Jack Weinstein; p. Teleketics; FRACOC.

EASTER CAROL, AN (28m C 1978, c1979)
Depicts mission/ministry in the synod of the Northeast of the United Presbyterian Church, United States of America. p. Robin Miller; UNIPCH.

EASTERN MYSTICS OF THE GOLDEN WEST (28m C p1980, r1980)
Explores the life-styles of the Hare Krishna cult and gives a rare glimpse inside a highly regimented Krishna school. The inequality of the sexes is reflected in the education of the children and there are candid interviews with women devotees who accept the sexist philosophy of the cult. A mother expresses her frustration about losing her daughter to the cult and explains why she believes her child was brainwashed. d./p. Josette Bonte; CAROUF.

EASY PILL TO SWALLOW, AN (30m C 1978)
Examines prescription drug abuse through interviews with doctors and patients, concentrating on the creation of "legal" addicts by physicians who are quick to prescribe tranquilizers for symptoms of stress. Looks at the expensive promotional techniques used by drug companies to encourage doctors to prescribe mood-altering drugs for a variety of nonexistent diseases, such as the empty-nest syndrome, car-itis, and picky eater-itis. Interviews doctors who state that physicians need to take more time with their patients and use community service groups to help counsel patients as alternatives to tranquilizers. Includes interviews with a current tranquilizer user, a former user, and a user who had been simultaneously addicted to drugs and alcohol. NFBC; CRM; IU.

EASY STREET (16m C p1979, r1980) (also Video)
Presents four Afro-American health professionals who are channeling their talents and ambitions into satisfying careers that make life a little better for others: a male and female physician, a public health nurse, and a respiratory technician, all true humanitarians. These four people comment about their careers and the hard work and long preparation necessary to become proficient. They also explain that many people are needed to keep others well but that, contrary to some belief, the path to helping does not lie on "Easy Street." An excellent career film. p. Blackside, Inc. in cooperation with United States Department of Health, Education and Welfare; NAVC.

EAT, DRINK, AND BE WARY (21m C 1975)
A critical examination of our eating habits, of nutritional losses in food processing, of food additives, and the role of food manufacturers in changing our diets. p. Churchill Films; CF; WSU, UM.

EATING ON THE RUN (16m C 1975)
This humorous fast-moving film shows how it is possible to have

a well-balanced diet even while "eating on the run." Examples of
nutritious breakfasts that can be prepared in seconds are shown.
Suggestions are made as to how to select a properly balanced lunch.
Also shown are nutritious snacks. HIGGIN; CORNELL, IU, UNEV,
WSU, UM.

EATING WITHOUT MEAT (20m C 1980) Think Nutrition Series
    Today, more and more people are turning to vegetarianism as
both an alternative to high prices, and a way towards better health.
But, with the new popularity of the meatless diet comes the attendant
danger of poor nutrition. This film presents a comprehensive overview of vegetarianism. Among the health factors discussed are cholesterol levels, the importance of fibers, processed meat analogs,
vegetable protein sources, and cancer frequency data. Interviews
are conducted by Judy Dean (registered dietician) with two nutritionists and four practicing vegetarians. NATFVC.

EBB AND FLOW, THE (52m C 1979) The Magic of Dance (Series)
    Dance has almost always moved freely across frontiers. Margot
Fonteyn calls this the ebb and flow of dance which theme she explores by visits with various people around the world. Includes
unique film of Pavlova, as well as Mikhail Baryshnikov dancing Pe-
trushka. Also features Yoko Morishita, Tetsutaro Shimizu, Vyvyan
Lorrayne, Desmond Kelly, Wayne Sleep and Esbart Dansaire de Rubi.
BBC/TIMLIF; TIMLIF; UMN.

ECOLOGY OF PRONGHORN, MOUNTAIN SHEEP, AND MOUNTAIN
    GOATS (15m C 1966) (also Video)
    The life cycles and habitats of antelope, mountain sheep, and
mountain goats are presented and illustrated by specific examples of
mammals from each category. For each type, the feeding habits,
physical structure, and defense mechanisms are briefly described,
and physical differences, especially horn structure, are shown. p.
Myrna I. Berlet, Walter H. Berlet; IFB.

EDGE OF SURVIVAL (58m C p1981, r1982)
    In-depth examination of the problems and solutions to world hun-
ger. Shows by dramatic examples positive and negative effects of
multinationals, government help, international aid programs, "grass-
roots" projects. Filmed in India, Brazil, Ecuador, the United States
of America and England, with Mother Teresa, Swami Muktananda,
United States Secretary of Agriculture and others. Sees cause for
celebration in man's ability to end World Hunger. d. Leigh Wharton;
p. L. Wharton/Barbara A. Gordon; WHARTN; FI.

EDHOLMS, THE (BLENDED FAMILY) see FAMILY PORTRAIT: THE
    EDHOLMS

EDITH HEAD (28m C 1981)
    Edith Head was the one Hollywood studio costume designer whose

name became a household word. This little dynamo dressed nearly all of the American film industry's biggest stars for almost half a century. Head worked with the greatest of directors. She was awarded a wheelbarrow full of Oscars, which got heavier nearly every year. This docu-drama focuses on the private world of this fascinating woman. In fact, we hardly leave Casa Ladera, the house designed by her late husband, Bill Ihnen. p./d. Christian Blackwood; Blackwood Productions; BLACKW.

EFFECTIVE USE OF POWER AND AUTHORITY, THE (32m C r1979)
Illustrates the variety of shapes and forms power takes and shows how the misuse of power can lower the productivity and self-esteem of workers. Also presents a general framework for using power in personal and organizational settings, and demonstrates how to "empower" others by sharing power. CRM; UMO, CWU, WSU, SILU, IU.

EFFI BRIEST (140m B 1974) (German/Subtitled)
Adapted from the nineteenth-century German novel. Recreates the nineteenth century and offers a modern analysis of it in terms of the rise of fascism and the oppression of women. Effi Briest, a vivacious mixture of nonconformity and mediocrity, is married when very young to a Prussian diplomat. Taken to a remote Baltic port by her pedagogical husband, Effi drifts into a brief, passionless affair with a local womanizer. The full effects are felt only six years later, in a chilling manifestation of the Prussian code. d. Rainer Werner Fassbinder; NYF.

EGG, THE (5m C 1971)
This swift-paced animated essay on the meaning of the egg in myth, history and art is a humanities feast for the eye as well as the mind. d. Clorinda Warny; p. Pierre Moretti, NFBC; WOMBAT.

EIGHT JELLY ROLLS (59m C/B 1974) (Video)
Presents Twyla Tharp's work Eight Jelly Rolls to the music of Jelly Roll Morton. Also, demonstrates choreographic techniques employed by Tharp and her company. Voted the best videotape at the 1978 Dance Video and Films Festival. Dancer/Choreographer: Twyla Tharp; d. Derek Baily; THARPT.

EIGHT MINUTES TO MIDNIGHT: A PORTRAIT OF DR. HELEN CALDICOTT (60m C p1981, r1981)
This profile of pediatrician, activist and author Dr. Helen Caldicott follows her over a two-year period as she struggles to alert the public to the medical hazards of nuclear power and weapons. The film's intimate approach reveals both the personal and public dimensions of a passionately committed, complex woman. d./p. Mary Benjamin; DIRECT.

EIGHTH WORLD WINTER: GAMES FOR THE DEAF, THE (29m C 1975) (Video)

Coverage of the Eighth World Winter Games for the Deaf, held in Lake Placid, New York. Contestants from around the world participate in men's and women's downhill races, slalom, ice hockey, speed skating, figure skating and cross-country relay. Highlights of the round-robin hockey tournament between the United States, Canada and the U.S.S.R. are included. Captioned for the deaf and hearing impaired. p. WGBH-TV, Boston; PBSV.

ELDERS, THE (59m C 1973) (Video)
Examines the difficulty of aging in a youth-oriented society and the attendant problems of an inflationary economy, acclerating technology, and inadequate medical care. Film segments include scenes from a nursing home, a look at the self-sufficient Amish, older people listening to Rep. Dick Clark (D-Iowa) explaining his position on the elderly and the foster grandparent plan at Woodward State Hospital. Syndicated columinist Sidney Harris discusses medical care for the elderly and Dr. Donald Cowgill, co-editor of Aging and Modernization, explains the history of Social Security. Other guests on the program include Dr. Terence Philbald, Professor Emeritus, University of Missouri; Philip Hauser, Director of the Population Research Center at the University of Chicago; Helena Lopata, author of Widowhood in the American City; George A. Sachar of the Argonne National Laboratory; and actor Arthur Ellison. p. Iowa Educational Broadcasting Network; PBSV.

ELECTRA TRIES TO SPEAK (30m C 1980-83) (Video, Beta, VHS) Concept Series
All women are trying to speak in this modern interpretation of the classic Greek tragedy. Through the sharp, cogent script and the vital, infinitely varied plane of Sondra Siegal, Electra becomes as much experience as performance. Coherence overlaps with freeze-frame confusion; the clear, determined statement is always blurred with flitting doubts, images passing through images to be frozen an instant before another anxiety or mask wipes them out. d./p. Doris Chase; s.w. Clare Coss, Sondra Siegel, Roberta Sklar; CHASED.

ELECTRIC GRANDMOTHER, THE (32m C 1981)
Ray Bradbury's classic story "I sing the Body Electric" is the source of this gentle and affecting film starring Maureen Stapleton and Edward Hermann. A young father and his three children lose their wife and mother. The harried father hires an electric grandmother with human qualities to care for his youngsters, and she pulls the family together. d. Noel Black; p. Dora Bachrach; LCA.

ELECTROSHOCK THERAPY (14m C 1980) (also Video)
Even its opponents concede that electroshock therapy is a safe and almost always an effective means of treating severe clinical depression. This film is a concise report on ECT (Electro Convulsive Therapy) with commentary by doctors and patients on the treatment and its results. One patient is anesthetized). Risk is minimal; the

major side effect is loss of memory, usually temporary. There are those who argue against ECT, but on the whole research has shown it to be a viable procedure when used appropriately. p. Christine Huneke; NBC News; FI.

ELEGY (7m C 1981) (also Video)
This extraordinary dance film will be a valuable program starter in workshops or seminars on grief, bereavement, and death and dying. Choreographed and danced by Debra Zalkind, it is a beautiful visual interpretation of understanding the loss of a loved one. p./d. Debra Zalkind, Jay Cohen; FILMLB.

ELIZA (27m C 1977) (also Video)
Depicts the life of an extraordinary woman in American history. Eliza Lucas was the personification of eighteenth-century enlightment in land use. Eliza was 17 years old when she took over the management of a South Carolina plantation. Eliza experimented with raising indigo plants, but her first efforts were sabotaged by an unscrupulous overseer. Later Eliza married Charles Pinckney and continued her experiments on his estates. By 1747, through her efforts, South Carolina was exporting more than 135,000 pounds of indigo annually. Eliza lived to the age of 80. d. Don Fouser; FI.

ELIZABETH (10m C r1978) People You'd Like to Know Series
Elizabeth, born with cataracts, had an operation when she was two years old that left her with very little vision. She explains that the disability causes her to see things as through a cloud, and she draws a sketch to show exactly what she sees. She wears thick glasses, uses a monocular aid, and she uses special machinery that enlarges what she is reading by projecting it on a screen. Elizabeth's goal is to become a singer. Shows her learning to play the guitar. EBEC.

ELIZABETH R (SERIES) (90m ea., 540m series C 1979) (Great Britain)
The mystery and power of Elizabeth I is recreated in this powerful and colorful drama, which stars Glenda Jackson in the title role and depicts one of the most exciting and colorful periods in English history. The episodes follow Elizabeth, Henry VIII's daughter by Anne Boleyn, through her gradual transition from a young pretty princess to a wrinkled, ugly, thumb-sucking old woman. Although Elizabeth never married, the drama is based on her relationships with the many men in her life. Five Emmy Awards. FI.

1. THE LION'S CUB
Portrays the young Elizabeth during the brief reigns of her brother Edward and her sister Mary and through her exile to the Tower of London because of her suspect relationship with Thomas Seymour, a courtier and political intriguer.

2. THE MARRIAGE GAME
Realizing that England needs a male heir to the throne, Elizabeth

embarks on a romance with the Earl of Leicester. He became her constant companion, but she couldn't bring herself to marry him and eventually tried to match him up with her cousin, Mary, Queen of Scots.

3. SHADOW IN THE SUN
Elizabeth is now Europe's most eligible lady. She flirts with the Duke of Alençon, heir to the throne of France, with whom she is pledged to form an alliance. However, she does not marry and placates him with 60,000 pounds instead.

4. HORRIBLE CONSPIRACIES
The Babington Plot is launched to assassinate Elizabeth, and Mary, Queen of Scots, is executed for her suspected role in the intrigue. Elizabeth is deeply upset and frightened by Mary's death.

5. THE ENTERPRISE OF ENGLAND
To avenge Mary's death, Philip of Spain prepares to launch his fleet against Elizabeth. On her astrologer's advice, Elizabeth mobilizes and defeats the Armada.

6. SWEET ENGLAND'S PRIDE
In her old age Elizabeth flirts with the handsome and ambitious Earl of Essex in a futile attempt to regain her youth. He later attempts to raise a rebellion against her, and she has him executed. Elizabeth dies a lonely death as her countrymen abandon her to greet the new monarch.

ELIZABETH SWADOS: THE GIRL WITH THE INCREDIBLE FEELING
(39m C 1977)
Presents Elizabeth Swados, composer, author and performer, and a highly imaginative and creative young woman. Shows her conducting a large group of people in a choral work. Numerous segments of home movies are interspersed throughout the film. Swados discusses the influences and experiences that affected her musical development. Paramount among those influences were the native music and sounds of nature to which she was exposed on a visit to Africa. It was there that she learned to regard the human voice as an objective instrument. That attitude is evident when she performs several of her compositions in which the voice is called on to imitate bird calls, carry on a "dialogue" with a drum, and create other nonstandard vocal sounds. One extended sequence provides an animated version of Swados' children's book, The Girl with the Incredible Feeling. p./d./ed. Linda Feferman; PHOENIX; VIEWFI; PAS, UIL, UM.

ELIZABETH II: WINDS OF CHANGE (24m C 1980) Leaders of the Century: Portraits of Power (Series)
Using rare documentary footage, this film shows Queen Elizabeth II as a symbol of national unity, a focus of patriotism and a living link with what remains of the Commonwealth and the Empire. Narrated

by Henry Fonda with commentary by Harrison Salisbury, Drew Middleton and Turner Catledge of the New York Times. p. Nielsen-Ferns International; LCA; IU.

ELLE (6m C 1978)
ELLE is the enigma of the face. It is constantly dissolving masquerade of color, ornamentation, concealment, cosmetic preparation, representation, protection and disguise, moving to the sound of primitive percussion instruments and flutes. p. Maxine Martell; MEDIAP.

ELOISA (14m C n.d.)
A flamenco performance "Solea" by Eloisa Vasquez. d./p. Simon Edery; CCC.

ELSA AND HER CUBS (25m C n.d.)
A unique documentary that the filmmakers made themselves in Kenya which records their five-year friendship with the lioness Elsa from the time she was a cub, until she in turn had cubs. Of that singular friendship between human and wild animal, Joy Adamson wrote Born Free and other famous books. p. Joy Adamson, George Adamson; BENCHMF.

ELSA DORFMAN: IMPRESSIONS (29m C 1975) (Video) Woman Series
Photographer Elsa Dorfman discusses her philosophy and career and shows some of the photographs from her book Elsa's Housebook: A Woman's Photojournal. Her subjects have included poets Allen Ginsberg, Gary Snyder, Robert Creeley and the late Anne Sexton, as well as people she spots on the streets of Boston. She has received critical acclaim for her unposed, unretouched photographs. Sandra Elkin is the moderator. p. WNED-TV, Buffalo, New York; PBSV.

EMERGENCE OF EUNICE (6m C 1980)
A strong and beautifully animated film depicting an adolescent girl's struggle for personal and sexual identity and the problems of achieving independence. p. Emily Hubley; SERBC.

EMERGENCY OBSTETRICS (21m C 1979)
Demonstrates the basic procedures for healthy, normal childbirth that must be followed wherever a baby is born ... in the hospital, at home or in the field. Covering all phases of birth from crowning to delivery of the placenta. It can be used for childbirth classes as well as professional medical training. p. Medi-Cine Productions, Inc.; PF; UCEMC, UMN.

EMERGING WOMAN ATHLETE, THE (58m C 1980)
James Michener reviews the history of women in sports and examines the current status of women athletes and women's athletics. Shows the progress that women have made in the sports world, progress paralleled in American society as a whole. It looks at myths, barriers and inequities faced by women athletes, contrasting these

problems with the rewards of physical performance and the success enjoyed by many of today's women athletes. Rare footage of historic "firsts" and fascinating conversations with pioneers of women's sports highlight the film. In addition, coaches, journalists, young athletes and current superstars like Chris Evert Lloyd, Janet Guthrie and Nancy Lopez offer intriguing commentary on the past, present and future role of women in sports. p. Cappy Productions, Inc.; PF.

EMILY DICKINSON see AUTHORS: EMILY DICKINSON, THE

EMILY DICKINSON: A CERTAIN SLANT OF LIGHT (29m C 1977, r1978)

Julie Harris takes the viewer on a tour of Dickinson's environment--a place of natural grandeur, devotion to religion and education and a toleration of individuality which inevitably shaped the poet's thoughts and feelings. Reciting "A Certain Slant of Light," "To My Small Hearth," "Safe in Their Alabaster Chambers" as well as other poems and prose, Harris tries to see Emily Dickinson's world as she did. Emphasizes both the personal contacts which sustained the very private but also dependent "Miss Emily" and authentic objects alluded to in her poems. p. Jean McClure Mudge; d. Bayley Silleck; PF; KENTSU, UMN.

EMITAI (101m C 1971, r1978--U.S.) (French and Diola/Subtitled)

A historical film that serves as a timeless allegory. Depicts the clash between French colonialists and a mystical African tribe in the closing days of World War II. Interestingly, it is the women of the village who provide the true voice of resistance, a voice that has nothing to do with the current notion of women's liberation and everything to do with the instinctual knowledge of how to survive. The myth, ritual, and history of this Senegalese tribe are hauntingly visualized. p. Ousmane Sembene; New Community Cinema; NYF.

EMOTIONAL ASPECTS OF PREGNANCY (20m C 1978)

Prepares the expectant mother and father for emotional changes. Dramatizations emphasize that understanding and honesty are qualities most needed to ease the way through emotional stresses of pregnancy. There may be doubts over wanting the responsibility of a child. An expectant mother is likely to experience intensified emotion and moodiness, vivid dreams, and sexual needs may vary greatly in intensity. The father may feel left out and unneeded in early pregnancy; and then, later overwhelmed by responsibility and mother's increasing needs, and seek escape in other activities. In later months, pregnant women feel increasingly helpless and need extra attention and reassurance from their mates. d./s.w. Sally Marschall, p. Joshua Productions, Ltd.; PEREN; UM.

EMPEROR'S NEW CLOTHES, THE (11m C 1977)

Video effects give the ageless fairy tale many magical moments. Choreographer Jonathan Hollander and dancer Nancy Cohen move to a musical score of George Kleinsinger and script of Ellen Schecter in this ballet/drama. p. Doris Chase; CHASED.

ENDOMETRIOSIS (13m C n.d.)
Explains the nature of endometriosis and the problems it causes. Discusses the variable nature of the symptoms along with the various treatment options available. Explains how drug therapy is most often the successful method of treatment. Where necessary, surgery offers an effective alternative. Also available in Spanish. p. Milner-Fenwick, Inc. MIFE.

ENEMY ALIEN (27m C p1975, r1977)
A historical documentary of Japanese who came to Canada and the United States in the late nineteenth and early twentieth centuries. They arrived poor, expecting to work a few years and return home. Instead, most stayed and fought their way through legal and social discrimination to become established in the Western world. A fine collection of visual materials have been used to illustrate this documentary on a dark period in Canadian history. d. Jeanette Lerman; p. Wolf Koenig; NFBC.

ENERGY AND MORALITY (35m C p1979, r1979)
New ideas about energy and information as major social forces. Dramatic, documentary and animated sequences are used to entice viewers to think about the relationship between varying levels of energy use and freedom, aggression, responsibility and "the patterns that connect our lives to other lives." p. Lynne Wolfe, Michael Gall, Richard Boylan; d. Swain Wolfe; BITROT.

ENERGY CRUNCH: THE BEST WAY OUT (51m C 1979) (also Video)
This documentary is an informative and practical approach for energy conservation. It outlines specific ways energy can be conserved, thereby drastically reducing dependence on oil from foreign markets. How-to-do-it demonstrations are shown in homes and industries on methods to conserve energy. also looks at what local governments and community groups are doing and have done to increase conservation. Explores the potential of solar and other alternative energy sources. p. Jane Bartels, Bernard Birnbaum, Hal Haley for CBS News with correspondent Dan Rather; CAROUF.

ENGINEERED FOODS: WHAT ARE THEY? (29m C 1976) (Video)
Woman Series
Nutritonist and author Beatrice Trum Hunter (Food Additives and Federal Policy: The Mirage of Safety, Consumer Beware: Your Food and What's Being Done to It) discusses reconstituted foods and additives we may be eating without knowing it. She also explains the possible loss of nutrients caused by pre-cooking and extended storage. Sandra Elkin is the moderator; p. WNED-TV, Buffalo, New York; PBSV.

ENGLISH FAMILY: LIFE IN SHEFFIELD (19m C 1975)
Depicts the daily life of a British steelworker and his family, and provides a brief introduction to the cultural and historical background of the region. Sheffield, in Northern England, is noted for the production of steel cutlery and machine tools. Jim and Emily Birch live in Greenmoor, a small rural village just outside of Sheffield. Shows the children attending classes in a one-room schoolhouse and visiting grandparents, Jim conducting his actor friend on a tour of the steel plant, and the family attending the theatre performance of a classical Greek tragedy. EBEC; UIL.

ENGLISH IS A WAY OF SPEECH (10m C n.d.)
Fusion of English grammar and dance movement. Students perform an original work describing in words and action all of the parts of speech. d./s.w. Sheila Hellman; HELMNS.

ENOUGH TO SHARE: A PORTRAIT OF KOINONIA FARM (28m C
p1982, r1983)
A documentary portrait of Koinonia Farm, a 1,500-acre farm in Sumter County, Georgia where some 100 members, employees and volunteers live a simple life-style based on the New Testament concepts of sharing and nonviolence. Founded in 1942 by scholar/theologian/farmer Dr. Clarence Jordan, author of The Cotton Patch Gospel, Koinonia stands as living testimony to Dr. Jordan's belief that "faith is the turning of dreams into deeds." Shows people who shaped its history being interviewed. d./p./ed. Gayla K. Jamison; IDEAIM, LTFTF.

EQUAL OPPORTUNITY (22m C 1977)
Designed to help viewers and managers come to grips with the crucial issue of equal employment opportunity in America today. By participating in a dramatized case history, viewers will understand better the Civil Rights Act of 1964 and 1966. Guide included. BFA; UMN.

EQUAL OPPORTUNITY (22m C 1982) (also Video) The Bill of Rights
in Action (Series)
Is it reverse discrimination or equal opportunity when Solomen Jones, who is black, is promoted over Phil Richards, who is white? Both men are presented as equally qualified, but Richards has seniority. The film shows the arbitration proceedings of this case--the union attorney argues for the contractually agreed seniority while the company attorney argues for the company's affirmative action program. The film states as fact that the major problem of equality is equality between races. Open-ended. d./p. Bernard Wilets; BARRF.

EQUAL RIGHTS AMENDMENT, THE (5m C 1981)
Parade footage from a rally for the ERA. American marching music and various readings of the ERA text join to offer the viewer an entertaining experience of the movement to ratify the Equal Rights Amendment. d./p. Marie Ashton; ed. Lori Kranz; NOW.

EQUAL RIGHTS AMENDMENT see WOMEN AND THE LAW, THE (SE-
RIES)

EQUAL RIGHTS TO THE SUN (25m C p1979, r1980) (also Video)
Shows people of Boston working together on low-cost solar energy options. Irene Smalls built a breadbox water heater from scrap
materials. John Ellertson converted the south-facing part of his attic
into a heat and food producing solar greenhouse. Don Lubin enclosed
his south-facing porch for $100 and created a winter sun-room. The
Lankys added seven passive wall collectors that save them 400 gallons
of oil per year. With study guide. d./p. Bonnie Symansky; BULFRG.

EQUALITY (60m C p1976, r1977) (also Video)
What is "equality"? Is there real equality of age, race, ethnic
origin, or economic opportunity in the United States? This multi-
award-winning sociodocumentary examines practically every side of the
the myriad of issues through interviews with nationally known figures
and dozens of other men and women from all walks of life. Juxtaposed commentary, live action, animation, and other special effects
lend an enlightening, entertaining perspective to the subjects. Discussions include equal rights for women, Afro-Americans, children,
the aged, and ethnic groups. Also included are the subjects of economics, alternate life-styles and political beliefs. p. New Jersey
Public Broadcasting; BESTF; PBSV.

EQUALITY AND THE CONSTITUTION: MYTH AND REALITY see
WOMEN AND THE LAW, THE (SERIES)

EQUATIONS IN ALGEBRA (11m C 1963) (also Video)
The ancient use of balances is reviewed and becomes the basis
for explanation of the nature of equations and the idea of solving
problems by putting numbers in balance. "Members," "terms," and
"signs" as used in algebra are defined. The use of letters for unknown quantities and the use of axioms in finding roots are explained
and illustrated. p. Katharine Cornwell, Bruce Cornwell; IFB.

ESCAPE (5m C 1956)
A visually abstract interpretation of a dramatic struggle between
two geometric forms. Based on the Toccata from Bach's "Toccata
and Fugue in D Minor." (Museum of the City of New York, November 12, 1978.) p. Mary Ellen Bute; EXCIN.

ESKIMO ARTS AND CRAFTS (22m C 1944)
The activities of Eskimos of Baffin Island are filmed by a noted
ethnomusicologist. Sequences include women preparing skins, men
and women sharing the tasks involved in building a kayak, women
preparing clothing, men carving ivory, and women practicing finger
weaving learned from nuns at Chesterfield Inlet. For relaxation men
and women tell stories with string figures and two old men prepare a
tambour drum, a somiac, for the men's dancing which follows. Though

some of the narration is dated stylistically, the film shows a wide range of handicrafts. Especially interesting is its rare emphasis on the significance of the role of women in Eskimo life; it represents their domestic work as the complement of the men's work as hunter. d. Laura Boulton; p. NFBC; IFB, PAS.

ESSENTIAL EXERCISES FOR THE CHILDBEARING YEAR (20m C 1980)
Childbearing puts unusual demands on key areas of a woman's body: the abdominal muscles, the backbone, and the muscle floor of the pelvic cavity. Hormonal changes which allow the body to stretch during pregnancy can leave muscles weak, causing misalignment. Explains these changes and teaches five simple exercises to help prevent the most common health problems resulting from childbearing: bulging abdominal wall, chronic backache, leaking urine, and lack of feeling during intercourse. Elizabeth Noble, R.P.T., author of the book with the same title as the film, teaches these five exercises to pregnant and postpartum women. p./d. Alvin Fiering; POLYMR.

ESSIE (55m C p1981, r1982)
A portrait of a vibrant, open and vigorous woman, suddenly faced with terminal cancer. Essie's feelings about her mother, her husband and her friends are all revealed as she struggles for health. Also revealed is this spunky woman's resolve to take responsibility for her own treatment and not passively accept the dictates of the medical profession. In her fight for survival she is willing to try new therapies despite serious side effects. At each step of the way she questions and reassesses her progress, determined to make the most of her time. Though the original prognosis gave her only one year to live, her constant energy and positive attitude extends her life by four years. A valuable film on death and dying, since it shows the patient as questioning, assertive and life-affirming. d./p. Gerald Wenner; FILMLB.

ESTAMPA FLAMENCA (28m C p1978, r1978) (also Video)
A documentary about the great American flamenco dancer Maria Benitez and her Estampa Flamenca dance company. The company is featured in rehearsal and performance in New Mexico, and Benitez is seen working to master the intricate rhythms of the dance. d./p. Dave Ellis; p. KNME-TV, Albuquerque, New Mexico, ELLISD; PBSV.

ESTROGEN AND THE MENOPAUSE (29m C 1977) (Video) Daniel Foster, M.D. Series
Dr. Daniel Foster and his guest Dr. Paul C. MacDonald, Director of the Cecil and Ida Green Center for Reproductive Biology Sciences at the University of Texas, discuss the causes and symptoms of menopause and the use of estrogen in treating postmenopausal women. A filmed interview with a woman who has had surgical menopause and estrogen treatments is shown. She describes her physical and emotional reactions to menopause, as well as the effects of her treatment. p. KERA-TV, Dallas; PBSV.

THE ESTROGEN QUESTION, PART I (29m C 1976) (Video) Woman
   Series
   The nature and function of estrogen is explained by three ex-
perts: Dr. Takuma Nemoto, Associate Chief of the Department of
Breast Surgery at Roswell Park Memorial Institute in Buffalo; Dr.
Rose Ruth Ellison, Vice-President for Medical and Scientific Affairs
at the Leukemia Society of America; and Rose Kushner, author of
Breast Cancer: A Personal History and an Investigative Report.
The women also discuss the use and possible side effects of the con-
troversial hormone. Sandra Elkin is the moderator. p. WNED-TV,
Buffalo, New York; PBSV.

THE ESTROGEN QUESTION, PART II (29m C 1976) (Video) Woman
   Series
   Dr. Takuma Nemoto, Associate Chief of the Department of Breast
Surgery at the Roswell Park Memorial Institute in Buffalo; Dr. Rose
Ruth Ellison, Vice-President for Medical and Scientific Affairs for
the Leukemia Society of America; and Rose Kushner, author of Breast
Cancer: A Personal History and an Investigative Report discuss the
uses of estrogen for birth control and during menopause. They also
explain the problem of "DES daughters" that resulted from estrogen
use during pregnancy. Sandra Elkin is the moderator. p. WNED-
TV, Buffalo, New York; PBSV.

ETOSHA: PLACE OF DRY WATER (60m C p1979, r1981)
   Extraordinary animal behavior, in some cases unknown even to
zoologists and ethologists, is observed in this documentary which
focuses on the wildlife in Etosha National Park, a preserve surrounding a huge dry lake bed in the Southwest African country of Namibia.
Nature's interplay of life and death is presented as it happens. A
zebra attacked and killed by lions, the birth of a wildebeest, and
young bullfrogs devouring each other are only a few of the unforgettable sequences shown. p. Carol Hughes, David Hughes; NGS.

EUDORA WELTY (29m C 1979) The Writer in America (Series)
   A filmed interview with Eudora Welty who ranks among America's
finest writers, living or dead. Ms. Welty received the 1973 Pulitzer
Prize for her novel The Optimist's Daughter. She expresses her
views about art, life, self-discipline, the creative process, inspiration
and the challenges as a writer. p./d. Richard O. Moore; CORONET;
UIL, PAS, IU.

EUGENIE (16m C 1977)
   Examines the emotional conflicts of a 12-year-old girl, Eugenie,
caught between the last remnants of her childhood and the awakening sense of womanhood. From an original story by Christine Schutt.
p. Susan Sussman; KPF; PHOENIX.

EUREKA! MEASURING TEMPERATURE (5m C 1981) (Video)
   Explanation of heat and temperature that demonstrates how

molecules move faster when the temperature of a substance rises.
Also explains how temperature is measured in Celsius degrees. d.
Denise Boiteau/David Stansfield; TVONT.

EVELINE (14m C 1981, r1982)
Based on a short story by James Joyce, EVELINE examines the
dilemma of a young woman in 1910 who must choose between her Catholic family and the romance of a life abroad offered by her new-found
suitor. d./p./ed. Margaret Ganahl; Music by Rick Epping; GANAHL.

EVERY REVOLUTION IS A ROLL OF THE DICE (11m C 1978) (French/
Subtitled)
A reading of Mallarmé's famous poem "A Dice Roll Will Never
Abolish Chance," staged near the Commune memorial at Père Lachaise
Cemetery in Paris and spoken by assorted filmmakers and critics,
among them co-director Daniele Huillet. d. Jean-Marie Straub, Dan-
iele Huillet; NYF.

EVERYBODY RIDES THE CAROUSEL--"THE LATER YEARS" (9m C
p1975, r1980)
Presents in animation two elderly couples who are living out their
last days in very different ways. Shows one couple complaining and
bickering as they stand in a cafeteria line. The other couple is
shown preparing for an enjoyable Halloween evening, serving "trick-
or-treaters" and commenting enthusiastically on children who come to
their house. They show affection for each other and joy of living
in all they say and do. p. Faith Hubley, p. Hubley Studios; PF;
UMN, UMO.

EVERYDAY MIRACLE: BIRTH (30m C 1981)
Follows the development of a baby from conception to birth.
Advanced techniques in microphotography provide stunning pictures
of a living human embryo within the womb. Combined with ultrasound recordings, they yield a comprehensive record of life before
birth. The excitement culminates in the birth of the child. p. Andrew Neal for BBC Enterprises; FI; IU.

EVERYDAY PARENTING (29m C 1978) Look at Me--A Series
A sensory game for a bus ride; color, size and shape discrimination at the grocery store; talking together on a park bench; math
concepts with tin cans; experimenting with bathtub boats; and role-
playing in a "dress-up" sequence. p. WTTN-TV; PEREN.

EVERYONE, EVERYWHERE (11m C 1979)
"Do we really know the poor in our own house ... in our family,
in our own community?" With this question, Mother Teresa challenges
us to recognize the poor in all those who are abandoned, unwanted,
alone. In this film, the words and the voice of Mother Teresa bring
depth and compassion to the camera's impressions: first, of India's
poor and the Sisters of Charity who share their lives; second, of

our own destitute and elderly in the West. Mother Teresa reminds us that we are all called to be missionaries of charity right where we live and work. p. Teleketics Production; MMM.

EVERYTHING YOU ALWAYS WANTED TO KNOW ABOUT SUPERVISION
(28m C 1980)
Dramatizes the story of a young woman who thinks knowledge of the job is sufficient to be an effective manager to point out the supervisory skills and techniques necessary to manage for positive results. Suggests steps for organizing and delegating work, communicating with employees, disciplining effectively, and motivating employees by helping them to see the importance of their work to the total benefit of their company. Simulates work situations to demonstrate the positive effects of feedback, effective listening, asking open-ended questions and being direct and factual. p. Arthur Bauer; AMMED; IU.

EVOLUTION (3m C p1980, r1980)
Through the use of humorous animation, the evolution of life on earth is traced--from prehistoric animal species to modern civilization. d./p. Sheila Graber; TEXFM.

EVOLUTION OF A YOGI (28m C 1970)
This film shot when Ram Dass first returned from India in 1969 gives insight into his past, the events leading to his metamorphosis, the concepts of Raga Yoga and practical suggestions for its practice. When first released few had heard of Ram Dass. Now this is one of our most popular films. p. Elda Hartley, p. Hartley Film Foundation; HARTLEY.

EXHIBITION (118m C 1975) (French/Subtitled)
In an attempt to explore, in documentary fashion, the life-style and philosophy of France's leading pornography star, EXHIBITION was the first "hardcore" film to play the New York Film Festival. Christine Beccarie emerges as a complex woman with numerous contradictions. d. Jean-François Davy; CORINTH.

EXITS AND ENTRANCES (28m C 1979) Begin with Goodbye Series
Deals with personal relationships which endlessly come into being or cease to be. Personal profiles include Deborah Wade, a Native American woman who leaves home to attend nursing school on a large and impersonal campus, and a family facing the trauma of divorce. With guide. MMM.

EXPANDING AIRPORT, THE (9m C 1958)
An animated film presenting Eero Saarinen's concept for the then proposed Dulles Airport in Washington, D.C. p. Ray and Charles Eames; PF.

EXPANDING THE LIMITS OF CONSCIOUSNESS (32m C 1977)
The desire to have peak experience is a basic drive. Doctors,

educators, artists, and psychics who have learned how to produce
altered states of consciousness (ASC) are now using them to effect
changes in perception. Dr. Jerry Jampolsky helps children with
learning problems. Dr. Joseph Spear uses meditation and guided
imagery to help recidivists. Dyveke Spino uses sports to produce
ASC's. Paul Solomon goes into trances and diagnoses illnesses, as
does Annette Martin. With a divining rod Christopher Hills helps
the police find stolen goods. Unwanted, repetitive patterns of behavior as well as new levels of creativity are unveiled to help individuals
develop their potential. p. Elda Hartley, p. Hartley Film Foundation;
HARTLEY.

EXPERIMENT IN EQUALITY--THE WOMAN'S VOTE see WOMEN AND
    THE LAW, THE (SERIES)

EXPLORATIONS (22m C 1969)
    A demonstration of the application of body movement taught and
used as an approach to dramatic expression and in developing an
awareness of one's body in space and in relation to other persons.
Simple and more complex exercises emphasize cooperation and trust
of participants. p. Veronica Sherbourne; NYU.

EXPLORING AND ACCEPTING INDIVIDUAL TRAITS (30m C 1980)
    (also Video) Look at Me Series
    Highlights: Recognition of physical bodies; understanding as-
sertiveness; coping with fears; developing individual traits. Children express their individuality and cope with the world around them
in various ways. Play-acting and make-believe are important in the
development of identity. Children's opinions of themselves depend
upon a parent's attitudes in helping their child feel "I am someone
very special." p./s.w. Jane Kaplan, Wendy Roth; p. WTTN-TV; FI.

EXPLORING THE WORLD TOGETHER (30m C p1979, r1980) (also
    Video) Look at Me Series
    Highlights: Seeing the world from the child's perspective; pro-
viding a safe environment; providing a creative environment. This
episode follows real parents and their children through a series of
typical family activities which broaden children's grasp of their environment and motivate them to continue to explore and to learn.
Emphasis is on providing a safe environment as well as a creative
one. p./s.w. Jane Kaplan, Wendy Roth, p. WTTW-TV; FI.

EXPONENTS (3m C 1973)
    A study in generalization. Algebraic equivalencies are presented
in simple terms at high speed. p. Ray and Charles Eames; PF.

-F-

FACE TO FACE (136m C 1976) (Swedish/Subtitled)
    Bergman's vision probes deep into the human psyche of a female

psychiatrist (Liv Ullmann) who is a helpless witness to the degenera-
tion of her family, career, marriage--and ultimately herself. Liv Ullmann is unforgetable as the woman facing up to her own emotions,
fears, and dreams. d. Ingmar Bergman; Paramount; FI.

FACE VALUE (40m C 1982)
Three facially disfigured people discuss their emotions and exper-
iences in a culture where beauty is valued. p. Perennial Education,
Inc.; PEREN.

FACES OF LOVE (91m C 1977) (French/Subtitled)
Three women actresses, each exemplifying a precise facet of femininity, ultimately blend into a single and individual entity which
defines the life of a movie director. d. Michel Soutter; NYF.

FACES OF MAN (SERIES) see FACES OF MAN: INDIA; FACES OF
MAN: FRANCE; FACES OF MAN: GERMANY; FACES OF MAN:
JAPAN

FACES OF MAN: FRANCE (25m C 1978) (also Video) Faces of Man
Series
Human geography is the focus of this film. The camera visits
five families in France--each in a different region, and each with a
different mode of living. All are deeply attached to their land and
to their unique way of life, as the French people have been for centuries. d. Harold M. Weiner; p. Marilyn Weiner/Harold M. Weiner;
SCRESC.

FACES OF MAN: GERMANY (25m C 1980) (also Video) Faces of Man
Series
Presents an informative picture of the life-styles that are com-
prised in present-day Germany. Although geographically and politically divided, Germany remains a marriage of individual regions. On
an island near the German-Denmark border, there are people living the
same life-style as their ancestors of 250 years ago. Forty-four families, on 2,500 acres, reveal a face of Germany that is strong-willed
and timeless. There, only the first son can remain to carry on the
traditions; the scarcity of land denies a livelihood to the other children. Also, shows the people of the industrial heartland as well as
Düsseldorf, the commercial center of Germany. d. Harold M. Weiner;
p. Marilyn Weiner/H. M. Weiner; SCRESC.

FACES OF MAN: INDIA (25m C p1979, r1979) (also Video) Faces of
Man Series
To understand India today, one must look carefully at the day-
to-day life of her numerous villages and teeming cities. This film
aims to evoke sympathy and understanding for that which all Indians
have in common--religion, mysticism, love for the land, a sense of
the epic, poverty, and hope for a dignified future. p. Marilyn Weiner, Harold M. Weiner; d. Harold M. Weiner; SCRESC.

FACES OF MAN: JAPAN (25m C 1981) (also Video) Faces of Man
Series
Once a closed feudal society, Japan now ranks near the top of
the world's industrial giants. Evidence of the West is everywhere,
but Japan's traditional customs and codes continue to thrive. Meet
three families who balance their ancient and modern ways. d. Harold
M. Weiner; p. Marilyn Weiner/H. M. Weiner; SCRESC.

FACING DEATH (30m C 1980) Coping with Serious Illness Series
Documentary on the last years of Joan Robinson, a woman who
was dying of cancer. Deals with the difficult issue of terminal illness and facing death. The Robinsons are shown going through the
painful process of realizing that Joan is going to die. Psychiatrists,
doctors, clergy and others who have experience in dealing with the
dying talk about the current knowledge of how we all face death
and the various choices the ill and their families may need to make:
whether to die at home, in a hospital, or in a special hospice hospital for the terminally ill. TIMLIF; PAS, UMN.

FACING DEATH (30m C 1980) (Video)
Although the subject of death is not easily discussed in our society, health care professionals have begun to talk more openly about
death, and to recognize the emotional stages brought on by an impending death. These stages--denial, bargaining, anger, depression,
and acceptance--may be experienced in various orders and to various
degrees, not only by the patient, but by relatives and health care
staff as well. In this film, various emotional stages are discussed by
people who have life-threatening diseases. The staff of an oncology
unit and the daughter of a patient also discuss their own reactions
to death. NETCHE.

FACTORIES FOR THE THIRD WORLD: TUNISIA (43m C 1979) (also
Video)
Until recently, the role of most Third World countries, such as
Tunisia, in the international division of labor was to serve as a sup-
plier of raw materials for the industrialized countries of Europe or
North America. The standard of living in these countries did not
rise very high, and labor costs remained low. But now, with improved communications and transportation on a world scale, and with
the greatly increased automation and fragmentation of the production
process, it has become profitable for multinational corporations to
make use of this large pool of mostly unskilled, but cheap labor.
These countries see a chance for them to escape from the status of
underdevelopment; thus, they adopt policies to actively encourage
foreign investments. This film analyzes the extent and consequences
of this new international division of labor and the pattern of development associated with it. This film is a provocative attack on an all-
too-common concept of progress and development. p. Marie Claude
Deffarge, Gordian Troeller; ICARF.

FACTORY (56m B n.d.)
Explores the world of the blue-collar worker and the psychological and economic bind in which he or she is caught. It captures the dreariness and monotony of the wedding-ring factory in which it was filmed, and the frustration of the worker who comments, "It's a treadmill going nowhere." A powerful statement of the need for better communication between management and labor. d./p. Evelyn Barron, Arthur Barron; FILMLB.

FACTS ABOUT SEXUALLY TRANSMITTED DISEASES, THE (25m C n.d.)
Factual information about today's increasing list of widespread sexually transmitted diseases is presented in clear non-medical narration, animation, and brief interviews with young people telling of their experiences with the diseases. Moralist and frightening overtones are absent. Information for each of the diseases presented covers the organism responsible, symptoms, treatment, and responsibility for advising partners of possible infection. BENCHMF.

FACTS OF LIFE, THE (28m C p1981, r1982)
"The blues tell about the facts of life." On location in Chicago and rural Alabama, the film features the life and work of blues musician Willie Dixon--composer, producer, and performer who has written some 700 songs, many of which were hits for other singers. He talks about his childhood, some of which is reenacted, and shows a scrapbook full of legendary figures "that even most blacks today have never heard of. If we don't uphold our own heritage, who will?" Dixon asks. d. Gilbert Moses; p./s.w. Carol Munday Lawrence; ed. Paul L. Evans; Original Music: Willie Dixon; BEACON.

FAILING MARRIAGE, THE (20m C 1978) (also Video)
Charlie and Caroline do not communicate well, and their lack of communication stems from deeper problems: the fear of being dominated and thus the need to manipulate. The film opens with a classic argument between husband and wife and then, by use of replayed and stop-scene photography, analyzes the forces behind each one's inability to feel and hear what the other is saying. It shows how anger, hostility, frustration and fear block successful communication and thus destroy marriages. In this case both partners are skilled manipulators, each trying to protect individual sensitivities. Manipulation replaces love; divorce replaces marriage. Demonstrates rather clearly some of the obstacles to good communication. A good discussion film. p. Alan Summers; TRANSDYI; CWU, PAS, UNEV.

FAIR EMPLOYMENT PRACTICE: RECRUITMENT, SELECTION AND PLACEMENT (19m C 1979)
Shows when word-of-mouth recruiting is illegal, the criteria for job tests, the dos and don'ts of interviewing, how to avoid charges of discrimination based on race, ethnic origin or sex, plus four key points to remember when hiring. Producer not given. UW.

FAIR EMPLOYMENT PRACTICE SERIES see PREVENTING SEXUAL
HARASSMENT

FALL IS HERE (2nd ed.) (10m C p1979, r1979) The Seasons (Series)
A film which gives children a feel for the changes that take place
in the fall. Shows the leaves changing color, birds flying south,
fruits ripening and being harvested and stored. Also, shows frost
arriving and children preparing for Halloween and Thanksgiving. p.
Myrna I. Berlet, Walter H. Berlet; IFB.

FALL 1976 (15m B 1976)
Traipsing through the underbrush of her life in cowboy boots,
Carla as camera-person creates this unique autobiography composed
of interviews with the key individuals in her life, and musing of her
own. Her wry sense of humor combines with her disconcerting willingness to expose herself and the viewer to all angles of her life.
p. Carla Dantzig; TEMPLU.

FALL OF THE ROMANOV DYNASTY, THE (105m B si 1927)
Events of the February Russian Revolution are brought back to
life by Esfir Shub using footage that had hitherto been regarded as
having only the nature of historical fragments. By juxtaposing these
"bits of reality," she was able to achieve effects of irony, absurdity,
pathos, and grandeur that few of the bits had intrinsically. Superb
editing by Shub. Available with either Russian or English intertitles.
FI, MMA.

FALL RIVER LEGEND (10m C 1971)
Excerpts from Agnes de Mille's ballet based on the Lizzie Borden
story. Filmed at Sturbridge, Massachusetts. Choreographer: Agnes
de Mille; d./p. Bob Shanks; p. Camco Productions, Inc. for Group
W. Westinghouse Broadcasting, in association with Griffin Productions.
PARAMOUNT; BU, BUDGF, KENTSU, NYU, SYRACU, UIL, UMN, PSU.

FAMILIES: GROWING AND CHANGING (14½m C p1980, r1981) (Video)
Explores the functions and importance of families of all types,
and the effects that changes in families have on the children. We
visit three different families: Lisa and Jason, whose mother and
father have promised them a new baby brother; Christian and Haley,
who live with their mother and only see their divorced father on
weekends; and Ade, whose mother has recently remarried. d. J.
Sampson, G. Parker, R. Macnee; p. P. Lee; ex. p. R. Abelson;
TAKE.

FAMILY (14m C 1972)
Probes people's needs for family ties. Even though we grow and
become individuals and independent, the need for family ties remain.
What are the ties that bind? And what are those that strangle?
WOMBAT.

FAMILY AFFAIR, A (28m C 1981)
Follows a middle-class family with a history of violent interaction through a violent encounter and into the criminal justice system. The common attitude is that family violence is something that happens behind closed doors and is therefore exempt from moral and criminal codes. Specifically addresses the issue of the battered woman and should be useful to all people who may become involved in this issue. d. Susan Shadburne; p. Shadburne/Vinton Production; VISUCP; MEDIAP.

FAMILY BIRTHING (19m C 1982)
Illustrates an alternative birth experience at the Hennepin County Medical Center in Minneapolis, Minnesota, where nurse-midwives deliver babies in the presence of their families. p. Parenting Pictures; PARPIC.

FAMILY ENCOUNTER (8m C 1970)
Presents a series of seven vignettes which explores various aspects of family relations. Projector may be stopped after each spot for discussion. 1) Some good news a husband has saved for his wife falls on inattentive ears. 2) The daily activities of a married couple are brought to fulfillment and symbolized in their embrace at the end of the day. 3) Children become spectators at a vivid family argument following a wife's error in a bridge game. 4) A father lies about his son's age when purchasing a movie ticket, and the son says "I wish I could cheat like you." 5) Pressures of time and work reveal their toll as a father returns home greeted as stranger. 6) A father's indifference alienates his son. 7) An understanding father and a loving child surmount everyday distractions to create a moment of affirmation. p. Franciscan Communication Center; FRACOE; TKF; UIL.

FAMILY IS BORN, A (27m C n.d.)
Begins with the birth of an infant. It then presents the anatomy and physiology leading to ovulation and fertilization of the ovum, as well as a study of the male and female reproductive organs, physiology of reproduction and embryonic development. A family is carried through the pregnancy, labor and delivery--magnificently shown in a human manner without loss of any clinical aspects. Recommended for demonstration and instruction for expectant mothers and classes in sex education. AF.

FAMILY KRISHNAPPA, THE (18m C 1977)
From the first stirring of their rural village at dawn in southern India, to their peaceful relaxation that evening, we share one ordinary day in the life of the Krishnappas, a farm family of seven. The day begins at dawn with farm chores, cooking over a fire, bathing, school for some children, planting rice in the fields, tending the cattle, harvesting sugarcane and making sugar, threshing and winnowing wheat, doing laundry outdoors, a blacksmith at work, and ends with prayers, dinner, and relaxation. BENCHMF.

FAMILY LIFE (108m C 1972)

Based on an actual case study. Dramatizes the struggle of a young woman who wants to break away from the overpowering influence of her well-meaning possessive parents. The conflict with her family is heightened when she begins psychotherapy, and her parents' rigid conformity to conventional, middle-class values is called into question. "The need for the truth is a basic human need that our society denies. This film satisfies that need."--R. D. Laing. p. Tony Garnett, p. Anglo-EMI Production; d. Kenneth Loach; s.w. David Mercer; ALMI.

FAMILY LIFE: TRANSITIONS IN MARRIAGE (Pt. 1: 16m; Pt. 2: 14½m; Pt. 3: 13m C n.d.) (also Video)

This three-film set deals with the timely issues of divorce, the single-parent family, and the stepfamily with emphasis on the adjustment problems of each member of the family. One family is followed through the set of films in a case-history approach; however, usage of grandparents, friends, and others in a discussion group helps illustrate the diversity of family responses to each problem. The first film, DIVORCE, illustrates from personal perspectives of family members the difficulties of communication, feelings of guilt, fault-finding, reactions of grandparents, child support, property settlement, and visitation rights. The second film, THE SINGLE PARENT FAMILY, focuses on financial problems, part-time parenting, new parental relationships, loneliness, day-to-day coping, and feelings of inadequacy. STEP FAMILY, the third film, emphasizes the complexities of relationships and feelings in families where remarriage with the addition of new children calls for many adjustments in relationships. The content of the films is accurate, current, and appropriate, and the idea of following one family could be workable; however, the dialogue is stilted and the acting poor. There are also noise interference and sound distortion in spots. Cutting from the father and his problems to the mother and hers, and back again, throughout each film is effective. The factual material is appropriate for junior high through lower-division college level and parenting groups. p. Gordon-Kerckhoff Productions; CENTEF.

FAMILY MATTERS (WHAT IS A FAMILY?) (15m C 1975) Self-Incorporated Series

Shows some of the problems a young woman faces when her parents are divorced. Examines the attitudes and feelings about the concept of family and the variety of forms a family may take. p. Agency for Instruction Television; AIT; IU, KENTSU.

FAMILY OF MAN, THE (SERIES) see MARRIED LIFE

FAMILY OF STRANGERS (31m C p1980, r1980)

When her mother remarries, 12-year-old Carrie Mills suddenly finds herself with a whole new family--and she doesn't like it. She doesn't like sharing a room and she certainly doesn't like sharing

her mother with these strangers. In fact, it's a difficult adjustment
for them all. It takes a major confrontation before they realize that
being a real family means more than just sharing a house or a name--
it means learning to respect each other as people. d. Robert Fuest;
ex. p. Linda Gottlief; LCA; IU, KENTSU, UMN.

FAMILY PLANNING (30m ea. C 1970) (Video)
    When you get down to it, controlling a nation's or world's popu-
lation begins on the individual family level. This three-lesson series
examines this complex problem on several levels: 1) Quality of Life,
2) Modern Fertility Control, 3) Abortion: Woman's Right. NETCHE.

FAMILY PLANNING IS NO PRIVATE MATTER (30m B 1980) (Video)
    Population control methods are discussed with health and govern-
ment officials; field trips to hospitals, communes, and factories are
made. p. George Stoney, p. Electronic Arts Intermix; ELARTI.

FAMILY PORTRAIT: SEAN'S STORY (12m C 1979) (also Video)
    American Family: An Endangered Species? (Series)
    Sean is a bright, black twelve-year-old who divides his time
between his recently divorced mother and father. Although well-
adjusted, Sean nevertheless endured a period of depression and
confusion before his parents' understanding and help minimized his
initial trauma over their divorce. p. Stanley Losak/Marion Lear
Swaybill for NBC-TV; FI; UMN; PAS.

FAMILY PORTRAIT: SHARE-A-HOME (9m C 1979) (also Video)
    American Family: An Endangered Species? (Series)
    The Florida-based Share-a-Home program brings together small
groups of elderly people in a family environment. The "family" is
intergenerational because it includes the staff members and their
children. Residents are enthusiastic--they feel they have a real home
and a haven in their old age. p. Stanley Losak/Marion Lear Swaybill
for NBC-TV; FI; UMN; PAS.

FAMILY PORTRAIT: THE EDHOLMS (9m C 1979) (also Video) Amer-
    ican Family: An Endangered Species? (Series)
    Remarriage often creates "blended" families: the Edholms, for
example, have five children--three of hers and two of his. On the
whole, they get along well, but acceptance of stepparents and jealousy among step-siblings create pressures with which the Edholms
are dealing successfully. p. Stuart Schulberg; p. Stanley Losak/
Marian Lear Swaybill for NBC-TV; FI; PAS.

FAMILY PORTRAIT: THE GLEGHORNS (8m C 1979) (also Video)
    American Family: An Endangered Species? (Series)
    John Gleghorn loses his job in a factory shutdown, shattering his
family's dreams for the future and creating financial and emotional
pressures. The Gleghorns, however, are determined to weather the
crisis, and their commitment to one antoher remains strong despite

their difficulties. p. Stanley Losak/Marion Lear Swaybill for NBC-TV; FI; UMN, PAS.

FAMILY PORTRAIT: THE HARTMANS (8m C 1979) (also Video)
    American Family: An Endangered Species? (Series)
Maria Hartman is forced to return to work by mounting expenses in her family of nine. Adjustment to the new situation has been difficult for Maria, her husband, and the seven children, but all of them agree that the sacrifices they have made have, in many ways, created a stronger family unit. p. Stanley Losak/Marion Lear Swaybill for NBC-TV; FI; PAS.

FAMILY PORTRAIT: THE KREINIK AND BOSWORTH FAMILIES (7m C 1979) (also Video) American Family: An Endangered Species? (Series)
Changes in societal attitudes have made adoption possible for unmarried adults such as Ms. Kreinik, who adopted two infant daughters, and Bruce Bosworth, who adopted two Vietnamese boys and a handicapped youngster. Makes clear the potential for satisfaction in single-adult parenting. p. Stanley Losak/Marian Lear Swaybill for NBC-TV; FI; KENTSU; PAS.

FAMILY PORTRAIT: THE MARINOS (8m C 1979) (also Video) American Family: An Endangered Species? (Series)
Charges and countercharges fly as Diane and Richard Marino engage in a custody fight. Both insist they want only the best for their three children, but the question remains as to how their parents' anger will affect them. The battle rages while the children strive to maintain a normal life. p. Stanley Losak/Marion Lear Swaybill for NBC-TV; FI; UMN; PAS.

FAMILY PORTRAIT: THE SCHUSTER-ISSACSON FAMILY (8m C p1979, r1979) (also Video) American Family: An Endangered Species? (Series)
This is a family of two parents, both women, and six children. Madeline and Sandy talk frankly about their life-style and about homosexuality in general. They are convinced their relationship does not affect the children adversely, and, in fact, the children say they are happy with their parents. p. Stanley Losak/Marion Lear Swaybill for NBC-TV; FI; PAS.

FAMILY PORTRAIT: THE SORIANOS (9m C 1979) (also Video) American Family: An Endangered Species? (Series)
Pedro and Eloisa Soriano, parents of sixteen children, exemplify the "extended" family, with parents, grandparents, children, uncles, aunts, and cousins all sharing joys and sorrows together. They are poor, but they have provided love, faith, and direction for their children. p. Stanley Losak/Marion Lear Swaybill for NBC-TV; FI; PAS.

FAMILY TALKS ABOUT SEX, A (29m C 1977)
Several parents and their children, of various ages, dramatize incidents that lead to discussions of sex and related matters. Illustrates the importance of maintaining an open and straightforward attitude. Young children are taught proper terminology for their genitals and are given honest answers to whatever questions they pose. A child using obscene language is handled by her father who explains the word's meaning and asks that she refrain from using it. Pregnancy, puberty, and menstruation are discussed candidly. In other scenes, parents of older children discuss wet dreams, masturbation, pornography, premarital sex, contraception and marriage. Delicate situations and questions are handled with sensitivity. d./ s.w. Larry Yust; p. Wexler Films for the E. C. Brown Foundation; PEREN; UMO.

FAMILY TEAMWORK (15m C 1979)
Emphasizes how cooperative teamwork and an effort to understand the feelings and viewpoints of others can lead to a happier, more productive family. Includes narration by five children who deal with conflicts between their desires and the desires of other family members. Presents multicultural one- and two-parent families. HIGGIN; IU.

FAMILY THAT DWELT APART, THE (8m C 1974)
A tall and salty Yankee story about a family done in by do-gooders is narrated by the author, E. B. White. Yvonne Mallette's animation matches the wry humor of his tale originally published in the New Yorker in 1937 as one of White's famed "Preposterous Parables." d. Yvonne Mallette; p. Wolf Koenig; NFBC; LCA.

FAN AND BUBBLE DANCES (9m B 1942)
Features Sally Rand and Faith Bacon in fan and bubble dances. p. Dance Film Archive, University of Rochester; DAN/UR.

FAR SHORE, THE (104m C 1978)
A story of a young Canadian woman who marries one man and loses her heart to another. The consequences are tragic. The story, set in Canada in 1919, is as much about the social, political and artistic spirit of the times, as it is about love and lovers. d. Joyce Wieland; LIBERTY.

FARM SONG (58m C p1978, r1979)
A year in the life of a farm family deep in rural northeast Japan, four generations under one ancient roof. We see the Kato family harvesting in the autumn, celebrating the New Year, sitting out the long winter and planting rice in the spring. Seeks to disclose how each member of the family comes to terms with the role in life enforced so relentlessly by tradition. d./p. John Nathan; JAPANS.

FASHION FORECASTING (30m C 1982) (slt)

A good introduction to the range of career choices available in fashion, and good though less-successful discussion of the process of fashion forecasting. The emphasis is on forecasting at the retail level, particularly on the role of the fashion director. It would be quite useful in college-level courses in fashion merchandising, general textiles and apparel, and career seminars as an introductory overview of the fashion process. d. Rita Perna; p. Fairchild Visuals; FAIRCHD.

FAST AND CLEAN (37m C p1980, r1980)
Explores the growing sport of whitewater slalom racing. Two world champions, a young man and young woman, become the best in the world in a demanding and exciting amateur sport. d. Russ Nichols; p. Louise Nichols; Nichols Productions; NICHOLSS.

FAT CHANCE! (30m C 1977)
Effects of the home environment on weight control. Dramatized scenes of one family's activities depict how individuals are influenced in their eating habits by other family members. Emphasis is on eating patterns, their long-term effect on obesity, and how habits can be generally changed to insure permanent weight control. p. The Pennsylvania State University; PAS.

FAT FILM, THE (11m C r1977)
A revealing film by four women filmmakers who undertook the project to provide themselves with the incentive to lose weight, but they had no more success than Kate in their film. Kate vowed to systematically diet, so she sets about removing temptation but the will power was just not there, much as those of the four women who made the film. p. Muffie Meyer, Aviva Slesin, Nancy Schreiber, Kathleen Dougherty; PHOENIX, IU.

FATHERS (23m C p1980, r1980)
About being a father in our culture and some difficulties in being a good one. Filmed in three families: the busy-at-work father, the authoritarian, and by contrast, a father sharing childcare responsibilities. d. Linda Jassim; CF; IU, UCEMC, WSU.

FATHERS (26m C 1980)
Portrait of American men revealing their needs, hopes, and worries. They are talking about their feelings about pregnancy and childbirth, nurturing and showing affection, masculine behavior, job vs. home life, changes in roles of women and men, etc. Includes comments from Dr. Henry B. Biller, distinguished clinical developmental psychologist, professor of psychology at the University of Rhode Island, and author of Father Power. p. Durrin Films, Inc. for American Society for Psychoprophylaxis in Obstetrics; NEWDAY; UMN.

FATSO (94m C 1980)
Dom DeLuise is irresistibly funny as he portrays a big man

obsessed with eating. "In an appealing writing and directing debut,
Bancroft's funny, pertinent Fatso is an affectionate ethnic comedy
and romance."--Kevin Thomas, Los Angeles Times. d. Anne Bancroft; FI.

FEAR THAT BINDS US: VIOLENCE AGAINST WOMEN, THE (52m B
    1981) (Video)
    The moving personal stories of six women who have experienced
various kinds of violence in their lives are combined with the varied
perspectives of historians, activists, social service workers and men
who have perpetrated this violence. It is an exploration of the history, extent and reasons for violence against women and how American values of individualism, success, power and freedom affect it.
d. Kathy J. Seltzer; p. New Front Films; NEWFRF.

FEEDING SKILLS: YOU BABY'S EARLY YEARS (24½m C 1981)
    Explains the role of parents in feeding their children from in-
fancy to two years. Content includes breast and bottle feeding
where oral reflexes control, the transition to solid foods as reflexes
fade, and helping the child to develop self-feeding skills. There is
instruction on food and nutrition. d. Ruth Arens; p. Churchill
Films/UAP, Children's Hospital of Los Angeles; CF.

FEELING GOOD, FEELING PROUD (27m C 1981)
    Twenty-seven-year-old Heidi Hennessy articulately describes her
experiences as an actress with performance ensemble Theatre Unlimited. Although epileptic and mentally retarded, Heidi has become
more independent since participating in this unique group which nur-
tures assertiveness and self-esteem. Raises important and complex
questions about the integration of the mentally disabled into society.
d. Richard Heus; p. R. Heus/R. Marinaccio; DIRECT.

FEELINGS (SERIES) see CHILD ABUSE, Pts. 1 and 2; DIVORCE;
    SEXUALITY, Pts. 1 and 2

FEET FIRST (22m C p1980, r1981)
    A nostalgic yet ironic look at partner-dancing from the viewpoint
of the filmmakers' fantasy search for Fred Astaire, the perfect partner. We witness the frustrations of dance students and the joys of
the competition winner with the backdrop of the romanticism of the
ideal dancer. d./p./s.w./ed. Ann Tegnell; TEMPLE UNIVERSITY;
TEMPLU.

FEMALE CYCLE (8m C 1970)
    The story of menstruation, simply and understandably told. An-
imation illustrates the development of the oocyte (immature egg), its
passage down the Fallopian tube, the preparation of the Fallopian
tube, the preparation of the uterus in the event of fertilization and,
finally, the disintegration of the vascular walls of the uterus. NFBC;
FI.

FEMALE EJACULATION (12m C 1981)
The first documentary film to depict expulsion of a clear fluid from the female urethra during orgasm induced by digital stimulation of the "Grafenberg" spot, a sensitive area in the anterior vaginal wall. This film is described in "Female Ejaculation: A Case Study," in the February 1981 issue of The Journal of Sex Research, which contains four articles on the subject. The filmmakers narrate the film. d. Beverly Whipple, RN, MED, ACS; Edwin Belzer, Jr., Ph.D.; John Delbert Perry, Ph.D., ACS; p. Richard Price, Inc. for Perry and Whipple, Ltd.; MMRC.

FEMALE LINE, THE (58m C 1980)
The Peabody family name has been synonymous with independence: and this independent spirit has not been restricted to the male members of the clan. Witness Mary Parkman Peabody, the grandmother, who at the age of 72 was arrested and jailed for her participation in a civil rights demonstration; Marietta Tree, the mother, New York businesswoman and Democratic Party insider who was this country's first woman to serve as Ambassador to the United States Mission to the United Nations; and Frances Fitzgerald, the daughter, Pulitzer Prize winning author of Fire in the Lake, a book which helped change the attitude of the American public to the war in Vietnam. This film explores the positions of these excellent representatives from three different generations on such topics as abortion, politics and the role of women in today's society. Even more important, it documents the passing of the torch from generation to generation, ever continuing "The Female Line." p. Pamela Peabody; d. Robin Hardy; CORINTH.

FEMALE PRISONER, THE (10m C 1978) (Video)
Derived from the Clouzot film La Prisonnière, the tape uses a variety of representational elements. Brettschneider "re-creates" the film or visualizes her memory of it. The result is an abbreviated but tortuous story, as well as a witty analysis of certain storytelling conventions. p. Jane Brettschneider, Whitney Museum of American Art; WHITNEYM.

FEMININE HYGIENE AND YOU (14m C 1982)
Designed to take the mystery out of feminine hygiene. It begins with a simple explanation of how a woman's body works--her reproductive system, menstrual cycle, vaginal secretions; then moves on to explain douching--what it will and will not do. Discussion materials available with this film. Free loan. p. Beecham Products; MTPS.

FEMININE MISTAKE, THE (24m C 1977)
Presents the effects of smoking on a woman's body. Evidence of constriction of the bronchial tubes, a sharp rise in blood pressure, is shown on a woman who has smoked heavily for 17 years. Study shows that heavy smokers tend to develop earlier and deeper facial wrinkles than do non-smokers. A pregnant woman is monitored as

she smokes a cigarette to show its effect on the normal quasi-breathing chest motion of the fetus. An interview with a 43-year-old woman dying of lung cancer is revealing and is one of the film's most disturbing and compelling sequences. A successful high school's stop-smoking program is surveyed. An excellent account of a growing problem, the number of male smokers have decreased in recent years while female smokers (especially among teenagers) has risen dramatically. p. Arnold Shapiro for Dave Bell Associates; PF; KENTSU, UIL, UMN.

FEMINIST PRESS (29m C 1976) (Video) Woman Series
Nancy Borman, co-founder and assignment editor of Majority Report (a bi-weekly feminist newspaper published in New York City), and Janis Kelly, a member of the Off Our Backs Collective, which publishes a monthly news journal for women in Washington, D.C. and Chicago, discuss the Feminist Press--an outgrowth of the Feminist Movement. Both journalists comment on the need for Feminist Press to offer a woman's point of view that cannot be found in the "establishment press" and to offer ideas for social change. Sandra Elkin is the moderator. p. WNED-TV; Buffalo; PBSV.

FEMINIST VISIONS OF THE FUTURE (50m C 1980) (Video)
Interviews with Phyllis Birkby, architect; Dorothy Bryant, novelist; Z. Budapest, High Priestess-author; Baba Copper, futurist; Dr. Mary Daly, philosopher-author; Barbara Hammer, filmmaker; Dr. Ron Hirschbein, philosophy professor; Dr. Pat Huckle, women's studies professor; Ruth Iskin, art historian; Robin Morgan, poet, essayist; Marge Piercy, novelist and poet; Arlene Raven, art historian; Dr. June Singer, Jungian analyst-author; Margaret Sloan, activist-poet; Starhawk, High Priestess-author; Merlin Stone, author; Philip Suntree, poet; Mary Beth Edelson, artist; Dr. Warren Farrell, author, men's liberationist.
The content describes goals for a healthy and egalitarian future society. Sources for the feminist visions include examination of two works of future fantasy novels by Peircy and Bryant; introduction to a spiral rather than linear thought process by Daly; reclamation of Wiccan spirituality; examples of the women's renaissance in art; exploration of women's architectural fantasies; possible futures in human relationships and the role of economic, physiological and political self-determination. p. California State University at Chico; CSUCHI.

FENCE IN THE WATER (44m C p1980, r1981)
This documentary shows the use of weirs and large fish traps used off the coast of Maine to catch small Atlantic herring. Hardly a new technique, ancient weirs 4,500 years old have been found by archaeologists, and a painting done in 1585 shows Indians using weirs in Virginia. Maine fishermen spend their spring days repairing pilings and nets, adding branches to help reduce the need for nets, scraping and repainting boats, buying new nets and installing lead

weights to hold the nets down. May to November, the fishermen go out each evening to look for fish in the harbor. p./d. Peg Dice; BODFIL.

FESTIVAL OF DANCE (60m C 1973)
A film about the creation of a company that includes students at the Connecticut College School of the Dance to perform dances choreographed by Doris Humphrey, Martha Graham, Charles Weidman, and José Limón, at the 1972 American Dance Festival at the college. Includes a brief history of modern dance as well as shots of auditions, rehearsals, and performances of excerpts from Emperor Jones, Flickers, New Dance, and With My Red Fires. d. Ted Steeg; p. Steeg Productions; DAN/UR.

FIBERGLASS CHAIRS, THE (9m C 1970)
The design concepts and the production of fiberglass chairs. p. Ray and Charles Eames; PF.

FIESTA (8m C 1978)
Shows the blending of ancient Indian and Spanish cultures in a Mexican celebration. No narration. Original song by Holly Graham enhances the visuals. p. Diana Colson; MCFI; UIL.

FIFTEEN JOYS OF MARRIAGE, THE (11m B n.d.) (Video)
In a humorous yet revealing manner, this program examines some of the predominant medieval attitudes toward women. Illustrated with medieval sculpture and scenes from medieval drawings, it shows how women were often protrayed as inherently evil and as the cause of the downfall of men. The title of the program is from a fifteenth-century French satire on wives. Narrated by Jan Tennant; s.w. Professor Roberta Frank of University of Toronto and Carolyn Eisen; Media Centre, University of Toronto; UTORON.

56½ HOWARD STREET (13m C n.d.)
For many years Marguerite Osborn, 84, of Indian and Black ancestry, was the subject of harassment, ridicule, and neglect in her Cambridge, Massachusetts neighborhood. She was called the voodoo woman. To reduce this tension, John McGannon, an independent filmmaker living nearby, approached several adolescents with the idea of making a movie about their courageous neighbor. As a result, an afternoon's visit is documented in this film. Shows Marguerite Osborn an articulate woman of great enthusiasm and spirit. She speaks of her ancestry and recites some of her poetry. She is sharp, witty, and provocative as she entertains her new guests. The film raises issues of aging, quality of life, community relations and services, and the role of women in society. p./d. John McGannon; EDC.

FIGHT FOR LIFE (67m B 1940) (also Video)
Classic film about the Chicago Maternity Center produced in 1940 for the Roosevelt Administration. It presents a bitter indictment of

slum conditions and a gripping plea for better and safer obstetrical care as was practiced by the Chicago Maternity Center. d. Pare Lorenta; p. United States Film Service; CINMD, VIEWFI.

FIGHTING CRIME: WE CAN DO IT (23m C 1980)
Presents numerous practical techniques designed to help the elderly participate in crime prevention and reduce their fear of being victimized, both at home and in public places. MTITI; UCEMC.

FILM ABOUT A WOMAN WHO ... (105m C/B 1974)
The film is a multilayered composite of images, tests, music, and speech. The story is a passage across an unspecified length and order of time, dealing with oppositions of emotional life set off against the appearances of everyday leisure activity. On a literary level the story is sustained via an intermittent narration by two off-screen voices that read, in both the past and present tense, discrete paragraphs about the experiences of someone referred to only as "she." On screen, two men and two women, and occasionally, a child, "play out" the valences of their interdependencies in word and gestures, gaze and stillness. Correspondence between image and narration at any given moment ranges from metaphoric cohesion to calculated incongruity. Subtitles and intertitles function as both counterpoint and connective tissue between sequences. The subjective, obsessive eye of the camera combined with the dry impersonal tone of the narration creates a constant flux of tension, absurdity, intense drama, and pathos. d./s.w. Yvonne Rainer; FLMKCO.

FILM ABOUT SHARON, A (19m C 1976)
Presented with a mixture of documentary and erotically explicit sexuality. Explores the very personal experiences of an attractive, educated and well-spoken woman who has achieved commercial success, public recognition and personal satisfaction as an actress in "pornographic" films. Can be used for discussion of female roles and sexual attitudes in a changing world. d./p. Barry Spinello; MMRC.

FILM WITH SEVEN DANCERS (7m B 1972)
A dance entitled "Cool Sun" is performed by students at the Ohio University School of Dance. The original work serves as the raw material for a specifically cinematic end-product rather than a record of the dance itself. Choreographer: Ginny Freeman; d. Jill Demby, Paul Halpern; p. Ohio University, Audio-Visual Dept.; OHIOU.

FILMS ABOUT ALTERNATIVE SERIES see THAT OUR CHILDREN WILL NOT DIE

FINAL PROUD DAYS OF ELSIE WURSTER, THE (58m B 1975)
A moving portrait of a woman who was undespairing and full of dignity in the face of death. Filmed in a nursing home during the last 44 days of Elsie's life as she interacts with visitors and nursing home staff, undergoes therapy, and shares her feelings, fears and

memories. p. P. J. O'Connell; p. The Pennsylvania State University Television; PAS; UMO.

FINAL SOLUTION, THE see HOLOCAUST

FINANCES (33m C 1980) Coping with Serious Illness Series
Documentary on the last years of Joan Robinson, a woman who was dying of cancer. Examines ways of coping with the financial aspects of being seriously ill. The Robinsons handle some of the problems bureaucratic and otherwise, of meeting their expenses and making the most of their insurance policies. Lawyers and consumer advocates discuss patients' rights and legal issues. TIMLIF; PAS, UMN.

FIND THE ONE THAT'S DIFFERENT (15m C p1977, r1977)
Shows how teachers can identify students with learning disabilities and demonstrates how to work with them positively and effectively. Good teacher training film, well dramatized and illustrated. p. Ann D. Clark; HUBBARD.

FINDING A VOICE (57m C 1982) (Video) Nova Series
What is it like not to be able to communicate? Examines the speech disabilities of Dick Boydell, born with cerebral palsy and unable for 30 years to say more than yes or no. In this program, we see how technology has provided Dick with a "voice." d. Sheila Hayman; s.w. Dick Boydell; ed. Graham Massey; p. WGBH-TV/BBC, Martin Freeth; TIMLIF.

FINNISH AMERICAN LIVES (47m C 1982) (also Video)
Explores the personal meaning of ethnicity, aging, and family relationships. The story of the Vuorenmaas family represents mainstream Finnish-American experience, yet viewers of all ethnic backgrounds will identify with people in the film. By delving deep into the emotional bonds between generations, the film touches on the universal. Family members talk of values and events, aspirations and regrets. These interviews blended with scenes from their daily lives reveal a close-knit family proud of its heritage and struggling to preserve it. Folk crafts and music, the rich Finnish language, and long-held traditions of hard work and care for the elderly are all documented here. Sponsored by The Michigan Council for the Humanities, The National Endowment for the Humanities. d./p. Michael Loukinen; ed. Deborah Dickson; NMICHU.

FIRE (54m C r1974)
This hard-hitting documentary examines the economics that industry and government allow themselves when it comes to protecting people from fire. Open and unprotected polyurethane insulation is still in interior use despite the fact that it can turn a small fire into an inferno. Also examined are the design and structure of high-rise buildings, manufacture of children's clothing that is not flame-

resistant, and inadequately reinforced automobile tanks responsible for deaths after relatively mild rear-end collision. p./d. Pamela D. Hill for ABC Close-Up; PHOENIX.

FIRE IN THE WATER (49m C 1981) (also Video)
This documentary examines hydrogen energy--what it is and its potential as an answer to our planet's energy crisis. p. KMGH-TV, Denver; Linda Howe; CRM.

FIREWOOD (10m C 1975) Yanomamo Series
Daily wood collecting in South American Indian tribe: a woman patiently and strenuously chops up a large log for firewood. Graphically demonstrates cultural differences in the concept of "women's work." Directed by Timothy Asch and Napoleon Chagnon; p. The Pennsylvania State University; PAS.

FIRST ASCENT (12m C 1982) (also Video)
In an inspiring account of adventure and achievement, two daring young women set out to conquer the Naked Edge, a 1,000-foot rock near Boulder, Colorado that sets a standard of great difficulty for experienced climbers. As they endeavor to become the first team of women climbers to reach its summit, Beth Bennett and Lynn Hill scorn mechanical aids, using only hands and feet to scale the rock's sheer face. When their first attempt at free climbing ends in failure, Bennett and Hill spend the summer developing the strength and stamina needed for another ascent. Upon their return to try again, the camera records each near miss and precarious hold in their suspense-filled climb, as they pass the point of their first failure to stand triumphantly at the top. p. Robert Carmichael, Greg Lowe; PF.

FIRST CHILD--SECOND THOUGHTS (29m C 1979)
A positive, intimate and realistic view of first-year parenting as experienced by four different couples. MILPIC.

FIRST DAYS OF LIFE, THE (24m C n.d.)
Through fiberoptic photography, the viewer is transported inside the womb to see life develop, from conception to natural birth. p. Cinema Medica; CINMD.

FIRST EDITION (31m C p1977, r1980) (also Video)
The film follows reporters and editors as they go about the business of discovering, investigating, writing and rewriting national and local stories in time to meet an uncompromising deadline. Tom Wicker of The New York Times has called it "The finest and truest documentary about a newspaper that I've seen...." p. Helen Whitney/Sage; FI.

FIRST ENCOUNTERS: A RUSSIAN JOURNAL (18m C p1978 r1978, c1979)
Reveals aspects of Russian life rarely seen in the West, especially

provincial cities and villages, and several ordinary homes. A documentary filmed inside Russia without the customary official permission. d./p. Laura Morgan; p. LSM Film Production; BENCHMF.

FIRST FLIGHT REPORT--STS-1 POST FLIGHT PRESS CONFERENCE (17m C 1981)

Commander John Young and co-pilot Robert Crippen provide narration for this official NASA footage, describing flight preparations, in-flight activities, and dramatic close-ups of the takeoff and landings. As the mission unfolds, the astronauts recount their adventure with humor, understatement, and candor. d. John Young/Bob Crippen; p. Margaret Hastings; NAVC.

FIRST FOODS (14m C 1976)

Dr. Jean Mayer offers advice on how solid foods should be introduced to babies in their first year of life. Spanish version also available. Guide book included. p. Jamil Simon Productions, Inc.; SNUTRE.

FIRST IT SEEMED KINDA STRANGE (6m C 1977)

Lee's parents are divorced and he lives with his mother. He visits his father and stepmother on weekends and vacations. Lee finds that now he can be more open about his feelings to each of his parents and that, for the most part, things are better for him since the divorce. He no longer feels in the middle of his parents' arguments. p. Mary Benjamin, WGBH-TV; FI.

FIRST LADY OF AMERICAN DANCE: RUTH ST. DENIS, THE (26m C n.d.)

Ruth St. Denis talks about and then performs four solos filmed late in her life: "White Jade," "Black and Gold Sari," "Cobra," and "Yogi." Choreographer: Ruth St. Denis; p. William Skipper; SKIPW.

FIRST LOVE (92m C 1977)

A beautiful, tasteful and refreshing film about the pangs, the excitement and the glory of the "first time." A mature picture any college student can relate to. d. Joan Darling; p. Lawrence Turman, David Foster; p. Paramount; FI.

FIRST POSITION (90m C 1972)

A fictionalized documentary about the onstage and offstage life of young dancers in the American Ballet Theatre School. With excerpts from Petrouchka and from rehearsals and classes featuring Yurek Lazowsky, Madame Valentina Pereyaslavec, and Leon Daneilian. CANTOR.

FIRST STEP, THE (13m C 1981)

Shows the importance for both mother and child of a playgroup for young mentally retarded children. Elizabeth Ashton, a specialist in retardation, runs such a group in Australia. She believes that children develop much faster with socialization and the repetitive music and movements that are part of the program. Mothers derive support from one another which help them deal more effectively with their children and their lives. p. Barbara Chobocky; FILMLB.

FIRST STEPS (26m C p1980, r1981) (also Video)
    Shows inner-city children of New York, principally black and Puerto Rican, as they participate in dance auditions conducted by American Dance Center or New York Circus School/Big Apple Circus. About 20 of the fortunate ones are chosen after intensive training. They are judged on natural aptitude, coordination, personality, enthusiasm, and ability to do what is asked of them. p. Pamela Emil, Ted Haimes; d. Ted Haimes; REVOF; WSU.

FIRST STEPS: CARING FOR THE VERY YOUNG (12m C p1981, r1981--U.S.)
    This animated film focuses on appropriate prenatal care, delivery, breast-feeding, safe learning environment, infant feeding, toilet training and the importance of exposing toddlers to others their own age. Proper nutrition for the pregnant woman as well as the dangers of drugs, alcohol and cigarettes are pointed out, and a natural birth scene involving the father is shown. The advantages of immediate maternal contact and early breast-feeding are considered, and the psychological benefits of close bodily contact with the mother during the early months of life is stressed. Individual differences in babies' eating habits and development are discussed, as is the need for parents to express special concerns to the child's doctor. Also covers toilet training, the need for neighborhood play groups, and the importance of good parental attitudes in raising healthy children. p. John Halas for Educational Film Center Ltd., London; SCRESC.

FIRST SWALLOW (80m C [Scope] 1976)
    An exuberant comedy about the coming of soccer to a small Georgian village at the turn of the century. The film really deals with the behavior of men. The viewpoint is affectionate, but objective. Soccer has become an obsession in the town of Poti. The bachelors play the married men, to the consternation of wives. The team, dubbed First Swallow, plays other teams, compiling one win after another, until the British arrive--the ones who invented the game. p. Nana McHelidze; CORINTH.

FIRST TUESDAY SERIES see ABORTION: LONDON'S DILEMMA

FIRST TWO WEEKS OF LIFE (17m C n.d.)
    This is the story of Jane, Fred and Rebecca during the two weeks of life after Rebecca joined the world. A fascinating, day-by-day visual "diary" of a natural childbirth and the practical guidance given to both parents in the care and handling of their first baby. In addition, the film is aimed at reducing the anxiety often felt by young couples concerning the birth of their first child. p. Pampers

Professional Services Division of Procter and Gamble. Approved by American Journal of Nursing. AF.

FIRST VISIT TO THE DOCTOR (29m B 1956) Months Before Birth-- A Series
Discusses the initial visit to the doctor after pregnancy is suspected. Includes a step-by-step description of the pelvic examination. p. WQED-TV; AF.

FIRST YEAR, THE (21m C p1980 r1980)
Looking at the important role that fathers can play in the growth of their child, this film shows different stages of development in three children between three and twelve months. The families involved are from widely differing social and cultural backgrounds. d./p. Barbara Chobocky; AFC.

FIRST YEAR (14m C 1975)
Eight-year-old Brian reacts to his parents' divorce and continued hostility with acute asthma in a believable and effective Emergency Room drama. d. Bernard Selling; p. Teleketics Films; TKF.

FISHING PEOPLE: THE TULALIP TRIBE, A (17m C 1980)
The Tulalip Tribe, whose reservation is near Seattle, tell the story of their history as a fishing people and provide an overview of the tribe's current involvement with fishing as an industry. Ray Fryberg, assistant director of the Tulalip Fisheries, tells the history of the tribe's efforts to retain fishing rights guaranteed to them by mutual treaties with the United States government. Until the Boldt Decision reaffirmed Indian fishing rights in the Supreme Court, these rights were not generally honored. Tulalip culture has always revolved around fishing and their respect for life is reflected in a tradition of good ecological practices. Fryberg describes the tribe's concern about pollution from the logging industry and other sources which threaten the salmon spawning grounds. Tribal elder Cyrus James recalls an earlier time when this was not the case. Today the Tulalip Tribe works with the State of Washington on salmon rearing ponds which are helping to replenish the salmon of Puget Sound, and young tribe members are being trained for jobs in the expanding fishing industry. p./d. Heather Oakson, The Tulalip Tribe; TULALIP.

FITNESS FOR PARENT AND CHILD (20m C n.d.)
Fitness expert Maurita Robarge and her daughter demonstrate how parents and children can join together in an exercise program. Eight exercises are demonstrated. UWI.

FITNESS IN THE NEW AGE (30m C 1980)
Millions of Americans would like to improve their health but are put off by the grueling routines, competition and pain. Dyveke Spino, co-founder of Esalen Sports Center, says no to all this and instead presents a joyful, spiritual approach to total health. A clinical

psychologist and professor at the University of California, Dyveke
shows how to move to a personal life-style which leads to specific
training programs and exercises suitable for individual personalities,
including running, tennis, structural alignment, endurance, nutrition,
flexibility, and spiritual well-being. Dyveke is both a physical and
a spiritual guide, demonstrating the most progressive and scientific
regimens for the body. But inspirational techniques--relaxation, inner awareness, visualization--also play a dramatic role in the rejuvenation of her clients. Recommended for everyone interested in maximum
health. p. Elda Hartley; HARTLEY.

FIVE DAYS WITHOUT NAME see TAJIMOLTIK

FIVE FORTY-EIGHT, THE (60m C 1979) (also Video)
    The story's protagonist is an "ordinary man" whose daily routine
is shattered when he finds himself in a situation of mortal danger.
Blake is commuting home from Manhattan as usual when he finds himself up against a life-threatening adversary, a desperate young woman
bent on revenge against her former lover and boss. p. Ann Blumenthal, Peter Weinberg; d. James Ivory; WNET-TV; FI.

FIVE WOMEN, FIVE BIRTHS (29m B p1978, r1978)
    Intimate and informative study of the choices and alternatives
open to women about to give birth. Superb photography shows five
different births (three in the hospital and two at home) and sensi-
tively illustrates the mothers' decisions and experiences. p. Suzanne
Arms, DAVFMS; MMRC.

FIXIN' TO TELL ABOUT JACK (25m C 1974)
    Ray Hicks is a mountain farmer with a genius for telling traditional
folktales, each with specific details and histories that have been
passed down in his family from generation to generation. Master of
storytelling, Ray tells the tale "Whickity-Whack, into My Sack" at
home and to a group of school children. p./d. Elizabeth Barrett;
APPAL.

FLICKERS (19m C 1978)
    A spoof of the silent movies. In four parts: "Hearts Aflame,"
"Wages of Sin," "Flowers of the Desert," "Hearts Courageous." The
work was choreographed in 1941 with Doris Humphrey and Charles
Weidman in the leading roles. Dance Company: Professional Reper-
tory Company at Connecticut College School of Dance; Choreographer:
Charles Weidman; d. Ted Steeg; p. Steeg Productions; DAN/UR.

FLIGHT OF THE GOSSAMER CONDOR (27m C p1978, r1978)
    The saga of Dr. Paul MacCready, who made aviation history by
building a man-powered aircraft capable of flying a difficult prescribed source. Fittingly, the plane is now in the Smithsonian Institution between the Wright Brothers' plane and Apollo II. d. Ben
Shedd; p. Jacqueline (Jackie) Phillips Shedd; CF.

FLOATING CLOUD (123m B 1955) (Japanese/Subtitled)
Illuminates the problems of post-war life as it tells the story of
an affair between a young woman and a married man she met during
the war. Accepting humiliation from him, she follows him from place
to place, until she succumbs to pneumonia on a remote island, just as
as he realizes his love for her. d. Mikio Naruse; CORINTH.

FLOW OF ZEN, THE (14m C 1969)
"The waters before and the waters after, now and forever flowing, follow each other." Thus Alan Watts begins his talk on the philosophy of Zen Buddhism with the Zen poem, comparing the qualities
of water with the qualities produced by following Zen. His talk prepares the viewer for meditation which is a structural part of the film.
p. Elda Hartley; HARTLEY.

FLOWERS IN THE SAND (28m C p1981, r1981--U.S.) (also Video)
Presents the story of one mentally retarded young man, Daniel,
and his endeavors to participate in the world around him. Daniel
finds courage to take a ferry to a training school only after meeting
a visiting young lady on the beach near his home. One day, Daniel
takes Grace up to the stone lighthouse tower where he performs a
ceremony over a skull and candles and they make wishes: Daniel
for courage to ride the ferry and she for flowers in the sand. Then,
Grace helps Daniel to understand that only he can make his wish come
true. The following day, Grace sees Daniel off on the ferryboat, and
she finds the flowers in the sand that Daniel had planted as she is
leaving. p. Christine Cornish, Leon Marr, Konkino Films, Canada;
PHOENIX.

FLOWING WITH THE TAO (14m C 1973)
Alan Watts explores the nature of reality as illustrated in the
flowing forms of water. Not didactic, it gives the essence of Taoism
through the synthesis of beautiful photography, a special musical
score by Iasos, and Alan Watts' inspired narration. This was Alan
Watts' last film ... it is one of his best. Especially valuable to those
interested in developing greater flexibility to life's rhythms and sensitivity to the beauty around them. p. Elda Hartley; HARTLEY.

FLUTE OF KRISHNA (9m C si 1923)
A work composed by Martha Graham during the year she was with
the Eastman School in Rochester, New York. Filmed by Eastman Kodak to experiment with a new two-color process. Graham does not
dance in the work herself. The unheard music was by Cyril Scott.
Choreographer: Martha Graham; Eastman Kodak; DAN/UR.

FLYAWAY DOVE (18m C 1982) (also Video)
An imaginative, nonverbal tale about Eva, a fledgling circus performer, who is frustrated when her "trained" dove refuses to fly back
to her. She dreams that the dove's dancing feather leads her on a
breathtaking airplane ride to a prince's palace. She then captures

the dove both in her dream and in life--and begins to understand that to possess something also involves the ability to set it free. Inspired by James Sage's The Boy and the Dove. p. Jill Fairchild, Edmond Sechan; d. Edmond Sechan; LCA.

FOLK GUITAR PLUS (SERIES) (30m ea. C n.d.) (Video, Beta, VHS)
Laura Weber instructs viewers in advanced guitar technique and introduces the Autoharp, banjo and recorder. The series is designed to stimulate interest in simple musical instruments which can be learned fairly quickly and played solo or ensemble. p. KQED-TV; PBSV.
The series includes these film lessons:
FIVE NOTES ON THE RECORDER; INTRODUCTION TO EACH IN-STRUMENT
BANJO CHORDS G, D7, C; GUITAR CHORDS D7 SUSPENSION AND G; C and G CHORDS ON THE AUTOHARP
SONGS FOR THE RECORDER, BANJO, GUITAR AND AUTOHARP
NEW BANJO STRUM FOR THE BANJO, GUITAR AND AUTOHARP
NEW SONGS, AND RECORDER NOTE F SHARP
MELODY PLAYING AND THE NEW CHORD OF F FOR BANJO
BANJO G TUNING; NEW BANJO CHORDS A MINOR AND E7 MINOR
NEW BANJO STRUM; BRUSH STRUM FOR AUTOHARP; RECORDER NOTE G SHARP
TWO NEW SONGS FOR ALL INSTRUMENTS
C SCALE ON THE AUTOHARP
BANJO TECHNIQUES OF PICKING, HAMMERING AND PULLING; NEW SCALE FOR AUTOHARP; BOSSA NOVA EXERCISE FOR GUITAR
THREE FINGER PICKING FOR THE GUITAR; DOUBLE THUMBING TECHNIQUE FOR THE BANJO
GENERAL REVIEW

FOLK SONGS AND FOLK DANCES OF PAKISTAN (18m B n.d.)
The dances of East Bengal in Pakistan represent the people's way of life, including the hardships and good times. The first dance, performed by men, makes effective use of swords and scarves and shows formation effects. Along the Punjab several women are shown performing a dance which tells the story of a princess. Also shows dances done at harvest time. All these are done in full costume to authentic music. p. Pakistan Pictures; STEREF; UIL.

FOLK SUITE (7m C n.d.)
Spirituals arranged by John Wilson are sung by the dancers as they interpret the music through dance. Dance Company: Harriette Ann Gray Dancers; Choreographer: Harriette Ann Gray; p. Portia Mansfield Motion Pictures; MANSPR.

FOOD ADDITIVES: HELPFUL OR HARMFUL? PART I (29m C 1976) (Video) Woman Series
Beatrice Trum Hunter, author and investigator of the food industry, discusses the effects of vested big business interests, deceptive

practices and public misconceptions about testing of food additives. She expresses her belief that additives are merely economic shortcuts for the food industry and do not really benefit the consumer and talks about the inability of federal agencies to regulate the industry as they should. Sandra Elkin is the moderator. p. WNED-TV; PBSV.

FOOD ADDITIVES: HELPFUL OR HARMFUL? PART II (29m C 1976) (Video) Woman Series

Beatrice Trum Hunter, author and investigator of the food industry, offers advice on ways to avoid food additives and increase nutritional value when shopping for food. She talks about the hidden additives in highly processed and "convenience" foods and explains that the human threshold of tolerance for various chemical substances cannot be decisively determined since some reactions may not appear for long periods of time. Sandra Elkin is the moderator. p. WNED-TV; PBSV.

FOOD FOLLIES (23m C 1977) (also Video)

A unique exposition of the problems facing today's supermarket shopper, FOOD FOLLIES is a thought-provoking look at the food marketplace as seen from consumer, government, and industry points of view. Packaging is often misleading, grading is sometimes confusing, labeling is frequently bewildering. Worse, some foods lack the nutrition they purport to provide and some are even hazardous to health. FOOD FOLLIES lays down guidelines to help the shopper obtain wholesome, nutritious food at full value for the food dollar. Consumers Reports. UCEMC, UIL, UM.

FOOD: GREEN GROW THE PROFITS (52m C 1973)

Explains that the entrance of industrial giants into the food business does not always coincide with sound nutrition, good taste or consumer economy. Vertically integrated agricultural systems, particularly in the chicken market, have generated several critical problems among the growers. Violations in production, processing, illegal use of arsenic in chicken feed, and slipshod inspection of the fowl are some of the points examined. Threats upon the lives of federal inspectors to pass diseased or contaminated chickens are revealed. Secretary of Agriculture Butz disclaims such allegations in a filmed interview. p. ABC-TV; MACMFL; UIL.

FOOD LABELING: UNDERSTANDING WHAT YOU EAT (11m C 1973)

By examining the process of labeling foods, this film raises some fundamental questions concerning nutrition. How can you know what you are eating? What should you be looking for in a given product, and how can a label help you find it? Explains that our reasons for eating go beyond nutrition and satisfaction of hunger, and shows how certain factors such as cultural background, group pressure, convenience and advertising influence our eating habits. p. Gilbert Altschul Productions; JOURVI; UIL.

FOOD: MORE FOR YOUR MONEY (14m C 1974)
When two detectives decide to enter a contest sponsored by a local newspaper on "how to get the most food for your money," they welcome the help of Sandy, a checker at the local market. Sandy advises all consumers to start with a shopping list, avoid impulse buying, use coupons, compare and evaluate both price and quality. She also warns about the additional expense of convenience foods. HIGGIN; UIL.

FOOD PREPARATION (2nd ed.) (15m C 1978)
A thorough introduction to the art of planning and preparation of delicious and nutritious meals. The film begins with an emphasis on value-conscious shopping for food and cooking utensils. It develops the practice of menu planning and the need to follow specific recipes. It demonstrates the methods of cooking each of the various food groups. Finally, it shows that the fundamentals of food preparation can be mastered. JOURVI; UIL, UMO.

FOOD SHOW, THE (47m C r1980)
Combining documentary techniques, dramatic sketches, and animation, the film provides solid information on reading and understanding labels, how to select foods for nutritional value, fact and fiction in advertising, the pros and cons of fast foods. p. Consumers Union Film Library; FI.

FOOD: SURVIVING THE CHEMICAL FEAST (17m C 1975) Coping with Tomorrow Series
Dr. Ann Noble, Robert Choate, and other specialists discuss their particular visions of the future of food, and some promising current projects are shown in action. Explains that increasing food requirements and decreasing acreage for agriculture and livestock may make necessary fish farms, food concentrates, and new sources of nutrients. The move to organic foods is likely to accelerate as more and more chemical fertilizers, pesticides, additives, and processes pollute and dilute the foods we eat. p. Hobel Leiterman Productions/Document Associates; PARACO; UIL.

FOOD--THE INSIDE STORY: NUTRITION AND THE HUMAN BODY (21m C p1980, r1980)
This film takes a close look at nutrition and the human body, focusing on food and its role in maintaining health. Follows food and nutrients through several body processes and shows how food is used for cells, energy and building and repair. It's a straightforward, clearly illustrated look at the science of nutrition. d. Tina Engleman; p. Tony Peters; TUPPRH.

FOODS: FADS AND FACTS (18m C 1973)
This informative film promotes good nutrition derived from fruit, vegetables, meat, grain and dairy products (not necessarily obtainable at a health foods store). The claim that organically grown food

is better than that grown commercially has been attacked by agricultural scientists. They have proved that there is no such thing as organic fertilizing and that without dependable, properly balanced fertilizers, it would be impossible to grow sufficient foods to meet human needs. Pesticides, processed foods and additives are also examined, and the beneficial uses of each are explained. HIGGIN; UIL.

FOOTBINDING (6m B 1978) (Video)
A reenactment of the ancient footbinding ritual is combined with historical stills and contemporary documentary footage to provide a comprehensive view of the dynamics which force women to accept male-defined standards of beauty. p. Laurie Meeker; MEDIAP.

FOR BETTER, FOR WORSE (25m B 1967)
The problems of teenage marriage are illustrated by an evening in the life of a young couple, parents of a baby. Contrasts the realities of their married life with the romanticism and freedom of courtship (flashbacks) and with the glamorous "happily ever after" marriage which they see in a movie newsreel. No narration, very little dialogue, permitting a wide range of interpretation and reaction. PARACO; UNEV, UMO.

FOR COLORED MEN WHO'VE HAD ENUF! (5m B 1981)
Though the film is narrative from a subjective point of view, it is also a metaphor, reflecting the consciousness of black men who have been rejected in relationships. d./p. Ilene Sands; CCC.

FOR OLD AND YOUNG ALIKE (25m C 1981) (Video)
A portrait of Boulder, Colorado's poet laureate, Florence Becker Lennon, in her 86th year as political activist, author and writer, children's poetry workshop organizer, and humanitarian. We see Florence conducting poetry workshops, speaking at International Women's Week, and her scrapbooks of 85 years. Florence, with her history, quips and anecdotes, revitalizes the child within all of us. d./p. Ron Taylor; TAYLORR.

FOR OUR CHILDREN (24m C 1981) (Video)
A narrative documentary examining the psychological effects two years after the Three Mile Island accident. Presents on-location interviews with area residents and authorities on nuclear regulation and psychological stress. p. Arna Susan Vodenos; p. A.F. Enterprises; RADIM.

FOR PARENTS ONLY: WHAT KIDS THINK ABOUT MARIJUANA (28m C p1979, r1980)
Seeks to alert parents to the reality of drug use by children. Candid interviews with 13- to 17-year-olds in three different cities provide a unique look at the use of marijuana by young people. Forthright about their use, how they pay for it and how it influences

their school, social and family lives, these young people represent a growing number of adolescents who are regularly using large amounts of marijuana and who usually are not aware of its effects on their lives. d. Lee Bobker; p. Vision Associates; p. Mary Carol Kelly; MTPS.

FOR THE LOVE OF AN EAGLE (22m C 1982--U.S.) (also Video)
Presents Jeanne Cowden, a courageous ornithologist, and her lonely five-month vigil with a Black Eagle family in South Africa's rugged, barren cliffs. Her work over those months is photographed in detail. p. Free to Live Productions, Toronto, Canada; LUCERNE.

FOR THE SPIDER WOMAN (16m C si n.d.)
Jane Comfort in a short solo repeated at various times during her pregnancy. p. Dance Film Archive; DAN/UR.

FOR TOMORROW ... AND TOMORROW (18m C 1971)
Uses brief sketches of the lives of five widows in the United States, Canada and England to point out the problems of widows and the solution of those problems. p. Sun Life Assurance Company of Canada; SLACC.

FORBIDDEN WOMEN: PAINTINGS BY PAUL DELVAUX, THE (18m C 1970) (Video)
As the camera moves across details of Delvaux's Surrealist paintings, many of the recurring themes and psychological undertones of his work are brought into focus. Memories and objects from the artist's childhood fill his canvases, giving the viewer a unique blend of Realism and Surrealism. Delvaux's paintings show the Elysian Field of Woman.... Women who do not see or hear each other, their eyes turned to the interior world, far away in time.... Women dressed in feathers, flowers, ribbons, jewels.... Women forever forbidden. IFB.

FOREVER YOUNG (58m C p1980, r1980)
Presents a positive point of view as it takes the stigma off of growing older. Academy Award winning director Robin Lehman goes to the true experts on aging--the generation over 65, and dispels many of the fears and prejudices normally associated with growing old. The 26 subjects of this film range in age from 66 to 100 and in participation from skydiving to beekeeping. Their excitement, their candor, and their wit are treasures to behold. Recommended by the White House Conference on Aging. d./p. Robin Lehman; LCA; PAS, UCEMC.

FORTINI/CANI (86m C 1977) (Italian/Subtitled)
This is the filmmakers' third film dealing with anticonventional trilogy on Zionism, here using Franco Fortini's text The Dogs of Sinai. d. Jean-Marie Straub, Daniele Huillet; NYF.

FORTNIGHT AT NINE FATHOMS, A (14m C 1970)
A research report on a part of the Tektile II Program in which five pioneering women aquanauts lived and worked for two weeks underwater ... studying sea water chemistry ... reef ecology and pollution ... and marine animal behavior. p. Hearst Metrotone News; KINGF.

FOUR ARTISTS, LIVE SERIES see ANTON RASMUSSEN, PAINTER: ABSTRACTIONS FROM NATURE; V. DOUGLAS SNOW, PAINTER: THE CONTEMPORARY LANDSCAPE

FOUR CHAIRS, SPINS (30m B 1975) (Video)
"Four Chairs" with Jennifer Muller. "Spins" with Jacqueline Smith-Lee. Choreographer/p. Doris Chase; CHASED.

FOUR JOURNEYS INTO MYSTIC TIME (52m B 1978)
Four individual, visually distinct dance films combining the pure form of dance with the surreal and experimental interplay of film. "Mysterium" explores the dynamics of the union of masculine and feminine. "Initiation" examines the mystery of ancient rites. In "Trance" a dancer, through video electronics, attempts to create the aura surrounding a soul in transition. "One-Two-Three" is a comic waltz. "One-Two-Three" received an honors award at the 1979 Dance Video and Film Festival. Dance Company: UCLA Dance Company; Choreographer: Marian Scott; d. Shirley Clarke; p. Shirley Clarke, Marian Scott; p. Spiral Productions; SPIRAL.

FOUR WOMEN ARTISTS (25m C p1977, r1978)
Presents a documentary of four Mississippi women artists. Shows them informally discussing their lives, careers, and art as they display portions of their works. Eudora Welty, the Pulitzer prize-winning novelist, also a photographer, shows some of her photographs and reads a brief selection from her works. Pecolia Warner tells how she learned to quilt and explains the process of harmonizing colors and materials to effect a balanced finished product. Ethel Mohammed discusses the importance that her family and home played in creating her embroidered pictures and how each "stitch picture" is a permanent document of an important event in her life. Theora Hamblett paints her "visions" which some people consider "weird" but she says they are very real and true to life to her. p. Judy Peiser for Center for Southern Folklore; d. Bill Ferris; SOFOLK; PAS.

FOUR WOMEN: BREAST CANCER (55m C p1978, r1979)
Examines the physical and psychological effects of surgery. This is the personal story of four women with breast cancer who underwent mastectomy. They and their families speak about their fears, uncertainties and the kinds of adjustments they had to make. A remarkable testimony to the ability of people to find strength and comfort in crisis. d. John Kastner; p. Ron Haggart, Brian Denike, CBD; FILMLB; PAS, UMN.

FOUR WOMEN OVER 80 (10m C 1979)
Four older women who demonstrate successful responses to aging through physical activity, continuing education, social involvement, and gainful employment. These women have found fulfilling life-styles even after the aging process forced them to modify their activities. p. Greenberg and O'Hearn Productions; MTITI; UCEMC, WSU.

FOUR WOMEN OVER 40 (10m C p1979, r1979)
Shows four older women demonstrate successful responses to aging through physical activity, continuing education, social involvement and gainful employment. A film with positive role models emphasizing the importance of physical and mental activity at all ages. p. Greenberg and O'Hearn Productions. MTITI.

FOUR YOUNG WOMEN: A FILM ABOUT ABORTION (20m C 1973)
Presents four situations in which women decide to have abortions for very different reasons. Focuses upon the people involved and lets them speak for themselves. Liz and Rob, unmarried college students, were not emotionally and financially prepared to raise a child. Patsy discovered too late she was not compatible with the expected baby's father, broke off the relationship and had an abortion. Mary and Steve were married and already had a five-month-old baby when Mary became pregnant again. Vicki, a high school student, was supported by her mother in the decision to have an abortion. In the film epilogue, Dr. Sadja Goldsmith provides a concise explanation of the medical abortion procedure and ends with the comment about the importance of effective contraception. p. Leonard Schwartz/Variation Films; PEREN; UIL.

"14 AMERICANS: DIRECTIONS OF THE 1970'S" (90m C p1979-80, r1980) (also Video)
Explores the multifaceted art scene in the last decade. Raises important issues about the nature and function of contemporary art. Six women and eight men, members of the New York art scene, comment about their work and exhibit some examples. Good enrichment material for students in art and art appreciation classes. p./d. Nancy Rosen, Michael Blackwood; BLACKW.

FRAGILE MOUNTAIN, THE (55m C 1982)
Describes the lives of the mountain people of Nepal as they struggle to survive in a collapsing environment. As they farm their terraces and cut trees for fuel, the monsoon rains sweep whole mountain sides away and flood valleys far below. The Nepali people know what's happening, and they show a tenacious courage in their attempts to build a stable future on the fragile mountains. d./p. Sandra Nichols; s.w. Carol Mon Pere; ed. David Gladwell; orig. music: Ed Bogas; NICHOLSS.

FRAGMENTS: MAT/GLASS (19m B 1976) (Video)
Two tapes from the 1975 video event performed in New York City.

The selections, MAT DANCE and WATER DANCE, are intended to be shown synchronously. They feature dancer Ben Dolphin. The video cameras of Richard Leacock and Ann McIntosh capture subtleties of the dancer's skills invisible to the naked eye. p. Amy Greenfield; EXPIF.

FRAME LOOMS (11m C p1977, r1977)
Erika Semler shows how to use simple frames as looms to create woven decorations and squares of fabric. Illustrates use of shed stick, needle, netting shuttle and comb. d. John Gray; p. Ken Widdowson; CENTEF.

FRANCESCA BABY (46m C 1976) Afterschool Specials Series
Deals with the impact of alcoholism in the family. Francesca James is 16 years old and her mother is an alcoholic whose problem is pulling the family apart. Through a series of events, Francesca discovers that there is help to be found, people who care. Designed to stimulate discussion about the physical, social and emotional effects of alcohol and alcoholism. Based on the novel by Joan Oppenheimer. p. Martin Tahse; Walt Disney Productions; DISNEY; UIL, UM, UMN, UMO, WSU.

FRANKENTHALER--TOWARD A NEW CLIMATE (30m C 1977) The Originals: Women in Art Series
Traces the background and evolution of the work of American artist Helen Frankenthaler, from the forceful color and form in her pioneering early "stain paintings" to the controlled strength of her most recent canvases. Shows her working, captures her personality, and relates her work to her life. d./p. Perry Miller Adato, p. WNET-TV; FI; PAS, UM, UMO.

FRANK FILM (9m C 1973)
Presents 11,592 separate shots of common objects that either appear alone or in repetition, primarily forming complex, rapidly moving patterns accompanied by two continuous narrative sound tracks played simultaneously. Created by Frank Mouris, p. Caroline Ahlfours Mouris; DIRECT.

FRANK LLOYD WRIGHT'S FALLINGWATER (23m C p1973, r1977)
American Life-Style--Cultural Leaders Series
Presents the life and career of a creative architectural genius, Frank Lloyd Wright. One of the greatest statements of Wright's architectural thought was Fallingwater in western Pennsylvania. Fallingwater, now open to the public, points out the ways Wright's unique ideas helped to blend the house to its environment and maintain a feeling of openness within closed space. p. Ann Zane Shanks. p. Comco Productions; PARACO.

FRAUD? YOU LOSE! (34m C 1973) Community Protection Series
A film to educate the public about fraud and thereby cut down

on the chances of fraudulent businessmen, confidence men and fraud
artists being successful. Experts discuss the problem and give advice. Dramatized incidents include charity frauds, phoney contests,
the professional con man, hearse chasers, bait-and-switch operations,
home repair frauds, phoney warranties, door-to-door pitches, child
model schemes, social and date clubs. p. Summerhill Productions;
PARACO.

FREE MOVEMENT EXPRESSION (12m C 1957)
    Dancers individually and in a group, through improvisation, show
qualities of movement and forms of personal expression. Dance Company: Barbara Mettler Dance Group; Narrator/Dance Teacher/d.
Barbara Mettler; p. Will Carbo; METTLER.

FREE VOICE OF LABOR: THE JEWISH ANARCHISTS (55m C 1980)
    Eastern European Jews fleeing oppression in the late nineteenth
century immigrated to the United States only to find sweatshop conditions as appalling as those they had left behind. Revolted by
American materialism, these idealists became anarchists, forming a
counterculture that would last until the echoes of the Yiddish language and culture fade away. This film documents their history and
philosophy, told in the words of surviving anarchists and interpreted
by historian Paul Avrick. Interviews by the filmmakers Steven Fisch-
ler and Joel Sucher blend with historic footage of Ellis Island immigrants, vintage Yiddish feature films, and soulful Yiddish songs and
poems heard over period headlines and photographs. Ahrne Thorne,
last editor of Free Voice of Labor (1870-1977) speaks of the newspaper's role in relieving sweatshop conditions and perpetuating Yiddish
literature, drama, and culture. Thorne and others explain how these
anarchists were dedicated to a society of voluntary cooperation and
opposed to what they viewed as the twin repressions of the state
and religion. d./p. Steven Fischler/Joel Sucher; CINGLD.

FREEDOM OF CHOICE (18m C p1982, r1983)
    Using a variety of locations, various recreational activities are
profiled to encourage the disabled to participate in recreational pursuits. The role of the recreational service providers, both volunteer
and professional, are shown as a positive force aiding in the integration process, as the disabled and the general public come together in
a recreational environment. d. Helene B. White; p. G. S. Toth/W.
L. Campbell; Sponsor: City of Calgary; CALGARY.

FREEDOM TO DEFINE MYSELF (14m C n.d.)
    The concepts of "mainstreaming" and "barrier-free access" for
the disabled in our education, business and social structure are explored in this film. The camera follows Judy Taylor, a quadriplegic
since the age of eight, as she manages her busy day as director of
the Handicapper Program at Michigan State University. We observe
Judy in her office as she works on plans and issues of importance to
the handicapped. We observe her in leisure, see some of her

paintings, and watch her participation in sports. Judy's goal is the objective of bringing new opportunities to all handicapped people everywhere. Judy discusses with the filmmaker the critical need to improve the public's image of the disabled, and the need to help the public rid themselves of misconceptions and preconceived, often negative, ideas about those with handicaps. A very positive film. p. Elizabeth C. Kay Camp; ARNPRO.

FREEZE, THE (25m C 1983) (Video)
Robert McNamara, Paul Wamke, Rear Admiral (Ret.) Gene R. LaRoque, Dr. Jack Geiger, Dr. Herbert Scoville, Jr. and Dr. Helen Caldicott are among the notable speakers to present detailed information and balanced viewpoints on the nuclear arms race, including excerpts from five award-winning films on the nuclear disarmament issue. p. Barbara Zheutlin; DIRECT.

FRENCH LIEUTENANT'S WOMAN, THE (124m C 1981)
A classic Victorian love story and an ironic look at the double-standard morality. Meryl Streep plays Sarah Woodruff in this film based on the best-selling novel by John Fowles. Sarah Woodruff's chance meeting with Charles Smithson (Jeremy Irons), a young man-about-town who subsequently discards his pretty young fiancée in a wave of passion, sets into motion a series of events that disrupts the quiet fishing and seaside village in England and profoundly affects the lives of its residents. d. Karel Reisz; UAS.

FRENCH PROVINCIAL (95m C 1955) (French/Subtitled)
A novelistic family saga whose central character is Berthe, played by Jeanne Moreau. Berthe's rise to power begins when she becomes mistress, then wife of one of the three sons of the old Spanish immigrant Pedret, whose factory dominates the small town. Berthe gradually asserts herself in the family; the patriarchy of Pedret gives way to matriarchy of Berthe. d. André Techine; NYF.

FROGGIE WENT A-COURTIN' (8½m C p1980, r1981) (also Video)
The film opens with a group of small children clustered around a folk singer-guitarist. They are singing about the adventures of the beloved amorous Froggie. As the song continues, the picture dissolves to Froggie--a young child dressed in tights, a ruffled shirt and hat with feather. The drama begins. In full costume, with props they made themselves, the children act out the entire song in mime. The cast is ethnically mixed and includes handicapped children in key roles. p./d. Wendy Hershey; BARRF.

FROM HARLEM TO HARVARD (28½m C 1982)
A documentary about George who is 18, black and the first person from his high school to go to Harvard. He attempts to reconcile personal dreams with extreme academic and social pressures and his interactions with three precocious roommates from different backgrounds. Combines verité footage with pointed interviews. Reveals

much about the issue of minorities in upper-class educational institutions. p. Carole Markin, David Gifford, David Lewis, Marco Williams;
LEWISDC.

FROM OUT OF THE ASHES (30m C p1981, r1983)
   This historical documentary was shot on location in Israel during
the World Gathering of Holocaust Survivors during June 1981. Itka
Zygmuntovich, a survivor of Auschwitz, discovers Joshua Kalfas, an
old friend from her home town. In a remarkable reunion, Itka tells
Joshua how she and her mother were tortured in an effort to save his
father's life. d. Ruth Lefkowitz; ed. Ruth Lefkowitz; PHOENIX.

FROM SOCIABLE SIX TO NOISY NINE (21m C 1954)
   The film looks into the meaning of various forms of conduct in
children from six to nine years old and suggests ways in which parents
may guide them through a challenging, often trying, phase of development. In a family with three children we observe how the parents cope with situations that often baffle grown-ups. d. Judith
Crawley; NFBC.

FROM SPIKES TO SPINDLES (50m C 1976)
   A somewhat schizophrenic production which aims to strengthen
the Chinese-American image outside of and within the Chinese-
American community today. Of relevance here because it touches
not only on the historic brutalization of coolie labor during the Western expansion of the United States, but also on the growing numbers
of Chinese-American women now employed in New York City's garment
factories, where they are apparently the major immigrant group.
Smashes the Chinese-American stereotype of passivity by including
anti-discrimination protest and job marches, unionizing and better
wage discussions, and talk of the spread of the garment and other
light industry within New York's Chinatown. d. Christine Choy for
Third World Newsreel; TWN.

FROM TEN TO TWELVE (25m B/C 1957)
   Quite far removed from infancy, yet not across the threshold of
adolescence, children aged 10 to 12 present an absorbing study of
adults-in-the-making. We watch the children of one family in various
situations in the home, at school and in group play, and find that
much of their conflicting behavior is actually a normal part of the
growing-up process. d. Edmund Reid; p. Judith Crawley; NFBC.

FROM THE ASHES ... NICARAGUA TODAY (59m C 1981)
   Shows how a revolution transformed a country and gave a new
dimension to daily life for a shoemaker and his close-knit family.
Also documents the importance of the United States in Nicaraguan
history, and shows how United States foreign policy continues to
play an influential role in Nicaragua today. A rare opportunity for
people in the United States to see a revolutionary crisis in a Latin
American country through the eyes of the people who are living it.

d. Helena Solberg Ladd; p. Helena Solberg Ladd/Glen Silber; p. International Women's Film Project; DOCUA.

FROM THE CLOUD TO THE RESISTANCE (105m C 1979) (Italian/Subtitled)
The filmmakers have chosen two unrelated texts by Cesare Pavese to make this film. In the first, "Dialogues with Leuco," mythological characters like Oedipus and Tiresias argue about the fate of man at the hands of gods, concluding that justice must be sought by man among men. The second part, "The Moon and the Bonfires," provides a historical context: a man returns to his hometown after the war to face the same questions and the same despair, a realization made all the more poignant by the Arcadian setting of these Italian hills. d. Jean-Marie Straub/Daniele Huillet; NYF.

FROM THE FIRST PEOPLE (45m C 1976) Alaska Native Heritage Series
A community-produced film about the Eskimo village of Shungnak. Documents early winter subsistence activities, following one family as they harvest fish, and captures the community's ambivalence towards the changes taking place in their culture. p. Sarah Elder, Leonard Kamerling; DER.

FROM THE HEART (58m C p1982, r1983) (Video)
Explores twentieth-century art portraying the feminine attitude and demonstrating the strength of women artists in America. Fosters a deeper understanding of the art by acquainting the viewer with nine artists--Lynda Benglis, Nancy Chambers, Clyde Connell, Janet Fish, Hermine Ford, Dorothy Hood, Mary McCleary, Gael Stack and Dee Wolff. The artists provide the dialogue, which ranges from family background to philosophy of art, to self-criticism and success. d. Nancy Schreiber; p. Carolyn Schroeder; s.w. Victoria Trostle; ed. Lisa Jackson; GIHON.

FROM THE MOUNTAINS TO THE BUNKER (40m C 1981)
The filmmakers accompany the supply unit bringing medicine, weapons, and ammunition to a guerrilla camp in the homeland of A.C. Sandino, the father of the Nicaraguan Revolution, who fought the United States Marines in 1933. In the camp the film documents the everyday life, democratic structure of command, training and education, history of philosophy of the Sandinistas. Scenes cover the last press conference of Somoza, the escape of the dictator and the occupation of his bunker on July 19, 1979. p./d. Christine Piotter, German Tellez; SUNDMN.

FRONTIER WOMAN, THE (36m B si 1923)
To portray the sacrifices of the women of the frontier and the part played by them in the making of our nation, this film recreates the story of the settlement of Watauga in the Tennessee mountains in 1780. Cornwallis had sent Ferguson to destroy the power of the

frontier patriots. John Sevier and his mountain men set out from
Watauga to oppose him. The women of the settlement, left with the
old men and boys, refuse to recall their warriors in the face of an
impending Indian attack. Sevier defeats Ferguson at King's Mountain, the turning point of the Revolution in the West. On their return several of the men are killed by Cherokees. The joy of the
Watauga women is turned to grief. After but two hours at home Sevier and his mountain men again swing into their saddles, determined
to remove forever the menace of the Indians. YALEU; UMN.

FULFILLMENT OF HUMAN POTENTIAL (18m C p1979, r1979)
    Live classroom sequences illustrate the process of teacher sensi-
tization to the handicapped child for teaching science and art to deaf,
blind, and emotionally disturbed children in a mainstream setting.
d./p. Dr. Doris E. Hadary; CRM.

FULL MOON LUNCH (57m C 1977--ed. rel.)
    Tells of the Sugiura family and their very successful catering
service. Mr. Sugiura was a chef for a Japanese admiral during
World War II. When he came back to Tokyo, he changed the family
business from a fish store to producing box lunches in the Japanese
tradition that are surpassingly attractive, and no doubt as appetizing.
The film conveys a wealth of information about the Sugiura family and
their country. p./d. John Nathan; JAPANS.

FUN WITH DAD (29m C 1978)
    Depicts various activities shared by children and fathers: think-
ing game for waiting in the clinic; comparing footprints at the beach;
sick-at-home activities--play dough, macaroni jewelry and printing;
parent/infant interaction; growing a kitchen garden; dealing with
fear of the water; a sampling of self-help experiences; helping grandma. p. WTTW-TV; PEREN.

FUNDI: THE STORY OF ELLA BAKER (63m C 1981) (Video)
    Fundi, a Swahili word meaning "master of a craft," describes
Ella Baker's involvement in the civil rights struggle over several
decades--as field secretary and president of the New York chapter
of the NAACP in the early 1940's and as first director of the Southern
Christian Leadership Conference in the 1950's (a position she resigned
in 1960 to work more directly with students). Her mission was to
enlighten, nurture, and motivate students toward nonviolent action.
Baker was also instrumental in the recruitment of churches and ministers into the movement in the early 1960's. This documentary is
also the story of SNCC (Student Non-Violent Coordinating Committee),
the Mississippi Freedom Democratic Party, and the Voting Rights Conference of 1960 which resulted in voter registration of southern blacks.
Actual film footage of voter registration in Jackson, Mississippi; the
bus boycott in Birmingham, Alabama; scenes of early civil rights
demonstrations; and appearances of veteran civil rights activists
such as James Foreman, Julian Bond, Stokely Carmichael, and Vincent
Harding are shown. d./p. Joanne Grant; NEWDAY.

FURI ZUTSUMI (9m C 1966)
A classical Japanese dance performed by a young woman in tra-
ditional costume, accompanied by Japanese music on the samisen.
The music is performed by Shofuku Kineya and Fukusuzu Okawa.
No narration. Dancer: Shizuko Inbe; d./p. William Kay; RADIM.

FURIES (3m C 1977)
Petty employs charchoal and pastels to create Cubist and Art
Deco-inspired designs which evoke the grace and beauty of two cats
in constant motion. The feline romp is set to Ned Rorem's "Trio for
Flute, Cello, and Piano." p. Sara Petty; SERBC.

FUTURES FOR WOMEN IN SCIENCE (88m C 1979) (Video) Women in
Science Series
Features an interdisciplinary panel of women scientists at the
"Futures in Science for Women" conference at Washington State University in Pullman, Washington. Shows the panel discussing their
work and their lives in Parts I and II. The panel answers questions
from the audience of undergraduate women science majors in Part III.
Conference keynote speaker Sally Ride, NASA astronaut, is interviewed in Part IV. p. Kelly Frederickson and KWSU-TV; WSU.

-G-

GAIA'S DREAM (3m C 1981) (Video)
A lively example of direct animation (a process which bypasses
the camera). GAIA'S DREAM is a series of visually pleasing transformations. Starting from lines and circles reminiscent of the sun,
a frolicking horse materializes and evolves into a Pegasus before returning to the sun. The film draws upon the concept of Gaia as the
ancient life force. The soundtrack is a traditional piece of music
from Zimbabwe and its repetitions complement the visual motion of
this cyclical film. p. Rose Bond; MEDIAP.

GALE IS DEAD (37m C 1971)
Gale Parsons is nineteen when she dies of a drug overdose. Her
story unfolds in flashbacks, flitting among the three or four persons
who tried to love this troubled girl. Gale is a very bright child, a
pretty youngster and initially a person with laudable and feasible
ambitions. But, she moves from one institution to the next, and each
stop is a step backward. Her rapid decline and predictable premature
death is a plea for more intensive investigation of the phenomena of
adolescence. TIMLIF; UNEV, KENTSU.

GAMES OF THE XXI OLYMPIAD (117m C 1977)
This official record of the 1976 Montreal Olympics is more than a
gallery of medal-winners. We see Olga Korbut's agony on the side-
lines as Nadia Comaneci effortlessly replaces her as queen of gymnastics, Soviet weightlifter Vaily Alexeev, Bruce Jenner's decathlon

victory, sprinter Sylvio Leonard coping with bitter defeat, Hungary's pentathlon team, and the West German cycling team. p. National Film Board of Canada; NFBC; PAS.

GARDEN METHODS: VEGETABLE GARDENING (15m C 1971)
The progress of a fine home garden is shown in detail, from the planning stages with the seed catalog through the harvest of colorful vegetables. Methods appropriate to each variety and the advantages of home gardening are discussed. p. Double Sixteen Production for Chicago Horticultural Society; PEREN; UIL.

GATHERING DARKNESS, THE see HOLOCAUST

GAY WOMEN SPEAK (15m B 1979)
An intimate discussion among three professional women active in the gay community. They share anecdotes of childhood, careers and many delights of being lesbian women. Non-explicit. p. Laird Sutton, National Sex Forum; MMRC.

GEISHA, A (87m B 1953) (Japanese/Subtitled)
Set amid the alleys and paper-lanterns of the Gion District in Kyoto, the story tells of a young beautiful girl who becomes the protégée of an older geisha. The geisha, no less than Mt. Fuji, is the postcard image of the beauty of traditional Japan, but underneath the trappings, the heroines find the following message: a woman must sell herself to live. A remarkable psychological and social insight into the position of woman vis-à-vis a materialistic society. "Quite simply a masterpiece of the highest order."--George Morris, Take One. d. Kenji Mizoguchi; NYF.

GENDER V (7m C 1977)
An effective teaching film for demonstrating the gender phenomenon of two names, two wardrobes, and two personalities. As a female entertainer lip-synching Charles Asnavour's song "What Makes a Man a Man?" and as a male actor delivering a monologue paraphrased from the Broadway show For Colored Girls Who Have Considered Suicide When the Rainbow Is Enuf, Logan Carter demonstrates the extraordinary degree to which sex-stereotyped behavior bears no relationship to the sex of the genitals. In so doing, he also makes a plea for tolerance of bisexuals and others who do not rigidly fit the stereotypes. This film should be previewed before showing a young audience. p. Focus International Inc.; CWU.

GENETICS AND RECOMBINANT DNA (60m C 1980) (Video) Better Health (Series)
Advances in genetic research have brought recombinant DNA research issues to the attention of the public. Dr. Phillip Leder, chief of the National Cancer Institute's Laboratory of Molecular Genetics gives us a fascinating glimpse into DNA research and its future potential in this presentation. Free loan. p. National Institute of Health; AF.

GEORGE SAND (15m B 1965) (French Dialogue)

Traces the life of George Sand through Nohant. The film deals with her youth in Nohant and then her life in Paris. She returned to Nohant to write her works, forget Musset, install Chopin, and entertain Parisian society. The film takes the form of a frank interview between a young man and George Sand, who is played by Sylvia Monfort. d. J. de Casembroot; p. Court Film Production; FASCEA.

GEORGES OF NEW YORK, THE (52m C 1976) Six American Families Series

The Georges are upwardly mobil black Americans. Bob is a New York City policeman whose tense and often dangerous job has brought material rewards but also a strain on family life. Peggy works as a supervisor for an insurance company. The Georges have successfully reached into the middle class but as blacks they are still painfully aware of second-class citizenship. p. Elinor Bunin Productions; WBCPRO; CAROUF; PAS, UIL, UM, USFL, KENTSU.

GEORGIA O'KEEFFE (60m C r1977) The Originals: Women in Art Series

Sensitive biographical portrait of one of America's major artists, revealing a warm earthy woman full of gaiety, humor, and wisdom. Employs old stills and newsreel footage to trace her life and shows a large selection of her paintings. d. Perry Miller Adato; p. WNET-TV; VIEWFI; KENTSU, UCEMC, UMO, UIL, UM, PAS, UFL, UMN.

GEORGIA SEA ISLAND SINGERS (12m B r1980)

Pure spirituals are sung as they were 100 years ago on St. Simon's, an isolated island off the Georgia coast. Each song is introduced by explanatory titles and is first sung unaccompanied by two men and three women, later with a tambourine, a broom handle on a board, and dancing. p. Bess Lomax; UCEMC.

GERHARDT KNODEL: AN ARTIST AND HIS WORK (13m C p1980, r1981)

Gerhardt Knodel, internationally acclaimed fiber artist, is seen working in his studio. No ordinary weaver, Knodel is interested in massive, woven, architectural sculptures ... shimmering fabrics that seem to clothe the architecture. His samples and models are translated into hundreds of yards of fabric by a group of folk weavers in Kentucky where we see him supervising their work. p. Sue Marx; p. Marx/Handley Productions; LREDF.

GERMAINE GREER'S SYDNEY (25m C 1980)

"This is a city where the poorest people can be millionaires. Where for nothing, practically, you can do the same things that in other countries you have to join select clubs to do, and pay enormous membership fees and qualify in all kinds of obscure ways." Before the publication of her first book, The Female Eunuch, Germaine Greer held teaching positions at the Universities of Sydney and Warwick. Since then, owing to the demands on her time as a writer/broadcaster, Dr. Greer has given up full-time teaching and accepts only lecture tours and visiting fellowships. LCA; UCEMC.

GERONTOLOGY: LEARNING ABOUT AGING (13m C 1979) Aging in
    Our Times Series
    Defines gerontology. Through interviews and on-site observations, the documentary focuses on men and women who are preparing for interesting new jobs with the elderly. It then moves to the laboratories and institutions where skilled and semi-skilled professionals are now working with the aging. STEREF.

GET A JOB (18m C 1978)
    This drama gives an opportunity to see both negative and positive job interviewing techniques. Within each sequence, the attitudes, manners of dress, and degrees of skill exhibited by the actors indicate why that person will or will not be offered a job. An excellent film to be used as an aide in career counseling situations. Highly recommended. p./d./s.w. Hugh Thompson; TRUEP.

GETTING AHEAD: THE ROAD TO SELF-DEVELOPMENT (28m C 1979)
    This motivational documentary includes interviews with a number of successful people who describe the techniques, education and preparation they needed for success in their present positions. An excellent film for programs on employee development, equal opportunity, affirmative action, career development and orientation. p. Roundtable Films, Inc.; RTBL.

GETTING OFF WELFARE (15m C p1980, r1981) (also Video)
    Documents the success of a nonprofit educational corporation in San Antonio, Texas in training divorced and deserted mothers to find jobs in private industry. Notes that the women are highly motivated to escape the humiliation and poverty of welfare, and can be trained in as little as three weeks. p. Jim Jackson for CBS News, from "60 Minutes"; UCEMC, KENTSU, UIL.

GETTING THE FACTS (12m C p1980, r1980) Comprehensive Skills
    Series
    Illustrates to young learners how enjoyment can be increased by reading all facts in a story. Shows how Rosie allows herself to be pulled into the story. It is suggested that, like Rosie, boys and girls remember to sort through the facts, answering the questions who? what? where? when? and how? then disappear into the story to avoid being disturbed. p. Marjorie Bean, Norman Bean; BFA; PHOE-NIX.

GETTING THE JOB DONE (30m C 1981) Professional Skills for Secre-
    taries Series
    Because an organized secretary can assure maximum efficiency in the everyday functions of a business, this course emphasizes the need

for structure and order. Viewers learn how to plan their activities and establish priorities, especially useful when working for multiple bosses. Special time-saving measures, such as keeping "to-do" lists and "blocking out" time for similar activities, are offered. Exercises are given to help secretaries determine their most productive periods of the day. Once these peak periods are identified, participants learn how to schedule their most challenging activities at these times. Leader's manual and participants' handbooks included. TIMLIF.

GIFT OF KATHARINE DREXEL, THE (28m C n.d.)
A profile of Mother Katharine, devout and energetic, who dedicated her inherited wealth to the cause of Native Americans and blacks. She found the Order of Sisters of the Blessed Sacrament to serve this desperate need. Traces events from her early life in a wealthy Philadelphia family to her last illness and death at the age of 96. Also shows how successfully the works she began are continuing today. p. Teleketics Films; TKF; AF.

GILBERTO--SHARK BOY OF THE SEA OF CORTEZ (23m C n.d.)
(also Video)
A true story of a teenager who lives a different life-style. Gilberto lives where his grandfather settled over half a century ago. In Pardito on Mexico's Sea of Cortez, there is no fresh drinking water, electricity, markets, schools, telephones or television. Gilberto's school is the sea, the teachers are his father and his uncle. The large family still honors the philosophy of the founding grandfather: "Live simply, do your work well, be kind to one another, and be friendly to all." Narrated by Charles Kuralt. p. Sarah Dixon, Peter Dixon, Diego Echevemia for CBS News; CAROUF.

GINGER ROGERS (30m C 1978) (Video)
Dick Cavett interviews Ginger Rogers, actress and dancer. p. WNET-TV; FI.

GINGERBREAD MAN, THE (13m C p1979, r1979)
Presents in animation the story of a mischievous gingerbread man. A narrator reads the story of the "gingerbread man," and the characters on the pages come alive and enact the tale. d. Lillan and J. P. Somersaulter; p. Pajon Arts; CORONET.

GIRL FRIENDS see GIRLFRIENDS

GIRL IN A BROKEN MIRROR (55m C 1975)
Follows Karen Hutton, lead ballerina in the first European production of a Sir Arthur Bliss ballet, through rehearsals and performance, as well as a tryout for London Ballet School, showing how the study of ballet has influenced her life both in and out of school. Performers in the ballet are the Ballet Group of the New Park's Girls' School in Leicester, England. p. Thames TV; UIL.

GIRL ON THE EDGE OF TOWN (30m C p1980, r1981)

A story of human growth. A teenage girl becomes pregnant and is faced with the responsibilities this entails. Features Sherry Hursey, Patty Duke Astin, Brad Wilkin, Billy Green Bush. d. Mike Rhodes; p. Ellwood Kieser for Capital Cities Television; CAPCT.

GIRL STUFF (22m C p1982, r1983) (also Video)

Using live action, animation and interviews with girls 11 to 15 years old, this is a film study of feminine hygiene and normal problems associated with growing up. Suggestions on the use of feminine products and ways to prevent vaginal infections are offered. Girls talk about menstruation, normal age of onset, length of cycles, how it is caused and different parts of the female reproductive system. An animated segment suggests the importance of daily bathing during menstruation and sanitary pads and tampons are discussed. d./ed. Barbara Noble; p. Robert Churchill; s.w. Jennifer Pirie; Animation: Diane Franklin; CF.

GIRL WITH THE INCREDIBLE FEELING, THE see ELIZABETH SWADOS--THE GIRL WITH THE INCREDIBLE FEELING

GIRLFRIENDS (86m C 1978)

An in-depth and realistic film which shows women struggling to attain and adjust to complete liberation. They succeed in various ways with differing degrees of success, learning that any free choice by a woman carries inherent limitations. d./p. Claudia Weill; s.w. Vicki Polon; ed. Suzanne Pettit; Warner Bros.; SWA.

GIRLS BEWARE (12m C 1980) (3rd ed.)

Awareness that sexual attacks exist is seen as a responsibility of growing up. Four vignettes show typical situations that can lead to danger; as importantly, it shows how those situations can be avoided. The final vignette points up the most common situation-- danger from someone already well known and trusted. Emphasizes early signs to beware and concludes with the importance of reporting incidents to responsible adults. AIMS; UMN.

GIRLS' DANCES (7m C 1964-65)

Thai girls' dances including "Kasatcho," "Sabumina," "Selung-mo," two round songs and "Amupatsala," from Chieng-Rai Province, Thailand. p. H. Manndorff, F. Scholz, K. Volprecht; p. Institut für den Wissenschaftlichen Film, Göttingen; PAS.

GISELLE (90m B 1964)

A not-too-well-filmed version of the ballet Giselle with Alicia Alonso as Giselle. Her performance when she was in her prime makes the film worthwhile. Dance Company: National Ballet of Cuba; Choreographer: Jean Coralli; d. Enrique Pineda Barnet; ex. p. Raul Canosa; p. Cuban Film Institute; UNIFILM.

GIUSTINA (28m C p1980, r1981) (also Video)
How a young woman learns to not be afraid of standing up for what she believes is right when she publicly challenges her matriarchal grandmother in order to defend the safety of her aunt. d./p. Rachel Feldman; WOMBAT.

GIVE OVER, AIR MY MIND (6m B si 1979) (ed.)
The use of optical printing techniques to achieve dance-like sequenced movements is applied to a narrative of a ritual courtship between a man and a woman. The title is from "On Being Young and Green" by Edna St. Vincent Millay. p. Marcelle Pecot; WMM.

GIVING BIRTH (16m C p1978, r1978)
A documentary study of a woman's labor and delivery at home, assisted by two midwives. Using synchronized sound, the camera explores the qualities of love, pain and joy in the birth experience. d./p. Allen Moore; PICTS.

GIVING BIRTH: FOUR PORTRAITS (60m C 1976) (Video)
Based on the birth experiences of four couples, the film covers the range of choices available in America: the high technology birth, complete with computers, anesthesia and forceps; a home birth with a "Leboyer" delivery; a natural childbirth which eventually becomes a Caesarean section; and a midwife delivery in an innovative maternity center. Includes long, uninterrupted sequences from the pregnancies and births and interviews with each couple; the extraction of a baby with forceps; a newborn in a "Leboyer" bath; a jubilant father after the Caesarean section; and a couple who cry when handed their baby after birth. Dr. Leboyer, interviewed at his home in Paris, makes a plea for the humanization of the birth experience. Included with the portraits are comments by Elizabeth Bind, Dr. Stanley James, and Dr. Margaret Mead--Global Village; p. WNET-TV; UM.

GLADYS KNIGHT AND THE PIPS WITH RAY CHARLES (75m C 1979)
Concert performance of Gladys Knight and the Pips, and Ray Charles. Includes off-stage interviews. p. Home Box Office; TIMLIF.

GLASS CURTAIN (30m C 1980-1983) (Video, Beta, VHS) Concepts
Series
GLASS CURTAIN explores a woman coping with the dimming mind of her mother who suffers from Alzheimer's disease. She struggles between the need to help and its futility. Love and memory render her incapable of letting go. d./p./s.w. Doris Chase, performed by Jennie Ventriss, with music by Katherine Hoover. CHASED.

GLEGHORNS, THE (UNEMPLOYED FATHER) see FAMILY PORTRAIT:
THE GLEGHORNS

GOD'S GRANDEUR (4m C 1976)
This visual interpretation of Gerard Manley Hopkins' poem is

narrated as the camera leads us to contemplate what unfolds before
us: "The world is charged with the grandeur of God." This lyrical
film sings of the earth ... the breath and presence of the Spirit.
Spectacular photography captures the majesty of the earth, sea, the
sky, still life, and contemporary city scenes. Our attention is called
to the ordinary, in an extraordinary way. A truly moving and heart-
warming visual experience. p. Mary Williams, p. St. Francis Productions; TKF.

GOING HOME (28m C p1979-80, r1980)
Explores a common dilemma: how to feed a large family properly
on a low budget. Tom Paige must return home from camp early when
his father loses his job. Tom learns that his poor eating habits are
the result of family patterns and emotional stress, and he helps his
family to change their eating habits and save money. d. Alan Seeger;
p. Yanna Kroyt Brandt, Judy Seeger for New York State Education
Department; Sponsor: United States Department of Agriculture;
NYSED.

GOLD BUG, THE (41m C p1979, r1979) (also Video)
Presents film adaptation of Edgar Allan Poe's famous story.
Shorter version also available. p. Dora Bachrach; d. Robert Fuest;
teleplay by Edward Pomerantz; LCA.

GOLD PIT, THE (23m B p1981, r1982)
Trading in the gold pit of New York's financial futures market
is a high-stakes, high-risk game. This film follows two traders into
the organized chaos of the gold pit. It reveals the competition and
the stress the traders face in the pit and shows how they carry the
intensity of their work into their personal lives. d./p. Pauline Spiegel; MIRROR.

GOLDEN FLEECE, THE (25m C si 1941)
A dance legend depicting a medieval alchemist who dreams that
he is able to extract gold from the earth's elements. Mercury, the
chief element in the process, is portrayed by Hanya Holm. Dance
Company: Hanya Holm and Company; Dancer/Choreographer: Hanya
Holm; d./p. Thomas Bouchard; BOUCHT.

GOLDEN MOUNTAIN ON MOTT STREET, THE (34m C 1968)
Considers the problems of Chinese Americans as they attempt to
identify with a new culture. Presents the history of the Chinese in
America, pointing out how centuries-old ethics and family ties are
breaking in the face of the fast-changing urban life. Discusses the
work of community action groups, teachers, and social workers. p.
WCBS-TV; CAROUF.

GOLDWOOD (21m C 1975)
Goldwood is the search for the early self. A woman describes
the look and feel of her childhood to an artist friend. This story

unfolds through the use of his paintings and live footage of their visit to the site. Nature has reclaimed the land. The adult attempts to reclaim the child. The film evokes the universal feelings of a child in an adult's world and the awareness of self. d. Kathleen Shannon; ex. p. Bob Verrall; NFBC.

GOOD DAY CARE: ONE OUT OF TEN (30m C 1978)
By looking at a variety of day-care centers, the film shows some of the benefits of good day care and suggests the reasons, historical and contemporary, why day care is at the bottom of the educational heap. Through example, it shows how active organization by parents can provide this valuable asset to a child's development. d. Martineau/Rasmussen; p. Good News Productions; RUSMUS.

GOOD GIRL (45m C 1979)
A reenactment of a diary kept by the filmmaker during her 13th year. The cheerful entries reflect her everyday life: proper girls' school, a summer at the Cape, sports, exams, clothes. But the real impact comes from the film's ability to read between the lines--loneliness and self-doubt, since a "good girl" from a middle-class environment did not admit to such emotions. Now, 25 years later, the hidden anxieties and fantasies are subtly brought out into the open. Juxtaposed with the scenes from the past are conversations with today's school girls. The emotions engendered by coming of age are surprisingly similar for both generations: the awkwardness, the yearning for approval, the friendship and rejections, the confusions of body changes. An extraordinary film about adolescence and growing up. p. Phyllis Chinlund; FILMLB.

GOOD WORK, SISTER! (20m C 1982) (Video/slt)
Tells the stories of women who went to work in the shipyards of Portland, Oregon and Vancouver, Washington from 1942-1945. The women talk about their successes and problems, and the context in which skilled shipbuilding jobs were opened, then closed, to women. p. Northwest Women's History Project; MEDIAP.

GOOSE HOLLOW (28m C 1982) (also Video)
Bunker's film looks at a section fo the city of Portland, Goose Hollow, which has a strong neighborhood identity, to see what has united its residents. Changes in the neighborhood, such as the new freeway, which threaten to disrupt this community are examined. A warm tribute to the concept of neighborhood. p. Elizabeth Bunker; MEDIAP.

GORILLA (60m C 1981)
The largest of the great apes--the gorilla--is quietly disappearing from the wilds ... and the world. This special takes a look at the dedicated conservationists, zoo directors, and scientists who are working to assure that these magnificent animals will not fall victim to the ultimate fate--extinction. Also examines the brutal acts of

poachers and the effect encroaching human populations have on these misunderstood and often maligned creatures. d./p. Barbarà Jampel; s.w. B. Jampel; NGS.

GOTTA DANCE (6½m B 1978)
Filmed on location in the studio of Camden Richman, a San Francisco Bay area tap dancer and dance teacher. Shows the dance form itself as well as answering the question, Why tap dance? d./p. Margaret Ganahl; GANAHL.

GRANDMA DIDN'T WAVE BACK (24m C 1982) (Video)
Grandma is the most important person in the world for 11-year-old Debbie. She has taken care of Debbie most of her life. They are constant companions. As senility sets in and gradually worsens, Debbie becomes confused. How can Grandma be fine one minute and be so forgetful the next? There is talk of putting Grandma into a nursing home. Debbie is shocked and angry. No matter what happens Grandma must stay in her familiar surroundings with those she loves most. d./p. Tom Robertson; s.w. Rose Blueed, Don Regensburger; MULTPP.

GRANDMA MOSES (22m C 1950)
A documentary about Grandma Moses, a self-taught artist who began painting in her seventies. An intimate visit, narrated by Archibald MacLeish. p. Jerome Hill, Erica Anderson; Museum of the City of New York, October 29, 1978; MUSNYC; UM.

GRANDMA'S BOTTLE VILLAGE (28½m C 1982)
Grandma Tressa Prisbrey built her first bottle house to hold 17,000 pencils. Now 84, Grandma is a vivacious guide to her brilliant houses crammed with objects scavenged from the country dump. She also sings, jokes with her older sister, and combs through the dump. The interiors of her 15 houses are documented and displayed as vivid examples of twentieth-century folk art. d. Allie Light/Irving Saraf; LISARF.

GRANDMOTHER AND LESLIE (29m C 1978) Look at Me Series
Word game for a long car ride; sorting the groceries; imaginative shadow play between a father and son; home math experiences; infant sibling/grandmother interrelationships; language development through story-telling and puppetry. p. WTTW-TV; PEREN.

"GRANNY'S QUILTS" (16m C 1974)
Mrs. Catherine Scott demonstrates the making of patchwork quilts and shows examples of work she did both as a teenager and in her advanced age. Mrs. Scott describes the proper stitches, fabrics, and tools she uses in making quilts with and without designs, and shows how to create a pattern and use a quilting frame. p. Highlight Productions, Ltd.; HILITP; UIL.

GREAT ANIMAL STORIES SERIES see GREATER SANDHILL CRANE
   STORY, THE; LIFE OF THE BIG HORN SHEEP

GREAT COVER UP, THE (12m C 1978)
   Focuses on clothing as an expression of our most crucial concerns:
sexuality, politics and professional roles, and aesthetics. In live-
action and animation, the film makes a number of witty and original
observations about dress.--About revealing and concealing--from
Adam and Eve to unisex.--About trousers as a revolutionary state-
ment--from the French Revolution to today's People's Republic of
China.--About dress as part of the total design of an age--and the
uncanny resemblance clothes have to the architecture of their time.--
About the dramatic responses clothing has made to war and peace,
intellectual ferment, social upheaval, the industrial age, contraception,
and the generation gap. THE GREAT COVER UP is a look at clothing as a powerful statement about ourselves and our world. p. Henriette Montgomery and Sonja Friedman; TEXFM; CWU.

GREAT EXPECTATIONS (22m C 1976)
   This film on nutrition for pregnant and nursing women portrays
women and infants from a variety of social and ethnic backgrounds
in real-life situations. Valuable information is conveyed by Howard
Jacobson, M.D., former Chairman, Committee on Maternal Nutrition,
Food and Nutrition Board, National Research Council; Eileen Buckley,
R.D., M.P.H., tells about the importance of wise daily food selection; and Maryellen Avery, M.D., pediatrician, talks about the advantages of breastfeeding. Possible solutions to common diet-related
problems of pregnancy and nutrients of special concern to pregnant
and nursing mothers are specifically discussed. Guide-book included.
Awards. p. Jamil Simons, Productions, Inc.; SNUTRE.

GREAT FEATS OF FEET (115m B 1977) (Video)
   A documentary exploring the tradition of jazz and tap dance.
Features the members of the Copasetic Club, who dance and speak
of their lives and their art. Dance numbers are taped in rehearsal,
workshop, and performance. d. Brenda Bufalino. p. Brenda Bufalino
Dancing Theatre; BUFALINO.

GREAT GODDESS, THE (25m B n.d.)
   A child, two youths, a mother and three crones spin spirals,
joining rituals of birth, death, and rebirth. Filmed in Mendocino,
California, where the water snake, a feminine symbol, appeared on
each shooting day, where the river flooded the sand spiral, where
earth, air, and water meet. p. Barbara Hammer; IRIS.

GREAT GRAND MOTHER (29m C 1975, r1978--U.S.)
   Depicts the lives of the pioneer women who settled western Canada
in the 1800's; includes reenactments of diaries, letters, books, and
newspaper accounts, as well as interviews with women who recall

those days. p. Anne Wheeler, Lorna Rasmussen; NFBC; NEWDAY:
UCEMC.

GREAT HORSESHOE CRAB FIELD TRIP, THE (28m C 1982)
    Reveals ways of both learning and teaching as students in a
seventh grade science class from Harlem take a field trip to the
shore. p. Grania Gurievitch/Ann Schaetzel; d. Grania Gurievitch;
sponsor: VIDDA Foundation; TOGGFI.

GREAT PERFORMANCE IN DANCE (29m B 1960) A Time to Dance
    (Series)
    Discusses and illustrates the importance of the dancer as the
creator of a dance and an interplay between choreographer and
dancer. Shows how individual interpretation can vary the effect of
the same choreography by presenting two sets of distinguished dancers performing the same roles from the ballet Le Beau Danube. Uses
rare film clips of outstanding dancers: Anna Pavlova, Irene and
Vernon Castle, and Argentinita. Features Alexander Danilova, Fred-
rick Franklin, and dance critic Walter Terry. NET; IU.

GREAT PRETENDERS: THE NEW FOODS, THE (29m C 1977) (Video)
    Woman Series
    Food expert and author Beatrice Trum Hunter discusses the danger
of saccharin, the appearance of substances such as wood pulp in
"high fiber breads" and "butterless butter" and the nutritive value
of some food substances. Trum Hunter, who wrote Consumer Beware:
Your Food and What's Been Done to It and Food Additives and Federal Policy: The Mirage of Safety, reviews laboratory tests that have
been conducted on artificial sweetners and talks about the increased
use of reconstituted foods. Sandra Elkin is the moderator. p. WNED-
TV; PBSV.

GREATER SANDHILL CRANE STORY, THE (17m C 1980) Great Ani-
    mal Stories Series
    Study of the life history of the Greater Sandhill Crane. Shows
a pair of cranes courting, nesting and rearing their young. Shows
some of the world's rarest cranes being studied by researchers at
Crane Foundation near Baraboo, Wisconsin. Shows how the proper
management and conservation of the wetlands is a crucial point in
the survival of the Greater Sandhill Cranes. p./d. Myrna I. Berlet,
Walter H. Berlet; BERLET.

GREENAWAY (50m C 1982)
    Portrait of an aristocratic American couple living on their own
island (Greenaway Island), exploring wealth and its manifestations
from an "inside" perspective. Old values predominate; the poignant
ending stems from the couple's realization that they are part of a
vanishing breed. p./d. Sue Gilbert; ABRAKA.

GREENBERGS OF CALIFORNIA (58m C 1976) Six American Families
    (Series)

Jackie and Arne Greenberg of California were married in 1960. They bought a showcase home north of the Golden Gate and set out to achieve the American dream of prosperity and happiness. Fifteen years and two children later, they are divorcing. Arne, a lawyer, has moved out and is now a weekend father. Jackie and the children represent a single-parent family. p. Elinor Bunin Productions; WBCPRO; CAROUF; KENTSU, UM, UIL, USFL.

GREETINGS FROM WASHINGTON, D.C. (28m C 1981)
Shows the more than 100,000 lesbians and gay men who marched on the nation's capital on October 14, 1979, to call for their rights. GREETINGS is a moving, often hilarious, vibrant film which combines the highcamp romance of underground gay culture with the on-the-spot vitality of the new non-fiction film. p. Lucy Winer, Greta Schiller, Frances Reid, Robert Epstein; d. L. Winer; IRIS.

GRETA'S GIRLS (18m B 1978)
Presents a day in the life of two young women who are just beginning their relationship together. The paradox of the human experience is conveyed without clichés. Uncertainties about themselves and one another, and the realities of daily existence in a harsh urban environment, counterpoint the deep warmth and affection they feel for each other. p. Greta Schiller, Thomas Seid; music by Diane Davies; WMM.

GRIEVING: SUDDENLY ALONE (26m C 1982) (also Video)
Illustrates the pattern of loss, grief and recovery to help the bereaved understand the pattern of grief and realize they are neither alone, nor unique. A middle-aged woman, Kate, is followed as she goes through the stages of grief over her husband's death to emerge a new person with strengths she did not know she possessed. Kate joins a widow-to-widow support group and shares her feelings and insights with others experiencing the same problems. The narration emphasizes the need for support and understanding from family and friends as the bereaved come to terms dealing with grief. d. Mortro Zarcoff; p. University of California, Division of Cinema-Television in association with the Journey's End Foundation and the Andrus Gerontology Center; CF.

GRIST MILLER (15m C 1976)
By horse and wagon, a local farmer brings a load of corn to be ground at a mill in Stillwater, New Jersey. The mill was renovated in 1844. Not many small farmers grow grain as their ancestors did and, with high taxes, this mill barely manages to survive. The miller likes his independence so he operates and maintains the mill by himself. p. Gay Courter, Phil Courter; PARACO.

GROSSFELD ON GYMNASTICS (30m ? 1972) (Video)
Ms. Grossfeld and Ms. Myslak combine talents and experience to outline the fundamental drills and skills which combine to create

Olympic quality gymnasts. That experience includes Olympic competition three times, 18 National Championships and judging for six major competitions for Grossfeld. NETCHE.

GROUNDSTROKES WITH BILLIE JEAN KING, THE (15m C 1969) On
    Tennis, a Series
Outlines the basic techniques for developing and improving the forehand drive and the backhand drive. Details are broken down into slow motion segments that illustrate Billie Jean King's commentary. Erik van Dillen and Vic Braden assist. FI; UIL.

GROUP DANCE IMPROVISATION (34m C 1977)
Thirty-five students attending the intensive summer course at the Tucson Creative Dance Center under the direction of Barbara Mettler perform on the lawn. Dance Teacher/d. Barbara Mettler; p. Mettler Studios; METTLER.

GROUP OF WOMEN OR WOMEN UNDER BAOBAB, A (5m B p1957-58,
    r1961) (also Video) San Series of John Marshall
Shows Kung women resting, talking and nursing their babies in the shade of the baobab tree. With flies lighting on their arms, faces and lips, the women seem unconcerned as they suckle their young under the baobab tree. Maternal concern is reflected in the women's desire to have the young nurse to the point of contentment, even when it interrupts their own sleep. After a time of rest, they turn to thoughts of subsistence, as one of the women begins grinding grain on a rock. p./d. John Marshall; DER; PAS.

GROW OLD ALONG WITH ME (12m C n.d.)
Two adults, about 60 years old, explore ways to revitalize their marriage after raising their children and grandchildren. p. Constance (Coni) Beeson; BEESON.

GROWING OLD see GROWING OLD: SOMETHING TO LIVE FOR

GROWING OLD IN AMERICA (29m C 1980)
May Sarton, author of the novel As We Are Now, talks with University of Michigan gerontologist Dorothy Coons and sociologist Karen Mason about her experiences in nursing homes while researching her book. They discuss the quality of life in custodial settings and the importance of warmth and caring. Shocked at seeing the power that people have over other people in such places as nursing homes and hospitals, Sarton states that "it's but a short step from degradation to disintegration." UMMRC; UM.

GROWING OLD: SOMETHING TO LIVE FOR (16m C p1977, r1978)
    Developmental Psychology Series
Today, 31 million Americans are over 60 years of age--14 percent of our population. The film examines the general attitudes toward growing old, working versus retiring in old age, and the development

of distinctive housing for aging people. Interviews with Margaret Mead and Gray Panther Lydia Bragger, along with a variety of active working older people, are included. They emphasize the fact that the elderly can be lively, useful members of society if they are allowed to be. p. ABC-TV; CRM; UIL, UCLA, CWU, WSU.

GROWING OLDER: A TIME FOR GROWTH (15m C 1981) (also Video)
Illustrates the wide range of occupational careers that are open to people who may be launching their first occupational career or to the retired person who would like to develop a new skill. The film is directed to anyone who wants to learn a new occupation, find employment, or start a business. It is designed to stimulate a new interest and incentive in the person who needs a new career or extended growth in a present career. Constructive ideas are given to help one realistically assess oneself and possible future job opportunities and then make the decision to take advantage of occupational education and training opportunity. NAVC.

GROWING PAINS: RURAL AMERICA IN THE 1980'S (29m C p1980, r1980)
For one hundred years, Americans were leaving rural areas and moving to the cities in search of a better life. Ten years ago this migration reversed itself with many city people deciding that rural life had more to offer. The film studies rural areas of Tyler (Texas), San Luis Obispo (California), and Plainfield Township (New Hampshire), stressing that by early, positive intervention, people can direct growth in a way that will retain the desirable qualities of rural life for the future. A thought-provoking study of rural America in 1980. p./d. Janet Mendelsohn, Rob Whittlesey; p. The Conservation Foundation; CONSF.

GROWING UP FAST, WHAT EVERY SERVICE PROVIDER SHOULD KNOW ABOUT PARENTHOOD (31m C 1979) (Video)
Through discussion and feedback from service providers and teenage mothers themselves, this tape provides excellent guidelines for designing a program to aid this population, or to add to or improve existing programs. It is also valuable as a general source of information in this social service area. This tape is a valuable tool to those involved with youth in the health/mental health field as it offers a good foundation for providing enlightened choices filled with information to the teenage parents. ex. p. Janet Kahn, p. Joseph Blatt, Adolescent Parent Project, American Institutes for Research; MMRC.

GROWING UP TOGETHER: THREE TEEN MOTHERS AND THEIR BABIES (28m C 1980) (Video, Beta, VHS)
A documentary in three segments featuring three teenage mothers who are raising their children as single parents. There was no script or rehearsal for the film: the young women describe their lives and experiences in their own words. The film is designed to encourage

students, parents, teachers and others to discuss frankly the realities of being a single parent and the development needs of children.
The mothers are Anne, 16; Criss, 16; and Lynn, 19. p. Crommie
and Crommie Productions; PBSV.

GROWING UP YOUNG (22m C p1979, r1980)
Explores the special problems of teenage sexuality and the need
for friendship and approval in the context of the teenager's everyday world. Emphasizes the need to take responsibility for one's own
actions and to make the decisions that are right for oneself. Especially made for teenaged audiences. d. Sally E. Marschall; p. Phillip
Koch; PEREN.

GUESS WHO'S PREGNANT? (60m C 1977) (also Video)
Combines the discussions of a group of sex-education experts
and other professionals with two case studies to center on the subject of pregnancy among unmarried teenagers. Explores possible
corrective measures, which are largely preventive, and their relative
or probable success. Examines the multiple influences of sexual openness in society, public attitudes, and the positions of local and federal government. Concludes with unwanted teenage pregnancies comprise a problem largely unattended and worthy of concern and action.
p. WTTW-TV; IU, UIL.

GUESS WHO'S PREGNANT?--AN UPDATE (59m C 1980) (Video, Beta,
VHS)
Combines segments from the documentary GUESS WHO'S PREG-
NANT? with new materials. This program re-examines the problem in
light of recent trends and revisits many of the experts who participated in the original program to gather current assessments of the
original program. p. WTTW-TV; PBSV.

GUILTY, THE (18m C 1978)
A young, single girl living away from home finds out she is pregnant. She returns home and realizes she must do more than just ask
for forgiveness. p. Brigham Young University; BYU.

GUILTY BY REASON OF RACE (53m C 1972)
Documents the plight of Japanese Americans during World War II,
when fear and prejudice led the United States Government to take
110,000 American citizens of Japanese ancestry away from their homes
and businesses. They were detained in relocation centers by Executive Order 9066 signed by President Franklin Roosevelt. Through
use of old newsreels, and through interviews with some of these Japanese Americans still living today, this report covers the effect this
uprooting had on these people and chronicles their lives in the detention camps where they were held for over three and a half years.
Only after the war, and after many Japanese Americans had served
with distinction in the United States Army, were they permitted to
leave the camps. States that Executive Order 9066 has never been

repealed and could be put into effect again today. p. NBC-TV; FI; UIL, PAS, UMN.

GUILTY MADONNAS (52m C 1981) (also Video)
Women are returning to the work force in ever increasing numbers. Many never left, except for brief maternity leaves. Now, some of these women who are also mothers are feeling guilty about leaving their children and their homes. Some have no other choice; they're the single breadwinner. Some are bored at home with the kids, but are ashamed to admit it. This revealing documentary discusses contemporary studies that show day care centers can have a very positive influence on a child's social and personal adjustment while allowing a mother to pursue her work ambitions ... if she can accept the fact that another person may be qualified to help raise her child. p. KMGH-TV, Denver; CRM; UCEMC.

GURDEEP SINGH BAINS (12m C n.d.)
Gurdeep's family runs a dairy farm in British Columbia. In many ways he is like most other 13 year olds. The difference is that he is a Sikh. His grandparents came from Northern India earlier in this century. Although Gurdeep is kidded about his turban and other practices, he is proud and happy to be who and what he is. d. Beverly Shaffer; p. Yuki Yoshida, Kathleen Shannon; NFBC; MEDIAG.

GWENDOLYN BROOKS (30m B [16mm], C [Video] n.d.)
Features Gwendolyn Brooks reading several of her poems accompanied by scenes of the Chicago environment, the source of material for much of her work. p. Indiana University Radio and Television Services and Afro-American Arts Institute; IU.

GYMNASTICS ... CATHY RIGBY TEACHES (33m C 1977)
Olympic Medal-winner Cathy Rigby demonstrates proper form for the vault, uneven parallel bars, balance beam, and floor exercises. Also shown are film clips of Olga Korbut on the balance beam, Nadia Comaneci on uneven parallel bars, and Nellie Kim performing floor exercises and the vault interspersed with Cathy demonstrating each routine broken down in separate movements. An excellent film for training in gymnastics. p./d. Stanford Blum for the United States Gymnastics Federation Films; BARRF.

-H-

HAD YOU LIVED THEN: LIFE IN A MID-WESTERN SMALL TOWN IN THE 1910's (17m C 1976)
Dramatizes the life of a family in a small midwestern town in the 1910's as a woman reminisces about her childhood. Illustrates the daily events--cooking, washing, school, working at a general store-- which provided the needs of everyday life. Points out the important changes taking place as electrical appliances, the automobile, packaged

goods, ready-made clothes, and other items began to become part of
American life. ACI; AIMS; IU.

HAD YOU LIVED THEN: LIFE IN AN EASTERN SEAPORT TOWN
1870's (16m C 1976)
Re-creates daily life in a New England seaport town by focusing
on Joshua and his family the day before his father and older brother
are due to ship out on a whale hunt that will keep them away from
home for as long as five years. Follows the family around town as
they make last minute preparations, visiting the ship's Chandler, the
General Store, and the Ship Carver's store. Considers the clothing
fashions of the day, navigation instruments, a brief maritime history,
and the lonely existence of the women. ACI; AIMS. IU.

HAIKU (28m B 1966)
Shows a suite of dances based on traditional Japanese poetry,
choreographed and performed by students in the graduate dance curriculum at Teachers College, Columbia University, directed by Jane
Dudley. It combines the study of literature, theatre production,
music and dance. Accompanied by electronic music. d./p. Leo Hur-
witz, Manfred Kirchheimer; p. Columbia University, Center for Mass
Communications; DANCFA; UMN.

HAITIAN SONG (49m C p1980, r1982)
A lyrical portrait of the rituals of daily, weekly and seasonal
life in a small village in rural Haiti. Narrated by a peasant in his
own language (Creole), with songs interwoven throughout. d. Karen
Kramer; KRAMERK.

HANDLING BABYSITTING EMERGENCIES (16m p1979, r1980) Babysitter Series
Teaches babysitters' first-aid procedures and safety precautions.
Stresses the value of participating in a first-aid course to learn the
basic steps to follow in case of intruders, bleeding, choking, poisoning or stoppage of breathing. d. Tom Solari; p. Film Communications;
FILMCO; UMN.

HANDMAIDENS OF GOD, THE (90m C p1979, r1979)
Focuses on a little-known order of nuns devoted to domestic service in the Church. Five hundred and fifty nuns (average age, 60)
belong to the community of Les Petites Soeurs de la Sainte-Famille;
200 must stay in the infirmary. But this is not a house of despair.
They cheerfully accomplish their tasks with a determination that
would defy an army. d. Diane Letourneau; p. Claude Godbout, Marcia Couelle; LIBERTY.

HAPPILY UNMARRIED (23m C 1977)
At 46, Joyce reflects on 20 years of marriage and offers advice
to those experiencing divorce. Joyce and her daughter candidly discuss marriage and single life. d. Lorna Rasmussen; NFBC.

HAPPINESS OF BEING LOVED: PAINTINGS BY FELIX LABISSE,
    THE (12m C n.d.)
    The metamorphosis of Surrealist Woman is illustrated through the
most memorable paintings of Felix Labisse. His models, Claude Bessy
and Jean-Louis Barrault pose in the positions in which they appear in
the extraordinary portraits of them. These and other portraits, as
well as the painters' friends--Lise Deharme, Cesar, Man Ray, Pierre
Seghers, Eugene Ionesco, Patrick Walbert--bring his world, both real
and magical, to the screen. The commentary by Pierre Seghers includes a poem by Paul Eluard as well as comments by Labisse himself. p. Henri Storck; IFB.

HAPPY BIRTHDAY (17m C n.d.)
    This couple decided to have their first child in a home-like hos-
pital setting. Shows the couple as they go through early labor,
transition, and the delivery of the child. The woman delivers in a
sitting position. The father coaches his wife through the difficult
contractions. As he cuts the cord, the father is told that he has
"just assumed full responsibility for his child." p. Cinema Medica;
CINMD.

HAPPY TO BE ME (25m C 1979) (Video)
    A documentary based on a survey of more than 600 students (K-
12) that provides an objective view of young people's attitudes toward gender, or male and female roles. With candid interviews and
spontaneous scenes of young people interacting at school, at play,
and in the community, this film reveals the freshness and vigor of
youthful attitudes and helps create an awareness of one's own assumptions about "maleness" and "femaleness." A good discussion
film on the feminist trend today. Award. MOKINA.

HARD CHOICES SERIES see BOY OR GIRL: SHOULD THE CHOICE
    BE OURS?

HARD WORK (29m C p1977, r1978) (also Video)
    Presents Margot St. James and her fight to decriminalize prosti-
tution. Revolves around the Hooker's Convention in Washington, D.C.
Over a five-day period, the action includes a visit to the Women's Detention Center, TV and press interviews, a congressional cocktail
party, the Hooker's Ball and a peaceful demonstration around the
White House. Raises legal, religious and sociological aspects of this
issue. p. Ginny Durrin, Durrin Films, Inc.; MTITI; UCEMC.

HARRIET (10m C n.d.)
    For most of her life Harriet Kerr was the wife of a minister whose
career was central to both their lives. When they learned of his illness, their first reaction was anger; life had been a struggle and
they were "just beginning to live." After her husband's death, Harriet was still angry--angry at him for leaving her with responsibilities she didn't know how to handle, angry at herself for not being

able to cope, and angry at the church for having taken up so much of his time in their lives together. For a long time she felt withdrawn and depressed and cried easily at small things. She forced herself to cook meals; she began a small quilting business to earn money; she went back to school to try to discover a meaningful vocation for herself. Decisions are forcing Harriet to face the fact that she's now single. Not without difficulty, but Harriet is gradually carving out her new life. p. United Methodist Communications; MMM.

HARRISON'S YUKON (23m C p1979, r1981)
Presents Ted Harrison, painter, and his personal view of the Yukon. Filmed in Whitehorse, Corcross, Tagish and Vancouver, Canada, this film reveals the primitive art of Ted Harrison who developed that bold, nontraditional personal style only after settling in the Yukon in 1968. Ted Harrison is photographed and interviewed as he travels to several areas of the Yukon sketching people and things that interest him and creating deceptively simple paintings of the Yukon and the people. d. Shelah Reljic; p. Peter Jones, National Film Board of Canada; WOMBAT.

HARTMANS, THE (MOTHER RETURNS TO WORK) see FAMILY PORTRAIT: THE HARTMANS

HARVEST COMES HOME, THE (18m C p1977, r1978)
Shows ways consumers can work cooperatively with urban as well as rural neighbors to reduce the market price of farm products. Prices have climbed steadily on produce at the market while the farmer's share of the food dollar has decreased. Recently, a number of alternative marketing plans are becoming popular. In many areas, farmers have established produce stores; others allow customers to harvest their own food in the fields. In urban areas consumers have set up produce cooperatives which buy food in bulk directly from the farm and sell to members at less than market prices. Co-op members work a few hours a month in the stores to eliminate the need for employees. The narrator points out that the consumer gains a sense of community with his/her urban and rural neighbors through such marketing system. d./ed. Kristine Samuelson; p. Whitney Green; p. Cine Manifest Productions; RAMFLM; UM.

HATS, BOTTLES AND BONES (22m C 1977)
A film portrait of the life and work of Sari Dienes, a 79-year-old avant-garde artist who has influenced many areas of the art world since the 1940's. (Museum of the City of New York, October 29, 1978). p. Martha Edelheit; MUSNYC.

HAUNTING OF SEVEN DRAGON AVENUE, THE (23m C p1978, r1978)
Depicts the process new home owners and house builders use to settle conflicts under the Home Owners Warranty System. Demonstrates the conciliation procedures between a new home owner and a home builder. d. Peter E. Wittman; p. Francine Rudine; HOMOWC.

HAVE A HEALTHY BABY: LABOR AND DELIVERY (28m C 1978)
Shares the experiences of two couplies about to have their first child through natural childbirth. Follows both from the onset of false labor through the stages of labor, delivery, and post examinations. Defines and discusses terms associated with childbirth and uses animated diagrams to explain labor. Views the importance of the husband's role during labor and delivery. CF; IU, UIL, UMN.

HAVE A HEALTHY BABY: PREGNANCY (22m C 1978) (rev. ed.)
Depicts, through animation, the growth of the human embryo from conception to term. Warns about possible damaging factors and promotes good nutrition as the single most important thing an expectant mother can do for her child. Interviews expectant parents on their feelings toward the baby and the joys and discomforts of each stage of pregnancy. CF; IU, UIL, KENTSU.

HAVING TWINS (22m C p1978, r1979)
Covers basic information on common problems in caring for newborn twins--feeding, preferring one to another, sibling rivalry, getting help from husband and others, scheduling, the need for getting out of the house, day care, returning to work, and the problems of the single parent. Shows the delivery of fraternal twins with the attending obstetrician explaining what is going on during labor and delivery. A number of parents of young twins share their experiences. p./d. Alvin Fiering; POLYMR; UM.

HAZARDOUS WASTE: WHO BEARS THE COST? (28m C 1981)
Examines Woburn, Massachusetts, America's oldest chemical waste dumpsite, as a case study of an affected community. The impact of the hazardous waste issue is discussed in interviews with public officials, business representatives, and concerned citizens. Proposed solutions, such as Superfund and new technologies for treatment and disposal of toxic chemicals, are explored, as is the need for siting treatment facilities across the country. d. Ann Carol Grossman; p. D. A. Smith/M. Kelsey/A. C. Grossman; EMERSC.

HEAD OVER HEELS (90m C 1979)
John Heard plays a young government worker who is hopelessly and obsessively in love with his ex-girlfriend, played by Mary Beth Hurt. The problem? She is now married to someone else. To make things worse, Heard is deluged with other people's problems. His boss needs advice about a troubled teenage son. His secretary is lonely. His best friend loses his job. His stepfather doesn't know how to help Heard's neurotic suicidal mother. Based on the novel Chilly Scenes of Winter by Anne Beattie. d. Joan Micklin Silver; MGMUAS.

HEALING (57m C p1977, r1978)
This documentary portrait of the late Kathryn Kuhlman explores the question of faith healing. Scenes from her dramatic performance

at the Ottawa Civic Center are interspersed with interviews of articulate professionals that reflect the many sides of the faith-healing issues. d. Pierre Lasry; p. M. McKennirey; NFBC; FILMLB.

HEALING AND WHOLENESS: HOLISTIC HEALTH IN PRACTICE (35m
    C 1978)
    A childhood bout with polio and a football injury sent Bob Keck into a deepening spiral of pain. The doctor's prognosis: permanent confinement to a wheelchair probable. Yet Keck emerged 80 percent triumphant over the unrelenting back pain by learning medical hypnosis. Acupuncture, biofeedback, and other altered states of consciousness were explored by the young minister as he sought a road to physical wholeness. What he learned he is passing on now in a holistic health center set up at his church, First Community Church in Columbus, Ohio. p. Elda Hartley; HARTLEY.

HEALTH AND LIFESTYLE: POSITIVE APPROACHES TO WELL-BEING
    (28m C 1980)
    Profiles people who report a new sense of well-being by changing their life-styles and improving their health. Demonstrates that it's never too late to start this process of self-renewal. p. Spectrum Films; SPECTR.

HEALTH CARE: YOUR MONEY OR YOUR LIFE (60m C 1977) (also
    Video)
    Follows hundreds of patients in two New York hospitals to illustrate the vast differences in health care that money can buy. It is a comprehensive look at America's medical system, exploring the role of government, the health product industry, health insurance and Medicaid, rising costs and shrinking budgets. Health care has become one of our most serious problems. Is health care a right or a privilege? In Part II, a panel of health professions, government officials and consumers from all over the United States explore these issues raised on health care. Proposed solutions ranged from eliminating all government programs to the establishment of socialized medicine. "A devastating commentary on the state of health in urban America ... a piercing study of hospitals and the business of medicine."--The New York Times. p. Keiko Tsuno, Jon Alpert, p. WNET-TV; DOWCTC.

HEALTH CARE OR QUACKERY: HOW CAN YOU TELL? (24m C r1979)
    Acquaints the viewer with common types of health quackery and explains ways to protect oneself and obtain genuine health information. The interviewer talks with people in medical, legal, and consumer areas, and with some victims of unethical practices. HIGGIN; IU.

HEALTH FOOD MOVEMENT, THE (17m C r1973)
    The increasing interest in organically grown and unprocessed foods is seen as a reaction to, first, the possible pollution of foodstuffs by use of agricultural chemicals, and second, to the values of what is seen as an over-consuming and overrefined society. The

movement's basic terms are defined. For example, "organically grown" refers to "food that comes from soil that has not been treated by chemical fertilizers, chemically sprayed or fumigated, or refined after harvest." Activities of three typical health food advocates are used to explain details of the movement. p. Norman Siege; FLMFR.

HEALTH MAINTENANCE AND CARE (11m C 1982)
Assumes that "sick care is costly; health care is cheaper and better." Older people are shown learning about health in the later years, visiting a community geriatric clinic, and taking measures to care for their own health. The Health Maintenance Organization (HMO) and similar programs are discussed along with the need for a national health policy. p. International Center for Social Gerontology, UMMRC; UM, UIL.

HEALTHY MOTHER, HEALTHY BABY (16m C 1975)
Offers valuable advice to pregnant women and teenagers on the importance of good eating habits. HIGGIN; UM, WSU, CORNELL.

HEART ATTACKS (60m C 1980) (Video) Better Health (Series)
Dr. Robert I. Levy, Director of the National Heart, Lung, and Blood Institute, talks about heart attacks and the magnitude of the problem--symptoms, causes, risk factors, treatment and research. He discusses encouraging evidence showing the cardiovascular death rates have decreased due to people's willingness to change diet and life-style. Free loan. p. National Institute of Health; MTPS.

HEART BEAT (15m C 1976)
An interview with Ms. Vija Vetra, who learned Indian dancing, especially "Kathak." INDIACG.

HEARTBREAK TURTLE, THE (58m C p1981, r1982) (Video)
Documentary describing international effort to preserve and protect the endangered Kemp's Ridley Sea Turtle. Videotaped on location in Mexico and the Texas Gulf Coast. Includes rare film shot in 1947 depicting 40,000 adult turtles on a Mexican beach, also unique new video of turtles laying eggs, interviews with recognized scientists in the field of sea turtle biology. d. Bruce Aleksander; p. Miriam Korshak; sponsor: Pel-Tex Oil Co.; s.w. Miriam Korshak; ed. Bruce Aleksander; KUHTTV.

HELEN FRANKENTHALER (28m C n.d.) The Originals: Women in Art Series
Profile of an artist who invented the "stained canvas" at the age of 24. p. Perry Miller Adato; FI; UMO.

HELEN HARDIN: see AMERICAN INDIAN; ARTISTS: HELEN HARDIN

HELEN HAYES AND MILLIE see OLD FRIENDS ... NEW FRIENDS ... HELEN HAYES AND MILLIE

HELEN KELLER CENTENNIAL (1m C p1980, r1980) (Video)
Celebrates one of history's most courageous women in her centennial year, combining graphic animation and voice-over from Miss Keller's inspirational writings. d. Harvey Bellin; p. Global Concepts; MTPS.

HELEN KELLER: THE LIGHT OF FAITH (30m C n.d.)
Although deaf and blind from early childhood, Helen Keller became a legend of our times. Produced by CBS-TV as part of the series "For Our Time," this feature salutes the centennial of her birth. Emphasis is on the part her faith (she was a Swedenborgian) had on her many accomplishments as a scholar, humanitarian and philosopher. Discussion guide available. Free loan. p. Swedenborg Foundation; MTPS.

HELEN McGEHEE TEACHES A DANCE STUDY (30m B 1974)
Helen McGehee shows students a dance sequence, assisted by three other dancers, then breaks it down. Dancer/Choreographer/Teacher: Helen McGehee; UMANA.

HELEN: QUEEN OF THE NAUTCH GIRLS (30m C/B r1973)
A behind-the-scenes and on-stage profile of the Indian movie goddess Helen. "Nautch" is an old Anglo-Indian word for professional dancing. Watching Helen sing and dance will stimulate discussion about how the mass media reveal extravagant fantasies. d. Anthony Korner; p. Ismail Merchant, Ivory Productions; NYF.

HELLO IN THERE (21m C n.d.)
A lonely widow creates imaginative ways to escape the monotony of retirement home living. p. Teleketics, Franciscan Communications Center; TKF.

HELP! I'M A NEW PARENT (24m C 1979)
Shows three young couples expecting their first child expressing rather naive expectations of what the baby will mean in their lives. Comment from the same couples following the births of their babies reveal new-found realizations of the heavy responsibilities involved in being a parent. An excellent realistic look at what being a parent really involves, especially recommended for teenage parents. d. Linda Jassim; s.w. L. Jassim, Lyn Della Quadri; ed. Barbara Noble; camera, Joan Churchill; CF; IU, KENTSU, UIL, UM.

HELP, I'M SHRINKING (12m C 1975)
An animated fable about Carie, a defeatist child. Every time Carie says, "I can't" she actually shrinks until she becomes small enough to ride on a butterfly's back. Eventually, encouraged by the butterfly, she learns to say, "I can," and begins to grow until her developing self-confidence restores her to her natural size. Awards. p./d. Barbara Dourmashkin. FI.

HELP YOURSELF TO BETTER HEALTH (16m C 1976) (also Video/S8)
Nutrition Education Series
A warm positive film that shows older people can enjoy food for
good nutrition, not only for health reasons, but also because it can
be an avenue to a richer, more enjoyable life in other ways. For example, it demonstrates how cooking and eating can be a pleasant social experience, even for people with limited resources. It includes
advice on how older people can shop wisely for their food, and it
deals with health problems and diet restrictions. Uses live action,
still animation, and original music. Guide-book included. p. Jamil
Simon Productions, Inc.; SNUTRE; KENTSU, PAS, UMO, WSU.

HER SOCIAL SECURITY SERIES (29m ea. C 1977)
A look at the Social Security system from a woman's perspective
finds women at a disadvantage. Some of the reasons are found in the
nature of women's employment: low paying jobs and interrupted careers. Other reasons for the inequity are with the system itself:
the benefit computation formula and the noncovered labor of housewives. This series examines these problems from the perspective of
both the Social Security professional and those who are taxed. Guests:
Wilbur J. Cohen, former United States Secretary of Health, Education,
and Welfare and former Dean of the School of Education, The University of Michigan; and Nancy Kehoe, former administrative official with
the United States Department of Health, Education and Welfare. p.
UMMRC; UM.

1. IN SEARCH OF TOMORROW. "Man-on-the-street" interviews
reveal the depth of concern that Americans have for the Social Security system.

2. WORKING WOMAN, THE. A discussion of the importance of
Social Security benefits for the working woman.

3. WIVES AND MOTHERS. A look at the benefits available to
women who have not earned benefits on their own but are eligible for
them under their husband's account; a discussion of benefits to widows, young dependent children, and divorced spouses.

4. IN SENIOR YEARS. An examination of the benefits to senior
citizens.

HERBS: USE AND TRADITION (18m C 1979)
Demonstrates thoroughly how to prepare herbs, how to make a
pomander, lavender sachet, and potpourri. An interesting miscellany
of the benefits of herbs throughout the centuries is presented along
with practical knowledge about herbs and their uses today. p. Ian
Clark for Brooklyn Botanic Garden; PEREN.

HERDING CASTES OF CENTRAL INDIA: LIFEWAY, CEREMONY,
DANCE (25m C 1978)

Shows daily life of the Mathura, a cattle breeding group, a group of pack bullock carriers and a blanket-making seminomadic group living in south central Maharastra. Also shown are their dances. d. Margaret Kennedy Fairlie, Mack Travis; p. School of Communications, Ithaca College; ITHACA.

HERE ARE LADIES (60m C 1974)
The international star Siobhan McKenna is brilliant in this film version of her New York and London stage success, Here Are Ladies. Supported by players of the world-famous Abbey Theatre in Dublin, McKenna appears in excerpts from the works of eight of Ireland's major writers: Sean O'Casey, George Bernard Shaw, W. B. Yeats, John Millington Synge, Samuel Beckett, Lennox Robinson, James Stevens and James Joyce. p. Sedgemon Production, Ltd., London; CANTOR.

HERE TODAY ... HERE TOMORROW: RADIOACTIVE WASTE IN
   AMERICA (28m C p1980, r1981) (Video)
A look at the current state of radioactive containment technology and some of the plans and theories of disposal. Includes a short history of the nuclear power industry, interviews with leading researchers as to the current status and potentials for the future, and an examination of government directives which delay the creation of a permanent repository for spent fuel. d. Frank Christopher; p. Jeffrey Kirsch/Rita Pastore; CRM.

HERMAN MELVILLE: CONSIDER THE SEA (28m C p1981, r1982)
A portrait of the mind and world of America's great novelist. Poet Richard Wilbur retraces the locales and sites associated with Herman Melville's career as sailor, author and customs official. Interspersed are mini-dramatizations and passages from Melville's works, including poems, short stories and novels culminating in Moby-Dick. d. Chuck Olin; p. Jean McClure Mudge; FFHUM.

HERPES: 400,000 NEW CASES EACH YEAR (15m C 1981)
Herpes II virus is a sexually transmitted disease believed to be active in at least eight million men and women. Deals with the physical and emotional traumas experienced by those infected. p. Paul Loewenwarter for CBS' "60 Minutes"; WOMBAT; IU.

HERPES SIMPLEX II (18½m C 1983)
Explains how this disease develops and what the short- and long-term problems can be. Long-term management techniques that can help both the physical and emotional upset are also discussed. Actual comments from herpes victims are especially convincing. MIFE.

HE'S NOT THE WALKING KIND (29m C 1973)
A documentary study that provides insight into the daily challenge that faces the physically handicapped, the private struggle and the victory that comes with each new obstacle met and overcome. Although

Brian Wilson is a spastic and confined to a wheelchair, he remains cheerful and optimistic and gives those of us with good health and no handicap a different perspective on the ordinary problems encountered in our lives. d. Sandra Wilson; p. Shelah Reljic, Peter Jones; NFBC; CENTEF.

HIDDEN ALCOHOLICS: WHY IS MOMMY SICK? (22m C p1977, r1978)
Presents actual case histories of two courageous women who have disregarded the usual anonymity and have dedicated themselves to helping other female alcoholics: actress Jan Clayton, known from her role as the mother on the "Lassie" television series, and Margaret Fleming, a former teacher. Provides viewers with facts and alternatives, the danger signals, and ways in which help is available. p. WLS-TV, Chicago; ABC-TV; CRM; UMN.

HIDDEN IN PLAY: LEKOTEK (28m C 1981)
The experiences of eight children as they discover the joy of achievement during visits to local Lekoteks. They come with their parents to borrow toys especially chosen for their particular developmental needs. Filmed in Norway and Illinois to show the first American Lekotek. d. June Finfer; p. J. Finfer, Filmedia Ltd.; LEKOTEK.

HIDDEN STRUGGLE, THE (25m C 1981) (also Video)
Chronicles one organization's success in helping moderately retarded individuals secure a place for themselves in the mainstream of adult life. It tells the story of Clausen House, a residential and educational facility serving about 80 mentally retarded adults which offers a positive alternative to state institutions. Its goal is to foster self-confidence, social and academic skills, and ultimately, the dignity of independence. These people offer living proof that the mentally retarded can move into the mainstream, living rich, meaningful lives. p./d. Claire Wiles/Lawrence Lansburgh for Dawn Flight Productions; PF.

HIDING PLACE, THE (150m C 1975)
A biographical documentary on the life of a Dutch Christian woman, Corrie Ten Boom, who with her family, aided Jews during Holland's resistance movement and, as a result, nearly faced death in the Nazis' Ravensbruck concentration camp. Based on Boom's autobiography; by James and Elizabeth Sherrill. Exec. p. William F. Brown; p. Frank R. Jacobson; d. James F. Collier; WORWIP.

HIGH CLASS HIGH (23m C 1977) (also Video)
Study of cocaine and its use, covers the historical background, and the cultivation of the coca plant from which it is derived. Tons of cocaine pour into the United States annually and is widely available, despite narcotic squads and police whose efforts seem to be exercises in futility. Users discuss on camera the pros and cons of cocaine use. Doctors point out that it is highly dangerous. But, its use continues to grow, especially among the well-to-do, who attend,

the proliferating cocaine "clubs" to enjoy a "high class high" on this champagne of drugs. p./d. Patricia Lynch; FI.

HILDEGARDE KNEF'S BERLIN (25m C 1980)
"Because there is so much life here, one hardly notices the absurdities. Most Berliners feel that the very limitations of the city help keep it alive. Having lost its status as a national capital, Berlin has become an international city open to the world." Hildegard Knef's career started in German theatre and has covered the areas of film, singing and lyric-writing. She has become a Broadway star and best-selling author. LCA; UCEMC.

HINDU FAMILY CELEBRATION; 60TH BIRTHDAY (9m C 1969) The India Image (Series), No. 11
Records the fire-offerings performed by the celebrating elderly couple aided by their hereditary family Acharya priest; their ritual baths and the performance of other subsidiary rituals; the renewal before their offspring of their original wedding vows, accompanied by the tying of a second gold pendant around the mother's neck; and the giving and receiving of gifts and blessings. p. Film Marketing Division of Syracuse; FILMDS; UW.

HINDUISM AND THE SONG OF GOD (30m C 1975)
The physical beauty of India is the background for the Hindu concepts of self-realization as expressed in the Bhagavad Gita, or Song of God ... our purpose in life, the four yogas, the law of Karma, the four stages of life. p. Elda Hartley; HARTLEY.

HISTORICAL OVERVIEW I: 1776-1870 see WOMEN AND THE LAW, THE (SERIES)

HISTORICAL OVERVIEW II: 1870-1920 see WOMEN AND THE LAW, THE (SERIES)

HISTORY LESSONS (85m C 1973)
Based on Bertolt Brecht's novel The Affairs of Mr. Julius Caesar. Revolutionary historical film: four Roman witnesses describe Julius Caesar's rise to power. d. Jean-Marie Straub; NYF.

HITCHHIKING (23m C 1973) Community Protection Series
Alerts potential hitchhikers to the types of crimes that have been committed against hitchhikers. It includes interviews with people who have had firsthand experiences with the dangers of hitchhiking, and an interview with the mother of a 14-year-old girl hitchhiker who disappeared and has never been found. Dramatized sequences are based on actual occurrences. Advice is given to those who will hitchhike in spite of warnings. Summerhill Productions; PARACO.

HITCHHIKING: TEENAGE RISK (10m C 1981) (also Video)
Teenagers who thumb their way across town or country say it's

the unexpected elements that make hitchhiking an exciting adventure. But what is the gamble they take? Made in Colorado, the crossroads for interstate hitchhiking, this film interviews young hitchhikers who reveal some of the highs and lows of being "on the road." p. CBS News; CRM; UCEMC.

HITCHHIKING: THE ROAD TO RAPE (14m C 1983)
A young woman, friendly and independent, has always felt safe hitchhiking. But she learns the hard way that experience is no guarantee of safety. She escapes an attack with her life; police and emergency medical staff are concerned and kind. But that help can never erase the agony of the rape itself. The message is clear without preaching that hitchhiking is dangerous. AIMS.

HOLE IN THE ROCK (12m C p1981, r1982) (also Video)
Documents a genuine piece of Americana, a tourist attraction in the southwest United States. In 1926, the enterprising Albert and Gladys Christensen began blasting caves into the side of a canyon. Today guides lead tours through the cavern-like structure, which has served as a home, restaurant and novelty shop. Celebrates the sometimes absurd results of American ingenuity. d. Suzanne Pastor; ex. p. Bill Couturie; DIRECT.

HOLISTIC HEALTH: THE NEW MEDICINE (35m C p1977, r1978)
Mind/body relationship is the theme of many of the holistic doctors. Others stress a better relationship between traditional and Western methods. All stress treating the whole person--body, mind, and spirit. This film shows the following doctors, leaders in the field, at work and demonstrates their methods for controlling pain, healing cancer, and promoting optimum health: David Bresler, Ph.D.; Cindy Chang; Milton Estes, M.D.; Rick Kozlenko, D.P.M.; Evarts Loomis, M.D.; Sandra McLanahan, M.D.; Kenneth Pelletier, Ph.D.; Effie Poy Yew Chow, Ph.D.; Ilana Rubenfeld; Leni Schwartz, Ph.D.; Norman Shealy, M.D.; Carl Simonton, M.D. p. Elda Hartley; HARTLEY.

HOLOCAUST (453m C 1978)
    Part I: THE GATHERING DARKNESS (144m)
    Part II: THE ROAD TO BABI YAR (99m)
    Part III: THE FINAL SOLUTION (94m)
    PART IV: THE SAVING REMNANT (116m)
A unique dramatization of one of the most horrifying periods in history--the Nazi occupation of Europe--and the effect it had on two German families, one Jewish, one Catholic. d. Rosemary Harris, Marvin Chomosky, Fritz Weaver, Michael Moriarity, Meryl Streep. LCA.

HOLY KORAN, THE (18m C p1978, r1978)
Presents a historical survey of the calligraphy of the Koran. The Koran was written down after the death of Mohammed, and this film traces the many writing styles used since A.D. 600. The various

styles reflect the extraordinary Moslem blending of art and religion, for many of the editions shown are unique and beautiful art objects, with the calligraphy itself intended to convey a sense of spiritual energy. Although many different writing styles have been used, the actual text of the Koran has remained unchanged since the time of Mohammed. Many of the illustrations used in this film are rare books, antique and stunningly beautiful examples of calligraphy. p. Frances Cockburn; p. Inca Films; PHOENIX.

HOME (90m C 1979) (Video)
Examines in portrait style, the significance of the family at critical life moments. Part I, THE BIRTH OF A CHILD, looks into the factors that lead a couple to decide to have their second child in a child-bearing center rather than a hospital. Shows the actual midwife-assisted birth. Part II, GROWING OLD, examines the conflicts felt by a 94-year-old widow and her children when the mother is placed in a nursing home. Part III, MARRIAGE, focuses on a young couple who feel, despite the woman's earlier failed marriage and an increasing trend toward informal relationships, that the depth of their commitment to each other can best be expressed through a traditional wedding. Part IV, THE DEATH OF A PARENT, examines the decision of a young man to care for his terminally-ill mother at home rather than send her to a hospital or a nursing home. HOME should be seen in its entirety by any group concerned with the study of the family. Individual segments may be rented also. Awards. d./p. Julie Gustafson/John Reilly; EDC.

HOME AND PROPERTY PROTECTION (35m C 1973) Community Protection Series
Demonstrates how members of the community can protect themselves, their homes, small businesses, and other personal property from theft and damage as a result of burglary. Explains how the criminal functions in preying on homes and businesses and suggests common sense security measures. Many different types of security hardware are also demonstrated. p. Summerhill Productions; PARACO.

HOME FREE (20m C 1978)
Presents a film that reverses the traditional story of the ethnic child assimilating into North American culture by placing a white child in a new cultural environment. For primary, elementary and intermediate level. p./d. Rebecca Yates, Glen Saltzman for Fruits and Roots Productions; PHOENIX.

HOME, SWEET HOMES: KIDS TALK ABOUT JOINT CUSTODY (20m C 1982)
A fresh perspective on custody and divorce is provided as five articulate children share their thoughts and feelings about joint custody with Dr. Mel Roman. Recommended as a training film, as a discussion starter for kids and as a must for all parents going through divorce. d. Josephine Dean; p. Josephine Dean Productions; FILMLB.

HOMEBOYS (60m C 1978)
A film about Chicano youth gangs in East Los Angeles, HOME-
BOYS explores the forces which shape the gang members' lives: police harassment, the school system, the search for identity within
Anglo society. The filmmakers met with the youths for eight months
before filming actually began, and they worked closely with the gangs
during production, showing the work as it progressed and receiving
criticism and suggestions. (Whitney Museum of American Art, December 5, 1978). p. Bill Yahraus, Christine Burrill, David Davis;
FOCALP.

HOMETOWN, THE (5m C 1980)
"This memory piece is a delicate gem, beautifully structured despite its seeming simplicity. The past unfolds sequentially; ultimately,
it stands before us in full visual summary, allowing us to pick out,
as we do in reality, the individual components of days gone by, within
the single all-encompassing canvas of the present."--Amos Vogel. p.
Bettina Matzkuhn; NFBC.

HONEYMOON (10m C 1974)
When her mother marries a widower with a little boy, the daughter shows her resentment and feeling of desertion. While the couple
is away on their honeymoon, the daughter becomes fond of her step-
brother and his grandmother. When the couple returns from their
honeymoon, she accepts her stepfather and is ready to help in the
new family. p. Gordon Kerckhoff; PARACO; KENTSU.

HOOLAULEA: THE TRADITIONAL DANCES OF HAWAII (20m C 1961)
Iolani Luahini performs seven hulas, seated and standing, to
various kinds of accompaniment including drum, wooden sticks, gourd,
and pebbles. Each dance is explained by Luahini, one of the most
respected of hula dancers. The granddaughter of dancers at the
court of King Kalahaua, she began her apprenticeship at the age of
three. She has served as the curator of the Iolani Palace and was
Hawaii's representative at the National Folk Dance Festival in 1945.
p. Francis Haar; p. Honolulu Academy of Arts; DANCFA.

HOPE IS NOT A METHOD (17m C 1977) (1973 ed. rev.)
Combines animation, diagram, and live-action sequences to impart
medical and scientific information about seven types of contraception:
withdrawal, rhythm, spermicidal foams, condom, diaphragm, pill, and
intrauterine devices. Also discusses vasectomy, tubal ligation, and
abortion. The language about legal entanglements of abortions con-
forms with current laws. p. Planned Parenthood Center of Syracuse,
Inc.; PEREN; UIL.

HOPI WAY, THE (22m C 1972)
The Hopi Way is concerned with traditional values and religion--
a respect for the land and the growth of crops is at its core--and,
historically, it is based on the Hopi's having lived for 1,300 years in

remote settlements on three mesas in the Arizona desert. The history of the Hopi is briefly surveyed by David Mongnongyi, who shows pictographs he says were made by Hopi ancestors. Peabody Coal Company is strip-mining at Black Mesa now. The tribal Chief describes how its presence can boost the economy; but at the same time it threatens their traditional way of life. p. Shelly Grossman, s.w. Mary Louise Grossman; FI; UAZ, UMI.

HORRIBLE HONCHOS, THE (31m C r1977) The Teenage Years (Series)
Presents a story of friendship and growing up. Hollis, a new boy in the neighborhood, has an unfortunate encounter with one member of the "Horrible Honchos," a semi-secret club of youngsters who make a pact to avoid befriending a newcomer at all costs and harass him whenever possible. The episodes that follow convince the "Horrible Honchos" they were wrong, they like Hollis, and decide to disband. Based on the book Seventeenth Street Gang. p. Fran Sears; d. Larry Elikann; p. Daniel Wilson Productions; TIMLIF; UIL.

HORROR DREAM (10m C n.d.)
Choreographic interpretation of a dancer's anxiety before starting her theatre routine. Choreographer/dancer: Marian Van Tuyl; p. Sidney Peterson; GROVE.

HORROR OF IT ALL (58m C 1983) (also Video)
Presents an entertaining look at the horror films of twenties through the present time. Narrated by José Ferrer, this documentary contains vintage film footage, on-camera interviews and live action as it focuses on outstanding horror films from the past 60 years that have frightened and delighted audiences. Several actors, directors, producers, writers, and other filmmakers discuss their roles. Shown are film clips from outstanding horror films. This study of horror films provides the rare opportunity to see some legendary actors briefly performing in their most famous roles, and it analyzes the evolution of that genre. d./s.w. Gene Feldman; p. Gene Feldman/Suzette Winter; WOMBAT.

HORSE FLICKERS (10m C 1977)
Film collage of horses created by using paint, feathers, dried leaves, mattress covers, chalk, rope, fabric, colored paper, and found objects, singly and together, assembled on the deep blue wooden floor of a bar, apparently photographed from above the rafters. d. Bill Stitt; p. Rhonda Raulston/Jim Gruebel; music by John Reubourn, Jack Nitzsche; TEXFM.

HOSPICE (13m C 1978) (also Video)
A documentary showing a new concept in caring for the terminally ill. Filmed at Hillhave Hospice in Tucson, Arizona. Staff members explain how they help their patients on a day-to-day basis with special medical and therapeutic care. They try to make life for the patient as easy as possible, free of physical and emotional pain, and

with constant care and attention given in a homelike atmosphere.
Although the hospice prepares patients and the families for the in-
evitable end, the patient is encouraged to live out the final weeks,
months or years to the fullest extent. p. Mary Drayne for CBS
News with correspondent Sharron Lovejoy; CAROUF; KENTSU, UMN,
PAS, USFL, WSU.

HOSPICE (26m C p1979, r1979)
Depicts an alternative way to care for the dying. Unrehearsed
scenes are filmed in actual hospice settings. Emphasis is on control
of pain and symptoms as well as the psychological, social and spiritual dimensions. Includes care of family as well as patient during
sickness and after death. Hospice is professional care and human
caring. d./p. Frank Moynihan; p. Billy Budd Films; MMM.

HOUSE (11m C 1955)
Presents a visual poem evolving from the four walls of a house
and accumulations of beloved objects that make a house and reflect
the lives of the people within. With Elmer Bernstein score. p. Ray
and Charles Eames; PF; UCEMC.

HOUSEHOLD TECHNICIANS (29m C 1981) (also Video) Are You Listening Series
Ten household workers talk about their experiences and their efforts to organize for better pay, benefits, and improved working conditions. d./p. Martha Stuart; STUARTM.

HOUSEHOLD WORKERS (29m C 1975) (Video) Woman Series
Josephine Hulette, who was a domestic for 20 years and Edith
Barksdale Sloan, an attorney, discuss their work with the Committee
on Household Employment. Both women are involved in the Committee's efforts to improve household working conditions through educating employers and employees about coverage by federal minimum
wage standards and the necessity of withholding Social Security.
Also, they are concerned with providing guidelines for specific job
requirements, sick leave, and paid vacations. Sandra Elkin, moderator. p. WNED-TV; PBSV.

HOUSEHUSBANDS (29m C 1976) (Video) Woman Series
Reese Sarda and Ross Bachelder, two men who have chosen to
remain at home to raise their children, discuss their experiences as
"househusbands" and how they have dealt with the emotions and circumstances commonly associated with the life of a housewife. They
comment on the reactions of friends and the community at large.
Sandra Elkin, moderator. p. WNED-TV; PBSV.

HOUSING: A PLACE TO LIVE (56m C 1973) Choices 1976 Series
Some questions are raised regarding how to get more housing
built and how to save housing from being abandoned. Possible answers: equitable tax schedules, better zoning and building codes,
closer supervision of the real estate market. STEREF; UNEV.

HOUSEWIFE, THE (6m C n.d.)
A study, in animation, of a day in the life of a housewife. There is no narration, and the film makes no judgments. A good discussion starter on the role of women and the value of their work. d. Cathy Bennett; p. Guy Glover, Wolf Koenig; NFBC.

HOW ABOUT SATURDAY? (20m C p1978, r1979)
Dramatic presentation of child's point of view in divorce situations. Deals with anger, frustrations, peer problems, sense of guilt, abandonment. Presents divorce as a total family problem and indicates the importance of dealing with the child effectively. p. Richard Steinbrecker; MTITI; IU.

HOW DO YOU COUNT? (12m C 1963) (also Video)
Shows that our familiar number system based on ten (decimal system) is but one of many possible number systems that could be used in counting. Illustrates how items could be counted and notated in systems with a base 3, base 4, base 10, base 12, and finally base 2, or binary system. p. Katharine Cornwell, Bruce Cornwell; IFB.

HOW DO YOU FEEL? (8½m C 1977)
A video animation "commercial" on body movement and self awareness. Charming musical score of George Kleisinger gives a "singalong" pattern for dancers Lloyd Ritter and Kei Takei. Narration by Mal Pate. p. Doris Chase; CHASED.

HOW DO YOU FEEL?/EMPEROR'S NEW CLOTHES/ROCKER (29m B 1977) (Video)
Three of Doris Chase's productions. Choreographer/p. Doris Chase; CHASED.

HOW FAR IS A ROUND? (8m C 1979) (also Video)
The concept of a circle as a limit is presented by a succession of regular polygons. The area is shown as the limit of a set of triangles. Finally, the visualization of the quantity pi is shown. p. Katharine Cornwell, Bruce Cornwell; IFB.

HOW THE KIWI LOST HIS WINGS (12m C p1980, r1980)
This New Zealand folk tale tells how the ancient forest god called on the birds to save the forest from a plague of insects. All were punished except the kiwi which sacrificed its beautiful plumage for a life in the gloom, cleaning the forest floor. A visualization of the book of the same name. d./p. Kathleen Houston; CF.

HOW THE LEOPARD GOT HIS SPOTS (10½m C 1982--U.S.) (also Video)
Presents in animation a film version of Kipling's story of how the leopard got his spots. d./animator Sheila Graber; p. Marble Arch Film, Ltd.; CORONET.

HOW TO BE EFFECTIVE (8-part Video Series 1983)
   Teaches life-planning skills through a filmed workshop and real
life experiences of eight different women. Viewers will learn how to
build confidence, how to decide what skills they have, how to make
decisions, and how to make plans for the future. They will see real
women learning "how to get what they want out of life" and then doing it. The series is accompanied by a workbook, which can stand
alone or be used in conjunction with the programs. It is suitable
for self-study, discussion groups, facilitator-led sessions, or as an
organizing framework and supplement for a skilled career-planning
instructor. p. New Environment for Women; NEWEFW.

HOW TO DIG A HOLE TO THE OTHER SIDE OF THE WORLD (11m C
   p1980, r1980)
   An adventure-in-geology story takes us on an amazing educational
journey from the topsoil to the limestone, through the granite to the
geysers, from the basalt into the molten core. As each layer of the
earth is passed, the geological terms are fully explained. Based on
a book of the same title by Faith McNulty. p. Polestar Productions
for LCA; p. Ira and Don Duga; LCA.

HOW TO GET A JOB (58m C p1979, r1979) (also Video)
   The unemployed in this film are enrolled in a program by the
federally funded Self-Directed Placement Corporation which teaches
job hunting as a skill. A series of confidence-raising sessions emphasize the assessment of personal skills, strengths, and accomplishments. Interview training utilizes videotaping and analysis by both
the instructor and other students. The film follows students into
actual employment interviews where the lessons learned are put into
practice. d./p. Wayne Ewing; p. WNET-TV; FI; UMN.

HOW TO KEEP FROM CATCHING VD (20m C 1979)
   Features Dr. Walter H. Smartt, M.D., M.P.H., Chief of V.D.
Control, Los Angeles County, California, talking in a straightforward
manner to an audience of young people about VD symptoms, effects
if untreated, how a doctor examines a person for VD, and how VD
is cured. Most importantly, stresses how one can avoid catching VD.
p. Jarvis Couillard Associates; TCAFMS.

HOW TO START YOUR OWN BUSINESS, PART I (29m C 1976) (Video)
   Woman Series
   Claudia Jessup and Genie Chipps, co-authors of The Women's
Guide to Starting a Business, discuss the risks, procedures and re-
wards for women starting a business on their own. Sandra Elkin is
the moderator. p. WNED-TV; PBSV.

HOW TO START YOUR OWN BUSINESS, PART II (29m C 1976)
   (Video) Woman Series
   Ann Smith, founder and owner of Annie's Firehouse and Soup
Kitchen, Inc. in New Haven, Connecticut, and Ava Stern, editor and

publisher of "Artemis for Enterprising Women" (a national newsletter
for women business owners), recount their experiences in starting
and operating businesses. Sandra Elkin is the moderator. p. WNED-
TV; PBSV.

HU HUNG-YEN: ASPECTS OF PEKING OPERA (30m C n.d.) (Video)
    Hu Hung-yen, a Chinese dancer, demonstrates Peking Opera
makeup. She then performs various dance patterns and presents a
scene from "The Butterfly Dream" and the "Scarf Dance." p. Performing Arts Division of Asia Society; PERFAAS.

HUCKLEBERRY FINN (29m C 1976) (also Video)
    When first published, Huckleberry Finn was considered by many
to be immoral, vulgar and coarse. Twain defends his novel and his
choice of style and use of the vernacular. Scenes from the novel
are interspersed with Twain's commentary to illustrate his philosophies
and literary theories. Some say Huckleberry Finn is a classic. Twain
says they are wrong, "a classic is something that everybody praises,
but nobody reads." d. Susan Murgatroyd; OECA.

HUMAN BODY SERIES see REPRODUCTIVE SYSTEM

HUMAN FACE OF CHINA, THE (SERIES) see IT'S ALWAYS SO IN
    THE WORLD; SOMETHING FOR EVERYONE; SON OF THE OCEAN

HUMAN GROWTH III (20m C 1979)
    Presents in a generally acceptable fashion and in a clearly educa-
tional and inoffensive way the biological facts of sex as an integral
part of human growth and development. p. E. C. Brown Foundation; PEREN; UMN.

HUMAN REPRODUCTION (3rd ed.) (20m C 1981)
    Features elegant, stylized animation that clearly shows the func-
tioning of reproductive organs. Includes interviews with youngsters
who answer the question, How are babies born? Shows prenatal development within the womb. CRM; IU, UCEMC.

HUMAN REPRODUCTION (20m C p1980, r1981) (also Video)
    Provides an overview of the factors involved in starting a family.
Emphasizes the continuous long-term responsibility of parents in caring for their children. Introduces the various aspects of reproduction using microphotography, animation, interviews and live action.
The fertilization process is explained and illustrated with animation,
and month-by-month fetal development is graphically demonstrated.
The narration stresses the importance of good nutrition and mental
and physical health of the mother. A group of parents-to-be are
seen as they participate in a childbirth education class. Scenes in
delivery rooms are presented and a live birth sequence is shown.
Brief interviews with parents and prospective parents. The film
focuses on parental responsibility in the areas of safety, education,

health, friends and habits as well as the joys and rewards of parenting. p. Wexler Films for E. C. Brown Foundation; PEREN; IU.

HUMANOIDS FROM THE DEEP (82m C 1980)
The odds are against the humans in HUMANOIDS FROM THE DEEP when salmon accidentally feed on fish that have been injected with growth and mating hormones. The resultant mutants emerge from the depth in search of mates among the local lasses including lucious Ann Turkel. d. Barbara Peeters; FI.

HUMOR BY WOMEN (29m C 1976) Woman Series
Anne Beatts, Emmy Award-winning writer for NBC's "Saturday Night," and writer Deanne Stillman share their experiences as author-editors of Titters--the first book of women's humor. They explain the concept of the collection and describe women's special appreciation for certain topics, such as "recipes" and "washing instructions." Sandra Elkin is the moderator. p. WNED-TV; PBSV.

HUNTERS OF THE SEAL (30m C 1976) (also Video)
The Netsilik Eskimo (Inuit) used to hunt seal by crouching motionless over an air hole until the chance for the kill came. Once the seal was caught, the hunter called together his hunting partners to celebrate and honor the dead seal's soul and to divide it among all the hunters and their families. This is no longer so. The effort of the Canadian government to provide the Netsilik social services has succeeded at the expense of their nomadic life. They now inhabit a year-round community at Pelly Bay. The building of the MacKenzie pipeline has stopped the caribou herds from migrating to where they hunted. They depend on store-bought food. As there are no jobs being developed here, the community must receive cash in the form of welfare payments from the Canadian government. The changes are well illustrated by footage of traditional activities from the Netsilik series intercut with interviews and scenes of daily life at Pelly Bay. p. Barbara Holecek; p. BBC/WGBH-TV; TIMLIF.

HUTTERITES, THE (28m B 1964)
Produced without shooting restrictions by the National Film Board of Canada in a northern Alberta colony to show the true nature of colony life and to alleviate some of the misconceptions and misunderstandings about the Brethren. The Hutterites, named after Jacob Hutter, are one of three Anabaptist groups surviving from the Reformation period. They live in complete community with all property held in common. Although not focused on social role behavior, this film can be utilized to illustrate sex-based occupational/social roles as followed in a variant of traditional Western society. NFBC; PAS.

HYMN TO ATON (15m C p1976, r1978--U.S.)
Tells the history of Egypt's Pharaoh Akhenaton, who worshipped the Sun-God Aton. Eartha Kitt introduces briefly the history of Egypt's Pharaohs and explains the radical change that was made by

Pharaoh Akhenaton in the ancient Egyptian religion. He abolished the worship of many gods, established one god, Aton, the Sun-God. Much dissension was caused by this act so that when Akhenaton died in 1357 B.C. his tomb was desecrated by the Egyptians and his mummy defiled and all the prior gods were reinstated. Over selected visuals of Egyptian culture, its people and its land, Eartha Kitt introduces and John Huston dramatically recites Akhenaton's prayer to Aton. d. Nadine Markova; p. Miguel Aleman Velasco for Televisa of Mexico; PHOENIX.

HYPOCHONDRIACS AND HEALTH CARE: A TUG OF WAR (38m C p1977, r1978)
Presents Dr. Robert Rynearson's thesis that hypochondriacs have a need to hold on to their symptoms. Actors re-enact actual case histories to point out some realistic goals for treating hypochondriacs. The hard-core hypochondriacal patient is described as a person with a life-style of sickness beset with continual symptoms, who has never been well. Dr. Rynearson explains that treating a hypochondriac is essentially protecting that patient from unnecessary surgery, costly tests, and phasing out addictive medications. He contends that the physician must have, in advance of treating the patients, the understanding that they will not get well and that a long-term relationship will be required. These patients do poorly in therapy because they need to remain sick. Further, Dr. Rynearson says, the doctor's responsibility is to prescribe an allotment of his time to talk with the patient about his/her problems. Techniques and methods are shown. d./p. Marilyn Felt, Henry Felt; p. Workshop Films; FAMINS.

HYSTERECTOMY (11½m C n.d.)
After an extensive explanation of just what a hysterectomy entails, the film follows a hysterectomy patient from hospital admission through her complete recovery weeks later. Anatomical animation is used to illustrate the reasons and methods of this procedure. The film is very reassuring on the outcome. Also available in Spanish. MIFE.

-I-

I AM A RUNNER (21m C p1979, r1979)
Using regular and slow motion, several runners' styles are analyzed and suggestions are offered for improving running techniques. A group of women are shown doing stretching exercises before running. Scenes filmed at Bonne Bell race show 4,500 women runners. Obviously, they all enjoy what they are doing. p. Yvonne Hannemann, Coronet; PAS.

I AM ALSO A YOU (14m C 1970)
Visuals of contemporary life are enhanced by quotations which span different societies, religions, age groups and centuries. By

relating the wisdom of the past to the problems of the present, the
reality of a generation gap is brought into serious doubt. Quotations
are read from the Bible, Buddha, the Talmud, Disraeli, Thomas Wolfe,
Dwight Eisenhower, Justice William O. Douglas and others. p. Wonderful Films; PF; UIL.

I AM NOT WHAT YOU SEE (28m C 1975)
    Interview with Sondra Diamond, who is so severely crippled with
cerebral palsy that she is completely confined to a wheelchair, unable
to perform such routine tasks as dressing or bathing. Despite this
disability, she is a practicing psychologist and an outspoken champion
of the rights of the handicapped. Film also provides insights into the
psychology of the physically fit when confronted with the disabled.
p. CBC; PAS, UIL.

IBM AT THE FAIR (8m C 1965)
    Captures the spirit of the IBM Pavillion at the 1964-65 New York
World's Fair: exhibits, media presentations, architecture and spectators (sometimes pixillated) reveal aspects unique to the filmic presentation. p. Ray Eames, Charles Eames; PF; UIL.

I CALL IT WORK (22m C p1977, r1979)
    A documentary exploring men's changing attitudes toward work.
It focuses on the relationship between the traditional male role and
how the work one does affects relationships with other men, with
women, and with children. Men from various class and cultural backgrounds discuss problems they have with their work, and ways they
are attempting to find resolutions. In so doing they are changing
the meaning of masculinity. d. Kathi Lipcius; p. Robert Dunn, K.
Lipcius; s.w. K. Lipcius, R. Dunn; FI.

I CAN MAKE MUSIC (18m C 1982)
    Focuses on the process in musical experiences. The children are
shown delighting in the joy of discovering, exploring and playing
with sound as they chant, stamp, clap, sing, play instruments, improvise dance movements and actively listen. The underlying premise of the film is that music is essentially patterned sound and that
through child-centered exploratory activities a sense for pattern in
sound is developed. d. Tom Zubrycki; p./s.w. Ursula Kolbe; ed.
Jim Stevens; orig. music: Michael Atherton; CORORI.

I DON'T HAVE TO HIDE (28m C p1982, r1983)
    Anorexia nervosa is a psychosomatic syndrome characterized by
an obsessive preoccupation with food and an intense desire to be
thin. Anorexics typically lose over 25 percent of their body weight.
Medical and psychological consequences include cessation of menstruation, disrupted endocrine balance, insomnia and depression. The
producer, Anne Fischel, who has herself experienced anorexia and
who now counsels other anorexic women, recalls her own experience
with anorexia and explores the private world of her friend, Cope,

who is bulimic, as she speaks openly abut her symptoms and the
fears and feelings which inspired them. p./d. Anne Fischel; Fanlight Productions; FANLP.

I HAD A DREAM A COUPLE OF MONTHS AGO (7½m C 1978) (Video)
  This is a story about the artist's imaginary four selves and about
the choices that women make between children, husband, friends,
work and school. p. Jeanne Hollenback; WMM.

I HAD A STROKE (28m C 1979) (also Video)
  This film will be valuable to anyone concerned with stroke reha-
bilitation--professionals, patients, and families of patients. It focuses on the emotional factors of recovery, including the stress placed
on a marriage. The film concentrates on Laura, a 36-year-old professional woman. We see her first angry response to being incapa-
citated, her satisfactions and setbacks, and her conflicting feelings
upon returning home. With understanding and support from her husband, she is gradually able to resume a full life. Besides Laura,
several other people who have had strokes, are shown. p. Grania
Gurievitch, Dr. John Downey for the Department of Rehabilitation
Medicine, Columbia University; FILMLB.

I NEVER PROMISED YOU A LONG RUN (11m C 1972)
  A flip on the double standard. The young man wants a relationship. The young woman asks, "Don't you realize there's a revolution going on?" She wants the right of the "one night stand." p.
Paul Leaf; p. Short Ends Productions; FI; KENTSU.

I SPENT MY LIFE IN THE MINES (40m C p1977, r1977)
  Through Juan Rojas' autobiographical account, this film investigates the way of life of the Bolivian miners. A few scenes are dramatizations, but most are documentary and show the inside of the mines
and communities. The cultural traditions and ties that constitute the
base for the strength of the miners' organizations are revealed within
the context of the grim reality of daily life. Also available in Spanish.
p. June Nash; d. J. Nash, Juan Rojas, Eduardo F. Banez. Awards.
UNIFILM.

I STAND HERE IRONING (20m C/B p1978, r1979)
  A thoughtful reverie of a mother performing the ritual chore of
ironing, as she reevaluates her relationship with her 19-year-old
daughter. Inspired by the autobiographical short story by Tillie Olsen. d./p. Midge Mackenzie; FILBOS.

I THINK I'M HAVING A BABY (29m C p1981, r1982) (also Video)
  Designed to help teenagers learn the difference between love and
sex and that it is not immature to say "no." A teacher in an Adult
Living Class speaks to students about the need for intelligent decisions regarding sex. She talks about conflicting pressures from television, magazines, parents, churches and from their own bodies. A

realistic portrayal of a major concern of our times. d. Arthur Allan Seidelman; p. Eda Godel Hallinan/Keetje Van Ben Shoten; p. Dan Curtis Associates; s.w. Blossom Elfman; LCA.

I WAS BORN AT HOME (59m C 1977) (Video, Beta, VHS)
Explored are the advantages and disadvantages of giving birth at home. Presents the views of midwives, obstetricians and an expectant couple in Detroit. Examines the reasons for the growing interest in home birth and the kind of training, experience and licensing required of a midwife. The birth of Pam and Paul Regan's child, at home, in the presence of family and friends and without any licensed medical personnel or equipment on hand, is shown. p. WTVS-TV, Detroit; PBSV.

IDA MAKES A MOVE (28m C p1979, r1979)
The story of a young girl, Ida Lucas, who, with her friend Cookie and brother Fred, makes a movie about pollution. Their movie is entered into a contest and wins--but, for the wrong reasons. The judges think the film is a protest against war. Ida has a serious decision to make. The film culminates when Ida musters up the strength to tell the truth. Based on a story by Kay Chorao. p. Linda Schuyler; d. Kit Hood; s.w. Amy Jo Cooper; LCA.

IDEAS, IMPRESSIONS, IMAGES: AMERICAN WOMEN IN THE VISUAL ARTS (29m C 1980)
Eleanor Munro discusses the factors and discoveries which led her to publish her book Originals: American Women Artists. She notes that American women artists have not been very visible because of a centuries-old tradition in America not to take women artists seriously; they have attracted little notice, not for lack of artistic ability, but for lack of public support. Host: Charles Eisendrath, University of Michigan Communications professor. UMMRC; UM, UIL.

IF IT HAPPENS TO YOU: RAPE (14m C n.d.) Something Personal Series
This docudrama simulates the situation of a young woman, who, having been raped, goes through counseling and examination procedures. She is brought to a Rape Crisis Intervention Center at a Boston hospital where the personnel--counselors, nurses, doctors, and specially trained members of the local police force--are supportive, sympathetic, and effective. The victim is encouraged to express her feelings of anger and fear and to realize that, as a victim, she should feel no shame. p. Nancy Porter, p. WGBH-TV; EDC.

IF TREES CAN FLY (12m C r1976)
A visual essay on the random thoughts of two 10-year-old children as they witness nature unfolding--bird eggs hatching, swans preening themselves and birds in flight. Through the fantasies they create, they relate how they think about birth, death, and life. p./d. Judith Kress, s.w. Marcia Tomkins, George Max Ross; ed. Jane Hernandez; PHOENIX.

IF YOU DON'T, WHO WILL? (28m C p1980, r1980) You Can Do It ...
  If Series
  Shows that people who excel and achieve have literally trained
themselves to push negative thoughts out of their minds. Motivational expert Marilyn Van Derbur uses illustrations of successful celebrities and sports figures in this film to show the necessity for positive thinking in reaching a goal. p./s.w. Marilyn Van Derbur;
VDBER.

IF YOU KNEW HOW I FEEL: BRAD'S LEARNING DISABILITY (17½m
  C 1982)
  Kristi was the last to be picked on the kickball team. Brad, on
the other hand, was a good player. But when it came to reading,
Kristi did well, but Brad was a disaster. Kristi thought Brad was
lazy, but when she was asked to help him she learned that Brad has
dyslexia--a learning disability. Kristi discovered what a learning disability is, and learned about handicaps--those that can be seen and
those that can't. d. Linda Haskins; CENTEF.

IF YOU LOVE THIS PLANET (26m C 1982) (also Video)
  In a campus talk, Dr. Helen Caldicott, noted author and pediatrician, clearly emphasizes the perils of nuclear war and reveals a
frightening progression of events which would follow a nuclear attack.
d. Terri Nash; NFBC: DIRECT.

I'ISAW: HOPI COYOTE STORIES (20m C 1978) (Video) (Hopi/Sub-
  titled)
  Hopi tribal elder Helen Sekaquaptewa tells traditional stories of
Coyote, the Trickster, to adult and young members of her Eagle clan.
The setting is her home at New Oraibi, Arizona, on the Hopi Third
Mesa. Also shown is author Leslie Marmon Silko talking about her
poetry and telling other Coyote tales. p. Larry Evers in cooperation
with the Arizona Film and Television Bureau; d. Denny Carr; CLRWP.

I'LL FIND A WAY (26m C r1978)
  Shows that being handicapped isn't the end; it can be the beginning of a challenging life. Nine-year-old Nadia De Franco, who has
had spina bifida since birth, is shown in therapy and in a special
school for the handicapped. Nadia expresses appreciation for ramps
provided at a circus and wishes more places had them. She is grateful to her family for their support and their willingness not to feel
sorry for her, and feels that others should react to a handicapped
person just as they would to anyone else. Nadia anticipates the possibility of being able to attend a normal public school in the near future. Though some kids may tease her, she expresses complete confidence that whatever arises she will find a way to deal with it. A
very positive film. Academy Award. d. Beverly Shaffer; p. Yuki
Yoshida, Kathleen Shannon; NFBC; MEDIAG: PAS.

I'LL NEVER GET HER BACK (24m B 1965)
  Documents the feelings and impressions of a young unwed mother

who is giving her baby up for adoption. Reveals her involvement
with the father of the child, her adjustment to her temporary resi-
dence in a home for unwed mothers, her awareness of the child growing inside, social scorn, and the loneliness of bearing a child which
must be given away. p. Tom Ashwell; p. NBC-TV; FI; KENTSU,
UMN.

ILLEGAL ABORTION (25m B 1968)
    Dramatized to illustrate the situation of a young couple, particu-
larly of the young woman, faced with an unwanted pregnancy and
desiring an abortion forbidden by law. Portrays her dilemma from
the time pregnancy is confirmed by her doctor, until her pregnancy
is terminated by an illegal practitioner. Not recommended for viewing by anyone under the age of 16. d. Robin Spry; p. Guy Glover;
NFBC; CRM.

ILLUSION OF SEPARATENESS (28m B n.d.)
    A filmed lecture by Ram Dass on universal oneness. Produced
by Bucks County Seminar House. Cinematographically poor, but it
captures Ram Dass's charisma and his delightful sense of humor.
p. Elda Hartley; HARTLEY.

I'M GOING TO BE (15m C 1977) I'm Going to Be Series
    Imaginative, colorful, and upbeat introduction to the career of
engineering. Free of racial and sexual bias and designed to interest
elementary students in the many and varied branches of the engineering profession. At a carnival, a boy and a girl are transported to
the world of engineers where they learn how exciting engineering can
be. p. Women's Resource Center, University of CAlifornia, Riverside;
UCEMC.

I'M MICHAELA'S FRIEND (10m C p1978, r1978--U.S.)
    An animated story shows Michaela watching a nature program on
television about a mother monkey and her children when suddenly the
little one jumped out of the set and into the room. The monkey and
Michaela became friends. Despite all the fun they were having, the
monkey soon became homesick so the next time the television was turned
on, he jumped in and rejoined his family. p. Romania Film; d./s.w.
Nell Cobar; PHOENIX.

I'M NOT ONE OF 'EM (3m B 1974)
    A woman spectator at the roller derby talks about her unique ex-
periences with lesbianism. Hilarious and also painful. p. Jan Oxen-
berg; IRIS.

IMAGE BEFORE MY EYES (90m C 1980)
    Jewish Poland before its destruction was the largest and most im-
portant center of Jewish culture and creativity in the world. Ironically, those of the last generation of Polish Jews are better known
for their annihilation in the Holocaust than for their achievements in

life. Through rare films as well as through photographs, memorabilia, music and interviews with survivors of this lost culture, the
film vividly recreates Jewish life in Poland from the late nineteenth
century through the 1930's--a unique and now vanished era. Funded
by the National Endowment for the Humanities. A YIVO Institute
for Jewish Research Presentation. d. Josh Waletzky; p. Susan Lazarus, Josh Waletzky; s.w. Jerome Badanes; NYF.

IMAGINARIUM, THE (15m C p1978, r1978)
   Presents the imaginarium, a team of artists, arts specialists and
museum educators who design unique participatory experiences for
children, integrating movement, music and visual arts. d. Tara
Alexander Curry. p. Museum of Art, Carnegie Institute; CARNIMA.

IMANI (7m C p1976, r1979) The Seven Principles Series
   Demonstrates the universality of the human experience through
the folklore of people of African descent using animation. p. Nguzo
Saba Films; p./s.w. Carol Munday Lawrence; BEACON.

IMPASSE (10m C 1978)
   An aggressive red arrow tries to get rid of a little white dot from
a totally black field. The little white dot triumphs through passive
resistance and the ability to change into other forms. The artwork
for this film is made entirely with self adhesive Avery labels attached
to the standard acetate cels of traditional animation. d./p. Caroline
Ahlfours Mouris, Frank Mouris; PHOENIX.

IMPERIAL CITY (50m C r1980--U.S.)
   Describes the building of the city of New Delhi, explores some
of the cultural and political conflicts that arose over it, and explains
the ideas and thoughts of the architects who undertook the project.
When King George announced the transfer of the seat of government
in India from Calcutta to Delhi, there was a great deal of resentment
and disapproval. Edwin Lutyens was chosen to be the architect and
asked for Herbert Baker to work with him. The Indian people wanted
native Indian style architecture, but the King wanted the Mongol style
with tile floors and pools. The architect urged compromise combining
the best of East and West. Taking almost 20 years to build, New
Delhi is the only complete city entirely designed and built by the
British. p. Margaret Williams/Arts Council of Great Britain; d. David
Rowan; CANTOR.

IMPROV (19m C 1973)
   A day of rehearsal with twelve actors, working without a script
toward an experimental play that will stretch the concept of improvisation into the final production. Starting only with a theme, the actors are, at the point of filming, working out ideas of improvisation
and a form of control of the action through the use of interrogation
of their personal and professional motives and competence. Shows
the struggle and moments of failure as well as success inherent in

improvisational work. In effect, the process of making the play becomes part of the play. This film can be used to assist teachers in
developing classroom drama or as a discussion on the psychology of
play-acting or group action. NOTE: Contains language that may be
offensive. d. Joan Henson; p. Tom Daly; NFBC; MACMFL.

IMPROVISATION (5m C 1977)
Using special video equipment, Doris Chase gracefully composes
and re-composes dance and movement, color and design, into a har-
monic imagery that combines the abstract and the recognizable. Kei
Takei dances to a rhythmic drum beat. Choreographed for television.
Funded by National Endowment for the Arts; p. Doris Chase for
WNET-TV; CHASED.

IMPULSES (30m C 1974)
Margaret Beals and Impulses Company in a performance demonstrating the art of improvisation. The company consists of three
musicians, a singer, a monologist and a dancer. Introduction by
dance critic Walter Terry. d. Peter Powell; p. Impulses Foundation;
BROOKSV.

IN CONTINUO (12m C r1973)
Focuses on the red-leather face of a woman scrubbing tiles; chains
clank and the camera pulls back to reveal the blood-stained tile walls
of a slaughter house. The filmmaker captures the strength and terrible beauty in the daily preparation for slaughter. The sound track
echoes with hard metallic knives being ground, tested and sharpened.
Testing the huge metal hanger, the butchers parallel the cattle that
will be killed and hung there; their muscular arms and blood-red
faces mirror their occupation. Water flushes away the blood and runs
down to the river that flows mysteriously clear. Thus water purges
but never really cleans the walls of the slaughter house. p. Dunay
Film; d. Vlatko Gilic; PHOENIX.

IN DARK PLACES (THE HOLOCAUST) (58m C r1978)
Explores the attempts of a few individuals to come to terms with
the Holocaust. Among them are the survivors of the ghettos and
concentration camps and their children; members of the New Artef
Players performing and disucssing their play based on the experiences
of the survivors; and writer and social critic Susan Sontag, who
places the event in a social and historical context, showing how the
imagery of the Holocaust has become part of our cultural fads and
fashion. This film does not attempt to reconstruct the actual history
of the period. Rather, this is a film concerned very much with the
present, with the ways in which the past reverberates in our current
consciousness. p./d. Gina Blumenfeld; ed. Sara Fishko; PHOENIX;
UCEMC.

IN FOR TREATMENT (99m C p1979, r1981)
A pleasant, cooperative middle-aged man checks into the hospital

unaware that he is fatally ill and eventually realizes, amidst the hypo-
crisy of the doctors and institutional personnel, he is losing his identity. Produced by the 11-year-old Het Werkteater of the Netherlands,
this film not only explores the meaning of illness and death to patients,
relatives, doctors and nurses, but also protests the dehumanizing
quality of contemporary life. d. Eric van Zuylen/Marja Kok; p. Het
Werkteater; IFEX.

IN GOOD COMPANY (20m C p1981, r1982)
 A film about Pratt and Whitney Canada, the world's leading manufacturer of small gas turbine engines. Briefly outlines the history
of the company and explains why Pratt and Whitney Canada puts so
much emphasis on research and development of aero-engine components.
It reveals the long road between initial engine concept and finished
product and introduces some of the people who are involved in the
process. d. Werner Volkmer, p. Tina Horne; PRATWHIT.

IN HER HANDS: WOMEN AND RITUAL (20m B 1979) (Video)
 Offers an unusual view of Syrian Sephardic Jewish women living
in New York City. Adolescent girls and young married women discuss their attitudes about themselves, their roles as wives and mothers, and the mikvah law they follow. A mikvah attendant explains
the ritual for purification and the laws governing sexual relations
between married couples. The interviewers' respectful curiosity elicits the trust and inner feelings of the women as well as the viewer's
serious appraisal of women's roles, family life, and sexuality within
the context of a strong religious tradition. d./p. Faye Ginsburg,
Lily Kharrazi, Diane Winston; p. Jewish Media Service/JWB; WMM.

IN LOVELAND: STUDY OF A TEENAGE SUICIDE (28m C p1981,
 r1982) (also Video)
 Presents a program that examines the tragic course of events
leading to the death of Mark Cada, a 15-year-old who killed himself
in Loveland, Colorado, and stresses the urgency of paying close attention to signals transmitted by potential teenage suicides. d./p.
Herbert Danska; p. ABC News Production from the ABC Directions
Series; ABCWWL.

IN NEED OF SPECIAL ATTENTION (16m C 1981)
 A docudrama, with narration by Loretta Swit, to assist emergency
room personnel in establishing procedures for the treatment of battered women. Based on protocols developed by Brigham and Women's
Hospital in Boston, the film focuses on the identification of patients
as victims of domestic violence and provides a model of intervention.
d. Christina Crowley; p. Nancy Graham; ODNPRO.

IN OUR OWN BACKYARD (59m C 1981) (Video)
 Focuses on events surrounding the Love Canal controversy, 1978-
1980. Examines how government officials handled the complex questions of what government should do and what it could do in the first

environmental emergency of its kind. Shows how residents formed their own views of these questions and then used public protest and the power of the media to influence the government. d. Lynn Corcoran for Buffalo Documentary Group; BULFRG.

IN OUR OWN BACKYARDS: URANIUM MINING IN THE UNITED STATES (29m C 1981)
Mining and milling of uranium, a delicate and dangerous process, involves release of radioactive gases into the air and the creation of millions of tons of radioactive waste. This film explores the impact of this process on the environment and on the health of workers and nearby residents. The filmmakers visit a Navajo Reservation and a plant in Vermont, and interview the representative of the Nuclear Regulatory Commission in Washington, D.C. p. Pamela Jones, Susanna Styron/Eleventh Hour Films; BULFRG.

IN OUR WATER (58m C p1981, r1982)
An investigative documentary based on a case study of chemical pollution in local drinking water reflecting a serious state and national problem. South Brunswick, New Jersey, Spring 1975: Frank Kaler and his family are convinced there is something wrong with their water: vegetables cooked in it turn colors and skin lesions appear after bathing in it. d./p. Meg Switzgable; NEWDAY.

IN PARIS PARKS (15m C 1954)
Children's rhythms as they play during an afternoon in the parks of Paris. d. Shirley Clarke; MOMA.

IN PLAIN SIGHT (3m C 1977)
Uniquely inventive film on paradoxes of life vs. art, and real vs. synthetic time. A paper rectangle taped inside the windshield of a moving car displays an animated cartoon of the passing landscape. A roadsign with hand drawn clouds drifting across it stands along a real country road. Animated chickens strut across an easel set against a coop of their real counterparts. Only American entry to win an award at the 1978 Zagreb Film Festival. d. Jane Aaron; music: Larry Packer, Richard Grado, Steve Silverstein; SERBC.

IN THE BEGINNING (15m C r1979)
Documents the abilities that take place in a child's development from birth to the age of two. The narrator describes the experiences from sucking as an infant to coordination at around 12 weeks, motor skills around seven months, forming special relationships and attachments at one year, and forming sentences by the age of two. It is noted that nurturing during this period is most important in the child's development since it will affect the behavior patterns throughout life. d. Roy Cox; p. Mark Krighaum; p. Eclipse Films; DAVIDSF.

IN THE BEST INTERESTS OF THE CHILDREN (53m C 1977)
Eight lesbian mothers are talking of their experiences as lesbians

and mothers. Their statements show them to be both the same as, and different from, other mothers. Their children are shown in inter-action with their mothers. In a rap group the women discuss how they feel about the court's right to decide where they will live and what they think about their own sexuality. Also presented are an attorney and a clinical social worker, both of whom have done exten-sive work with lesbian mothers. What the film says, ultimately, is YES, lesbians are good mothers; YES, lesbians do have problems, but those problems come from the attitudes of our society and the courts toward them. A direct challenge to the prevailing myths about lesbians as mothers. IRIS; PURDUE, UCLA, UM.

IN THE REALM OF THE SENSES (115m C 1977) (Japanese/Subtitled)
This is the true story of Sada, a geisha, and her lover, Kichi. Almost all the film's action takes place within their closed world of eroticism. Their lovemaking steadily increases in erotic intensity as they deliberately isolate themselves from society until a crime of pas-sion is committed. According to director Oshima, Sada was one of the first women in Japan to have her sexuality made public. During her trial, she attracted much sympathy and was finally sentenced to only six years in prison. The mention of her name is still synony-mous with the breaking of sexual taboos in Japan. Please note that this film contains scenes of explicit sex and other material that may be offensive. p. Anatole Dauman; d. Nagisa Oshima; NYF.

IN TIME (44m C r1977)
A number of interesting and vital elderly people describe their lives, reminisce, and respond to such questions as: Would you want to be young again? Do you consider yourself old? What are the ad-vantages and disadvantages of growing old? Are you a more interest-ing person now than when you were young? Scenes of their lives today are intercut with rapid-fire clips illustrating each decade of this century. Shows some youthful fads of the recent past and today-- fads already slipping into past. Demonstrates that old age is merely a part of the life process. Sensitive and thought provoking. UCEMC.

IN WHICH WE SERVE (113m B 1942)
This is the story of the H.M.S. Torrin, a British destroyer, and of those gallant men and women who served aboard her during World War II until she was sunk off Greece. A testament to human faith. d./p./s.w. Noel Coward; LCA.

IN WINTERLIGHT (18m C 1974)
Two women share their space and sexuality in a tender and lov-ing manner. Their warmth comes through in the conversations and their way of relating. On pillows, they relax with each other in the soft winter light. They use their hands and a vibrator to enjoy and pleasure each other's bodies, and one reaches a marked orgasm. Some post-orgasmic interaction is included. Explicit. p. Laird Sut-ton, National Sex Forum; MMRC.

INCAS, THE (59m C 1980) The Odyssey Series
Examines the Inca Empire through the work of anthropologists
and archaeologists currently involved in research in Peru. One archaeologist directs research that has led to the restoration of modern
irrigation canals on the basis of ancient Inca engineering. This restoration is part of an attempt to alleviate the abject poverty of Quechua Indians, who live in this once-prosperous land and from whom
the archaeologist is learning about relationships between ancient and
contemporary subsistence activities. p. Ann Benson-Gyles; DER.

INCENSE (5m C 1953)
An excerpt from RUTH ST. DENIS BY BARIBAULT. Features
Ruth St. Denis in a solo choreographed in 1906. Her particular kind
of sensual, ritualistic dance displays her sinuous arm movements.
DAN/UR.

INCEST: THE HIDDEN CRIME (16m C 1979)
Much of this interview-style discussion centers around a real family which has dealt with an incestuous relationship and managed to
stay intact. Provides statistical information: average age of victim
is eight years, all social classes are affected, sexual intercourse and
violence do not always occur, and because of the power structure in
the family, the father is usually the offender. In the case studied,
the nine-year-old daughter blamed herself because she had asked her
father a question about sex. After the situation was exposed, the
wife agreed not to seek a divorce and opted for compulsory therapy
sessions for the husband. The repercussions of the incest on the
future of the family members is discussed. p. CBS-TV; UIL, UCEMC,
UMN.

INCREASING JOB OPTIONS FOR WOMEN (10m C 1975) (slc)
Job options for women are increasing. This slide presentation
shows that the variety of jobs open to women is greater today than
ever before. Women have better opportunities to make a contribution,
use their abilities, and work in jobs that hold their interest and meet
their needs. Script included. Produced by the Center for Human
Systems, University of Minnesota, in cooperation with the Women's
Bureau, United States Department of Labor. UMN.

INCREDIBLE SAN FRANCISCO ARTISTS' SOAP BOX DERBY, THE
(24m C p1975, r1977)
Documents an unusual and memorable events which took place in
spring of 1975, when 104 San Francisco Bay area artists combined
their talents in a unique soap box derby. A creatively rewarding
and fun occasion helped raise $20,000 for the San Francisco Museum
of Modern Art. p. Amanda C. Pope; PHOENIX; UIL.

INCREDIBLE SARAH, THE (105m C 1976)
An oppulent drama of Sarah Bernhardt's flamboyant career. The
tempestuous and eccentric French actress dominated European theatre

toward the end of the nineteenth century. Glenda Jackson stars as Sarah Bernhardt. Musical score by Elmer Bernstein. Review by Judith Christ praises Glenda Jackson's portrayal of Sarah Bernhardt. d. Richard Fleischer; FI.

INDEX (5m B n.d.)
Multiple exposure of a duet turns it into a sextet. Dancers: Judith Dunn, Tony Holder; Choreographer; Gene Friedman, Judith Dunn; d./p. Gene Friedman; EASTEND.

INDIA AND THE INFINITE: THE SOUL OF A PEOPLE (30m C p1979, r1981) (also Video)
A picture of India as paradoxes and extremes: the country's many religions--Islam, Parsiism, Jainism, Buddhism, Sikhism, Christianity, and, of course, Hinduism; its love of ritual and what it symbolizes; its great art and architecture and the extraordinary leap of consciousness that birthed the concept "You are God." Images are gathered from Kashmir to Benares, from Bombay to Bangalore, d./p. Elda Hartley; HARTLEY.

INDIA IMAGE SERIES, THE see HINDU FAMILY CELEBRATION: 60TH BIRTHDAY

INDIAN RIGHTS, INDIAN LAW (60m C 1978) (also Video)
In recent years American Indians have been asserting their rights in court and demanding the fulfillment of the nation's long-standing obligations to them. Focuses on the work of the native American Rights Fund (NARF) in such cases as the fight between 14 tribes and Washington State officials over treaty rights along the Puyallup River; the struggles of the Paiute tribe against the diversion of water from Pyramid Lake in Nevada; the religious rights of prisoners; more equitable treatment for Indian school children; and the land-claims suit of the Passamaquoddy and Penobscot tribes in Maine. Provides a rare glimpse of the litigation process and insight into why the land resources, and tribal sovereignty are so important in preserving Indian identity. p. Ford Foundation; d./p. Sandra Consentino, Joseph Consentino; FI.

INFANT CARRIER (½m C p1980, r1980) (Video)
Urges parents to use an infant carrier restraint seat in their automobiles. d. Phil Schulman; p. Wendy Mayer; MTPS.

INFERTILITY IN MEN AND WOMEN (22½m C 1983)
A young couple, unable to conceive, agree to seek medical help with their infertility problem. The husband consults a urologist. The wife visits her gynecologist. Both undergo full workups. Animation is skillfully used to explain the various procedures. Emphasizes the close cooperation required to assure accurate test results and optimum chances for conception. MIFE.

INNER SPACES (28m C 1973)
Captain Mitchell, the sixth man to set foot on the moon, conducted telepathy experiments from outer space and now explores the inner spaces of the human mind. Recent scientific findings ... the daily use of ESP by executives, the effects of telepathy on the body, the "out-of-body-experience" ... combine with ancient religious and meditational practices to illustrate Captain Mitchell's contention that intuitive and religious ways of knowing are just as important as objective or scientific approaches. p. Elda Hartley; HARTLEY.

INNER STRENGTHS (28m C n.d.) Prime Time (Series)
A visit with some older Americans whose attitudes about life and living can serve as examples to us all. They show us something about growing, as well as growing older. Narrated by Don McNeill. Free loan. p. Sears-Roebuck Foundation; MTPS.

INNER VISIONS/BEAH RICHARDS (29m C 1975) (Video, Beta, VHS)
Actress-playright-poet Beah Richards, known for her roles in GUESS WHO'S COMING TO DINNER and GREAT WHITE HOPE, reads from her book A Black Woman Speaks and Other Poems and talks about her life with host David Crippins. She expresses her strong feelings about women's liberation and illustrates with several of her poems, including "Black," "Wanna Bet" and "A Black Woman Speaks." p. KCET-TV, Los Angeles; PBSV.

INNER WOMAN, THE (SERIES) see BREAST SELF-EXAMINATION; CONCEPTION AND PREGNANCY; MENSTRUATION AND SEXUAL DEVELOPMENT; PHYSICAL SIGNS AND EFFECTS OF VENEREAL DISEASES; PHYSIOLOGY OF MISCARRIAGE AND ABORTION; QUESTION OF SELF CONCEPT, THE

INQUIRY: YESTERDAY'S CHILDREN (48m C p1978, r1978)
In our society, old age is a time of loneliness in the uncaring urban world which caters almost exclusively to the young and their fast-paced life-style. Takes a sensitive and probing look at our old people and how we treat them. More important, it asks why we treat them in the manner we do. d. Ron Carlyle; p. Jack McGaw; CTV.

INSIDE, I ACHE (17m C 1982)
Explores teenage suicide. For young people, the visual presentation provides an opportunity to talk about a guarded subject with their peers and with a caring adult. For educators and counselors, it offers an entry into a sensitive subject with carefully prepared suggestions for discussion, related activities and additional reading materials. p. Rabbi Daniel A. Roberts; d. Elaine Rembrandt; MMM.

INSIDE LOOK NORTH (4m C p1978, r1979)
An overview of the media world set to music that increases in tempo as the deadline for "airtime" approaches. The fast-paced animation presents a television news team conducting their daily assign-

ments of reporting and writing the news of the day, through its con-
version to tape, and finally, in split-second timing, going on the air!
p. Sheila Graber; STEREF.

INSIDE-OUT SERIES see BREAKUP

INSIDE WOMEN INSIDE (28m ? 1978)
    Provocative interviews with women at the North Carolina Correc-
tional Center for Women and the Correctional Institute at Rikers Island, New York. Testimonies are heard from women who have suffered miscarriages and improper medical care. Shows glimpses of inhumane conditions ranging from feudal wages and overcrowded cell
blocks to lack of nutritional meals. p. Christine Choy, Cynthia
Maurizio; TWN.

INSIGHT VIGNETTES SERIES see KINSHIPS: FINDING VALUES IN
    FAMILY RELATIONSHIPS

INTERDEPENDENT RELATIONSHIPS (28m C n.d.) Prime Time (Series)
    Shows a few examples of the kinds of interdependent relationships
we have as we grow older and how they affect the quality of our lives.
Narrated by Don McNeill. Free loan. p. Sears-Roebuck Foundation;
MTPS.

INTERFACE: REFLECTIONS IN TIME AND SPACE (28m C 1981)
    (Video)
    The three-dimensional arts of dance, sculpture and architecture
are explored. This collage of visual images reveals how the elements
of space, shape, scale, and time--when interfaced--create new perceptions of three-dimensional art forms. d./p. Mary Ellen Brown;
ICAP.

INTERLOPERS (24m C 1979)
    A landowner and his neighbor finally face each other, having
been made enemies by the land on which they stand. Suddenly the
winter wind pins them side by side under a fallen tree. The enemies slowly recognize their shared bond and the futility of their
age-old family dispute. They wait for rescue, anxious to publicly
display their new friendship. Adapted from short story by H. H.
Munro (Saki). d. Zack Taylor; p./s.w. Karen Taylor, Z. Taylor;
p. A Touch of the Sun Production; BARRF.

INTERNAL TRIP WITH DOROTHY HEATHCOTE, THE (54m C 1975)
    (Video)
    Speaking before a group of drama instructors, Dorothy Heathcote
gives a detailed analysis of her methods of instruction and presents
a film of a children's drama workshop that she recently conducted.
p. Robert Miller; UNEWB; UMN.

INTERNATIONAL TRIBUNALS ON CRIMES AGAINST WOMEN (29m C
    1977) (Video) Woman Series

The investigation of crimes against women by two international tribunals is discussed by their organizers, Diana Russell and Judith Friedlander. Russell was one of the founders of the International Tribunal on Crimes Against Women held in Brussels in March of 1976 and is the co-author of Crimes Against Women: The Proceedings of the International Tribunal. Friedlander helped organize the New York Tribunal, which was established as a support council for the world meeting. The tribunals considered subjects ranging from forced motherhood to the workload of working women to medical crimes. Sandra Elkin is the moderator. p. WNED-TV, Buffalo; PBSV.

INTERVIEW (13m C n.d.)
The filmmakers reveal something of their lives through use of collage and fingerpaint animation techniques respectively. There is a special paradox connected with the animator's lonely art--caught between frustrating aloneness and the joy of solitude--which this film captures beautifully. d. Veronika Soul/Caroline Leaf; p. David Verrall/Derek Lamb; NFBC; SERBC.

INTERVIEW: READY OR NOT (24m C 1975)
An animated film satire presents an imaginary interview between two so-called knowledgeables of the music world, poking fun at the pretensions that often surround a "cultural discussion." "Well, yeah man, you know" is just about as articulate as Shorty Petterstein, jazz musician, ever gets. p. Dimension Films; CF; UIL, UM.

INTERVIEW: WOMEN CANDIDATES, THE (35m C n.d.) (Video)
Presents an interview with a woman and dramatizes ten potentially unfair employment practices. Features a discussion of the implications of those practices. XICOM.

INTERVIEW FILM: WHAT TO KNOW AND WHAT TO DO, THE (21m C 1977)
An analysis and dramatization of the interview procedure from the point of view of the employer. Shows five candidates for a position (cashier in a restaurant chain) during the interview procedures and enumerates the elements which provide the interviewer with clues for rating and comparison. p. CBS-TV; BFA; UIL, PAS, IU.

INTERVIEW WITH BARBARA JORDAN (29m C 1980) (Video, Beta, VHS)
Congresswoman Barbara Jordan is now a professor at the Lyndon B. Johnson School of Public Affairs in Austin, Texas. In the wide-ranging discussion with host Ben Wattenberg, Jordan reflects on the changing political and economic status of blacks, and on the changing face of American liberalism. She looks back on her years in Washington, and discusses her reasons for abandoning Congress for the classroom. And she offers brief assessments of a number of prominent political figures. The program also visits Jordan's classroom for an animated discussion of the ethics of politics. p. WETA-TV, Washington, D.C.; PBSV.

INTERVIEWING SKILLS (42m C 1980) (Video)
Preparation for the job interview, dos and don'ts pertaining to
the interview itself, and follow-up procedures are presented by Robert Chersi, the corporate college relations and recruiting representative for IBM. p. College of Business Administration at The Pennsylvania State University; PAS.

INTERVIEWING THE ABUSED CHILD (21m C 1978)
Interviews children who have been abused by their parents. Explains that teachers, doctors or social workers must gain the child's
trust, listen intently to what the child says and just as carefully note
the child's nonverbal expression. p. Cavalcade Productions, Inc.;
MTITI; CORNELL, CWU.

INTO THE MOUTHS OF BABES (28m C 1978)
Report on the infant formula conflict in the Dominican Republic.
For example, multinational corporations selling and encouraging the
use of powdered milk by mothers who have inadequate resources to
use it properly. The result: infant malnutrition and death. d./p.
Janet Roach for National Council of Churches; CBS-TV; NCCHS; PAS.

INTOXICATING DREAMS: THE ADVERTISING OF ALCOHOL (30m C
1982) (slt, Video)
Examines the images used by advertisers to sell alcohol. Based
on the lectures, slide presentations and research of Jean Kilbourne,
nationally known media analyst and educator, who has spent many
years studying the advertising and alcohol industries. Jean Kilbourne
is also available as a guest speaker. Write for information on her
slide presentation "Under the Influence: The Pushing of Alcohol Via
Advertising." p. Cambridge Documentary Films, Inc.; CAMDOC.

INTRODUCING JANET (27m C p1981, r1982)
Janet hides her insecurities behind a boisterous and self-deprecating
facade. Her friends know her as "Big J." Her mother wants her
to lose weight, be more active and outgoing. When she meets Tony,
an aspiring comic, her life begins to change and their friendship
helps her to strive for a more positive self-image. d. Glen Salzman;
p. Rebecca Yates; BEACON.

INTRODUCTION TO ARNOLD SCHONBERG'S "ACCOMPANIMENT TO A
CINEMATOGRAPHIC SCENE" (15m C 1973) (German/Subtitled)
Examination of an artist's political commitment: Schonberg's let-
ters justifying his decision to leave Nazi Germany. d. Jean-Marie
Straub; NYF.

INTRODUCTION TO DUNCAN DANCES (15m C 1965-67)
The Isadora Duncan dances performed are "Three Graces," "Lullaby," "Cossaise," and "Scarf Dance" (Schubert); "Springtime" (Gret-
chaninoff); "Tanagra" (Corelli); "Waltz Studies" (Strauss). Dancers:
Hortense Kooluris with students of the Philadelphia Dance Academy;

Choreographers: Isadora Duncan, Irma Duncan; Project d. Nadia Chilkovsky Nahumck; a.d. Fai Coleman; p. Calvin De Frenes Corporation; FRANDA.

INTRODUCTORY PRINCIPLES OF NUTRITION SERIES see NUTRITION IN INFANCY; NUTRITION IN PREGNANCY; NUTRITION ON AGING; VITAMINS I; VITAMINS II

INVENTION IN DANCE (29m B 1960) A Time to Dance (Series)
     Alwin Nikolais and Martha Myers discuss modern dance pioneers Isadora Duncan and Ruth St. Denis, and the Denishawn school, whose students included Martha Graham, Charles Weidman and Doris Humphrey. Slides of these dancers, film clips of St. Denis in an excerpt from her dance RADHA, and a demonstration of the Duncan Technique by Sima Boriosivana are shown. Members of the Henry Street Playhouse Dance Company demonstrate various methods used in order to portray emotions, height and weights in modern dance technique. Dances include excerpts from "Web," "Discs," "Noumenon" and "Fixation." Choreographers: Alwin Nikolais, Martha Myers; Commentator: Martha Myers; p. Jac Venza; p. WGBH-TV; IU; IU, AFI, UIO, UUTA, PSU.

INVESTIGATION OF RAPE (20m C 1977)
     Dramatizes an actual rape investigation to demonstrate the victim's emotional needs from the first call for help through the medical examination. MTITI; UCEMC.

INVESTMENT PICTURE, THE (27m C 1981)
     A country's economic health is largely dependent upon the investment decisions of the individual citizens. The investment cycle is explored via one such individual and Telidon animation to illustrate the process. d. Roman Bittman; p. Marilyn A. Belec; MOBIUS.

IRENE MOVES IN (25m C p1981, r1981--U.S.) (also Video)
     Shows the danger in snap judgments and first impressions and points out the value of friendships. d. Londa Schuyler, Kit Hood; p. Playing With Time, Inc., Canada; s.w. Amy Jo Cooper; LCA.

IRISH, THE (26m C 1974) A Storm of Strangers (Series)
     Authentic period photographs chronicle the arrival of Irish immigrants in the United States, the economic conditions they left behind, problems of the early settlers, and the contributions to American government and culture. Narrated by Edmund O'Brien. d. Chris Jenkyns; p. National Communication Foundation/Elaine Attias, Paul Attias under a grant from National Endowment of the Humanities; NCOMF; PAS.

IRONING (16m C p1977, r1980)
     Faced with a possible judgment by a visiting social worker, a mother recollects the rearing of her daughter. In spite of economic

deprivation, the child blooms into a comedienne. Inspired by a partial rendition of "I Stand Here Ironing," a short story by Tillie Olsen. d. Lynne Conroy; s.w./ed. L. Conroy; IRIS.

IS IT O.K.?--WOMEN AND THE CRIMINAL JUSTICE SYSTEM see
   WOMEN AND THE LAW, THE (SERIES)

IS MY BABY O.K.? (24m C 1979)
   Presents four case histories showing the various complications which can occur during pregnancy and the birth process. Illustrates how the medical sciences are dealing with the problems that can arise during pregnancy. p. WABC-TV; BESTF.

IS THAT WHAT YOU WANT FOR YOURSELF? (13m C p1980, r1980)
   Presents a realistic look at today's social scene. Fifteen-year-old Debby Edwards suspects she may be pregnant, a dilemma that creates numerous questions and problems for her and her boyfriend Tony. The problems remain unresolved in this film, allowing viewers to reach their own conclusions and prompting further discussion concerning teenage sexuality, child and parental relationships, expectations, and what each person wants for his or her own life. p. Peggy Stevens, Diane Smook; p. Health Video Services; d. J. Philip Miller; LCA; IU, KENTSU, UMN.

ISABEL BISHOP: PORTRAIT OF AN ARTIST (29m C 1979) (also
   Video)
   Master of romantic realism, Isabel Bishop's preoccupation with the ordinary has produced a style of painting uniquely her own. She is a highly individual exponent of the art of painting and a distinctive personality. This film portrait is studied and knowing. Scenes out of her paintings and from her life have been re-created to expand the viewer's understanding of her translations to canvas. p. John Beymer; d. Patricia Depew; FI.

ISABELLA AND THE MAGIC BRUSH (14m C 1977)
   An animated fantasy, adapted from a Chinese tale. Tells of little Isabella whose desire to be an artist is thwarted by poverty, a tyrant king, her own parents (who think she should be a cook), and the court painter who fears competition. However, Isabella wishes for and receives a brush--a magic one that gives life to whatever is painted with it. Her fame spreads throughout the kingdom. p. Barbara Dourmashkin; FLMFR.

ISADORA DUNCAN AND THE ART OF THE DANCE (20m C 1960's)
   (SFS)
   Illustrated lecture on Isadora Duncan and the Art of the Dance by Julia Levien, lecturer, solo artist, and teacher who performed in the companies of Irma and Ann Duncan (they were members of Isadora Duncan's original school). Narrator: Julia Levien; p. Dance Films Association; DANCFA.

ISADORA DUNCAN: BIGGEST DANCER IN THE WORLD (63m B 1966)
Ken Russell's BBC film reveals the beginnings of an erratic-style dance especially suited to the material. Vivien Pickles assays the role of the notorious, eccentric and doomed dancer with obvious relish if not downright glee. Much of the screenplay is Russell's embellishments on fact carried to their cinematic extreme. p. BBC; KPF; DAN/UR.

ISADORA DUNCAN: TECHNIQUE AND CHOREOGRAPHY (29m C 1978)
Shows Isadora Duncan Centenary Dance Company with soloists Gemze de Lappe, Hortense Kooluris and Julia Levien. Included are technique class excerpts as well as performances of "Three Graces," "Water Study," "Mazurka for Two," "Two Scriabin Etudes," and "Chopin Polonaise." p. Virginia Brooks; BROOKSV.

ISLAND OF THE RED PRAWNS (53m C 1977)
Documents the culture of one of the Fiji Islands by recording the traditional wedding of the children of two important chieftains. Intersperses scenes of the wedding preparations and ceremony with scenes of many local customs, such as the making of tapa cloth; planting, growing, and harvesting food; fishing methods; and walking over burning coals. Visits the sacred site of rare red prawns and recounts the legend of the red prawns during the wedding feast. p. William Geddes; IU, UCEMC.

ISSEI, NISEI, SANSEI (18m C 1975)
Portrays three generations of a Japanese-American family. Reveals the changing values of each generation as they attempt to live within the system. p. UCLA; UCLA.

ISSEI: THE FIRST FIFTY YEARS (17m B 1978)
A history of Japanese Americans from first immigration over 100 years ago to the present; their various roles in agriculture, domestic employment, railroad building and general business; also the legislative disadvantages and discrimination they have experienced. p. University of California, Berkeley; WSU; UCEMC.

ISSUES FOR WOMEN IN MANAGEMENT (18m C 1978) (Video)
Presents ten scenes portraying unresolved situations that may be experienced by women managers. These scenes are intended to provoke discussion through the use of role playing. Includes training manual. Presented by the School of Social Work, University of Washington. UW.

IT ONLY HAPPENS NEXT DOOR (35m C 1977) (Video)
Incest has long been a taboo subject and consequently is seldom discussed and rarely reported. Yet it does occur, and this film provides startling evidence of its prevalence. Points out the far-reaching and life-long effects on these victims. Social workers believe jailing offenders is not the answer; rather, attempts should be made to solve

their psychological problems. Above all, they say, the message must get to the public--incest does happen. d. Gerald Polikoff; FI.

IT WORKS FOR US (20m C p1980, r1980)
Uses three totally different types of food-buying cooperatives in New York City to offer ideas that could be implemented anywhere in the United States to make cooperative food-buying work for you. d. Gary Wachter; p. David Handwerker; Cornell University AV Center; CORNELL.

ITALIAN AMERICAN (ed. rel.) (26m C 1977) A Storm of Strangers (Series)
In this film interview, director Martin Scorsese used motion pictures and early family photographs to richly illustrate the recollection of his mother and father whose parents came from Italy and settled in New York in an area called Little Italy in the early days. They recall with gusto their childhood, their parents, sisters and brothers, and all things Italian. Catherine Scorsese is the epitome of the Italian mother whose warmth and ebullience is infectious. Charles Scorsese is at first reticent but in the telling of his stories he becomes the typical cavalier, holding the reigns on his family. d. Martin Scorsese; p. Elaine Attias, Saul Rubin under a grant from the National Endowment for the Humanities; NCOMF: MACMFL.

IT'S A NEW DAY (9m C 1981) (also Video)
Shows new attitudes and technologies for disabled persons to increase their integration into the mainstream of life. Highlights new devices such as vertical-lift wheelchairs, talking calculators, Opticonscan, Porta-printer. Disabled persons are shown in challenging lifestyles: riding dirt bikes, playing tennis, working as forest ranger, school teacher, airline reservation agent. Free loan. d. Annett Wolf; p. Fern Field; South Bay Mayors Committee for Employment of the Handicapped; SBMAYC.

IT'S A THOUGHT (22m C p1980, r1980) (also Video)
A dramatic story of a junior-high girl desperate to be "popular" and trapped in a nightmare of social rejection. Offers practical advice and hope. d. Linda Haskins; p. Centron Films; CORONET; UIL.

IT'S ALWAYS SO IN THE WORLD (28m C p1979, r1980) (also Video)
The Human Face of China Series
Shows the new life-style which has emerged in China since liberation in 1949. Numerous housing complexes, light industry, state subsidation of medical expenses and new opportunities in education reveal the country's accelerating development program. Chinese conversation with English subtitles introduces the Sun family with three generations living together in a two-room apartment in a new residential area. p. Suzanne Baker, Film Australia; d./s.w. Bob Kingsbury; LCA.

IT'S MY TURN (19m C 1974)
Describes in detail the most common methods of contraception; their effectiveness, safety and side effects; and the pros and cons of each in the group's opinion. Featured is a young woman seeking information from a professional counselor and an informal group discussion by married women. Presented by the Department of Obstetrics and Gynecology, Washington University School of Medicine. p. Linda Martin Enterprises; FLMFR.

IT'S NOT A ONE PERSON THING (30m C n.d.)
A moving film about the Federation of Southern Cooperatives, a service, resource and advocacy association of 30,000 Blacks and low-income families in 100 co-ops across the rural South. An outgrowth of the civil rights movement, the Federation was chartered in 1967 to help Blacks and poor people produce an income and solve employment, education, housing and health care needs for its members. The film examines these people who joined this self-help economic development movement. p. Sally Heckel; GRNMTP; UM.

IT'S NOT AN ILLNESS (23m C 1980) (Video)
Presents the concept that pregnancy is a natural experience and that with proper medical attention, women can continue normal exercise and fitness programs. Through a combination of dramatization, discussion and documentary techniques, we follow several women through their pregnancies and through the culmination of a natural delivery. Positive, multi-cultural presentation which features women in professional roles. Healthy participants demonstrate the benefits of exercise during pregnancy. Good demonstration of Lamaze breathing. Natural delivery scene shows spouses who are warm and supportive. p. Patter of Little Feet Film; JOURVI.

IT'S SNOW (6m C 1974) (also Video)
Delicate cut-out animation transforms the fragile snowflake designs into shining patterns of airy magic in cadence to a jingling melody. p. Gayle Thomas, NFBC; IFB.

IT'S SPRING MICHAELA (10m C p1978, r1978)
Without narration, this animated film tells the story of Michaela and her little puppy who were responsible for a butterfly's losing its wings and how they were able to finally restore the wings on the butterfly. p. Romania Film; d./s.w. Nell Cobar; PHOENIX.

IT'S UP TO LAURIE (21m C 1979)
Focuses on interpersonal relationships and attitudes toward sex, especially dating and premarital sexual intercourse. Shows how interpersonal relations and sexual attitudes and behavior may affect each other in their positive or negative ways. Also deals with the reactions and attitudes of parents. Raises many questions and provides a stimulus for a good discussion. With guide. p. Gordon-Kerckhoff; CENTEF.

-J-

JACK LEVINE (23m C 1964)
An at-work profile of one of America's leading artists, Jack Levine. Gives a terse history of Levine's work, and follows Levine throughout his major, complex painting, Witches' Sabbath, a devastating portrait of the McCarthy era. p. Zina Voynow, Peter Robinson, Herman J. Engel; TEXFM.

JACKSON COUNTY JAIL (85m C 1976)
An exploration of rape--both a reality for women and a metaphor for male-female relations in contemporary American society. Rave reviews from national critics. Starring Yvette Mimieux, Tommie Lee Jones. d. Michael Miller, p. Jeff Begun; FI.

JAIL (25m C p1979, r1979)
Motivational film to get young people thinking about the importance of keeping out of trouble. Dramatization show on the streets and in prison; makes its case without use of scare tactics or rough language. A straight message from young people who have done time to those who think they never will. p. Isabel Brenner, Michael Laurence; d. Michael Laurence; ex. p. Henry Brenner. ARTVIS.

...JAIL FOR WOMEN, A (57m B 1977) (Video)
Life in a residential cottage at the State Correctional Institution at Muncy, Pennsylvania. Focuses on a matron, three resident counselors and inmates. Variety of everyday situations: a room search, cottage meeting, overnight lock-in, arguments between inmates, an inmate's telephone call to her family, and discussions of sentences, sex and "doing time." p. P. J. O'Connell; PAS; IU.

JAMES MICHENER'S WORLD SERIES see WOMEN IN SPORTS

JANE SEYMOUR (102m C 1976) (The Six Wives of Henry VIII (Series)
Portrays Jane Seymour, a shy, devout girl whom Henry VIII invites to court and eventually marries. Uses a flashback technique to reveal events, feelings, and fears experienced by Jane. Examines Jane's influence on Henry's position on monasteries and her request that his daughter Mary be allowed to return to court. Arouses sympathy for Henry as he sees the birth of his son Edward and the consequent death of his dear Jane. p. BBC-TV; TIMLIF; CWU, IU.

JANET FLANNER (29m C p1978, r1978) The Writer in America (Series)
In her usual spirited manner, Flanner--who wrote for five decades as Genet, the Chronicler of an era--discusses her world. Through her eyes and sensibilities, we again see Hemingway, Picasso, Braque, Stein; we share her friendships and come to know her as a friend, journalist, artist and certainly, constantly, as a woman. d./p. Richard O. Moore; CORONET; IU, PAS, UIL.

JANIS IAN (40m C 1979)
   Janis Ian emerged in 1966 at the age of 16 with the hit song
"Society's Child." Shortly thereafter, she slipped into obscurity,
reappearing in 1975 with another smash composition, "At Seventeen,"
again meeting instant popular acceptance (and a Grammy Award).
Her creative output has since continued on a prolific wave of success.
Selections include: "This Is My Song," "Boy, I Really Tied One On,"
"At Seventeen," and "Tea and Sympathy." p. BBC-TV; TIMLIF.

JAZZ DANCE (26m C 1976)
   Synthesizing dance and video technology, the filmmaker uses linear figure drawing in animation. The upbeat lively mood is set by
the Dixieland rhythms and gaiety of Jelly Roll Morton's music performed by the Uptown Lowdown Jazzband. With Gay De Langhe; d.
/p. Doris Chase; CHASED.

JAZZ OF MARIAN MCPARTLAND, THE (28m C 1973) (Video)
   Jazz singer-pianist Marian McPartland presents a program of old
favorites, including "All the Things You Are," "Time and Time Again,"
"A Night in Tunisia," "Blues for B," and "While We're Young." Ac-
companied by Joe Corsello (drums) and Rusty Gilder (bass). p.
WLIW-TV, Garden City, NY; PBSV.

JEANNETTE RANKIN: THE WOMAN WHO VOTED NO (29m C 1983)
   (Video, Beta, VHS)
   Profile of Jeannette Rankin, the first woman to be elected to
Congress and the only Representative to vote against American entry
into both world wars. Chronicles Rankin's life from 1916. A short
epilogue covers the years prior to her death in 1973 when she be-
came a symbol of the contemporary women's and anti-war movements.
Original newsreels and photographs are used in addition to interviews
with friends, associates, and historians. p. Nancy Landgren, Susan
Regele, Ronald Bayly; p. The Fine Tuning Co.; FINTNC.

JENNIFER: A REVEALING STORY OF GENITAL HERPES (28m C 1982)
   Follows a young woman striving to cope with her own case of genital herpes. Through conversations with medical virologist Stephen
Straus, M.D., and nurse practitioner Susan Bachrach, R.N., both
of the National Institute of Allergy and Infectious Diseases, Jennifer
begins to understand the nature of this widespread viral infection.
She also begins to deal with her anger, feelings of social isolation
and increasing concern with her health. These conversations are
intercut with interviews with leaders in the field of genital herpes
research and photographs and other illustrations of the disease process. Jennifer offers an objective educational message for the general
public while providing emotional support for persons already suffering from genital herpes. Free loan. p. National Institute of Allergy
and Infectious Diseases; MTPS.

JENNY (19m C p1977, r1978)
   Profile of a Japanese-American family who teach their eight-year-

old daughter the traditions and arts of their ancestors. They are
not affiliated with a traditional Japanese religion in which many customs have their origin, yet they do not deny their ethnic heritage--
rather they incorporate it into their American life-style. p./d. Ginny
Hashii; CAROUF; ADL; UM.

JEN'S PLACE (52m C p1982, r1983)
     Fourteen-year-old Jen returns from summer camp to learn that
her parents have separated and agreed that Jen will live with her
mother during the week and her father on weekends. She is unable
to get either parent to listen to what she thinks about it so she ac-
quires the services of a child advocacy lawyer. She is able to get
the case reopened and the family gains a new perspective about one
another's feelings. D. Glen Salzman; p. Rebecca Yates; BEACON.

JERO ON JERO: A BALINESE TRANCE SEANCE OBSERVED (17m C
     1980)
     Jero Tapakan, a spirit medium, was invited to view herself in
trance filmed by the filmmakers Linda Connor and Timothy Asch.
Presents some of Jero's reactions and her comments as she watched
herself. Her comments provide insights into how she feels while
possessed, her understanding of witchcraft, and humility in the presence of the supernatural world. p. Linda Connor, Timothy Asch;
DER.

JERSEY DINER (47½m C 1980) (Video)
     A trip through the night along New Jersey's truck routes. Fol-
lows truckers to those fading pieces of Americana--the old "tin can"
diner. This is a story of eggs over easy, hard-working waitresses,
America's truckers, and life along the highway. d./p. Amanda Kissin; METROT.

JERUSALEM PEACE (57m C r1977)
     This film on Jerusalem deals with its present through montages,
city scenes and its past history as seen through the eyes of a leading archaeologist. d. Mark Benjamin; p. Elizabeth Fink Benjamin;
PHOENIX.

JESSE JACKSON AND CAROLYN SHELTON: PUSHING FOR EXCEL-
     LENCE (17m C p1978, r1978)
     United States Health, Education and Welfare awarded Jessie Jack-
son a grant to start programs on excellence in schools. Exhorting
an Afro-American high school audience, he brings this message:
"You're not a man because you can make a baby--you're a man because you can raise a baby." He believes that schools are a necessity for "upward mobility." Carolyn Shelton, a young Afro-American
stewardess, brings a similar message to minority girls: the importance
of "knowing the right things in the right places." Both seem to emphasize a new determination to help minorities transform their careers
and their lives. p. CBS-TV; PHOENIX; UIL.

JEWISH AMERICAN (ed. rel.) (26m B 1977) A Storm of Strangers
(Series)
Records the arrival of the first great wave of Jewish immigrants
to America, telling of their origins, their experiences in the new
land, and their contribution to the culture. Actor Herschel Bernardi,
portraying an elderly man, narrates this story of the early Jewish
experience in America. d. Ben Maddow; p. Elaine Attias, Saul Rubin;
p. National Communication Foundation under a grant from the National
Endowment of the Humanities. NCOMF; PAS.

JIGSAW FIT (29m C 1976) (also Video)
Unique model animation illustrates geological changes and processes such as mountain building, earthquakes, volcanoes, etc. These
sequences are highlighted with scenes from around the world that exemplify the actions of plate tectonics. d. Penny Crompton; OECA;
FI.

JILTING OF GRANNY WEATHERALL, THE (57m C 1980) American
Short Story Series
Katherine Anne Porter's story illustrates one of her major themes,
the human propensity for self-deception, through the painful memories that intrude upon Ellen Weatherall during the final hours of
her life. She had been jilted on her wedding day, and it becomes
clear that her lifetime of hard work and obsession with order were
ways of suppressing the hurt and proving she could succeed without
the man she loved. d. Randa Haines; CORONET; PAS, UMN, UMT,
UM.

JOAN OF ARC (10m B 1970)
The patron saint of France is brought to life as a secular person
through the use of beautiful and specially-commissioned artwork and
animated maps. Whether viewers believe Joan was a saint or a patriot
or both, her life is made meaningful. p. Connecticut Films, MACMFL;
UFL.

JOAN OF ARC: A PROFILE IN POWER (25m C r1977)
Sandy Dennis dramatically and forcefully portrays Joan of Arc.
Placed in an adversary position by interviewer Patrick Watson, Joan
counters emphatically, telling of the dramatic episodes and trials she
endured in her desire for the liberation of France. LCA.

JOAN ROBINSON: ONE WOMAN'S STORY (165m C 1979)
After 22 months of battle against ovarian cancer, Joan Robinson
died in 1975. It is a battle Joan waged--at her suggestion--before
cameras; it was a way, she felt, to make her final days useful. This
resulting documentary is an intimate and powerful record of a woman,
her husband, doctor and friends trying to cope with the anguish of
terminal illness. The camera follows Joan's stages of her illness and
adjustments: questioning, fear, resolution, rage and finally tran-
scendence. It explores significant and difficult questions of medical

capability, pain management, the patient's right to know, family relations and the right to die. p. Red Cloud Productions; TIMLIF.

JOAN WESTON (ROLLER DERBY) (22m C 1973) Women in Sports--A Series
Joan Weston, queen of the roller derby skaters, is featured in a candid, in-depth, behind-the-scenes look at the violent, often ridiculed world of roller derby. A look into her professional and personal life shows the excitement of her career, and what she gave up to pursue it. p. Tele-Sports; PARACO.

JOB DESCRIMINATION: DOING SOMETHING ABOUT IT (50m C 1977)
Examines several cases of sex discrimination in employment, with Harriet Rabb, Assistant Dean of the Columbia University Law School, offering a step-by-step analysis of how to recognize, document, and combat such cases. Discusses the need to organize for group action, the desirability of legal help, and the emotional strain involved in any prolonged fight against discrimination. Includes such topics as adverse working conditions, low-status jobs, and unequal pay for women. NET; IU, PAS, UIL, UIO, UM, UCEMC.

JOB HUNTING IN THE 1980's: SKILLS FOR SUCCESS (73m C 1981)
(slc) Job Opportunities for the 1980's Series
Provides students with guidelines to job hunting: Deciding what type of work to look for, where to look, how to write an effective résumé and cover letter, how to fill out a job application and prepare for an interview. p. Guidance Associates; COMPVF; UMN.

JOB INTERVIEW: I GUESS I GOT THE JOB (13m C 1975) Conflict and Awareness Series
Portrays how the course and outcome of the job interview are influenced by various factors that may have nothing to do with an applicant's qualifications for the job or with how well he or she could perform in it. The focus is on the subtle cues that affect the interviewer's overall impression of the applicant ... treating different interview strategies in an open-ended fashion. CRM; SILU.

JOB INTERVIEW: WHOM WOULD YOU HIRE?--FILM A: LARGE BUSINESS (20m C p1980, r1980)
Shows the key qualities employers look for, such as strong motivation, reliability, and appearance. Actual interviews are filmed with Rosie, Alex and Donna. Following each interview there is an opportunity to stop the projector to discuss and evaluate the applicant. p. Dimension Films; CF; UMO, IU, PAS, KENTSU, WSU, UM.

JOB INTERVIEW: WHOM WOULD YOU HIRE?--FILM B: SMALL BUSINESS (22m C 1980)
Shows the key qualities employers look for, such as strong motivation, reliability, and appearance. Four young people are interviewed for various restaurant jobs, a hidden camera records the interviews

without their knowledge. Following each interview, the projector may be stopped for discussion and evaluation. p. Dimension Films; CF; IU, KENTSU, UM, UMO, WSU.

JOB OPPORTUNITIES FOR THE 1980's <u>see</u> JOB HUNTING IN THE 1980's: SKILLS FOR SUCCESS; JOBS FOR THE '80's: WHERE THE OPPORTUNITIES ARE; WORKING FOR A LIVING: JOB SKILLS FOR THE REAL WORLD

JOBS FOR THE '80'S: WHERE THE OPPORTUNITIES ARE (60m C 1981) (slc) Job Opportunities for the 1980's Series
Part I takes a look at a variety of jobs and demonstrates the procedure to predicting job markets. Parts 2 through 6 each deal with one broad career field. Also reviews the training required for specific jobs in these fields and outlines why the field is promising. p. Guidance Associates; COMPVF; UMN.

JOCELYN (28m C 1980) (also Video)
About a girl with such enormous spiritual resources that she is able to face her untimely death with equanimity and her remaining days with cheerfulness. Shows a sensitive portrayal of a loving family, steadfast friends, and above all, a remarkable girl whose inner light shows through. Jocelyn's father is a minister. Faith is a natural part of family life. Her parents see their role as three-fold: to explore all medical advances, to encourage Jocelyn to live each day as normally as possible, and to help her accept her coming death. An unforgettable family that deals openly with emotions and is not afraid to show affection. Although Jocelyn's life will be short, her impact on others has been deep. d. Bill Kendrick; p. Leo Rampen/ CBC; FILMLB; PAS.

JOE AND MAXI (80m C 1981)
An unusually intimate and revealing documentary portrait of one family, but human relationships and emotions portrayed are universal. Within the immediate family situation, however, the film touches on a broad range of issues, including the emotionally constrictive nature of stereotypical sex roles, the psychological barriers to expressing or accepting love, the pressures facing a young woman who opts for a non-conventional life-style, and even the ethical considerations involved in documentary filmmaking. Also, this is a film about the filmmaker, Maxi Cohen, and her father, who learns he has cancer shortly after the filmmaking began. Cohen also lost her mother to cancer a short time before the filmmaking started. p. Maxi Cohen, Joel Gold; FIRRNF.

JOE DAVID/SPIRIT OF THE MASK (24m C 1982)
A look at West Coast native artist Joe David--his personal reflections and scenes from his life. Follows the creative process of carving and finishing a magnificent wolf headdress from a block of cedar to its ultimate use as a ceremonial mask worn by the artist himself in a

haunting dance which ends the film. A highly personal picture, it is also a look at the vitality of the cultural revival now underway in many native communities in North America. d. Jennifer Hodge/Robert Lang; p. Seawolf Films; KENSCOM.

JOHN GLICK: AN ARTIST AND HIS WORK (9m C 1981)
John Glick, major American ceramist, is visited in his studio as he creates new pieces. We see him prepare the clay, throw at the wheel, decorate, bisque fire, glaze and final fire his works. During the process, Glick describes himself, his feelings, and his work. Original music by Chris Birg enhances the gentle quality of this sensitive film portrait. p. Sue Marx/Robert Handley; LREDF.

JOHN JACOB NILES (32m C r1978)
Portrait of 86-year-old John Jacob Niles, who played an important part in the revival of folk music of the Appalachians during the twenties and thirties when he and noted photographer Doris Ulmann traveled the mountain region. Shows Johnny Niles in concert, at home, at work arranging his music and explaining the historical place of balladry in American music. p. Mimi Pickering, Bill Richardson, Ben Zickafoose; APPAL.

JOHN RINGLING'S CA D'ZAN (23m C p1973, r1977) American Lifestyle
  --Cultural Leaders Series
A biographical sketch of the life and career of circus owner John Ringling. E. G. Marshall narrates as he conducts this filmed tour of Ringling's elegant Florida home, Ca D'Zan. p. Ann Zane Shanks; p. Comco Productions; PARACO.

JOJO'S BLUES (? C 1982) (also Video)
Using animated puppets, the film tells the story of two teenage boys who are asked to take a dangerous test before they would be allowed to join a club, the Rockets. After their narrow escape during this caper, the boys decline to join the Rockets telling the group the price of their friendship is too high. p. Jane Warrenbrand for the Scott Newman Foundation; p. Peter Wallach Production; d. Peter Wallach; s.w. Steven Molton; animation by Peter Wallach, Jimmy Picker; CF.

JOLO SERPENT-HANDLERS, THE (40m C 1978)
This documentary focuses on a small snake-handling church in rural West Virginia. The film is an in-depth portrait that not only shows two fascinating serpent-handling services, but also answers many of the questions that viewers have about this religion and the people who practice it. Varied scenes shown are the rattlesnake hunt through the mountains; the washing of the serpents; the annual outdoor homecoming service; colorful exteriors of the countryside; a very rare documentation of an all-night prayer vigil, held for the victim of a rattlesnake bite; and many interviews taken with the people inside the relaxed and natural setting. p. Karen Kramer; KRAMERK.

JONAH HAS A RAINBOW (19m C p1982, r1983)
"My son Jonah was born three months premature, weighing three pounds, and suffering from weak lungs. Yet, through the miracle of the intensive care nursery and the strength of our affirmations, he is now a bright, healthy, two-year-old. This film celebrates his conception, birth, hospital experience, and first two years of life." d. Ron Taylor; p. Jude Bea; TAYLORR.

JONATHAN AND THE ROCKER (34m B 1977) (Video)
Jonathan Hollander performs a duet with a sculpture which is animated by the Rutt-Etra synthesizer. p. Doris Chase; CHASED.

JONATHAN AND THE ROCKER, OP ODYSSEY, ROCKER (60m B 1977) (Video)
A combined version of three Doris Chase performances. Choreographer/p. Doris Chase. CHASED.

JONATHAN HOLLANDER AND VIDEO SYNTHESIZED ROCKER (34m B 1977) (Video)
Dancer: Jonathan Hollander. Choreographer/p. Doris Chase. CHASED.

JOSHUA AND THE BLOB (7m C 1977) The Joshua Trilogy (Series)
Joshua finds himself confronted by a form of unknown--a "blob." For most individuals, as with Joshua, the unknown is threatening and filled with many anxious moments. Useful in identifying barriers to effective work relationships. p. Kandi Lange, John Lange; d. John Lange; BOSUS; PSU.

JOSHUA AND THE SHADOW (10m C 1977) The Joshua Trilogy (Series)
Animated story demonstrating that when individuals begin to accept, understand and shed their real or imagined fears, the process of realizing their potential can begin to take place. Emphasizes the benefit derived by the individual and the organization. p. Kandi Lange, John Lange; d. John Lange; BOSUS; PSU.

JOSHUA TRILOGY, THE (SERIES) see JOSHUA AND THE BLOB; JOSHUA AND THE SHADOW

JOURNALISTS AT INTERNATIONAL WOMEN'S YEAR (29m C 1975) (Video) Are You Listening Series
An international group of journalists covering the 1975 Mexico City conference of women bring lively and conflicting points of view to bear on the complicated but crucial questions concerning press coverage of women's issues. The discussion opens with arguments over whether a journalist should function as a teacher, whether objective journalism exists as a practical reality, and whether the individual journalist really has any control at all over what is or is not printed. From there talk moves on to a consideration of the tactics of the worldwide feminist movement and the responsibilities of the

journalist to help women understand and stand up for their rights. An indispensable background for anyone wishing to understand the progress of the international women's movement. p. Martha Stuart; STUARTM.

JOURNEY FROM ZANZIBAR (24m C p1978, r1978)
For hundreds of years, skilled shipbuilders on the west coast of Africa have been using simple hand tools to fashion magnificent sailing ships. Fourteen-year-old Slima learns these ancient skills in the setting of his fishing village on the island of Zanzibar. The completed ship is then launched, with a huge village celebration. d. Paul Saltzman; p. Deepa and P. Saltzman; SUNRIF.

JOURNEY TO THE CENTER OF A TRIANGLE (9m C 1977) (also Video)
A series of animated constructions determine the "center" of a variety of triangles. These centers include circumcenter, incenter, centroid and orthocenter. The technique of the constructions uses a variety of dynamic and graphically fascinating devices, such as expanding circles and traces of loci. p. Katharine Cornwell, Bruce Cornwell; IFB.

JOURNEY TOGETHER (22m C p1980, r1980) (also Video)
Set in an urban Black neighborhood during a harsh winter, when many senior citizens had to cope with subfreezing temperatures, this story describes how a young girl mobilizes her peers to help secure rebates on fuel bills for senior citizens with limited incomes. The drama is based on the true-life accomplishments of 14-year-old Shawn Leach, who was elected as the youngest delegate to the National Women's Conference in 1977. Tina Andrews and Esther Rolle are featured. p. Diane Asselin, d. Paul Asselin; Guenette-Asselin Productions; FI.

JOURNEYS FROM BERLIN/1971 (125m C/B 1980)
Deals with moral/political questions while exploring parameters of an "alternative" cinema. Contains both finely directed nuances of characterization and extremes of narrative disjunction. Attests to the on-going vitality and necessity of the search for alternatives to the thralldom and aridity of much commercial and avante-garde cinema. A fascinating and unusual film. d. Yvonne Rainer; FLMKCO.

JOY UNSPEAKABLE (58m C p1980, r1981) (Video)
Captures the faith and spirit of the Pentecostal religion and portrays the importance of the church in daily life. The program focuses on Oneness Pentecostals in and around Bloomington, Indiana and follows one local Pentecostal congregation to three different church services. In particular, explores the active role of women as primary participants in the church. d. John Winninger; p. J. Winninger, Elaine J. Lawless, Elizabeth Peterson; IU.

JOYCE CHEN'S CHINA (59m C 1975)
A personal view of China by cookbook author and television

personality Joyce Chen, who returned to her homeland in 1972 after an absence of 20 years. Accompanied by her daughter Helen and son Stephen (a Boston University student, who shot the film of the journey), Chen traveled through Canton, Shanghai, Suchow, Hangchow and Peking. The film includes scenes of the Little Red Soldiers school in Shanghai, a sandalwood fan factory in Suchow, Chen's reunion with her family and a trek to the Great Wall. The second part of the program shows the Chen family at a Chinese banquet held several years later in Boston. Economist John Kenneth Galbraith and Edward Klein, foreign editor of Newsweek magazine, joined the Chens to view the film and discuss their experiences in China. Captioned version for the deaf and hearing impaired also available. p. WGBH-TV; PBSV.

JUBILEE (23m C p1978, r1978)
Shows how Macomb County, Michigan provides educational services to children who have moderate to severe mental impairments, including those with physical handicaps and those requiring 24-hour nursing care. d. Merlin Peck; p. Marjorie Leach, M. Peck; PEACH.

JUDY CHICAGO ON FEMINIST ART (29m C 1975) (Video) Woman Series
Artist Judy Chicago tells of her struggle to bring feminist consciousness into art and shows slides of her work. She explains her concept of feminist art and her belief that women have been dependent on images made by men. She also describes her efforts to fuse traits traditionally attributed to men with feminine qualities in her art. Sandra Elkin is the moderator. p. WNED-TV; PBSV.

JULIA (117m C 1978)
A true story of loyalty, courage and love. JULIA is acclaimed playwright Lillian Hellman's tribute to her remarkable friend and childhood idol. The surface story relates an incident in Hellman's life, when at Julia's request, Hellman smuggled money through Nazi Germany to help secure freedom for Jews and other political prisoners. Underneath this exciting adventure story, Julia's many layers examine the nature of friendship; strongly independent but enduring relationships; the personal agony of creativity; the loss of friends and family as one grows old; political and personal commitments; the precariousness of survival in times of danger. A film of great depth and beauty with a perfectly timed sense of direction. Cast: Jane Fonda, Vanessa Redgrave, Jason Robards, Hal Holbrook. p. Richard Roth; d. Fred Zinneman; p. Fox; FI.

JULIA CHILD AND COMPANY SERIES (29m ea. C 1978) (Video)
French chef Julia Child shows how to plan and prepare complete meals for a variety of special occasions in this series. She draws from a number of cooking traditions and concentrates on menus that allow flexibility and advance preparation. For each program, she has chosen an event and presents a meal from start to finish--including serving and wine suggestions. p. WGBH-TV, Boston; PBSV. These are films in the series:

1. Holiday Lunch (Chicken Melon and Apple Turnover)
2. Buffet for 19 (Fresh Oysters; Turkey Orloff and Ice Cream Goblet)
3. New England Potluck Supper (Fresh Fish Chowder and Indian Pudding)
4. Birthday Dinner (Roast Duck and Los Gatos Gateau)
5. VIP Lunch (Choulibiac and Pear Sherbet)
6. Kitchen Cocktail Party (Puff Pastry; Ham Pithiviers; Gravlaks, dilled fresh salmon and bass; and Puffed Cheese appetizers)
7. Dinner for the Boss (Timbale of Fresh Corn; Standing Rib Roast of Beef and Chocolate Truffles)
8. Breakfast Party (English Muffins; Poached Eggs; Eggs Benedict and Corned Beef Hash)
9. Lo-Cal Banquet (Chicken Bouillabaisse with Rouille and Caramel Steam-Baked Apples)
10. Sunday Night Supper (Corned Beef and Pork Boiled Dinner; Homemade Noodles and Sherbet with Strawberries en Chemise)
11. Informal Dinner (Casserole Roast of Veal; Wok Saute of Grated Zucchini and Fresh Spinach; and Floating Island)
12. Indoor/Outdoor Barbeque (Roast or Barbequed Butterflied Leg of Lamb; Homemade Pita Bread and Pita Pizzas)
13. Chafing Dish Dinner (Steak Diane; Fresh Green Peas and Le Gâteau Victorire au Chocolat, Mousseline)

JUMPING AND HURDLING (15m C 1976) The Track and Field Series for Girls
Demonstrates the high jump and long jump. The girls demonstrate the different styles and their principles are discussed. p. Ryan Films; MACMFL.

JURY OF HER PEERS, A (30m C p1980, r1981) (also Video)
Adapted from the story written by Susan Glaspell in 1917. It uses the murder of a farmer as the backdrop for exploring the oppression of a farm woman in 1905 rural America. The farmer's wife is accused of murder and arrested. Two women, her neighbors, discover the incriminating clue the sheriff and attorney are looking for. They must decide whether or not to reveal the evidence to the lawmen. (The author rewrote her one-act play Trifles into this story). d./p. Sally Heckel; photographer: Janet Meyers; TEXFM; UIL, UM.

JUST A LITTLE LOVE SONG (10m B n.d.)
A caustic commentary on rural life, performed to a gay barn dance, but with action that is sometimes sombre and even violent. Animated illustration is in the form of heavy black line drawings. d. Viviane Elnecave; p. Gaston Sarault; NFBC.

JUST LIKE AT HOME (108m C 1978) (Hungarian/Subtitled)
Tells about a curious and touching liaison between an unstable male writer and a golden-haired ten-year-old peasant girl. Combines

an acute sensitivity to the quirky, unpredictable paths of human emotions with a rich, often overpowering lyricism. The director is noted for her treatment of offbeat female relationships. d. Marta Meszaros; NYF.

JUST POSING (33m C p1979, r1981) (also Video)
A commentary on values and the current syndrome of emphasis on youth in advertising. Tracy is a beautiful 12-year-old model whose parents are divorced. With the aggressive help of her agent, Bobbi, she is being primed to be an actress and sex symbol. But Tracy is at an age when she needs love and guidance. Finding none from her parents, she turns to Bobbi, whose own ambitions as an agent overshadow any warmth and understanding of Tracy. Tracy must learn to deal with an adult world without either the experience or familial support to do so. d./p. Lynda Sparrow; CAROUF.

JUVENILE JUSTICE SERIES see CHILDHOOD SEXUAL ABUSE: FOUR CASE STUDIES

JUVENILE JUSTICE SYSTEM see WOMEN AND THE LAW, THE (SERIES)

JUVENILE LIAISON (88m C 1974)
This controversial documentary records the work of an experimental counseling program within the Juvenile Liaison Department of the Lancashire Police Force in England. In cinema-verité style, the film follows first-time offenders over a seven-week period. It reveals the program's serious flaws and although the filmmakers tried to present an unbiased view (there is no interpretive commentary and editing is minimal), the Police Department's reaction was negative and the film's distribution was initially blocked. d. Joan Churchill, Nick Broomfield. MMA.

-K-

KALEIDOSCOPE ORISSA (37m C 1967) (also Video)
A cultural study of Orissa, a state in India renowned for its intricately beautiful artifacts. Included in the film are the molding and baking of ceramic pottery, and weaving with extraordinary beauty of color and design. Awards. p. Mary Kirby; p. Pilgrim Films; IFB.

KANOJO TO KARE see SHE AND HE

KAREN KAIN: BALLERINA (54m C 1977)
A detailed portrait of the life and art of a contemporary ballerina. Rehearsals, performances and interviews convey the flavor of a life dedicated to dance. Roland Petit, French choreographer, directs and comments on her style. p. Nielsen--Ferns Ltd.; HERVSL; UIL.

KATE CHOPIN'S "THE STORY OF AN HOUR" (24m C 1981)
This dramatization based on Kate Chopin's celebrated and daring short story of the 1890's is narrated by Elizabeth Ashley. Upon hearing of the death of her dear husband, Mrs. Mallard is shocked to discover that for the first time in her life, she is free to live for herself--a discovery which leads to tragedy. A glimpse into the thoughts and milieu of Kate Chopin precedes the story. d. Marita Simpson; p. Martha Wheelock; ISHTAR.

KATHERINE DUNHAM PROFILE (30m C 1978) (Video)
A look at the work of this gifted dancer/choreographer and the dance troupe she has founded in the slums of East St. Louis. Part of the McNeil/Lehrer report. Choreographer: Katherine Dunham; p. WNET-TV; FI.

KATHLEEN WARE, QUILTMAKER (33m C 1980)
"Capturing both the folk art of quiltmaking and the personality of a folk artist, and including interactions with customers and family members, this is clear, carefully-detailed, well-structured ethnographic work."--Amos Vogel. p. Sharon Sherman; UORFE.

KATHY (27m C p1981, r1981)
Shows how one young girl has managed to go beyond her handicap. We learn a lot about Kathy; we also learn a lot from her about ourselves. With determination, humor and a disarming modesty, Kathy teaches us all a little about self-determination, courage and the human spirit. She reminds us about the untapped potential we all possess. d./p. Kier Cline; FLMID; UIL.

KATHY'S DANCE (28m C p1977, r1979) (also Video)
An aesthetic study of the beauty of dance. Kathy Posin, a modern dancer/choreographer, allows the audience to witness the steps of the creative process as she generates a new dance alone in her studio in New York, in rehearsal with her dance troupe, and finally, in an ingeniously photographed stage performance. p. Anne Drew for Drew Associates; DIRECT.

KAY SAGE (20m C p1977, r1979)
The surrealist painter Kay Sage, one of the numerous artists whose work is now re-emerging as a result of the women's movement and feminist scholarship, is introduced through her paintings, readings from her poems and journals, and the recollections of her closest friends. d. Marilyn Rivchin, Kells Elmquist; p. H. F. Johnson, Museum of Art; AFA.

KEEPING YOUR TEETH HEALTHY (8m C p1981, r1981)
Using special dental equipment, X-ray photography and models of teeth, this film provides a positive view of important twice-a-year visits to a dentist and emphasizes that people need their teeth all their lives and must take good care of them and eat proper foods.

A well-illustrated introduction to teeth care for children. p. Suzanne Johnston, High Johnston for Encyclopaedia Britannica Educational Corporation; EBEC.

KEI TAKEI'S MOVING EARTH COMPANY AND KEI TAKEI'S SOLOS (30m B 1975) (Video)
    Dancer: Kei Takei, Choreographer: Doris Chase, p. Doris Chase; CHASED.

KENNEDYS OF ALBUQUERQUE, THE (58m C 1976) Six American Families (Series)
    Jim and Joan Kennedy are an upper-middle-class professional family in Albuquerque. Jim, epitome of the American overachiever, designs nuclear weapons and Joan, at 40, is making an effort to enlarge her experiences beyond the role of housewife. Jim crusades for the rights of the retarded, but spends so much time traveling that he has little time for his retarded son. p. Elinor Bunine Productions; WBC-PRO; CAROUF; PAS, KENTSU, UIL, UM, USFL.

KEVIN ALEC (17m C n.d.)
    Kevin lives on the Fountain Indian Reserve in British Columbia. He is an 11-year-old Indian boy whose parents are dead; he lives with his grandmother, who is in her 80's. Kevin learns from his grandmother and other relatives such ancient arts as skinning and tanning. He shows great pride in his heritage. d. Beverly Shaffer; p. Yuki Yoshida, Kathleen Shannon; NFBC; MEDIAG.

KEY WOMEN AT INTERNATIONAL WOMEN'S YEAR (29m C 1975) (Video)
    Are You Listening Series
    A historical landmark discussion among women leaders attending the 1975 Mexico City women's conference. Participants include members of parliaments, cabinet officers, ministers, UN representatives, and women in special advisory roles in governments around the world. Their discussion develops around the critical question of how attitudes can be changed worldwide to advance equality to women. Special attention is paid to the problems of reaching rural or village women on issues such as family planning and women's rights, and convincing male-dominated national governments to act in ways that advance the cause of women. The program is a unique and invaluable resource for anyone concerned with the worldwide women's movement and its current status in a cross-section of developed and undeveloped countries. p. Martha Stuart; STUARTM.

KHETURNI BAYO: NORTH INDIAN FARM WOMEN (19m C 1980)
    An introduction to the daily life of peasant women in one extended family in Western India. Shows their relationships with their children, men, and each other, and how they integrate the artwork they make-- dowry embroideries--with their other work in the home and fields. d. Sharon Wood; p. San Francisco Matching Service; SFMATS; PAS.

KICKING THE LOOSE GRAVEL HOME: A PORTRAIT OF RICHARD
    HUGO (56m C 1977) (also Video)
    A rare and candid portrait of Richard Hugo, an American poet.
The film follows him from his childhood home in Seattle to his teaching post in Missoula, from tavern to picnic, and from highway to lecture hall. Hugo reads some of his best-known poems. He talks about
the craft of poetry and the role of writing in his life. Because Hugo
proves himself an unusually open and generous subject, one leaves
the film with deeper feeling for his work and his life as an artist.
p. Beth Chadwick Ferris, Annick Smith, Ron Carraher; NWMP.

KIDS TODAY (22m C 1981) (Video)
    Vignettes of four "special" kids, ages 6, 11, 14, and 17. Grow-
ing up in widely varied areas and circumstances in Pennsylvania, each
is "making it" in spite of mental retardation, child abuse, emotional
trauma or teenage pregnancy. The way each finds help from family,
friends and community services shows that each, although considered
"special" has needs that are universal to all kids today. d. Tim
Swartz; p. Anne Stanaway for Sunlight Productions; PAS.

KIKI CUTTER BEATTIE (SKIING) (22m C 1973) Women in Sports--A
    Series
    Sometimes shy and often impatient, Kiki is featured competing for
first-prize money in the first women's professional ski race in history.
She shows the skill and determination that enabled her to be the first
American ever to win a World Cup ski race. p. Tele-Sports; PARACO.

KILLING TIME (60m C p1980, r1981)
    Takes viewers behind the walls of four Massachusetts' prisons
(maximum, medium, minimum security, and pre-release) for a close-
up look at the problems and conditions. Includes cinema-verité footage and interviews with inmates, guards, and staff who tell their
stories. p./d. Ellen Boyce, Sam Kauffmann; KAFBOY.

KILLING TIME (9m B p1978, r1979)
    This is a suicide's guide on how to live forever. It is a day out
of the life of Sage Brush, a kind of anti-heroine, who is trying to
find a way, which she can "live with," to die. d. Fronza Woods; p.
F. Woods, Women's Interart Center; s.w./ed. F. Woods; WOODSF.

KILLING US SOFTLY: ADVERTISING'S IMAGE OF WOMEN (30m C
    1979) (Video)
    A unique analysis of one of the most powerful forces in our so-
ciety. Using hundreds of ads from magazines, newspapers, album
covers and store front windows, Jean Kilbourne has produced a concise and important analysis of a 40-billion-dollar industry that preys
on the fears and insecurities of every consumer in America. With
an intriguing mixture of fact, insight, humor, and outrage, Kilbourne
brings her audience to see that although ads may seem harmless or
funny by themselves, they add up to a powerful form of cultural

conditioning--and their message is deadly serious. p. Jean Kilbourne; d. J. Kilbourne, Margaret Lazarus, Renner Wunderlich; CAMDOC; PURDUE.

KINGDOM COME SCHOOL, THE (22m C 1973)
Portrait of a one-room schoolhouse, grades one through eight, taught by middle-aged Harding Ison, combined with cultural heritage of Appalachia. "An interesting and instructive film on the educational and social values of the small rural school. Receives an excellent student response and is a good starting point for discussion of educational policy for rural areas."--Dr. Richard E. Withers, Alderson-Broaddus College. d./p. Dianna Ott; APPAL.

KINSHIPS: FINDING VALUES IN FAMILY RELATIONSHIPS (12m C 1974) Insight Vignettes Series
Four sketches dramatize the attempts of parents and teenagers to reach across the chasms between them. Most are caused by the conflict between individuality and "role." What would you think of your parents if they were not your parents? p. Paulist Productions; MEDIAG; UIL.

KIRTLAND'S WARBLER: BIRD OF FIRE, THE (10m C 1980)
Relates the life-history of the rare Kirtland's Warbler. Shows management efforts to create habitat by planting jack pines and also by burning specific areas to allow natural jack pine growth. Also shows efforts to control nest parasitism by cowbirds, which are probably the greatest threat to the Kirtland's Warblers' survival. p. Myrna I. Berlet, Walter H. Berlet; IFB.

KISHA'S SONG (3m C p1978, r1978)
A simple anatomy showing the related functions of touch, sound, motion, and gesture in the creation of a lullaby and sleep. First in a cycle of short films about family. d./p. Elizabeth Nadas Seamans; FAMCOM.

KITCH'S LAST MEAL (60m C 1973-78) (S8)
A three-segment film (20 minutes each) in which events are captured through the eyes of the filmmaker's cat. Other experiments relate to the size and shape of the film image itself. p. Carolee Schneemann, Upstate Films; UPSTF.

KITTY: RETURN TO AUSCHWITZ (73m C p1979, r1981)
Kitty revisits Auschwitz with her grown son, to whom she recounts her experiences while there. Kitty was inmate #39934 as a teenager; 34 years later she has consented to leave her home in England for the recording of these painful recollections, to counteract the fact that there are people who disbelieve the events she lived. A revealing account of an incredible experience, and a meeting with a person of strength of character and humanity. d. Peter Morley; p. Michael Deakin/Yorkshire Television Ltd.; FI; UIL.

KLAN YOUTH CORPS (11m C p1980, r1980)
Reveals how leaders of the controversial Ku Klux Klan are expanding its membership by recruiting and training teenagers. p. Catherine Olian for CBS "60 Minutes"; CAROUF; UM.

KOREA: PERFORMING ARTS--THE WONDERFUL WORLD OF KIM SUNG HEE (21m C p1979, r1979)
Kim Sung Hee, a professional dancer in the National Theater in Seoul, reveals her personal feeling towards her art as we see famous, colorful traditional dances of Korea. d. Harold Harvey; p. Centron Films; CENTEF; PSU.

KOREA: THE FAMILY (18m C 1980)
Presents a detailed examination of the changing family structure in a nation undergoing rapid urbanization and industrialization. p. Centron Films; CENTEF; PSU.

KOREA: THE CIRCLE OF LIFE--TRADITIONAL CUSTOMS AND RITUALS (35m C 1980)
Set in ancient Korean villages where the architecture, clothing and life-styles have remained unchanged for centuries. This film surveys the elaborate customs and ceremonies attending birth, childhood, matchmaking, marriage, aging, death, interment and mourning. p. Centron Films; CENTEF; KENTSU, PSU.

KREINIK AND BOSWORTH FAMILIES, THE (SINGLE ADOPTIVE PARENTS) see FAMILY PORTRAIT: THE KREINIK AND BOSWORTH FAMILIES

KRISTINA TALKING PICTURES (90m C 1976)
A narrative film inasmuch as it contains a series of events that can be synthesized into a story if one is disposed to do so. The film can also be viewed in terms of its discussions from a strict narrative line via reflections on art, love, and catastrophe sustained by the voices of Kristina, the heroine-narrator, and Raoul, her lover. Within a form that allows for shifting correlations between word and image, persons and performer, enactment and illustration, speech and recitation, explanation and ambiguity, the film circles in a narrowing spiral toward its primary concerns: the uncertain relation of public act to personal fate, the ever-present possibility for disparity between public-directed conscience and private will. Having just put your check to Amnesty International into the mailbox, you are mugged ... or discover you have cancer ... or perhaps you betray an old friend. Nothing can ensure that we remain honorable, nor save us from betrayal and death. In the next-to-last shot a love letter is recited. Life goes on. d./s.w./ed. Yvonne Rainer; FILMKO.

KUJICHAGULIA (5m C p1979, r1980) The Seven Principles Series
Presents an animated folktale to illustrate the principle of self-determination. p. Nguzo Saba Films; p./d. Carol Mundy Lawrence; BEACON.

KUUMBA: SIMON'S NEW SOUND (7m C p1978, r1978)
An animated folktale illustrating the concept of "Kuumba" ("creativity" in the Swahili language). A boy named Simon from the Island of Trinidad uses his creative gifts to develop a new musical instrument. d. R. Bloomberg; p. Carol Mundy Lawrence; SABAN.

-L-

LA LA MAKING IT IN L.A. (58m C 1979) (also Video)
Views the race for work in the Los Angeles entertainment industry, featuring aspiring actors, actresses, musicians and filmmakers talking about themselves. p. Caroline Ahlfours Mouris; d. Frank Mouris; DIRECT.

LA PLAGE (4m B p1978, r1981--U.S.) (also Video)
Presents an animated short story by Rock Carrier in which a man foresees the drowning of a lone sailor. p. Suzanne Gervais; NFBC; PHOENIX.

LABOR MORE THAN ONCE (52m C 1983) (Video, Beta)
Documents a lesbian mother's three-year struggle to regain parental rights to her son and the judicial system's denial of those rights solely on the grounds of her sexual preference. The filmmaker chronicles events as Marianne appeals the case right up to the Supreme Court of Virginia leading to a landmark court trial in 1981. While breaking stereotypes about motherhood, lesbianism and parenting, the film explores pervasive homophobia of our society as it is institutionalized in the legal system, and in the favored status of the heterosexual household and child-raising structure. p./d. Liz Mersky; WMM.

LABOR OF LOVE: CHILDBIRTH WITHOUT VIOLENCE (27m C 1978)
The subject of this film is the controversial and somewhat radically new technique of birth popularized by Dr. Frederick Leboyer. The focus is on the newborn child rather than the mother, the father, or the doctor. Contrasts a traditional delivery with a Leboyer delivery. Concludes with a well-balanced series of pro and con statements from physicians representing various medical specialties. Narrated by Dr. Art Ulene. Emmy award. PEREN; WSU.

LACEMAKER, THE (108m C 1977) (French/Subtitled)
A moving and nuanced story about a shy 19-year-old girl (Isabelle Huppert) on holiday in Normandy who begins an idyllic romance with a student. Her inability to express her feelings, to assert her needs, results in a tragic break and her mental collapse. Based on the prize-winning novel La Dentellière by Pascal Lane. Themes for discussion: How does the heroine conform to the stereotype of the "nice" girl? Is it her passivity and undemanding behavior that victimizes her, her lover's insensitivity, or social class difference? In

what ways are women reared to be "lacemakers"? d. Claude Goretta; NYF.

LADY AND THE OWL, THE (28m C 1976)
Documents a Canadian woman's efforts to study the behavior of owls, dispel the many widely-held myths concerning them, and save the species from threatened extinction. Sensitive and humanistic. NFBC; WOMBAT; UCEMC.

LADY FISHBOURNE'S COMPLETE GUIDE TO BETTER TABLE MAN-
NERS (6m C 1976)
A hilarious animated film about the dos and don'ts of table man-ners. Demonstrations include how to hold a fork, how to handle a knife, and what to do when a parrot lands in your plate. d. Janet Perlman; p. Wolf Koenig, Derek Lamb for NFBC; CAROUF.

LADY IN MOTION: A PORTRAIT OF MISS AGNES HAMMOND AND
FRIENDS (29m C 1982)
Explores the life and times of an independent woman rancher and artist living in the foothills of the Canadian Rockies. A compilation of interviews with 72-year-old Agnes Hammond, her work with her herd of horses, her 150 dogs, her horse museum and her earlier life of art study, deb balls and sports competition. Presents a woman who (from many available choices) chose a life of hard work and con-tentment. d./p./s.w. Helene B. White; ed. Bill Campbell; WHITEH.

LADY NAMED BAYBIE, A (60m B p1980, r1980)
A documentary about the indomitable 64-year-old Baybie Hoover, born blind, who "pitched" her way from Wichita, Kansas to New York City by singing religious songs with tin cup in hand. d. Martha Sandlin; a.p. Hsienli Tan; SANDLIN.

LADY VANISHES: WHERE ARE THE WOMEN IN FILM?, THE (29m C
1976) (Video) Woman Series
Midge Kovacs, coordinator of the National Organization for Women's Image of Women in Film Task Force, and Marjorie Rosen, film critic and author, assess the contemporary role of women in film. They both believe that films have not reflected the struggle and the chang-ing status of American women, but have relegated them to secondary roles as victims of violence or on the brink of madness. Sandra El-kin, moderator. p. WNED-TV; PBSV.

LAILA (12m C 1981)
Shows one woman pursuing the nontraditional trade of drywall taping. Her experience with low-paying traditional female jobs prior to her training and her unsuccessful attempts to get a position with a contractor following the training period highlight the types of work-related problems many women face. Laila's determination to use her skills by opening her own business and her ability to cope with the problems encountered provide an inspiring example for other women.

The viewer follows Laila through her activities while listening to pertinent and interesting information and comments. d. Diane Beaudry; Cowling, Diane; p. Margaret Pettigrew; PHOENIX.

LAMENT (20m B 1956)
This dance piece premiered in 1947 and was staged especially for the film. It is based on a poem by Federico García Lorca titled, "Lament for Ignacio Sanchez Mejias." The dancers act out the death of the bullfighter as the words of the poem are spoken. Choreographer: Doris Humphrey; p. Walter P. Strate; DANCFA; PSU, PAS, SILU, SYRACU.

LAMENTATION (10m C 1943)
John Martin, former dance critic of the New York Times, gives a brief history of modern dance and talks about dance as a medium of expression. Martha Graham performs excerpts from her work Lamentation to music played by Louis Horst. Throughout the dance, Graham is seated on a bench. Dancer/Choreographer: Martha Graham; p. Harmon Film Foundation; National Archives and Records; DANCFA; PAS, UIL.

LAND CALLED PECONIC, A (47½m C 1980) (Video)
The story of the eastern end of Long Island, an area rich in natural resources and beauty, and of the residents' struggle to preserve the land in the face of haphazard development. d./p. Amanda Kissin; METROT.

LAND OF COOL SUN, THE (28m C 1981) (Video)
The story of Maria and Arnie Valdez of the San Luis Valley of southern Colorado who, by their hard work and example, have inspired the most solarized community in the United States. This achievement is remarkable because of the extreme poverty of the area, which is populated largely by Spanish-speaking people. The solar collectors were built in the old barn-raising fashion--with neighbor helping neighbor--and the result has been the revitalization of the unique Spanish culture, economy and spirit of the area. d./p. Pamela Roberts; PROGP.

LAND OF IMMIGRANTS (rev. ed.) (16m C 1981) (also Video)
Shows in animation a historical overview of the waves of immigration that populated the United States beginning in earliest Colonial times to the end of the great period of immigration. Shows the principal causes that impelled people to leave their homes and come to the new land. Animated by Spencer Peel, p. Diane MacDermott; CF.

LANDLORD-TENANT LAW (23m C 1978) Law and the Citizen Series
Examines, through dramatization, the relationships and potential points of dispute between landlords and tenants. A young couple agrees to take an apartment needing repairs in return for lower rent. A dispute arises later when the repairs exceed their ability to deal

with them. Reenactment of court scene brings out rights of tenants and landlords, necessity of full contractual agreements. Open-ended to invite discussion. p. Bernard Wilets/CBS-TV; PHOENIX, UIL.

LANDS'S EDGE (28m C 1974)
LAND'S EDGE is what might be called a poetic documentary, a film essay and a very thoughtful one about the land's edge, the sea-coast. Filmed in Newport area and on a fishing boat, the film is a three-part study of coastal life, including plants and animals. The first shows the surf and sea creatures which live close to shore.... The middle part shows fishermen at work and features interviews with a few, including one by a man who tells how CBS-TV made a fisher-man don a rain slicker for an interview because he hadn't dressed like the stereotype. The last part shows only a little of the storm itself, although it is still an exciting segment; but it shows the build-up, the shore waiting and the aftermath of the storm. p. Susan Shadburne, Richard Blakeslee, Tom Chamberlin; NWMP.

LANGUAGE OF MODERN DANCE, THE (22m B 1958)
Dance sessions teaching modern-dance movement, pattern and rhythm. Also demonstrates the value of practice. Dance Teacher/ p. Lila Cheville; UIO.

LAS TURAS (16m C 1979)
Depicts the celebration of las turas, an ancient fertility rite still practiced by Indian peasants in Venezuela. The film's sensitive por-trayal of the ritual is complemented by an explanation of its back-ground and meaning which utilizes the words of the Indians them-selves. English language narration. d. Ana Maria Enriques; UNI-FILM; UMN.

LASER IN GYNECOLOGY: VAGINAL VAPORIZATION AND BULVAR
EXCISION, THE (17m C 1982) (Video)
A teaching tape for medical personnel to demonstrate the use of the laser for both vaporization and excision of vulvar vaginal lesions. The laser is demonstrated in the handheld and the coloposcopic appli-cations. Its advantages and limitations in the care and removal of intraepithelial neoplasia and of viral lesions are stressed. p. C. Stark/R. Temple; BAPMEMH.

LAST CRY FOR HELP, A (32m C 1980)
Alienated, depressed, unable to communicate with her parents or make close friends, a young girl attempts suicide. We see her ex-perience both before the attempt and her emerging strength after-ward as she attempts to take control of her life with the help of her psychiatrist. LCA; CWU, IU, UCEMC, USC, KENTSU, WSU.

LAST DAYS OF LIVING, THE (58m C 1980)
Illustrates, through case histories, the special types of care and unorthodox approaches used in palliative care of terminally ill patients

and their families at Montreal's Royal Victoria Hospital. Uses interviews with patients and staff, on-site footage of hospital procedures.
Summarizes aims and philosophy of palliative care. NFBC; UIL.

LAST GREAT RACE, THE (50m C p1979, r1982)
    The annual 1,200-mile dog-sled race across the frozen wilderness
of Alaska--the Iditarod--is a grueling test of human endurance. A
BBC camera crew followed 56 mushers and 800 dogs in the three-week
trek across some of the world's most torturous terrain. For many
competitors, the Iditarod has become a way of life, as they spend
much of the year breeding and training sled dogs and planning for
the next great race. d. Susan Ruddy, p. Northrim Associates; FI.

LAST MONTHS OF PREGNANCY, THE (29m B 1956) Months Before
    Birth--A Series
    Discusses fetal development during the later months before birth
and gives suggestions for the care and well-being of the expectant
mother. p. WQED-TV; AF.

LAST OF LIFE, THE (28m C p1977, r1978)
    Revealing study of cell biology of a young person and of an el-
derly person. Geriatric specialists discuss the various "annoying"
attitudes projected at the elderly and stresses the fact that old people
must be seen as individuals. One geriatrician sums up his work with
the comment that it should be the concern of geriatrics to add life
to the final years, rather than simply add years to life. d./p. Die-
drik d'Ailly for CBS-TV; FILMLB; UM, UMO.

LAST POWDER PUFF DERBY, THE (ed.) (28m C p1979, r1980)
    Presents an absorbing film about some very special women and
their love of a unique sport. In 1947, Amelia Earhart and 25 other
women were participants in the original women's air race from Palm
Springs, California to Tampa, Florida, dubbed the "Powder Puff
Derby" by Will Rogers. Continuing for 30 years, the final Powder
Puff Derby on July 1, 1977, was a commemorative flight to honor
those who went before. Although the final flight was not a race,
each pilot hoped to arrive first in Tampa and to perform well on special skill tests required of them along the way. Several women who
flew many of the early races talk about both the history and future
of women in aviation. p./d./s.w. Joyce Young; MACMFL.

LAST RITES (30m C 1979)
    The mystery of death and its incomprehensibility to a child is
the subject of this drama. A young boy is unable to cope with the
loss of his mother. He tries to fantasize his mother back in various
ways. Although this effort fails, solace comes from a stranger who
at last helps him to accept reality and come to terms with his loss.
p./d. Joan Vail Thorne, Anne Macksoud; FILMLB.

LAST SUMMER (17m C p1978, r1979)
    Three women, at the end of pregnancy, pass some time together

being silly, hopeful, happy, and scared. They meet again that fall
with their babies to see how their lives have changed. A funny/
serious fictional film. p./d. Miriam Weinstein; PEREN.

LAST TABOO (30m C 1977)
     Documents a dramatic week-end therapy session in which six vic-
tims of early childhood sexual abuse work through some of the pain
they carry from this mistreatment. Designed for public awareness
building, the film alerts the viewer to the reality of the incest experience. Deflates the position of well-intentioned incest. Shows the
long-term personality damage resulting from the experience while demonstrating that victims can overcome the damage and lead reasonably
normal and full adult lives. p. Cavalcade Productions; MTITI; UIL,
UMO, UM, UMN.

LAST TO KNOW, THE (45m C 1981)
     Nearly one half of the 10 million alcoholics in this country are
women, yet their special problems are totally ignored. Concealed by
families, protected by friends, betrayed by physicians, these women
are kept invisible. Through the intimate stories of women's lives,
we see how the medical community, the media and the values of society at large perpetuate alcoholism and prescription drug abuse in
women. The film combines scholarly, social and historical analysis
with poignant personal interviews, bringing to public attention a hidden and denied aspect of women's health. p./d. Bonnie Friedman,
p. Pandora Educational Film Center, Inc.; NEWDAY.

LAST TREE, THE (10m C r1975)
     An ecological parable which traces the evolution of matter from
the first amorphous blob right up to the emergence of man. All
through the many stages of the development of living things, the
many species coexist and interact to maintain the delicate balance of
nature, taking only what is necessary for them to live, not destroy-
ing life wantonly. It is not until the final stage is reached, and man,
the "superior" animal emerges, that the all-important balance of nature is threatened through his monumental disregard for the other
living things that surround him. In this atmosphere, all living things
die, until only one tree remains on earth as a reminder of the life
that has been destroyed. p./d. Chris Bryant, Ceevah Sobel; PHOE-
NIX.

LAST WOMAN, THE (111m C 1976) (French/Subtitled)
     Focuses on the relationship of a young Parisian couple. Deals
uncompromisingly with the nature and roots of sexism. p. Edmondo
Amati; d. Marco Ferreri; CORINTH.

LATER THAT NIGHT see ANIMATED WOMEN

LAW AND THE CITIZEN SERIES see LANDLORD-TENANT LAW

LE PAYSAGISTE see MINDSCAPE

LE REGARD PICASSO (27m C 1966)
In November 1966 the most complete exhibit of all times concerning a single creative artist opened in Paris--that of Pablo Picasso. The film retraces the various productive periods of the greatest artist of the twentieth century. French and English sound. d. Nelly Kaplan; FACSEA.

LEADERS OF THE 20TH CENTURY: PORTRAITS OF POWER see
    ELIZABETH II: WINDS OF CHANGE

LEAP OF A THOUSAND YEARS, A (25½m C 1982)
Thousands of Southeast Asians have fled the war in their homeland and found refuge in North America. They have come to make their home here. Building a new life is not an easy task. Both sponsors and refugees have had to make efforts to bridge the gap between their two cultures and have learned a lot from each other. d. Laurette Deschamps; p. Cine-Contact; CINCONT.

LEARNING: A HAPPY EXPERIENCE (16m C p1978, r1979)
Shows how teachers can create a successful learning atmosphere. When a child is loved and accepted, she/he will have a high level of self-esteem and is likely to be a quick learner; however, once the child experiences negative feelings about himself/herself (or one's school), a pattern of failure can be established that is difficult to reverse. Emphasizes young children's need for frequent personal experiences of success. Suggests that the teacher's task is to assess the student's needs and guide her/him into that atmosphere. It is pointed out that students need to be involved in investigation with all their senses in order to retain information and make it meaningful. d./p. Carolyn Sue Benson; FILMFR.

LEARNING TO BE HUMAN SERIES see MAKE-BELIEVE MARRIAGE;
    MR. GIME; SHOESHINE GIRL

LEARNING TO BREASTFEED (22m C 1979)
Provides useful information and role models for facilitating successful initial breastfeeding experience. For all its advantages and apparent simplicity, breastfeeding requires learning. Shown is a hospital class on breastfeeding for pre- and post-partum women, with discussion of cesareans, sore and inverted nipples, engorgement, and the role of oxytocin. Hand and breast pump expression of milk are clearly demonstrated, as is the use of a breast shield. Returning to work and the importance of the psychological aspects of breastfeeding are discussed. Ideal teaching tool for mothers as well as hospital and professional staff. d. Alvin Fiering; produced in collaboration with Childbirth Education Association of Seattle; POLYMR.

LEARNING TO COPE (25m C 1979)
Introduces several persons who are all learning to cope with the stress and tensions of their daily lives. Shows how they struggle

to master the transitions and painful times. Presents successful strategies for coping and analysis of the actions seen on the screen. In conclusion, the film comments that the goal is not to eliminate tension but to control it. p. Screenscope, Inc.; SCRESC; CWU.

LEARNING TO DIAGNOSE ARTHRITIS (26m C 1978) (Video) The Physicians Update Series
Dr. Mary E. Moore, associate professor of medicine at Temple University's School of Medicine, explains how to diagnose osteoarthritis, rheumatoid arthritis, gout, and other variants by use of live model, clinical slides and superimpositions. PSUAVS; PAS.

LEARNING TO ENJOY (28m C n.d.) Prime Time (Series)
Shows people who have found that the later years can be a most satisfying time of your life if you make your own choices, let go, take a risk and allow yourself to pursue the things that bring enjoyment. Narrated by Don McNeill. Free loan. p. Sears-Roebuck Foundation; MTPS.

LEAVING HOME: A FAMILY IN TRANSITION (28m C 1981)
An honest and intimate portrait of four sisters and their parents who are ending one phase of their lives and beginning another. It documents the experiences of the Bar-Din family, Californians with Israeli roots. LEAVING HOME is seen through the eyes of Ilana, the oldest daughter, and also the filmmaker. Ilana watches her sisters' attempts to define themselves as women in this film. Ilana says she made this film because, "I realized that the difficulties my family was having in making this important transition are common to families everywhere. LEAVING HOME gains power from its subjective point of view. It is a touching film which will be especially beneficial to groups concerned with family relations and women's issues. p./d. Ilana Bar-Din; DIRECT.

LEE KRASNER: THE LONG VIEW (30m C p1978, r1978)
Critic Barbara Rose's film portrait of the seminal Abstract Expressionist artist focusing on Krasner's life, including her studies with Hans Hoffman and her marriage to Jackson Pollock. Krasner is also seen completing work for and hanging a show at New York's Pace Gallery. Awards. d./p. Barbara Rose; AFA.

LEFT-HANDED WOMAN, THE (119m C 1978) (German/Subtitled)
Tells of a German housewife, living in an anonymous-looking suburb of Paris, who decides to become "unmarried." The narrative goes on to record her quiet "war with the world" over three months of loneliness, near-breakdown, and adjustment. The subject of the film, however, is not upbeat feminist coping, but the struggle to locate oneself in a universe that often seems as difficult and alien as the other side of the moon. d. Peter Handke; NYF.

LEGACY (90m C 1976) (Rated R)
Joan Hotchkiss plays an attractive, wealthy and spoiled Pasadena,

California matron. In a course of a day, Joan visits her senile mother and drives to her own well-appointed home to prepare for dinner guests. In the meantime, she talks on the phone, talks to herself, recalls her out-of-town husband and children, and her first love. She relieves herself sexually in the bathtub to thoughts of the Japanese gardener. She finds the right decorations for a table centerpiece. Gradually she comes apart at the seams. "Clitoris ... I can't pronounce it. He can't find it," she says in a soliloquy about her husband. Later she calls her analyst. "I feel I'm going to commit suicide. I thought I ought to inform you." p. Karen Arthur; s.w. and star, Joan Hotchkiss; KINO.

LEGACY: CHILDREN OF HOLOCAUST SURVIVORS, THE (23m C p1979, r1979)
More than 30 years after the Holocaust of World War II, the children of Holocaust survivors are looking back at the generation behind them. This film integrates the attitudes, memories, and feelings of five children of survivors, and delves into how they have been affected by their legacies. d./p./s.w. Miriam Strilky Rosenbush; p. Rosenbush Productions; FLMST.

LEGACY OF THE NEW DEAL (28½m C p1980, r1980) (Video)
Whether Democrats or Republicans have controlled the executive and legislative branches since 1945, basic New Deal programs remained intact. The expectation that the national government can respond to national concerns is the legacy of F.D.R. and the New Deal. Though by the late 1970's there was skepticism about the ability of Big Government to deal effectively with many issues, critics offered few viable alternatives. Contemporary film and analysis by Arthur Schlesinger, Jr. highlight this program. d. William Anderson, p. Cheri Simon; DALLASCO.

LEGAL RESPONSIBILITIES FOR AFFIRMATIVE ACTION AND EQUAL EMPLOYMENT (12m C 1975) (slc)
Explains the need for equal opportunity employment and affirmative action laws and how these laws help women. Discusses the Equal Pay Act of 1963, Title VII of the Civil Rights Act, and guidelines enforced by the Equal Employment Opportunity Commission. The program emphasizes that knowledge of the law is vital for people who are working toward fair employment opportunities for everyone. Script included. p. Center for Human Systems, University of Minnesota in cooperation with the Women's Bureau, United States Department of Labor. UMN.

LEGAL RIGHTS OF WOMEN WORKERS (6m C 1975) (slc)
More and more women are getting jobs that have been considered unusual for women. Explains how the equal opportunity laws help women get the best jobs possible. The program stresses "It's up to you to make sure that the laws work for you." Script included. p. Center for Human Systems, University of Minnesota, in cooperation with the Women's Bureau, United States Department of Labor; UMN.

LEGEND OF PAULIE GREEN, THE (29m C 1976) Dial Alcohol Series
Presents the story of Paulie Green, from the film HOTLINE, who turns out to be a problem drinker, and Karen, a young lady with an alcoholic mother. p. National Institute on Alcohol Abuse and Alcoholism; NAVC.

LEGISLATIVE REPORT (29m C 1976) (Video) Woman Series
Carol Burris, President and founder of Women's Lobby, Inc., discusses current proposed legislation that would benefit women. She covers child care credit, various national health insurance plans, displaced homemakers' legislation and the Humphrey-Hawkins Bill. Sandra Elkin is the moderator. p. WNED-TV; PBSV.

LEGISLATIVE REPORT UPDATE (29m C 1977) (Video) Woman Series
Washington lobbyists Carol Burris, President and founder of Women's Lobby, Inc. and Susan Tenenbaum, editor and founder of "Women's Washington Respresentative," discuss their efforts on behalf of women's issues. They describe the role of the lobbyist, the attitudes they encounter and the progress of courrent legislation affecting women. Sandra Elkin, moderator. p. WNED-TV; PBSV.

LEMONADE SUITE (30m C 1982) (Video)
An interpretation through music and dance of the works of black poet Gwendolyn Brooks. The poetry tells of a young girl who, longing to be grown-up and independent, meets a young man, falls in love, finds herself pregnant and abandoned and then rebuilds her life. Original music by Kenneth Ware of Indiana University, Afro-American Arts Institute; choreography by Iris Rosa, Director of the I.U. Afro-American Dance Company. With study guide. p. Indiana University Radio and Television Services and Afro-American Arts Institute; IU.

LEON "PECK" CLARK: BASKETMAKER (18m C 1980) (Video)
Presents Leon "Peck" Clark one of the few remaining hand basketmakers in the South still working at an art he learned from an early American artisan. Traces the steps he goes through to create his unique white oak baskets. Mr. and Mrs. Clark talk about their life together. But, it is the basketmaking that keeps him engrossed and involved today along with farm chores. d./p. Judy Peiser, Bill Ferris; p. Center for Southern Folklore; SOFOLF.

LESBIAN MOTHERS AND CHILD CUSTODY, PART I (29m C 1977) (Video) Woman Series
Attorneys Barbara Handschu and Margot Hagman discuss lesbian mothers' struggle for custody of their children. Hagman describes a 1970 case that established a precedent when a San Jose, California mother stated in court that she was a lesbian but did receive custody of her children. Handschu explains the controversy surrounding the question of parental fitness and its relationship to sexual preference. Sandra Elkin is the moderator. p. WNED-TV; PBSV.

LESBIAN MOTHERS AND CHILD CUSTODY, PART II (29m C 1977)
(Video) Woman Series
Mary Jo Risher and Ann Foreman describe their efforts to reclaim custody of Mary Jo's ten-year-old son, who was taken from the Risher-Foreman home and placed under his father's guardianship as the result of a jury trial. Mary Jo's lesbianism was the central issue in the trial. Sandra Elkin is the moderator. p. WNED-TV; PBSV.

LESS AND MORE (20m C p1978, r1978) Trade-offs Series
Introduces the general concept of increasing productivity and the accompanying advantages and disadvantages. It defines productivity as the amount of output (or production) per unit of input. Designed to help students think through economic problems and increase their understanding of economics. p. Maggie Stratton; d. Eric Jordan, Paul Stephens; AIT.

LET'S EAT FOOD (35m C r1976)
Informative but entertaining look at American eating habits and nutrition, exploring such topics as processed foods, cholesterol, and the role sugar plays in tooth decay, diabetes, and coronary disease. Experts offer guidelines for healthier diets and how how to prepare a varied menu of low-fat dishes. Narrated by Tony Randall. Top award. CRM; UCLA, UNEV.

LET'S KEEP IN TOUCH (28m C n.d.)
Uses intriguing fantasy characters to introduce viewers to the workings of the Medicare system. A glib carnival barker, a jovial game show host, and an eccentric pharmacist add to the fun as the film's principal characters, Arnie and Millie Harper, learn entertainingly how Medicare, with recommended supplementary insurance, can serve the needs of senior citizens. Free loan. p. Bankers Life and Casualty Company; MTPS.

LET'S WRITE A STORY (2nd ed.) (11m C 1978)
Presents imaginative episodes that will stimulate a class of young children to write--first, a lively descriptive phrase, a vivid sentence, and last, a story of their own. Several situations and characters are presented to stimulate imaginations in describing what they have seen, conceive possible endings for situations, and to match characters and locations to create a story. d./p. Susan Shippey; CF.

LETTER FROM AN APACHE (11½m C 1982)
An animated dramatization of the true story of an Apache who was born in 1866, captured in 1871, sold and brought to Chicago where he became a doctor and returned to help his people. Drawn in nineteenth-century, Indian style, the film reveals the tragic fate of many Indians of the period. d./p./s.w./ed. Barbara Wilk; WILKB.

LETTER TO MY UNCLE (15m B 1981)
The filmmaker pays tribute to her uncle's struggle to create

meaning in his life when faced with imminent death. Excerpts from tapes which he recorded during his illness are juxtaposed with images reflecting his thoughts. These images are simple and direct, so that his concerns can be understood within the context of everyday life. d. Deborah Lefkowitz; p. Harvard University LEFKOF.

LIES (30m C 1980-1983) (Video, Beta, VHS) Concepts Series

LIES uses cost accounting to dramatically emphasize the spoken lie (the everyday garden variety that we use to stay civilized) and lists its price in subtitle. s.w. Lee Breuer, performed by Ruth Malaczech, both founding members of Mabou Mines, with music by Bob Telson. d./p. Doris Chase; CHASED.

LIFE AFTER DEATH (35m C p1978)

Brings into focus the question of the persistence of consciousness after biological death. Dr. Lawrence LeShan presents the scientific view. At a session at the Monroe Institute with Robert Monroe, author of Journeys Out of the Body, participants learn that they are more than their physical body.... Dr. Kenneth Ring interviews four who were "clinically dead...." Margaret Flavell, British medium, communicates with the late A. D. Mattson, who describes the hereafter. This film reviews historical beliefs about immortality and concludes with the view of modern physicists that at one level of reality we are indeed immortal. p. Elda Hartley; HARTLEY.

LIFE AND TIMES OF ROSIE THE RIVETER (65m C 1980)

Reconstructs the experience of women workers during World War II through interviews with five former "Rosies." Rare archival recruitment films, stills, posters, ads and music from the period contrast the reality of their experiences with the popular legend of Rosie the Riveter. p./d. Connie Field; p. Clarity Educational Productions; CLARITY; UM, UMN.

LIFE CAREER PATTERNS OF WOMEN (30m C 1974) (Video) Career Development of Women Series

Presents a glimpse of seven women in different life patterns, including a married active volunteer, a single adoptive parent, a professor in an equal partnership marriage, a psychologist living in a commune, a Black married woman who is in a mid-career shift, a young married college student, and a divorced re-entry woman, mother of six. The program is an introduction to the problems in career patterns of women. p. University of Minnesota; UMN.

LIFE, DEATH AND THE AMERICAN WOMAN (54m C 1977)

"Ten thousand times a day in the United States one of life's most poignant dramas is reenacted--the drama of birth." Following this opening statement, the film traces the lives of ten women as they face various health-related crises most common to women. First part examines various cancer problems: cervical, breast and spinal. Balance of the film examines hypoglycemia, menopause, complications of pregnancy, sickle-cell anemia, mongolism, RH incompatibility, and career hazards. Problems, alternatives, solutions, and conclusions are discussed through patient and professional commentary. Narrated by Patricia Neal. BEST; UIL.

LIFE HISTORY OF MARY (45m B 1952)
Case history of female child's development over a 15-year period. Psychological analysis follows filmed sequences that date from 1938 to 1953. Shows a child born with superior biological capacities who nevertheless develops a neurosis through interaction with those in her environment. NYU; UFL.

LIFE IN A MIDWESTERN SMALL TOWN IN THE 1920's see HAD YOU LIVED THEN: LIFE IN A MIDWESTERN SMALL TOWN IN THE 1910's

LIFE IN AN EASTERN SEAPORT TOWN 1870's see HAD YOU LIVED THEN: LIFE IN AN EASTERN SEAPORT TOWN 1870's

LIFE OF OHARU (133m B 1952) (Japanese/Subtitled)
Set at the turn of the eighteenth-century in Japan, the film paints a vast and intricate canvas of feudal Japan, a world which brutally links women with property, and one where a woman must always play her assigned role. From the vast panorama of the heroine's life-- courtesan, breeder, working woman, bourgeois wife, fugitive, common prostitute, and finally not even that--it becomes clear that Mizoguchi, the director, sees her as not just a woman but all women. Mizoguchi is known for his remarkable and special insight into the social conditions of women. d. Kenzo Mizoguchi; NYF.

LIFE OF THE BIGHORN SHEEP (16m C p1980, r1981) (also Video)
Great Animal Stories Series
Filmed on location in Yellowstone, Jasper, Banff, and Glacier National Parks, this is a film study of the Rocky Mountain bighorn sheep from spring when new lambs are born through the following winter when the next generation is on its way. p. Myrna I. Berlet, Walter H. Berlet; BERLET; IFB.

LIFE OF WOMEN IN JAPAN, THE (20m C n.d.)
An investigation of the roles of women in Japan today, using statistics, interviews with women's rights leaders, and footage of women from all walks of life. Touches on the lives of schoolgirls, working women, mothers, and senior citizens. p. Japan Foundation; PAS.

LIFE THAT'S LEFT, THE (29m C r1980) (also Video)
A study of bereavement; focuses on personal experiences of ordinary people. p. NETCHE Video Tape Library; NETCHE.

LIFELINES: A CAREER PROFILE STUDY (26m C 1977)
Dr. Edgar Schein of the Sloan School of Management at the

Massachusetts Institute of Technology discusses some of the results of his research in career formation and explains that each of us has a "career lifeline"--a path that directs our choice of work.   p. Hobel-Leiterman; DOCUA; UM.

LIGHT (15m C p1979, r1979)
    A pictorial history of lighting from Genesis to Edison. Emphasis is placed on Thomas A. Edison's invention of the lightbulb, and how a lightbulb is made. d. Ellen Hovde, Muffie Meyer; p. Middlemarch Films; DIRECT.

LIGHT, PART V (20m C 1975)
    Presents an extraordinary dance trio by choreographer Kei Takei. Shows a slow, fluid dance, whose setting is an isolated pool of light. The two men (Maldwyn Pate and John de Marco) assume sixteen different poses, and the woman (Takei) has her own correlated ritual. Interpretation of the images is left up to the viewer and the descriptive words applied by observers have varied widely. DAN/UR; UIL.

LIGHT FANTASTIC PICTURE SHOW, THE (7m C 1974) (also Video)
    Ten different styles of animation provide the viewer with the unusual experience of seeing art created before one's very eyes with no human being present. The images emerge "without hands," as yarn dances, paper cutouts move about, line figures appear and, in a stunning final sequence, an oil portrait of a lady is created--step by step. Musical sound track by jazz pianist Marian McPartland. d. Lillian Somersaulter, J. P. Somersaulter; p. Pajon Arts; FI.

LIGHT IS MANY THINGS (12m C 1977)
    The importance of light is discussed by a group of young people in their classroom. They bring what they know about the importance of light as the source of life and energy to plants and animals, and try to answer the question, "Why is light important to you?" p. Glenda Fillinger, Paul Fillinger; MACMFL; UIL.

LIGHTS, ACTION, AFRICA! (55m C p1982, r1983) (also Video)
    Filmed on location in Tanzania National Park, Kenya National Park, and Maasai Mara Game Reserve, this film captures the skill and daring of two renowned African wildlife filmmakers, Joan and Alan Root. More at home in tents on the plains of Africa than in their lakeside African house, the Roots grew up in Kenya where Alan was more interested in filming animals than going to school and Joan was the daughter of one of the originators of photographic safaris. Emphasizing natural cycles of death and rebirth in their photography, Alan and Joan Root apply their special skills with deep love and understanding to preserve on film what may never be captured again. p. Joan and Alan Root for BBC-TV; BENCHMF.

LIKE ANY CHILD ONLY MORE SO (29m C 1978)
    Provides some medical opinions, opinions of parents of youngsters

who are active in the extreme and others concerned with the treatment and education of such children. There is considerable controversy over what hyperactivity is and how it should be treated, as
opinions expressed by various people in this film show. A good exploration film for parents and others who work with hyperactive
youngsters. Narrated by Belva Davis. p. Catharine Allan, Maile
Ornellas; IU, UCEMC.

LILA (28½m C 1980) (also Video)
    Profile of Lila Bonner-Miller, an 80-year-old practicing psychia-
trist who is also an artist, a church leader, a mother, grandmother
and a great-grandmother. Aims to show how one elderly individual
maintains an active, productive schedule. p./d. Fran Burst-
Terranella; Cheryl Gosa; IDEAIM.

LILLIAN LAROO (1m C 1980)
    Lillian is a peace-loving, mind-her-own-business woman who is
out for a breath of fresh air in the mountains. But Lillian can take
care of herself and provides the audience with a simple and delightful sense of our own power. In animation. p. Lorraine Weese; IRIS.

LINDA AND JIMMY (17m C 1978) The Changing Scene (Series)
    Provides insight into one woman's changing feelings about her-
self and her family, and discusses the impact of those changes on her
husband and daughter. Linda Fox and her family are interviewed
about changing roles and shared responsibilities involved in modern
marriages. Linda felt that in order to be a good wife and mother,
she must first be happy with herself, and for her a career was necessary to achieve that. She discusses her choice, its rewards, and
difficulties with her family when she decided to pursue a career.
Linda's husband, Jimmy, explains how her career affected his role
as husband and father. He admits that at first he felt threatened
but as Linda became more secure and self-sufficient, their marital
relationship has actually become closer and healthier. p. Coronet
Instructional Media; CORONET; PAS, UMN.

LINDA VELZY IS DEAD (13m C p1979, r1979)
    Deals with the dangers of hitchhiking. Television's "60 Minutes"
program followed the police investigation into 18-year-old Linda Velzy's
disappearance. Shows the stark reality of her brutal killing. Prosecutor makes the case that if young people can't be talked out of hitchhiking, legislative changes should be made to keep them from endangering their lives. d. Arthur Bloom; p. David Lowe, Jr., CBS-TV
"60 Minutes"; MTITI.

LION AND THE MOUSE, THE (5m C 1977)
    Aesop's fable done in brilliantly colored, cutout animation. The
compassionate lion catches, and then releases a grateful mouse. The
lion is later rewarded when he is trapped in a rope net, and the
mouse chews through the rope to free him. Moral: One good turn
deserves another. p. Evelyn Lambart; NFBC; BENCHMF.

LIPSTICK (88m C 1976)
An uncompromising portrayal of a legal system which seemingly regards a rape victim with less feeling than it shows the criminal. The tragedy of a beautiful model begins when she (Margeaux Hemingway) is raped. Events thereafter lead the viewer to sympathize with her final act of vengeance. d. Lamont Johnson, p. Freddie Fields; PARACO.

LISA: THE LEGACY OF SANDRA BLAIN (21m C 1979)
Dramatizes Lisa's road to alcoholism as, three months after her mother's funeral, she is drinking heavily herself. Observes how her progressive inability to cope affects nearly every aspect of her life and a combination of pills and alcohol nearly kills her. Shows how a young woman at work, herself a recovered alcoholic, helps Lisa enter a recovery program. Uses voice-over narration to discuss the unique problems confronting young women alcoholics and the need for a total mental, physical, and spiritual recovery program. p. Charles Cahill and Associates, Inc.; AIMS; IU.

LISTEN LISTEN LISTEN (83m C n.d.)
A look at the controversial educational community in Southwestern Ontario where people of all ages come, either freely or referred by the courts, the psychiatric wards and training schools. Focuses on the "referrals," and their struggle to find a new meaning to life. d. Barbara Greene; p. Cynthia Scott, Roman Kroiter; NFBC.

LISTEN TO THE DANCE (10m B 1977)
Depicts a group of about 20 men and women who weekly attend a dance movement therapy session in a mental health day treatment center for people who are experiencing emotional difficulties. Stresses interaction between therapist and clients and cooperation between psychotherapist and dance therapist. Filmed at Miramonte Mental Health Services. Dance Therapist: Patricia M. Burbank; p. Wendy Roth; PEREN.

LITTERS (9m C 1981)
A live-action, slow-motion documentary film footage of Coney Island as it is today has been transferred frame-by-frame onto paper via a special xerographic process. These ghostly grey, surreal images are augmented with neon intensity dyes and inks to suggest the glittering dazzle of Coney Island. The film demonstrates how a passive environment can be overrun and destroyed by litter, violence and neglect. p. Caroline Ahlfours Mouris, Frank Mouris; DIRECT.

LITTLE INJUSTICES: LAURA NADER LOOKS AT THE LAW (59m C
    1981) (also Video) Odyssey Series
An anthropological study comparing the way legal systems in Mexico and the United States settle minor disputes and consumer complaints. The film focuses on the Zapotec Indians in the Mexican village of Talea and illustrates how the local legal system handles certain

cases, such as a merchant who has his basket of chilies run over by a truck driver, or two drunken teenagers who drive their truck off the road into a house. The emphasis is on negotiation and settling the dispute locally without resorting to outside authorities. To demonstrate the contrasting style of the United States legal system, the proceedings in the Mexican courtroom are frequently interrupted by interviews with American consumers describing their long, unsuccessful attempts to get some type of action for defective products. The film illustrates how such disputes in large, industrialized societies are often characterized by escalating conflicts between strangers in which these "little injustices" often go ignored and unresolved. p. Terry Kay Rockfeller; DER, PBSV; PAS.

LITTLE LULU (24m C 1979)
The famed comic strip character comes to life to prove that girls are not the weaker sex. p. ABC-TV; MEDCON.

LITTLE SISTER (45m C p1975, r1978)
A reunion of friends evolves into an emotional crucible for Ellen, a young woman who has stalwartly committed most of her adult energy to maintaining her dialogue with a mythified past. Now, as the group's dynamics threaten to clamp off that umbilical cord, Ellen must react; she is impelled into a painfully direct confrontation with her oldest and most cherished friend. d./p. Mellena Bridges; BRIDGES.

LIVE OR DIE (29m C 1979)
Demonstrates the effects of life habits on one body in a way that is dramatically and scientifically authentic, and conveys the vital message that our health is our own responsibility. Different stages in the lives of two people are shown in great detail (by use of flashbacks), and pathologists indicate the effect of life-style, work habits, eating habits, exercise routines (or lack of it), personal relationships, stress build-up, and competition on the human body. A good introductory film for all health education situations. d./s.w. Larry Yust; p. Wexler Foundation for the E. C. Brown Foundation; PEREN; CWU.

LIVED TIME (15m C n.d.)
Through a flow of silent images, this film describes the passage of experienced time as much by its edited rhythms as by its pictorial subject matter. As you play the film back (or remember it), it may take on narrative level, or it may persist without supporting story, depending on your needs. On its narrative level, two characters flow in opposition to (or in parallel with) the flow of events. On its nonnarrative level, it concerns foreground and background, proximity and pace. p. Martha Haslanger; CCC.

LIVES OF FIRE CRACKERS (11m C n.d.)
A hilarious parody of the "Me" generation's search for identity. The film track is crowded with competing voices: the erotic, academic, schizophrenic, political, and paranoid "fire crackers." p. Sandy Moore; BELVFF.

LIVING AMERICAN THEATRE DANCE (11m C 1981)
The American Dance Machine is a company specifically devoted to preserving Broadway theatre dances and choreography. Led by Lee Theodore, an extraordinarily energetic dancer/choreographer/teacher, the troupe practices and performs numbers from such plays as West Side Story, as well as lesser known plays from the thirties and forties, adding their own flavor to these classics. d. John Alper; p. Ruth Caplin; PHOENIX.

LIVING ARRANGEMENTS AND SERVICES (15m C 1982)
Briefly traces the historical development of specialized housing and projects expected future changes in living arrangements in relation to lengthening longevity. It illustrates older people already adapting (shared, congregate and cooperative housing) to mounting costs, loneliness, and need for social and health services in order to retain their independent life-style. p. International Center for Social Gerontology, UMMRC; UM, UIL.

LIVING GODDESS, THE (30m C 1979)
The Kumari are virgin female children selected by ancient rites among the Newar people of Kathmandu in Nepal to be living embodiments of traditional goddesses. Focuses on three of several Kumari in existence. Raises valuable questions, including the role played by the goddess in society once she loses her status as such. The ending is particularly good in that it ties in what at first seems to be a very strange concept with broader beliefs in other ares, for example, the veneration of purity. An excellent study of a little-known aspect of religion. d. Frank Heimans; WOMBAT; UCEMC.

LIVING THE GOOD LIFE WITH HELEN AND SCOTT NEARING (30m C p1976, r1977)
Forty-five years ago, Helen and Scott Nearing quit city life and moved to Vermont. He was a brilliant economist; she a concert pianist. Today, Forest Farm is synonymous with the ideal homestead. At 74 and 93, Helen and Scott are self-subsistent, involved, balanced, and healthy. They grow their own food, cut firewood for fuel, and have just built a large stone home by themselves. Through books and public appearances they remain effective critics of the market economy. But their greatest contribution lies in the example of their day-to-day living. p. Bullfrog Films; BULFRG; CWU, PAS.

LIVING TIME--SARAH JESUP TALKS ON DYING (15m C p1979, r1980)
Sarah Jesup, 41, in her last three months of life, faces the tragedy of death as a reality. She begins to define her priorities and realizes the importance of being able to go on living while dying. In an interview three weeks prior to her death, Jesup discusses important issues which dying patients must confront and the outrage some feel. Explaining her approaching death to her children, speaking about dying to friends, the importance of the doctor/patient/nurse relationship, and the Living Will are among the topics which Sarah

Jesup discusses in this short but powerful film. d. Hilary Harris;
p. Keneholistic Foundation; CONCFD.

LIVING TREASURES OF JAPAN (ed.) (59m C p1981, r1981) (also
    Video)
    Features nine of the seventy "Living Treasures of Japan," artists
designated by the Japanese Government as "Holders of Important In-
tangible Cultural Properties" and charged with publicly exhibiting
their works and teaching and training apprentices to carry on their
skills in the artists who have honored their country and themselves
with their creative ability. p./s.w. Miriam Birch; p. National Geographic Society, SQED-TV, Pittsburgh; NGS.

LIVING VIGNETTE SERIES see CLOSE FEELINGS

LIVING WITH FEAR (52m C 1974)
    Extent to which fear flavors American life today. Explores the
country's unshakeable commitment to the private possession of fire-
arms and the tradition of vigilante justice. Fear of rape as a special
anxiety of women. Crime and fear in the inner cities is represented
by the Harlem ghetto. Variety of ways Americans seek to foster their
sense of security, including self-help Black associations. p. Gateway
Educational Films, Ltd.; GATEWF; PAS.

LIVING WITH STRESS (22m C 1976)
    A fast-moving look at typical daily stress-producing situations
that everyone can relate to. Emphasizes that stress is a personal
problem that each individual must first understand then deal with in
a personal way. p. Trio Productions; Xerox Films; AF.

LIVING YOGA: FOUR YOKES TO GOD (20m C 1976)
    From head to heart to feet this is a film about the four classic
pathways of "union" (yoga), revealed to us through the lives of dis-
ciples of Swami Satchidananda: hatha, the yoga of physical postures
and breathing techniques; raja, the path of meditation and introspec-
tion; karma, the way of selfless service; and bhakti, the yoga of
love and devotion. p. Elda Hartley; HARTLEY.

LOIS GOULD ON WOMEN WRITERS (29m C 1977) (Video) Woman Series
    Novelist and journalist Lois Gould (Such Good Friends, Necessary
Objects, Final Analysis, A Sea Change) explains some traditional assumptions about women writers and describes the limitations they impose on writers of fiction. She discusses her feelings about the responsibility contemporary women writers have to other women. Sandra
Elkin is the moderator. p. WNED-TV; PBSV.

LONESOME TRAIN, THE (21m C r1973)
    Using history, anecdote and legend, this tribute to Abraham Lin-
coln shows the problems of the times and the powerful symbol of freedom Lincoln represents. p. Barbara Begg, Norman Rose; FLMFR.

LONG ISLAND WILDERNESS--THE PINE BARRENS (24m C 1981)
A detailed exploration of a fire-climax ecosystem on Long Island and a look at the many adaptations plants and animals living there have made in order to survive in dry soil and frequent fire. d. Michael Male/Judy Fieth; p. Michael Male; MLINS.

LONG LIFE AND PROSPERITY (29m C n.d.)
For 5,000 years, the extended family has been the basic unit of Chinese society. Historically an agricultural people, their traditional farm home represents the values of Confucius, Lao-tse, and the other sages whose teachings have directed Chinese life. Today, with rapid industrialization and westernization in the Republic of China in Taiwan, the people are undergoing significant changes in their way of life. Shows a traditional birthday party in honor of the family's 82-year-old grandmother. For the reunion, the younger family members arrive from the city to observe the ancient rites of ancestor worship and honor their obligations of filial piety. p. University of Georgia; UGA.

LONG MARCH OF THE SUFFRAGISTS, THE (50m C 1981) Yesterday's Witness in America Series
In 1916, a group of suffragists who paraded, lobbied and argued for the vote for women decided to try British "suffragette" tactics. They gained considerable publicity by picketing the White House, being imprisoned, going on hunger strikes and being forcibly fed. With the aid of rare film and photographs, six fine old suffragists relate the final, dramatic years of their battle for the vote, which culminated in victory of 1920. p. BBC-TV/Time-Life Video; TIMLIF.

LONG VALLEY: A STUDY OF BEREAVEMENT, THE (59m C 1978)
Dr. Colin Murray Parkes, a social psychiatrist who has devoted his life to helping those who have suffered loss, talks to a group of doctors, clergy, social workers and six bereaved people about the process of grief. p. BBC-TV/OCEA; TIMLIF; PAS, UIL.

LOOK AT LIV, A (67m C p1979, r1979)
Presents a film portrait of Norwegian actress Liv Ullmann, who was born in Japan. Still photographs trace her childhood; her father's death; her years in London, Düsseldorf, and Oslo; and her school years. Shows clips from her motion pictures. Ullmann talks candidly about her personal relationship with director, friend and lover Ingmar Bergman as well as about her daughter, whom she is raising alone. p. Win-Kap Productions; p./s.w. Jerry Winters, Richard Kaplan; d. R. Kaplan; MACMFL.

LOOK AT ME--A SERIES see CHILD/PARENT RELATIONSHIPS; EVERYDAY PARENTING; FUN WITH DAD; GRANDMOTHER AND LESLIE; SINGLE PARENT, THE; WORKING MOTHER, THE

LOOK AT ME SERIES see BUILDING FAMILY RELATIONSHIPS;

DISCIPLINE; EXPLORING AND ACCEPTING INDIVIDUAL TRAITS; EXPLORING THE WORLD TOGETHER; RESPONSIBILITIES AND REWARDS OF PARENTING; SEPARATION; UNDERSTANDING SEXUALITY

LOOK AT ME--UNDERSTANDING SEXUALITY see UNDERSTANDING SEXUALITY

LOOK BEFORE YOU EAT (22m C 1978)
Surveys the role that advertising and food industry promotion play in what foods are available in recent years. The introduction of hundreds of new food items through promotion and advertisement has led to a shift away from basic foods. The effects of processing and its nutritive values are examined. Consumers are urged to examine food labels closely when shopping. People's eating habits affect their health greatly. p. George H. McQuilkin; CF; CWU, UIL, UMO, WSU.

LOOK OF AMERICA, 1750-1800 (26m C 1977) (also Video)
Shows the richness and diversity of our historical heritage. Wilderness settings unchanged in 200 years blend with live-action re-enactments of busy craftworkers and settlers to give us a sense of what life was like in early colonial times. Contrasts the austere Puritan settlements of New England with the plantation life of the Cardinas, etc. p. Ray Eames, Charles Eames; PF.

LOOK! WE HAVE COME THROUGH (11m B p1978, r1978)
Presents an expressionistic view of a dancer's art. There is no narration, just a musical accompaniment. Choreographed and performed by Stephanie Avon. p. R. Bruce Elder; PHOENIX.

LOOKING AHEAD (30m C 1981) Stress Management: A Positive Strategy Series
Designed to help managers with their personal strategic planning. It examines physical fitness and nutritional awareness as they dovetail with effective stress management. Viewers learn how to make time for fitness and why a sensible diet is "an investment in their physical capital." For those who want to change some aspect of their lives--and also avoid a sense of punishment for making that change-- this program provides guidelines for increasing the odds for success. How the skills of day-to-day stress management transfer to larger issues in life also is presented. Participants discover how controlling stress in their lives will result in an across-the-board improvement-- in their priorities, commitments and life satisfaction. Leader's manual and participants' handbooks included. p. Time-Life Video; TIMLIF.

LOOKING FOR MR. GOODBAR (136m C 1977)
A young woman breaks away from her restrictive family to search for her identity. She wanders into the world of dope, singles bars and discos, where she is forced to seriously examine choices concerning

her own mental and sexual development--choices today's woman must face. d. Richard Brooks; p. Freddie Fields; p. Paramount; FI.

LOOKING FOR ORGANIC AMERICA (28m C 1971)
A powerful contrast between the organic way of farming and agri-business. Without narration, the film allows audiences to tour the world's largest feedlot and egg ranch, and juxtaposes their "economies of scale" with organic family farms. Some of the latter turn out to be extensive operations, and the contrast is really not in size, but in approach. Where conventional agriculture is simplistic in its under-standing of the soil, insects, and weeds, organic farmers take the whole picture into account and attempt to come up with creative, non-destructive solutions to agricultural problems. The story is told in the words of those involved, including John Todd of the New Alchemy Institute, Frank Ford of Arrowhead Mills, Eddie Albert, Fred Rohe, Robert Rodale, and Gaylord Nelson who points out that "Revolutions have been fought for centuries over individual ownership of land, and now our country is going in the other direction." The film ends with the inspiring example of Virginia Benz, who reversed the farm-city trend by leaving a city factory to set up her own successful organic farm. p. Rodale Press/Amanda and Burton Fox, John Hoskyns-Abrahall, Winifred Scherrer; BULFRG.

LOOSE PAGES BOUND (1979)
Documentary on the Asian Americans living in the Delaware Valley, conveying their heritage, the struggle for identity and the racial and generational cultural alienation they experience. p. Christine Choy; TWN.

LORANG'S WAY (69m C 1979) (Turkana/Subtitled)
A multifaceted portrait of Lorang, the head of the homestead in East Africa. Because they are relatively isolated and self-sufficient, most Turkana (including Lorang's own son) see their way of life con-tinuing unchanged into the future. But Lorang thinks otherwise, for he has seen something of the outside world. A study of a man who has come to see his society as vulnerable and whose traditional role in it has been shaped by that realization. Explores Lorang's person-ality and ideas through his conversations with the filmmakers, the testimony of his friends and relatives, and observation of his behav-ior with his wives, children, and men of his own age and status. Awards. d. Judith MacDougall, David MacDougall; p. University of California, Berkeley; UCEMC.

LOST CONTROL (50m B 1980)
Men and women in a federal drug program speak with startling candor of the forces that drove them to drugs, how they supported their habit, and their feelings about how this program has helped or failed them. Shot on location at a state prison in Philadelphia and Philadelphia Community Mental Health Center. d./p. Edie Lynch; BLACKFL.

LOTTE EISNER IN GERMANY (34m C 1980) (in English)

When Werner Herzog heard that Lotte Eisner had suffered a heart attack in Paris in 1975, he went to her bedside. This is the interview portrait of Eisner. At various points in her long life, she has been participant, refugee, critic and savior to those whose muse is Film: she knew Brecht, Lang, and Pabst; she hid in the south of France during World War II with Henri Langlois' prints of THE GREAT DICTATOR and POTEMKIN; she championed the young filmmakers of the New German Cinema. Horowitz's portrait reveals the great and modest woman--and her relationship with Germany--in this fascinating series of conversations shot at her home in Paris and at the Cinémathéque Française. d. S. M. Horowitz; NYF.

LOUDER THAN OUR WORDS: WOMEN AND CIVIL DISOBEDIENCE
(36m B 1983) (Video, Beta, VHS)

Follows the experience of one women's affinity group, from their discussions through their arrests, at the June 14, 1983, action, United Nations Special Session on Disarmament. Examines the historical use of civil disobedience by women to gain political rights, from the suffragists through the anti-war and civil rights movements. Featured are interviews with experienced activists and footage from the 1982 Women's Pentagon Action. Many issues are critically addressed--political and personal conflicts surrounding civil disobedience; the relationship between feminism and nonviolent resistance; and the significance of women organizing for social change. d. Lydia Dean Pilcher, Harriet Hirshorn; WMM.

LOVE AND LEARN (10m C p1980, r1980) (Video)

Records a planned program of warm and satisfying visits between nursing home residents and preschool children. This unique program pairs an older adult with a child, fostering a growing relationship that enriches both. d. Daniel Wetherbee; p. Maria Oliva; p. Adelphi Productions, Inc.; ADELPHIP.

LOVE AND LONELINESS (59m C n.d.) (Video, Beta, VHS) Young and
Old: Reaching Out (Series)

The satisfaction of all kinds of love, and coping with the anguish of its absence, are the themes of this program. Love of work, the joys of friendship, the current emphasis on "self-fulfillment" and more are discussed. The guests include Pulitzer Prize-winning playwright Marc Connelly. p. Communications Resource Foundation, Inc.; PBSV.

LOVE CAREFULLY (17m C n.d.) (also Video)

Birth control information for women and men who are educated to the eighth-grade level or below, for foreign-born who have difficulties in English, and for slow learners. p. Perennial Education, Inc., PEREN.

LOVE IT LIKE A FOOL (28m C 1977)

At age 76 Malvina Reynolds performs, provokes, and proves that age has only increased her integrity, insight and humanism. She records an album, gives a concert, rehearses with young musicians, and manages her record and publishing companies with vigor and excitement. d. Susan Wengraf; p. S. Wengraf, Charles Rudnick, David Dobkin; p. Red Hen Films; REDHEN; UMN.

LOVE 'N' LACE (10m B 1978)
Chris is an accomplished dancer who practices Yoga and healing. Her husband, Steve, devotes his time to playing, composing and recording music. She is seven months pregnant and continues to enjoy a sensuous sex life with Steve. With voice overlay. p. Laird Sutton, National Sex Forum; MMRC.

LOVE TAPES (30m B 1980) (Video)
Against background music of their own choosing, people from all walks of life record their feelings about love. Among those you will meet are Darrell, a black student, afraid of love; Frieda, a disabled professor, who struggled for self-worth; Rose, in her eighties, recalling her changing needs; Jorge, speaking lyrically in Spanish of his mother; Darlene, unloved as a child, who finds that men treat her callously. The net result is both an increased self-awareness and a growing ability to empathize with the common humanity of "strangers." In this exploration of the basic need for love there is a wealth of material for discussions on aging, parenting, the handicapped, and cultural diversity. p. Wendy Clarke; FILMLB; PAS.

LOVING HANDS (23m C 1976) (English narration)
Touching is the primary language of the newborn. Frederick Leboyer shows how a mother can transmit love, energy and well-being to her infant through massage. Shantala, a young mother, seated outdoors with her baby, demonstrates the soothing, rhythmic movements of the traditional Indian art of infant massage. With hands working in harmony upon her child's body, she releases the tensions along his back, liberating his chest for breathing and gently but firmly animating the extremities. The baby responds to his mother's touch with quiet sounds of satisfaction. d. Frederick Leboyer; NYF.

LOVING PARENTS (24m C 1978)
This sex education film is designed for parents, but its style and content make it extremely appealing to young people as well. Brief "trigger" sequences are used to raise questions which concern parents: How should we project our own sexuality to our daughters and sons? What image would we like them to have? What kind of guidance should we provide for their sexual development? How should we talk with them about sex? What kind of information about sex do they need? Immediately after each trigger sequence there is a spontaneous discussion among a group of parents. This is followed by a short animated sequence which helps place the particular issue in perspective. d./p. Herman J. Engel; TEXFM; CWU, PAS, UM.

LUCK OF ROARING CAMP, THE (27m C 1982) (also Video) Short
   Story Library Series
   Presents a film version of the Bret Harte short story. Recom-
mended for creative writing students and cinema classes. d. Kevin
Hynes; p. Anne Kimmel; LCA.

LUCKILY I NEED LITTLE SLEEP (8m C 1974)
   Kathy worked as a nurse in Greece and then came to Canada.
She and her family live in northern Alberta where they are developing a farm. Kathy nurses, sews for children, maintains the house,
and helps with the farm work. d. Kathleen Shannon; p. Len Chatwin; NFBC.

LUCY COVINGTON: NATIVE AMERICAN INDIAN (16m C 1978)
   Tells the story of Lucy Covington, granddaughter of Colville Indian Chief Moses. Lucy spent most of her life tending herds on the
Colville reservation. Recently, however, she has taken a leadership
role as her people fight for their heritage and their land. As chair-
person of the Colville Tribal Council, she lobbied at home and in
Washington, D.C. against termination, a legal process by which the
United States government buys back reservation land from Indian
tribes. Following her victory in this legal battle, Lucy Covington
presides over the Tribal Council attempting to revitalize the Colville
Indians and preserve their culture. On behalf of the 6,000 who live
there, she vows to fight against giving up her people's land and heritage. p. Odyssey Productions, Inc.; EBEC; KENTSU, SCC, UCEMC,
UMN, WSU.

LUISA TORRES (WITHIN AMERICA) (43m C c1980, r1981) (Video)
   This well-crafted documentary follows one day in the farm life
of Luisa Torrês. Weaving carefully chosen scenes with a combination
of Spanish and English narration, the film watches this 79-year-old
woman take care with all that she does, from gathering medicinal herbs
to making goat's-milk cheese, from washing out a wool mattress to selecting the tree from which her casket will be made. Each of her actions has been honed by experience to be perfectly attuned to the
task at hand. Luisa and her husband, Eduardo, wear their ages
gracefully, not greedily. Luisa's homemade casket is already prepared with mementos from her past, and she waits with a love of the
land for her own return to the soil. The film would be most useful
in a bilingual class studying aspects of rural New Mexico. But it
would also be useful in Spanish classes, courses on the problems and
processes of the aging, and in any course seeking to show the beauty
of careful work. Levels: community college, lower- and upper-
division undergraduate. d. Michael Earney; p. Jack Parsons; CENTRE.

LUMIERE (95m C 1976) (French/Subtitled)
   Jeanne Moreau's directorial debut is a woman's frank, personal
vision of herself, other women, and their relationship to the world
at large. This is an intelligent celebration of the choices available

to women. Cast: Jeanne Moreau, Francine Racette, Lucia Bose, Caroline Cartier, Keith Carradine, Bruno Ganz. p. Claire Duvall; d. Jeanne Moreau; FI.

LUNA TUNE (2½m C 1979)
This sand animation celebrates women's spirituality with 80-year-old lesbian poet Elsa Gidlow reading her work, "What If ... the Million and First Meditation." Flute music by Kay Gardner accompanies the ocean's sounds, creating a gentle and sensual experience. Excerpted from Musereel #1. p. Carol Clement; WMM.

-M-

MACHETANZ: AN ARTIST'S JOURNEY (28m C p1981, r1982)
Traces painter Fred Machetanz's early years in Alaska, making use of archival film footage shot by Fred in the 1930's and 1940's of his adventures, the Alaskan wilderness and native people. Contemporary scenes show Fred at work in his Mantanuska Valley studio, explaining his techniques and the sources of inspiration for his paintings and lithographs. d./p. Kristine Samuelson; UALASKA.

MACHORKA-MUFF (18m B 1962) (German/Subtitled)
Based on a Boll story: concise satirical attack on the revival of militarism in West Germany. d. Jean-Marie Straub; NYF.

MADAME DERY (102m C 1976)
An intimate look at the fears and anxieties of a famous nineteenth-century actress as she approaches a crucial stage in her career. Based upon the life of Madame Rosa Dery, who was a very popular theater actress. A masterful performance by Mari Torocsik, a Hungarian actress. d. Gyula Maar; LIBERTY.

MADE FOR EACH OTHER see ANIMATED WOMEN

MADE IN THE BRONX--A WORKSHOP IN CREATIVITY (30m C p1979, r1980)
Documents a vital community-oriented arts program in the South Bronx. It focuses on an intensive workshop, designed to give adults with no background in art a direct understanding of the creative process. The purpose: to allow them to transmit the same experience to children. The film intimately explores this process in dance, music, poetry and the visual arts. d./p. Susan Fanshel; SULANI.

MADNESS AND MEDICINE (49m C r1977)
Investigates the use in mental institutions of three controversial types of therapy: drugs, electroshock, and psychosurgery. Probes the validity of these methods and questions whether they violate the rights of patients. Howard K. Smith, Commentator. p. ABC-TV; CRM; UIL.

MAGGIE (24m C p1981, r1982)
Dramatic portrayal of a young woman struggling to maintain her sanity. Charts the progression of Maggie's disillusionment to her final self-reliant realization: "Things are set in motion over which you have no control. Once you accept that you are lost, you are free to enjoy the ride." d. Barry Healey; p./s.w. Katherine Neilsen; ed. Haida Paul; original music: Michael C. Baker; CANFDC.

MAGIC FLUTE, THE (8m C p1977, r1978--U.S.)
An animated story with a special message. A young boy finds an abandoned flute whose music reflects the true nature of the flute player. d. Gayle Thomas; p. Derek Lamb; NFBC.

MAGIC OF DANCE, THE (SERIES) see SCENE CHANGES, THE; EBB AND FLOW, THE; WHAT IS NEW; ROMANTIC BALLET, THE; MAGNIFICENT BEGINNING, THE; OUT OF THE LIMELIGHT, HOME IN THE RAIN; REFLECTIONS

MAGIC WORLD OF WHISELPHASOON, THE (12m C 1975) (also Video)
Using cutout animation techniques, tells the story of Leander, a little boy whose fertile imagination could always be depended upon for stories, ideas, and solutions to problems. Through a series of adventures and misadventures, Leander falls into the clutches of a wicked king. Leander almost loses his imagination, but in the nick of time Leander awakens the king's dormant imagination and shows him how to use it for the good of his subjects. d. Lillian Somersaulter, J. P. Somersaulter; p. Pajon Arts; FI.

MAGNIFICENT BEGINNING, THE (52m C 1979) (also Video) The Magic of Dance (Series)
The first real ballet school was founded by King Louis XIV of France in 1669, and it is from Louis's great palace at Versailles that Margot Fonteyn introduces this program. At Drottningholm in Sweden, she visits the Court Theatre and sees ballet performed in the original settings and under the original conditions. Shows performances of parts of La Fille Mal Gardée (first performed in 1789 just two weeks before the outbreak of the French Revolution) and a much more recent ballet--Roland Petit's Carmen (1948). Features Roland Petit, Zizi Jeanmarie, David Wall, Wendy Ellis, Ronald Emblem, the Royal Ballet, the Royal Swedish Ballet and the Dance Academy of Peking. p. BBC/TIMLIF; TIMLIF; UMN.

MAHALIA JACKSON (34m C r1974)
A portrait of the late Mahalia Jackson, queen of the gospels, who spread the religious music of Afro-Americans from congregations in small churches to vast audiences throughout the world in concert halls and stadiums, and on radio, television and records, until her death in 1972. Emphasizes the joys and triumphs of Jackson's life as she communicated them in her songs, with noted author and broadcaster Studs Terkel providing the commentary. Includes footage of Mahalia

Jackson's funeral in Chicago in 1972 attended by more than 40,000
persons; her birthplace in New Orleans; and eleven songs sung by
Jackson (taken from old performances). p./d./s.w. Jules Victor
Schwerin; PHOENIX, UFL.

MAHANAGAR (122m B 1964) (Bengali/Subtitled)
    A dramatic crisis occurs when a young couple in Calcutta agree
that the wife should take a job. The traditions of family structure
are upset. Despite scandalized grandparents, an uneasy husband,
and her own terror, Arati starts working and meets Edith, an Anglo-
Indian woman who befriends her. A humanistic comedy that takes a
sympathetic but satirical look at the older generation and the new
Indian woman. d./s.w. Satyajit Ray; FI.

MAHATMA GANDHI: SILENT REVOLUTION (38m C 1970)
    Documents the record of Gandhi's plan for basic education. Shows
this plan operating at a basic school in South India, in the areas of
agriculture, education through handicrafts, and industrial training.
d. Mary Kirby, Robert Steels; p. Pilgrim Films Production; IFB.

MAI ZETTERLING'S STOCKHOLM (50m C r1978--U.S.) (also Video)
    Mai Zetterling presents a film of Stockholm that is a provocative
testament to the spirit of that city. Filmed in the winter, Mai Zetterling portrays Queen Christina, and Swedish novelist and playwright
August Strindberg as she strolls through the city. As Strindberg,
with wig and mustache, she quotes at some length from Strindberg's
writings in an imaginary interview that covers his many fears: the
devil, the war, and caustic remarks about women. As Queen Christina, Zetterling wears a wig of long curls, a feathered hat, and a
black cape; is accompanied by attendants; and speaks on a number
of subjects--notably marriage, which the queen saw as the desperate
action of a coward. Viewers may feel in the end that this is more of
a film about Zetterling and Strindberg than about Stockholm. p.
Nielsen-Fern Ltd./John McGreevy Productions; LCA; UCEMC, USC.

MAILBOX, THE (24m C 1977) (also Video)
    Older persons know loneliness when families fail to communicate
meaningfully with them. This film tells the story of an elderly woman
who hopes each day to receive a letter from her children bringing her
some warmth and happiness. p. Brigham Young University; BYU;
KENTSU.

MAINSTREAM (24m C 1976) (Video, Beta, VHS) The Real People
        (Series)
    The story of a young Coeur d'Alene Indian woman's rediscovery
of her ties to family, land and tribe is told. It is a story common
to many young Indians in today's mainstream who are seeking and
finding new pride in their own tribal values and identities. As the
young woman recalls her father, her childhood and her tribe's history, she becomes aware that the reservation she grew up on and

her past remain a source of energy and inspiration in her life. Filmed on the Coeur d'Alene Reservation in Idaho and in the city of Spokane, Washington. d. Larry Littlebird, George Burdeau; p. KSPS-TV, Spokane; PBSV.

MAINSTREAMING IN ACTION (27m C 1979)
Due to new civil rights legislation, handicapped youngsters all over America may now be a part of regular classes. Designed to make teachers aware of both the risks and heart-warming success involved in "mainstreaming"; also, to increase awareness among teachers and administrators of the variety of disabilities that children who enter their classrooms may have. p. Ellen Barnes, Grania Gurievitch; d. G. Gurievitch; EBEC.

MAINSTREAMING TECHNIQUES: LIFE SCIENCE AND ART (18m C p1979, r1979)
Illustrates the involvement activities, the interactions, and responses of handicapped children in a mainstreamed life science and art program. Features are classroom experiments with live organisms and art which provide science education for both ordinary and handicapped students. d./p. Dr. Doris E. Hadary; CBM.

MAKAH SONGS BY HELEN PETERSON (15m C 1981)
A brief introduction and performance of three songs of the Makah Indians of the Pacific Northwest with background discussion. p. Chvany Films; WSU.

MAKE-BELIEVE MARRIAGE (50m C 1979--unabridged; 33m C 1979-- abridged) Learning to Be Human Series
Can you practice marriage? Mr. Webster's high school marriage class did practice marriage. They were paired off, took vows, drew up a budget, had a make-believe baby, learned to deal with unemployment and car accidents. Eventually, they decide whether to continue their marriage or get a divorce. They learned that being married requires patience, communication, and above all--a sense of humor. p. Evelyn Barron; d. Robert Fuest; LCA; KENTSU, PAS, UCEMC, UIL, WSU.

MAKE IT HAPPEN (22m C 1982)
Women are rejecting traditional reward patterns connected with being female. Reaching for alternatives, risking, trying to achieve in nontraditional areas for women, initiating career moves, discovering training avenues. Carpenters, engineers and stockbrokers--they are making it happen for themselves. d. Donna Preece; p. Carol Horne; s.w. Fiona McHugh; ed. Daniel Dutka; music: Nancy White; Sponsor: Toronto Board of Education; MOBIUS.

MAKE ME PSYCHIC (8m C 1979)
The trio of Quasi, Anita and Rollo return in this highly stylized, Art Deco-looking sequel to QUASI. Full of intrigue and irreverence. p. Sally Cruikshank; SERBC.

MAKING DANCES (90m C p1980, r1980)
Explores the post-modern dance scene through the work of seven New York-based choreographers: Trisha Brown, Lucinda Childs, David Gordon, Douglas Dunn, Kenneth King, Meredith Monk and Sara Rudner. Because it was filmed at rehearsals, performances and during interviews, the film is a unique primary source that reflects the rich diversity of contemporary dance. d./p. Michael Blackwood; BLACKW.

MAKING DECISIONS ABOUT SEX (25m C 1981)
A Planned Parenthood representative and a group of teenagers discuss the difficulties and decisions facing young people concerning sex, and their own feelings and views about their developing sexuality and sexual expression. The teenagers represented in the film differ widely in their viewpoints, but they frankly relate their own decisions and thinking on this very important and controversial subject. d. Barbara Noble; CF.

MAKING IT HAPPEN (17m C n.d.)
Portrays the lives of three female athletes. Examines past and present cultural attitudes surrounding women's participation in competitive sports. Music by Cris Williamson. p. Women's Educational Equity Act; EDC.

MAKING OF A CHAMPION (12m C 1977)
Encourages young children to practice good eating habits, physical exercise and work at positive self-identity. p. Walter Klein; d./s.w. Laura Andrus; SUNRIEM.

MAKING OF CANADIAN WHISKEY, THE (16½m C p1982, r1983)
A four-part description of the making of Canadian Whiskey--I: Grain and Malt; II: Yeast and Fermentation; III: Distilling; IV: Maturing and Blending. Designed for educational use, with animated sequences illustrating the action of the malt enzyme and the yeast during the fermentation process. Provides an inside look at the whiskey-distillation process, treating the scientific aspects and also the craftsmanship that is part of distilling tradition. d./s.w. Tina Horne; p. Werner Volkmer; SEAGRAM.

MAKING OF THE FROG KING, THE (11m C p1981, r1982)
A documentary about filmmaking and film acting, narrated by Tom Davenport and Ann Clark, the 14-year-old actress of THE FROG KING. An entertaining supplement to THE FROG KING that tells how this fairy tale was brought to life with real people and live frogs. p. Mimi Davenport, Tom Davenport; DAVNPT.

MAKING POINTS (11m C p1980, r1981)
In this short film, the differences in expected behavior between men and women are subtly and wittily expressed by reversing them. A female television correspondent interviews a group of adolescent

boys about their future plans. The answers given are from the female point of view. One boy's answer is: "I'd like a really good job--legal secretary--make it to the top. The pervasive effects of sex-role stereotyping are vividly emphasized in the topsy-turvy world of MAKING POINTS. ex. p. Ellen Hovde/Muffie Meyer; p./d. Charlotte Zwerin; p. Middlemarch Film Production; DIRECT: UMN.

MAKING TELEVISION DANCE (60m C/B p1976, r1977) (also Video)
    Dance in America TV Series
    Presents Twyla Tharp and her dance company. Fuses visual art with the mastery of dance. Choreographer: Twyla Tharp. p. WNET-TV; PHOENIX; UCLA.

MALADY OF HEALTH CARE, THE (57m C 1980) Nova Series
    Most people aren't concerned with health care until they get sick. This program examines how two societies--Great Britain and the United States--have organized health care delivery for their inhabitants. A comparable community in each country is studied and compared. In Britain, the National Health Service is paid for through taxes and covers an individual's needs from cradle to grave. In the United States, similar care can cost a patient hundreds of thousands of dollars. Health care administrators in both countries are paying greater attention to preventive techniques and public education. NOVA raises the question, Should limited funds be devoted to ever more sophisticated technology, or to public health programs? p. WGBH-TV; TIMLIF.

MALE AND FEMALE SEXUAL ANATOMY (22 color slides n.d.)
    Depicts male and female anatomy. Included are fetal development of the male and female sex organs, adolescent development of secondary sexual characteristics, the external and internal sex organs, the four phases of the sexual response cycle (external and internal) and the three phases of the menstrual cycle. Produced by the author of The Sex Atlas, Erwin J. Haeberle; MMRC.

MALE-FEMALE RELATIONS (50m C 1980) (Video)
    The content includes relationship problems caused by sex role socialization and myths of romantic love, how the differences manifest in sexual difficulties and solutions achieved through effective communication. Goals of egalitarian relationships are explored.
    Interviewed are Dr. Jessie Bernard, sociologist and author; Dr. Rosalie Chapman, clinical psychologist; Dr. Nancy Chodorow, sociologist-author; Ilene Dillon, counselor; Dr. Warren Farrell, author and leader of men's liberation; Dr. Herb Goldberg, psychologist-author; Thea Lowry, counselor; Dr. Tom Lowry, psychiatrist; Jo Ann Nicola, child development professor; Shirley Radl, author of books on motherhood; Isolina Ricci, counselor-author; Dr. Lillian Rubin, sociologist-author; Dr. June Singer, Jungian analyst-author; Dr. Arlene Skolnick, psychologist-author. p. Women's Studies Program, California State University, Chico; Coordinator: Dr. Gayle Kimball; CSUCHI; UMN.

MALE PERSPECTIVES ON WOMEN'S CHANGING ROLES (30m C 1974)
(Video) Career Development of Women Series
This program attempts to create an awareness of the effects of
women's changing career patterns on significant others in their lives;
for example, on husbands, children, friends, family and life-styles.
It presents some male viewpoints about the impact of female career
goals and decisions on their own roles and goals. The implication is
that counselors have to consider the total life space of a person and
the interrelationships of career decisions. p. University of Minnesota; UMN.

MALNUTRITION IN A THIRD WORLD COMMUNITY (26m C 1979)
To document malnutrition in the Third World countries, the film
surveys the conditions of the poor in the Philippines. With an inadequate supply of food, improper sanitation and scarce water, impoverished people all over the world, like those seen in this film will continue to suffer from malnutrition. p. Helen A. Guthrie, George M.
Guthrie; PSUPCR; PAS.

MAN, A (21m B 1976)
Members of a workshop for men share their personal experiences.
Focuses on the difficulties men have in expressing personal loss and
grief, particularly in regard to the death of a loved one. p. About
Men Workshop; POLYMR; PAS, MN.

MAN AND WOMAN: MYTHS AND STEREOTYPES (36m C 1975) (slc)
Examines the ways that men and women throughout history have
regarded themselves and each other. Explores various methods of
breaking down these stereotypes and dealing with people as individuals. Commentary includes excerpts of literature and music. (160
slides in carousel tray with audiocassette tapes). p. Center for Humanities, Inc.; CEFH; UMN.

MAN WHO LOVED WOMEN, THE (119m C 1977) (French/Subtitled)
Bertrand Morane is a bachelor obsessed with women. In an effort
to understand his obsession, Bertrand writes his memoirs and remembers all the women he has loved. This film is François Truffaut's
love letter to womankind. d./s.w. François Truffaut; p. Les Films
du Carrosse/Les Productions Artistes Associés; ALMI.

MANAGE YOUR STRESS (60m C 1980) (Video)
Covers characteristic stress tolerance levels in various personality types and stress responses. Describes effects of diet, nutrition, physical exercise and such abuses as tranquilizers, smoking
and alcohol on stress levels. Other topics include self-monitoring
techniques, stress inoculation, behavior styles and occupational stress.
Strategies offered for managing stress are stress support systems,
self-regulation contracts and tension relaxation exercises. Workbooks
available from CRM/McGraw-Hill Films. CRM; UMN.

MANAGEMENT OF RECURRENT BREAST CARCINOMA (27m C 1979)
Physician Update Series
Carl Strodes, M.D., assistant clinical professor of medicine at the
University of Pittsburgh School of Medicine, reviews the latest infor-
mation on the diagnosis and treatment of breast carcinoma. p. Penn-
sylvania State Television; PAS.

MANAGEMENT OF SEXUALLY ASSAULTED WOMEN (29m C 1975)
(Video) College of Medicine Presents (Series)
Rape crisis center services, rape victims and the courts, obtaining
patient consent and examining the patient, laboratory tests and rec-
ords needed for court cases, statistics on rape. Features Dr. David
R. Halbert, assistant professor of obstetrics and gynecology, College
of Medicine, The Pennsylvania State University. p. Pennsylvania
State Television; PAS.

MANAGEMENT TRAINING SERIES see CAREER DEVELOPMENT: A
PLAN FOR ALL SEASONS

MANAGING STRESS (35m C p1978, r1979) Organizational Development
Film Series
Designed to help the viewer recognize common sources of stress,
assess her or his own capacity to tolerate stress and become more
aware of alternative means for coping with stress. Includes a Stress
Reduction seminar which delineates the main issues in stress research.
d./p. Stephen Judson; CRM; CWU, IU, KENTSU, PAS, UCEMC, UCLA,
SILU, UMO, UM, UMN, USC, UIL, WSU.

MANAGING YOURSELF (30m C 1981) Stress Management: A Positive
Strategy Series
No one would dispute the fact that it's better to face a pressure
situation with your nervous system more or less under control. In
the program, viewers study how to manage their thoughts feelings and
reactions to stress by using relaxation skills and behavioral techniques.
To reduce anxiety, participants learn to structure their mental train
of thought, or "self-talk," with positive connotations. They discover
what the common elements of frustration are--and how a verbal anti-
dote to frustration works. On-camera consultants describe ways to
foresee stress, suggesting methods to change behavior when coping
with stressful situations. Also presented are the merits of deep relaxation as a combatant against stress, as well as ways to monitor individual progress toward relaxation. Leader's manual and participants' handbooks included. TIMLIF.

MANIFESTATIONS OF SHIVA (61m C p1980, r1980)
Shows the worship of the Hindu god Shiva on a personal level
through dance, art, music and ritual. Without narration, its aim is
to convey a feeling for the events represented through experience
rather than didactic exposition. d. Malcom Leigh; p. Muriel Peters;
ASIAS.

MAN'S PLACE, A (24m C 1979)
Documents the lives of men who live and/or work in a setting that requires them to expand their conception of the traditional male role. Focuses primarily on five men: a homemaker, a nurse, a father raising an infant, a man sharing household responsibilities with a working wife, and a man in equal partnership with a woman. These sequences are alternated with person-on-the-street interviews which address the issues raised by the life-styles of the five men featured. p. Case Institute for Research and Development in Occupational Education, City University of New York; KENTSU.

MAN'S RELIGIOUS QUEST SERIES see THREE FAMILIES: JERUSALEM

MANUEL JIMENEZ--WOOD CARVER (22m C n.d.) Mexico's Folk Artists Series
Shows how a rural Mexican folk artist represents the sights and scenes of his daily life. Jimenez carves with an infallible eye, striking swiftly at the rough, green branches with an ordinary farmer's machete; finishing the work with a common kitchen knife; and completing the piece in a wild whimsy of character and color. Available in English and Spanish. p. Judith Bronowski; WORKS.

MANY HEAR, SOME LISTEN (12m C 1975)
"People differ in the ways they possess information received.... Some of these ways are more effective than others." Uses a series of vignettes to describe various listening styles in different situations. Three types of characters are introduced to depict individuals having difficulty in accurate listening; a non-attender, an assumer, and a word picker. Portrays sequentially what these styles sound like within a classroom, a business office, and a marriage counselor's office. CENTEF; UIL.

MANY WORLDS OF INDIA: GESTURES AND GODS: THE STORY OF INDIAN DANCE, THE (29m B 1967)
Four classical Indian dances demonstrate the characteristics of dance form: Bharata Natyam, Kathak, Kathakali, Manipuri. Chants in Sanskrit and music recorded in India accompany the dancers. Dancer: Betty Jones; d. Priscilla Travis; p. Alfred Slote; p. UMMRC; UM.

MARAGOLI (58m C 1977)
Insightful document on the social and economic problems of village life in Third World countries; using the Maragoli region of western Kenya--one of the world's most populated rural areas--as a case study. In discussion with a sympathetic African interviewer, the men and women of Maragoli tell their side of the story. A perceptive portrayal of interlocking problems of high fertility rates, food shortages, land scarcity, lack of education and employment, and migration --the elements that must be considered when devising or evaluating any rural development program. d./p. Sandra Nichols; UCEMC.

MARATHON WOMAN, MIKI GORMAN (28m C p1980, r1981)
Profiles extraordinary Miki Gorman, who set the women's world marathon record at the age of 38 and went on to become the only woman to win the Boston and New York marathons twice. The film not only explores the making of a world class athlete--following her from training through competing in the New York marathon--but reveals the determination to achieve, which has shaped Miki's life. d./p. Ellen Freyer; p. Freyer Productions; FILMLB.

MARCELO RAMOS--THE FIREWORK MAKER'S ART (23m C p1980, r1980) Mexico's Folk Art Series
Shows how an extraordinary Mexican Folk Artist, in fleeting images of fire, executes his work. Intricate procedures all done by hand result in highly complex structures that are also heart-stopping works of art. In the context of a traditional fiesta in rural Mexico, the film documents cultural traditions and unchanging human concerns. d./p. Judith Bronowski; WORKS.

MARGARET MEAD (30m B 1964)
Noted anthropologist discusses her "modified optimism" for the survival of the human species even with its potential for complete self-annihilation. p. University of Southern California; MODNLA; PAS, KENTSU.

MARGARET MEAD: PORTRAIT OF A FRIEND (27m C p1978, r1978)
Using a handheld camera, Jean Rouch creates a close up, intimate approach supplemented by his own friendly, almost bantering relationship with "Margaret," with whom he reflects aloud on subjects of mutual interest and of whom he frequently asks spontaneous, casual questions, as well as well-considered ones about anthropology. Filmed in her office and the various halls in the American Museum of Natural History, Mead is revealed as a loving, open person behind the legend. d. Jean Rouch, John Marshall; p. Emilie de Brigard; AMUSNH.

MARGARET MEAD: TAKING NOTE (59m C 1980) The Odyssey Series
This filmed portrait of Margaret Mead, probably one of American anthropology's most popular and public figure, interweaves her personal history and intellectual contributions, based on interviews held shortly before her death, on old family and field photographs, and on conversations with a variety of her friends, family and former students. Born in 1901 in Philadelphia, Mead was first drawn to anthropology as a student at Barnard, where she was influenced by Franz Boas and Ruth Benedict. Her field trips took her to eight different societies, from Bali to New Guinea. p. Ann Peck; DER.

MARGINAL PEOPLE (28m C 1978)
Shows dire living conditions of the people of Bangladesh; how they exist as a severely overcrowded population with insufficient food production, no technology above a subsistence level, no natural resources, and no investment capital. Describes a small foreign aid

project aimed at birth control and outlines the role of women. Narrated by Cliff Robertson. p. United Nations; WSU.

MARGOT FONTEYN (53m C 1978)
    Presents a combined documentary performance biography of the
ballerina Margot Fonteyn. Shows her at work, exercise, rehearsal,
and at rest and play at her home in Panama. Fonteyn began her
serious training at 15 in London, studying with a legendary Russian
teacher whose influence lasted throughout her long and brilliant career.
Also shows her performing the "Gayaneh" with Viktor Rona, Swan
Lake with David Wall, and the Rose Adagio from Sleeping Beauty.
d./s.w. Keith Money; p. Degamo Production, London; UIL.

MARGOT FONTEYN DANCES (10m B 1947)
    An excerpt from the feature film LITTLE BALLERINA. Margot
Fonteyn, with Michael Somes and the Corps de Ballet, dances the
first movement of Les Sylphides. The performance is intercut with
backstage scenes. Dance Company: Royal Ballet; Choreographer:
Michel Fokine; THUDRBD.

MARIA (46½m B p1976, r1980)
    In the form of a drama, fictitiously but authentically, this program outlines the typical problems of organizing a labor union in the
garment industry, which in most respects are similar to problems in
organizing any union. d. Allan King; p. Stephen Patrick; CBC.

MARIA AND JULIAN'S BLACK POTTERY (11m C 1938/1977) (si)
    Documentary on the famous Pueblo potter Maria Martinez and her
husband, Julian, at San Ildefonso Pueblo, New Mexico. Complete
process of making the black pottery from beginning coils through
the final firing and polishing. Produced by Arthur Baggs, Jr.; PAS.

MARIA CALLAS IN CONCERT (60m B n.d.) (Video)
    This is the only visual recording of Callas in concert. One of
the most colorful and exciting opera singers of our time is seen in
this rare 1959 appearance. She sings from Spontini's The Vestal,
Verdi's Macbeth and Don Carlos, Rossini's The Barber of Seville, and
Bellini's The Pirate. Captures the 36-year-old Callas in peak form.
p. TeleCulture Inc.; TELCULT.

MARIA MONTESSORI: FOLLOW THE CHILD (48m C 1978)
    A view of Dr. Maria Montessori's struggle to become a physician
and, as such, her observations of early childhood development that
were to make her famous as an educator. First person accounts by
those who worked with her together with scenes from contemporary
Montessori classrooms. Features Jane Alexander as the voice of Dr.
Montessori. d. Joseph De Francesco; p. Douglas Clark; CLARKD.

MARIAN ANDERSON (20m B n.d.)
    A documentary study of Marian Anderson. Anderson began her

career singing in her church choir. Includes some of her career's
highlights. Shows her singing "Ave Maria," "He's Got the Whole
World in His Hands," and "Crucifixion." p. World Artists, Inc.,
BUDGET.

MARIANNE AND JULIANE (106m C 1981) (German/Subtitled)
This is a story of two sisters; it also is a story of the political
turmoil of Germany in the 1970's. Growing up in the "leaden times"
of the 1950's, the two sisters turn to radicalism, Juliane working
within the system as the editor of a left-wing feminist journal, Marianne becoming a notorious terrorist, the character based on an actual
member of the Baader-Meinhof group. It is Juliane's resistance to,
compassion for, and eventual obsession with her doomed sister that
forms the center of the film. d. Margarethe von Trotta; NYF.

MARIE CURIE (1867-1934): A LOVE STORY (32m C 1978) The Prize-
    winners (Series)
Story of Marie Sklodowska and Dr. Pierre Curie, two dedicated
scientists, who met, fell in love and married. Their life together is,
to them, a blissful combination of love and hard work. The couple's
incredible dedication to scientific research culminates in the discovery
of the new elements Polonium (named after Marie Curie's homeland,
Poland), and Radium. They were awarded the Nobel Prize for physics in 1903. Shortly after returning from the award ceremony, Pierre
was killed in a tragic street accident. Marie conquers her consuming
grief and continues her work. In 1911, the Swedish Academy of Science, in an unprecedented move, awards Marie Curie a Nobel Prize
in chemistry. She thus became the only person ever to win two Nobel Prizes. p./d. Richard Marquand, p. Chatsworth Film Production,
England; CENTEF, KAROL; KENTSU, PSU, UIL, UMN, UMO; WSU.

MARINOS, THE (DIVORCING PARENTS) see FAMILY PORTRAIT:
    THE MARINOS

MARK TWAIN: BENEATH THE LAUGHTER (58m C 1979) (also Video)
Authentic dialogue and dramatized incidents from Mark Twain's
fiction and life highlight this examination of the writer's darker side.
Dan O'Herlihy stars in a richly crafted and carefully researched look
at the pessimism underlying Twain's celebrated humor. p. Marsha
Jeffer, Larry Yust; d. Larry Yust; s.w. Gill Dennis, Larry Yust;
PF.

MARK TWAIN'S HARTFORD HOME (23m C p1974, r1977) American Life-
    styles--Cultural Leaders Series
A biographical outline of Mark Twain's life. E. G. Marshall narrates the tour through Twain's Victorian home in Hartford, Connecticut. d./p. Ann Zane Shanks, p. Comco Productions; PARACO.

MARK TWAIN'S HUCKLEBERRY FINN (29m C 1976)
Presents Twain scholar Gordon Pinsent as he gives a convincing

delineation of Twain's character and defends the novel <u>Huckleberry</u> <u>Finn</u> and his choice of style and use of the vernacular. d. Susan Murgatroyd; p. Philip Nixon for the Ontario Educational Communications Authority, Canada; s.w. Jed Mackay; FI.

MARKET PLACE IN MEXICO (13m C 1975)
Shows how people are dependent on one another's skills to meet their basic needs. Features a serape maker, a potter, and a rope maker in a small Mexican village. Tells something of an ancient Aztec marketplace and points out that although many things have changed in the 500 years since the days of the Aztecs, people's dependence for their basic needs on each other's skills has not. p. Judith Anne Perez, Severo Perez; FILMFR.

MARRIAGE see WOMEN AND THE LAW, THE (SERIES)

MARRIAGE: IS IT A HEALTH HAZARD? (30m C 1979)
Examines one of New Zealand's most disturbing health statistics: married women make up the largest percentage of first admissions to psychiatric hospitals suffering depression. They are the group consuming the greatest quantity of tranquilizers and sleeping pills. These women suffering depression initially cannot understand what went wrong. Gradually, says an experienced woman psychologist, the married woman comes to feel that she's being devoured by all those dependent people, very often, and very sadly. New Zealand women describe their stages of the journey from isolation, to the general practitioner, to the psychiatrist, and finally, to the psychiatric institution. Two professionals in the mental health field question the use of drugs and shock treatment to "cure" what may be a healthy protest and not an illness. d./p. Deirdre McCartin; LUCERNE.

MARRIAGE UNDER STRESS (48m B 1969)
Examines the causes of divorce, the pressures that force a couple to consider a future apart from each other. This study shows that it is not always "the other woman" or "the other man." Interviews with several couples reveal that often the first real stress of marriage comes with the arrival of children. Other difficulties cited include jealousy, money, and division of work at home. Also discusses what happens when a marriage is finally over. p. BBC/TIMLIF; TIMLIF; UIL.

MARRIED LIFE (52m C 1970) The Family of Man (Series)
Compares five different marriages in five different societies to point out that marriage takes many forms and is, in many respects, dependent upon where one lives. Shows a wife and three husbands in the Himalayas, a couple in an affluent English community, a man with three wives in New Guinea, a man with two wives in Botswana, and a young couple in Lancashire, England. Interviews the married couples and discusses the roles assigned to men and women in each society. p. BBC, TIMLIF; CWU, IU, KENTSU.

MARRIED LIVES TODAY (20m C 1975)
Explains that various styles of marriage are possible today, points out some of the advantages and disadvantages of each, and distinguishes between some of the fantasies and realities of married life. Juxtaposes a young couple who operate a business together and see themselves as completely equal; another couple who are more traditional in outlook; and a third couple who, although separated, continue to share the parenting responsibilities of their daughter. As different as they are, all three couples continue to function creatively in their married lives. p. CBS-TV; PHOENIX; KENTSU, UIL.

MARTHA (111m C 1973)
MARTHA tells the story of a woman's subjugation by the men in her life. In a glittering succession of visual images, director Fassbinder injects his customary irony by depicting Martha as a willing slave. In the eyes of a society structured on male authority, Martha embodies the perfect daughter and wife. Through the radical example of a woman, crippled physically and emotionally, Fassbinder seems to be challenging all women to assume responsibility for and control over their own fate. d. Rainer Werner Fassbinder; p. Tele-Culture, Inc.; TELCULT.

MARTHA CLARKE: LIGHT AND DARK (54m C p1980, r1980) (also Video)
Portrays an artist's imaginative sources and the process through which she creates an original evening of threatrical dance. The film departs from traditional dance films by looking behind finished performance to its creative source and development. We follow Martha Clarke, a former member of Pilobolus Dance Theatre, and her collaborators over a one-year period during the development of four new dance pieces. d. Joyce Chopra, Martha Clarke; p. Joyce Chopra; PHOENIX; UMN.

MARTHA GRAHAM DANCE COMPANY (90m C 1976, r1977) Dance in America Series
Beautifully filmed tribute to and portrait of Martha Graham, one of the most important and influential dancers and choreographers of the twentieth century. In interviews, she relates her dance philosophy and discusses the development of her intensely dramatic style. Her company is shown performing six of her creations: Diversion of Angels, Lamentation, Frontier Adorations, Cave of the Heart, Appalachian Spring. p. WNET-TV; IU, PAS, UCEMC, UIL.

MARVA (17m C 1979)
Marva Collins, veteran public school teacher, became disillusioned with the school system, its rules, unions and failures. She resigned from her school and, using her retirement funds, started her own school. Located in a black, low-income area of Chicago, her back-to-basics teaching method is being praised by teachers, administrators, and parents all over the country. p. CBS-TV, "60 Minutes"; d. Suzanne St. Pierre; CAROUF; UMN, UCLA, CWU, IU, PAS, USFL.

MARY CASSATT: IMPRESSIONIST FROM AMERICA (30m C r1977)
The Originals: Women in Art Series
Intertwines Mary Cassatt's personal story--her years in Paris,
her relationship with Degas, the influence of her family--with views
of her paintings, drawings, and aquatints to demonstrate the quality,
variety, and originality of her art. d. Perry Miller Adato, p. WNET-
TV; FI; UMN, UMO, PAS, UM.

MARY JANE GROWS UP: MARIJUANA IN THE 70s (52m C 1976)
(also Video)
The control of marijuana has become the subject of national controversy. The trend is toward decriminalization, but many argue for
complete legalization, while others for stricter enforcement of present
laws. It is clear that marijuana use is a part of contemporary life
and must be dealt with for the benefit of society. p. NBC-TV; FI.

MARY KATE'S WAR (25m C 1975) The American Revolution (Series)
Mary Katherine Goddard is postmistress of Baltimore and publisher
of the newspaper The Maryland Journal. This presentation dramatizes
the events which occur in February of 1777 after she publishes a letter suggesting that the colonies surrender by accepting a British
peace proposal. While intended as a satire, some factions construe
this as serious, and demand the identity of the author from Mary
Katherine. In her refusal to reveal the author, she demonstrates
great courage in upholding one of the basic freedoms which helped
guide the American Revolution. p. WQED-TV; NGS; KENTSU.

MARY WIGMAN: FOUR SOLOS (11m B si 1929)
Mary Wigman performs "Seraphic Song," "Pastoral," and "Dance
of Summer" from the "Shifting Landscape" cycle. Excerpts from her
famous "Witch Dance" are included. These dances are seen as choreographed and performed in the late 1920's. With Danish introduction
and titles, no narration. Musical background. MMA; DAN/UR; UIL.

MASAI WOMEN (51m C 1979) Disappearing World Series
The Masai are animal herders in the East African Rift Valley.
This film is about the women of the tribe--from childhood through
marriage to old age. The women are totally dependent on the Masai
men and, here, they talk about their feelings, marriage, love and
children, and the structure of society that is as far from female emancipation as any in the world. d./p. Chris Curling for Granada TV,
England; Institute for the Study of Human Issues; ISHI.

MASCULINE, FEMININE AND ANDROGYNY (29m C 1976) (Video, Beta,
VHS) Woman Series
Psychologist Joan Bean, co-author of Beyond Sex-Role Stereotypes: Readings Toward a Psychology of Androgyny, discusses the
meaning of an androgynous personality and its significance to the
women's movement. She explains the benefits of broadening characteristics previously defined as masculine or feminine in view of the

changing roles of men and women. Sandra Elkin is the moderator.
p. WNET-TV; PBSV.

MASK (30m C 1980-1983) (Video, Beta, VHS) Concepts Series
MASK charts the subconscious journey of a black woman unravel-
ing history and discovering her true source of strength. The mask
of her painted face returns hauntingly through the narrative and
hints at her buried rage. Theatrical performance is combined with
dance in a uniquely expressive form. s.w. Bonnie Greer, performed
by Pat Patton, with music by Craig Gordon. d./p. Doris Chase;
CHASED; CHASED.

MASTERS OF THE PERFORMING ARTS: MAUREEN FORRESTER (30m
C 1981)
A rare voyage behind the curtain to see one of Canada's great
musical stars enthrall a student group as she teaches, discusses her
art, and performs. d. T. Robinow/ N. Campbell; p. T. Robinow;
INTELFE.

MASTRI--A BALINESE WOMAN (78m C 1975) The Asian Neighbors--
Indonesia Series
Explores the lives of a Balinese couple in their village. Contrasts
their day-to-day activities and religious beliefs with the Bali known
to tourists. p. Film Australia; AVIS; UMO.

MASTURBATORY STORY, A (15m C 1978)
Designed to educate and enlighten any adult who is in regular
contact with a developing child. Excellent discussion starter. It
would also be a good program to introduce into a senior citizen's
club, as many are baby-sitting grandparents. p. Chris Morse, Judy
Doonan; PEREN; UM.

MATCHLESS (54m B 1974)
This fictional narrative is built around an unlikely threesome:
an alcoholic, a suicidal schizophrenic and an epileptic. They live
together harmoniously until the outside world interferes. d. John
Papadopoulos; s.w. Sally Blake; MMA.

MATH: A MOVING EXPERIENCE (30m C 1981)
Kindergarten children exploring mathematics concepts including
numbers, counting, curves, shapes, and vocabulary through a series
of classroom experiences integrating mathematics, movement and imagination. In the humanistic environment which develops, children and
teacher feel free to work, cooperate, laugh, touch, and dance together. d. Richard Gaughan; p. Teresa B. Benzwie; NYU.

MATH-SCIENCE CONNECTION: EDUCATING YOUNG WOMEN FOR
TODAY, THE (17m C n.d.)
Four examples of model programs that stimulate and support the
efforts of women at different age levels to pursue scientific and technical areas of study. p. Abromowitsch Films; ABROMWF.

MATHEMATICS FOR PRIMARY: ADDITION (9m C 1978) Mathematics
for Primary Series
Illustrates, in animation, the basic math concepts of addition.
p. Anna Keating, Lawrence Levy; PARACO, AIMS.

MATHEMATICS FOR PRIMARY: DIVISION (8m C 1978) Mathematics
for Primary Series
Illustrates, in animation, the basic math concepts of division. p.
Anna Keating, Lawrence Levy; PARACO; AIMS.

MATHEMATICS FOR PRIMARY: MULTIPLICATION (7m C 1978) Mathematics for Primary Series
Illustrates, in animation, the basic math concepts of multiplication.
p. Anna Keating, Lawrence Levy; PARACO; AIMS.

MATHEMATICS FOR PRIMARY: SUBTRACTION (8m C 1978) Mathematics for Primary Series
Illustrates, in animation, the basic math concepts of subtraction.
p. Anna Keating, Lawrence Levy; PARACO; AIMS.

MATHEMATICS FOR PRIMARY SERIES see MATHEMATICS FOR
PRIMARY: ADDITION; MATHEMATICS FOR PRIMARY: DIVISION;
MATHEMATICS FOR PRIMARY: MULTIPLICATION; MATHEMATICS
FOR PRIMARY: SUBTRACTION

MATRIOSKA (5m C 1970)
A dance of Russian dolls, as lively in its way as any performance
of the Moiseyev Company. These are painted dolls, hollow inside and
of graded sizes so the largest holds all the rest. They twirl, swing
and sway to gay Russian tunes but never lose their fixed reserve.
When the dance ends they hop up in turn into the mother figure and
hurry off the scene. d. Co Hoedeman; p. Dorothy Courtois, Joseph
Koenig; NFBC; CRM.

MAUD LEWIS: A WORLD WITHOUT SHADOWS (10m C r1978)
Maud Lewis of Yarmouth County, Nova Scotia, didn't own a paint-
brush until she was thirty, never saw a work of art or took a painting lesson. Crippled with arthritis, she rarely strayed far from
home. Maud lived with her husband in a small house covered with
her paintings of birds, butterflies and flowers. "A World Without
Shadows" is the world that Maud Lewis saw around her and transferred onto canvas. Maud's world is filled with freshness and joy
of discovery, and a hint of remembrances of things past. d. Diane
Beaudry-Cowling; p. Kathleen Shannon; NFBC; PHOENIX; UIL.

MAX (20m C p1974, r1979) (also Video)
The scene opens at a Broadway theatre. Shows Max, the door-
man, reading Variety while on a bare stage a director works with an
actress. The rehearsal is not going well. In frustration, the director dismisses everyone for the night. As Max is cleaning up, he

discovers Lynn, rehearsing the same scene the director was having
trouble with. He reveals to Lynn that he had once been a juggler
and dancer in vaudeville for 52 years and had worked with great
stars including Al Jolson, George Burns and Judy Garland, and perhaps he could help her. His performance is so compelling that Lynn
concedes that maybe he can help her. An extraordinary performance
by Comedian Jack Gilford. Recommended for all theatre arts and
cinema students. p. Joseph Gilford, Jennifer Lax, Joel Silver; d.
J. Gilford; CAROUF.

MAXINE (13m B 1975)
    A documentary portrait of a woman who is dying, isolated in her
rural home with her husband and two sons--an eloquent celebration
of a woman who, although her body fails her, remains strong. p.
Sarah Snider; IRIS; PAS.

MAYA FAMILY TODAY (23m C 1973)
    Chronicles the life of one Mayan family in Chiapas, a village in
southern Mexico, where the Indians live much as their ancestors did.
p. Elda Hartley; PARACO, HARTLEY.

ME, A TEEN FATHER (13m C 1980)
    Explores the pressures, the moments of nostalgic tenderness,
the guilt, ambivalence, anguish and anger of a teenage boy who has
just learned that his girlfriend is pregnant. Randy's mind roams
back to his past romantic relationship with Carol, struggles with the
choices that they both must make in the present, and casts forward
to try to glimpse the shape of their future with--or without--the baby.
p. Gordon-Kerckhoff Productions, Inc.; CENTEF; PSU, KENTSU, IU.

ME AND STELLA: A FILM ABOUT ELIZABETH COTTON (24m C 1977)
    Presents Elizabeth Cotton, who sets an example of courage and
determination and proves that neither age nor race need be impedi-
ments in the world of folk music. Elizabeth, an elderly black woman,
spent most of her life as an amateur guitarist, singer and songwriter,
only to gain recognition in her later years. Cotton, now in her
eighties, recalls her girlhood working as a domestic to earn enough
money to buy her guitar, which she named Stella. In 1943, she and
her husband moved to Washington, D.C., where she cleaned government buildings and later went to work for Charles and Ruth Seeger.
The Seegers discovered her abilities and encouraged her to play in
clubs and festivals. One of her songs, "Freight Train," written when
she was 12, became a major hit of the 1960's folk movement. Unfortunately, her copyright claim was never recognized, and she received
no royalty from it. Accompanying herself on the guitar, she sings
the song. p./d. Geri Ashur; PHOENIX; UIL.

MEADOW, THE (8½m C p1974, r1980)
    Introduces children to the insects commonly found in the summer
in a country meadow or city park. Intended to help increase their

awareness of the enormous variety and beauty to be found in a simple natural setting. p. Catherine Mercier, Clayton Rawson; p. Geode Film Production; TEXFM.

MEANINGFUL COMMUNICATION WITH OLDER ADULTS (43m C 1982)
(Video)
Basic elements of communication and its breakdown are discussed during the introduction of this taped seminar for nurses, social workers and general staff of any nursing facility. "For sending messages to anyone, we need to remove roadblocks, be brief and make ourselves understood." The second rule is to listen. Put the person you're talking to at ease. Avoid distracting behavior. Listen to understand and not just to reply. Specific problems in communicating with older adults are discussed. Lecturer: Marty Richards, M.S.W., A.C.S.W., Director of Social Services, Foss Nursing Home, Seattle. Presented by the Institute of Aging, University of Washington; UW.

MECHANICAL KNEE, THE (22m C 1971)
A medical biography of a young office secretary who is threatened by a giant cell tumor of the leg. Faced with three alternatives (amputation, fusion of the knee joint, or an experimental prosthesis), she chooses the mechanical knee. Shows the various stages of this surgical procedure. This surgery along with physiotherapy enabled her to return to work and a reasonably normal life. d. Claudia Overing; p. Jean Roy, Tom Daly; NFBC.

MEDICAL RESIDENCY: YEARS OF CHANGE (30m C 1982) (Video)
Examines the final stage of physician training in light of the impact of recent technological and social change. Two young doctors, a man and a woman, are the focus upon which this videotape examination of medical residency is based. In interviews throughout the tape, young doctors talk about their residency and their lives devoted to that work isolated from the world outside medicine. They realize that they are not infallible, question their judgment, and admit that the pressures often cause them to lose their ideals. Very useful introduction to medicine for laypersons and for those contemplating a career in medicine. p. David Shapiro/Selma Thomas; p. Watertown Productions Inc. and KWSU-TV, Washington State University; KWSUTV.

MEDICINE AND MONEY (ed.) (48m C 1977)
Examines abuses in government-funded medical programs and discusses the issue of accountability for both money spent and quality of medicine received. Frank Reynolds hosts this study with a look at a New York Medicaid Clinic and California's Medical program. In closing, Reynolds calls for stricter government control and scrutiny of the cost and quality of tax-supported medical care. p. ABC-TV; CRM.

MEDICINE FLOWER AND LONEWOLF see AMERICAN INDIAN ARTISTS: MEDICINE FLOWER AND LONEWOLF

MEDICINE IN AMERICA, PTS. I, II, III (3 hrs. C 1978) (Video)
A comprehensive examination of the quality and economics of
health care. Part I includes a brief history of medical science and
modern trends in health care; a sampling of medical schools and
training of physicians; discussion of surgical procedures and controversial techniques. Part II discusses malpractice as it affects doctors
and patients; details the cost of hospital care--who pays and why it
is so expensive. Part III examines proposals of health insurance
programs; discusses health maintenance organizations and preventive
medicine; looks at the future of medical research and treatment. d.
Joel Banow, Darold Murray; FI.

MEDITATION CRYSTALLIZED: LAMA GOVINDA ON TIBETAN ART
(14m C 1973)
Mandalas, paintings, and sculpture of Tibet are combined with
the music and chants of lamas to create an experiential understanding
of an art which is the crystallization of centuries of meditation. Lama
Govinda, a leading interpreter of Tibetan Buddhism, explains the
paintings as guides to the deeper strata of the human psyche. p.
Elda Hartley; HARTLEY.

MEDITATION IN MOTION (11m C p1978, r1979)
Introduces the ancient Oriental discipline of Tai Chi. Over 4,000
years ago in China, Emperor Yu ordered that exercises in the form
of a dance be performed that would build body fitness and health.
By the fifteenth century those dances had evolved into Tai Chi
Ch'uan, slow movements that bring the body and mind into harmony.
Shows Tai Chi being practiced in both China and the West. d./ed./
s.w. Irene Angelico; NFBC.

MEDITATION: THE INWARD JOURNEY (20m C 1977)
From the opening sequence--an arresting call to prayer from a
Moslem minaret--to its closing footage showing a young man meditating
as he walks through the woods, the atmosphere is conducive to meditation. The film explores some of the techniques developed through
the ages for this journey inward ... the importance of posture, the
use of mantra, the imageless silence of the Buddhists, the Sufi's use
of dance and a meditation, the Christian's use of the Jesus prayer.
An excellent introduction to the essence of meditation. p. Elda Hartley; HARTLEY.

MEDIUM IS THE MASSEUSE: A BALINESE MASSAGE, THE (35m C
1982)
Unlike many spirit mediums, Jero Tapakan of Bali practices as a
masseuse once every three days, when possession is not auspicious.
Shows Jero treating Ida Bagus, a member of the nobility, for sterility
and seizures. Jero begins work this day with religious preparations
and the assembling of traditional medicines. Treatment includes a
thorough massage, administration of eye drops, an infusion, and special paste for the chest. The dialogue, which is subtitled, includes

a detailed discussion between anthropologist Linda Connor, Ida Bagus, and Jero, about the nature of the treatment of her illness, as well as informal banter between Jero, her other patients, and people in her houseyard. A broad view of Jero's practice is given in the film's conclusion, which shows excerpts from the treatments of other patients. p. Linda Connor, Timothy Asch; DER.

MEET ME IN ST. LOUIS (2m B 1962)
A sequence done for a 1962 television special. p. Ray and Charles Eames; PF.

MEET THE PRESIDENT (25m C p1978, r1979)
Acquaints students selecting a college with an overview of Cornell and the aim and purpose of the university as seen through its President, Frank Rhodes. p./d. Laurel Fox Vlock; p. Eden Film Group for Cornell University; CORNELL.

MEETING IN PROGRESS (43m C 1969) (also Video)
Looks at the role of the conference leader as he or she faces 12 critical points that can arise in any meeting and deals with the six basic "task" functions. p. Roundtable Films, Inc.; RTBL.

MELI (21m C 1983)
A story of an artist's struggle to balance her personal life and her career. Meli Davis Kaye, a dancer/mime in her sixties, made choices 30 years ago that led her in directions other than fame and fortune. Today she is director of an innovative dance/mime workshop, directs professional dancers and mimes, performs in her solo retrospective, spends time with her family and discusses her art and her views. p. Fran Burst-Terranella, Cheryl Gosa; IDEAIM.

MELINA MERCOURI'S ATHENS (25m C p1978, r1980) (also Video)
Presents Greek actress Melina Mercouri's view of Athens. Actress-politician Melina Mercouri expresses her deep love for Greece and the Greek people as the camera accompanies her around Athens. Exiled for her open defiance of the fascist military junta in Greece until 1974, she became a deputy of the Greek parliament in 1977. She says that 51 percent of her vote came from women. She enjoys fighting for her people and against all kinds of tyranny in the country she loves. An emotional, highly personal view of Athens as Melina Mercouri knows it. p. John McGreevy Productions/Nielsen-Ferns International; d. John McGreevy; LCA, UCEMC.

MELODY see OLD FRIENDS ... NEW FRIENDS ... MELODY

MEMAW (28m B 1981)
Filmed on the last day Memaw spent on her farm; Memaw is an 88-year-old woman with Alzheimer's disease. The day marks a passage in the lives of Memaw, her daughter, and granddaughter as well as the 200-year-old farm. At the heart of the film is a dilemma faced

by many people with aging parents. d./p. David Carnochan; CARNCHAN.

MEMENTO MORI (3m B 1982)
An image of a 1,500-year-old Indian burial is used as springboard for examining the ethics of ownership and of responsibility for cultural artifacts. The issues of who owns images, who owns art, and who owns bones--the fragments of life itself--are addressed within the context of the impermanence of all things. d./p. Karen Nulf/ Joseph Marshall; s.w. Joseph Marshall; ed. Karen Nulf; NULFMAR.

MEMORIES FROM EDEN (57m C p1977, r1978) Nova Series
Once primarily exhibition areas, zoos are now regarded as principal conservators of programs on genetics and pathology with creative new animal habitats to ensure successful captive breeding and the reintroduction of animals to their natural environments. p. Barbara Holececk/WGBH-TV; TIMLIF.

MEN WHO ARE WORKING WITH WOMEN IN MANAGEMENT (29m C 1979)
Are You Listening Series
Shows a group of male executives at AT&T exploring the changes in their personal and corporate awareness brought about by their women colleagues. They discuss the differences in attitude reflected by language, the value of activism on the part of women and the advantages of intelligence and competitive instincts, and the awkwardness of changes in their own life-styles at home and at work required by women's new status. There is information about how these men have coped with training, advancing, advising and criticizing women. p. Martha Stuart; STUARTM.

MENOPAUSE (23½m C 1983)
Explains in detail the menopausal experience of an individual woman. A realistic seminar featuring eight other women discussing their menopause interspersed with the main story line. Cause of hot flashes is explained. Mild estrogen therapy is discussed. MIFE.

MENOPAUSE: A TIME OF TRANSITION (20m C n.d.) (slc)
Menopause has long been a mystery, and myths are widespread about loss of womanhood connected with menopause causing many women to suffer needlessly. This slide set provides information that can help to eliminate fears and worry through thorough, concrete and objective information about menopause. p. Sheryl Brown, Planned Parenthood of Alameda/San Francisco; MMRC.

MENOPAUSE: MYTHS AND REALITIES (22m C p1980, r1980) (also Video)
Throughout history, a woman's usefulness was measured by her childbearing years, but now it is recognized as the opportunity for women to bring a new way of living. The cessation of menstruation for at least one year signals the onset of menopause. It is a normal

process of life, but it may, through the imbalance of hormones, cause hot flashes, night sweats and weight gains. Good nutrition, avoiding sugar and salt, and getting enough exercise, are ways to minimize the discomfort. Hormonal replacement therapy that helps replace estrogen and progesterone is discussed. Attitude is noted as the real key to accepting the changes that are occurring during menopause. Six women experiencing menopause are seen interviewed revealing how they have managed to come to grips with this normal occurrence which signals a new period in their lives. p. Zelda Burnford, Paul Burnford; d. Brian Gaffikin; PEREN.

MENSTRUATION AND SEXUAL DEVELOPMENT (28m C 1978) The Inner Woman (Series)
An informative and reassuring film for young women concerned about changes occurring in their bodies. The development of internal reproductive organs, from birth through first menstruation and ovulation, is illustrated. Marilyn Poland, R.N., moderator. CRM; WSU.

MENTAL HEALTH CARE: ONE PATIENT'S VIEW (29m C 1976) (Video) Woman Series
Janet Gorkin shares insight from her ten years as a patient in the mental health care system which included drug treatments, electro-shock therapy and periodic confinement. She feels the need for greater respect for the patient and discusses her desire to lessen what she feels is the coercive nature of the system. She urges formation of patients' rights groups for those involved in counseling and treatment. Narrator Sandra Elkin. p. WNED-TV, Buffalo; PBSV.

MENTAL PATIENTS' ASSOCIATION (29m C n.d.)
One of eight Canadians will at some time in their lives be admitted to a mental institution. This film shows how ex-mental patients and their friends formed the Vancouver Mental Patients' Association, a unique, democratically organized self-help group to assist people during the critical post-release period. Members' comments afford some insight into what has been called the "mental health industry." d. Richard Patton; p. Shelah Reljic, Peter Jones, John Taylor; NFBC.

MERCE BY MERCE BY PAIK (30m C 1977) (Video)
The first part shows BLUE STUDIO: FIVE SEGMENTS by Charles Atlas and Merce Cunningham. With Chromakey and mirrors, Cunningham's movements are transposed against various realities. The second part shows MERCE AND MARCEL by Nam June Piak and Shigeko Kubota using material from BLUE STUDIO: FIVE SEGMENTS as well as from other sources, including Russell Connor's 1964 interview with Marcel Duchamp. d. Charles Atlas, Nam June Paik, Shigeko Kubota; p. Electronic Arts Intermix, Inc.; ELARTI.

MERCE CUNNINGHAM (13m B 1973)
Cunningham and his company perform. He "moves like no other

dancer ... during the last decade, his choreography has been the most influential (and controversial) development in the world of modern dance."--Calvin Tomkins, The New Yorker. d./p. Patrice Wyerse/ Merce Cunningham; MACMFL.

MESTIZO MAGIC (27m C p1980, r1980)
A young Hispanic schoolboy meets a magical flute lady, who takes him on a fantastic journey through Chicano art. Featuring eleven artists in various mediums; special effects include a simple explanation of the Aztec calendar. d. Juan Salazar, Daniel Salazar; p. Susan Salazar; CHISPA.

META MAYAN II (20m C p1981, r1982) (Video)
An impressionist documentary that dispenses with conventional methods of narration and interview techniques to create a portrait of Guatemala through images of the people, the landscape and the implications of social and political upheaval suggested by the different levels of the society. d. Edin Velez; p. Ethel Velez/Edin Velez in association with WNET-TV; MMA.

METADATA (10m C 1971)
Presents a story of a man and woman, love and joys and pains of the modern world using computer animation. Emphasizes an awareness of life and the fast proliferating complexity of the technical world. Employs provocative jazz and electronic music as "narration." NFBC; FI; IU.

METAMORPHOSIS (10m C 1977)
A presentation of an aesthetic and scientific film on the transformation of a caterpillar. No narration. p. Catherine Mercier, Timothy Wallace; TEXFM.

METAMORPHOSIS OF MR. SAMSA, THE (10m C p1977, r1979)
An animated film adaptation of Franz Kafka's classic short story "Metamorphosis." d./p. Caroline Leaf; p. NFBC; TEXFM.

METHADONE ALTERNATIVE, THE (18m C 1974)
Candid discussion by methadone clinic patients and open observation of their activities reveal the hopelessness that heroin addiction brings and the optimism that methadone offers. Although methadone is a drug, its substitution for heroine makes it possible for the symptoms and struggles of addiction to be overcome and gives the addict a new chance to live a productive life. p. Leonard Wood III; p. Oxford Films; UIL.

METHADONE CONNECTION, THE (27m C 1973)
Centered around the methadone maintenance program operated by Beth Israel Medical Center in New York City, the film explains how methadone works and tells what prospects it holds for rehabilitation of heroin addicts. Several addicts are followed from preliminary interviews and screenings through admission and extensive

medical and psychiatric treatment, to their release as out-patients, cured of their addiction and able to function normally so long as they continue their daily methadone dosage. Also presents varying views on methadone maintenance held by some authorities on heroin addiction and addict treatment programs. Narrated by Herbert Kaplow. p. ABC-TV; KAROL; UIL.

MEXICAN DANCES: PTS. I and II (18m ea. C 1972)
Traditional Mexican dances, from the early Aztec period to dances of today, performed by school children who are colorfully and authentically costumed. English narration. Dance Company: Ballet Folklorica Estudiantil, Lincoln High School, Los Angeles, CA.; Dance Director: Anita Cano; AIMS.

MEXICO'S FOLK ARTISTS SERIES see MANUEL JIMENEZ--WOOD CARVER; MARCELO RAMOS--THE FIREWORK MAKER'S ART; PEDRO LINARES--ARTESANO CARTONERO; SABINA SANCHEZ-- THE ART OF EMBROIDERY

MICHAEL HALL: SCULPTOR (10m C p1980, r1980)
Large sheets of steel and I-beams, welded and braced and bolted, take on images, provoke questions and become more understandable as Michael Hall speaks of his kind of constructivism, derived from his American and Midwestern roots. Trestles, billboards, fences, objects in the landscape, become sculptural ideas and pieces as images explore Hall's interpretation of urban/rural environments. p. Sue Marx/Robert Handley; p. Marx/Handley Productions; LREDF.

MIDDLE AGES: A WANDERER'S GUIDE TO LIFE AND LETTERS, THE (27m C 1971)
It is the year 1350. In church, where illiterate masses learn from morality plays, part of "Everyman" is presented; the game of love, from contrasting views is played in quotations from Dante's "Love Sonnets"; and the role of women is seen in earthy prologue to the "Wife of Bath" from Chaucer's Canterbury Tales. p. Helen Jean Rogers, John Secondari; LCA.

MIDDLE MONTHS OF PREGNANCY, THE (29m B 1956) Months Before Birth--A Series
Discusses birthmarks and deformities, morning sickness, changes in clothing, and relaxation and rest. Discusses ways of relieving constipation, shortness of breath and dizziness. p. WQED-TV; AF.

MIDDLE OF THE WORLD, THE (115m C 1974) (French/Subtitled)
Describes a love affair between Paul, a Swiss engineer running for political office, and Adriana, an Italian immigrant working as a waitress. The filmmaker takes the materials of a classic "femme fatale" tragedy and refashions them into a subtly observed but invigorating tale of the growth of a woman's consciousness. Set in "a period of normalization" and punctuated with landscapes of startingly original

beauty. This cool, highly erotic, teasingly ambiguous film is one of the few convincing, truly modern treatises on the nature of love-- but a love not divorced from the contexts of society and politics. "... The movie takes a profound, though subtle stand against treating women as objects: it really is a feminist statement." --Nora Sayre, The New York Times. d. Alain Tanner; NYF.

MIDWIFE (26m C p1979, r1979)

Focuses on two young women who are making careers as midwives in the San Francisco area. They are licensed by the state, backed by local pediatricians and obstetricians, and allowed hospital privileges at some Bay area hospitals. Both women are university graduates with majors in midwifery and have worked as registered nurses in obstetrics at hospitals before becoming a team as midwives. All their clients are pre-screened to determine whether the expectant mother is emotionally and physically suited for home birth. The women counsel the prospective parents on diet, exercise, birth control and perform examinations to determine the position of the baby, take blood pressure and coach the husband and wife on how to breath and work together to make the delivery as comfortable as possible. Both midwives enjoy working in the home atmosphere. Two births are graphically filmed from the onset of labor to the delivery of the baby. p./d. Michael Anderson; ANDRSM.

MIDWIFE: WITH WOMAN (28m C 1982) (also Video)

Traces the uneasy history of midwifery and illustrates how, with the modern concept of the nurse-midwife, the profession has regained a small but tenacious foothold in American maternity care. Interviews with families, nurses, and physicians reveal the safe care provided by nurse/midwives, usually in hospitals backed by physicians. Several birthing centers are shown and discussed, and an obstetrician speaks of the need for midwives. Also see DAUGHTERS OF TIME. Recommended for planned parenthood courses and nurses training classes as well as hospital staffs. Narrated by Mariette Hartley; d. Mary Paul Wells; p. Cooperative Birth Center Network and Maternity Center Association; FANLTP.

MILES TO GO (80m C 1982)

Eight women with no previous wilderness experience undertake a two-week adventure in the Smoky Mountains of North Carolina. Through a series of outdoor challenges that include backpacking, orienteering, rock climbing and rappeling, and whitewater rafting, explores how people grow--or don't grow--through the way they respond to challenge and adversity. d. Deborah Boldt/Sarah Stein; p. Hilary Maddux/Deborah Boldt; MADBOLT.

MILES TO GO BEFORE I SLEEP (78m C 1974)

Problems of the aged and the adolescent are highlighted in this drama about two people who, through each other, discover something worth living for. Martin Balsam portrays 70-year-old Ben, a man

surrounded by memories of yesterday and little interest in tomorrow.
His granddaughter Maggie, who works at Dartmouth Place, a treatment center for delinquent girls, tries to wake him up by arranging
a foster grandparent experiment between him and a 15-year-old car
thief named Robin, played by Mackenzie Phillips. She hates old people and he hates teenagers, but each finds a grudging respect and
affection creeping into the days they spend together, walking around
Boston and touring in his vintage Oldsmobile. Robin and Ben end
up as each other's best friend and their future, once uncertain and
bleak, now looks much brighter. Also stars Kitty Winn and Elizabeth
Wilson. p. Tomorrow Entertainment, Inc.; LCA; UIL, UM.

MILES TO GO BEFORE WE SLEEP (58m C 1979)
A documentary about the physical, emotional and financial consequences of mandatory retirement. Actress Helen Hayes, host and
narrator, guides viewers through the debate surrounding the forced
retirement issue. Visits to Bankers Life and Casualty Company in
Chicago and Mature Temps, which show hundreds of examples of
employees over 65 who are productive, integral participants in their
company's operations. Also profiles a number of exceptional older
workers, including a 105-year-old George Zerkas who holds a full-
time job in a grocery store. p. WTTW-TV, Chicago; PBSV; KENTSU,
UM.

MILLIONS OF US (17m B 1935)
An early American-made labor drama with sound. The story concerns a discouraged, unemployed worker who finds no solace in the
empty platitudes of traditional charity and official government rhe-
toric. He crosses a picket line to get work as a scab, but the union
leader (a George Raft type) offers him a meal and some solid advice
about unions, about "millions of us getting together, that's the answer"--Film Forum, October 26, 1978. p. Tina Taylor, Slavko Vor-
kapich; MOTPIC.

MILLSTONE SEWING CENTER, THE (13m C r1972)
Tells how this rural community in Letcher County, Kentucky,
organized the Millstone Sewing Center under the effective and successful leadership of Mabel Kiser. The center employs women as
seamstresses, gives away clothes to needy families, operates a lunch
program and serves as an information and referral center. The program is designed to teach as well as feed. Mabel's resourcefulness
is always strained by lack of funds. For a period, the Office of
Economic Opportunity (OEO) provided some funds, but even this is
now being cut off; however, Mabel believes the Lord will help them
again. A very positive film for use in community organizing as well
as for use in schools for better understanding the elderly and their
plight. p./d. Mimi Pickering; APPAL.

MIND, BODY AND SPIRIT (28m C 1979)
Illustrates the various medical techniques used for the rural

Chinese. Mao Tse-Tung campaigned vigorously for better health care for his people. The "barefoot doctors" program began in the 1960's with six months to two years of training for selected rural people from each commune. The camera follows the work of one barefoot doctor in Chienchou People's Commune as she diagnoses and treats simple illnesses and injuries, gives injections, works to improve health conditions and carries out government propaganda campaigns. p. Film Australia; p. Suzanne Baker; d./s.w. Bob Kingsbury; LCA.

MIND MACHINES, THE (57m C p1978, r1978) Nova Series
Explores artificial intelligence, a branch of computer science which may yield computerized machines that are smarter and more efficient than people. Scientists are at work on programs that can communicate with human beings in every day language as well as programs that machines can "learn." p. Paula Aspell, p. WGBH-TV, BBC; TIMLIF.

MINDSCAPE (LE PAYSAGISTE) (26m C 1977)
Dory Previn, lyric writer and composer, writes subjectively after years of writing for films in a mostly objective way. Her themes are personal, humanistic and often bittersweet. A poet and playwright, Previn writes finely chiseled lyrics, full of perceptive irony and haunting melancholy. d. Don Thompson; NFBC; UMN, IU, KENTSU.

MING-OI, THE MAGICIAN (25m C 1979) (also Video)
Sixteen-year-old Ming-Oi has studied 2½ years with a master magician, Mr. Wong, one of the only two magicians in Hong Kong still perfecting the "old ways." Shows her efforts at becoming a master magician as she prepares to substitute at a supper club. She admits to some stage fright. She easily establishes rapport with her audience. p. Sunrise Films, Ltd., in association with CBC; d. Deepa Salzman, Paul Salzman; CORONET.

MINI-MARATHON (25m C p1977, r1978)
Explains why some women have started to run as a form of exercise. It shares their motivations and experiences in training for the Mini-Marathon, a ten-kilometer race (6.2 miles) in New York's Central Park. In the race there were 2,500 participants and 2,500 individual goals. d./p. Yvonne Hannemann; WOMBAT.

MINNESOTANOS MEXICANOS (61m C 1978)
Shows Minnesota Mexicans working to close the gaps existing in areas of education, economic power and political voice. To put the present in perspective, the film includes a concise history of their ancestors, beginning with the pre-Columbian civilization in Mexico. The Spanish Speaking Cultural Club of St. Paul spent more than two years making this film a reality, working with all the elements in the community, as well as sending their filmmakers to film throughout the state, and in Mexico, Texas, New Mexico and Arizona. In Spanish and English. Funded by Northwest Area Foundation, Jerome

Foundation, and St. Paul Foundation. d./p. Kathleen Laughlin, Don Morstad; SPANSCC; UMN.

MINOR ALTERCATION, A (30m C 1976, r1977)
    Designed to open a dialogue on the race issue, this film is already being used to promote greater understanding and ease race tensions in communities throughout the country. The film attempts to get to the roots of the crisis by viewing it from both white and black perspectives. Dramatizes a real-life incident involving a fight between two high school girls--one white, one black--in a dispute over placement in a special source that will admit only one of them. It then traces in parallel fashion the response of the two families to the incident, revealing the real feelings underlying racial tensions as well as the existence of common interests. Although addressing a volatile issue, it avoids antagonizing any audience since it recognizes the complexities of the issues involved. Highly recommended for use by any group interested in developing an understanding of racial tensions and conflicts. p. Jackie Shearer, Terry Signaigo, Mary Tiseo; d. Jackie Shearer; p. The Black Filmmaker Foundation; UINFILM; PAS.

MIRACLE OF LIFE, THE (12m C 1977)
    Examines the early stages in the development of an embryo using special microphotographic techniques. Adapted from the documentary THE BEGINNING OF LIFE. p. Cine-Science Company, Japan, in association with Pyramid Films; PF; UIL, PAS, UMN.

MIRROR, MIRROR ON THE WALL (28m C 1979) Begin with Goodbye
    Series
    Examines the seldom-discussed topic of physical loss and bodily changes, which involve not merely our vanity, but our very identity. Interviewed are Quinby Schulman, who recently underwent a radical mastectomy, and Island Matthews, who experienced a heart attack. With guide. MMM.

MIRROR PHASE (46m C 1978)
    Records the filmmaker's daughter's first encounter with her own image in the mirror. Her use of split-screen techniques allows several views of her experience simultaneously as it raises questions about identity and developing self-awareness. d. Carola Klein; p. British Film Institute; MMA.

MIRRORS--REFLECTIONS OF A CULTURE (16m C p1979, r1980)
    (also Video)
    Three Chicano artists, Manuel Martinez, Carlota Espinoza, and Carlos Sandoval, are shown creating murals on buildings in Denver, Colorado, that tell what Chicano people once were, are now, and will be. As work on the mural progresses, the artists talk about their own experiences. The colorful, bold designs are said to tell a story of their own and to put pride in people's hearts about their own heritage. p. Millie Paul; CF.

MISA COLOMBIANA (20m B 1977)
The developed countries of the West strive to cut back on their economic and resource waste at the same time as many emerging countries try to gain the "better" living conditions and increased supply of consumer goods they envy. Here we see a shanty town in Colombia, which seeks to find a better way of life for its 370 families. Living next to the town dump, they spend much time reclaiming materials from it in order to supply both food and hardware in the struggle to improve their life-style. p. Anne Fischel, Glenn McNatt; d. Anne Fischel, DER.

MISCHIEF (8m C r1974)
A felt-cut tale for very young children. The protagonist of this film is a naughty boy punished for his mischief by animals in the yard. The malicious boy played dirty tricks on the animals. For example, he spread glue on the fence to catch the doves on it. Finally, he had to pay for his malicious pleasure from this "amusement." d./s.w. Hermina Tyrlova; p. Short Film Prague; PHOENIX.

MISS JULIE (37m B 1964)
An excerpt from SWEDEN: FIRE AND ICE. Birgit Cullberg's 1950 ballet interpretation of the Strindberg play Miss Julie is performed by members of the Royal Swedish Ballet. Choreographer: Birgit Cullberg; p. Dance Film Archive, University of Rochester; DAN/UR.

MISS LARSEN: REBEL AT 90 (17m C 1976)
This story of an indomitable ninety-year-old woman dramatically traces her path of revolt, her struggle for self-determination, through hospital and nursing home situations with their imposed tranquilizers, restraints, and other indignities to which old people are subjected "to keep them from hurting themselves." Extracted from NOBODY EVER DIED OF OLD AGE. p. Herbert Danska; UM.

MISS UNIVERSE 1965 (14m C 1965)
The international beauties grace the screen against the backdrop of Miami and Miami Beach. A brief look at the colorful events leading up to the selection of Miss Universe 1965, plus behind-the-scenes activities as the world lovelies demonstrate the friendliness and international understanding that this annual summer event promotes. p. Florida Development Committee; UFL.

MISSING PERSONS (26m B p1979, r1981)
A documentary on the question of disappeared political prisoners of Chile, the implications for the international human rights debate and the current United States policies toward Chile. A firsthand account of repression in Chile today related by three Chilean women, wives and mothers of missing prisoners. The film presents an insight into the personal drama of the disappearance. Spanish version, Spanish dialogue and English voice-over. A co-production of Chile Demo-

cratica, Donna Bertaccini; p. Pennee Bender, Donna Bertaccini, Monika Villaseca, Jaime Barrios; WMM.

MISSOURI: PORTRAIT OF THE PEOPLE (27m C r1976)
Depicts the history of Missouri through the enduring works of its major painters, sculptors, architects, composers, musicians, and writers. Focusing on the history of Missouri, this film illustrates the suggestion that "the greatness of a people is revealed in their art." Shows the Osage Indians, painter George Caleb Bingham, architect Lewis Sullivan, artist Thomas Hart Benton, poet Eugene Field, as well as architectural styles which includes French, Italian, Romanesque, Byzantine and Gothic. p. Mary A. Nelson, John Altman; p. Pentacle Films under the auspices of Missouri Arts Council; CF.

MR. FROG WENT A-COURTING (5m C 1976)
A delightful rejuvenation of an old classic children's story interpreted in animation. Lyrics sung by Derek Lamb to lute accompaniment. d./animator Evelyn Lambart; NFBC; FI.

MR. GIMME (28m C p1979, r1979) Learning to Be Human Series
A story of a youngster who has his heart set on buying drums, but has no money to do so. Tony gets involved in get-rich quick scheme that backfires and nearly lands his father in the midst of a lawsuit. Tony's father dips into his own hard-earned savings and rescues his son, but is repaid twofold when Tony learned his lesson and takes on the responsibilities of a "real" job. p. Dolores Danska; d. Peter Schifter; s.w. Carolyn King; LCA; KENTSU.

MR. PREBLE GETS RID OF HIS WIFE (17m C p1980, r1981)
Based on James Thurber's short story with the same title. In typical Thurber style, satiric exaggeration is used to create a metaphor for domestic politics. A good discussion film in areas of literature, film adaptation, humor, human relations, marriage counseling, sociology, psychology, and women's studies. A teaching package is available for use with film production, directing, writing and editing students. It includes the script, storyboards and camera plots, script notes, and approximately 3,000 feet of selected sync dailies with music and sound effects. d. Ellen Hovde/Muffie Meyer; p. Tom Simon; p. Middlemarch Films; DIRECT.

MISTER ROGERS TALKS WITH PARENTS ABOUT DIVORCE (59m C 1981) (Video)
Fred Rogers and Dr. Earl Grollman host a studio conversation to help families cope with the problems of divorce. d. Hugh Martin; p. Sam Newbury for Family Communications, Inc. Sponsored by Sears, Roebuck Foundation and Public Television Stations; p. Family Communications, Inc.; FAMCOM.

MR. SPEAKER: A PORTRAIT OF TIP O'NEILL (58m C p1978, r1978)
Profile of the man who wields awesome clout as the second most

powerful person in the nation. The cinema-verité excursion behind
Washington's closed doors captures facets of the O'Neill character
that are rarely seen. d. Nancy Porter; p. Nancy Porter for WGBH-
TV; FI.

MR. STORY (28m C r1973)
A study of old age. Lips aquiver with the palsy that denotes
impotence, Albert Story describes his life and attitudes with that
captivating forthrightness that so often characterizes the very young
and the very old. He has conquered no worlds and claims no great
achievements--except perhaps that he has never been responsible for
a "good girl going bad." p. Anita Thacher, DeeDee Halleck; PHOE-
NIX; KENTSU, UMO.

MITSUYE AND NELLIE (58½m C 1981) (also Video)
Creates a moving and challenging double portrait of two women
whose poetry expresses with dramatic clarity the immigrant experience of Asian-American women in a society contemptuous and suspi-
cious of "orientals." A film about tenderness and anger between
daughters and mothers, generational conflicts, and the breaking of
stereotyped images of Asian-American women. p./d. Allie Light, Irving Saraf; LISARF.

MIXED MARRIAGES: HOMOSEXUAL HUSBANDS (13m C 1977)
What occurs when a wife discovers that her husband is homosexual? Mike Wallace interviews two such couples in Great Britain. He
also speaks with the founder of Sigma Society, a self-help group of
women who are/were married to homosexuals, revealing tragedies and
some self-acclaimed happy survivors of such marriages. p. CBS-TV,
"60 Minutes." CAROUF; FI; PAS, UM, UCEMC.

MIXING THE MEDIA WITH DR. CAROLINE FELLER BAUER (30m C
1979) (Video)
Caroline Bauer demonstrates how to use effectively a variety of
media--including handmade craft items, puppets, toys, and other
simple props--to bring stories alive for audiences of all ages. She
tells more than a dozen stories--each dramatized in a different way.
The viewer is told how to create the media used where possible and
in all cases how to relate them to various stories. Recommended for
the experienced storytellers as well as the inexperienced. PSBV.

MODERN DANCE I (8½m C 1965-67)
Dancers demonstrate what the narrator discusses, that "You and
your own energy make Dance...." They perform basic studies on
the floor and improvise on a motif. Produced under the auspices of
the Department of Health, Education and Welfare, the University of
Pennsyvlania and the Philadelphia Dance Academy as part of a comprehensive dance curriculum program. Project Director: Nadia Chilkovsky Nahumck; Associate Director: Fai Coleman; p. Nicholas Nahumck;
p. Calvin De Frenes Corporation; FRANDA.

MODERN DANCE II (18m C 1965-67)
Extension of the basic concepts introduced in Part I to study at
the barre. Shows use of the circular barre (invented by Nicholas
Nahumck) and modern studies, by Nadia Chilkovsky Nahumck, at the
linear barre attached to the wall. Also, original studies for barre introducing spiraling progressions and conscious manipulation of body
energy organically woven into dance design. The barre, freed from
the wall, was used as an aid in choreographing. Excerpts from "No
Hiding Place" and "Flight," choreographed by Nadia Chilkovsky Nahumck, are performed. Project Director: Nadia Chilkovsky Nahumck;
Associate Director: Fai Coleman; p. Nicholas Nahumck; p. Calvin De
Frenes Corporation; FRANDA.

MODERN DANCE: CHOREOGRAPHY AND THE SOURCE (20m C 1967)
Illustrates that the source of creativity is within us and that
subject matter for dance exists in the world around us. Four complete dances are performed: "Summer Is Icumen In," "Farandole,"
"Greensleeves Duet," and "Boxes." Dancers: Students of San José
State College (California). p. Hildegard L. Spreen, Margaretta Fristoe; PHOENIX; BU, NILLU, UIL, UIO, PSU, USFL.

MODERN DANCE COMPOSITION (rev.) (13m B 1963)
Dance students at the University of Colorado are shown practicing basic techniques to prepare the body for dance movement. Shows
how compositions start with an idea and develop as movements are
improvised. Two dances--"Celebration" and "Lament"--demonstrate
the points made. Dance Director: Patricia Eckert. p. University
of Colorado; KENTSU, UCEMC, UIL, UIO.

MODERN DANCE: CREATIVE IMAGINATION AND CHOREOGRAPHY
(17m C 1967)
Four complete dances are performed to illustrate how the chor-
eographer with a creative imagination discovers new relationships and
concepts in common subject matter. Dancers: Students from San
José State College (California). p. Hildegard L. Spreen, Margaretta
Fristoe; PHOENIX; BU, KENTSU, NILLU, SYRACU, UIL, UIO, USFL,
PSU.

MODERN DANCE TECHNIQUES IN SEQUENTIAL FORM (12m C 1962)
Demonstration of basic expressive dance movements, showing how
they lend themselves to numerous variations. Shows how technique
is developed from natural body movements combined with skill, adding
imaginative deviations and giving meaning to then studies by expressing personal feelings. When these combine it is possible to achieve
exciting, artistic and dramatic results. Dancers: Students of San
José State College (California). p. Hildegard L. Spreen, Margaretta
Fristoe; BU, Budget, KENTSU, UIL, NILLU, PAS, SYRACU, PSU.

MODERN DANCE: THE ABC OF COMPOSITION (13m C 1962)
One of a series of dance studies to create interest in composing

dances. Studies include the use of rhythmic pattern of a round based on creative use of children's games. Shows functional use of architectural shapes as the base of the folk idiom and the use of a duet pattern with complementary movement. Dancers: Students of San José State College (California). p. Hildegard L. Spreen, Margaretta Fristoe; PHOENIX; BU, NILLU, SYRACU, UIL, UIO, USFL, PSU.

MODERN EGYPTIAN FAMILY (17m C 1977)
On grandfather Mahmoud Allam's 78th birthday, there is a family party. Through the eyes of his children and grandchildren we see some of the changes that have taken place in Egypt during his lifetime. p. International Film Foundation; IFF; PSU.

MODERN WORLD HISTORY, THE (SERIES) see QUEEN VICTORIA AND BRITISH HISTORY (1837-1901)

MOHAWK POTTER (18m C p1978, r1979)
Sara Smith, a Mohawk Indian from the Six Nations Reserve in Ontario, Canada, uses contemporary methods to make pottery of exceptional beauty. The designs she uses on her work are drawn from age-old cultural symbols, such as the "Tree of Peace," so exquisitely recreated on the vase she makes in this film. d. Geoff Voyce; p. B. T. Film Sound; NAINDF.

MOIRE (4m C 1977)
Made without a camera by applying layers of self-adhesive dot patterns to clear 16mm film and then handcoloring it with felt pens. When projected, the dots appear to dance in time with the music, merging to form constantly sifting moiré patterns that seem to live in a three-dimensional space. Colorful and upbeat. p. Sharon Niemszyk; NWMP.

MOISEYEV DANCERS IN "THE STROLLERS," THE (6m C 1952, 1978-- U.S.)
A film of exciting artistry featuring lively folk dances vibrant with high spirits, gaiety, beauty of movement and the complicated steps for which Russian folk dancing is noted. The Moiseyev dancers made theater history in a tour of the United States in 1958. d. Igor Moiseyev; p. Lenfilm Studios, Russia; MACMFL.

MOLLY RUSH (28½m C 1981) (Video)
Molly Rush was a member of the Plowshares 8, a group of nuclear protesters including the Revs. Daniel and Philip Berrigan, who walked into a missile assembly plant in King of Prussia, Pennsylvania, and smashed the nose cones of two nuclear warheads with hammers. She is unique in that she is a mother of six who risked 30 years in jail for her act. This is a study of her motivations and the conflicts that developed in her family as a result of what she did. d. Arthur Kamell, Terence Williams; p. Booth Gallett; WITNESS.

MOM, I WANT TO COME HOME NOW (56½m C 1980) (also Video)
A searing portrait of a tragic contemporary problem. About teenagers who run away from home each year and wind up on the streets,
prey to pimps, drug pushers and child pornographers. Filmed entirely in San Francisco, the documentary looks at the problem through
the eyes of the young runaways, who escape emotional and physical
abuse at home, only to be exploited by the adults who become their
new "families." Includes scenes of male and female teenage prostitutes working the streets, playing a cynical cat-and-mouse game with
police, having mutually frustrating visits with their parents, and often just talking about themselves. A powerful social document, the
film contains mature subject matter and some graphic street language.
Narrator: Beau Bridges. d./p. Fleming Fuller; s.w. F. Fuller;
a.p. Lucille Kristofits, Marilyn Neckes; CORINTH.

"MOM AND DAD CAN'T HEAR ME" (47m C 1978)
This dramatized story deals with the relationship between Charlotte, a normal, lively and attractive 15-year-old, and her deaf parents. Charlotte and her parents communicate through sign language
and lip reading; her parents' occasional "speech" sounds strange.
A telephone ring or a doorbell is signaled by a flashing light; phone
conversations are conducted by a tele-typewriter. The script sensi-
tively treats Charlotte's anxiety regarding peer pressure approval
as well as the damage to her own self-esteem when she takes that
need too far. She concocts a series of lies to keep her friends from
meeting her parents and, at one point, she identifies her mother as
their deaf housekeeper. Ashamed and anguished, she finally tells
her friends the truth, and is afterwards able to integrate her friends
into her family's life. d. Larry Elikann; p. Fran Sears/Daniel Wilson
Productions Inc., TIMLIF; UIL.

MOMENT BY MOMENT (103m C 1978)
Trisha Billingsworth (Lily Tomlin) is a bored, pampered Beverly
Hills housewife whose life is coming apart at the seams. Then Trisha
meets Strip (John Travolta), a streetwise youth who parks cars for
a living when he isn't at the beach. Although Trisha's social position warns her not to become involved with Strip, he ultimately makes
her confront not only her own passion, but also her need for affection, tenderness and love. d. Jane Wagner; s.w. Jane Wagner; p.
Robert Stigwood; UNIVERSAL; CWF.

MONARCH (15m C p1978, r1978)
The magic cycle of a butterfly's life: The story starts in a
meadow where the cycle begins, and reveals the metamorphosis from
caterpillar to chrysalis to butterfly. The camera then follows the
monarch on its 3,000-mile journey to the forests where its ancestors
have wintered for centuries. d. Fran Mellen; p. Butterfly Production. CANFDC.

MONEY (29m C 1976) (Video) Woman Series
Business woman Elizabeth Forsling Harris discusses the extent

of women's economic clout and her belief that it is time women began
to appreciate their economic impact on society. She also warns of
the need for women to be careful of exploitation by marketing specialists. Narrator: Sandra Elkin. p. WNED-TV; PBSV.

MONEY AND THE SINGLE WOMAN (29m C 1976) (Video) Woman Series
Author Martha Yates ("Coping: A Single Woman Alone"), who
has supported her family since she became a widow in 1970, discusses
the problems facing single women who must manage their own finances.
She suggests that women running households establish credit in their
own names, that all women take out several manageable loans and
credit cards and keep accurate financial records. She also advises
women to learn about income tax preparation and to get comprehensive will and insurance policies. Sandra Elkin, moderator. p. WNED-
TV, Buffalo; PBSV.

MONEY TREE, THE (19m C 1971)
Traces the disintegration of marriage, which results from materialistic values and habits of financial management. Attempts to put
viewer into an "emotional" situation where one can identify with the
pain and reality of human experience, and be motivated into discussions about the monetary problems that can exist in a marriage; fra-
gility of contemporary family units; acquisitiveness and materialism
desire for immediate gratification; susceptibility to cultural, especially
media pressures; financial responsibilities of parenthood; credit, contracts, loans and credit ratings; job security. p. Hanna-Barbera
Productions, Inc. for Charles Cahill and Associates, Inc.; AIMS; UIL.

MONITOS: PORTRAIT OF AN ARTISAN FAMILY (11m C 1974)
Reveals the typical summertime daily life of the Garcia-Aguilar
family, and especially in the making of the "Monitos" people, the
small clay figures that have brought the mother fame in the world
of popular folk art. Shows the home process of forming, firing, and
painting the clay figures and the family's way of life in this small
village. A trip to the market to sell the "Monitos" shows the important role of the market in their rural Mexican life and completes the
picture of a family unit, its economy, and the skills involved in it.
p. Judith Anne Perez, Severo Perez; FLMFR.

MONTANA (3m C 1982) (Video)
A portrait of the state employing the imagery of video games and
computer graphics to construct a series of tableaux that suggest the
natural, economic and social fabric of that state. d. Jane Veeder;
MMA. MONTHS BEFORE BIRTH--A SERI

MONTHS BEFORE BIRTH--A SERIES see BEGINNING OF PREG-
NANCY, THE; BIRTH OF THE BABY, THE; FIRST VISIT TO THE
DOCTOR, THE; LAST MONTHS OF PREGNANCY, THE; MIDDLE
MONTHS OF PREGNANCY, THE; NUTRITION AND DENTAL CARE

IN PREGNANCY; PHYSIOLOGY OF REPRODUCTION, THE; WEEKS
AFTER BIRTH, THE

MOON GATES I (5½m C 1973)
The dancers perform in and around pieces of sculpture designed
by Doris Chase. Filmed in the Wadsworth Atheneum, Hartford, Connecticut. Dance Company: Mary Staton Dance Ensemble, Choreographer: Mary Stanton, Composer: George Kleinsinger, p. Doris
Chase; CHASED.

MOON GATES II (5½m C 1974)
Dancers perform in and around pieces of sculpture designed by
Doris Chase. Video synthesized at the experimental TV laboratory
of WNET-TV, New York City. p. Doris Chase; CHASED.

MOON GATES--THREE VERSIONS (15½m C 1974)
A dance film based on the kinetic sculpture designed by Doris
Chase for the Seattle Opera Company Ballet. The filming took place
in the Wadsworth Atheneum, Hartford, Connecticut. The first part
of the film is a documentary showing the dancers working with the
sculpture relative to space and form. In the second part of the film,
the first part is seen again in a synthesized version. It was put
through a video synthesizer at the experimental laboratory of WNET-
TV, New York City; the video tape was then transferred back to
film and optically printed by Brown/Olvey of Seattle, Washington.
Dance Company: Seattle Opera Company Ballet, Choreographer:
Mary Stanton, Composer: George Kleinsinger, p. Doris Chase;
CHASED.

MOON GODDESS (15m C n.d.)
Two women search for the feminine creative spirit guided by
moon power and mutual respect in a barren desert land. p. Barbara
Hammer, Gloria Churchman; IRIS.

MOON REDEFINED (5½m B 1980) (Video)
Chase uses the architectural forms of her sculpture as an integral
element in this film. The image is video synthesized and sequenced
at variable speeds to create a sensual rhythmic pattern. Produced
at the Experimental Television Center in Binghamton, New York with
Peer Bode; music is by Bruce Ditmas; p. Doris Chase; CHASED.

MOONCHILD (49m C p1981, r1982) (also Video)
Real life deprogrammers and ex-Moonies re-enact the story of
one person's journey into and out of the Unification Church in this
riveting documentary drama. Based on the actual experiences of a
former Moonie who plays himself in the film. MOONCHILD is an eye-
opening glimpse of a religious cult from an insider's point of view.
MOONCHILD exposes the questionable recruiting tactics and high
pressure methods of indoctrination that this cult uses with young
people who are searching for direction and purpose in life. It

documents the controversial practices of the Unification Church. And, by simulating the painstaking process of deprogramming, it demonstrates how the effects of cult brainwashing can be reversed. p./d. Anne Makepeace; PF.

MOORS PAVANE, THE (16m C 1950)
An episode from William Shakespeare's Othello told in dance with lines from the play spoken by Bram Nossem. Using the structure of a court dance, the passion and the tragedy in Othello is portrayed. Choreographer: José Limón; d. Doris Humphrey; MACMFL; BOSU, PAS, SYRAU, UIO, UM, USFLA, UU, PSU.

MORE THAN A DREAM: BEING YOUR OWN BOSS (27m C p1980, r1980)
Profiles a variety of characters who have shared the same dream: to continue their own destiny--to be free, independent and maybe get rich in the process. It explores the real world of the entrepreneur through their candid observations and experiences--separating the "dream" from the reality. First in a three-part series. p./d. Philip Gittelman, Deirdre Evans; GITFM.

MORE THAN HUGS AND KISSES (23m C 1981) (also Video)
In Alice Brogan's class, emotions, attitudes, and values are as much a part of the curriculum as learning skills. Born with spina bifida, she knows from her own experience the importance of being independent and feeling good about herself. Brogan uses the precepts of affective education in her mainstreamed classroom, where one third of the students are developmentally delayed. Filmed in a class of three- to seven-year-olds at the Jowonio School in Syracuse, New York. Observing each child individually, Brogan determines personal psycho-educational goals. Then, through sequential activities, and spontaneous intervention when called for, she helps her students improve their communication skills and their behavior. This film will be helpful to anyone concerned with mainstreaming when they observe how both typical children and children with special needs learn alongside each other and from each other. With discussion guide. p. Grania Gurievitch, Togg Films; FILMLB.

MORE THAN JUST A JOB (20m C p1980, r1981)
Interviews with youths ages 14 to 17 who talk about the value of work in their lives. Includes youths who've dropped out of school who say why and those still in school who talk about how learning about work and learning job skills has fit into the rest of their education--why it's been so important to them. All programs in the film were co-sponsored by public schools and local CETA youth programs. d. Derek Muirden; p. Marcia Douglas for Film Loft, Inc.; ORSTED.

MORNING NEWS, THE (7½m C 1981)
A funny, yet ultimately tragic commentary on the life of an "everyman" whose paranoid fantasies are provoked by the headlines

that greet him each day. After three successive encounters in which he is the victim of missiles, rioting refugees and a catastrophe of pollution, he attempts to control his anxieties by cancelling his subscription. He finds a brief and peaceful respite, but discovers fatally that there is no escape from bad news as he himself becomes his neighbor's morning news. p. Donna Salem; SALEM.

MORTAL BODY, THE (12m B n.d.)
This poetic film of the body's vitality and vulnerability can be used as a discussion starter or a summation piece in any workshop relating to aging and death. Projecting a series of powerful images-- the birth of a child, a couple making love, an old man contemplating eternity--the film capsulizes the life cycle. Nonverbal with music. FILMLB.

MOSES AND AARON (105m C 1975)
A meticulous production of Schönberg's opera; a radical film experiment. d. Jean-Marie Straub, Daniele Huillet; NYF.

MOSES COADY (58m C n.d.)
Moses Coady spearheaded Canada's cooperative movement from 1929 to 1950. He encourages his audiences to come together in "kitchen meetings" to discuss their situation and how co-ops could help. And they did. In one extraordinary two-year period in the Maritime Provinces mining, fishing, and farming families were galvanized into action, turned their backs on the "company store," and set up their own businesses, credit unions, and even built community housing. Today, the Coady International Institute continues the work by bringing people together from all over the world to learn the managerial skills and the philosphical principles of democratic cooperation for mutual advancement. p. NFBC; BULFRG.

MOSLEMS IN SPAIN, THE (39m C p1978, r1979)
Presents a history of the Moslem presence and influence on Spanish culture. Around the year A.D. 700 the Moslems landed in Spain and took control of the country. The legacy left behind by the Moslems can be seen in many areas, especially in the architectural style that dominates southern Spain. The Moslems made many advances in agriculture by introducing the water wheel and the laws assuring equitable distribution of water, a tradition that is followed today. But the Moslems, on the other hand, were influenced by the Spanish, particularly in the area of literature and the arts. Perhaps the film's most important contribution is in the imparting of knowledge about a subject that is little known. p./d. Mary Kirby, Catherine Blue/Pilgrim Films; IFB.

MOTHER, MAY I? (28m C 1981)
About sexuality and teenage pregnancy as seen through the eyes of 11-year-old Karen and her 16-year-old sister, Michelle, who thinks she's pregnant. The girls argue over whether to tell their parents,

who are embarrassed to talk about sex with each other and with their children. In the course of the film everyone begins to learn how to communicate about sexuality and how to act responsibly on sexual issues. d. Linda Feferman; p. Gina Blumenfeld/L. Feferman; CF.

MOTHER OF MANY CHILDREN (58m C 1978)
Agatha Marie Goodine, 108 years old, a member of the Hobbema tribe, contrasts her memories with the conflicts that most Indian and Inuit women face today. Traces the cycle of their lives from birth to old age in a series of sensitive vignettes. Sarah looks forward to a picnic of raw arctic char dipped in seal oil. Elizabeth is learning to make leaf dolls with one of her nine grandmothers. Sally, who was brought up by her grandparents in the bush, remembers that "it was a good life. I never felt like I was poor." Also available in French. p./d. Alanis Obomsawin; NFBC; UMT.

MOTHER TIGER, MOTHER TIGER (11m C 1975)
Dramatization of mother's struggle, despair, and eventual acceptance of her severely handicapped child. In a series of memory flashbacks, she relives her recent joy and expectation in giving birth, and the resulting anger and frustration when learning the doctor's diagnosis. p. Teleketics Films; TKS; PAS.

MOTHERLESS CHILD IV (3½m B 1978) (Video)
A dance piece designed for television. Choreographed by Celia Ipiotis, reconceived from original choreography by Geraldyne Blunden. Music is by Odetta. d./p. Celia Ipiotis, Jeff Bush; BUSHIPIO.

MOTHERS ALWAYS HAVE A REASON TO BE (7m C 1979) (Video)
A mother reflects on her children and her work. p. Jeanne Hollenbeck; WMM.

MOTHERS AND DAUGHTERS (29m C 1975) (Video) Woman Series
Singe Hammer, author of Mothers and Daughters, Daughters and Mothers, discusses some of the major conclusions she has reached about mother-daughter relationships. She explains that her research revealed that most women grow up without a strong sense of self or personal identity. She also found that the intensity of the mother-daughter relationship at an early stage strongly affects the daughter's later relationship with men. Sandra Elkin, moderator. p. WNED-TV; PBSV.

MOTHERS, FATHERS AND CHILDREN SERIES see ARE YOU LISTENING SERIES

MOTHERS IN CONFLICT--CHILDREN IN NEED (25m C p1979, r1979)
Concerns infant health and nutrition in developing countries. Through interviews with the Third World mothers, physicians and a nutrition-anthropologist, the film presents many of the factors contributing to a decline in breast-feeding in the Third World. Examines

from an anthropological/cultural point of view the plight of mothers and infants in the Third World with regard to their nutrition and health care. Free loan. d. Gunter Doetsch; p. Joyce Doetsch. SCNTIF.

MOTHERS WHO ARE PART OF SUPPORTIVE DAY CARE (29m C p1979, r1980) (also Video) Are You Listening Series
A group of mothers--from cities and farms; from all economic backgrounds; whites, blacks and Orientals--share their experiences about trying to create a responsible way to combine being a mother and holding a job. These women discuss some of the major issues of our time, such as a mother's responsibility to her children versus her responsibility to herself; the solitariness of parenting and the importance of creating parent support networks for sharing experiences; the economic necessity of women having to work, but the guilt mothers often feel when having to leave their children in someone else's care. d. Ivan Cary; p. Martha Stuart; STUARTM.

MOTHER'S WORRY, A (33m C p1978, r1979)
Shows parental anxiety and its effect on doctor-parent relationships. Robert, a two-year-old, suffers chronic diarrhea and has been brought to the hospital for tests. Days go by and nothing conclusive has been proven, and the wear and tear on the mother and staff becomes almost unbearable when the doctor proposes more tests. The mother is concerned about its effect on the weakened body, and she begins to fear for his life. After ten days, it is finally determined that Robert has a colon infection which will gradually clear up. Many viewers can identify with the mother's situation. p./d. Gary Schlosser, p. New Health Institute; LREDF.

MOUNTAIN FARMER (9m B n.d.)
Shows Lee Banks, a wizened mountain farmer, who uses a wooden plow and work horse to turn his ground. He grows a full supply of vegetables and keeps just enough hogs to feed his family. He says, "I never bought no meat nor lard in 50 years." Fiddle music is playing as the old man coaxes potatoes from the ground as he carefully guides plow and horse. A film for those desiring to see what honest-to-God rural America is. p. Shelby Adams, Mimi Pickering; APPAL.

MOUNTAIN LIFE ZONE COMMUNITIES (Replaces LIFE ZONE OF THE CENTRAL ROCKIES) (21m C 1976) (also Video)
Shows how the rapidly changing elevation of the Rocky Mountains drastically affects living conditions, creating distinct life zones. Examines the grassland, deciduous forest, coniferous forest, and alpine-arctic zones and investigates the plants and animals that have adapted to each region. Wildlife photographs include bison, prairie dogs, bears, woodpeckers, pelicans, swans, Rocky Mountain sheep and goats, and ptarmigans. Also shows animals that range through more than one life zone--mountain lions, antelopes, elk, moose, and several bird species. p. Myrna I. Berlet, Walter H. Berlet; IFB.

MOUNTAIN PEOPLE (52m C 1978)

Retirement is something the elderly of rural Dingess, West Virginia do not ever consider. John and Nora Sturgill, in their eighties, and Myrtle Thomas and Lula McCloud, in their seventies, know no way of life other than self-sufficiency. They grow their own food, tend to their small farms, maintain such disappearing crafts as quilting and even hold down jobs. The relationship between young and old is very important to all of these people. As opposed to the elderly in homes or retirement communities, they maintain and cherish daily contact with their children and grandchildren. However, things are changing in Dingess, old ways are dying and young people are moving away. p./d. Cinda Firestone; ALMI.

MOUSIE BABY (25m C r1978)

Tells of a strike in a big-city advertising agency during the Depression. Betty, a pretty young secretary from the Midwest is reluctant to strike with her co-workers. She imagines herself in love with her handsome, eligible boss, and dreams one day of being his wife. The strike is gradually defeated by the clever boss by threatening and intimidating each worker. The two who resisted are forced to quit their jobs. During the after-hour celebration, the triumphant boss attempts to seduce Betty, revealing the true nature of his feelings for her. Showing surprising courage and a new sense of self-worth, Betty walks out on her boss and her job. Based on a short story by Tess Slesinger, a Hollywood screenwriter of the thirties. p./d. Ann Zane Shanks. PHOENIX.

MOVE! (29m C 1974)

Shows Sue Cambigue and Bella Lewitsky in a Reno, Nevada elementary school as part of the Artists in Schools programs. p. Ted Steeg; STEEG.

MOVE: CONFRONTATION IN PHILADELPHIA (60m B 1980) (Video)

An investigative report on the eviction of a radical black political commune by Mayor Frank Rizzo of Philadelphia. Billed by the media as a "back-to-nature group," MOVE was a highly complex entity, and the producers document the intricate relationship of media bias, police harassment, and subtle economic motivation which led to MOVE's violent removal by the police in August 1979. Shifting from newspaper headlines to television newscasts to mayoral press conferences to on-the-street interviews with community residents, the filmmakers reveal how the media manipulated the news and how the Black Powelton community in Philadelphia proved to be the real pawn in a political and media chess game. d./p. Karen Pomer/Jane Mancini; TEMPLU.

MOVEMENT IMPROVISATIONS (19m C 1957)

Four areas of movement expression are explored: (1) "Free Movement of Separate Body Parts"; (2) "Three Duets and a Trio"; (3) "Designs in Movement"; and (4) "Heads, Hands, Feet." Dance Company: Barbara Mettler Dance Group; Dance Teacher/Narrator/Director: Barbara Mettler; p. Barbara Mettler; METTLER.

MOVEMENT STYLE AND CULTURE, THE (SERIES) see BAROQUE
DANCE, 1675-1725

MOVIE STAR'S DAUGHTER, A (33m C p1979, r1979)
Presents a story of how a young girl, Dena McKain, discovers
that she has choices to make and lessons to learn on the real meaning
of friendship. p. Dora Bachrach; d. Robert Fuest; s.w. Jeffrey
Kindley; LCA.

MOVING/MAKING/ME (28m B 1972)
Documentary film made at a public school of primary educable
mentally retarded children in a special education class. The children
(ages 6 to 10) are shown studying art and dance. The soundtrack
includes the children's descriptions of their original artwork and
dance and comments by the art and dance therapists. Teachers:
Carole Weiner (dance), Georgiana Jungles (art); p. William Jungels;
REAJUNG.

MOVING MOUNTAINS (27m C 1981)
Trumpets forth the message that women belong behind the driving
wheel ... not in the kitchen. It's one more sign of women's determination to take their place in the world, even if it's a world they
themselves might have made differently. p. Laura Sky and United
Steel Workers of America; MOBIUS.

MOVING ON (4m C 1977)
An animated introduction on history of transportation. No narration. Animation. p. Sheila Graber; FI.

MOVING TRUE (19m B 1973)
A demonstration of the use of dance therapy with a severely with-
drawn female patient. One actual dance therapy session is condensed
here. A professional training film for educators and clinicians.
Dance Therapist: Anne Olin; p. Creative Arts Rehabilitation Center;
CREARTRC.

MRS. BREADWINNER (12m C p1981, r1982) (also Video)
It is reported that a growing number of women in America out-
earn their husbands. Harry Reasoner interviews several women on
the results of role changing on the relationships between the wife
and husband and between the children and their parents. A good
discussion film. p. CBS News; MTITI.

MRS. GANDHI'S INDIA (55m C 1976)
A biographical documentary of Mrs. Indira Gandhi, Prime Minister
of India. Mrs. Gandhi movingly speaks of her childhood and the influence of her father on her political life; her rise to power; the controversial emergency which beset India and her hopes for India's future. The camera picks up the subtle personality traits of Gandhi,
offering insight into the truth behind her public image. The film

captures the mood of a country still searching for its own identity.
p. Document Associates Inc.; DOCUA.

MRS. WARREN'S PROFESSION (110m C 1976) (also Video)
     Mrs. Warren is a brothel madam. That's how she can give her
daughter an expensive education. George Bernard Shaw's play is
a highly feminist statement, full of emotion and dramatic tension, and
is as typical today as it was in 1905. BBC; FI.

MS.--THE STRUGGLE FOR WOMEN'S RIGHTS (14m B 1972) The Screen
News Digest Series
     An entertaining and informative cavalcade of the events, issues
and personalities which gave impetus and leadership to the struggle
for women's rights in the United States. p. Hearst King Features
Production; KINGF; KENTSU.

MURAL (5m C 1977)
     Shows the creation of a mural by sculptor Glen Michaels. Uses
animation of tile, stone, wood, wax, bronze and brass to show the
growth of segments of a mural piece by piece without the intrusion
of hands. Shows the finished mural in its architectural setting. Original music by jazz pianist Marian McPartland. p. Pajon Arts Ltd.;
p. Lillian and J. P. Somersaulter; WMM.

MURIEL NEZHNIE HELFMAN (17m B 1977)
     Tells about the work and family of a tapestry weaver and designer
in St. Louis. She works at home in order to balance home and family
life. p. Carol Greenfield; GRNFLDC.

MURIEL RUKEYSER (29m C 1979) The Writer in America (Series)
     Filmed interview with Muriel Rukeyser in her studio overlooking
the Hudson River. When asked to talk about obstacles a poet faces,
Rukeyser mentions misunderstanding--of one's self, one's family,
and the audience--and how she strives to overcome this. In a life
filled with the making of poems, she writes, she rewrites, she reads
extensively from her works, and encourages striving poets. d./p.
Richard O. Moore; CORONET; PAS, IU, UIL.

MUSEREEL NO. I: TAPESTRY OF WOMANSPIRIT (17m C n.d.)
     A documentation of the first women's spirituality conference,
"Through the Looking Glass: A Gynergetic Experience," a gathering
of over 2,000 women in Boston in 1976. Combining live action, still
photographs, animation and drawing with music and interviews from
conference participants, the film recreates many events of that weekend. p. Denise Bostrom, Carol Clement, Ariel Dougherty, Nancy
Peck, Marilyn Ries; WMM.

MUSIC BOX: BEAT AND TEMPO, THE (14½m C 1981) (Video)
     Hostess Heather Conkie and the Magic Music Box explore the mus-
ical elements of beat and tempo. They discover through song and

film that lots of things have a "beat" and that you can dance to the beat in many styles of music. They also show how the beat fits onto the rhythm pattern of a song, and how, if the beat slows down or speeds up, the tempo changes. d. Susan Murgatroyd; p. Heather Conkie; s.w. Barbara Boyden; original music: Heather Conkie; p. TV Ontario Marketing; TVONT.

MUSIC LESSONS (40m C 1981) (also Video)
    The Kodaly method of music training, aimed at developing mus-
ical literacy in all children, is illustrated in several United States
public schools. d./p. Joyce Chopra; written and narrated by Tom
Cole; sponsored by Ford Foundation; KAROL.

MUSIC OF AUSCHWITZ, THE (16m C 1978)
    Fania Fenelon recalls the atrocious acts committed by the Germans
at the Auschwitz concentration camp. Her life was saved from extermination because she was a musician. Fania and other inmates played
to sedate new arrivals and entertained German staff and guards. Includes actual film footage and photographs taken during the Holocaust. CBS-TV, "Sixty Minutes," d. John Tiffin; CAROUF; UIL,
UMN, USFL, RARIG.

MUSIC SEQUENCE (10m C 1960)
    A résumé of the popular music of the fifties, introducing what
later became a fashionable quick-cut technique in television. p. Ray
and Charles Eames; PF.

MUSICMAKERS (26m C r1978)
    An introduction to the world of music for children. Combining
their talents and experience, artists like actress/singer Carol Bur-
nett, singer Helen Reddy, pianist George Shearing, songwriter Jim
Webb, singer Al Jardine of the Beach Boys, and singer/songwriter
Johnny Rivers explain the basics of music-making. Children are encouraged to find the musical possibilities in even the most common-
place objects, and to join in the beautiful world of rhythm and melody. p. Joan Marks; s.w. J. Marks, Robyn Knapton; PHOENIX.

MY BRILLIANT CAREER (101m C 1980)
    Sybylla Melvyn (Judy Davis) is an exuberant young girl growing
up in the Australian outback during the turn of the century. She
admits to a solid streak of egotistical independence that prevents her
from engaging in the dusty struggle of becoming the wife of a dirt
farmer or of anyone else for that matter. She hates the thought of
milking cows, raising children and surrendering her dream of a career
to the reality of marriage. But her ethereal thoughts are weak weapons against the concrete block of tradition. Based on a semi-
autobiographical novel published in 1901, which was written by 16-
year-old Miles Franklin as a hymn to individuality. The film is notable because it marks the feature film debuts of director Gillian Armstrong and the leading lady, Judy Davis. Well received at Cannes.

Reviews by notable critics excellent. d. Gillian Armstrong; p. Margaret Fink; s.w. Eleanor Whitcomb; a.p./p.s. Jane Scott. p. The South Wales Film Corporation and GUO; ALMI.

MY CHILD IS DEAD (15m C 1981)
Profile of Compassionate Friends, a group organized in Buffalo, New York to help parents come to terms with the death of their children through peer counseling. States that because symptoms of grief can be similar to mental illness, bereaved parents often think they are losing control. Shows Compassionate Friends reassuring parents and helping them deal with their friends and relatives. p. CBS News; PAS.

MY DAD LIVES IN A DOWNTOWN HOTEL (34m C 1975)
Through the eyes of Joey Grant, age 10, the film portrays the dilemma faced by a child as he attempts to resolve his conflicting feelings about his parents' separation. Assuming that the divorce is his fault, Joey decides to write up a contract. He believes that if he mends his ways, his dad will come back home. Finally, he understands that, although they no longer live together, they both still love him. p. Multimedia Producers Corporation; PHOENIX; UIL, UMN.

MY FRIENDS CALL ME TONY (12m C 1975)
Since he was three, when he had an operation to remove a brain tumor, Tony has been blind. Now ten years old, this alert, energetic and otherwise normal boy is learning to live a full and fulfilling life despite his handicap. d. Beverly Shaffer; p. Yuki Yoshida, Kathleen Shannon; NFBC; MEDIAG.

MY HANDS ARE THE TOOLS OF MY SOUL (54m C r1978) (also Video)
Illuminates the cultural landscape of the American Indian. They have no word for "art" in their languages. Their masks and carvings, pottery, sand paintings, songs and dances are part of the activities of their lives, along with eating and sleeping, hunting, talking and praying. The film is permeated by the Indian sense of the harmony of nature, the intimate relationship between man and his environment which people today are trying so hard to rediscover. p. Arthur Barron, Zina Voynow; TEXFM.

MY LOVE HAS BEEN BURNING (84m B 1949) (Japanese/Subtitled)
The story is set in the 1880's, a crucial period in the modernization of Japan, when both liberalism and feminism were nascent under the Meiji Restoration. The conflicts of the era are embodied in the struggles of a determined young women, a schoolteacher, who leaves home and becomes politicized in Tokyo. The film ends with a hauntingly simple image of two women forming a mystical bond that includes and transcends politics. d. Kenji Mizoguchi; NYF.

MY MOTHER WAS NEVER A KID (ed.) (46m C p1980, r1981) (also Video)
Francine Pascal's popular teenage novel Hangin' Out with Cici

is the source of this adventure about a girl who takes a meaningful
trip back in time. The film reminds us that sometimes it's hard to
remember that all grownups were young once. What happens when
13-year-old Victoria witnesses some of the events of her mother's
adolescent years makes for an eye-opening story revealing that understanding can go a long way in closing the generation gap. p. Dora
Bachrach, Linda Gottlieb; d. Robert Fuest; ABC Afterschool Special;
LCA; IU.

MY SON, KEVIN (24m C 1975)
    There are over 400 children in England born malformed because
of the drug thalidomide. The film is about such a child--as seen by
his mother: a woman who communicates her strength to 11-year-old
Kevin and to the rest of the family as well. p. Granada International
Film; WOMBAT.

MY SURVIVAL AS AN ABORIGINAL (55m C p1978, r1980)
    Directed by an aboriginal activist and Country/Western singer,
this film shows the history and meaning of the fight for black identity on Australia's outback reserve. d. Essie Coffey; p. Martha An-
sara; Australia Films; ICARF.

MY VERSION OF THE FALL (12m C si 1978)
    Originally shot in 35mm black and white positive using an old
camera with a hand-crank. The film was completely hand-painted,
frame by frame, using liquid watercolors, brush and magnifying
glass. The images are seen once forwards and once backwards,
highlighting the illusionary qualities of the film medium. The characters of the woman and the devil are both played by Diana Barrie.
p. Diana Barrie; WMM.

MYSELF, YOURSELF (30m C p1980, r1980)
    Different people perceive others in different ways. Recalling
their childhood and school experiences, three adults and two teenagers reveal how the attitudes of others affected their own sense of
identity. d. Jennifer Hodge; p. Jenfilms Inc.; MOBIUS.

MYSTERIUM (11m C p1978, r1978)
    The enigma of the masculine/feminine is explored from its pri-
mordial beginnings. The filmmaker takes the choreography and gives
it a new existence as a dance film. Choreographer: Marion Scott.
d. Shirley Clarke; p. Shirley Clarke, David Cort; p. Spiral Productions; SPIRAL.

MYSTERY OF THE MAYA (58m C 1974)
    An archeological expedition to Rio Bec in Campech, Guatemala,
near the border of Quintana Roo was organized by two professional
filmmakers and a Princeton historian to rediscover a temple photographed in 1912 and then lost from outsiders' knowledge. The film
shows the search for the temple and its discovery. In focusing on

this research, the film emphasizes its interest in examining the ancient
Maya through the research being done by archeologists at many sites.
Connections are made between these ancient city-states and contemporary Maya-speaking Indians. p./d. Suzanne Johnston/Hugh Johnston; WNET-TV; FI.

MYTH CONCEPTIONS: A TEENAGE SEX QUIZ (18m C 1980)
     This amusing and entertaining film portrays peer group education
program for junior high and high school age youth. Explores traditional questions about sex and parenting. Issues included are birth
control, parenting as a teen, venereal disease, and the decision to
be or not to be sexually active. It is straightforward and provides
a great deal of information, in a manner that is neither condescending
nor threatening, by teens themselves involved in this program. Sexually non-explicit. p. Darrell Sevilla; MMRC.

MYTH OF THE HAPPY CHILD, THE (29m C 1976) Woman Series
     Author Carole Klein (The Myth of the Happy Child) discusses
her research on childhood and the discovery that children are totally
aware of their inadequacy to handle life on their own and are therefore often afraid. She explains society's misconceptions about childhood and the need for parents to understand their own limitations.
She also talks about groups of children's advocates who support a
children's liberation movement and understand that childhood is a
time that needs a great deal of honest examination. Sandra Elkin is
the moderator. p. WNED-TV; PBSV.

MYTHS OF SHOPLIFTING, THE (16m C p. 1979, r1980)
     A look at the myths commonly believed by America's teenagers
about shoplifting: it doesn't hurt anyone, you won't get caught,
you won't be prosecuted, etc. In a dramatic presentation, the audience is shown what can--and does--happen. A good discussion film.
p. Doris Storm, Frank Jacoby; d. Doug Jacoby; p. National Retail
Merchants Association; NATRMA.

-N-

N!AI, THE STORY OF A !KUNG WOMAN (59m C p1979, r1980) The
     Odyssey Series
     Told in her own words and song, the film covers 27 years in the
life of N!ai, a !Kung San woman from Namibia's Kalahari Desert.
Film footage of N!ai's early years, when her small band still roamed
freely as gatherers/hunters over 15,000 square miles of desert, contrasts sharply with her present, and radically different, life on a
government-run reserve. It provides a comprehensive and historical
look at a traditional culture that is rapidly disappearing. d. John
K. Marshall, Adrienne Miesmer; p. John K. Marshall, Sue Marshall-
Cabezas, A. Miesmer. DER; PAS, UMM; UW, UMT, UM.

NAKED KISS, THE (90m B 1964)

Reveals attitudes and inner feelings of a hooker (Constance Towers) as she travels the road from prostitution to respectability, and then to disillusionment with the facade of the "respectable" life as she found it. A very perceptive film describing the conflict between personal emotional interests and the more impersonal, mechanical responses social and environmental superstructures demand. d. Samuel Fuller; p. Allied Artists; ALMI.

NANCY ACOSTA see OLD FRIENDS ... NEW FRIENDS ... NANCY ACOSTA

NANCY ASTOR SERIES (9 episodes/55m ea. C 1981)

Nancy Langhorne, an American who became the wife of English millionaire Waldorf Astor and later the first woman elected to the British House of Commons, was one of the most fascinating and powerful among women of her time. This nine-part series covers Lady Astor's life from the post-Civil War period in Virginia where she spent her childhood through the "Gilded Age" of New York in the 1890's, to Edwardian England and ends shortly after World War II, when she was 80. Filmed in Charlottesville and Richmond, Virginia, as well as England, the series stars Lisa Harrow as Lady Astor, James Fox as Waldorf Astor, Dan O'Herlihy and Sylvia Syms as her parents and Nigel Havers as her son. TIMLIF.

NANDUTI: A PARAGUAYAN LACE (17m C p1978, r1978)

Nanduti is a lace-making technique found only in Paraguay. The basic shape of this lace is a "solar disc" in which cobweb-like threads radiate from a central hub. On these rays are laced patterns that represent a rich diversity of objects from everyday life. The film first explores the source of these patterns in the daily life of a typical farm woman; then it shows how the lace is made. d. A. Sanjurjo; p. A. Casciero; CKPRO.

NAN'S CLASS (30m C 1978)

Explores the joys of prepared childbirth. Nan's class has eleven people, therefore eleven different ways of anticipating, of hoping, of dreaming. Shown are five couples and one single parent. We see the Lamaze techniques effectively used through many different types of births. We see a Leboyer delivery and the role of the coach. Produced by Durrin Films, Inc.; NEWDAY.

NAP, THE (13m C p1978, r1978)

A well-earned afternoon nap turns into a nightmare. p./d. Joan Rosenfelt; ROSFTJ.

NAPOLEAN CONQUERS AMERICA (52m C 1981)

A documentary on the rediscovery of Abel Gance's 1927 silent film masterpiece, NAPOLEON. Includes interviews with Kevin Brownlow and Robert Harris on the reconstruction of the lost film and with

Carmine and Francis Coppola on its presentation with a live orchestra. Excerpts from NAPOLEON are used to illustrate Gance's innovations in the art of filmmaking. d. James Paiten; p. Mary Bell;
IMAGES.

NARAKASURAVADHA: THE KILLING OF THE DEMON NARAKASURA
(60m C 1979) (Video)
A performance of the Indian Kathakali dance-drama, featuring
M. P. Sankaran Namboodiri of Kerala, India. This award-winning
video program captures all the color and music of the spectacle.
Voice-over narration in Indian, translated into English. p. Judy
Susillo, Bernie Mitchell; UCLA.

NATHALIE (32m B 1970) (also Video) (French/Subtitled)
In the story of a single day of Nathalie's life is the story of a
child's confrontation with her own maturing. We follow the girl at
school, in the street, and on the subway. Unexpectedly, she is confused, suddenly aware of mute gazes of others. We see her at home,
misunderstood and in revolt. In the intimacy of her own room she
is alternately a little girl, or a young woman with an awakened body.
The film is a poetic and sensitive evocation of the pain and uncertainty of adolescence and the inner evolution from child to woman.
Awards. d. Anne Dastree; p. Filmex; FI.

NATHALIE KREBS (12m C n.d.)
Camera follows Nathalie Krebs, chemical engineer and creator of
unique stoneware glazes, in her workshop where the famous glazes
are mixed according to her own secret formulas. Magnificent close-
ups of glazed stoneware, reminiscent of the ancient Chinese ceramics,
but inspired by nature's own shapes and colors. AUDPLS.

NATHANIEL HAWTHORNE: LIGHT IN THE SHADOWS (23m C 1981)
(also Video)
Portrays Nathaniel Hawthorne's life. Shows every building of
significance in his life--from the Salem Athenaeum to the House of the
Seven Gables to the Old Manse. Accompanied by words from his jour-
nals and essays, spoken by either his "voice" or that of the narrator.
Several of his works are mentioned, including Scarlet Letter, The
House of the Seven Gables and many short stories. These themes
of Hawthorne are illustrated rather than tediously discussed. d.
Mary Norman; p. Unicorn Productions, Inc.; IFB.

NATIONAL CRIME AND VIOLENCE TEST: RAPE, THE (40m C 1982)
(also Video)
Hosts Art Linkletter and Jane Kennedy use a quiz format to bring
information about rapes. Through test questions and explanation of
the answers it is shown that a large percent of victims know their
attacker, that rapes occur most often in the victim's home, with the
rapist having entered by stealth or having been admitted by a trust-
ing person. Two women officers discuss the question of how, when,

and whether or not to fight an attacker, and what to do after having been raped. The myths about rape which have made women feel shame and guilt are dealt with and, it is noted, that rape is an act of violence and that victims may be of any age, attractive or unattractive, and that rapists come from many economic and educational levels. The narration stresses that rapes should be reported because rapists often repeat their crimes. p. Warren V. Bush Productions, Inc.; MTITI.

NATIONAL FISHERIES CENTER AND AQUARIUM (11m C 1967)
Shows the architecture of the new National Aquarium, something of what it contains and general philosophies and disciplines involved. p. Ray Eames, Charles Eames; PF.

NATURAL FAMILY PLANNING (22m C n.d.) (also Video)
Shows two midwives and two home births. "The supportive attitudes of the midwives and the father, the gentleness of the environment, the naturalness of it all, make the film work as a statement for natural birth and home birth."--Richard Chew, Film Editor. p. Cinema Medica; CINMD.

NATURAL HISTORY OF LOWER MANHATTAN, A; PTS. I, II (13hrs., 30m C si 1976-78) (S8)
Everyday for the past 15 years, the filmmaker has filmed scenes from her window and on the routes she travels frequently. PART 1 (A YEAR OF THE DAY/LIGHT) concerns itself with light: the geometry it creates and its salutary effect on mind and body. PART 2 (A YEAR: EVENING/NIGHT) records the real and imagined images found in the night. (Collective for Living Cinema, November 19, 1978.) p. Susan Harmett; COLIVC.

NATURE OF MILK, THE (10m C 1981)
Compares the animal kingdom's nursing habits to those of humans. The film encourages breast-feeding and stresses careful consideration of feeding whole cow's milk to infants. Free loan. d. Joseph Pipher; p. Linda Ingram Spalazzi; ROSLAB.

NATURE'S FOOD CHAIN (14m C p1978, r1979)
The hierarchical ordering of predator and prey in the natural environment. d. Marie-Paule Henot; p. NFBC; BENCHMF.

NATURE'S WAY (22m C 1975)
An old-time midwife in Appalachia delivers twins with confidence, warmth and efficiency in this beautiful and technically excellent film about home remedies, folk cures and midwifery. p. Elizabeth Barret; APPAL.

NAVAJOS AND ANNIE WAUNEKA, THE (30m B 1965) Twentieth Century Series
Documents the work of Mrs. Annie B. Wauneka, who was awarded

the Freedom Medal by President John F. Kennedy for her achievements in public health education among her fellow Navajo Indians.
Follows Wauneka as she visits the scattered homes of her people, instructing them in simple health measures. CBS News; AF.

NEAR AND FAR AWAY (90m C 1978) (Swedish/Subtitled)
     A young woman starts working as an attendant at a mental hos-
pital and soon becomes deeply involved in the fate of a young mental
patient--a mute. She is also confronted by two doctors having ut-
terly disparate views of psychiatry. To one, she is merely a scientific case, while the other attempts to understand the human being
involved. d. Marianne Ahrne; s.w. M. Ahrne, Bertrand Hurault;
p. Swedish Film Institute; ALMI.

NEIL AND BETSY (27m C 1979)
     This is a story of Neil, who has cerebral palsy; his parents; and
Betsy, an able-bodied woman. Neil remembers the rehabilitation center where he was told to forget all about women and all about sex.
Neil's parents reveal their anxiety and anguish as they confront the
guilt and fears they experienced as parents. Years later, Neil met
Betsy who says, "I've always been attracted to extroverted people
who are really positive and optimistic." Neil and Betsy were married
in 1976. They view marriage as "a haven where each can reveal secrets and grow independently." p. University of California, Davis;
UCDAV.

NELLI KIM (29m C p1979, r1980--U.S.)
     Presents Nelli Kim's participation in the 1976 Montreal Summer
Olympics, where she won two gold medals for the U.S.S.R. gymnastic
team. The pressures of Olympic competition and the discipline required to participate in world-class events are explored in this personal portrait. p. Jacques Bobet; d. George Dufaux; NFBC; MACMFL.

NELLIE BLY (97m C 1979)
     Tells of the exciting adventure of the first woman newspaper re-
porter whose courage and nose for news made her a legend in her
own time. LUCERNE.

NELLIE'S PLAYHOUSE (14m C p1981, r1982)
     Provides an overview of Nellie Mae Rowe's art--her sculptures,
dolls and paintings. But it does more, capturing the high spirits
that moved her to create, a process she describes with animation and
humor as she tells of the spontaneity of her art and of her passion
"not for high things but for just junk." A moving examination not
only of an individual artist but of the joy of creation and the spirit's
triumph over adverse personal circumstances. Although Nellie says
she "had to go to work in the fields and so never had the chance to
be what I wanted--an artist," she became just that with her work
being featured in an important black folk art exhibit. d./p. Linda
Armstrong; SOFOLK.

NERMISH GOTHIC (9m B 1980)
A woman sits alone in a dramatically lit room, looking like one of those odd, self-absorbed heroines of a 1930's surrealist film. She adjusts her gloves. Her gloves adjust themselves. Her clothing twitches around on its own. Suddenly, into the room bursts an assortment of strange, cone-shaped glowing creatures, one of them trailing an extension cord. The Nermishes have arrived. Using stop-motion photography, Janice Findley has created a luminous and dream-like world that is sure to entertain and amuse almost everyone. p. Janice Findley; NWMP.

NEVELSON IN PROCESS (30m C 1977) The Originals: Women in Art Series
Insightful biographical portrait of sculptor Louise Nevelson; captures her charisma and iconoclasm and shows how she transforms discarded wood and other unlikely materials into an innovative "environmental" art. d. Jill Godmilow and Susan Fanshel; p. WNET-TV; FI; PAS, UCEMC, UMO.

NEW AGE COMMUNITIES: THE SEARCH FOR UTOPIA (40m C r1978)
Humankind's dream of living in harmony with the rest of humanity is as old as memory itself. In some ages there has been a flowering of this search for utopia and the present era is one of them. From Scotland to India, Virginia to California ... Twin Oaks, Koinonia, the Farm, Ananda, Finhorn ... we see functioning, practical attempts at the utopian life, both secular and spiritual. We hear what brings them there and what holds them together--the economic, philosophical and spiritual beliefs that are the building blocks of new models for a better life. p. Elda Hartley; HARTLEY.

NEW AGE FOR THE OLD, A (27m C p1979, r1980)
Traces the social, cultural, economic, and political influences that have determined attitudes toward the old from classical times to the present. In Greek and Roman times life expectancy was 30 years, while today that has expanded to 70 years. In Puritan England, the old were venerated for their wisdom and experience. Then, for a short time old and young were thought of equally, before the emphasis began to focus on youth. By the late eighteenth century, contempt and scorn for the elderly replaced respect. Maggie Kuhn, founder of the Gray Panthers, an aged-rights group, emphasizes the need to develop a mutual respect between youth and aged members of society. p. Dan Klugherz; s.w. D. Klugherz, Arthur Zitrin; ALTANA.

NEW ALCHEMISTS, THE (28m C 1975)
Near Falmouth, Massachusetts, a small group of young scientists and their families are successfully working an experimental plant and fish farm using only organic fertilizers in an efficient self-contained ecosystem with solar heat and windmill for energy. Nothing is wasted and all is provided naturally. d. Dorothy Todd Henaut; p. Colin Low, Len Chatwin; NFBC; BENCHMF; CWU, UCEMC, UIL, UM.

NEW AMERICAN WOMAN, THE (B n.d.) (SFS)
   A look backward at the American woman's place in history and a
look forward to her long-range objectives. p. Educational Enrichment
Materials; EDENM.

NEW BABY, THE (20m C 1963)
   An overview film that visits a home where a third child is expected.
It shows the family preparing for the baby's arrival, with emphasis
on the mother's prenatal medical supervision. After the birth, the
film centers on the baby, his emotional needs and his daily care.
Also shown is the way parents anticipate and cope with the reactions
of the two older children to the new arrival. NFBC; STEREF.

NEW BEGINNINGS: WOMEN, ALCOHOL AND RECOVERY (21m C 1977)
   Presents case studies of three women who have successfully overcome alcoholism. Features Dona-Marie, a young woman recovering
from alcohol and drug abuse; Chaney, author of I'm Black and I'm
Sober; and Muriel, a career woman and grandmother. Emphasizes
the importance of a total commitment to healing aimed at earlier awareness, identification, and effective treatment for women. AIMS; IU.

NEW CONCEPTS IN HOUSING FOR OLDER ADULT SERIES (C 1978)
   This series takes a close look at the housing needs of the elderly
and offers some innovative and well-considered solutions. Host:
Marie McGuire Thompson, consultant. International Institute of Social Gerontology. Consultant: Dr. Wilma Donahue. Director: International Institute of Social Gerontology. UMMRC; UM.

   1. ASSISTED RESIDENTIAL LIVING--A FORM OF CONGREGATE
      HOUSING (14m)
   Congregate housing makes economic sense and enables older adults
to live with dignity and privacy, yet receive the help that the frail,
but not ill, need. Facilities examined include communal dining areas
and personal and housekeeping services.

   2. DESIGN MUST BE HUMAN, THE (18m)
   The necessary planning and design needed in providing housing
for older adults. High vs. low rise housing, important facilities (such
as mail and laundry rooms) and interior and exterior design considerations are covered.

   3. FINANCING (21m)
   Various methods of financing housing for the elderly. Sponsor-
ship, sources of capital, how to apply for loans. Industrial Revenue
Bonds, costs, and consumer tips are reviewed.

   4. ARCHITECT'S VISION, AN (22m)
   Shot on location at an award-winning housing project, this program discusses how to choose an architect, fees charged, the economics of using an architect, and architectural principles to be

considered in designing housing for older adults. William Kessler, a nationally known architect, is interviewed at the housing unit.

NEW DANCE--RECORD FILM (30m C 1978)
    A Doris Humphrey classic of modern dance, choreographed in 1953. This is a record film (single fixed camera) of the 1972 reconstruction as performed by the professional Repertory Company at the American Dance Festival at Connecticut College. Choreographers: Doris Humphrey, Charles Weidman; DAN/UR.

NEW DIRECTION IN DANCE, A (58m C 1978)
    Seventeen men and women, members of the Barbara Mettler Dance Company, demonstrate dance as a language of movement and an expression of group feeling. Dance Company: Barbara Mettler Dance Company; Dance Teacher/Narrator/Director: Barbara Mettler; p. Mettler Studios; METTLER.

NEW HARMONY: AN EXAMPLE AND A BEACON (29m C 1971)
    Traces the history and significance of New Harmony, Indiana, from its communal origins--first as a settlement in 1814 by German religious refugees led by George Rapp, and then replaced by Robert Owen's attempt in 1825 to establish a model socialist society--to its contemporary renaissance as a historic landmark. Members of the Harmony Society (Rappites) held property in common, practiced celibacy, and prepared themselves for the second coming of Christ. When the Harmonists moved to Pennsylvania, they sold the community's holdings to Owen, who recruited freedom educators in an effort to create a new social environment emphasizing intellectual freedom. Although Owen's experiment did not meet his expectations, many of his group remained in New Harmony making valuable contributions to the Midwest and the nation. NET; IU.

NEW IMAGE FOR BLACK WOMEN (29m C 1976) (Video) Woman Series
    Marcia Ann Gillespie, editor-in-chief of Essence, discusses the new directions her magazine has taken, her philosophy of women's magazines in general and her views of the relations between blacks and whites in American society. She explains why she changed the emphasis of Essence from high fashion to service and talks about her attempts to enhance the black woman's image of herself and to encourage more awareness of a woman's power as a consumer, family member, employee and citizen. Sandra Elkin is the moderator. PBSV.

NEW IMAGE FOR NURSES, PART I (29m C 1976) (Video) Woman Series
    Dr. June Rothberg, Dean of the School of Nursing at Adelphi University; Dr. Jean Spero, Dean of the School of Nursing at the State University of New York in Buffalo; and Dr. Jo Ann Ashley, author of Hospitals, Paternalism and the Role of the Nurse, discuss the struggle of nurses to attain professional recognition. They explain the historical role of nurses and the re-socialization that is

currently taking place. Sandra Elkin is the moderator. p. WNED-
TV; PBSV.

NEW IMAGE FOR NURSES, PART II (29m C 1976) (Video) Woman
    Series
    Dr. June Rothberg, Dean of the School of Nursing at Adelphi
University; Dr. Jean Spero, Dean of the School of Nursing at the
State University of New York in Buffalo; and Dr. Jo Ann Ashley,
author of Hospitals, Paternalism and the Role of the Nurse, discuss
efforts to provide a political voice for nurses. They explain the work
of the Nurses Coalition for Action in Politics--a group formed by Dr.
Rothberg and others to organize nurses and raise their awareness of
the potential for the nursing profession. Sandra Elkin is the moderator. p. WNED-TV; PBSV.

NEW KLAN: HERITAGE OF HATE, THE (58m C p1977, r1978)
    A startling portrait of a movement within the Ku Klux Klan which
is bent on bringing the Klan into the mainstream of American politics.
Focuses on David Duke, the movement's spokesman, and his goal of
bringing the Klan to a greater national visibility through sophisticated
media techniques. d. Eleanor Bingham; p. Leslie Shatz; CORINTH.

NEW MAID, THE (35m C p1980, r1981) (also Video)
    Dramatizes the problems faced by a young boy when his mother
returns to work and hires a maid to care for him and his brother.
Maria, a Guatemalan woman, comes to work as a maid for the McGrath
family. The tension between employer and maid increases when Maria's friendship with the youngest boy, Joey, deepens. Conflict
boils over when Mrs. McGrath is unable to treat Maria well. Film
promotes talk about family and values. d./s.w. Christine Burrill;
p. Randi Johnson; p. American Film Institution Productions; BURRILL;
LCA.

NEW OPIUM ROUTE, THE (54m C 1973)
    A remarkable study of a society that is seldom observed and little
understood. This is the story of the Pashtus, who have lived for
centuries in the wild regions of the Khyber Pass, on the border between Afghanistan and Pakistan. Since the days of the British Empire, they have had complete control over their own affairs, and no
government has ever dared to change their autonomous status. Shows
the daily lives of these people: growing and harvesting poppies,
making weapons, working for professional smugglers, etc. p. Catherine and Marianne Lamour; ICARF.

NEW RELATIONS: A FILM ABOUT FATHERS AND SONS (34m C 1980)
    As his son's first birthday approaches, the filmmaker explores
the costs--both economic and emotional--as well as the rewards of
having decided to become a father in his mid-thirties, and of choosing
to share childcare responsibilities equally with his wife, who also has
a career. He and his wife share a frank discussion of some of the
conflicts that have arisen between them since the birth of their child.

With his own father, the filmmaker reflects on differences in fathering styles between the two generations. This unusually sensitive
film realistically confronts many of the problems facing parents today:
changing sex roles and parenting styles, new images of masculinity,
childcare options and alternatives, conflicts between work and family
roles. It is honest about the problems, but concludes with a positive
message about this couple's decision to become parents. p./d. Ben
Achtenberg; PLAINSG; UMN.

NEW ROLES FOR WOMEN IN SPORTS (29m C 1977) Woman Series
    Author and athlete Lynda Huey (A Running Start) and women's
sports instructor Jane Fishman discuss the changing roles of women
in athletics. They talk about the traditional attitudes of women toward sports and describe historical conditions that have been responsible for them. Sandra Elkin is the moderator. p. WNED-TV; PBSV.

NEW SEXUALITY, THE (26m C 1981) (Video)
    Nude encounter groups, bisexuality, open marriages--all unmen-
tionable a generation ago--are now discussed and experienced openly.
This sensitive exploration of changing attitudes, especially in urban
areas, deals not only with the outward expressions of the new sexuality, but also with possible causes: sex in media, the women's
liberation movement, and others. People involved in alternative life-
styles talk frankly about their activities and personal relationships:
behavior experts discuss sex therapy, surrogate sex, and counseling.
The focus is on the effect changing patterns of sexual behavior have
on individuals and society. FI, KENTSU.

NEW YORK HAT, THE (10m B 1912)
    Mary Pickford's last film for Biograph, written by 16-year-old
Anita Loos, co-starring Lionel Barrymore and Charles Hill Mailes.
Young village minister becomes object of scandalous gossip when he
purchases an expensive New York hat for a pretty but poor young
girl at request of her dying mother. d. D. W. Griffith. p. Eastin-
Phelan Corporation; PAS.

NEWBORN (26m C 1972)
    Unique documentary on the beginning of life, helping to give new
and future parents confidence through understanding. Covers the
first three months of life and the dynamic process by which the baby
develops into a separate, original being. Free loan. p. Johnson and
Johnson Baby Products; MTPS; PAS, UMN, UM.

NEWBORN: READY FOR LIFE (28m C 1977)
    Beginning with a natural childbirth sequence and the first tender
moments of mother and child, the film captures the beauty and wonder
of newborns. Dispels notions of infant helplessness, showing the
child's highly developed responses to light, sound and taste. Shows
that reflexes used later for crawling, walking and exploring the environment are already present at birth. Makes a strong appeal for

allowing mothers and babies to be together in the first hours after birth. Features the neonatal research of Dr. Barry Brazelton, Dr. Lewis Lipsitt, Dr. Louis Sanders and Dr. Klaus Minde. CBC; FILMLB; IU, UCLA, UIL.

NEWTON'S EQUAL AREAS (8m C 1968) (also Video)
Animation is used to show how only forces which act on the bodies are short powerful blows. The early sequences develop Newton's laws without naming them. The heart of the film is Newton's proof, from Principia, that if all of the forces on the body act toward a fixed point, the line connecting the moving body and that point sweeps out equal areas in equal times. Elementary geometry is used to obtain the point. p. Katharine Cornwell, Bruce Cornwell; IFB.

NEWTON's METHOD (3m C n.d.)
An introduction to differential calculus. p. Ray Eames, Charles Eames; PF.

NEXT YEAR COUNTRY (57m C 1981)
The rush to develop the vast mineral and energy resources of the West is changing the face of the region--and the lives of the people who live there. Large-scale industrialization of the West conflicts with the long-established, rural, agricultural way of life and the environmental concerns long identified with the region. d. Beth Farris; AXLTRE.

NIAMBI, SWEET MELODY (25m C 1980) (also Video)
A strong sense of heritage and family warmth is present in this story of Niambi Robinson, a little black girl who at the age of five broke the world's record in her age group for the 100-meter dash. Not only the story of a remarkable young athlete, the film explores the values and constant nurturing of a loving family. Niambi is seen at school, at ballet class, on the track, and at home. Her parents speak of their commitment to active family involvement in school, athletics, and cultural activities. p. Carol Rosenbaum; FI.

NICHOLAS AND THE BABY (23m C p1980, r1981) (also Video)
Nicholas, a four-year-old child, is expecting a birth in his family. Through his perspective, the film follows the family through the stages of pregnancy, labor, birth and bringing home the newborn. Includes an animated sequence depicting fetal development and is scored with original music created by the Carl Orff Schulwerk Society. Designed to prepare children for involvement in the prenatal experience as well as to acquaint them with the sights and sounds of birth. d./p. Victress Hitchcock; p. P. J. Vest, R. Elias; CENTRE; UM.

NICHOLAS COPERNICUS (10m C 1973)
A visual essay showing the environment in which Nicholas Copernicus, founder of modern astronomy, lived and worked. The viewer

travels with Copernicus as he moves from city to city during his lifetime. Provides the viewer with a real sensitivity to the life of Copernicus. d. Ray Eames, Charles Eames; PF.

NIGENDL--A JEWISH FAMILY PORTRAIT (10m C 1976)
Begins with a still of 13 dancers in a picture frame. As they are mentioned in the song accompaniment they step out of the picture frame and dance (grandparents, mother and father, bride and groom, rabbi and children). Choreographer/Director: Edith Segal; NIGENDL.

NIGHT BEFORE: THE MORNING AFTER, THE (14m C p1979, r1979)
A depiction of the humor and futility of the modern day phenomenon, the "one night stand," as seen from the woman's point of view. In the dim, night light of her bedroom, a man and woman fumble, psychologically, in a hurried attempt to achieve immediate intimacy. Then, in the cold light of morning they part, neither having gained a lasting relationship. d. Barry Healey; p. Phillip G. Borsos; MERCURY.

... NIGHT FULL OF RAIN (104m C 1978)
This, Lina Wertmuller's first English language film, couches humankind's oldest conflict--the battle between the sexes--in Marxist and feminist terms. Married for ten years, Giancarlo Giannini and Candice Bergen are in constant conflict. He's a Communist chauvinist who likes his shirts hand-laundered, while she is a feminist photographer who feuds with him in flashback against a chorus of friends straight out of Wertmuller's previous association with Fellini. The complete title is "The End of the World in Our Usual Bed in a Night Full of Rain." d./s.w. Lina Wertmuller; FI, TWY.

NIGUN (9m C 1977)
Uses the story of a primordial couple and the birth of their child as the vehicle for the retelling of a myth. The couple is portrayed as a composite of races and cultures, and their pains, joy and bewilderments as part of the universal experience set to soundtrack by Harry Partch. Uses some 2,500 separate watercolor paintings. p. Andrea Gomez; SERBC.

NIKKOLINA (27m C p1977, r1978)
Nikkolina is dismayed when her old-world aunt arrives from Greece for a wedding, and her dismay turns to anger when she realizes the wedding conflicts with an important skating competition she had planned to enter. Nikkolina, however, decides to give up her competition for the sake of the family occasion. Later, she has a second chance at the competition where she combines the newly-learned Greek dance with her figure-skating in a climactic winning performance. p./d. Rebecca Yates, Glen Salzman; LCA.

NINE MONTHS (93m C 1977) (Hungarian/Subtitled)
A story of love affair between a strong-willed young woman and an

impulsive, often arbitrary fellow-worker in a chilly industrial city. Director Marta Meszaros' feeling for environment--stunning factory-scapes of snow and smoke--is matched by her sensitivity to the sensual chemistry and emotional ups-and-downs of the central relationship. Her style leans heavily toward close-ups, and hands and faces are used with an expressiveness and intensity rarely encountered in the cinema since the films of Carl Dreyer. d. Marta Meszaros; NYF.

NINE MONTHS IN MOTION (19m C p1977, r1977)
Shows that expectant mothers can greatly benefit both physically and mentally from exercising. Key exercises that will benefit expectant mothers are clearly demonstrated. d./p. Patty Moore; PEREN.

9 TO 5 (110m C 1980)
Taking on the giant Consolidated Corporation in general and their despicable boss Frank Hart, Jr. in particular, the three modern musketeers (Jane Fonda, Lily Tomlin, and Dolly Parton)--abused and harassed secretaries all--decide to make their secret fantasies come true: they're going to get rid of their chauvinistic superior. With endless creativity the trio considers different schemes to accomplish their deeds. One of the funniest, biting and entertaining comedies. d. Colin Higgins; FOX; FI.

NINE VARIATIONS ON A DANCE THEME (13m B 1966)
A modern dancer performs a simple set of dance movements in a bare room. The performance is filmed and edited in nine different ways and is accompanied by nine musical variations. p. Hilary Harris; UPSTF.

1981 WOMEN'S ALL-AMERICA BASKETBALL TEAM (17½m C 1981)
Highlights the outstanding college women basketball players selected annually by the Association of Intercollegiate Athletics for Women. Shows Lynette Woodard from Kansas (who has been selected for the team four years in a row), Denise Curry of U.C.L.A., and Pam Kelly of Louisiana Tech. Free loan. p. Eastman Kodak Company; EASTK.

NO APPLE FOR JOHNNY (9m C n.d.)
This documentary cartoon is the visual enactment of the year-long obstacle course run by a teacher trainee. Rich in humor and anecdote, it is a comedy of educational manners seen through the autobiographical eye of the trainee-turned-filmmaker. d. John Weldon; p. Dorothy Courtois, Wolf Koenig; NFBC.

NO CRYSTAL STAIR (12m C 1975) (Video)
Montage of black music, dance, poetry and images on black creativity in the United States from 1900 to 1950. Features the poetry of Langston Hughes, the voices of Dr. Martin Luther King, Jr. and Ossie Davis, and performance by the Marla Blakey Dancers. p. Ithaca College; ITHACA.

NO EXCEPTIONS (24m C 1977)
Provides suggestions for attempting to avoid rape from happening.
Illustrates effective methods which can prevent rape, and what to do
if rape should occur. Concludes by stressing that prevention is the
best course, and that a well-informed, prepared woman is her own
best guardian. d. Thom Eberhardt; p. Jeanette Stirdivant, Christine
Vasques; s.w. Debbie Edwards; FLMFR; UIL, IU.

NO EXCUSE, SIR (53m C p1979-80, r1981) (also Video)
Examines the role that the United States Military Academy at
West Point plays in our national defense. Traces the history and
looks into the current goals and expectations of the Academy. Interviews with cadets, professors and officers trained at West Point
are played off against critics of the Academy. In its 178th year,
cadet life goes on amidst the timeless setting of the Hudson River
Highlands. d./p. Sonja Gilligan/Mike Gilligan; p. KERA-TV; HUDRFV.

NO FITTING HABITAT (29m C p1980, r1980)
The story of the city: its origins, its development and the factors that have contributed to its growth and style. Beginning with
human evolution from nomadism, the film continues right up to our
contemporary urban problems and their possible solutions. d. Tina
Viljoen; p. NFBC; TEXFM.

NO MORE SECRETS (15m C 1981)
Presents sexual abuse within the family from the child's point of
view. An afternoon of play provides the backdrop for four good
friends to talk about sexual problems they have with adults in their
families. Animated vignettes depict the problems while the children
speculate about solutions. Each vignette finishes with a comfortable
sense of resolution. The film is a catalyst for discussion among children, and a tool for professional use in identifying and preventing
incest-related problems. Film Guide contains prevention strategies.
d. Peter Barton; p. Oralee Wachter; ODNPRO.

NO PLACE LIKE HOME (60m C 1982) (Video, Beta, VHS)
Traces the origins and development of nursing homes in America
--from the almshouses of the 1800's to the more than 18,000 institutions that today constitute a 21 billion dollar industry. It also examines some desirable alternatives. Helen Hayes, who recently celebrated her 81st birthday is narrator as she travels throughout the
United States reporting on nursing homes and a range of alternative
approaches to long-term care for the aged, including home care, day
care and congregate living. p. WNET-TV; FI.

NOBODY'S VICTIM II (24m C 1978)
Presents a positive approach to women's self-protection as well
as the latest expert advice on preparedness and personal responsibility. The film is divided into three parts: Part 1 deals with crimes
of opportunity. Part 2 analyzes confrontation. Part 3 discusses rape

and ways of handling rape. The importance of remaining as calm
as possible is stressed. If rape does occur, specific instructions as
to the dos and don'ts until after the crime is reported are outlined.
A good discussion film. d. Alan Barker; p. Vaughn Obern; RAMFLM;
BUDGET, CWU.

NOEL'S LEMONADE STAND (8m C 1981) (also Video)
Illustrates in animation one of the Swahili "Seven Principles," or
the principle of "Ujamaa"--cooperation in order to profit together in
business. p. Carol Munday Lawrence, p. Nguzo Saba Films; BEACON.

NON-VERBAL GROUP PROCESS IN DANCE THERAPY SESSIONS (30m
    B 1977) (Video)
Includes three different dance therapy sessions at an adult psychiatric facility. The first session focuses on the interaction process
in movement. The second session focuses on the enlargement of movement repertoire with particular attention to one chronic schizophrenic
patient; and the third session illustrates the structure and development of an entire dance therapy session in a ward setting. Produced
at the Bronx Psychiatric Center, New York City. Available only to
professional audiences connected with the field of mental health and
mental health education. p. Miriam Roskin Berger, Bonnie Eggena;
NYSBPC.

NORA EPHRON ON EVERYTHING (29m C 1976) (Video) Woman Series
Journalist and author Nora Ephron (Crazy Salad) comments on
a number of issues surrounding the women's movement: that it lacks
a sense of humor; what it has and has not accomplished; whether it
can survive close scrutiny; and the need for women to take responsibility for their own lives. Sandra Elkin is the moderator. p.
WNED-TV; PBSV.

NORMA RAE (115m C 1979) (Reg./Scope)
Sally Fields portrays a courageous textile worker who fights for
the right to better conditions and unionize the mill in which she works.
Although most workers would like to see better working conditions,
they are reluctant to join the union because of well-founded fears of
management reprisal. But once Fields decided to join the cause, the
more pressure exerted against her by the management, the tougher
and more determined she became. An indelible portrait of an unforgettable woman. d. Martin Ritt; p. Tamara Asseyev, Alex Rose;
FOX; FI.

NORTH INDIAN VILLAGE (32m C 1958) (also Video)
The village of Khalapur has many features which have changed
little over the centuries. The relationships between men and women,
the hereditary occupations of castes, and forms of worship and ceremony are explored in this film. p. Patricia Hitchcock, John Hitchcock;
IFB.

NORTH STAR, THE (106m B 1943)
A powerful drama about an idyllic Russian village overrun by the German army during World War II. In advance of the assault, the men of the village retreat to the hills to form a guerrilla brigade, leaving the women, children, and elders at the mercy of the invaders. The New York Times praised this film as a "tribute to the tenacity and courage" of those who resisted the Fascists, yet this film was one for which writer Lilliam Hellman and others were attacked politically less than a decade later. Starring Anne Baxter, Dana Andrews, Erich von Stroheim, d. Lewis Milestone; s.w. Lillian Hellman; p. Goldwyn; FI.

NORTH WIND AND THE SUN: A FABLE BY AESOP, THE (3m C n.d.)
An animated ancient Greek fable in which the warm sun proves to the cold wind that persuasion is better than force when it comes to making a man take off his overcoat. d. Rhoda Leyer, Les Drew; p. Robert Verrall; NFBC.

NORTHERN IRISH PEOPLE'S PEACE MOVEMENT, PART I (29m C 1977)
(Video) Woman Series
Betty Williams and Mairead Corrigan, leaders of the woman's peace movement in Northern Ireland, explain the purpose of the nonsectarian and nonpartisan People's Peace Party they founded after three Belfast children were killed during a gun battle between Irish Republican Army and British troops. They identify the terrorist groups and tell how the violence affects the everyday lives of people on both sides of the political question. Sandra Elkin is the moderator. p. WNED-TV; PBSV.

NORTHERN IRISH PEOPLE'S PEACE MOVEMENT, PART II (29m C
1977) (Video) Woman Series
Betty Williams and Mairead Corrigan, founders and leaders of the nonsectarian, nonpartisan People's Peace Party in Northern Ireland, discuss their goals for peace. They describe the source of support for prisoners' families, the state of Irish social life and the status of new Irish womanhood. They also read their "Declaration of the Peace People," a document recently introduced to the United Nations by delegate Connor Cruse O'Brien. Sandra Elkin is the moderator. p. WNED-TV; PBSV.

NORTHERN IRISH QUESTION: ANOTHER VIEW, THE (29m C 1977)
(Video) Woman Series
The Irish Republican movement's political plans for peace are discussed by Patricia Davidson, Press Officer for the Ulster Provisional Sinn Fein (a political wing of the Republic movement), and Mary Mc-Nicholl, Secretary of the United Brooklyn Irish. The women explain how funds contributed by Americans to the people of Northern Ireland are being used, their assessment of President Carter's concern about the deprivation of human rights, and the part they would like to play in resolving the Irish conflict. Sandra Elkin is the moderator. p. WNED-TV; PBSV.

NORTHWEST VISIONARIES (59m C 1979)
Focuses on the work of painters Mark Tobey, Kenneth Callahan, Morris Graves, Margaret Tomkins, Guy Anderson, Paul Horiuchi, Helmi Juvonen, and George Tsutakawa. Filmmaker Ken Levine has fashioned a historically informative yet contemporary documentary which broadly examines the regional characteristics of Northwest art from the 1930's to the near present. Weaving together statements from artists, patrons, and articulate members of the art community with historic footage and rare photographs, NORTHWEST VISIONARIES presents a highly personal account of the evolution of artists and their environment. p./d. Ken Levine; IRIS; WSU.

NOT A LOVE STORY: A FILM ABOUT PORNOGRAPHY (69m C 1981)
(also Video)
The world of explicit spectator sex is explored by the filmmaker. Through a combination of interviews and documentaries from a variety of sexually explicit presentations, she explores how participants and spectators feel about pornography. Presents a panorama of what is available today in most major cities. It also offers an examination of that variety in interviews with publishers, producers, photographers, actors and actresses, and observers. The point is made frequently that pornographic imagery is abusive of both male and female sexual identity. The explicit scenes may require previewing for acceptability for certain college and adult audiences. A shorter (29-minute) version and less explicit program is PORNOGRAPHY AND FANTASY (PBS VIDEO, 1972) NFBC.

NOT BY CHANCE (22m C n.d.)
Shows an unmedicated mother as she experiences the different phases of labor, the birth of her child, and the delivery of a placenta. The main purpose of the film is to show that even with a great deal of discomfort during labor if there's a good support for the mother, no pain medication is needed in the normal birth. Dr. Eisenstein describes each part with clinical commentary. p. Cinema Medica; CINMED.

NOT IN VAIN: A TRIBUTE TO MARTIN LUTHER KING, JR. (28m C 1982) (Video)
A dramatic interpretation of two of Dr. Martin Luther King, Jr.'s most significant speeches: "I've Been to the Mountaintop" and his "Eulogy." Both were delivered shortly before his assassination on April 4, 1968. The setting is a southern Baptist Church and gospel music is featured. The purpose is to preserve the spirit, words and philosophy of Dr. King. Reenacted by Portland School Board Chairman Herb Cawthorne. d. Doug Rice; p. Karen Lee Rice; KOIN-TV; KOINTV.

NOT MY PROBLEM (18m C 1979)
Explores the dilemmas and responsibilities of sexually active boys. Dave is the usual gregarious 16-year-old. Baseball, homework and

Susan, his current love, take most of his time. When Susan suspects she is pregnant, he felt at first that it was not his problem until one of Dave's buddies convinces him that it is his problem--his and Susan's. Confronted by Susan at the ball field the reality of the situation suddenly becomes clear. They have some very important decisions to make together. Openended. p. Ann Vracin, Dan Bessie; BARRF; UIL.

NOT ONE OF THE CROWD: DAVID LINCOLN (29m C 1981) (Video)
David Lincoln is President of People First, an organization of mentally retarded individuals who are seeking to be regarded as people in their own right. David, a charismatic leader, is introduced at People First's first provincial conference, where members talk about issues such as labelling, sterilization and institutionalization as they have been affected by them, and about their desire to be a part of the wider community. d. Phil Desjardins; p. Babs Church; p. TV Ontario Marketing, Canada; TVONT.

NOT ONLY STRANGERS (23m C p1980, r1980)
Tells the story of Sarah, a rather plain college co-ed who is brutally raped by a classmate. Presents a realistic portrayal of Sarah's emotional shock, revulsion, guilt and ultimate anger, and of the painful but necessary process leading up to the filing of criminal charges. d. Edward Dmytryk; p. Not Only Strangers Company; CENTEF; IU, KENTSU, PSU, WSU.

NOT RECONCILED (51m B 1965)
Lengthy Boll novel of Nazism's effects on three generations severely condensed and paradoxically expanded--a turning point in modern cinema. d. Jean-Marie Straub; NYF.

NOTHING BUT THE BEST (43m C 1982) (also Video)
Stating the goal of Ort Schools all over the world, this film focuses on Latin America and the creative education Ort offers Jewish children. Black and white pictures and the narration tell the history of Jews in Brazil with their first organized community formed in 1630. Ort schools help Jewish children have a sense of who they are by knowing their roots. A Harold Mayer Production; p. Lynn Rhodes Mayer, Harold Mayer. Presented by Women's American Ort, Israel; ALDEN.

NOTRE JEUNESSE EN AUTO-SPORT (OUR SPORTS CAR DAYS) (3m C n.d.)
Here the motor itself becomes animated with the pulse and passion of wheeled competition and of love. Words and music by Christian Larsen, Claude Gauthier. d. Viviane Elnecave; NFBC.

NOVA SERIES see ARE YOU DOING THIS FOR ME, DOCTOR, OR AM I DOING IT FOR YOU?; ARTISTS IN THE LAB; FINDING A VOICE; MALADY OF HEALTH CARE, THE; MEMORIES FROM

EDEN; MIND MACHINES, THE; PINKS AND THE BLUES, THE; TEST TUBE BABIES; WOMAN REBEL, THE

NOVEMBER 1977 (3m C 1978)

Crayon drawings with a childlike simplicity engagingly record a month with reference to a birthday, Thanksgiving, and adolescent romance. p. Susan Rubin; SERBC.

NOW THAT YOU'RE POSTPARTUM (21m C 1980)

Explains the physical changes a new mother faces after the birth of her baby. Fatigue, vaginal flow, hair loss, care of episiotomy and hemorrhoids, contraception and resuming sexual relations, the importance of outside help and support, all are discussed. Also explains the need for emotional closeness during this time of greater dependency. Suggests ways of achieving better communication and building a stronger, closer relationship with one's partner. A class for new mothers being taught by Kris Leander at Group Health Cooperative Hospital in Seattle is shown in which questions of concern to a new mother are answered. The film follows one of the women in the class home with her four-day-old baby. The audience experiences first-hand those initial hours of caring for two older siblings as well as the newborn, all while a new mother is not yet fully recovered herself. A group of recent mothers discuss their experiences and feelings about the first weeks of mothering and offer valuable insights. p./d. Alvin Fiering; POLYMR.

NOWHERE TO RUN (20m C 1977)

A documentary on the vanishing American mustang. The first horse was brought to America by the early Spanish conquistadors; some of them escaped, banded together, multiplied, and large herds developed. The estimated two million horses in 1900 has been reduced to 40,000 in 1976. While some citizens' groups lobby for legislative action to protect the mustangs, ranchers want measures to reduce their numbers. Federal Bureau of Land Management catches hundreds each year and give them to people who will care for them. Those for which no homes are found are destroyed. The future outlook for the mustang is not bright, the fight to save them is an up-hill battle. p. Jeanne Rosenberg, Max Trumpower; d. J. Rosenberg; p. AJ/Max Film; PHOENIX.

NUCLEAR WATCHDOGS, THE (ed.) (13m C p1979, r1980)

This well-documented exposé reveals that unsafe practices are routine and widespread in the construction of nuclear reactors, endangering untold lives in the process. Interviews with individuals on both sides of this problem provide interesting comments and points of view. This is a disturbing look at a condition that has unthinkable consequences for now and for future generations. p. Esther Kartiganer, CBS News; CAROUF.

NUER, THE (75m C 1971)

Depicts, with minimum of narration, the harmony and rhythm of the present-day dry season life of the Nuer, a people native to Ethiopia and the Sudan. Shows them caring for their cattle and training their young warriors, and captures the subtle patterns of their collective interaction in work, play, and ritual. p. Robert Gardner, CRM; UCEMC, WSU, KENTSU.

NEUVA VIDA (NEW LIFE) (14m C 1980)
Expresses the feelings of two fathers as they discuss the pros and cons of their involvement in the birth process and the adjustments of the post-partum period. In Spanish with English transcript. p. Terry Looper; SERBC.

NUMBER OUR DAYS (29m C 1978) (also Video)
A moving portrait of a community of elderly Eastern European Jews sustaining their vivid culture in the face of poverty, loneliness and extreme old age, by the Pacific Ocean in Venice, California. Free loan from Pierce County (WA) Library. d./p. Lynne Littman; based on the field work of anthropologist, Dr. Barbara Myerhoff, p. Hackford/Littman; HACKLT; UMO.

NURSE, WHERE ARE YOU? (49m C 1981) (Video, Beta, VHS)
A revealing documentary about the critical shortage of hospital nurses and how they are overworked, underpaid and disillusioned. Fewer than half of the nations 1.4 million nurses stay in hospitals because they can't find better pay elsewhere, and hospital nurses often become disillusioned when they find they have little authority and awesome responsibilities--this sometimes leads to a conflict with doctors and interns. Also shown is an effort to unionize nurses at the University of Pennsylvania Hospital where they have been met with resistance from hospital administrators. Prospects for correcting the nursing shortage are uncertain unless hospital administrators respond to the needs of nurses. p./d. Judy Towers Reemtsma for CBS News with correspondent Marlene Sanders; ex. p. Howard Stringer; CAROUF; UCEMC, UIL, PAS.

NURSING HISTORY INTERVIEW WITH A RECENTLY SOBER ALCO-
   HOLIC WOMAN (50m C 1982) (Video)
Nada J. Estes, R.N.M.S., Associate Professor, Alcohol and Drug Abuse Nursing Program, University of Washington demonstrates the interview for the purpose of obtaining a history with a 25-year-old alcoholic woman. Explains the six major purposes of doing such a history, including verbalizing identity problems, determining if and how problems affect daily living activities, building trust and understanding. p. University of Washington Press; UW.

NURSING: THE POLITICS OF CARING (ed.) (22m C p1977, r1978)
   (also Video)
Explores the evolution of nurses' attitudes towards their work, their relationship with the medical profession, and their right to take an active role in the shaping of health care in America. A revealing

film that brings to the forefront major issues affecting health professionals and patients alike. p. Joan Finck, Timothy Sawyer in collaboration with Karen Wolf, R.N., Ilex Films; FANLTP.

NURTURING (17m C p1978, r1978)
Demonstrates the important role of the care-giver in infant de-
velopment and shows how babies can be gently encouraged to learn.
Stresses the importance of a free and stimulating environment as well
as the infant's need for emotional and verbal support. With Dr.
Bettye Caldwell. d. Roy Cox; p. Marc Krigbaum; DAVFMS; UCEMC.

NUTRIENTS AND NUTRIENT LABELING (8m C 1976)
Gives an overview of nutrition, showing that there is no single
most important nutrient and that all nutritional needs can be met with
a balanced diet. Includes tips on how to read and use nutritional
labeling charts. An excerpt from Food ene. p. WPSX-TV, The
Pennsylvania State University, Audio Visual Services; PAS.

NUTRITION AND DENTAL CARE IN PREGNANCY (29m B 1956) Months
    Before Birth--A Series
Discusses dietary needs for maintaining the mother's dental health
as well as for developing the baby's teeth. p. WQED-TV; AF.

NUTRITION AND FAD DIETS (29m C 1978) (Video) Daniel Foster, M.D.
    Series
Dr. Daniel Foster and his guest Dr. George F. Cahill, Jr., Professor of Internal Medicine at Harvard University, discuss controversial questions surrounding nutrition and fad diets. They examine
synthetic proteins sold for weight control and the nutritional value of
the so-called "fast foods" and "natural foods." Dr. Cahill talks about
the reasons for current concern over cancer-causing foods and emphasis on adequate vitamin supplies. p. KERA-TV; PBSV.

NUTRITION EDUCATION SERIES see HELP YOURSELF TO BETTER
    HEALTH

NUTRITION FOR SPORTS: FACTS AND FALLACIES (20m C 1981)
Provides answers to questions commonly asked by athletes and
others interested in nutrition for active people. Misconceptions are
dispelled and rational nutritional guidelines for athletes are communicated. Explains in a question-and-answer format general diet and
carbohydrate loading, proteins, water intake and dehydration, caloric
requirements, weight control, and supplementing vitamins and other
nutrients. The points are made by athletes themselves and nutritionists through the use of narration and visual displays. The educational messages are interspersed with good action shots of athletic
competitions. d. Stephen Wallen; HIGGIN.

NUTRITION IN AGING (42m C 1978) (Video) Introductory Principles
    of Nutrition Series
Examines physical and physiological factors influencing food

choices and nutrient utilization by the elderly. p. The Pennsylvania State Univeristy, Audio Visual Services; PAS.

NUTRITION IN INFANCY (50m C 1977) (Video) Introductory Principles of Nutrition Series
A comparison of human's and cow's milk, the introduction of the infant to solid foods, nutritional considerations during childhood, food likes and dislikes, and establishment of food habits. p. The Pennsylvania State University, Audio-Visual Services; PAS.

NUTRITION IN PREGNANCY (60m C 1977) (Video) Introductory Principles of Nutrition Series
Examines nutrition as one factor influencing the outcome of pregnancy, including physiological adjustments, stages of fetal growth, nutrient needs, pregnancy during adolescence, physiological and psychological aspects of lactation, and interviews with nutrition experts. p. The Pennsylvania State University, Audio Visual Services; PAS.

NUTRITION IN PREGNANCY (24m C n.d.)
Dr. Tom Brewer, a nationally recognized authority on nutrition, tells couples how to eat well. Emphasis is placed on simplicity. Questions are answered as to how much weight to gain, what to include in the daily meals, and the importance of this to the developing baby. Nutrition more than any other factor dictates a healthy outcome to pregnancy. p. Cinema Medica; CINMD.

NUTRITION: THE ALL-AMERICAN MEAL (11m C 1976)
Combines on-the-street interviews, lively kinestasis, and sequences at the local fast food emporium, with a meaningful analysis of the nutritional and sociological implications of our fast food culture. As hamburgers, fries, and soft drinks are prepared, the nutritional value of the "All-American Meal" is discussed along with suggestions for improvement. States that very real problems of the "quick meal" are loss of variety in the diet, too much fat and too many calories, and the loss of leisurely companionship at the dinner table. p. William Crain; BARRF; UIL.

NUTRITION: THE CONSUMER AND THE SUPERMARKET (15m C 1976)
The maze of food items offered in our supermarkets creates for the buyer a problem of gigantic proportions--how do we know what to buy? Using consumer interviews and visual analysis of the products and merchandising techniques in the supermarkets, this film will help the shopper to select the best nutritional value for her/his dollar. It provides an in-depth consideration of the basic food groups available, the role of advertising that influences our buying decision, and special tips on getting the maximum nutritional value at the lowest possible cost. p. William Crain; BARRF; UIL.

NUTRITION: THE INNER ENVIRONMENT (17m C 1973)
Shows that good eating makes good sense, and emphasizes the

fact that eating habits influence physical and mental fitness. An animated sequence illustrates the process of digestion. Pictures results of a diet lacking in essential nutrients--tiredness, restlessness, inability to concentrate, poor posture and improper growth. Concludes with a picnic as teenagers, who earlier selected good foods in the supermarket, now share them at the beach. Narrated by Rafer Johnson (U.S.A. Olympic Gold Medal Winner). p. American Educational Films; AMEDF; UIL.

NUTRITION: WHAT'S IN IT FORM ME? (26m C r1976)
Factors that affect our physical and emotional well-being when we eat. Many health problems can be prevented by knowledge of body's basic nutritional needs. Consumer concerns for getting true value for the food we purchase and eat. p. Macmillan Films, Inc.; DOCUA; PAS, KENTSU.

- O -

O YOUTH AND BEAUTY (60m C 1979) (also Video)
Introduces one of Cheever's favorite themes, the American male's fear of losing his identity and social equilibrium. The fact that he is no longer young frustrates middle-aged executive Cash Bentley (Michael Murphy) to the point that he attempts to recapture the glories of his college years, attempting to demonstrate his athletic prowess by hurdling the living room furniture. The results are dire! p. Ann Blumenthal, Peter Weinberg; d. Jeff Bleckner; p. WNET-TV; FI.

OBESITY (8m C 1976)
Explores the reasons for obesity and the idea of energy balance (the relationship between the number of calories eaten and the number of calories spent for energy). An excerpt from Food ene. p. WPSX-TV; PAS.

OBESITY (60m C 1980) (Video) Better Health (Series)
Dr. Lester B. Salans, Associate Director of the National Institute of Arthritis, Metabolism and Digestive Diseases, explains our energy metabolism. We find out that too much food and lack of exercise results in an expanded waistline, and learn how this affects our health. A question and answer session is included in the program. Free loan. p. National Institute of Health; AF.

OBSTETRICAL INTERVENTION (43m C n.d.) (also Video)
Conference report of American Foundation for Maternal and Child Health by Dr. Roberto Caldeyro-Garcia. Film is scientifically oriented. Excellent for medical schools, nursing schools, in-service workshops. p. Cinema Medica; CINMD.

OCCUPANT IN THE SINGLE ROOM, THE (21m C 1974)
Explains that more than 200,000 elderly people are living a grim

existence in New York City on fixed incomes below the national poverty level. Many of them can only afford to live in one of the city's
remaining single-room occupancy hotels. Reveals the deplorable living conditions of the 123 hotels, many of which have been cited with
numerous fire and health code violations and provide no heat or hot
water to their tenants. In interviews, the unfortunate old people
living in one such place express their worst fears that the hotel will
be closed and they will have nowhere else to go except the streets.
p. Richard Kotuk, p. WNET-TV; CWU, IU, UIL.

OCEANS (16m C 1980)
    This experimental narrative completes an ironic circle as it inves-
tigates the curiously indirect effects of a well-known political mystery.
The conflicts between the personal and the political, the meditative
and the active, interplay with circumstantial repetition. Photographed
with strikingly lush colors and images. An intriguing film. p. Patricia Quinn; NWMP.

ODALISQUE (12m C 1980)
    A sensual and humorous study of male/female relationships done
in an animation style that is a cross between Matisse and Saturday
morning cartoons. p. Maureen Selwood; SERBC.

ODYSSEY SERIES see DADI'S FAMILY; INCAS, THE; LITTLE IN-
    JUSTICES: LAURA NADER LOOKS AT THE LAW; MARGARET
    MEAD: TAKING NOTE; N!AI THE STORY OF A !KUNG WOMAN;
    OTHER PEOPLE'S GARBAGE

ODYSSEY TAPES, THE (29m C p1980, r1981) (Video)
    Richard Dyer-Bennet, noted folksinger, storyteller and concert
artist, at work on his newest project--the recording of the 24-hour
long, 2,000-year-old epic poem, Homer's Odyssey. His exquisite performance makes clear the power of the storyteller's art and reaffirms
the relevance of this age-old tradition for our times. d. Jill Godmilow/
Susan Fanshel; p. Research Foundation/State University of New York;
ODYTPS.

OF BIRTH AND FRIENDSHIP (29m C p1980, r1981)
    The story of Susan, who chooses to have her baby at home with
80 of her friends present. It is also a deeply moving account of
friendship and support between people who live a new, exciting and
courageous life-style. d. Geoff Parr; p. Environmental Films; ENVFMS.

OF SUGAR CANE AND SYRUP (15m C p1978, r1978)
    As was done long ago, the Stribling family in Louisiana still make
cane sugar using horse and manpower, simple procedures and equipment. Brady Stribling provides comment, sharing the methods his
uncle taught him. d./p. Luella Snyder and Steve Knudsen; CORONET.

OFF MY ROCKER (30m C n.d.) (Video)
    Clara Cassidy, a 78-year-old West Virginia newspaper columnist,

shares her positive, upbeat approach to growing old. p. Opequon
Productions; OPEQUON.

OFF YOUR DUFF (ed.) (30m C p1979, r1979)
Demonstrations by celebrities, doctors, professional athletes, and
others of their favorite form of exercise. Shows viewers a wide range
of ways to achieve physical fitness. Also, common sense advice is
given about how to start, problems that should not be ignored and
the importance of enjoying the exercise you choose. p. Kate Taylor,
Kim Prince; p. WGBH-TV; Boston; LCA, CWU.

OFFICIAL DOCTRINE, THE (3m B 1967)
Solo by Judith Dunn is photographed with special film to create
an avant-garde style in which the film techniques are part of the
creative approach to the dance. With narration by Gene Friedman.
Choreographers: Judith Dunn, Gene Friedman; d./p. Gene Friedman; EASTEND.

OH BROTHER, MY BROTHER (14m C 1979)
Captures the normal conflicts of early childhood ... the quick
changes from happiness to sorrow, from cooperative play to fears
and arguments ... all the while keeping these conflicts in perspective;
showing them within the framework of the joy that the two young
brothers find in each other's presence. A delightful film on family
relationships. p. Carol Lowell, Ross Lowell; PF.

OH DEAR: A HISTORY OF WOMAN SUFFRAGE IN OHIO (38m C
1978)
An important history of the woman suffrage movement focusing
on the people and events in Ohio which initiated and reflected the
struggle for women's votes across the nation. Supported in part by
a grant from the Ohio Program in the Humanities. p. L. Thornburg;
THRNB.

OISIN (17m C 1973) (also Video)
The filmmakers invite us to share with them the glories of Ireland
which was inspired by the hero-poet of the myths of early Celtic literature. Oisin "set the blackbird's song above the bells. That music
is the sweetest in the world. It is a pity not to listen to it for a
while." p. Vivien Carey, Patrick Carey; IFB.

OKLAHOMA! (148m C 1955)
This famous musical of the Southwest has dances choreographed
by Agnes de Mille, who integrated her dances with the drama. The
work was founded on Lynn Riggs' play Green Grow the Lilacs. Choreographer: Agnes de Mille; p. Arthur Hornblow, Jr.; BUDGET, FI.

OLA BELLA REED: MEMORIES (14m C 1975)
Utilizes two expressive forms--dance and film--to interpret a third
form, music. Three traditional Anglo-American ballads are sung by

Ola Belle Reed accompanied by her familial musicians. Modern dances based on traditional dance movements are used to interpret each song. Three experimental film methods are used to integrate the songs and the dances. Choreographer: Nadia Chilkovsky Nahumck. p. Gei Zantzinger, Nadia Chilkovsky Nahumck; ZANTAG; PAS.

OLD AGE (45m C 1971) Family of Man Series, No. 7
   Here we learn how different societies deal with death. On a hillside in north India a corpse burns slowly on an open fire. At a Surrey crematorium the nasty side of death is tucked out of sight behind the rose bushes in the garden of remembrance. In Botswana a witch doctor dances. In New Guinea a sorcerer fights a duel with a nasty-minded ghost. In Hong Kong paper money and incense are burned to help the dear departed on their way. TIMLIF; CWU.

OLD BELIEVERS (29m C 1981) (also Video)
   A portrayal of the Russian Old Believers of Oregon's Willamette Valley, who have preserved their way of life for three centuries. Unchanging religious ritual intertwines with a rich heritage of folk tradition--embroidery, belt weaving, folk songs, and foodways--as a family prepares for a wedding and its community celebration. Perspectives are given from different generations as cultural values pass on. p./d. Margaret Hixon; MEDIAP.

OLD, BLACK AND ALIVE!--A PORTRAIT OF AGING (28m C 1974)
   Contrary to its title, this portrait of half a dozen elderly blacks in Macon County, Alabama seems remarkably representative of the variety of life-styles and attitudes of the aged in rural and small-town ambiences. Although unavoidably poignant at times, this film as a whole is uplifting. These are not, with one exception, people living out their final days in misery and loneliness (as do perhaps most urban poor blacks), but ingratiating individuals who have variously reached some accommodation with being old. In a society in which both age and blackness still provoke negative stereotypes, this film should be useful for the elderly (as well as for those working with them). With study guide. d. Frank Cantor; p. Christopher Knight, NEWFLM; UM.

OLD FRIENDS ... NEW FRIENDS ... GERALD JAMPOLSKY, M.D. (29m C p1980, r1980) (Video)
   Dr. Jampolsky is a physician and caregiver to children with catastrophic diseases. In his Center for Attitudinal Healing in California, he introduces Fred Rogers to some of his patients and their families. Here, caring is the most important part of treatment. Loving support, Dr. Jampolsky believes, is the primary component in overcoming illness, pain and the fear of death. d. Arthur Barron; p. Carolyn King, Arthur Barron; FAMCOM.

OLD FRIENDS ... NEW FRIENDS ... HELEN HAYES AND MILLIE JEWETT (28m C 1981)
   Fred Rogers visits with the first lady of American theatre Helen

Hayes and with Millie Jewett, a Coast Guard warrant officer on Nantucket Island, who has been caring for people, animals and boats for most of her life. p. Family Communications, Inc.; PBSV.

OLD FRIENDS ... NEW FRIENDS ... LEE STRASBERG (28m C p1980, r1980) (Video)
Octogenarian Strasberg displays his fiercely demanding teaching techniques, talks with Fred Rogers about his philosophy, and reminisces about his daughter, Susan, his own childhood. Insights about the man are contributed by Susan and actress Shelley Winters. d. Arthur Barron; p. Carolyn King, Arthur Barron; FAMCOM.

OLD FRIENDS ... NEW FRIENDS ... MELODY (28m C 1981) (Video)
Portrait of Lesley Frost Ballantine, daughter of poet Robert Frost and herself a poet and author, and of famous, black blues singer John Jackson. p. Family Communications, Inc.; PBSV.

OLD FRIENDS ... NEW FRIENDS ... NANCY ACOSTA (28m C 1981) (Video)
Nancy Acosta is a 21-year-old teacher in the barrios of La Puente outside of Los Angeles, where crime and violence are common. In this hostile environment, Acosta is providing an alternative: a school for dropouts where the atmosphere offers uncompromising love and respect. p. Family Communications, Inc.; PBSV.

OLD FRIENDS ... NEW FRIENDS ... RUTH ELLEN PATTON TOTTEN/ HELEN ROSS (28m C 1981) (Video)
In this two-part program, two women reflect on their lives. Daughter of General George S. Patton, sister of General George S. Patton III, wife of General James W. Totten and a descendant of generations of military families, Ruth Ellen Patton Totten talks about influence of the Army in her life. In a rare television interview, noted child development expert Helen Ross talks about her work with children and her remembrances of her own childhood. p. Family Communications, Inc.; PBSV.

OLD FRIENDS ... NEW FRIENDS ... TOM COTTLE (29m C p1980, r1980) (Video)
Psychologist, author, TV interviewer Tom Cottle today is compulsively busy and productive, doing what he likes to do and doing it well. In frank conversation with Fred Rogers, however, he tells why he doesn't consider himself a success and confesses to basic human fears and insecurities. By doing so, he sheds much light on the subtle and troublesome dynamics of human relationships. d./p. Phyllis Chinlund; FAMCOM.

OLD HOUSE, NEW HOUSE (27m C 1981)
Documents the transformation of a drafty, Victorian home in downtown Toronto into an energy efficient showplace called Ecology House. d. Barbara Sweete; p. David Springbett/Larry Weinstein; p. Fichman-Sweete Productions; FILMLB.

OLD IS ... (13m C 1979) Aging in Our Times Series
Introduces four delightful men and women who remain vigorously active in their 70's, their 80's, and their 90's. The film reveals the challenges, the frustrations, the pleasures, and the satisfactions of aging. It disproves the weary methology that surrounds the elderly in a society where youth is revered. STEREF; CWU.

OLD ONES, THE (29m B 1964)
The pioneer work by Denmark, in programs for the old, has aroused interest throughout the world. The Danish Parliament passed its first old age assistance act in 1891. Since then, Denmark has tested many different approaches and systems: nursing homes, old people's towns, home care. The story of its success and failures is pertinent everywhere, since the problems are worldwide. CMC; UNEV.

OLD WORLD, NEW WOMEN (28m C 1975)
Women of the People's Republic of China are playing an important role in the nation's modernization, making inroads into positions women never held before. Presents a cross-section of the areas in which women have become successful. A journalist, a television director, a politician, an architect, and members of a modern dance troupe are among those singled out to be interviewed and observed. p. Chinese Arts Films, Ltd./Mass Communications, Inc.; CIS, UIL.

OLDER ADULT: THE CHALLENGE OF CHANGE, THE (29m C 1979) (2" HB tape)
A look at attitudes and legislation concerning older people and the increasing awareness of discrimination against these citizens. Host: Harold Johnson, Director, Inst. of Gerontology, University of Michigan. Guests: Brad Geller, Attorney and Penny Hommel, Inst. of Gerontology, University of Michigan. UMMRC; UM.

OLDER AND BOLDER (14m C n.d.) Something Personal Series
Focuses on a small group of older women in Cambridge, Massachusetts who meet weekly to talk, laugh, and share their joys and problems. These senior citizens are vital, amusing women who have all had to face problems and loneliness, but who have taken control of their own lives and continue to enjoy active outside interests. A very positive film. p. Nancy Porter; p. WGBH-TV; EDC.

OLDER PEOPLE (29m C p1975, r1976) (Video) Are You Listening Series
An exceptional glimpse into the lives of several senior citizens, this tape captures their fairly divergent views on such subjects as the right to work (specifically the relationship between the absence of active work and the growth of senility), leisure time, extramarital affairs, right to an income, and self-help. The people interviewed express more active political concerns. p. Martha Stuart; STUARTM.

OLDER WOMAN: ISSUES, THE (7m C 1978) (slt)
A slide-tape program to trigger discussion about issues and

attitudes on aging and older women, including remarriage, widowhood, retirement and sexuality. Intended audience for the four vignettes includes those who work with the elderly, students of gerontology, the general public and older adults. Includes synchronized audio-cassette and user's manual. p. Institute of Gerontology, University of Michigan; UM.

OLIVIA: BETWEEN TWO CULTURES (13m C 1973) Searching Years
 Series
Olivia protests the Mexican traditions in the family, which she feels are unjust and restrictive. Yet she wants her parents' love. How can she find out where she belongs? CF; UNEV.

OLIVIA RECORDS: MORE THAN MUSIC (28m C 1979) (Video)
Profiles a lesbian feminist collective formed six years ago to make "women's music" and set up a feminist business. Interviews with Meg Christian, Mary Watkins, and Linda Tillery, among others, explore Olivia's philosophy about supporting women. Shows recording sessions, members working on their distribution network and Olivia artists performing in concert. Filmed by an all-women video crew, this inside view of the music business from a feminist perspective is a thoughtful, positive look at women working together. d. Anita Clearfield; BAYAV.

ON A PAR, NOT A PEDESTAL (26m C r1977)
Discusses contemporary issues relating to the role, concerns, and prospects of women at various levels in the corporate structure. Documents what happened at Connecticut General Life Insurance Company of Hartford, Connecticut, when a group of women employees asked and got a meeting with management to present employment grievances against the company. Several executives discuss the event in filmed interviews and the group spokeswomen talk freely about what happened as a result of the meeting. A senior vice-president recalls that no one on his level realized the women's depth of frustration, or men's lack of understanding of women employees' problems, dreams, and wishes. As a result of this discovery, a series of workshops were held covering a wide range of things attended by more than 4,000 people from all levels of employment. At these sessions women achieved some dignity and understanding from men. One executive says what he learned there not only helped him at the company, but also at home. It is noted that as a result of this program, Connecticut General is not only retraining more of their high level people but attracting others from the outside. An experiment that has clearly been a success and can be a pattern for others to follow. p. Hobel-Leiterman, Ltd.; DOCUA; UIL.

ON AMERICAN SOIL (28m C 1983) (also Video)
Presents the complex nature and extent of the soil erosion problem in America today. Interviews with farmers, soil conservation experts, and photographic stills and motion picture clips are used in

this film discussion about America's soil conservation problem and why farmers are not utilizing soil in ways they know will help prevent erosion. d. Janet Mendelsohn/Rob Whittlesey; p. The Conservation Foundation; CONSF.

ON BEING AN EFFECTIVE PARENT (43m C 1972) The Distinguished
    Contributors to Counseling Series
    The basic tenents of Parent Effectiveness Training are presented by Thomas Gordon, the father of the training program, through lectures, role playing with a group of graduate students, and through a discussion with Dr. Thomas Allen. The rationale and techniques of active listening, "I" statements, and "no-lose" problem-solving are presented for the use of parents and other helping adults. AMERGA; UNEV.

ON DEATH AND DYING (58m C r1974)
    In-depth interview with Dr. Elisabeth Kubler-Ross, who discusses her experiences in helping the terminally ill face death without fear. Wide-ranging, sensitive, and moving. p. NBC-TV; FI; VIEWFI; PAS, UMN.

ON OUR LAND (55m C 1982)
    One in six Israeli citizens is a Palestinian Arab. After the dispersal of the Palestinian people, and the creation of the state of Israel in 1948, the lives of those Palestinians who stayed were greatly changed. This report tells the story of this forgotten section of the Palestinian population through portrayal of their daily lives and interviews with ordinary Palestinians. d. Antonia Cacia; p. Iain Bruce; ICARF.

ON TENNIS, A SERIES see GROUNDSTROKES WITH BILLIE JEAN
    KING, THE; SERVE WITH BILLIE JEAN KING, THE

ON THE LINE (ed.) (50m C r1977)
    Shows how the problems of this country's economy touch the lives of people and their communities. Interviewed are women in the Black ghetto, a middle-aged man in the employment line and others unemployed. The narrator discusses the current economic scene: employment down, declining buying power, and sustained increase in prices. Residents at a Bronx housing development are interviewed as they begin to strike to protest rents which doubled in five years. That strike is filmed through nine months, as court orders and criminal charges are brought against the strikers; the final outcome is not revealed. A vintage film of early Ford factory assembly line illustrates some of the evils that system has bred, the complaints of present-day automotive workers reveal that much of the evil has remained in the system. Two workers speculate that the only viable solution to current problems may be a reordering of the economy toward Socialism. d./p. Barbara Morgolis; CININF.

ON THE LINE (37m C p1981, r1981)
Shows a cross-section of workers from an American corporation
sent to Japan to observe Japanese businesses which have become a
major competitive threat and to bring back valuable information about
their methods and operation. Accompanied by a translator and with
instant translation equipment, the Americans are filmed as they watch
Japanese workers. At the end of this visit the Americans agree that
nothing magic is happening in Japan, but they need to appeal to their
people back home to work a full eight hours, take greater pride in
their work (as Japanese workers do), communicate more effectively,
and be highly motivated to accomplish daily goals. p. Carolyn King,
Arthur Barron; d. Arthur Barron; KINGA.

ON THE RUN (27m C 1977)
Youthful runaways discuss the situations and expectations that
led them to leave their homes. Also shows facilities designed to help
young runaways cope with the grim reality of their lives "on the run."
MTITI; UCEMC.

ON THE SPRING ICE, PTS. I & II (45m C 1976) (Eskimo/Subtitled)
The Alaska Native Heritage Film Series
Shows the hazards the people of Shungnak face hunting walrus
on ice. The first part shows the rescue of the hunters lost on ice;
the second highlights the walrus hunt and the preparation of the walrus for distribution. p. Sarah Elder, Leonard Kamerling; DER.

ON THE TRAIL: AN INTRODUCTION TO TRAIL WALKING (9m C
1975)
Hiking groups of different types and ages are seen on trails in
city, country, state parks, and on trails laid, by permission, through
private land. Demonstrates map and compass reading, trail maintenance, and finding the way by blazes and markers. Emphasis is on
day hikes, which require no expensive equipment, training, or great
physical strength. p. Acorn Films, Inc.; UIL.

ONA PEOPLE: LIFE AND DEATH IN TIERRA DEL FUEGO, THE (55m
C p1976, r1977)
Explores the culture, history and eventual decline of a now ex-
tinct group of hunters and gatherers in Tierra del Fuego. Using old
photographs and oral histories, the film recreates the Ona (Selk'nam)
Indians' once flourishing culture and chronicles its tragic destruction
in the early 1900's at hands of foreign explorers and immigrants. d.
Ana Montes de Gonzalez, Anne Chapman; p. Ana Montes de Gonzalez;
DER.

ONCE A DAUGHTER (58m C p1979, r1979)
A chronicle of the complexities of mother/daughter relationships.
Through a series of portraits we find that what these subjects lack
in sympathy they make up for in candor, reflecting interdependencies,
jealousies and, ultimately, the role reversal that comes with old age--
when daughter "mothers" mother. d./p. Lynne Littman; LITTMAN.

ONCE UPON A BOA (28m C p1978, r1978)
Mr. Elliott thinks he may like to have a pet boa. He visits his neighbor, Martin, who has a pet boa named Nigel. After listening to Martin tell about his experiences with Nigel, and having the boa around for a while, Mr. Elliott decides that he might like such a pet. p./ed. Lora Hays; d./s.w. Renata Stoia; PHOENIX.

ONCE UPON A CHOICE (15m C p1980, r1981) (also Video)
A humorous, original fairy tale in which an unconventional princess faces the conventional dilemma of deciding which prince to marry. She is expected to choose between Prince Premium of Upper Fiduciary, Prince Gauntlet of Skirmish-on-Avon, and Prince Rapport of Outer Begonia. Princess Frances, in striking contrast to the passive princesses of traditional fairy tales, is eager to explore the outside world. Her delightful and unexpected solution raises contemporary questions about sex-role stereotyping and stimulates discussion of parent/child relationships. d./p. Liane Brandon; s.w. Debra Franco, Liane Brandon; NEWDAY.

ONE BY ONE (30m C n.d.)
Stresses the difficult process of implementing the policies of Equal Economic Opportunity at the personal level in business and industry. Explains that emotional prejudice is hard to overcome. Dramatizes employer's efforts to deal with his own feelings about a minority employee. p. Cally Curtis Company; CALLYC.

ONE GOOD TURN (9m C 1976) (also Video)
Animated woolen puppets star in this fable of friendship where each one is richer for having met. d. Hermina Tyrolova; p. Whitehill Films; FI.

ONE HAND CLAPPING (9m C 1973)
Noise is seen as an aural enemy that assails us from all sides, with no regard for ear or nerve. No one seems to find a silencer for the clatter and clang of the world we build. Even communication, the openness of mouth and mind that is said to be a virtue, can swell to strident surfeit when a dozen tongues wag as one. We are overly tolerant of noise, and the film suggests what this does to reduce mind, spirit and hearing. It is time to make more noise about noise. d./p. Joan Henson; NFBC; MACMFL.

ONE HUNDRED ENTERTAINMENTS (28m C 1979--U.S.)
Illustrates the life of a Chinese artist and presents that aspect of Chinese culture. Set in Shensi Province of the People's Republic of China. A member of an acrobatic troupe is telling a young audience what life was like for performers before liberation of Mao Tsetung, and what life is like for them at the present. Several sequences show performers practicing difficult acts learned after years of perfecting skills. p. Film Australia; p. Suzanne Baker; d./s.w. Bob Kingsbury; LCA.

ONE IN ELEVEN (14m C 1981)
An encouraging look at an alternative treatment for breast cancer,
this film presents evidence that lumpectomy followed by high dose
radiation therapy is a viable alternative to mastectomy for early breast
cancer. An awareness of this method tends to encourage early self-
examination and prompt action. Specialists discuss development of
this radiation therapy, whose survival rate equals that of mastectomy.
d./p. Kate Spohr; PF.

ONE LITTLE KITTEN (3m C p1980, r1980)
With music and no narration this film follows a curious kitten as
he explores the world around him. He hides under a hat, explores
a paper bag, knocks over a box, etc. As the film ends, the kitten,
tired from his many adventures, heaves a big sigh and falls asleep.
Intended to encourage children to discover the world around them.
p. Tana Hoban, music by Peter Fish; TEXFM.

ONE OF A KIND (58m C p1977, r1978)
Diane Baker stars in the drama about the love and the conflicts
between a mother and her daughter. Lizzie is a special child who
desperately needs her mother's love and understanding, but mom has
troubles of her own. Filmed in a carnival atmosphere, the action
centers around the staging of a Punch and Judy show. d. Harry
Winer; p. Diane Baker, p. Artemis Productions; s.w. Marjorie Sigley;
music by Maurice Jarre; PHOENIX; IU, UMN.

ONE ON ONE SERIES see CHANGING ROLE FOR MEN; COUNSELING
CHANGES; WOMEN'S RIGHTS IN THE COURTS

ONE SINGS, THE OTHER DOESN'T (105m C 1977) (French/Subtitled)
Follows the friendship of two young women over a period of 14
years, a time when each seeks to take control of her destiny and
eventually finds contentment. "A handsome movie-movie, guaranteed
to be all things to all women and most men. A blend of fact, fiction
and feeling--the stuff of life."--Judith Crist, New York Post. p.
Cine-Tamaris; d./s.w. Agnes Varda; ALMI.

ONE THING AFTER ANOTHER (15m C p1980, r1980)
Presents a lightly spirited film that deals with the frustrations
of people caught in a "throw-away society." A thought-provoking film.
p. Jennifer Lewis, Town of Amherst Youth Bureau; d. Fred Keller;
TWNAYB.

ONE, TWO, THREE (33m C 1975)
Documents how a group of women in Britain organized to meet
their need for pre-school care and covers several issues involved in
cooperative childcare. Interviews with mothers deal with their objective to meet their own needs as well as their children's. There
are discussions of what they want the children to learn, budgeting,
and involvement of volunteers. The children are shown engaging in

activities as some of the mothers comment on the objectives they have in mind in programming these experiences. (LIBFI; CFCL) UIL.

ONE, TWO, THREE (14m C 1978)
One of the series of four dances from FOUR JOURNEYS INTO MYSTIC TIME, choreographed by Marian Scott and performed by members of the U.C.L.A. Dance Company. Dance Company: University of California at Los Angeles Dance Company; Choreographer: Marian Scott; d. Shirley Clarke; MAYERA.

ONE, TWO, THREE, ZERO: INFERTILITY (28m C p1979, r1980) (also Video)
One out of six couples has trouble having a baby. This film shows the stress placed on a marriage by infertility and the advances of modern medicine to help people have families. Useful for nursing in-service programs, psychology, marriage and family counseling, public library programs. d. Heather Cook; p. James Murray, CBC; FILMLB; UMN.

ONE WAY OR ANOTHER (78m B 1977) (Spanish/Subtitled)
A perceptive portrait of a Cuba in transition, providing an un-flinching honest examination of social problems still being resolved despite the profound transformation of the Cuban revolution. Equally important, its insights into the way human relations are shaped by social surroundings and background are equally valuable to both women and men here in the United States. d. Sara Gomez, p. Cuban Film Institute; UNIFILM.

ONE WOMAN'S DIVORCE (29m C 1975) (Video) Woman Series
Journalist and author Susan Braudy (Between Marriage and Divorce) discusses her book, which is a personal account of her divorce. She talks of her false expectations about marriage, which she believes are common to all people and taught by television, parents and peers. She also comments on the "perfect couple" myth and describes the feelings she had during the divorce process. Sandra Elkin is the moderator. p. WNED-TV; PBSV.

ONSET OF LABOR (14m C n.d.)
Deals with the real concerns woman have about labor. Discusses Braxton-Hicks contractions, thinning, dilation, lightening, the "show," false labor, breaking of water, contractions, going in for delivery, prepping and episiotomy, delivery (husband-coach attending) and bonding. Also available in Spanish. MIFE.

ONSTAGE WITH JUDITH SOMOGI (28m C 1981)
Opera and symphony conductor Judith Somogi welcomes us into a world which few of us have ever seen so closely. We witness the love she has for her music, the care with which she develops her craft, and the pleasure all of this brings to her life. Quickly we come to understand that music is more the pure sound. It is a

discipline, a life-style, and a comfort--as well as high cultural enrichment and enjoyment. Somogi shows us that success in any career
requires talent, hard work, sacrifice, tenacious dedication, and a
strong belief in oneself. Free loan. KAROL.

OP-ODYSSEY (15m B 1977) (Video)
An excerpt from a multimedia piece which involves dance, music,
sculpture and film. A work based on Diane Wakowski's poetry. For
a version in combination with other pieces, see JONATHAN AND THE
ROCKER. Choreographer: Valerie Hammer; p. Doris Chase; CHASED.

OPEN MIND: A TALK WITH MARGARET MEAD, THE (29m B 1972)
(Video)
Margaret Mead, noted American anthropologist, author, and critic
of the current world scene, offers her views on topics ranging from
women's liberation to the Vietnam War. UMMRC; UM.

OPENING NIGHT (144m C 1977)
Gena Rowlands portrays an aging actress suffering a middle-age
identity crisis using booze and sex to avoid facing up to age. d./s.w.
John Cassavetes; p. Paul Stewart; FACES.

OPUS I NUMBER I (21m C p1978, r1978)
A trio of youthful musicians shape a piece of classical music, developing a sensitive musical relationship through rehearsals, culminating in a vibrant final, performance. d./p. Barbara Sweete, Niv
Fichman. CANFDC.

OPUS-OP (20½m C 1967)
An experiment in interpretative dance and rock music (the latter
by Crome Syrkus). Young dancers act out their feelings while the
camera interplays the stage action with the varied audience reactions.
Dance Company: Joffrey Ballet Company; Choreographer: Anna Sokolow; d. Lazlo Pal; p. King Screen Productions; SYRACU.

ORBIS (5m B 1977)
A single figure in slow rotation, seen both in deep space and in
extreme close ranges so that the fall of light and shadow upon the
form becomes an abstraction. d./p. Christie Ann Piper; PIPER.

ORDINARY PEOPLE (25m C 1977)
Shows how normal stresses can combine to place an average parent in danger of behaving abusively toward his or her children.
Focuses on John, Rita, and their children, who have recently moved
from a major urban area to a small town. Shows John making exciting strides in his new job and Rita feeling isolated, locked into her
role as mother, and less able to cope with her nine-year-old son and
infant daughter. Points out the distress signals of child abuse: the
persistent, unexplained crying of the Miller baby, Rita's unrealistically
high expectations for her children, mysterious bruises on the son,

and Rita's ambivalence and recurring avoidance in her contacts with the public health nurse. p. University of Pittsburgh Parental Stress Center; MTITI; CORNELL, IU.

OREGON WOODCARVERS (24m C 1979)
    Covers the works, lives and philosophies of four very different Oregon wood artists. Ed Quigley, painter and sculptor of Western themes; Douglas MacGregor of Corbett is one of a vanishing few who repair, carve and create carousel animals; Gary Hauser lives by the sea and derives his inspiration and materials from the sea; Roy Setziol, actor, ex-chaplain, lives on a mountaintop near Sheridan and carves logs into abstract works. p. Jan Baross; NWMP.

OREGON WORK (30m C 1982) (Video)
    Explores creative solutions to recession through the cooperation of labor and industry. Dave Vincent, owner of a small mill in Philomath, Oregon, discusses how he is able to run his mill in the black while maintaining his responsibility as the town's primary employer. The film compares attitudes of corporate responsibility and examines the actions of larger companies. Provocative analysis is supplied by a labor economist and the Secretary-Treasurer of Oregon's AFL-CIO. p. Sharon Genasci; MEDIAP.

ORFEUS AND JULIE (7m C 1970)
    Danger and happiness expressed through modern choreography performed by Sorella Englund and Eske Holm. The film is a ballet abstraction using real film with animation effects. Dancers: Royal Danish Ballet. AUDPLS.

ORGANIC FARMING: CAN IT FEED THE MULTITUDES? (23m C 1972)
    Studies the effects of chemicals on food and the economic pressures that will be caused by the elimination of industrial processing. Presents the viewpoints of both those who maintain that scientifically produced substitutes and additives are legitimate and harmless, and those who show the average diet to be less nutritious today than ten years ago. p. Hobel-Leiterman Productions; DOCUA; UIL.

ORGANIC GARDENING: COMPOSTING (11m C 1972)
    Using live action and animation the film shows how to build a compost heap; what ingredients to use; in what proportions; how to layer the heap to ensure speedy and uniform decomposition. p. Rodale Press/Amanda and Burton Fox, John Hoskyns-Abrahall, Winifred Scherrer; BULFRG.

ORGANISM (20m C 1976)
    Makes a visual analogy between living tissue and the structure of cities. Traffic arteries are the bloodstream circulating through the urban body, and skyscrapers are the skeletal structure. To Harris, the city and the human body are both regenerating organisms (Upstate Films, October 17, 1978). p. Hilary Harris; PHOENIX.

ORGANIZATIONAL DEVELOPMENT FILM SERIES see MANAGING
STRESS; POWER OF POSITIVE REINFORCEMENT, THE

ORIGINALS: WOMEN IN ART SERIES, THE see ALICE NEEL--
COLLECTOR OF SOULS; ANONYMOUS WAS A WOMAN; FRANKEN-
THALLER--TOWARD A NEW CLIMATE; GEORGIA O'KEEFFE; HELEN
FRANKENTHALER; MARY CASSATT--IMPRESSIONIST FROM PHIL-
ADELPHIA; NEVELSON IN PROCESS; NEW CLIMATE; SPIRIT
CATCHER--THE ART OF BETYE SAAR

OSAKA ELEGY (NANIWA ELEGY) (71m B 1936) (Japanese/Subtitled)
At the end of Osaka Elegy the heroine, once goodhearted and
naive, walks into oblivion, guilty of some sordid schemes, but no
more so than the men who forced her into amorality. The difference
is that society tolerates such lapses from men, but will not forgive
identical conduct by women. Based on a story by Mizoguchi, with
Isuzu Yamada. d. Kenji Mizoguchi; s.w. Yoshi Kata Yoda. FI.

OTHER PEOPLE'S GARBAGE (59m C 1980) The Odyssey Series
Although written documents record more than 350 years of events
in North America, they reveal little about what everyday life was like.
The three segments of this magazine-format film explore the current
work of historical archaeologists at three sites across the United
States. Details of people's lives are revealed in excavations at slave
quarters on St. Simon Island, slag heaps in northern California mining towns occupied between 1859-1902, and subway construction sites
in Cambridge, Massachusetts where urban archaeologists devise new
methods to discover artifacts in land still used. p. Ann Peck, Claire
Andrade-Watkins; DER.

OTHER WORLD, THE (19m C r1976--U.S.)
Presents the biological ladder from the microscopic plants and an-
imals to the otter, a mammalian bridge between land and water. p.
Roman Bittman, Colin Low; d./ed./s.w. Claudia Overing; NFBC;
MOKINA.

OTHON (88m C 1969) (French/Subtitled)
Corneille's play staged in contemporary Rome, as a discourse on
power politics, classical tragedy, and filmic reality. d. Jean-Marie
Straub, Daniele Huillet; NYF.

OUR HIDDEN NATIONAL PRODUCT (25m C 1982)
A documentary that goes beyond the horrors of hazardous waste
to feature solutions and processes. Hazardous waste disposal and
treatment facilities around the country are seen, and procedures are
shown, such as tracking, laboratory analysis, resource recovery,
chemical treatment, a properly engineered landfill, and incineration.
A typical siting problem is documented through community hearings
and interviews held because of a confrontation between Groveland
Township in Michigan and Stablex Corporation over the company's

proposal for a waste treatment and land reclamation center. p. Durrin Films, Inc.; DURRIN.

OUR HOME (15m p1981, r1982)
A positive look at living in a Care Home, breaking down some of the stereotypes connected to living in a home. A look at the people in the German Canadian Care Home, and why they are living there: "We don't live here to die, we live here to live!" d./p. Eileen Hoeter; CANFDC.

OUR LITTLE MUNCHKIN HERE (12m C 1975)
A painful episode in the life of an adolescent girl who finds herself at odds with her family environment. p. Lois Tupper; IRIS.

OUR TIME IN THE GARDEN (15m B p1980, r1981) (also Video)
Tells the story of a young Jewish woman growing up in Berlin during the time of Hitler's rise to power. German footage of the era and a multilevel sound track are used to evoke a sense of those times and explore their effect on an individual. d./p. Ron Blau; CENSTU.

OUR TOWN IS BURNING DOWN (18m C 1982)
Examines the tragic effects of arson on its victims and the way one small rural community united to fight back. The postive actions taken by the citizens of Muncy, Pennsylvania can serve as model that other communities (rural and urban) can also use to combat arson. Free loan. d. Wendy Wood; p. Margaret Mick; AETNA.

OUT OF ROCK (30m C 1980) (also Video)
The creative process and the forces embodied in his work are the focus of this film about sculptor Boz Vaadia. Recently Vaadia has been working in Palisades Interstate Park and New York City, using materials he finds in the two environments, mountain rocks on the one hand and discarded building stones on the other. Vaadia is profoundly influenced by forces expressed in an uncultivated natural environment. But he is equally affected by the reservoir of strength and energy as manifested in the city. his works, primitive and urban, are juxtaposed, highlighting the interplay between the forces of nature and the dynamic technology of a great cosmopolitan city. p./d. Julia Keydel, Arik Bernstein; FI.

OUT OF SILENCE (38m C 1971)
Shows the Montreal Oral School for the Deaf. The school employs the method known as "Oralism" which adapts the child at an early age to live and communicate in the world of sound. Audiovisual equipment, modern electronics and specially trained teachers are all part of this new approach which enables children with impaired hearing to be integrated into regular school classes. p. Dorothy Courtois, Robert Verrall; d. Leonard Forest; NFBC.

OUT OF THE LIMELIGHT, HOME IN THE RAIN (52m C 1979) The
Magic of Dance (Series)
Margot Fonteyn explores the dancer's life. The rigors of ballet
class, the rehearsals and preparation, and finally the moment of judg-
ment when it's "out in the limelight" and on with the performance.
Shows Margot Fonteyn and Rudolf Nureyev performing Frederick Ash-
ton's Marguerite and Armand in its entirety. Also features Frederick
Ashton, Michael Somes and the Royal Ballet. BBC/TIMLIF; UMN.

OUTSIDE G.N.P. (8m C 1980)
Shows that women's labor in subsistence agriculture and in the
home is excluded from gross national product figures, and what this
means to the development planner, to the whole society and to women
as individuals. p. Bettina Corke, United Nations; WSU.

OVERTURE: LINH FROM VIETNAM (26m C p1980, r1980)
Linh Tran, a young Vietnamese immigrant, befriends her neighbor, José Aguilar, a young Mexican American, when they discover
their mutual interest in flute-playing. Their friendship is threatened,
however, when Linh wins the spot in the school band that José had
been counting on. The resentment of the community towards the Vietnamese adds further strain to the relationship. After Linh's flute is
stolen, the friendship falls apart. When they both realize what has
happened, the beauty of a shared relationship is caught in the music
each play to the other. d. Seth Pinsker; p. Elaine Sperber; LCA;
UCEMC.

OVERWEIGHT? (25m C 1980) Think Nutrition Series
Emphasizes the balance between calories taken in and calories
burned and provides the viewer with reliable information on the comparative caloric value of different foods; ways to combat the impulse
to eat; simple and effective exercises designed to burn off fat; and
how to keep weight off once it is lost. p. National Film and Video
Center; NATFVC.

-P-

P4W; PRISON FOR WOMEN (81m C/B 1981) (also Video)
A portrait of five women prisoners and their feelings about love
and loneliness. Provides powerful insight into prison life for women--
clears away the myths and misconceptions. Shows the sense of hope
they sustain in the face of a bleak future, also the possibility of
friendship and family ties on the outside. Shows intelligent prisoners
thinking out the problems within the system. The element of violence
in their lives is underplayed. Packs an emotional wallop: moving,
thorough, authentic. d. Holly Dale/Janis Cole; p. Pan Canadian
Film Distributor; FIRRNF.

P.M. (7m B 1980)
Depicts the quiet dismissal of those who are no longer able to

keep up with the relentless pace of consumer society. Tight editing. Leaves a powerful impact of how our society relates to the aged. Poignant. d. Jan Krawitz, Thomas Ott; KRAWITZ.

PM Magazine/Acid Rock (4m C 1982) (Video)
Features iconographic images from American broadcast television transformed by high technology, pop music and the artist's vision. By re-contextualizing the television image, the filmmaker allows the viewer to draw new conclusions about the role of mass media in contemporary culture. By invitation, Dara Birnbaum presented her video production at the prestigious contemporary art survey Documenta 7 in Kassel, West Germany. She was the only video artist so honored. p. Dara Birnbaum; ELARTI.

PACIFIC FAR EAST LINE (12m C si 1978-79)
The changing skyline of downtown San Francisco was photographed over the period of a year (Collective for Living Cinema, October 27, 1978). p. Abigail Child, COLIVC.

PACIFIC ISLAND FAMILY LIFE (16m C 1977) Pacific Island Life Series
Each family has its own field, usually on one of the more fertile islands. Teheilau and his family take a boat trip to attend to their plot where they grow taro and tumeric. Other plants, like bananas, sweet potatoes and papaya are also grown on the islands. No narration. p. International Film Foundation; PSU.

PACIFIC ISLAND LIFE SERIES see PACIFIC ISLAND FAMILY LIFE

PADENIYE DINASTI ROMANOVIKH see FALL OF THE ROMANOV DYNASTY, THE

PAIN (26m C 1980) Coping with Serious Illness Series
Documentary on the last years of Joan Robinson, a woman who was dying of cancer. Shows approaches to coping with both pain and the fear of pain. Explains the effect of suffering on the personality, the differences between types of pain, and methods available in treating pain. TIMLIF; PAS, UMN.

PAINFUL WAY, THE see VIA DOLOROSA

PALLADIO--THE ARCHITECT AND HIS INFLUENCE IN AMERICA (48m C 1981)
Surveys the major monuments of the Italian Renaissance architect, including Venetian churches, palaces in Vicenza, and country villas. Also shows Palladio's influence on American architecture of the Federal Period and on the buildings of Thomas Jefferson. d. Mildred Ackerman, John Terry; FOGG.

PALM PLAY (30m C p1977, r1978)
Shows that the degree of open palm display symbolizes the role

of women in culture, casting light upon an important aspect of non-verbal communication. d. Alan Lomax, F. Pauley; p. Alan Lomax; CHOREOP.

PANAMA CANAL: THE LONGEST SHORTCUT (28m C p1980, r1981)
Provides insight into the unique problems and solutions of one of man's greatest engineering achievements. The Panama Canal took decades and a great many lives before it was completed. A rich collection of early stills and motion pictures with contemporary footage illustrate the informative narration. p. Diana Colson, Mack Swain Productions; MCFI.

PANDORA'S BOTTLE: THE DRINKING WOMAN (40m C n.d.)
From benign overprotection to cruel and unforgiving over-reaction, the female alcoholic is frequently the victim of yet another double standard--the one of alcoholism. This film is not only for the female alcoholic but for her "co-alcoholics" which can extend from her immediate family to her work situation. Rather than a simplistic limitation of anatomy as her destiny, the social background and the behavior of the female alcoholic is explored for causes and solutions, now. This is a constructive, compassionate film for men and women, the female alcoholic, the alcoholism professional and all those involved in support systems for women and alcoholics. d./p. Mariette Hartley; MTVTM.

P'ANSORI (30m B n.d.) (Video)
Kim So-Hee, a leading Korean mime, is joined by three musicians in this traditional music and dance. The musicians play the kayageum (12-stringed zither-like instrument), kuhmoongo (6-stringed zither-like instrument) and p'iri (Oboe). The performance ends with a folk dance by Madame Kim. p. Performing Arts Division of Asia Society; ASIAS.

PAPA PEREZ (32m C 1980)
Gives a balanced view of Judge Perez's influence in this family-oriented sketch. Well-documented and edited. Good insight into the political structure of the region. Touches on the importance of oil to the southern structure. Subtle view of discrimination and power in Louisiana under the Perez family. d. Kathleen Dowdey; CECROPIA.

PAPA TAPE I (4m C 1982) (Video)
An expression of the artist's feelings for her father who has been in a nursing home for two years. It is electronically processed, using vertical rolling, sequencing, and layered source material. These alterations enhance both the inexorable condition of his existence, and the struggle to accept the irreparably divergent views of himself as a once vibrant person. p./s.w./ed. Mimi Martin; MARTIN.

PARALLELS--THE PROLOGUE (12m C si 1977)
An abstract film shot frame-by-frame. The landscape elements

were shot sidewise, forming vertical bands with a strong central axis. The filmmaker regards the axis as a path to higher consciousness (Museum of the City of New York, October 29, 1978). p. Vicki Z. Peterson; MUSNYC.

PARDON ME FOR LIVING (27m C 1982) (also Video)
Presents a film version of Jean Stafford's short story "The Scarlet Letter." The film title, "Pardon Me for Living," is taken from Virgil's habit of starting almost everything he says with those words. p. Elaine Sperber; p. Highgate Pictures; d. Stephen Foreman; LCA.

PARENT-TEENAGER COMMUNICATIONS (19m C 1981) (also Video)
Trigger Films on Human Interaction Series
"I should tell you more, right? So you can start putting me down for everything? You want me to be you." This film offers opportunity for parents to share experiences with each other, clarify values about teenage behavior, and practice ways to communicate with teenagers about these issues: independence and responsibility, drugs and alcohol, honesty and openness, boy-girl relationships, sex, schoolwork, household chores, sibling rivalry, depression, suicide, delinquency, futures. Guide included. p. Family Information Systems and Resource Communications, Inc.; MTITI.

PARENTING (50m C 1980) (Video)
Examines the impact of a child on the parent's relationship, the impact of the myth of super mother, the expanding role of the father, parental support systems including books and day care, how to build communication and discipline skills with children, and the pitfalls of rushing children through developmental tasks. Interviewed are Katherine Read Baker, early childhood educator-author; Dr. Nancy Chodorow, sociologist-author; Ilene Dillon, counselor; Dr. Warren Farrell, author of The Liberated Man; Dr. Richard Hanson, Assistant Professor, Home Economics, CSUC; Dr. Barbara Mahler, director of Child Development Lab, CSUC, Jo Ann Nicola, Child Development professor, CSU, Sacramento; Gayle Smith, organizer of single parent co-op; Dr. Benjamin Spock, physician and author of Baby and Child Care. Dr. Gayle Kimball, Coordinator Women's Studies Program, California State University, Chico; CSUCHI.

PARENTING CONCERNS--THE FIRST TWO YEARS (21m C 1978)
Explores common child-rearing problems encountered during the child's first two years. Includes information on discipline, a child's independence, toilet training, sibling rivalry. p. Perennial Education, Inc.; PEREN.

PARENTING EXPERIENCE, THE (19m C n.d.)
Introduces the concept of "parenting" as a means of enriching the parent/baby relationship. It presents two couples and shows how both mother and father carry out the basic "how-to" skills of infant care: bathing, feeding, diapering, etc. At the same time, the

spontaneous actions of these parents and discussion by the narrator help make viewers aware of the equally important skills and rewards of "parenting"--the emotional and physical closeness of parent and baby that has such a profound effect on the development of the baby and the happiness of the family. Approved by the Educational Services Division, The American Journal Nursing Company. p. Pampers Professional Services Division of Procter and Gamble. AF.

PARENTING: GROWING WITH CHILDREN (22m C 1976)
Looks at the realities, responsibilities and rewards of parenting as seen in the lives of four very different families: 1) a young couple struggling to adjust to the arrival of a new baby; 2) a large family in which each parent plays a distinct and clearly-defined role; 3) a household in which both husband and wife are seeking meaningful careers while sharing equally the parenting responsibility; and 4) a single mother, trying to raise her children with dignity and humanity in a difficult urban environment. Demonstrates that successful parenting involves many years of commitment, love, patience, and skill. It also shows that there is no one "right" way and that each family must find its own parenting style, consistent with the parents' personalities, values and life goals. p. Peter Schnitzler; FLMFR; UIL.

PARENTING THE SPECIAL-NEEDS CHILD (25m C 1981) (also Video)
Trigger Films on Human Interaction Series
Parents of special-needs children find they face many stressful situations in addition to the extra requirements of child care, and most of these situations come in the form of reactions of other people. Uses topical, dramatic vignettes to depict interactions with many of the people who affect the life of the parents of the special-needs child. Guide included. p. Family Information Systems and Resource Communications, Inc.; MTITI.

PARENTS AND CHILDREN: A POSITIVE APPROACH TO CHILD MANAGEMENT (24m C 1979) (also Video)
Presents an overview of reinforcement principles in easily understood, nontechnical language. It examines the parent-child relationship as a special learning experience in which the use of rewards can play a crucial role. Shows how to use positive reinforcement to teach children and improve their behavior. An excellent aid to teachers, psychologists, social workers, or other professionals involved in parent training. Features Dr. Richard M. Foxx. p. Dr. Gladys B. Baxley, Norman E. Baxley with Research Press; RESPRC.

PARENTS AND CHILDREN WHO HAVE ADOPTED EACH OTHER (29m C 1982) (also Video) Are You Listening Series
Producer Martha Stuart has gathered together a group of adoptive parents and children to share their feelings and experiences. Included in the group is a single adoptive father, couples who birthed children and then adopted, couples who adopted children from Southeast Asia

and Korea as well as interracial American children, and an adoptive family with teenage boys who were originally in foster care. These families, founded on choice, talk about the importance of listening to one another and about how the bonds of love can be willfully, consciously made. They discuss what to do with questions about the biological mother and how to handle insensitive comments from strangers and even friends. They also talk about the differences between adopting older children versus infants; the benefits of adopting children from other cultures and countries; and the designation of children as "hard to place." They stress the importance of hearing "success" adoption stories as a support mechanism for adoptive families. Produced with a grant from The Edna McConnell Clark Foundation. p. Martha Stuart; STUARTM.

PARK THAT KIDS BUILT, THE (19m C 1982) (also Video)
Shows how one dedicated young teacher and her sixth-grade class turned an unused strip of ground that had long been a dumping ground for thoughtless and inconsiderate people into a playground. By talking to civic leaders and with the help of media coverage, etc., they were able to raise the $60,000 for the land. In breaking ground for the park, the whole neighborhood came together, joined by city and school officials. The entire project took two years, not soon enough for that particular class to use very much, but they left a very fine gift of service to the neighborhood. It was a valuable experience for all concerned. d. Linda Jassim; CF.

PARTO POR CESAREA (CAESAREAN BIRTH) (11m C 1980)
A couple shares the experience of a Caesarean birth with the father present during the operation: In Spanish with English transcript. p. Terry Looper; SERBC.

PASCIAKS OF CHICAGO, THE (58m C 1976) Six American Families (Series)
Stanley and Lorraine Pasciak of Chicago are blue collar, second generation Polish Americans whose traditions and ethnic roots are challenged by the life-styles of their six children. Refusing to follow their father into jobs at the Department of Sanitation, the oldest sons choose careers in acting and rock music. p. Elinor Bunin Productions; WBCPRO; CAROUF; KENTSU, PAS, UIL, UM, USFL.

PAST, PRESENT, FUTURE--MARIA SANDOZ (30m 1961) (Video)
Maria Sandoz, author, tells about how she became inspired to write about the characters, their experiences and their stories around Nebraska, Missouri and others. NETCHE.

PATHWAY FROM WITHIN: THE SCULPTURES OF ELIZABETH FRASER WILLIAMSON, A (18m C 1975)
Elizabeth Fraser Williamson, who has attained recognition as an outstanding sculptor for her work in stone, concrete, clay and wood, is shown in her studio working on various pieces of sculpture. She

says that sculpting to her is an approach to self-expression and self-fulfillment, and explains how she gets inspiration from nature. p. Educational Film Distributors, Ltd.; JOURVI; UIL.

PATRICIA'S MOVING PICTURE (27m C 1978)
Patricia is first seen reminiscing over a box filled with old photographs, then talking about her wedding day 19 years ago, her husband, and family. She is one of many women who have to face the question, What do you fill your life with when the family is grown?-- Will life be as full and purposeful as when the children were little? Patricia shares the experiences of her adjustment. She had crying jags, felt like she was in a dark tunnel, and her marriage seemed rocky. Follows her discovery that she was mourning the death of a role, and her search for a new one. d. Bonnie Sherr Klein; p. Margaret Pettigrew, Ann Pearson; NFBC; MEDIAG; UCEMC, UIL.

PATTERNS, THE (SERIES) see WOMAN'S TOUCH, A

PAYMENT OF TERESA VIDELA (11m C/B 1979)
Graphic re-enactment of torture and murder of political prisoners, created from data acquired from Argentina. Depicts the sexual violation, torture, and murder of a young woman student by Argentina Army personnel. d. Niccolo Caldararo; CALDN.

PAYSAGISTE, LE see MINDSCAPE

PEACE: A CONSCIOUS CHOICE (4m C 1982) (also Video)
Provides a positive way of helping to inspire and create peace. As animated images appear and disappear on the screen along with English and then Russian subtitles, the voices of a Russian and an American each claim, "I don't want war, but if we are attacked we must defend ourselves." The narration explains that the first step toward peace is for opposing nationals to let each other know they do not want war. The film ends with a quote from Gandhi: "Almost anything you do will seem insignificant but it is very important that you do it." p. Dorothy Fadiman/Robert Pacelli; p. Fadiman Films; BULFRG.

PEDAL POWER (19m C p1977, r1978)
Demonstrates the energy potential of the human body using pedal-powered machines and questions our unthinking use of electricity. The use of pedal power in practical application is traced in this film as far back as the early sixteenth century to a screw-cutting lathe designed by Leonardo da Vinci. An interesting look at one imaginative energy alternative. p. John Hoskyns-Abrahall, Winifred Scherrer, p. Rosedale Press; BULFRG.

PEDOPHILE (20m C 1972)
Aimed at police, educators, and parents, this film sheds light into the world of a universally feared but little-understood criminal,

the pedophile--child molester. Who is the molester? How does he
entice his young victims? What drives him to commit his hideous
crimes? The film provides answers to these questions. p. Sid Davis
Productions; AIMS.

PEDRO LINARES--ARTESANO CARTONERO (23m C 1975) MEXICO'S
    FOLK ARTISTS SERIES
    Shows the beauty and skill of the work of Mexican papier-mâché
artist Pedro Linares. Linares describes his life and his work; how
he began with papier-mâché, and his deep feelings about the traditions which his art serves. Available in English/Spanish. p. Judith
Bronowski; WORKS.

PEGGY COLLINS (SINGLE MOTHER) (9m C 1979) (also Video) The
    American Family, An Endangered Species? (Series)
    A divorcee, Peggy Collins struggles to support herself and her
teenaged daughter on a waitress' salary. Her financial problems are
compounded by her daughter's uneasy adjustment to the divorce. p.
Stuart Schulberg; FI.

PELVIC INFLAMMATORY DISEASE (8½m C n.d.)
    Explains how pelvic inflammatory disease is an infection problem
caused in most cases by contracting a venereal disease. Describes
the symptoms, treatment and what the long-term effects may be if allowed to go untreated. Film is very positive in its message. MIFE.

PENCIL BOOKLINGS (14m C 1978) (SFS)
    Charming fantasy animation of the filmmaker and her assortment
of characters. Each of her characters has a unique personality as
they take turns doing solo performances. Then, they evolve in group
calisthenics inviting the filmmaker to join them. Excellent study in
the art of animation. p. Kathy Rose; SERBC.

PENNSYLVANIA DUTCH DANCING (15m C 1965-66)
    These dancers, filmed at the Kutztown Fair near Lancaster, Penn-
sylvania, demonstrate dances which have been performed by Amish
and other sects for over 200 years. Produced under the auspices
of the Department of Health, Education and Welfare, the University
of Pennsylvania and the Philadelphia Dance Academy. Dance Com-
panys: Lykens Valley Jiggers, Stone Valley Jiggers; Project Director: Nadia Chilkovsky Nahumck; Associate Director: Fai Coleman;
p. Calvin De Frenes Corporation; FRANDA.

PENNY SUITE, A (5m C r1977)
    A visual poem in animation where animals float aimlessly through
space; a large smiling face swallows the animals and they emerge as
a carousel. Originally attached firmly to their poles, the animals
slowly learn to relate to one another and develop greater freedom.
They dance and play games with and for each other as their independence progresses. Finally the animals transform from one shape

to another and ultimately end up as at the beginning, floating freely through space. p. Jody Silver; PHOENIX.

PENSIONS: THE BROKEN PROMISE (39m C 1972)
A hard-hitting documentary that looks at the fiction of pensions for many American employees who work long, hard years for a company, spurred on by the idea that their retirement years will be carefree, only to find this dream of security has faded along with their pension funds. Interviews with retirees reveal their bewilderment, resentment and bitterness. Comments by labor leaders, social workers, and others point out the need for some form of government legislation. Archive film footage is used to review the history of Social Security and retirement pension plans. p. NBC-TV; FI; OSU, PAS, IU, UCEMC, UIL.

PEOPLE AND ARTS (Two 30-sec. spots C 1977)
Public service announcements for the Architecture Program of the National Endowment for the Arts. p. Caroline Ahlfours Mouris, Frank Mouris; FRANKF.

PEOPLE ARE DANCING AGAIN, THE (28m C 1976)
A historical documentary of the Confederated Tribes of Siletz Indians in western Oregon from 1850 to the present. From 1850 to 1854 the coastal Indians were moved to Siletz when their status as an officially recognized Indian tribe was terminated by the government. All federal support was withdrawn and remaining tribal land sold off. In 1970, the Siletz people began working to regain federal recognition of their tribal status. In a long and difficult process of working for restoration, there has been a rebirth of the tribe's spirit and the people's own sense of their values as Indians in modern America. p. Harry Dawson Jr./John M. Volkman; CURBE.

PEOPLE OF THE CITIES (31m C 1979) The Russians, (Series)
Documents the daily lives of three Russian families in the cities of Moscow, Odessa, and Sochi. Provides insights into working conditions, housing, transportation, education, culture, recreation, and standard of living. Emphasizes the role of women in Russian society and points out the similarities of life in Russia with life in the West. p. Film Australia; LCA; IU.

PEOPLE OF THE COUNTRY (30m C 1979) The Russians (Series)
Examines life on the collective farms in Russia by visiting the new Bratsk Timber Complex in Siberia, the 50,000-acre Kirov Collective Farm in the Kuban, and a small collective farm in Byelorussia. Shows the people at work and observes their continuing efforts to industrialize agriculture, modernize housing, and provide better school, cultural, and sporting facilities for the farmers. Looks at the problems of insufficient work for the women of a collective. p. Film Australia; LCA; IU.

THE PEOPLE VS. INEZ GARCIA (88m C 1975) (Video)
A dramatization of the explosive trial of Inez Garcia, based on
an adaptation of the actual court transcription of the 1974 trial in
Monterey, California. In a decision her supporters termed "racist
and sexist," Garcia was found guilty of second degree murder of
the shooting death of the accomplice of the man she accused of rape.
The drama raises important questions about the American criminal
justice system and a woman's right to defend herself in the context
of an alleged rape. p. KQED-TV; San Francisco, California; PBSV.

PEOPLE WHO HAVE EPILEPSY (29m C p1979, r1979) (also Video)
Are You Listening Series
This film cuts through the fog of popular ignorance to present
an intimate and informative view of the disorder, the people who
have it, and how it affects their lives. Shows a diverse cross-section
of persons who have epilepsy. The discussion that emerges deals,
among other topics, with its onset; how to abort a seizure; the importance of feeling independent; how parents and children can best
deal with one another on the subject. People talk about how they
cope with jobs, schools, travel, marriage, driving, and other practical aspects. Recommended for people who have epilepsy and for
health care professionals and students. p. Martha Stuart; d. Ivan
Cury; STUARTM.

PEOPLE YOU'D LIKE TO KNOW SERIES see DIANA; ELIZABETH;
VISION OF THE BLIND

PEPPERMINT SODA (97m C 1978) (French/Subtitled)
The story centers on the friends, family, classes, vacations, and
sulks of a French-Jewish schoolgirl from summer to summer in the
epochal year of 1963. d. Diane Kurys; NYF.

PEPTIC ULCERS (60m C 1980) (Video) Better Health (Series)
What ulcers are and what to do if you have one are the topics
of this show. Dr. Denis McCarthy, senior investigator for the National Institute of Arthritis, Metabolism and Digestive Diseases, talks
about the kinds of ulcers, who gets them and why, and various treatments. Free loan. p. National Institute of Health; MTPS.

PERFECT TRIBUTE (19m B 1935)
Dramatizes the story of Mary Shipman Andrews, telling of Lincoln's composition of the Gettysburg Address, his subsequent disappointment at its reception, and its final appreciation by a wounded
soldier. MGM; UFL.

PERFECTLY NORMAL DAY, A (27m C 1978)
Alan Lakein says a normal day is like a jigsaw puzzle--it comes
in a lot of fragmented pieces. A lot of unexpected things happen.
A lot goes wrong. We have two choices: we can be pulled in a
dozen directions all day long and not accomplish "A" priorities--or

we can develop a new attitude toward crises and interruptions and learn to reduce and manage them. Fast paced, entertaining and informative. p. Cally Curtis Company; CALLYC.

PERIPATEIA 1 AND 2 (12m C si 1977)
Part One explores the movement of a forest and human body spiralling sunward. Part Two extends this exploration, contrasting more severely the fixed camera and the moving body. Both parts were filmed in the Oregon coastal rain forests. (Collective for Living Cinema, October 27, 1978.) p. Abigail Child; COLIVC.

PERMANENT WAVE (3m C 1967)
By rephotographing scenes from a "blue movie," director Thacher subverts its eroticism and builds a new, more distanced involvement through texture and motion. d. Anita Thacher; MMA.

PERSONAL FINANCES AND EFFECTIVE CONSUMERSHIP (11 programs, 17m ea. C 1981) (also Video)
Shows how to budget income, how to make informed decisions about large purchases, and how to survive financially on one's own. p. Centron Educational Films; CENTEF.

PERSPECTRE/PERSPECTRUM (6½m C 1981)
An animated film in which a simple geometric form, thin and flat as a playing card, is duplicated, arranged and rearranged into a flow of patterns and perspectives such as you might see in a kaleidoscope. Accompanied by koto music by Micio Miyagi; p. Dorothy Courtois for the National Film Board of Canada; NFBC; IFB.

PETEY THE PELICAN (9½m C r1978) (also Video)
Introduces the pelican to children in a fascinating way. p. Myrna I. Berlet, Walter H. Berlet; IFB.

PETRONELLA (13m C p1978, r1978)
An animated fairy tale in which a princess feels that she deserves equal opportunity to go forth and rescue a prince, suspected to be held captive. d./p. Barbara Dourmashkin; FLMFR; IU.

PHILADELPHIA QUARTET (5m C 1975)
Bartok is played by the Philadelphia Quartet. Technical collaboration on optical effects with Robert Brown. Original taping directed by Steve Welch at NET in Seattle, Washington. p. Doris Chase; CHASED.

PHOEBE (28m B n.d.)
About a teenage girl who allows herself to become accidentally pregnant. Dealing accurately with teen feelings, it shows her fantasy of what her father, mother, and boyfriend will do when they learn of the problem. The important thing is that she must not handle this serious problem alone. She must talk to someone. NFBC; VIEWFI.

PHOTOGRAPHY: MASTERS OF THE 20TH CENTURY (25m C p1981,
r1981) Americana Series, Art in America, PT. 10
Illustrates the works of the photographers of this era and their
approach to art as explained during personal interviews. Shown are
on-camera appearances and works of artists Ansel Adams, Barbara
Morgan, Harry Callahan, Eliot Porter, Gordon Parks, Patrick Naga-
tani, Betty Hahn, Robert Heinecken and Joel Meyerowitz. Early artists discussed in the film include Lewis Hine, Walker Evans, Paul
Strand, Dorothea Lange, Margaret Bourke-White, Edward Steichen
and Alfred Stieglitz. A montage of the works of a new generation
of artists discovering new ways of recording with the camera ends
the film. p./d./s.w. Irene Zmurkevych; HANDEL.

PHOTOGRAPHY: THE BEGINNINGS OF A NEW ART (25m C 1981)
(also Video)
Shows the developments and artists who endeavored to perfect
this mechanical medium--bringing it into the realm of fine art. Using
a splendid collection of early black and white stills and some of the
first cameras, this film explains and demonstrates how those first
photographs were made and tells of innovations that seemed to appear
simultaneously in different countries. Louis Daguerre of France developed a method of fixing images on a metal plate, Samuel Morse was
one of the first Americans to use his camera. America's Albert South-
worth and Josiah Johnson lent their artistic interpretations to photography, turning it into an art form. Many innovations and innovators
are discussed. p./d./s.w. Irene Zmurkevych; HANDEL.

PHYSIATRY: A PHYSICIAN'S PERSPECTIVE (26m C 1981)
Shows medical students why they should specialize in physiatry
(rehabilitation medicine) by presenting its unique challenges and rewards. Dr. Chuck Marshall is shown with six patients as he diagnoses, consults, and teaches. His responsibilities extend beyond narrow definitions of medicine as he finds ways to improve each patient's
quality of life. d. Grania Gurievitch; p. G. Gurievitch/John A.
Downey, M.D.; REHABF.

PHYSICAL FITNESS (19m C 1980)
A commitment to a well-planned exercise program helps attain
maximum working efficiency for the heart, blood vessels, lungs and
muscles, as well as increase strength and endurance. A well-planned
physical fitness program helps you to lose weight, stop smoking, reduce the risk of heart and blood vessel diseases, gives you greater
endurance and stamina and helps you cope with stress and life in
general. p. Professional Research, Inc.; FLMFR.

PHYSICAL FITNESS AND HEALTH (42m C 1981) (Video)
Jim White, a physiologist at the University of California, San
Diego, talks to viewers on how proper diet and regular exercise can
change one's life for the better. Clear and concise. Technical information is brief. A good training film for persons embarking on a

physical fitness program. p. University of California, San Diego, California; HUMRM.

PHYSICAL SIGNS AND EFFECTS OF VENEREAL DISEASES (28m C
    1978) The Inner Woman (Series)
    Stresses the critical need to acknowledge symptoms of venereal
disease and seek immediate help and the need for public education
about the causes, the symptoms and treatment of these diseases. Moderator: Marilyn Poland, R.N.; CRM.

PHYSICIAN UPDATE SERIES see LEARNING TO DIAGNOSE ARTH-
    RITIS; MANAGEMENT OF RECURRENT BREAST CARCINOMA

PHYSIOLOGY OF MISCARRIAGE AND ABORTION (28m C 1978) The
    Inner Woman (Series)
    Presents the signs and causes of miscarriage and mentions the
controversy about the effect of the IUD in causing abortions and infections. Also, discusses the induced abortion. Marilyn Poland, R.N.,
moderator, p. WXYZ-TV; CRM.

PHYSIOLOGY OF REPRODUCTION, THE (29m B 1956) Months Before
    Birth--A Series
    Uses charts to show and explain the function of the male and
female reporductive organs. p. WQED-TV; AF.

PIAF--THE EARLY YEARS (104m C 1982) (French/Subtitled)
    A superbly crafted biography of the late, great French singer.
The soundtrack includes 14 classic Piaf songs--five from original Piaf
recordings. Shows Piaf's early years in the poor Parisian quarter of
Belleville where she is put to work on the streets and must literally
sing for her supper. After years of poverty and hardship, Piaf finally achieves success. Included is her triumphant audition at the
famous ABC Theatre. A touching and sympathetic tribute to an extraordinary woman who was destined to become a legend. Cast: Bri-
gitte Ariel, Pascale Christophe, Guy Trejan; d. Guy Casaril; FI.

PICASSO--A PAINTER'S DIARY SERIES (C 1980)
    PART I, THE FORMATIVE YEARS (35m)
    PART II, CUBISM TO GUERNICA (34m)
    PART III, A UNITY OF VARIETY (21m)
    A diary in three chapters ... with intimate revelations by one of
our greatest contemporary artists, his children, his friends, his fellow
artists, his loves. But most importantly, this diary focuses on his
habitats throughout Europe and on a wealth of his drawings, paintings and sculptures. For, as Picasso "writes" in this diary, "My
works are a form of a diary. For those who know how to read, I
have painted my autobiography." In a deft mix of rare and unpub-
lished photos, painstaking cinematography and re-creation of past conversations and letters, Pablo Picasso illustrates the drive, explosive-
ness, influence, unceasing experimentations and vision of art that are

uniquely his. From the traumatic impact of his close friend Carlos Casegmas' suicide to the fond remembrances of total immersion in creative play with his children, Picasso shows us how an artist continually evolves and sees the world from his fertile perspective. p./d. Perry Miller Adato; p. WNET-TV; CORONET; UIL.

PICK ME UP AT PEGGY'S COVE (25m C p1982, r1983)
Based on the book by the same title by Brian Doyle. The story is about Ryan, who spends the summer at a seaside tourist town with his aunt after his father left home. In rebellion, Ryan becomes the accomplice of a local kid who rips off the tourists. When the police catch up with them, Ryan learns that he does have friends and a family-support system to help him through his crisis. d. Don Mc-Brearty; p. Janice Platt; BEACON.

PICTURES (3m C 1978)
A short animated film made to commemorate International Women's Year. Hundreds of images were collected, Xeroxed, hand-colored, and then photographed to create a montage. Photographs, art reproductions and images from the print media combine with music to trace the history of women. A definite dissatisfaction with the present is felt, the film ends with a dream for the future. p. Janet Benn; WMM.

PICTURES OF THE LOST (21m C si 1978) (Video)
Meshes representational imagery with colored kinetic abstractions in 22 evocatively titled vignettes, creating a subtle and mysterious world in which semi-recognizable figures seem to appear out of a pulsing and flowing colorized set of images. (For a fuller description see Film Library Quarterly, 1980, page 40, Volume 13, No. 1.) p./d. Barbara Buckner; BUCKNER.

PICTURES OUT OF MY LIFE (13m C 1973)
The drawings and memories of Eskimo artist Pitseolak, from the book of the same title written by Dorothy Eber. Now in her seventies, Pitseolak is one of the most famous of the graphic artists of the Cape Dorset (Baffin Island) artists' colony and cooperative. Her colored pencil and felt-pen drawings vividly illustrate her recollections of past life in the Arctic and of the birds, animals and spirits that figured so largely in the daily life of the Eskimo. d. Zina Heczko; p. Wolf Koenig; NFBC.

PIECE OF CAKE (23½m C 1981)
A film about the loneliness of old age. Two male old-age pensioners live in a semi-rural town. The daughter of one is expected home for Christmas from overseas. The father is unable to get credit to buy a goose for Christmas dinner. He plans to steal one and, in doing so, implicates his friend. d./s.w. Mitch Matthews; p. Pamela H. Vanneck; p. Australian Film Commission; LCA.

PILL AND I.U.D., THE (16m C n.d.)
   Dr. John Hillabrand, an OB-gynecologist and an expert on the
pill and I.U.D., discusses this topic with a panel of ten men and
women. Questions regarding the modes of action and side effects
of these methods of contraception are discussed and answered. p.
Cinema Medica; CINMD.

PIÑATA (24m C 1978)
   Country and city life in Mexico is revealed through the adventures
of a small boy whose imagination is captured by a beautiful and magical piñata. d./p. Diana Colson/Hank Swain Production; MCFI; UIL.

PINK TRIANGLES (35m C 1981) (also Video)
   Although the film is specifically about "homophobia"--the fear
and persecution of lesbians and gay men--it is also about the very
nature of discrimination and oppression. This film examines both
historical and contemporary patterns of persecution in which social,
religious, political, and sexual minorities are singled out as "different,"
"not normal" or "inferior" and become the victims of the scapegoat
mentality of societies under stress. As parents, educators, providers
of health care, medicine, mental health care and social services, the
effectiveness of our efforts is only as good as the quality of our human relationships. To be good at what we do, we must examine a
form of discrimination that affects an estimated 10 percent of the population. Includes the research of a German born historian who escaped the Nazi imprisonment of homosexuals and returned to investigate the plight of many thousands who suffered in the concentration
camps wearing the Nazi insignia for gay men--the pink triangle. Produced by a group of nine women and men, both gay and straight,
who work as health workers, mental health workers, historians, and
in photography, print, and film. Study guide also available. p.
Triangle Film Collective; CAMDOC.

PINKS AND THE BLUES, THE (57m C 1980) Nova Series
   Even after a decade of sex role redefinition, boys and girls today
are treated in stereotypical fashion. This program demonstrates that
"from the moment parents wrap a newborn baby in either a pink or
blue blanket, they start a socialization process that lasts a lifetime."
Furthermore, these patterns may be so subtle that parents and teachers responsible for the child's socialization may deny that distinctions
are made. p. WGBH-TV; TIMLIF; PAS, UMN.

PINS AND NEEDLES (37m C p1979, r1980--U.S.) (also Video)
   A personal film made by a young woman, Genni Batterham, who
was striken with multiple sclerosis. Genni refused to relinquish her
sense of purpose and dignity because of her disability. Realizing
how society has turned its back on the handicapped, Genni organizes
protests and speaks out in public. Teachers will find this film invaluable since so many major issues are expressed: sexuality, self-
esteem, dependency, denial of reality by family, the appropriateness

of occupational workshops, and the problems of access. d. Barbara
Chobocky, Kim Batterham; p. Genni Batterham, Kim Batterham;
FILMLB; PAS.

PIONEER GIRL (31m C n.d.) (Video) Voices of Early Canada Series
Based on a series of letters written by 14-year-old Maryanne
Caswell in 1887, this film vividly illustrates what it was like to build
a new life in the prairies. It uses original prairie film footage, photographs and archival material, and follows the long trip she and her
family made from Palmerston, Ontario to a fledgling community on the
Saskatchewan River. Maryanne is depicted in the program as an
older woman recalling her earlier journey. p. Media Centre, University of Toronto; UTORON.

PISTA: THE MANY FACES OF STEPHEN DEUTCH (28m C p1978,
r1979)
A searching portrait by his daughter of sculptor/photographer
Deutch spanning 70 years--his social and political attitudes and his
relationship to art, music and family through personal commentary,
family photos, interviews with fellow artists and critics (e.g. Studs
Terkel) and extensive footage of his own work. Sound track (recorded live) by The Fine Arts Quartet. d./p. Katherine Deutch
Tatlock; DEUTAT.

PIZZA PIZZA DADDY-O (18m B 1969)
A dozen fourth-grade Afro-American girls, playing singing games
in a school playground in a Los Angeles ghetto, are shown. The
film records eight of these games as examples of the tradition of singing games which have been handed down from one generation of school
children to the next. The main stylistic feature is call and response
with almost every phrase echoed in singing and movement patterns.
Organization of the games and group activity is done by the children
themselves. A study guide with complete texts of the songs is available. d. Bess Lomax Hawes, Robert Eberlein; p. Department of Anthropology, San Fernando Valley State College; UCEMC, IU.

PLACE THAT COMMA! (19m C 1980) (also Video)
Introduces, repeats and reinforces the rules of comma placement.
It clarifies and simplifies rules of punctuation. A study guide with
practice worksheet included. p. Marsha Jeffer; PF.

PLACE TO GO, A (ed.) (15m C 1981) (also Video)
Documents the widespread incidence of wife beating in America.
Two million women are said to be suffering this kind of violence which
is not limited to any social or economic strata, but rather, touches
every segment of the population. Laws that are ambiguous and wives
who are often hesitant to press charges compound the problem. Another thing that discourages these women is the fact that of the 400
battered women centers throughout the nation, most are housed in
run-down facilities and lack adequate staffing and funding to offer

real help. Discussions among victims offer new insight into the way beatings affect the lives of the women and their families. p. CBS News "60 Minutes"; MTITI; IU.

PLAGE, LA see LA PLAGE

PLANNING AHEAD SERIES, THE see BLACK GIRL; CHILE PEQUIN; SISTER OF THE BRIDE

PLANNING BABYSITTING (13m C p1979, r1980) Babysitter Series
Shows a babysitter how to handle a variety of duties relative to babysitting. Good communication between babysitter, parents and children is stressed as imperative if the experience is to be an enjoyable one for all concerned. d. Tom Solari; p. Film Communicators; FILMCO.

PLANT A SEED (3m C 1977)
Shows what an individual can do to bring floral beauty into the urban setting. Filmed in New York's Greenwich Village, it extols the virtues of the window box in brightening the urban scene. On roofs, balconies and windows and houses, window boxes are shown to liven up drab walls and bring some reminder of natural plant life into the city environment, varying from a few sparse sprigs to profuse floral covering an entire window, and the vines climbing up the ladder of a fire escape. No narration, lyrics are of an original song. d./p. Joan Rosenfelt; PHOENIX, KPF.

PLASTIC BODY, THE (20m B 1958) (Video)
This kinescope is the result of a master's thesis by Jane Josepian. This creative dance demonstration explains how the body is designed for movement; how movement can be made expressive by manipulating the elements of time, space and energy; how qualities of movement can be achieved in dancing. Dancers: Students at the University of Utah; Dance Teacher/Narrator/d./p. Jane Josepian; p. for TV: Harold Hickman; p. Dance Films Association; DANCFA; UIL.

PLEASE AT LEAST LEAVE ME THE SUN (9½m C n.d.) (also Video)
Animated film without words on children's drawings from the exposition called "The City of Tomorrow." These paintings show what the world might have in store for these children who will be the citizens of the future. p. Lydia Chagoll, Belgium; CAROUF.

PLEXI RADAR (7½m B 1981) (Video)
Plexi Radar involves the filming of a revolving, circular plexiglass sculpture which then is computer sequenced. The image of the sculpture alternates and divides into numerous horizontal planes--hypnotic in that the subconscious imposes the illusion of an ever-changing screen. p. Doris Chase; CHASED.

PNEUMONIA (1m C 1982) (Video)
To inform viewers of the symptoms and treatment of pneumonia.

d. Susan Marrone; p. Alvin Roselin; s.w. Susan Marrone; ed. Stan Redding; sponsor: Abbott Labs; PLANCS.

POET OF HIS PEOPLE, PABLO NERUDA (13m C 1978)
Mixes live action, still footage, computer images, dance and poetry to represent Chilean poet Pablo Neruda's life and his poem "Barcarola." p. Lillian Schwartz; LILYANP.

POISON IVY (13m C p1979, r1980--U.S.) (also Video)
Presents Ivy Granstrom, who lost most of her vision through insufficient care at birth. However, Ivy jogs every day, swims, skiis, bowls, curls and leads an active, happy and independent life. Shows Ivy doing her own dusting, vacuuming and plant care, depending much more on her sense of touch than on her nearly sightless eyes. One of 14 children, Ivy speaks of being taught how to do everything by her mother and her love of nursing when she served as a nurse's aid for years before retiring. Her comment about unusual and courageous lifestyle is "I manage pretty good." d. Richard James Martin; p. Jack Long/National Film Board of Canada; PHOENIX.

POLICE TAPES (49m B 1977)
Cinema-verité documentary showing interaction of New York police officers with urban ghetto over six-month period. Wide variety of incidents include responses to homicide, assault, drug abusers, domestic fights. Socio-economic problems of decaying urban centers are shown through the eyes of the police department responsible for "keeping the lid on." d. Susan Raymond, Alan Raymond; p. Video Verité; DIRECT.

POLITICAL PARTIES: WOMEN'S CLOUT (29m C 1976) (Video) Woman
    Series
Carol Burris, founder of Women's Lobby, Inc. and Susan Tolchin, director of the Washington Institute for Women in Politics, discuss the new awareness of political power on the part of women. Tolchin, who wrote Clout: Woman Power and Politics, attributes the real change to the national political conventions of 1972. She points out that while more women are seeking positions of political influence, few aspire to "high office," which she blames on society's disapproval of a woman's role in a male-dominated field. Sandra Elkin is the moderator. PBSV.

POLITICS OF AGING (15m C 1982)
Shows that although older people have never formed a political block, they are taking a very active role in the politics of age. Consumer advocacy and lobbying are important. Silver-haired legislators are shown in session; older people are seen learning the basics and art of advocacy; a state legislator advises older people to look after their own interests, which are in reality, those of all Americans. p. International Center for Social Gerontology, University of Michigan; UMMRC; UIL, UM.

POPOVICH BROTHERS OF SOUTH CHICAGO (60m C 1978)
Tells about the 1,100 Serbian-American families in South Chicago.
What connects them to their family, church and community and provides the deepest expression of their identity is their traditional Ser-
bian music, and the Popovich Brothers have been a constant source
of that music for over 50 years. These four brothers, now in their
sixties, represent the very best and most beloved expression of Ser-
bian cultural identity. Through their lives, past and present, the
film offers a picture of the classical immigrant experience in its most
positive manifestation: a small community of mostly blue-collar families who, years after their ancestors arrived in this country, still
maintained their affection and identification with their old-world heritage without isolating themselves from the values and life-styles of
mainstream America. d./p. Jill Godmilow in collaboration with Ethel
Raim and Martin Koenig of the Balkan Art Center, Inc.; BALKAC.

POPULATION AND POLLUTION (17m C 1971) (also Video)
Portrays the present environment crisis in North America caused
both by misuse of the environment and by the great demands of a
constantly growing population. Emphasizes the need for changes in
attitude and for a commitment to finding both short-range and long-
range solutions to the problems of air, water, and land pollution.
French version also available. p. Myrna I. Berlet, Walter H. Berlet,
IFB.

PORNOGRAPHY (29m C 1977) (Video) Woman Series
The effect of pornography on children, crime rates and morality
is discussed by Susan Brownmiller, author of Against Our Will: Men,
Women and Rape; Dr. Anke Ehrhardt, psychoendocrinologist and sex-
role researcher; and Loretta Darling, Secretary of the Citizens for a
Decent Community in Rochester, New York. The women explain their
individual definitions of pornography and talk about the kinds of controls they favor. Sandra Elkin, moderator. p. WNED-TV; PBSV.

PORNOGRAPHY AND FANTASY see NOT A LOVE STORY: A FILM
ABOUT PORNOGRAPHY

PORTRAIT: MAGGIE KUHN (29m C 1979) (2" HB tape)
Maggie Kuhn, National Convener of the Gray Panther Network,
discusses projects, issues, achievements, and aspirations of the Gray
Panthers and her hopes for younger Americans. Host: Carol Hollens-
head, Institute of Gerontology, University of Michigan. UMMRC; UM.

PORTRAIT OF A REBEL: MARGARET SANGER (96m C 1982)
At one time in this country it was illegal to disseminate information about birth control. This docudrama details the efforts of Margaret Sanger (Bonnie Franklin), a nurse who struggled to have that
law, the Comstock Act of 1912, repealed and to educate women to the
option of contraception. In her desperate battle, she endures ridicule, censorship, a prison sentence, and a fractured family life.

Her relationship with soulmate English psychologist Havelock Ellis detailed. Also starring David Dukes, Milo O'Shea, Richard Johnson and Francis Lee McCain. p. Marvin Minoff; TIMLIF.

PORTRAIT OF CHRISTINE (25m C p1977, r1978)
Twenty-eight-year-old Christine Karcza, orthopedically handicapped since infancy, proves that handicapped people can become fully involved members of society. p. Film Arts Production; d. Elizabeth MacCallum; WOMBAT; UCEMC.

PORTRAIT OF GRANDPA DOC (28m C r1977)
Explores the relationship of the young to the very old, and the special grief that death brings. As a young artist prepares his first one-man show, he struggles to complete a portrait of his maternal grandfather, who died several years earlier. He searches for the image which will capture his grandfather, recalling that it was Grandpa Doc who first encouraged him to express himself through art. The memories of the times he spent with his grandfather flow into his work until, finally, he captures the image he has been seeking. p. Diane Baker; ex. p. Barbara Bryant; d./s.w. Randal Kleiser; PHOENIX; UMO.

PORTRAIT OF MAYA ANGELOU, A (45m C 1982) (Video) Creativity Series
Maya Angelou is an internationally acclaimed poet, writer, actress and singer. As a black child, she grew up in Stamps, Arkansas before the days of civil rights marches and equal opportunity. We accompany her as she goes home and remembers her childhood. "I was terribly hurt here," she tells us, "and vastly loved." With Bill Moyers. p./d. David Grubin; s.w. Ronald Blumer; ed. Merle Worth; sponsor: Chevron USA, Inc.; PBSV.

PORTRAIT OF TERESA (115m C 1979)
The sexual politics of the marital relationship, especially the persistence of a "double standard" for extramarital sex, is the explosive subject of this drama. Teresa and Ramon, a young working class couple, have reached a crisis point in their marriage because of her after-hours involvement with a dance group. Her husband complains that she is disregarding her duties as wife and mother. Already overburdened with housework, factory job, and the care of their three children, Teresa nevertheless feels it is her right to have time for her own creative activities. Their confrontation over this issue-- including one knock-down, drag-out bedroom fight--provides the dramatic focus for a portrayal of modern married life that is as relevant in this country as it is in Cuba. d. Pastor Vega; UNIFILM.

PORTRAITS OF AGING (18m C p1979, r1979)
Presents a positive view of aging to deepen the understanding of aging among young people and to inspire older women and men. Shows people from all walks of life, active, vibrant and with zest for living. p. Fred W. Miller; CENTEF; KENTSU, WSU.

PORTRAITS OF AGING: A POSITIVE VIEW (28m C 1978)
Profiles of people who have found their later years most enriching and satisfying. Their backgrounds are different, but they have
learned to cope with their problems. An inspirational film. p. Miller
Productions, Inc.; CENTEF; UIL, PSU.

PORTRAITS: TWO MALE PROSTITUTES (23m B p1980, r1980) (Video)
Explores the lives and feelings of two young male (transvestite)
prostitutes, one of whom has been selling his body on the streets
since he was 13 years old. Issues such as family relations and personal goals are openly discussed. d./p. Aron Ranen; RANEN.

POSSIBLY SO, PYTHAGORAS (14m C 1963) (also Video)
Investigates the Pythagorean theorem through induction experimentation as well as through formal deductive proof. By use of animation, the student can watch triangles continually change. Gives
an insight into the meaning of mathematical discovery by observation
and experiment. p. Katharine Cornwell, Bruce Cornwell; IFB.

POSSUM LIVING (28½m C p1980, r1981) (also Video)
The story is told through the eyes of Dolly Freed, a remarkable
young woman who has authored the successful "how-to" book Possum
Living (Bantam Books, 1980). The film presents a unique family in
its quest for quality of life on a "no frills" budget. For the past
five years, 20-year-old Dolly Freed and her father, Frank, have
maintained a middle-class standard of living on less than $2,000 a
year without any government assistance. Spending only $270 on food,
$160 on fuel and $15 on clothing each year, the Freeds have perfected
a life-style in the suburbs of Philadelphia which is simple, practical
and instructive for millions of Americans caught in the inflationary
spiral. Whether or not someone chooses to become a nonconsumer,
Dolly will inspire independent thinking about how economics affects
the course of one's life now and in the coming age of shortages. p.
Nancy Schreiber, Peter Polymenakos; d. N. Schreiber; NEWDAY.

POSSUM TROT: THE LIFE AND WORK OF CALVIN BLACK (28m C
p1977, r1977)
Documentary on the life of American folk artist Calvin Black.
Shows the village Possum Trot inhabited by nearly life-sized dolls
created and carved by Calvin Black. Black's widow still lives there
and guards the legacy he left. Mrs. Black recounts events in her
husband's life and how he came to carving these dolls. People come
to Black's village located in the Mojave Desert to see Black's dolls
perform and hear his voice on tape recordings. A brief glimpse into
the life of an individualist who saw life in an original way and lived
it according to his own rules. p. Allie Light, Patricia Ferrero, and
Irving Saraf; PHOENIX.

POST PARTUM DEPRESSION (28m C p1978, r1980--U.S.) (also Video)
Presents postpartum depression and how it affected two couples.

Ten to 20 percent of mothers develop postpartum depression shortly after the birth of their baby causing them to temporarily lose the ability to cope with life. Two women who experienced postpartum depression after the birth of their second children discuss their thoughts and feelings during that crisis period which affected all their relationships and threatened life itself. They both discovered a lifeline back to health through postpartum groups which bring together women who have experienced the same thing, recovered, and are willing to help others. p. Jennifer Torrance; d. Margit Nance; NFBC; PEREN.

POSTPARTUM CARE (12½m C n.d.)
This film follows the new mother's recovery in the hospital and at home after the birth of her baby. Covers treatment of her physical discomforts, mental adjustments (including postpartum blues) and her return home to regain her strength. Includes resuming sexual relations and her postpartum check-up. Also available in Spanish. MIFE.

POWER OF POSITIVE REINFORCEMENT, THE (28m C 1978) Organizational Development Film Series
Documents on-site applications of behavior management in several organizations, where increased satisfaction and productivity were the results in all cases. Uses short film segments, animation and sharing of experiences to describe the use of behavior modification in business organizations and everyday life. d./p./s.w. Frieda Lee Mock; CRM; CWU.

POWER PINCH: SEXUAL HARASSMENT IN THE WORK PLACE, THE (28m C p1981, r1981) (also Video)
Examines many aspects of sexual harassment in business including what it is, why it happens, who is involved and how it can be prevented. Female victims of sexual harassment describe the anger and humiliation caused by their male bosses or co-workers and the repercussions that affect their jobs, economic earning power and self-esteem. Ken Howard admits to the fine line between flirting and sexual harassment, the latter is described as unwanted, unwelcome, and repeated attention from one person to another in the work place. Subtle sexual undertones in an office, peer power and subordination, innuendos, jokes and stage whispers about women are things noted as contributing to sexual harassment. Interviews and dramatizations illustrate political structure of offices and three types of sexual harassers. d. Victor Summa; p. Jane Kaplan, Peter Schnitzler; p. Integrated Video Services, Inc.; MTITI; UMN.

POWER VOLLEYBALL (22m C p1980, r1980)
The United States Women's Volleyball Team is featured. The world's best women volleyball players display their skills in international competition and demonstrate the game's latest techniques, using slow motion and stop action cinematography for easy learning. d. Kirk/Garrity/Ingram; p. Tenth Street Studios; VOLLEY.

POWERLESS POLITICS (28m C 1975) (Video)
Provides an overview of the legal relationship between the United
States and Indian tribes showing how shifts of emphasis in the government's "Indian policy" have had far-reaching effects on Indian
life. Specific examples, historical and contemporary, vividly illustrate
the legal relationship in action. At issue are Indian land, water, and
mineral rights, education and self-government. The relationship with
the Bureau of Indian Affairs is explained, emphasizing how Indian
people must deal with the BIA's complicated bureaucracy in all aspects of their lives. Includes archival photographs, diagrams and
a lively host-narrator who gives a clear and comprehensive overview
of the Indian-United States legal and political relationship. Written,
produced and acted by Native Americans. p. Sandra Osawa/KNBC-
TV; BYU.

POWERS OF TEN, A ROUGH SKETCH (9m C 1968) (also Video)
Illustrating the relationship between the number ten and the size
of the physical universe, the film takes as its reference frame the
one square meter view of a couple picnicking on the grass of Soldier's
Field in Chicago. The camera zooms outward; time and distance increase in increments of ten until we reach the outer galaxies. Returning to earth, we proceed from the human scale into the micro
world of cells, DNA molecules, and the nucleus of an atom. p. Ray
and Charles Eames; PF; UCLA.

POWERS OF TEN, 1978 (9m C 1978)
Shows a linear view of our universe. First, from the human
scale to the sea of galaxies, then directly down to the nucleus of a
carbon atom. With an image, a narration and a distance register,
it gives a clue to the relative size of things. The film has moved
in real time over its course of 40 powers of ten, from the cosmic
distances of the universe to the heart of an atom. p. Ray Eames,
Charles Eames; PF; UCEMC, UCLA, UIL, USC.

PREGNANCY AFTER 35 (22m C 1979) (also Video)
Deals with both the physical and emotional aspects of late pregnancy. Shown are a number of women in real life situations. Statistics relating to Down's syndrome and other birth defects in relation to mother's age are given, and a woman is shown having amniocentesis (a method of testing for Down's syndrome early in pregnancy). Narrated by Carole McCauley, author of the book with the
same title as the film. p. Alvin Fiering; d. Gwen Brown; POLYMR;
UM. Video available from PBSV.

PREGNANCY AND CHILDBIRTH SERIES see SPECIAL CASES

PREGNANCY IN MOTION (Not given)
A supple pregnant woman demonstrates nearly 20 postures and
principles of yoga, applying the yogic approach to natural childbirth.
The model gave birth two days after the film's completion. p. Cinema
Medica; CINMD.

PREGNANCY PREVENTION: OPTIONS (17m C 1980)
Teenagers discuss what they think they know about birth control
as well as the attitudes, feelings, questions, and doubts that many
students share. To answer that, the ethical aspects of sexual activity and the medical aspects of pregnancy and its prevention are
discussed thoroughly, with attention to the theory and use of the
various methods of contraception. Stressed is the importance of being responsible about their sexual relationships. AIMS; WSU.

PREGNANT BUT EQUAL (24m C 1982)
In 1978 Congress passed the Pregnancy Discrimination Act, making it illegal for employers to discriminate against pregnant workers.
However, some companies are failing to comply with the law, many
women don't know their rights and a majority of women workers have
inadequate benefits. Documents the fight for equal rights on the
job--highlighting the story of one group of workers and their fight
for maternity benefits. d./p. Judith Pomer; p. Women's Film Project;
ICARF.

PREGNANT: TOO YOUNG (29m C 1982) (Video)
An analysis of adolescent pregnancy in the State of Utah. A
look at teenage sexuality and the resulting pregnancy as outlined by
social service and health professionals. Teen mothers, a young couple
and expectant teens describe how sexual attitudes and pregnancy affect their lives. A single, expectant teenager is followed through
labor and delivery. d./p./s.w. Marilyn K. Toone; ed. Douglas Waters; p. KUED-TV; KUEDTV.

PREMATURITY (29m C 1978) (Video) Daniel Foster, M.D. Series
Dr. Daniel Foster and his guest Dr. Charles R. Rosenfeld, Associate Professor of Pediatrics at the University of Texas Health Science Center, discuss the recent advances in modern neonatology--a
new speciality dedicated to insuring the health survival of pre-term
newborns. The program includes a filmed tour of the Parkland Memorial Hospital nurseries, during which Dr. Rosenfeld points out the
major complications for the premature infant and how they may be
recognized and treated. p. KERA-TV; PBSV.

PRE-NATAL DIAGNOSIS: TO BE OR NOT TO BE (45m C 1981) (also
Video)
Modern medicine has developed techniques that allow doctors to
detect more than 80 biochemical abnormalities in utero. Shows how
amniocentesis, fetoscopy, and ultrasound can detect various birth defects. The bioethical questions raised are particularly challenging.
When Down's syndrome or spina bifida is detected, parents have the
difficult decision of whether to terminate the pregnancy. Doctors,
too, are faced with complex problems. This up-to-date presentation
will be very useful in in-service education, genetic counselling, patient education, and medical ethics programs. d. David Suzuki; s.w.
Tara Callis; p. CBC; FILMLB.

PREPARING FOR CHILDBIRTH: A NINE-MONTH EXPERIENCE (15m
 C n.d.)
 Emphasizes prenatal visits and covers birth preparation classes
on diet, exercise and relaxation techniques. In the third trimester,
the featured couple attend childbirth training classes, practice at
home and tour the hospital. Concludes with labor onset, birth, and
bonding. Also available in Spanish. MIFE.

PRESERVING EGYPT'S PAST (23m C p1981, r1982)
 Increased agriculture, population, changing weather conditions,
and tourists threaten to destroy monuments, temples and tombs, carvings and paintings of the ancient Egyptian legacy. Scientists are
now attempting to record and, if possible, to preserve the remnants
of this civilization. d. Norris Brock; p./s.w. Miriam Birch; Sponsor:
National Geographic Society/Gulf Oil Corporation; NGS.

PRETEND YOU'RE WEARING A BARREL (10m C p1978, r1979)
 On her 35th birthday, Lynn Ryan took stock of her life. She
had five children, no husband, no job, and the outlook for getting
off welfare was bleak. Shows how Lynn Ryan has taken control of
her life. A vivid portrait of a tough-minded, courageous woman.
d. Jan-Marie Martell; p. Shelah Reljic; ed. Christl Harvey; NFBC;
PHOENIX; IU.

PREVENTING SEXUAL HARASSMENT (24m C 1980) Fair Employment
 Practice Series
 Using a deft combination of commentary and dramatization, it explores sexual harassment from innuendo to blatant attack. Each vignette is based on an actual case. Points out management responsibilities and employee rights; presents guidelines for dealing with incidents involving sexual harassment; emphasizes the necessity for
management to act promptly and properly should such an incident
occur; and stresses the need to practice the principles of good management to prevent such incidents in the first place. BNA.

PRICE OF CHANGE, THE (26m C 1982) (also Video)
 For 60 years Egyptian women have been gradually entering all
sectors of the public work force. Work outside the home, once considered shameful, has today become a necessity. Today, nearly 40
percent of Egyptian women contribute in some way to providing the
family income. Examines the consequences of work for five women--
a factory worker with four children, a rural village leader involved
in family planning, a doctor, a social worker, and a member of Parliament who is also speaker for the opposition party. Presents a picture of changing attitudes toward work, the family, sex, and women's
place in society. Study guide included. Made by an all-women crew
(British, American, and Arab). p. Elizabeth Fernea; d. Marilyn
Gaunt; ICARF; WSU.

PRIME TIME (SERIES) see COPING WITH CHANGE; INNER STRENGTHS
 INTERDEPENDENT RELATIONSHIPS; LEARNING TO ENJOY

PRIMUM NON NOCERE (24m C n.d.)
Shows a couple going through natural childbirth at home under
the supervision of a birth attendant who is well trained and skilled
in the art of home obstetrics. These home-birth attendants follow
the medical dictum stated by Hippocrates' Primum Non Nocere ...
"Above all do no harm." p. Cinema Medica; CINMD.

PRIORY, THE ONLY HOME I'VE GOT (29m C p1978, r1979)
The majority of people living in extended-care hospitals suffer
from chronic geriatric illness. The priory is a public hospital designed to stimulate an interest in living and a sense of self-worth
for a person needing constant care. Treatment shows how even the
ordinary activities of a patient's life contain many elements of therapy.
d. Mark Dolgoy; p. A. Wheeler, M. Scott; NFBC; IU.

PRISONERS OF CHANCE (23½m C 1978)
Shows some of the problems of teenage pregnancy. Using three
couples, the film documents problems arising from teenage pregnancy.
1) A teenager becomes pregnant at 16, and unable to care for the
child alone, chooses to put the child up for adoption. 2) An unmarried high school girl decides to keep her child and the problem resulting from her decision is told. 3) A teenage marriage results
from pregnancy and the ensuing financial problems, the end of their
career goals, and their complete naivete of daily living with the responsibility of a child to raise are seen to be destructive forces with
which they are ill-equipped to deal. p. Thom Eberhardt, Marc Stirdivant; d. Thom Eberhardt; FLMFR, MMM; IU, KENTSU, UIL, UMN,
WSU.

PRIVATE LIFE, A (30m C p1980, r1980)
Explores the adjustments which immigrants must experience.
Tells the story of two people attempting to find love and companionship as they adjust to aging and the dislocations of the emigrant's
adapting to a new land. Dramatizes the story of Margot and Karl,
two aging German-Jewish immigrants living in New York City. Margot and Karl met each other through friends after the death of their
mates. Margot is a vital woman who exercises, studies a new language, works part time and is eager to build a future. Margot is
saddened because Karl needs to live in the past, spending much of
his time writing memoirs. Karl visits Margot to tell her that he is
leaving New York to live near his son, and Margot reminds herself,
"We must be archeologists of our own lives and think ourselves out
of the years of the dust others have thrown on us." Lotte Andor
plays Margo. p. Peter Almond in association with Film for Thought,
Inc.: d. Mikhail Bogin; photographed by Alicia Weber; MMA.

PRIVATE WORLD OF BEATRIX POTTER, THE (42m C p1978, r1979--
U.S.)
Examines the life of Beatrix Potter, whose books for children
are a household word, yet her life is almost totally unknown. Born

in 1866 in Kensington, England, Beatrix Potter's hopes of pursuing
a career in art centered around her splendid botanical drawings.
But the academic world refused to accept her delicately beautiful and
scientifically accurate re-creations because she was an untrained
woman. She grew up in a wealthy environment, rich in experiences
and opportunities. She retained a lifelong love for and curiosity
about the lakeland country of England where the excitements of nature
served as the setting of her books for children. When no one would
publish her stories, she did so herself, with the same fierce absorption for excellence that characterized all her works. Despite the success that came to her books they ceased to appear later in her life
when she married William Heelis. From that time on she devoted herself to her home and sheep farm. Old photos of family members, and
of Beatrix, as well as interviews with people who remember her, lend
credence to this film portrait of the famous author as a unique individual who loved her solitary moments almost as much as her art and
writing. p. Yorkshire Television, England; CANTOR.

PRIZEWINNERS SERIES, THE see MARIE CURIE (1867-1934): A
    LOVE STORY

PROBLEM? ... TO THINK OF DYING (59m C 1977)
    Personal experiences and feelings relating to death from cancer
are expressed by widow Lynne Caine and terminal cancer patient Orville Kelly. From their unique perspectives, they reveal the intensity
of emotions felt when facing death and how this affects the individuals
concerned, their spouses, their children, and others. In an open
discussion with the moderator, the two speak of emotional phases encountered, how they are coping with the question of death, mistakes
each believe were made, how to plan in advance for the transition,
and their revised philosophies of life. p. KCTA-TV; IU.

PROFESSIONAL SKILLS FOR SECRETARIES SERIES see COPING
    WITH CHANGE; GETTING THE JOB DONE; WE'RE COUNTING ON
    YOU; WORKING WITH OTHERS

PROFILE OF AN ARTIST: ANNA TICHO (25m C p1978, r1982--U.S.)
    (also Video)
    Presents a film portrait of Israeli artist Mrs. Anna Ticho in her
quiet home in the heart of Jerusalem where she speaks about her life
and art. As a young girl growing up in Austria she was not encouraged to pursue a career; in fact, she gave up her dowry to go to
Jerusalem where she met her husband, an army medical officer, who
became a distinguished ophthalmologist. She assisted her husband
until his death, and she spent time making many sketches while developing a great love for the Judean hills and the city streets. In
recent years she has traveled in Europe, but as subjects for her art
she finds the hills and people of Jerusalem most compelling. She
also does portraits, but seems to prefer subjects who might be called
old and ugly, her models are often beggars. Now in her eighties,

she no longer goes out into the streets, but continues to create at
home and tends her plants. Her work is widely exhibited and appreciated. p. Yigael Ephrati, Nathan Ben Ari; p. Israel Film Service,
Israel; ALDEN.

PROFILES IN LITERATURE SERIES see BETTE GREENE

PROFILES IN POWER SERIES see CATHERINE THE GREAT: A PRO-
FILE IN POWER

PROGRESSIVE RELAXATION TRAINING: A CLINICAL DEMONSTRA-
TION (21m C r1977)
Portrays the nuances and subtleties of progressive relaxation
procedures. Presents a clinically accurate view of the techniques
by taking one into a counseling session in which progressive relaxation is being used. Based on the book of the same title by Dr.
Douglas A. Bernstein and Dr. Thomas D. Borkovec. Film Consultants: authors of the book. p. Norman Baxley/Research Press;
RESPRC; IU.

PROJECT PUFFIN (13m C 1981)
Depicts efforts of an Audubon biologist to reestablish a breeding
colony of Atlantic Puffins on an island off the coast of Maine. Puffins, once common along the Maine seacoast, were breeding only on
two remote offshore islands. In 1981, for the first time in 100 years,
puffins were again nesting on Eastern Egg Rock, the third breeding
colony in Maine. d. Susan Oristaglio; p. Carol Lee Taylor: LCA.

PROLOGUE, THE (12m C 1978)
THE PROLOGUE is the 12-minute first section of a 50-minute film,
THE EVOLUTION OF THE PATH. Shot entirely in the camera, frame
by frame, it employs landscape elements shot sideways and usually
forming vertical bands with a strong central axis. The filmmaker
speaks of this axis as a path, and the evolution or development of
the film as parallel struggles leading from animal consciousness to a
higher consciousness, and eventually becoming that path. In simpler
terms and without the Zen philosophical overlay, the film can be seen
as a journey through life. d. Vicki Z. Peterson; PETERSV.

PROLOGUE (88m B 1969)
An exploration of the world of the drop-out. Concerns a young
Montrealer who edits an underground newspaper, and his female com-
panion, who are joined by a young draft dodger from the United
States. In the choices they make, the two rival philosophies of dis-
senting youth become evident: militant protest or communal retreat.
Includes the bloody rioting in Chicago during the 1968 Democratic
Convention. Also seen and heard is the anti-war and civil rights
spokesman Abbie Hoffman. d. Robin Spry; p. Robin Spry, Tom Daly;
NFBC.

PROMISE SHARED, A (29m C 1972) (Video) Woman Series
A documentary on the status of Israeli women, which explores
the results of the 1948 Israeli Proclamation of Independence promise
that Israel will maintain "equality of social and political rights ...
without distinction of creed, race or sex." To determine if this
promise has been kept, the program looks at women in the professions, the serious lack of day-care facilities and the universal military service. Prominent Israeli women evaluate their status and
rights: Beba Idelson, director of the Working Women's Council of
the Israel Federation of Labor; Colonel Dvora Tomer, commander of
the Women's Army Corps; Shulamit Aloni, attorney and politician;
Hanah Zemer, editor-in-chief of Davar, Israel's largest morning daily
newspaper; and a woman scientist who works on a water purification
project. The documentary was shot on location in Israel. p. WOSU-
TV; PBSV.

PROMISES (21m C 1978)
Presents the manipulation of advertising and its pervasive influence on our lives. An analysis of selected claims reveals how meaningless, misleading, and improbable they are. The same is true of
promises of more fun in life, and even a better love life resulting
from the use of certain products. Examines advertising schemes and
shows exactly why they are used, why they succeed, which helps to
put them in proper perspective. It reveals the masses buy without
thinking. This satirical film documents some of our buying foibles.
p. Vaughn Obern; d. Alan Barker; RAMFLM.

PROP DANCES #1 (1965-67)
Sheila Sun performs "The Chinese Ribbon Dance," for many years
a part of Chinese court festivities. Yoshiaki Morimoto performs a
Japanese version of the Chinese Ribbon Dance to twentieth-century
music. Dancers: Sheila Sun (Taiwan), Hoshiaki Morimoto (Japan);
Project Director: Nadia Chilkovsky Nahumck; a.d. Fai Coleman; p.
Calvin De Frenes Corporation; FRANDA.

PROP DANCES #2: THREE SATIRES ON FASHION (10m C 1965-66)
Eve Gentry performs one of her dances in three parts: "Cha-
peaux Are Definitely In," "Hemlines-Waistlines: The Everchanging
Shape," and "Weirdies--the New Look in Outer Space." Dancer/
Choreographer: Eve Gentry; Project Director: Nadia Chilkovsky
Nahumck; a.d. Fai Coleman; p. Calvin De Frenes Corporation; FRANDA.

PROP DANCES #3: TWO DANCES OF THE PHILIPPINES (10m C 1965-
67)
"Tinikling" (Bamboo Stick Dance) and "Pandango Sa Ilaw" (Candle
Dance) are performed. Dancers: Luz Umali, Chit Saniel, Eddie Al-
madrones, Roberto F. Enrilo; Dance Director: Florence J. Burns of
the Filipino Association of Philadelphia; Project Director: Nadia Chilkovsky Nahumck; a.d. Fai Coleman; FRANDA.

PROPER AUTHORITIES (21m C n.d.)
Documents the public's often confused and ambivalent attitude
toward the police.   d. Margaret Kenda; POLPUP.

PROPER PLACE: WOMEN IN THE CHURCH, THE (29m C 1976) (Video)
Woman Series
Author Mary Griffin (The Courage to Choose: An American Nun's
Story) and Patricia Hughes, a graduate divinity student and member
of the Executive Committee for Women in Future Priesthood Now, A
Call for Action, discuss the changing role of women in the church.
The guests, both ex-nuns, believe that the reality of the church in-
volves a need for women in the priesthood and in other important
functions in church structure.   Sandra Elkin is the moderator.   p.
WNED-TV; PBSV.

PROPERTY (89m C 1978) (also Video)
PROPERTY is about friendship and the politics of poverty--in
general and as it relates to this group.   It is also about the problem
of "living lightly" in an urban environment where attempts to protect
the quality of one's life can be destructive as powerlessness itself.
Why, after all these years, can't they just move on, find some new
houses, and start again?   Probably because they are older.   Probably
because they are remnants of a declining subculture, and their survival, as individuals, is more than ever dependent upon their survival
as a group.   Filmed in southwest Portland.   The film introduces the
people who live in these homes, the youth culture of the sixties grown
up--or, at least, older.   p. Penny Allen, Eric Edwards; MEDIAP.

PROTEIN AND MEAT SUBSTITUTES (7m C 1976)
Looks at whole and incomplete proteins and alternatives to meat
as a source of protein.   Also examines common deficiencies, such as
fiber and calcium loss, associated with high meat diets.   An excerpt
from Food ene.   p. WPSX-TV; PAS.

PSYCHEREEL (10m C 1978)
Forms play hide-and-seek, changing one's everyday perception
of form and effecting transformations of identity (Global Village,
December 29, 1978).   p. Olga Spiegel; GLOBALV.

PSYCHIC POWERS OF THE MIND: ENERGY FIELDS OF LIFE (55m C
n.d.) (Video)
Chronicles the growth of the science of parapsychology.   Dr.
Margaret Mead explains why she worked to get parapsychology accepted into the prestigious American Association for the Advancement
of Science.   Kirlian photography is discussed as a device that reveals
auras, or life energies.   The controversy about Uri Geller, both pro
and con is explored.   The psychic experiences of New York artist
Ingo Swann, Russian housewife Ninel Kulagina, and Philippine healer
Tony Agpowa and others are presented and analyzed in depth.   p.
Jeffrey Norton Publishers, Inc.; NORTONJ.

PSYCHICS, SAINTS AND SCIENTISTS (33m C 1972)
Psychic Magazine says: "The first documentary film in many
years on parapsychology, this one will be hard to top.... In a word,
this film is remarkable. Combining artistic style with scientific accuracy, Psychics, Saints and Scientists presents a unique visual introduction to today's fore-runners of tomorrow's world of mind."
Covers spiritual healing, biofeedback, ESP training, brain-wave conditioning, Kirlian photography, and much more. p. Elda Hartley;
HARTLEY.

PSYCHOLOGY OF EATING, THE (29m C 1978)
What motivates animals and humans to seek food? Why do we
choose some foods and avoid others? Why do some people eat more
than they need and become obese? What are some strategies for losing unwanted weight? These fascinating questions posed by Dr. Val-
enstein provide the framework for the consideration of the psychology
of eating in this film. p. Harcourt Brace Jovanovich, Inc.; HBJ;
CWU, UNEV.

PSYCHOSEXUAL DIFFERENCES: 1 (25m C 1975)
Concentrates on the sociocultural determinants of psychosexual
identity. Pursues the question of whether our social environment,
both in early childhood and in later life, plays a critical role in creating and maintaining masculine and feminine character traits. Interviews with three social investigators: Dr. Ann Oakley, a sociologist
engaged in research on women; Dr. Robin Oakley, an anthropologist;
and Juliet Mitchell, a writer and theorist who is particularly interested
in psychoanalysis. Considers the relationship between theory and
methods of data collection, demonstrates the value of comparative approaches, and raises questions as to the relationship between biological givens and social facts. BBC; UMMRC; PAS.

PSYCHOSEXUAL DIFFERENCES: 2 (25m C 1975)
Looks at the physiological and genetic origins of sexually differ-
entiated behavior. Jeffrey Grey talks about his research with rats
and the kinds of role reversals he can initiate by the manipulation
of hormones. BBC; UMMRC; PAS.

PUEBLO PRESENCE, THE (58m C 1981) (also Video)
Examines the continuity of ancient Pueblo civilization into the
present. Zuni historian Andrew Napetcha discusses the ancestry of
Pueblo people in sequence filmed at Pueblo Bonito, one of the important ancient cities. The ancestors are honored in a Hopi man's pil-
grimage to place a prayer plume in the sacred ruin of Kaweste. The
film makes extensive use of narration to discuss specific examples
from many different Pueblo tribes that represent common cultural
features. Pueblo art, religion and ceremonials, language, architecture and daily activities, and relationship to the natural world are
shown integrated parts of a unified conception of life. Carefully
researched with good photography. p./d. Suzanne Johnston/Hugh
Johnston, p. WNET-TV; JOHNSTS; FI.

PUEBLO RENAISSANCE, THE (26m C 1976)
This television documentary is concerned with the blend of the traditional and modern in a Native American community's life. People of San Juan Pueblo reflect on their traditions and interests. Sequences of Christmas celebrations show how Roman Catholic and ancient religions are combined. The impact of the wage economy is felt by members of the community. Some people work at a nearby nuclear physics plant. Others have formed a crafts cooperative that enables artists to practice traditional arts while taking advantage of modern marketing methods. Several points of view about how to maintain tradition in modern circumstances are articulated. p. Brenda Horsefield; ex. p. Philip Hobel; p. BBC; DOCUA; IU.

PUERTO RICAN WOMEN'S FEDERATION (29m C 1975) (Video) Woman Series
Teacher Lourdes Vasquez and social worker Sister Elidas Rodriquez discuss the goals of the Puerto Rican Women's Federation, which they helped found to change discriminatory laws and eradicate social inequities in Puerto Rico. The two women discuss the issues of employment, forced sterilization, women's consciousness toward Puerto Rican culture, male-female relationships, religion, family and social institutions. Sandra Elkin is the moderator. p. WNED-TV; PBSV.

PUFFINS, PREDATORS AND PIRATES (28m C p1973, r1979)
A close-up view of the dramatic struggle between two species of birds, the North American puffin and the herring gull. Their delicate population balance has been upset by man's pollution of the coastal waters. The barron rocks of Great Island, off Newfoundland, is the setting for this survival. The camera captures the life cycle of these birds. d. Nancy Archibald; p. CBC; FILMLB.

PUTTIN' ON THE RITZ (4m C 1974) (also Video)
Animation that is a tribute to Fred Astaire, including a tap-dancing silhouette who leads a chorus line of animated figures. d. Antoinette Starkiewicz; p. Contemporary Films; Composer: Irving Berlin; FI.

PUTTING IN THE BONE WITH DOROTHY HEATHCOTE (58m B 1975) (Video)
Dorothy Heathcote, eminent English drama educator, conducts a workshop for drama teachers at the University of New Brunswick. Participants present their problems, concerns and objectives for the conference, while Heathcote develops an outline for establishing a successful drama program. p. Les Blank; UNEWB; UMN.

PUTTING UP THE PICKLES (29m C 1981)
Allows a peek behind the scenes at the Pickle Family Circus. This circus is not just an occupation to its members, it is a way of life. The spectacular skills and infectious fun which are Pickle Family Circus trademarks are enhanced by seeing rehearsals and private

moments backstage as well as performances done for appreciative
audiences. d. Yasha and Carrie Aginsky; p. Steven Pinsky; DIRECT.

-Q-

QUACK (24m C 1976)
An experimental film about a young black woman who fantasizes
about becoming a documentary filmmaker. The obstacles she encounters symbolize her oppression by a white, male-dominated world. p.
Scott Guthrie, John Huckert; GUTHOR; PAS.

QUEEN ISABEL AND HER SPAIN (32m C 1978, r1979)
Isabel's story told through contemporary paintings, carvings,
castles, monasteries, and battlefields. When Isabel came to power in
1474, she inherited a kingdom torn by factionalism and on the verge
of civil war. By 1492, she had united her country, defeated Portu-
gal and Moorish Granada, expelled the Jews, and sent Christopher
Columbus on his famous voyage. When she died in 1504, Isabel left
a country united under one Crown and one Church and on the threshold of world dominion. p. Mary Kirby, Catherine Blue; p. Pilgrim
Films; IFB; PAS, PSU, IU.

QUEEN OF THE STARDUST BALLROOM (98m C 1974)
Presents the heartwarming musical melodrama of a middle-aged
woman whose life crumbles around her when her husband dies suddenly. Having no particular plans made, a friend finally invites her
to a local dance hall, where music and atmosphere of the 1940's are
recreated. There a stocky, middle-aged mailman invites her to dance,
a whole new relationship begins for them both. This late-blooming
romance is filled with tears of joy and happiness, until a bittersweet
ending. Stars Maureen Stapleton and Charles Durning. p. Tomorrow
Entertainment, Inc.; LCA, KENTSU.

QUEEN VICTORIA AND BRITISH HISTORY (1837-1901) (28m C 1977)
The Modern World History Series
Presents a biography of Queen Victoria. Includes a discussion
on the effects of the Industrial Revolution, the Crimean War, the
Indian Mutiny, and the expansion of the British Empire. p. Chats-
worth Film, London; CENTEF; USC, PSU, KENTSU.

QUEEN VICTORIA: THE ROYAL WIDOW (29m B n.d.)
This program concentrates on the latter half of Queen Victoria's
reign, ending with her death at the turn of the century. Life after
Albert's death was difficult for the Queen. It shows her bereavement being marked outwardly by frequent retreats from political and
social affairs, while in her journal she expressed the fear and loneliness of a grieving wife and the resolute determination to preserve
her duties as Albert would have wished. Illustrated with Victorian
photographs and drawings, the program also highlights the Industrial

Revolution, the Franco-German War and the garnering of India to the Empire. p. Media Centre; UTORON.

QUEEN VICTORIA: THE YOUNG QUEEN (31m B n.d.)
Follows Victoria from the night of her proclamation as Queen upon the death of her uncle William, through her marriage to Prince Albert and the establishment of her reign, and finally to the death of Albert in 1861. Actual photographs from the period document the social and political atmosphere and the national affairs of the day, including references to the Canadian boundary dispute, the Irish crimes, the Crimean War and the Great Exhibition. Based on the personal journals of Queen Victoria. p. Media Centre; UTORON.

QUEENS OF HARMONY (44m C 1977)
Reflects the week of fun and dedication by 5,000 women, from 18 to 80, who converged on Seattle for the 29th Annual Convention of Sweet Adelines, Inc. in October 1975. Sweet Adelines, Inc. began in 1945 in Oklahoma. Tulsa Chapter No. 1 emerged as the first club of Sweet Adelines with 41 members. There are now over 23,000 members all over the United States, Canada, Panama and England. BBC; TIMLIF; UIL.

QUESTION OF INTIMACY, A (19m C p1980, r1981) (also Video)
Explores the subject of intimacy. Keith Miller, a Christian writer and public speaker, leads a group of young adults in a discussion of intimacy and the complexities of human relationships. Dialogue includes fear of closeness, trust, commitment, acceptance, love, sex and becoming vulnerable to another person. Participants speak of the pain of rejection when an intimate relationship does not work out and of awkwardness experienced in initiating affection. Miller points out the frightening intensity when one looks for a mate and suggests changing the focus to building one's own life and identity instead. p. Kathy Dale, d. Jeff Weber; p. Umcom Productions; MMM.

QUESTION OF SELF-CONCEPT, THE (28m C 1978) The Inner Woman
(Series)
Examines the causes and effects of the woman's changing roles. Psychiatrist Judith Bardwick explores reasons why more women now seek counseling and therapy, and why such therapy is failing. Women are urged to accept challenges, explore alternatives, and develop positive self-image. Marilyn Poland, R.N., moderator. p. WXYZ-TV; CRM; PAS.

QUIET REVOLUTION OF MRS. HARRIS (21m C r1977)
Remarkably upbeat portrait of a woman--a housewife with four children--who grows dissatisfied with her life, enrolls in college, and eventually becomes a college placement counselor. Excellent production follows her progress for some five years. Shows the encouragement she receives from her husband and children; narration by the woman herself, in her own words. p. Lore Caulfield; MEDIAG; UCEMC.

QUILTED FRIENDSHIP (5½m C 1979) (Video)
   Two women have almost completed a quilt together when they discover that they have completely different views of their friendship.
p. Jeanne Hollenbeck; WMM.

QUILTING: PATTERNS OF LOVE (20m C p1979, r1979)
   A state of the art look at the craft of quilting: the origin and
history of this folk art, its decline and renaissance, the rural roots
of the craft and the people who practice it. d. Bill Johnston; p.
N. Stiliadis, R. Lillie; LAURON.

QUILTS IN WOMEN'S LIVES (28m C p1980, r1980) (also Video)
   Presents a series of portraits of seven quiltmakers while providing insight into the spirit of this traditional women's art form. With
candor and humor, women tell the stories about the importance of
quilts in their lives. One woman sees quilts as having "a great deal
of sorrow stitched into them." Another feels they "function as mandalas do, speaking to something very deep." Still another finds
her quiltmaking to be "a way of working through prohibitions of
touch." We see how women of different backgrounds and ages bring
the materials and experiences of their daily life to their craft; how
they learn the art and pass it on; how quilts function in their families and communities. Pat Ferrero has captured in a sensitive and
intimate way the broad range of motivations and attitudes that contribute to this traditional art form. Awards. d./p. Patricia Ferrero; NEWDAY; UMN.

-R-

RAANANAH: A WORLD OF OUR OWN (29m C p1980, r1980)
   The story of Raananah, a Jewish communal settlement in New
York State. Founded in 1937 by immigrant Jews who wanted to work
the land--for the summers only--Raananah still exists. Combining
historic stills, old home movies and current footage, the film looks at
Raananah past and present, and talks to its elderly founders of old
age, idealism, death and loss of a way of life. d./p. Marlene Booth;
RAPHAEL.

RADHA (19m C 1941, 1972)
   Ruth St. Denis performing her famous Hindu work at Jacob's
Pillow, Massachusetts, in 1941. The film was edited in 1972 to Ed-
ouard Lalo's music. Still photographs from early performances are
inserted between sections of the dance. Choreographer: Ruth St.
Denis; Narrator: Walter Terry; p. Dance Film Archive; DAN/UR.

RADHA'S DAY: HINDU FAMILY LIFE (17m C 1969) The India Image
      Series, No. 4
   Shows a girl in her late teens during a typical day: getting up,
decorating the threshold, putting on her makeup and jewelry, cooking,

washing clothes, shopping at the street market, worshipping at the local shrine and sitting at home with her sister as the day draws to a close. Abounds in ethnographic detail and in social and anthropological data that help lead to a comprehension of Hindu family life in a middle-class white-collar, urban setting. p. Film Marketing Division of Syracuse (FILMDS); UW.

RADIANCE: THE EXPERIENCE OF LIGHT (22m C 1978)
RADIANCE is a journey from the light in nature to the radiant spirit in all life. Using a stunning array of religious art, video images, nature photography and kinetic mandalas, the filmmaker communicates her own encounter with the phenomenon of inner light. Fadiman brings one to a deeper understanding of the special luminous quality in every living thing. p. Dorothy Fadiman, Michael Wiese; PF.

RADIATION: IMPACT ON LIFE (23m C 1982) (also Video)
Radiation is the stuff of nightmares. Undetectable by any of our senses, we have seen the havoc it can wreak on the human body and on the environment. Three leading experts, with the aid of imaginative animation, explain the most important physical and biological concepts, including ... stable and unstable elements, ionizing radiation, the "half-life" of radioactive materials, how radiation affects DNA and how low levels of radiation can be concentrated in the food chain. The three experts interviewed are Dr. Lauriston Taylor, past Chairman of the National Committee on Radiation Standards; Dr. Michio Kaku, a leading physicist who had relatives killed at Hiroshima; and Dr. John Gofman, Professor Emeritus of Medical Physics at the University of California, Berkeley. p. Kathleen Quaife, Sam Love/ Public Communications Incorporated; BULFRG.

RAGAS FOR SWAMI SATCHIDANANDA (15m C 1974)
Two dances choreographed and danced by Margaret Beals, based on yogic postures and forms with music by Ravi Shankar and Collin Walcott. Dancer/Choreographer: Margaret Beals. p. Virginia Brooks; BROOKSV.

RAINBOW BRIDGE, PTS. I, II (43m C si 1975)
"The Rainbow Bridge is a term used in metaphysics to describe the dynamics in meditation which link the intellect and the intuition. The film applies this metaphor in investigating the relationship between the creation in thought and the creation of form. The use of geometrical configurations and their symbolic values is one of the types of image-making which relates form to intuition."--Vicki Z. Peterson (Museum of Modern Art, Nov. 13, 1978). p. Vicki Z. Peterson; PETERSV.

RAINDANCE (8m C n.d.)
A fertility dance--a woman dancing through scenes of fruit and flowers bejeweled by raindrops. Traces woman's evolution and

emergence from bondage to self-discovery, creation and oneness with nature. The filmmakers have used double exposure. d./p. Marsha Ross; CFS.

RAINY DAY, A (35m C p1978, r1979)
Stars Mariette Hartley as a famous actress going home for her father's funeral and remembering an overprotected childhood. The film is painful recreation of childhood; of a mother determined her daughter should succeed; of a father who is a kind, ineffectual man; and of a woman who comes to grips with her hostilities, past and present. LCA; WSU.

RAISED IN ANGER (60m C r1979)
Documents the extent, nature, and causes of child abuse in America, showing that it cuts across all socioeconomic boundaries. Thorough, sometimes shocking, but ultimately optimistic production. Host and narrator: Edward Asner. MEDIAG; UCEMC, UIL, UMN.

RAISING A FAMILY ALONE (9m C 1976)
A Puerto Rican father moves his children to a new neighborhood and manages to care for them with help from the community. d. Henry Felt; p. Educational Development Center, Inc.; EDC.

RAISING CHILDREN (59m C n.d.) (Video, Beta, VHS) Young and Old Reaching Out (Series)
Explores contrasting views on discipline, religion, parental authority and loving support, and youthful rebellion. Dealing with violence and overcoming personal tragedy are illustrated by personal experiences. The guests include writers Emily Hahn and Sophia Collier. p. Communications Resource Foundation, Inc.; PBSV.

RAISING MICHAEL ALONE (17m C 1976)
A black mother demonstrates how she succeeds as a single parent of an 11-year-old in spite of the pressures. With guide. p. Henry Felt; EDC.

RANA (19m C 1976)
Provides a glimpse into the life and role of women in India. Rana is 21, Muslim and a college student living with her extended family in an overcrowded house of Old Delhi. Daily routine is simple, aided by few modern conveniences, and domestic work is shared among females of the household. Never alone, always veiled, Rana is permitted to walk through the neighboring streets, crowded with vendors, laborers, musicians and school children. However, Rana is a comparatively modern Muslim who puts aside the veil in co-ed university classes, but her parents still have full responsibility of selecting her husband, and thereby deciding her future. d. Debby Kingsland for Film Australia; WOMBAT; UCEMC, UIL.

RAPE see WOMEN AND THE LAW, THE (SERIES)

RAPE (35m C 1979)
Shows three rape victims speaking to the filmmaker and to each other about their experiences. Julia Lesage, feminist film critic and teachers says, "Of all the documentaries on rape, this is far the best. The film elicits a consideration of both the 'rape culture' we live in which shapes all women's lives and the agonizing personal and institutional problems which rape victims must deal with. Its open-ended format raises issues rather than presents answers." Emphasizes the sexual imbalance in our American culture. p. Jo Ann Elam; CCC, FLMKCO.

RAPE, PART I (29m C 1975) (Video) Woman Series
Author Susan Brownmiller discusses the major points in her book Against Our Will, an exhaustive study of rape. She explains the psychology of rape, the liberal viewpoint toward it and how to recognize early warning signs of potential rape situations. She describes Albert DeSalvo, known as the "Boston Strangler," as an individual who broke all stereotypes about the psychological makeup of a rapist. She also states her belief that rape victims have a right to kill their assailants. Sandra Elkin is the moderator. p. WNED-TV; PBSV.

RAPE, PART II (29m C 1975) (Video) Woman Series
Author Susan Brownmiller discusses the major points in her book Against Our Will, an exhaustive study of rape. She describes cultural images that promote the "woman as victim" idea and cites examples from children's stories as well as from standard newspaper accounts of rape-murder. She also states her views on the philosophies of pornography and rape. Sandra Elkin is the moderator. p. WNED-TV; PBSV.

RAPE: A NEW PERSPECTIVE (7m C 1976)
Examines the unique dilemma of the female victim of forceable rape by analogy with a robbery. The problem, "a double-edged sword," is placed in perspective at the opening of the film. The victim of the crime is the sole witness in the trial of the assailant. The audience, through the technique of a subjective camera point of view, finds itself in the position of the attorney defending the accused. p. Summerhill Productions; PARACO; UM.

RAPE ALERT (17m C 1975)
Being alert to the possibility of rape can help prevent an attack. Understanding the psychology of the rapist can limit the possibility of becoming a victim. Examines the dos and don'ts of the situation of rape. AIMS; UMO, KENTSU, UIO.

RAPE AND THE RAPIST (15m C 1978)
Uses a series of vignettes to examine the psychology of the rapist, including research which indicates that rapists are primarily motivated by the desire to dominate and inflict suffering. p. Sid Davis Productions; DAVISS.

RAPE: CARING FOR THE ADULT FEMALE VICTIM (44m C 1981)
This drama portrays the physical and emotional trauma of rape--
and demonstrates approaches that emergency services, medical personnel, and counselors should use in treating the victim. Physical examination, evidence collection, crisis counseling, and other important
areas are covered. The program emphasizes sensitivity to victim's
emotional needs and how to meet them. d. Dale McCaulley; p. Cavalcade Production; NAVC.

RAPE: ESCAPE WITHOUT VIOLENCE (18m C n.d.)
Outlines several methods of insuring one's security. Emphasizes
that a woman must be constantly on guard and use her head. PEREN;
UMO.

RAPE, INCEST AND ABORTION (28m C 1979) (Video)
Documentary on the incidence of rape and incest and the necessity for Medicaid coverage for them. Interviewed are victims and
members of Congress. p. Shirley Robeson, Everywoman, WDVM-TV;
NARAL.

RAPE: INVESTIGATIVE TECHNIQUES (10m C n.d.)
Emphasizes the importance of the police officer's attitude in gaining the confidence and cooperation of a traumatized victim. p. Harper
and Row Criminal Justice Media; HAR.

RAPE PREVENTION: NO PAT ANSWERS (16m C 1976)
Practical information concerning rape and how to deal with it.
Methods discussed include preventive measures. Also mentions sexual assault directed at children and handling its occurrence in one's
family. Stresses the necessity of being prepared in the event of a
violent sexual crime. p. University of Kansas/Douglas County Rape
Prevention and Victim Support Service; UIL, UM.

RAPE PREVENTION SERIES see DATE, THE

RAPE: VICTIM OR VICTOR (17m C 1979)
Uses a series of vignettes to illustrate that although there are
no hard and fast rules for avoiding rape a woman can take action to
protect herself and reduce risk. Presents a range of easy-to-learn
tactics (both active and passive) without advocating a single, simplistic approach. Urges viewers to develop their own personal rape
prevention program. Free loan. Los Angeles County Sheriff's Department; p. National Center for the Prevention and Control of Rape;
MTPS; IU.

RAPE VICTIMS: AN UNBLINKING LOOK AT A GROWING SOCIAL
    PROBLEM, THE (22m C 1978)
A revealing documentary on rape, explores the scope and significance of this social problem. The film opens with a uniquely informative historical and social analysis of rape. Examines the various

sorts of rape victims: women of all ages, children of both sexes, male and female inmates of prisons and mental institutions. Concludes with what women are doing to protect themselves, with advice to viewers on how to defend against rape. p. WABC-TV; MEDIAG; CWU, KENTSU, SILU, UIL.

RAPUNZEL (10m C p1980, r1980) (also Video)
A classic tale retold in animation, enhanced by an original musical score. Isolated in a tower by an enchantress, Rapunzel grows into a beautiful young woman. A young prince falls in love with her, but is discovered and blinded by the enchantress. The despairing prince wanders the world and comes at last upon Rapunzel, banished to a desert. Her tears restore his sight and they live happily ever after. p. Lillian Somersaulter, J. P. Somersaulter; CORONET.

RAPUNZEL LET DOWN YOUR HAIR (80m C 1978)
The filmmakers adapted this classic fairy tale to investigate issues related to female identity and sexuality. Rapunzel tells the story four times, each from a different character's point of view. The beautiful subtlety of Asa Sjostrom's animation sequence adds to the interest of this first feature film made by women in Great Britain, by London Women's Film Group; British Film Institute; MMA.

RAPUNZEL, RAPUNZEL (16m C 1978)
Grimm brothers' fairytale in live action. The cinematography is beautiful and severe. Shaker melodies help to liven the mood. p. Mini and Tom Davenport; DAVNPT.

RATIONAL SUICIDE? (15m C r1981) (also Video)
A discussion film to examine a controversial subject. To some perfectly rational people afflicted with pain and incurable disease, rational suicide has become a real and plausible option. Others, such as Dame Cecily Saunders, an articulate spokesperson for the hospice movement, believe that you don't have to kill the patient to kill the pain. Her viewpoint is contrasted by Derek Humphry, a British journalist, now living in California, who abetted his wife dying of cancer by giving her poison when the end was near. He and others campaign for the right to assist a death on request from rational, intelligent people. p. Barry Lando for CBS News "60 Minutes"; CAROUF; UC, UCEMC, UIL, PAS, IU.

RATTLE OF A SIMPLE MAN (95m B 1964) (Great Britain)
A 39-year-old bachelor from Manchester, in with his friends for a football match, wagers his motorcycle on his success with a girl they meet in a club. "This portrait of a simple man shows sobering truth"--New York Times. d./p. Muriel Box, Gerry O'Hara; FI.

RAYMOND LOEWY: FATHER OF INDUSTRIAL DESIGN (ed.) (15m C 1979) Reading: Self-Improvement Series
Presents a profile of Raymond Loewy, father of industrial design.

Loewy, a transplanted Frenchman, touched all American lives with his designs such as the Shell Oil sign, coke machine, International Harvester tractor, trains, buses, and United States Post Office symbol as well as Air Force One and Skylab. As Mr. Loewy strolls through a hardware store with Morley Safer, he points out good and bad design. At age 85, he is still working at his homes in Paris and Palm Springs looking for ways to improve ordinary objects. p. CBS News, "60 Minutes"; p. Suzanne St. Pierre; CAROUF.

REACH OUT FOR LIFE (11m C p1979, r1979)
The hero of this animation is an upwardly mobile man who has thrown all his energies into his career at the expense of his personal relationships. Life ultimately becomes meaningless to him and he attempts suicide. Older and wiser, he comes to some truths that may help other people. d. Irma Taina; p. Epidem Films; FILMLB.

REACHING OUT (32m C p1980, r1980--U.S.) (also Video)
Explores some of the problems and feelings dealt with by the physically and emotionally handicapped. Blake and Karyn are two teenagers who fall in love, but unlike most teenagers, they have extraordinary handicaps which create added burdens and needs on both their parts. Blake is confined to a wheelchair for life, the result of a childhood accident. When he meets the emotionally troubled Karyn living in a group home, he struggles to create the beginnings of a satisfying relationship, though Karyn's fears of abandonment create problems at first. Blake continues to retain his positive attitude throughout, though doubts about his sexual capabilities cause him to seek medical advice and professional guidance. Now happy, Karyn begins to write poetry, and because of that she faces the taunts and teasing of the other troubled children in the home. In anger, she runs away to a secret hiding place in the forest where Blake finds her and persuades her to face the reality of the situation. p./d. Rebecca Yates, Glen Salzman; s.w. Marc Rosen; p. Cineflics, Ltd., Canada; LCA; UCEMC.

READING: SELF-IMPROVEMENT SERIES see RAYMOND LOEWY: FATHER OF INDUSTRIAL DESIGN

REAL PEOPLE, THE (SERIES) see SEASON OF GRANDMOTHERS, A; MAINSTREAM

REBEL EARTH (50m B p1980, r1980)
Chronicle of a prairie voyage. Henry Martinson, 97, with a young farmer returns to the land of Henry's past. They visit the exact spot where Henry "proved up" his homestead in 1907, the old Socialist Party Headquarters, the North Dakota Senate Chambers, and an old farmhouse where Henry sings, dances and reads his poetry. Humanity, humor, patience and good will flow throughout the journey. d. John Hanson, Rob Nilsson; p. Diane Harris, Sandra Schulberg; NEWFRF.

RED KIMONO, THE (75m B si 1925) (with music track)
Dorothy Davenport Reid had a long, but largely unrecognized career in motion pictures beginning in the very early silent era when she co-directed films with her husband, silent star Wallace Reid. When he died of drug addiction in 1922 she combined her film work with a crusade against dangerous drugs and other social problems. This film deals with prostitution, and Reid appears in the prologue and epilogue asking for help for women who stray into prostitution to lead better, more productive lives. Priscilla Bonner stars as a young schoolgirl who becomes a hardened prostitute. She realizes the errors that she's made and attempts to regain her stature as a respectable woman. d. Dorothy Davenport Reid; p. Vital; THUDRBD; BUDGET, EMG.

RED SHOES, THE (134m C 1948)
The story of The Red Shoes is loosely based on the famous ballet Russes and its zealous impressario, Serge Diaghilev. Here he is called Lermontov, and the pupil he discovers, shapes, grooms and finally catapults to stardom is a beautiful young ballerina named Victoria Page. Vicky falls in love with the company's resident composer, and Lermontov demands she give up this romance and dedicate her life to her art. Refusing, she leaves his company but is drawn back for a performance that ends in tragedy as all the conflicting forces of her life converge in one frenzied evening. With Anton Walbrook, Marius Goring, Moira Shearer, Robert Helpmann, Leonide Massine, Albert Basserman, Ludmila Tcherina. Music by Brian Easdale with Sir Thomas Beecham conducting the Royal Philharmonic Orchestra. STEREF; UMN.

REDISCOVERING HERBS, PTS. I, II, III (28m, 15m, 15m, C 1981)

PART I, OVERVIEW
Here are herbs for home remedies, cooking, pot pourris, pest control in the garden, dyeing and home decorating.

PART II, CULINARY HERBS
An in-depth look at the different varieties of culinary herbs, cultivation technique, and how to use them in the kitchen.

PART III, DRIED FLOWER ARRANGEMENTS
Shows what varieties to select, how to grow them, dry them, and different flower arrangements. p. Rodale Press/Robin Miller; BULFRG.

REDUCING DIETS (8m C 1976)
Examines the effects of fad diets by contrasting nutritionally balanced weight reduction diets and fad diets with severely limited food choice. An excerpt from Food ene. p. WSPX-TV; PAS.

REFLECTIONS (52m C p1978, r1979) The Magic of Dance (Series)
Margot Fonteyn looks at the work of the pioneers of dance, from

the seventeenth-century Commedia dell'Arte to Martha Graham. A performance of Fokine's ballet Le Spectre de la Rose features Fonteyn dancing with Mikhail Baryshnikov. p. Patricia Foy; s.w. Margot Fonteyn; ed. Arthur Bennett; TIMLIF

REFLECTIONS (4m C 1979) (Video)
An abstract of nighttime water reflections. This mesmerizing and colorful film adroitly explores the use of hand-colored imagery. p. Sharon Niemczyk, Laura DiTrapani; MEDIAP.

REFLECTIONS: FROM THE GHETTO (28½m p1980, r1980) (Video)
A look at El Barrio from the inside out. Songs and sketches by the Family Theatre give added insight to interviews with J. J. Gonzales and Felipe Luciano. Their memories of ghetto life and the way it has influenced their vision of the outside world provide a perceptive interpretation of the Puerto Rican experience. d. Sonja Gilligan, Michael Gilligan; p. Hudson River Film and Video Co., New York State Education Department; NYSED.

REFLECTIONS: MARGARET MEAD (58m C p1975, r1979) (also Video)
A moving portrait of Margaret Mead, the internationally recognized writer, teacher, and social critic. Mead helped the world discover and appreciate the diversity of its peoples. In this film, she reflects upon her life in a world context, touching upon her educational experiences, career choices, and personal philosophy that guided her monumental research. She shares with us the experiences that molded her perspective on cultural advancements, technological change, and family life--and those that fueled her hope for humanity's survival. Includes her final visit to the cultures she studied several decades before. p. International Communication Agency; ex. p. Timothy White; NAVC; PAS.

REFLECTIONS OF A DANCER: ALEXANDRA DANILOVA (52m C 1981)
A portrait of Alexandra Danilova, the great Russian-American Prima Ballerina Assoluta, who was one of America's favorite ballerinas in the 1930's, 1940's and 1950's with the Ballet Russe de Monte Carlo. Today she is a famous teacher at George Balanchine's School of American Ballet in New York. The film provides a rare behind-the-scenes look at this great dancer passing on her art to a new generation of young dancers. Woven throughout is the story of her life, told in her words. d./p. Anne Belle; SEAHRS.

REFLECTIONS ON CHOREOGRAPHY (13m C 1973)
A documentary on the choreography of Marion Scott, who discusses her own work. Her work "Abyss" is performed by U.C.L.A. students. Choreographer: Marion Scott; p. Allegra Fuller Snyder, Department of Dance; UCLA.

REFLECTIONS: THE PROMISE AND THE REALITY (28½m C p1980, r1980) (Video)
An overview of Puerto Rican migration to the mainland from 1898

to the present. Includes contributions of representative members of the community from both the island and mainland. It shows the challenges of negotiating two societies and retaining an awareness of the past, while struggling to move into the future. d. Sonja Gilligan, Michael Gilligan; p. Hudson River Film and Video Co.; NYSED.

REGARD PICASSO, LE see LE REGARD PICASSO

REGROUPING (77m B 1976)
The film is a highly controversial, visually stunning, non-linear portrait of the evolution and deterioration of a women's group in the mid-seventies. Explores the tension between the need for autonomy and a sense of commitment to the group, the feminist questions of identification with women or men, and the artists manipulation of content for artistic purposes. The film is about the filmmaker's violation of the expectations of the group and her predicament in placing artistic needs first. Deals with the difficulties of making a film, particularly one involving people and their lives. The film takes on an experimental form in which the narrative is constantly disrupted, thereby providing an analogue for contradiction. "Lizzie Bordon's work is one of the few examples of successful experimentation with a radical methodology and form for narrative film. Her films are multi-leveled stories; partial fabrication, partial truth.... Continuity is established by on-going criticism of the film, its premises and assumptions, particularly in regard to the film's ability to deal with the political problems it is addressing. These problems are invariably the problems facing American women when attempting to define workable political tactics"--Becky Johnston, New Cinema. p. Lizzie Borden; WMM.

REHABILITATION: A PATIENT'S PERSPECTIVE (28m C 1975) (also Video)
Here is a film for sensitizing professional staff to the emotional needs of patients, which are often neglected as therapists concentrate on physical goals. The film follows Kathy, a young woman recovering from Guillan-Barré Syndrome, from her initial helplessness to her release from the hospital. Shows Kathy in many routines of the rehabilitation program, but its special value is in revealing her inner feelings during this process. It stresses the special relationship between patient and therapist that plays an important role in motivating progress. p. Grania Gurievitch, Dr. John Downey for the Department of Rehabilitation Medicine, Columbia University; FILMLB.

RELATIONSHIPS AND STRESS (25m C 1980) Coping with Serious Illness Series
Documentary on the last years of Joan Robinson, a woman who was dying of cancer. The Robinson family and friends show ways of handling the changing relationships with family, friends, and medical personnel. Experts discuss how serious illness can materially change relationships and how people can cope with the emotions and strain that inevitably follow diagnosis of a serious illness. TIMLIF; PAS, UMN.

REMEMBER THE LADIES (23m C n.d.)
A reexamination of historical records, touches on the extraordinary achievements of America's women during the period 1750-1815. Letters, diaries, crafts and artifacts combine to form a richly diverse memorial to women--at work and at war. Narrated by Celeste Holm. Free loan. p. Philip Morris, Inc.; MTPS.

REPOSSESSION (26m C p1979, r1979)
Information for American Indians on what their rights are regarding repossession on the reservation and what they can do to protect their rights under the law. Free loan. p. Barbara Alexander; d. Miles Watkins; ex. p. Ira Englander; USDL.

REPRODUCTIVE SYSTEM (15m C 1980) Human Body Series
Each human life is a link in a great chain of life stretching through time, a chain kept unbroken by the body's reproductive system. Through animation, the structures of the male and female reproductive systems and the bodily changes occurring during maturation (including the function of hormones, the process of fertilization and development of the embryo) are clearly and objectively investigated. CORONET; UNEV, UMN, IU.

RESCUE FROM ISOLATION (22m C p1973, r1977--U.S.)
Uses a series of interviews with old people to establish the need for some sort of half-way house between total isolation and total institutionalization. Points out that one answer to this need is a day hospital, an out-patient facility connected with a geriatric day hospital. Documents the activities of one such organization in the areas of physiotherapy and psychiatry. p. Gilbert Rosenberg, M.D., Canada; d. Ron Blumer; p. Transit Media, Inc.; POLYMR.

RESONANT (13m 1969)
Montage of still photographs depicting a day in the life of an elderly woman, the filmmaker's grandmother. A nostalgic look at the past history of her house. The memories of the past as the filmmaker had seen them on that particular day. p. Richard Shirley; UM.

RESPONSIBILITIES AND REWARDS OF PARENTING (30m C 1980)
(also Video)
In this episode, Donahue summarizes the importance of a parent's role and retraces the various stages in a young child's development. Beginning with a baby's first introduction to its parents and siblings, the film touches on the major issues that arise in most parent-child relationships. The overall idea that "Look at Me" strives to leave with its audience is that parents should relax and accept their children and themselves for what they are. p./s.w. Jane Kaplan, Wendy Roth; p. WTTW/TV; FI.

RESPONSIBLE ASSERTION: A MODEL FOR PERSONAL GROWTH (28m C 1978) (also Video)
Patricia Jakubowski and Arthur Lange, two of the most respected

people in the field of assertion training, define assertive behavior and demonstrate procedures which promote the development of assertive skills. The process of assertion training is demystified by their straightforward, nontechnical presentation. Includes documentary footage of an assertion training workshop conducted by Dr. Lange. p. Norman E. Baxley/Research Press in collaboration with Dr. Patricia Jakubowski and Dr. Arthur J. Lang; RESPRC; UIL, UNEV, UMN, IU, PAS, UMN.

RESURGENCE: THE MOVEMENT FOR EQUALITY VS THE KKK (54m C 1981)

The story of the recent rise in Ku Klux Klan terror and the growth of the movement for social and economic justice. Dramatic events and characters emerge to tell two sides of a political conflict raging in the United States today. Filmed in North Carolina and Mississippi, the film covers the new civil rights movement, labor issues and women in the workforce as well as the formation of the "United Racist Front" and the murders by Klan and Nazi members in Greensboro, North Carolina. d. Pamela Yates/Tom Sigel; p. Skylight Pictures Film Library; FIRRNF.

RETIREMENT (50m C 1978)

Examines the growing controversy concerning the ultimate damage that restricted adult retirement communities may have on our society. They isolate people who might still play important roles in our society and severely curtail much needed interaction between generations. Profiles three retirement communities and the feelings of residents about stopping work, sex, and prejudice against the elderly. p./d. Cinda Firestone; ALMI.

RETIREMENT INCOME SECURITY (14m C 1981)

Shows young people expressing their worry that there will be no Social Security for them when they want to retire. Others fear their parents may lose their Social Security income. An evaluation of their worries leads to the conclusion that if society plays its proper role, if older people engage in enlightened self-help and collective action, there will be social security and older people can live with dignity. p. International Center for Social Gerontology, University of Michigan; UMMRC; UM, UIL.

RETIRING? WORRIED ABOUT INFLATION? SO WHAT IF IT RAINS! (17m C 1979)

Finances are the number-one concern of most people planning for retirement. Shows men and women from varying backgrounds discussing their experiences with money and inflation. There are specific suggestions on how to plan for the future and how to protect a nest egg from inflation. p. Alternate Choice, Inc.; FILMLB.

RICH MAN'S MEDICINE, POOR MAN'S MEDICINE (43m C 1976)

Focuses on the complex realities of medical care in the developing nations. The setting is in Senegal and Gabon, West Africa. The filmmakers provide a glimpse into the conflict between Western medicine and the traditional medicine on the other hand. The views expressed by a European and a traditional doctor is that the two systems are now set against each other, but the two techniques could complement one another which could mean progress. p. Marie Claude Deffarge, Gordian Troeller, François Partant; ICARF.

RICHARD KARWOSKI: 1981 (45m C p1981, r1981) (Video)
A documentary on contemporary artist Richard Karwoski, offering a unique view of the world of fine arts from both the practical and creative side. The program's approach emphasizes that being a successful artist is as much a business as it is a talent. d. Ralph Toporoff; p. Leah Laiman; p. Xyrallea Productions, Inc.; XYRALEA.

RICHARD'S TOTEM POLE (25m C 1981)
Richard Harris is a 16-year-old Gitskan Indian living in British Columbia. His father, a master totem pole carver, asks for Richard's help in carving a 30-foot totem pole. Richard has never taken an interest in his heritage, but through his carving he discovers his roots, his culture, and the traditions of his family. p. Deepa Salzman/Paul Salzman; CORONET.

RIDDLES OF THE SPHINX (92m C 1977)
Shot in a series of virtuoso camera movements, the film weaves episodes from a woman's life with narration and music conjoining naturalistic story with avante-garde form. "By juxtaposing a fable of contemporary life, dealing with real and urgent personal and political problems, with the story of Oedipus and the Sphinx, we want to provide a framework within which we can begin to see new connections and ask new questions. The segmented and patterned way in which the story is told proposes ways of understanding which are not determined or presupposed by traditional ways of seeing traditional images of women on the screen"--Peter Wollen, Laura Mulvey. d. Laura Mulvey, Peter Wollen; p. British Film Institute; MMA.

RIGHT OUT OF HISTORY: THE MAKING OF JUDY CHICAGO'S DINNER PARTY (75m C p1979, r1980)
Surrounded by controversy, mammoth in size and scope, Judy Chicago's Dinner Party is generally considered the most significant art piece of the 1970's. The work required five years to complete and enlisted the aid of some 400 volunteers. Dementraka's sensitive yet objective documentary chronicles the communal process that brought Chicago's vision to fruition and provides a cogent illumination of the complexity of the monumental completed work. d. Johanna Demetrakas; p. Thom Tyson; PHOENIX; BUDGET, KPF, UCEMC, UMN, UIL.

RIGHT TO DIE (52m C 1974)
Examines the ethical questions involved in problems of euthanasia.

Is quality of life as important a factor as quantity? Whose is the decision to unplug the machine, when the patient is unable to make decisions? Includes interviews with a 12-year-old cystic fibrosis patient, a terminal cancer patient, with people who have made "living wills" (the written request not to sustain their life by artificial means), with doctors, including Dr. Elisabeth Kubler-Ross. Examines legal provisions in other countries assuring the "right to die." p. ABC-TV; MACMFL; CWU, IU, KENTSU, UIL.

RIGHT TO FIGHT (45m C p1981, r1982) (Video)
    An organizing/teaching tool which gives a strong voice to the needs of low-income tenants and shows a community organizing for affordable housing. Facts, music, theatrical satire and documentary footage combine to portray real people behind a real crisis. Canadians and Americans are fighting for affordable housing across North America. In telling Vancouver's (Canada) story, it also tells the story of every community where housing prices and rents have been driven beyond the reach of people who live and work there. d. Nettie Wild; p. Nettie Wild/David Diamond; ed. Bill Roxborough; original music: Jay Samwald; IDERAF.

RIGHT TO LET DIE, THE (28m C 1980)
    The film comes to grips with the ultimate questions of life and death. What is the meaning of death and dying? Can any human agency interfere with the natural process of dying? Does the patient in the agony of dying have the right to ask to be allowed to die? Does a physician have the right to respond to this appeal? Can a physician act affirmatively to end the suffering of one's situation? If not, who can? Is any life so useless that it should not be permitted to continue? These are the questions discussed by the panel members. The panel consists of David C. Abramson, M.D., Ph.D., Director of Newborn Services, Georgetown; Sydney Cornelia Callahan, M.A., L.L.D., author and columnist, Hastings-on-Hudson; Warren T. Reich, S.T.D., Kennedy Center for Bioethics, Georgetown. p. NBC-TV in cooperation with the Kennedy Institute for the Study of Human Reproduction and Bioethics at Georgetown University; KENJP.

RIPARIAN (30m C n.d.)
    Documents the debate over the case of Oaks Bottom, a 167-acre wetland several miles from downtown Portland, Oregon. Presents the attempts of city groups and industrialists to develop the area and the attempts by the community and natural science professionals to preserve it as a wildlife habitat. p. Diana Cuitanovich, Don Adams; CCC.

RITES OF WOMEN (11m B n.d.)
    Rites of Women is a feminist theatre collective which combines the techniques of theatre and modern dance in performance. The three women's anarchist philosophies are examined in relation to the

disciplines and difficulties of creation and performance. p. Sharyn
Blumenthal, Susan Curran; TEMPLU.

RIVER, THE (29m C p1977, r1977)
   Based on a short story by Flannery O'Connor about a neglected
little boy who is befriended by the poor woman who takes care of
him. Zealously religious, she introduces him to religion and this experience of baptism and religion has dramatic effects on him. p./d.
Barbara Noble, American Film Institute; PHOENIX.

ROAD I TOOK TO YOU: THE STORIES OF WOMEN AND CRAZINESS,
      THE (45m C p1980, r1981) (Video)
   A documentary of the pressures which make women "crazy" and
the potential of alternative programs such as the Elizabeth Stone
House, a residential program for women in emotional distress. Women
speak of the impact of violence, racism and poverty on their lives,
their experiences with traditional mental health care, and their experiences at the Elizabeth Stone House. d. Cindy Marshall; p. Brand
Cotter/Jennifer Holme; STONEHE.

ROAD NEVER ENDS, THE (15m C 1976)
   A truck driver's work and life are shown as they are--which is
not entirely what the driver or his wife imagined they would be. An
insight into a contemporary family life. p. ASD Arts; TEXFM.

ROAD TO BABI YAR see HOLOCAUST

ROAD TO KATHMANDU, THE (58m C n.d.)
   Documents an astonishing 11-week overland expedition from London to Nepal and across Asia via truck. Their first stop is Istanbul,
then to the archaeological sites of Ephesus, Temessos, and Aspendos,
followed by the spectacular coastline of Southern Turkey. Then north
to the valleys of Cappadocia and mountainous areas of Eastern Turkey. From there to Iran and Isfahan and across the Iranian desert
into Afghanistan, from Herat to Kabul, over the Khyber Pass, and
into Pakistan. After a brief rest at Lake Dal in Kashmir, they drive
into Delhi and the tourist spots of India. Finally, to the foothills of
the Himalayas, to Nepal, and the journey's end, Kathmandu. d./p.
Annie South, David South; DOCUA.

ROADS TO HELL (22m B si 1948)
   Dance in four parts: "Pride," "Sloth," "Envy," "Wrath"--depict-
ing four of the seven deadly sins. "Suite of Satires" performed without music. Dancer, Choreographer: Eleanor King; d./p. Thomas
Bouchard; BOUCHT.

ROBBERS, ROOFTOPS, AND WITCHES (46m C p1981, r1982) (also
      Video)
   Designed to inspire the study of the American short story and
to serve as a catalyst for creative writing. Tom Aldridge is shown

playing Washington Irving at Sunnyside, his 24-acre estate along the Hudson River, discussing the unique features of the short story. Dramatization of three short stories are presented. d. Mark Cullingham; p. Elaine Sperber, p. Highgate Pictures; s.w. Bruce Harmon; LCA.

ROBERT FROST'S "THE DEATH OF THE HIRED MAN" (21m C p1978, r1979)
   A dramatization of a poem by Robert Frost. Adapted for film using Frost's dialogue word for word, and visually translating the spirit and texture of Frost's poetry. d./p. Jeanne Collachia; EBEC; IU.

ROCKER (9m C 1976)
   The graphic image of one of the "Chase Sculptures for Dance" was synthesized with the assistance of Steve Rutt. The edited version was colorized with Brian Mattlin assisting at the Experimental Television Center of WNET-TV, New York City. Sculptor: Doris Chase, p. Doris Chase; CHASED.

ROCKING ORANGE (3m C 1974)
   A dance film based on Doris Chase's kinetic sculpture for a ballet commissioned by the Seattle Opera Company. Filming was done in the Avery Court of the Wadsworth Atheneum, Hartford, Connecticut. The first part of the film is a straight record of dancing. In the second part of the film, the record is video synthesized and the sculpture is optically printed. Choreographer: Mary Staton; Sculptor/ p. Doris Chase; CHASED.

ROCKING ORANGE IN THREE VERSIONS (12m C 1975)
   Based on kinetic sculpture designed by Doris Chase for the Seattle Opera Company Ballet, the first version is a straightforward presentation of dancers and sculpture in motion, showing inventive variety in space and form. The second part is the identical film put through a video synthesizer and transferred back to film. The third version is achieved with the creative use of optical processing. p. Doris Chase; music: George Kleisinger; choreography: Mary Staton; CHASED.

ROCKING ORANGE III (3m C 1974)
   Dance with sculpture. Dance Company: Mary Staton Dance Ensemble; Choreographer: Mary Staton; Sculptor/p. Doris Chase; CHASED.

RODEO RED AND THE RUNAWAY (33m ed.) (49m C 1979)
   Geraldine Fitzgerald portrays Ella, a strong-willed prairie woman in this film adapted from Shelter from the Wind by Marion Dane Bauer. A young girl who refuses to accept her stepmother runs away from home. She meets "Big Red," a former rodeo horse who becomes her companion and is owned by Ella. What she learns from

Ella enables her to return to her family newly aware of the understanding needed in human relationships. p. Dora Bachrach; d./s.w. Bert Salzman; NBC Special Treat; LCA.

ROLE OF WOMEN IN AMERICAN SOCIETY SERIES <u>see</u> SALLY GARCIA AND FAMILY

ROLE OF WOMEN IN THE MOVIES, THE (27m B p1978, r1979) The Art of Film (Series)
   Presents the history of the treatment of women on the screen from the beginning of the movies to the great depression. It is pointed out in the "Love Goddess" that movie heroines have always been a reflection of our social behavior, customs, manners and morals. The creation of the "Vamp," in motion pictures is explained and her distinctive webbed costumes and her power to leave a victim helpless are described. Later movies introduced the flapper-tease heroine and the rich, sophisticated heroine. When the film musical was born in 1929, the heroine was shown to be beautiful, cold, sexy and had the appearance of royalty. As moral attitudes relaxed, the blond bombshell combined with comedy became the rage. Includes brief scenes with all of the early screen goddesses, Lillian Gish, Theda Bara, Gloria Swanson, Clara Bow, Jean Harlow, Carole Lombard, Pola Negri, Greta Garbo, Marlene Dietrich, and Mae West. CORONET; KENTSU, UM, UMN, USC.

ROLL OF THUNDER, HEAR MY CRY (110m C 1979) (also Video)
   Based on Mildred Taylor's Newbery Award-winning novel of the same title. Told from the point of view of 11-year-old Cassie Logan (portrayed by Lark Ruffin). The film depicts the struggle of a fiercely proud and independent black family to hold onto the land that has been in its possession for three generations. Against the backdrop of rural Mississippi in 1933, the Logan family is pitted against various representatives of white racial oppression: the sharecropping system and the company store, unscrupulous bankers and landowners, poor whites and night riders. While the film is unsparing in its judgment of white racism, it nevertheless presents its story in human terms. Starring: Claudia McNeil, Morgan Freeman, Janet McLachlan. p. Jean Anne Moore; d. Jack Smight; LCA.

ROMANCE TO RECOVERY (36m C 1979)
   Dr. Joseph A. Pursch describes how alcoholism adversely affects the normal relationships of the family and turns other family members into co-alcoholics who operate to reinforce the alcoholism of one member. Follows an alcoholic/co-alcoholic family situation through cover-up, manipulation, medical complications, child abuse, remorse, separation, revenge, and reunion. Emphasizes that all family members need treatment, that solutions are available, and talks about how to find them. FILMSPRO; PAS.

ROMANTIC BALLET, THE (52m C 1979) The Magic of Dance (Series)
   Margot Fonteyn traces the story of the Romantic Ballet and its

greatest exponents. In 1832, the most famous ballerina in the world was Maria Taglioni; one of the first ballerinas to dance on the tips of her toes, she epitomized the Romantic Age--ethereal, sylph-like, in a white gauzy skirt with wings sprouting from her back. Her most famous role was La Sylphide. By mid-century, however, there were new styles--the waltz, the can-can--and the music-hall was in its prime. It was left to the Russians to revive the Romantic Age in 1909 when they brought to Paris Les Sylphides. Includes part of this ballet, danced in the original setting by Margot Fonteyn, Marguerite Porter, Yoko Morishita and Ivan Nagy. Also features Roland Petit, Mette Honningen, Flemming Ryberg and the Royal Danish Ballet. p. BBC/TIMLIF; UMN.

ROMANTICISM: THE REVOLT OF THE SPIRIT (24m C 1971)
The mood of nineteenth-century Romanticism--escape from an increasingly complex, industrialized world to the purity of nature--is revealed in dramatized excerpts from literary works. In a scene from Les Miserables, Victor Hugo sees society as the force that makes man evil. The Romantics' attitude toward death is typified in the death scene from Wuthering Heights and their love of heroic gesture in the flamboyant fire of Shelley's funeral pyre on the beach, as his friend Bryon swims out to sea for a better view. p. Helen Jean Rogers, John Secondari; LCA.

ROOM FOR ALL (23m C p1980, r1980)
Two refugee families entered the United States in 1975 and experienced job mismatch. In their homelands, these professionals, with education and expertise, had jobs with considerable responsibility. The doctor, an emigrant from the Soviet Union, found she had to pass relicensing exams to become an intern. The lawyer from Vietnam found that his knowledge was not applicable. Yet these refugees courageously endure. d. Midge Graves, M.K. Van Duyne; p. M. K. Van Duyne; p. Institute of Pluralism and Group Identity; IPLGPI.

ROSE, THE (134m C 1979)
Based loosely on the life of Janis Joplin. Bette Midler plays "The Rose," a hard-singing rock star who can't reconcile public adulation with her own deeply-rooted loneliness. On stage, she is vital and electric and her fans go wild for her. Offstage, she's burning herself out as she careens from crisis to crisis. Locked into an ironclad contract and managed by an unsympathetic promoter, The Rose leads a nomadic, self-destructive existence where ecstatic highs are followed by viciously depressive lows. Drinking heavily and popping pills, she desperately searches for someone to love her, but even love isn't enough. d. Mark Rydell; p. Marvin Worth, Aaron Russo; p. Fox; FI.

ROSE: A PORTRAIT OF ROSE FITZGERALD KENNEDY (12m C p1981, r1982)
A biographical film made entirely from stills which presents a

portrait of the life of Rose Fitzgerald Kennedy. The film is like a
walk through a family scrapbook as well as a look at 90 years of
American history and politics. The photographs selected are largely
from the family's private collection and many have not been seen before. d./p. Mikki Ansin Ehrenfeld; KENJP.

ROSE BLOOD (8m C 1975)
Images of a woman in dance, in flora, in picture, in eyes, in
architecture, in sunshine, in color, in crystal, in space, in confusion,
in danger, in disintegration, in her hand, in birth, in the Valley of
Sorrow, in the sea, in repetition, in sculpture and in herself. Won
a certificate of merit at the 1978 Dance Films and Video Festival.
Dancer/Choreographer: Carolyn Chave Kaplan; d./p. Sharon Couzin;
p. Augenlust Films; CCC.

ROSE BY ANY OTHER NAME (15m C p1977, r1979) (also Video)
A trigger film about the older person's search for closeness,
privacy and love. It fills the need for a sensitive, nonclinical, educational film that portrays the experiences of older people living in
long-term care facilities. Attitudes towards the elderly and their
sexual needs are explored in a tactful and delicate manner, using a
dramatic story rather than a documentary approach. The film is designed to help older people and their families, persons working with
the elderly and those with policy-making responsibilities develop informed judgments about lifelong needs for affection, privacy and
sexuality. Study guide included. p. Judith Keller; d. Rosanne V.
Allessandro; p. James D. Pasternak, p. Adelphi University Center
on Aging; ADELPHIP; PAS.

ROSES IN DECEMBER: THE STORY OF JEAN DONOVAN (55m C
p1981, r1982)
A documentary study concerning the brutal murder of four women
missioners in El Salvador on December 2, 1980. Examines the circumstances surrounding the deaths, the aftermath, and the political situation currently surrounding the events. Much of the story is told
in the words of Jean Donovan, the one lay missioner, whose life is
the focus of the film. d./p. Ana Carrigan/Bernard Stone; s.w. Ana
Carrigan; ed. Bernard Stone; original music: Chris Adelmann;
FIRRNF.

ROSEY GRIER: THE COURAGE TO BE ME (23m C 1982)
"It's your life--you can be the man or woman you really want to
be." With this attitude, Rosey Grier overcame painful shyness, rejection and failures in order to achieve success in sports, politics,
entertainment and in serving young people. d. Miles Watkins; p. A
Dimension Film; CF; WSU.

ROSIE RADIATOR (8½m C 1981)
Rosie Radiator is one of San Francisco's most famous street artists. Rosie demonstrates her unique style of tap dancing: the super

shuffle. She dances at the Bay Area Rapid Transit, in her studio, and across the Golden Gate Bridge. d./p. Ron Taylor; TAYLORR.

ROUNDABOUT (19m C p1978, r1978)
A non-narrated modern fairy tale on human relations between a young boy and an old man with a merry-go-round. p. Leah Miller, Pieter Van Deusen; CF, UIL.

ROYAL HERITAGE SERIES see VICTORIA AND ALBERT; VICTORIA, QUEEN AND EMPRESS

RUBY DUNCAN--A MOVING SPIRIT (15m C n.d.)
This documentary film depicts the concern, inspiration, and leadership of a Black woman in the Las Vegas ghetto. The story of Ruby Duncan and the women of Operation Life is commanding evidence of the ability of the poor to tackle their own problems with perception, know-how, and dedication. Ruby's actions peak cogently of what it means to be a prophet in your own back yard ... to stand against the powers of oppression and to communicate a message of hope that is tangible, and therefore, believable. d. Tom Rook. p. St. Francis Productions; TKF.

RUBY DUNCAN--CONFIRMATION STORYSCAPE (23m C n.d.)
The role of the Spirit in calling us to be all that we are capable of and the power of faith to help us grow through conflict and underlying themes of this documentary film on Ruby Duncan and the Women of Operation Life. p. Teleketics Films; AF.

RUFUS M., TRY AGAIN (13m C 1977)
A story illustrating the importance of perseverance based on the book Rufus M. by Eleanor Estes. Rufus encounters several obstacles as he tries to check out a library book. Determined, however, he overcomes these obstacles and reaches his goal. p. Martha Moran; PHOENIX.

RULE OF THUMB (16m C 1973)
During his radio show, a young disc jockey presents a documentary about hitchhiking. In the voices of the young people themselves, we hear the stories: Mark, the victim of a homosexual attack by a man who gave him a ride; Laura, raped by a driver who seemed to respect her as adult; Albert, who picks up a girl who has a gun in her purse and an accomplice down the road; and Ron, who falls in with a less-than-respectable group of fellow hitchhikers. p. Sid Davis Productions; AIMS.

RUMPELSTILTSKIN (2nd ed.) (11½m C 1981) (also Video)
Tells in animation, Grimm's fairy tale "Rumpelstiltskin." p. Pajon Arts, p. Lillian Somersaulter-Moats, J. P. Somersaulter; CORONET; UIL.

RUN TO LIVE (22m C 1980)
An inspiring documentary on the life of a remarkable black woman --surgeon, educator, and civic leader. Dr. Dorothy Brown's day begins and ends with a phone call about her patients. The hectic hours between are filled with crucial life-saving decisions, civic responsibilities, and giving of herself to all those whom she touches. Dr. Brown spent the first 13 years of her life in an orphanage in Troy, New York. In the early 1920's, she dreamed of becoming a doctor and pursued her dream. Her life and all her achievements are the culmination of hard work, determination, and miracles. From home to the hospital, to the medical school, to one of her many meetings, Dr. Brown must indeed "run to live." UMCOM; MMM; RARIG.

RUNAWAY: FREEDOM OR FRIGHT? (10m C 1980)
Examines the reasons children, especially teenagers, run away from home and some of the possible consequences of that decision. Urges viewers to consider what they already know--they aren't prepared to survive in the world yet and they can easily be taken advantage of by other people. Points out that everyone leaves home eventually and that the key to success is being prepared. Emphasizes the importance of staying in school and learning to live with problems at home by talking about them with a friend or teacher. p. Charles Cahill and Associates, Inc.; AIMS; IU.

RUNAWAY PROBLEM, THE (2nd ed.) (27m C 1979)
Portrays young people and parents struggling with separation and alienation brought about when a child runs away from home. The stories interweave--young people telling about life on the street, parents relating their feelings of anguish and helplessness, and the Peace of Mind Hotline volunteers who open doors of communication between parents and runaways. p. Miller Productions, Inc., CENTEF; IU, PSU, UIL.

RUNAWAYS (10m C n.d.)
The revealing accounts of two youngsters who run away from home: Danny, after a particularly upsetting day at school, and Alice, after an argument with her mother over dating. Both teenagers return home, but in Danny's case, only after a cold, hungry, and frightening journey. Alice is attacked by two older boys and found wandering down a lonely mountain road. The message is clear that when you run away from problems, you only create bigger ones. p. Sid Davis Productions; AIMS.

RUNAWAYS ... FROM WHAT TO WHERE (29m C 1976)
Explores actual case histories of runaways. A runaway is usually a female in her early teens, middle- or upper-class family, lives in the suburbs, feels unloved and misunderstood, lacks respect and understanding from her parents, and feels she has nothing to live for. There are no two cases alike, yet, a thread of consistency runs through all. Informs viewers what organizations are offering runaways

a place to think without pressure, peer interaction, and counseling. p./d./s.w. Ted Offret; UAZ.

RUNNING AWAY TO WHAT? (17m C 1979)
Looks at the predicament of the teenagers who run away to Fort Lauderdale, Florida, a popular East Coast refuge. Focuses on the hustling and prostitution that these young people usually turn to as a means of self-support. Since Florida is the worst state to be convicted in, many adolescents spend time in prisons or juvenile detention centers. Points out that although the orignal home conditions may have been rough, the street can be rougher. Interviews with teenagers who have run afoul of the law make the message clear: there are a lot of surprises out in the street, the chances of "making it" are better at home. One of the runaways, it turns out, is serving a life sentence for killing a man who picked him up. p. NBC-TV; FI; UIL.

RUNNING EVENTS, THE (15m C 1976) The Track and Field Series
for Girls
Events include sprints, middle distances and distance runs. In sprints, girls are shown the techniques used by world champions. In middle distances, girls and coaches are introduced to new techniques that have caused the track record explosion. Similar techniques are applied in distance runs. p. Ryan Films; MACMFL.

RUNNING, FOR THE BODY AND MIND (26m C p1978, r1979)
Introduces running as a form to lifetime fitness. Points out that running is the most popular, easiest, and least expensive form of exercise. Research indicates it may prevent heart and circulatory disease, fatigue, depression, insomnia, and overweight. Shows how to choose proper footwear, how to prepare mentally and physically for running, and the therapeutic benefits of running. Clearly, regular exercise is key to good health. p./d. s.w. Richard Sullivan; p. Belltown Films; LAWM.

RUNNING MY WAY (27½m C 1981)
A film about communication and sexuality as a common human experience. Focuses on issues, dilemmas, conflicting societal messages, parental denials, peer pressures, personal values and decisions confronting 14- and 15-year-olds. Shows adolescents' struggle to deal with their feelings, physical urges, feelings of parents and pressure from peers. Does not editorialize or make judgments. d./p. Lynne Littman; ex. p. Charlotte De Armond; CHSCA.

RUSSIAN BALLET AND FOLK DANCES (10m B 1944)
A rare Ulanova film, made in Russia, in which Galina Ulanova and K. M. Sergeyev perform an adagio from Swan Lake. Includes folk music by the Kirghiz artist Ogonbayev and two of his pupils, and the Ukrainian song and dance ensemble of the Don Bas Coal Miners. p. Central Documentary Film Studios, Moscow; MACMFL.

RUSSIANS, THE (SERIES) see PEOPLE OF THE CITIES; PEOPLE
OF THE COUNTRY

RUTH ELLEN PATTON TOTTEN/HELEN ROSS see OLD FRIENDS ...
NEW FRIENDS ... RUTH ELLEN PATTON TOTTEN/HELEN ROSS

RUTH PAGE: AN AMERICAN ORIGINAL (58m C p1978, r1979) (also
Video)
From a Midwest childhood and first lessons in "fancy dancing"
through her illustrious career as dancer, choreographer, and director, the film traces the life of a warm vital woman whose influence
on the dance spans three continents and more than half a century.
Page's sparkling reminiscences of her associations with Anna Pavlova,
Diaghilev, Adolph Bohm and others are interspersed with dance sequences which highlight her innovative choreography. Her talent
was not only technical excellence, but the ability to visualize a performance as a whole--the integration of movement, costume, scenery,
music, even the spoken word. Now in her seventies, Ruth Page
continues to teach and puts in her daily stint at the barre. d. David W. Hahn; p. Nicholas Prince, p. Otter Productions; FI.

RUTH ST. DENIS BY BARIBAULT (24m C 1940's-1950's)
Five numbers by Ruth St. Denis, filmed in color in the 1940's
and early 1950's by Phillip Baribault, a professional Hollywood camera-
man. Included are "White Jade," "Red and Gold Sari," "Gregorian
Chant," "Tillers of the Soil" (with Ted Shawn), and "Incense." See
also INCENSE, which is available separately. Dancers: Ruth St.
Denis, Ted Shawn; p. Dance Film Archive; DAN/UR.

-S-

SX-70 (11m C 1972)
The invention, technology and potential of a remarkable new
photographic system. p. Ray Eames, Charles Eames; PF; UIL.

SABINA SANCHEZ--THE ART OF EMBROIDERY (22m C 1976) Mexico's
Folk Artists Series
Shows the life and work of Sabina Sanchez, a Zapotec woman in
Oaxaco, Mexico, who still makes the embroidered blouses of her tra-
ditional village costume. Available in Spanish or English. p. Judith
Bronowski, Robert Grant; WORKS.

SACRED TRANCES IN BALI AND JAVA (30m C r1976)
In the sacred rituals of Bali and Java, invisible spirits are brought
down to enter the bodies of trancers, who perform supernormal feats,
such as walking on fire, piercing cheeks with pins, and rolling on
broken glass ... extraordinary examples of altered states of consciousness in animistic, Hindu, and Muslim rites. p. Elda Hartley; HART-
LEY.

SAEKO ICHINOHE AND COMPANY (30m B n.d.) (Video)
The Japanese choreographer-dancer Saeko Ichinohe and her company perform modern dance inspired by the Japanese tradition in such works as "Hinamatsuri" ("The Doll's Festival") and "Sun Dance" in which Ichinohe dances to Japanese poems recited by Joan Baez. Dancer/Choreographer: Saeko Ichinohe; Dance Company: Saeko Ichinohe's Company; Narrator: Joan Baez; p. Performing Arts Division of Asia Society; ASIAS.

SAEKO ICHINOHE DANCE: EAST AND WEST (30m C n.d.) (Video)
A comparison of Japanese and Western dance patterns. Also, works choreographed by Saeko Ichinohe, such as "Kitchen," "Goza" ("The Mat"), and "Fire-Eating Bird." Dancer/Choreographer: Saeko Ichinohe; p. Performing Arts Division of Asia Society; ASIAS.

SAFE STRANGERS (14m C 1982)
Through a series of dramatized vignettes, illustrates times and events when young people should turn to a Block Parent for help. The approach is positive and is directed at upper elementary school age children. The objectives are to instill a sense of responsibility in young students for their own safety and that of others. It educates young people about who Block Parents are and their role in community safety. d. Mark McCurdy; p. Nancy Johnson; ONTBPP.

SAGA OF SOULI (5m B 1981)
In the early 1800's, a group of Greek women, trapped on a mountaintop by invading Turkish troops, decide to dance over the edge of the mountain to their death rather than submit to their barbaric conquerors. This somber film poem retells the story of these women and their heroic and final, circle dance. p. Judy Mann; MEDIAP.

ST. JOAN (60m C 1978)
Shaw's heroic girl-soldier in conflict with the establishment of her day--military, royal, ecclesiastic. Clever twists of logic are developed by the wittiest playwright in English theater history. This version begins at the point of Joan's imprisonment, through her pretrial, recantation, and decision to face execution rather than to surrender belief. Guest artist Julie Harris discusses her role as Joan in "The Lark," and reenacts a stirring speech from an earlier episode showing Joan as a practical idealist. p. Miami-Dade Community College in Association with the British Open University and BBC; FI.

SAINTS AND SPIRITS (26m C p1979, r1979) (also Video)
Shows the dimensions of religious expression in Islam as viewed through the experience of one woman in Morocco. The rituals and events of Islam are tightly woven into the fabric of everyday life. This film shows several religious observances in the Moroccan city of Marrakech which has nearly a hundred shrines. In addition to the narration, subtitles are used in a short segment of dialogue, onsite sounds add realism to the action. A 16-page guide, including

map, history of Islam, complete film commentary, suggestions for discussion and bibliography is included. p. Center for Middle Eastern Studies, University of Texas. p./d. Melissa Lewelyn-Davies, Elizabeth Fernea; ICARF.

SALLY (25m C p1979, r1980) (also Video)
The time of adolescence is dramatized in this story about Sally at age 13. Reassures girls, in a gentle manner, that the traumatic experiences of adolescence are really very common. p. Patricia Russell; PEREN.

SALLY GARCIA AND FAMILY (35m C r1978) Role of Women in American Society Series
A study of the family, marriage, and the changing roles of women. Sally Garcia, of Chicopee, Maine, was busy raising her five children and taking care of the household. Her husband, Juan, was an Air Force pilot but now retired and is earning an advanced degree at the university where he works. So, Sally, now 40, has started a whole new career counseling young women who are trying to find careers for themselves. Part of Sally's job is to be an advocate to the Hispanic community of Springfield. Besides her work, evenings are spent taking college courses, or playing bingo or bowling. Although everyone cheerfully shares in the housework, Sally expresses her ambivalence at being torn between home and career, and her guilt at not spending all her time with her children. p./d. Joyce Chopra; EDC.

SALLY OSBORNE: MECHANICAL ENGINEER (10m C n.d.)
Follows a computerized-simulations engineer through a typical workday and looks at the education and training necessary for such work. Aims to stimulate interest in engineering careers for women. Free loan. MTPS.

SALMON PEOPLE (25m C 1977)
Shows re-enactment of the legend of Raven and Salmon Woman. Contemporary scenes of the salmon fishing industry and other salmon-related activities are interspersed with the re-enactment. The intercutting is visually disruptive but effective in communicating that the salmon's contemporary importance comes from a continuous link with the ancient past. The legend serves as an object lesson in ecology, and illustrates the Native American philosophy that humankind and the natural world exist together in a sacred relationship. Tribal or geographic placement of the contemporary action or the myth has been omitted. p. Shelah Reljic; ex. p. Peter Jones/NFBC; NFBC.

SALT: THE HIDDEN THREAT (21m C 1983) (also Video)
Designed to help viewers become aware of excessive sodium in their diets and its possible effects on health. Tells how one can control the amount of sodium consumed; how one can begin forming eating habits that reduce sodium intake, and gain knowledge of the

hidden sources of sodium in foods.   d. Stephen Wallen; s.w. Michael
Heldman; p. Alfred Higgins Productions; HIGGIN.

SAN SERIES OF JOHN MARSHALL see GROUP OF WOMEN OR WOMEN
    UNDER BAOBAB, A

SANDRA AND HER KIDS (26m C 1982) (Video)
    Shocked by the plight of Third World orphans, Sandra Simpson
adopted one and that was only the beginning.   She now has 20
adopted children in addition to her own four, operates an international adoption agency and orphanages in India, Bangladesh and So-
malia.   d./p. Tom Kelly; ed. John Gareau; CBC.

SAPPHO (7m C n.d.)
    Using the sixth century B.C. lyricist's poetry, a group of women
unwrap the papyrus gauze of the Lesbian poet and bring her to life.
p. Barbara Hammer and six students at the Women's Building in Los
Angeles.   p. Iris Feminist Collective, Inc.; CCC; IRISFC.

SARAH JACKSON: HALIFAX 1980 (10m C 1980)
    Shows Sarah Jackson, sculptor and experimental artist, at work.
Tells how she perceives herself and how others perceive her.   p.
Doomsday Studios; DOOMSD.

SARAH T ... PORTRAIT OF A TEENAGE ALCOHOLIC (97m C 1975)
    Examines one of today's most serious problems--increasing inci-
dence of alcoholism among teenagers.   Linda Blair portrays Sarah
Travis, a 15-year-old schoolgirl who begins drinking secretly when
she has difficulty adjusting to a new neighborhood, a new school and
life with her mother and stepfather after her parents are divorced.
Sarah steps up her drinking after failing to win selection to her
school's glee club.   Then, at a neighborhood teenage party, she gets
slightly drunk and becomes the life of the party when she loses her
inhibitions.   Ken Newkirk (Mark Hammill), a teenager railroaded into
taking her to the party on a blind date, begins to like her.   But
after several dates he becomes worried about her secret drinking.
Sarah's mother, her well-meaning stepfather and her charming but
irresponsible father are among the last to recognize the symptoms of
Sarah's disease, but Sarah is finally convinced that she is an alcoholic in need of outside help.   d. Richard Donner; s.w. Esther Shapiro, Richard Shapiro; Universal.

SATURDAY (5m B 1971)
    Three short films made by teenagers at the Lexington, Massa-
chusetts School of Modern Dance.   Three kinds of action: a slow-
motion circling movement; jumping and rolling in the snow; and fast
running, swinging, somersaults.   d. Karen Gil, Joyce Wolfson; p.
Cellar Door Cinema; CELRDC.

SATURDAY'S CHILDREN (36m C 1982)
    Shows the births of the four babies whose parents were admitted

to a Florida hospital on Saturday, June 12, 1982. All the parents
had attended natural childbirth classes and selected portions of their
labors are also shown. Emphasis is placed on family-centered birth
experiences with strong parent/child attachment in a hospital setting.
d. Philip Courter; p. Courter Films and Associates; PARPIC.

SAVING REMNANT, THE see HOLOCAUST

SAYING "NO": A FEW WORDS TO YOUNG WOMEN ABOUT SEX (17m
    C p1981, r1982) (also Video)
    Using a dramatization in which a girl does not know how to be
assertive toward a boy's sexual advances and repeating the scene
after she has learned to say "no" effectively, this film presents a
realistic look at decisions about sexuality facing teenage girls today.
A girl who was talked into having sex is told by a radio psychologist
that she has not really decided what she wants to do and needs to
make a personal decision about the best behavior for her, including
whether to smoke, drink, use drugs and participate in sex. The
risks of premarital intercourse, including venereal disease and teenage pregnancy, are discussed and a quiz is provided to familiarize
teenage girls with their real feelings. Several girls speak of their
personal experiences and their reasons for having or not having sex.
It is pointed out that other girls and the media, as well as boys,
pressure girls to have sex and that indeed they can learn to be assertive and say "no." p. Crommie and Crommie; s.w. Karen Crommie; PEREN; IU.

SCENE CHANGES, THE (52m C 1979) The Magic of Dance (Series)
    Margot Fonteyn explores her own world of dance--from the dom-
inance of the ballerina in the 1930's to the emergence of the great
male dancers of the sixties and seventies. Her story is illustrated
by some of the world's greatest dancers performing some of the era's
most enduring dances--from Swan Lake to Top Hat, and Pierrot Lu-
naires to Sleeping Beauty. Features Rudolf Nureyev, Natalia Maka-
rova, Fred Astaire, Sammy Davis, Jr., Michael Denard, Luigi Bonino
and Lynn Seymour. p. BBC/Time-Life Video; TIMLIF; UMN.

SCHEHERAZADE (10m C p1978, r1978)
    A production created by the expressive media of electronics. It
is the first time an analog hybrid computer has been used for the
animation of images which symbolize the characters in the familiar
story of Scheherazade. The symbolic story-telling is a collaboration
between the visual of Casey and Naschke and the music of Rimsky-
Korsakov. d. Susan Casey, Nancy Naschke. p. Celectronic Graphics; CELECG.

SCHOOL OF AMERICAN BALLET (43m B 1973)
    A documentary about the School of American Ballet. Guest teacher
Helgi Tomasson of the New York City Ballet appears teaching adagio
class. George Balanchine is seen working with Madame Danilova at

a rehearsal of the advanced students' workshop in which Fernando Bujones appears doing a variation from the first act of Swan Lake. Other teachers are shown instructing their students. p. Virginia Brooks; BROOKSV.

SCHOOL PROFESSIONALS AND PARENTS (25m C 1981) (also Video)
  Trigger Films on Human Interaction Series
  Presents some of the situations that commonly arise in parent-counseling. It is designed for use by school professionals in improving communication techniques. Open-ended. Guide included. p. Family Information Systems and Resource Communications, Inc.; MTITI.

SCHUSTER-ISSACSON FAMILY (LESBIAN MOTHERS), THE see
  FAMILY PORTRAIT: THE SCHUSTER-ISSACSON FAMILY

SCIENCE: WOMEN'S WORK (27m C p1981, r1982)
  By taking math and science courses in high school, young women keep a variety of choices open for satisfying, well paying careers later. The large numbers of women lacking these courses is a major factor in the small number of women scientists in the work force. Documents a wide variety of options through seven women at various stages of their science careers. Free loan. d. Bastian Wimmer; p. Image Associates; a.p. Jan Hatcher; NAVC.

SCORAFORM (10m C 1969)
  Presents a new contemporary art form developed from paper sculpture by Canadian artist Peggy Specht. Using a plastic material called Forbon, Specht bends and scores a flat surface plane into an object with both mass and volume. Shows the artist at work and many of her completed mobile lamps and sculpture. p. Halewyn Films; HALWNF; UIL.

SCOTT JOPLIN: KING OF RAGTIME COMPOSERS (15m C 1977)
  Scott Joplin's ragtime piano swept the world at the turn of the century. Dramatized biography traces roots of his music in New Orleans and Mississippi, his study of classical composition, his great initial success, failure of his opera Treemonisha, and his death in poverty and obscurity. Includes early film footage of the 1904 World's Fair in St. Louis. Narrated by Eartha Kitt. p. Amelia Anderson; PF; PAS.

SCREAM FROM SILENCE, A (96m C 1980)
  Rape is also an internal act: it attacks the soul. This film is about rape in all its horror. Suzanne, a nurse, is grabbed by a man with a knife and pushed into a van. The sequence that follows is explicit in its brutality. Suzanne escapes with her life, but something is irrevocably changed; she has lost the capacity to love. Spreadeagled on the gynecologist's table, she is systematically probed and photographed for medical and legal reasons. At the police station, the interrogating officer aims questions in accusing tones.

Already in a state of shock, Suzanne feels violated once again. Society's method of dealing with rape is coldly clinical. This docudrama explores, with unusual techniques, society's attitudes which cause the woman to feel guilty and responsible for an act she cannot control. (NOTE: This is a moving, shocking, compassionate film on a subject little discussed. The first section deals graphically with a brutal rape. The film should be previewed in order to assure that the material is suitable and that the audience will be adequately prepared for its presentation.) NFBC; UW.

SCREEN NEWS DIGEST SERIES, THE see MS.--THE STRUGGLE FOR WOMEN'S RIGHTS

SCREENTEST (20m C r1975)
A candid look at an unusually gifted group of actor/mimes. They made all their costumes, sets and makeup, and created and acted all the roles. p./d. Caroline Ahlfours Mouris, Frank Mouris; KPF, PHOENIX.

SCREW (3m C 1977)
A witty bedroom fantasy in animation set to the words of a "technical love poem" ("Screw" by Diane Wakowski). It is one woman's visual interpretation of the word "screw"; it is an attempt to examine love as a "techno-experience" with the final conclusion that it is not. d./p. Margaret Bailey Doogan; SERBC.

SCROLLS (30m C si 1978)
An exploration of oscillation. The film is single-framed, and the location of the axis within the frame is continually shifted (Museum of Modern Art, November 13, 1978). p. Vicki Z. Peterson; MMA.

SEA DREAM (6m C 1979) (also Video)
A young girl dreams her bed covers become rippling waves and she is diving deeper and deeper into this sea where she meets a congenial octopus who shares in a tea party with her. The two play games in rhythm with the undersea current. After awhile the girl starts back to the surface, but swirling waters return her to the embracing arms of the octopus for a final goodbye. Once again rising to the surface, she emerges through her bed comforter and is returned to quiet sleep. Adapted from a poem by Debra Bojman. d. Ellen Besen; p. Kathleen Shannon; NFBC; PHOENIX.

SEA TRAVELS (11m C 1978)
Using optical effects and the manipulation of live-action images, Thacher explores the theme of childhood memories: its dreams, fantasies, and unique landscapes. p. Anita Thacher; MMA.

SEAN'S STORY (DIVIDED CUSTODY) see FAMILY PORTRAIT: SEAN'S STORY

SEARCH FOR THE GREAT APES (55m C 1975)
Presents a look at two women's studies of the closest nonhuman relatives to people, the great apes. Documents Birute Galdikas-Brindamour's research project on the behavior of wild orangutans in Borneo. In the Virunga mountains of Rwanda, Africa, Dian Fossey has established a long-term research project observing mountain gorilla behavior. p. National Geographic Society; NGS; UW, PAS.

SEARCHING YEARS SERIES see OLIVIA: BETWEEN TWO CULTURES

SEASON OF GRANDMOTHERS, A (28m C 1976) (also Video) The Real
    People (Series)
The role of the grandmother in American Indian life is illustrated in this program, filmed by an all-Indian crew in Montana, Idaho and Washington. Grandmothers from the Spokane, Coeur d'Alene and Nez Percé tribes care for children, weave, sew and dance. A Kootenai grandmother and grandfather butcher and skin a deer, while talking about hunting and the old days. A Flathead Tribe grandmother tells how her family was massacred by a game warden in 1908, and a Colville Indian grandmother describes the old ways of discipline. Scenes from a "stick game" being played at the Kalispel Reservation are also shown. p. George Burdeau, a.p. Phil George; p. KSPS-TV, Spokane, Washington; PBSV.

SEASONS (16m C 1971)
Deals with the health and rehabilitation of older people including nursing and rest home conditions and effective programs in geriatric therapy. Used in the presentation which launched the 1971 White House Conference on Aging. USNAC; UM.

SEASONS, THE (SERIES see FALL IS HERE (2nd ed.); SPRING IS
    HERE (2nd ed.)

SEASONS OF THE BASQUE (29m C 1978) (Video)
The movements of the Basque sheepherders in Nevada are traced throughout the seasons' changes. An intimate look at a disappearing subculture, its camaraderie and isolation, this work records the sheepherders' skills and way of life. As engrossing as it is instructive. p. Suzanne Tedesko; MEDIAP.

SEASONS SERIES (2nd ed.) (11m C 1979)
Each film introduces the activities of people and animals and the alterations in nature as the seasons change. At the beginning of each film, it is explained why seasons occur. Series include FALL IS HERE, WINTER IS HERE, SPRING IS HERE, SUMMER IS HERE. p. Myrna I. Berlet, Walter H. Berlet; IFB.

SECRET OF NANCY DREW, THE (32m C p1981, r1982)
A profile of the late Harriet Stratemeyer Adams, octogenarian author and director of the Stratemeyer Syndicate, whose characters

include Nancy Drew, the Hardy Boys, the Bobbsey Twins, the Dana
Girls, and Tom Swift. Beginning with the books' colorful origins at
the turn of the century, the film explores their impact on an estimated
billion readers, through interviews with Adams, journalist Frances
Fitzgerald, critic George Woods, publisher Jack Artenstein, historian
Arthur Prager, and many others. d. Karl Harr III; p. Caroline A.
Jones; PROTNP.

SECRETS (8m C p1979, r1980) (also Video)
A dramatic sketch of a day in the life of an 80-year-old, who
outwits time every Sunday by returning to the scene of his former
grandeur and playing out his past with three of the ladies in it.
The first secret of the title is that his own wife arranges these adventures for him; the second is that he knows her secret without
letting on. Stereotypes of aging are shattered in the process. d.
Joan Vail Thorne; p. J. Vail Thorne, Bill Richards; FILMLB.

SECRETS OF THE MASTERPIECES (SERIES) (30m ea. B n.d.) (English sound only) p. Madeleine Hours; FACSEA.
JEROME BOSCH. Born at Bois-le-Duc circa 1450, Bosch continued
the traditions of the early Middle Ages. His painting contains all of
the imagery of the Gothic Cathedrals.

COROT. Corot as a landscape painter and portraitist.

JEAN FOUQUET. The greatest painter of the fifteenth century.

LEONARDO DA VINCI. A study of the work and technique of
Leonardo da Vinci.

MALADIES DES TABLEAUX ET LEURS REMEDES. The different
ways of preserving works of art.

EDOUARD MANET. A study of the painter who was one of the
last of the great classical painters and one of the first of the modern.

LE NAIN. A little known aspect of seventeenth-century painting.

REMBRANDT. An examination of Rembrandt's works in the laboratory of the Louvre revealed a great number of surprises. The
work of this painter is ideal for demonstrating the value of these
methods in art history.

LE RETABLE DE BEAUNE. A study of the most moving masterpiece to have come down to us from the fifteenth century: the Van
der Weyden reredos at the Beaune hospital in Burgundy.

LE TITIEN. A study of the considerable work of Titian.

VAN EYCK. A study of the work of Van Eyck, the most famous

of the fifteenth-century Flemish painters--often said to be the inventor of oil painting.

LES VRAIS ET LES FAUX. The discovery of fake paintings has always fascinated the public, but it is extremely difficult to tell a fake from a genuine painting. Here is how scientific analysis can help.

SEE NO EVIL (15m B 1975)
Bertha and Ralph, both in their seventies, live together (although unmarried) in a senior citizen hotel. Bertha, almost blind, is extremely bitter about her loss of independence. Ralph accepts growing old more readily. They provide a candid picture of the attitudes and feelings of their age. Although Ralph expresses strong commitment to Bertha, he leaves her in the end. Film is useful in programs dealing with adjustment to aging, marriage in later life, and counselling. Illustrates that the dynamics of relationships are similar regardless of age. p. Seth Pinsker; FILMLB; UM.

SEE WHAT I CAN DO (18m C 1976)
Designed for Art Education students and classroom teachers. Ten 11- and 12-year-olds work with modeling clay. Teacher encourages each child to develop a three-dimensional sculpture expressing a personal concept. The students discuss their own work, the work of classmates, and a sculpture by an adult artist. d./p. Dr. Alive M. Schwartz; PAS.

SEE WHAT I SAY (24m C p1980, r1981) (also Video)
The charismatic Holly Near, feminist folksinger, is breaking through the barrier that separates the hearing and the deaf communities. She shares her concert stage with Susan Freundlich, recognized American Sign Language interpreter, who incorporates mime and dance in the translation of the lyrics. Their synchronized performance heightens the impact of her vision of a better world. Holly Near's commitment to the hearing-impaired is underscored by the stories of four women who experienced the isolation of the deaf. As the film closes, Holly, Susan, and the concert audience sing and sign "Harbor Me," a ballad about women supporting one another. Holly then asks the audience to sign without singing. With the last piano refrain and audience applause, the film ends with a sense of shared communication between hearing and deaf cultures. p./d. Linda Chapman, Pam LeBlanc, Freddie Stevens; p. Crommie and Crommie; s.w. Karen Crommie; FILMLB.

SEEING DANCE (29m B 1970) (also Video) Contemporary Dance Series
Instructors Vera Embree and LaRainne Jones discuss the problems of seeing, remembering and preserving dance. Topics are how, when and where to see dance performance; film and TV recording of dance; and dance notation. Quin Adamson, Director of Music for the dance program at the University of Michigan, created the score for

"Moment" (danced by Mary Spalding). An original electronic score by Peter Klausmeyer, student at the University, provides the music for "Antibodies" (danced by Diane Elliott). Host: Robert Luscombe. d. Marshall Franke; p. Selma Odom; UMMRC; UM.

SEIZURE: THE STORY OF KATHY MORRIS (104m C 1983) (also Video)

Based on the true story of Kathy Morris, SEIZURE tells of a young music student suddenly afflicted with a tumor, the brilliant neurosurgeon in whose hands her life is placed, and the anguish and struggle both patient and doctor must endure when Kathy comes out of the operation unable to read or count. Determined to return to her career, Kathy overcomes these adversities and inspires her surgeon (whose wife has left him) to confront his problems with the same resolution. Starring Leonard Nimoy and Penelope Milford. p. Jozak Productions; TIMLIF.

SELF DEFENSE FOR WOMEN I.-X (40m C p1976, r1977)

Shows the many techniques women can use in self-defense. Defense techniques are shown in slow motion. Four basic principles are stressed: balance, focus, advantage and leverage. The application of these principles is illustrated. The narration stresses the fact that these techniques must be practiced and rehearsed continuously to be effective, and that the element of surprise is a woman's best weapon. From the book Personal Safety and Defense for Women by Patricia Stock. p./d. Herbert Dalmas; p. Survival Media, Inc.; SURVM.

SELF INCORPORATED, THE (SERIES) see FAMILY MATTERS (WHAT IS A FAMILY?)

SENIOR POWER AND HOW TO USE IT (19m C 1975)

Instructs older persons on how to protect themselves from purse snatching, armed robbery, and telephone harassment. Specific suggestions on how to make homes secure and whom to contact when problems arise are included. p. William Brose Productions; BROSEW; UIL, UM.

SENSE OF PRIDE: HAMILTON HEIGHTS, A (15m C p1977, r1978)

The Hamilton Heights neighborhood in Harlem is explored through interviews and visuals which show how the residents' sense of pride, struggle and pulling together make it the landmark area it is today. p./d. Monica Freeman; MUSNYC; MJPRO.

SEPARATION (30m C 1980) (also Video) Look at Me Series

Highlights: Laying the foundations for a healthy approach to separations; observations on coping with the different forms of separation a child may face. Separations from familiar people and places are part of the process of maturing. The episode focuses on various specific examples of separation--entering school; divorce; moving to a new home; death--and shows how a parent can help cope with children's anxieties over these separations. p./s.w. Jane Kaplan, Wendy Roth; p. WTTW-TV; FI.

SERENGETI SHALL NOT DIE (84m C n.d.) On Safari Series
Presents a documentary of life on the Serengeti Plain in Africa. d. Joan Root, Alan Root; p. Survival Anglia Television; HURCW.

SERGEANT TOM KELLER (17m C n.d.)
One day in the life of a police officer in Portland, Maine. d. Margaret Kenda; p. Police and Public Project; POLPUP.

SERIOUS MINDED STUFF (16m C 1983)
In this whimsical comedy, 16-year-old Amanda Sharpe discovers her natural talent for slapstick and becomes an overnight silent film star. To the disappointment of her parents she stops her ballet training in order to pursue her new career. Set in 1919 Los Angeles, this delightful film is for all ages. d. Mollie Miller; p. University of Southern California, Division of Cinema and Television; DIRECT.

SERIOUS UNDERTAKINGS (30m C p1982, r1983)
Explores film form and the politics of representation while examining Australian culture and the position of women. Images of terror and childcare collide, underlining the difficulties of representing "positively" or "realistically." Montage is used to interweave diverse elements, such as drama, "interviews," painting, literature, art, social history, film. Video special effects draw attention to the image's construction. d. Helen Grace, p. Erika Addis; AFC.

SERMONS IN WOOD (27m C p1979, r1980)
An evocative examination of the life and art of Elijah Pierce, a master craftsman who carves intricate relief sculptures in wood. p. Carolyn E. Jones Allport; SOFOLK.

SERVE WITH BILLIE JEAN KING, THE (15m C 1969) On Tennis, a Series
The serve is called the key attacking weapon of the game. The basic serve is demonstrated move by move, including grip, position of the feet, the toss, the swing, contact, and follow through. Slow motion gives a graphic representation to the instructions. The slice serve and twist serve are also detailed. Erik van Dillen and Vic Braden assist. FI; UIL.

SET-UP (17m B 1978)
Depicts a violent sexual interaction between two men. The first half presents the encounter using conventional cinematic exposition. This model is then visually and ideologically analyzed through the use of voice-over, split-screen and slow motion (Whitney Museum of American Art, November 21, 1978). p. Kathryn Bigelow; WHITNEYM.

SEVEN BRIDGES OF KONIGSBERG, THE (4m C 1965) (also Video)
Recreates Leonard Euler's analysis of the problem of crossing the seven bridges of Konigsberg in a single continuous walk. Drawings show that Euler condensed a real-life question into a mathematical problem and proved that crossing the bridges in a single continuous walk is impossible. The narrator explains the issue. p. Katharine Cornwell, Bruce Cornwell; IFB.

SEVEN PRINCIPLES SERIES, THE see IMANI; KUJICHAGULIA; UJIMA; UMOJA

SEVEN WISHES OF A RICH KID (ed.) (30m C 1979)
Calvin Brundage is a rich kid--lonely, unhappy, and disliked at school. Although he has everything money can buy, what he wants is social acceptance. One day while watching television, a video fairy godmother appears on the screen to grant him seven wishes, six of which he uses up before learning an important lesson. p. Dora Bachrach; LCA; KENTSU.

SEVEN WISHES OF JOANNA PEABODY (29m C 1978)
Joanna Peabody lives in an urban ghetto with her family. One day while watching television, a modern day fairy godmother appears on the screen and grants Joanna seven wishes. After wasting three of them, Joanna carefully uses the remaining ones for herself, her family, and even the fairy godmother. Based on the book by Genevieve Gray. p. Dora Bachrach; LCA; KENTSU, RARIG.

SEX AND THE SINGLE PARENT (98m C 1982) (also Video)
How do divorced parents re-establish themselves as unattached, available adults and still fulfill their responsibilities as parents? Divorced Sally (Susan Saint James) is ensnared in the treadmill of job, children and babysitters. George (Mike Farrell), likewise divorced, sells cars by day, then swings all night in singles' bars. This comedy-drama shows how they meet, how their romance develops and how their children create some funny and awkward barriers which Sally and George must surmount before attaining a new mature understanding of themselves. p. Time-Life Films; TIMLIF.

SEX FOR SALE: THE URBAN BATTLEGROUND (45m C r1977)
Explores the civic, moral, and legal controversies surrounding the growth of prostitution and pornography in most American urban centers. Focuses on massage parlors, sex theaters, and "adult" bookstores, contending that such businesses are factors in many types of crime, not merely victimless crimes. p. ABC-TV; CWU, PAS, UCEMC, UIL, UMN.

SEX MORALS (13m C p1977, r1977)
An unscripted filmed discussion on sexual ethics by a group of teenagers. Discussion are on spiritual aspects of sex as opposed to merely a physical experience; does one need to be in love to have

sex? should sex be reserved for marriage? the merits of marriage; possibility of being in love with many different people in the course of a lifetime, with each relationship as important as the last, etc. p./d. Kent McKenzie, p. Dimension Films; LREDF.

SEX THERAPY, PART I (29m C 1976) (Video) Woman Series
Helen Singer Kaplan, a sex therapist and psychoanalyst, discusses the need for people to carefully evaluate sexual problems and seek treatment. Kaplan, who is head of the Sex Therapy and Education Program at New York Hospital's Payne Whitney Clinic, explains sex therapy, behavior therapy, psychoanalysis, marital therapy and hormone therapy. She estimates that 50 percent of the people who come to the Clinic with sexual problems respond successfully to treatment. She also talks about the "new" sex therapy, which stresses open communication and education. Sandra Elkin is the moderator. p. WNED-TV; PBSV.

SEX THERAPY, PART II (29m C 1976) (Video) Woman Series
Helen Singer Kaplan, a sex therapist and psychoanalyst, discusses organic and emotional reasons for sexual problems. She explains that people who acknowledge problems and seek treatment generally find rewards. She talks about the role of anxiety in the failure to find sexual fulfillment. Sandra Elkin is the moderator. p. WNED-TV; PBSV.

SEXES: ROLES, THE (28m C 1972)
Surveys evolution of female/male roles from prehistory to current industrial age. Psychologist Judith Bardwick points out stresses caused by clash between traditional expectations and new realities, Matina Horner presents her classic studies on women's fear of success, and sociologist Jean Lipman-Blumen relates how "girls are socialized to destroy their own dreams at an early age." p. CBC; FILMLB; PAS.

SEXES: WHAT'S THE DIFFERENCE?, THE (28m C 1979) (also Video)
Addresses the sensitive question: Are "male" and "female" traits inborn or are they learned in childhood? Research methods of Dr. Jerome Kagan and Dr. Elinor Maccoby can be observed as they isolate biological from cultural factors. Surveys the evolution of male-female roles from pre-history to our current industrial age. Psychologist Judith Bardwick, feminist and dean at the University of Michigan, points out the stresses caused by the clash between traditional expectations and new realities. Matina Horner presents her classic studies on women's fear of success, and sociologist Jean Lipman-Blumen relates how "girls are socialized to destroy their own dreams at an early age." Can be shown independently or used in sequence for a comprehensive survey of the psychology and sociology of male and female behavior. p. CBC; FILMLB; UCLA, UMN.

SEXISM: AN INTRODUCTION (8m C 1982) (slc)
Presents a general introduction to sexism for teachers. Identifies

sex bias, sex discrimination, and sex stereotyping. Looks at the examination of personal beliefs and suggests actions the teacher can take to prevent sexism in the classroom. Includes guide and script. p. Kent State University; KENTSU.

SEXISM IN SOCIAL WORK PRACTICE (14m C 1978) (Video)
Presents six scenes portraying examples of sexism in individuals, couple and group therapy, and in professional staffing. These scenes are intended to stimulate discussion of what is sexist in each inter-action and how each situation can be handled differently. Includes training manual. Presented by the School of Social Work, University of Washington; UW.

SEXISM, STEREOTYPING AND HIDDEN VALUES (29m C 1978)
Educators experienced in identifying and dealing with sexism and other forms of unwanted stereotyping explain the sources of hidden values in the school setting and offer means whereby teachers can promote a climate of equal opportunity in their classrooms. Approaches and strategies for recognizing and avoiding hidden presumptions and biases in both materials and activities are described and demonstrated. Documentary scenes illustrate the comments of authors Nancy Reeves (Womankind: Beyond the Stereotypes) and Stephanie Waxman (What's a Girl? What's a Boy?). p. Media Five Film Distributors; MEDIAF; UMO.

SEXUAL ABUSE OF CHILDREN (29m C 1977) (Video) Woman Series
Social workers Linda Sanford (founder and director of Seattle's Rape Prevention Forum) and Florence Rush talk about the incidence of sexual abuse of children by family members and neighbors. They explain how to tell a child about molestation and discuss identifying the abuser. Sandra Elkin is the moderator. p. WNED-TV; PBSV.

SEXUAL ABUSE OF CHILDREN: AMERICA'S SECRET SHAME (28m C 1980)
The molestation of children has grown to epidemic size in the United States because it has been protected by its own silence, a silence of embarrassment and guilt. In a thoughtful, controlled, documentary-style, narrator Peter Graves takes the viewer through interviews with district attorneys, with Dr. Frank Osanka, the na-tion's leading child-abuse expert, with actual victims, and with con-victed molesters themselves. Revealed are the methods of the mo-lester, what about him appeals to his victims, how he lures his vic-tims, how he avoids detection, and why he is rarely recognized as a child molester. The complexity of the crime is what has made it hard to prosecute. Clearly the only way to solve a problem is with direct community involvement. AIMS; IU, UIL.

SEXUAL ABUSE: THE FAMILY (30m C 1977)
Features a discussion of sexual abuse in children by a physician,

social worker and a psychologist. Involves a role-play by professionals of interviewing a child sexual victim and her family in an emergency room setting. Not recommended for showing outside the training setting. Title No. 000612/BB. NAVC.

SEXUAL ASSAULT, PTS. 1, 2, 3 (30m ea. 1979)
Based on personal interviews, this three-lesson series explores the psychological implications of sexual assault, bringing into the classroom the assailant, the victim and the police officer. The series is aimed primarily at students in criminal justice programs as the role of the law enforcement officer is probed in depth in each instance. There are, however, applications outside the field of law enforcement. Each of the interviews provides insight in the thoughts and actions of both the assailant and victim, before, during and after the assault. Classes in human development, deviant behavior, and women's studies will find the series valuable. NETCHE.

SEXUAL FUNCTION AND DYSFUNCTION (29m C 1978) Daniel Foster, M.D. Series
Dr. Daniel Foster and his guest Dr. Kenneth Z. Altshuler, Professor and Chairman of the Department of Psychiatry at the University of Texas Health Science Center, discuss the concepts of normal and abnormal sexual behavior in physical and psychiatric terms. Dr. Altshuler, a noted authority on sexual dysfunction, comments on the results--both healthy and unhealthy--of sexual openness and talks about sexual identity. p. KERA-TV, Dallas, Texas; PBSV.

SEXUAL HARASSMENT (A LECTURE BY DR. JENNIFER JAMES) (31m C 1980) (Video)
In a lecture taped before a meeting of the United States Forest Service, Dr. Jennifer James discusses sexual harassment in the work environment: the reasons for it, why it is a problem, what it is, and what to do about it. p. Dr. Jennifer James; UW.

SEXUAL HARASSMENT: A THREAT TO YOUR PROFITS (19m C 1981) (also Video)
Uses a case study of a woman employee's charge that her supervisor is guilty of sexual harassment to trace what should happen at the management level to deal with such problems. Emphasizes preventive measures and discusses what constitutes sexual harassment and the negative impact it can have on an organization. p. Philip Office Associates; AMMED; PAS, WSU.

SEXUAL HARASSMENT: NO PLACE IN THE WORKPLACE (29m C 1979) (2" HB tape)
Gloria Steinem and Lynn Farley (author of Sexual Shakedown) discuss issues facing working women, offering insights as well as solutions to the problem of sexual harassment in the work place. In cooperation with the Institute of Labor and Industrial Relations. UMMRC; UM.

SEXUAL HARASSMENT ON THE JOB (29m C 1977) Woman Series
  Karen Sauvigne, Program Director of the Working Women United
Institute, and Susan Meyer, Executive Director of this program, discuss how to identify and deal with sexual harassment on the job.
Sauvigne explains the results of research carried out by the Institute
and both women talk about the implications of several court cases involving sexual harassment in the work place. Sandra Elkin is the
moderator. p. WNED-TV; PBSV.

SEXUAL HARASSMENT: THAT'S NOT IN MY JOB DESCRIPTION
  (19m C 1981) (also Video)
  Case studies of sexual harassment in the workplace include homosexual and male and female heterosexual harassment situations. Discusses preventive measures that can be taken by employees and points
out the difficulty in determining when sexual harassment has taken
place. Explains that the Equal Employment Opportunity Commission
guidelines state that "unwelcome sexual advances, requests for sexual favors, and other verbal or physical conduct of a sexual nature
constitute sexual harassment." p. Philip Office Associates; AMMED;
PAS.

SEXUALITY (30m C/B p1979, r1980) Coping With Serious Illness Series
  Deals with the difficult issue of sexuality and the need for loving
at critical times as well as during times of stress. Through a discussion by Joan Robinson, who is dying of cancer, and her husband,
we see the questions and difficulties with which such couples contend.
Hosted by Meryl Streep. TIMLIF; PAS, UMN.

SEXUALITY, PART I (29m C 1980) (Video, Beta, VHS) Feelings
  (Series)
  Despite the fact that children are bombarded with sexual images
from the time they are old enough to turn on TV sets, parents are
still confused about how and when to explain sexuality to them.
Just what do children know and how do they feel about sex? The
answers are surprising, as Dr. Lee Salk discovers from three young
teens--Laura, Eli, and Lisa--who have some very definite opinions
on subjects ranging from teen pregnancies to suggestive scenes on
television. PBSV.

SEXUALITY, PART 2 (29m C 1980) (Video, Beta, VHS) Feelings
  (Series)
  With Dr. Lee Salk, 13-year-old Lisa and 14-year-old Eli and Laura
continue their exploration of sexual attitudes and behavior. The discussion ranges from homosexuality and the double standard to parents' mistaken ideas about their children's sexual knowledge and behavior. PBSV.

SEXUALITY: A WOMAN'S POINT OF VIEW (30m C p1979, r1982)
  (Video)

Explores the world of women's attitudes about sexuality. It is divided into four parts, touching on the mirror technique of therapy; Judeo-Christian influence on sex and morality; a women's seminar where information and experiences are exchanged. It concludes that there must be evolution rather than revolution which will require courage and cooperation between women and men. Non-explicit. Narrated by Stefanie Powers. d. Amelia Anderson; p. Anderson and Brown; MMRC.

SEXUALITY AND COMMUNICATION (55m C 1971)

Drs. Avinoam and Beryl Chernick of Canada use role playing to explore the subjects of sexuality and communication as they relate to the doctor-patient and husband-wife relationship. Presents the physical and physiological aspects of sex in an informal and informative way. Demonstrates how attitudes and feelings affect sexual performance and how the anxieties of daily living interfere with family relationship, showing examples of positive and negative communications which can alter and improve relationships. AF; UNEV.

SEXUALLY ABUSED CHILD: A PROTOCOL FOR CRIMINAL JUSTICE, THE (26m C p1979, r1979) (also Video)

Provides information for professionals dealing with sexually abused children on how best to serve the child through the criminal justice system. Sandra Baker, a nationally recognized authority on the sexual abuse of children, and others, presents valuable suggestions for dealing with this widespread problem. A judge, a district attorney, physician, and a receiving home director all contribute their ideas for successful prosecution of offenders, as well as a sensitive approach to dealing with the victims. Also see the companion film A TIME FOR CARING: THE SCHOOLS RESPONSE TO THE SEXUALLY ABUSED CHILD. p. Sandra Baker, Richard Baker; Profile Films; LAWREN; IU.

SEXUALLY TRANSMITTED DISEASES (10m C n.d.)

A broad overview on the numerous, different diseases that can be sexually transmitted. Both the diseases and their symptoms are described with emphasis on the most prevalent ones. Stresses early detection and treatment. Also available in Spanish. MIFE.

SHADOW CATCHER (88m C r1975)

Tells about Edward Curtis--photographer, anthropologist and filmmaker--and the Indian people he worked with over 32 years of his life (1890-1930). Includes all of Curtis' recoverable film footage. Shown are the Kwakiutls, the Navajos, and the Hopis. Narrated by Donald Sutherland, Dennis Wheeler. p./d. T. C. McLuhan; s.w. T. C. McLuhan, Dennis Wheeler; PHOENIX.

SHADRAC (1½m C n.d.)

A continual metamorphosis of abstract shapes, faces and animal forms. p. Sara Petty; CFS.

SHAKER LEGACY, THE (20m C 1976)
    Shows how the indigenous American culture of the Shakers pro-
vides, for us in the twentieth century, a rich heritage represented
in the works of artists such as Charles Sheeler, Aaron Copland and
others. Founded in England in the mid-eighteenth century as a reaction against the dehumanizing effects of industrialization, the Shakers (or "Shaking Quakers," so named for the practice of exorcising
evil by shaking their bodies) combined their peculiar form of Christianity with a form of early Socialism. They were joined in 1758 by
a young woman, Ann Lee, who became their spiritual leader and was
regarded by followers as the reincarnated Christ; evidence of that
belief is found in the "spirit drawings" produced by later followers.
In 1774 Mother Ann, as she became known, led eight followers to
America where they established the first Shaker community in this
country in 1776. In a strict code of celibacy in communal living,
men and women were not allowed to touch. The ideals of simplicity
and functionality guided the development of Shaker furniture, art,
architecture and handicrafts. Evidence that the Shaker heritage
greatly influenced many twentieth-century creative personalities is
presented in the music, paintings, graphics, and still photography.
p. Patrick J. Sullivan, Judith Speidel, University of Massachusetts
School of Education; University of Massachusetts, Audio-Visual Department; UMA.

SHAKERS, THE (29m C 1974)
    A film incorporating old graphics and photographers as well as
narration to depict the life of Mother Ann Lee, founder of the Shaker
sect, and the sect's history of America. Filmed to the a capella singing of nineteenth-century Shaker hymns. A discussion guide is available. p. Tom Davenport; DAVNPT.

SHAKERS, THE (20m B si 1940)
    A dance interpretation of an early meeting of the American reli-
gious sect, the Shakers. Mother Ann Lee, founder and eldress of
the sect, is portrayed by Doris Humphrey. Dance Company: The
Humphrey-Weidman Company; Choreographer: Doris Humphrey; d./p.
Thomas Bouchard; BOUCHT.

SHAKESPEARE: A MIRROR TO MAN (27m C 1971)
    Two distinguished English actors, Eileen Atkins and Brian Cox,
use an authentic Tudor castle as the setting for a lively introduction
to Shakespeare. Playing all the roles in segments from three of his
plays, then stepping out of character to explain, analyze and question, they reveal the essence of Shakespeare's genius--and his remarkable understanding of the deepest motivations and darkest emotions of man. p. Helen Jean Rogers, John Secondari; LCA.

SHAKTI--"SHE IS VITAL ENERGY" (56m C n.d.)
    Through a succession of mini-portraits, this documentary portrays
the woman of rural India whose life, shaped by traditional and ritual,

still follows a predetermined course. Images of great visual beauty illustrate the various stages of her evolution, from childhood into old age. Her marriage to a young man of her parents' choice is a turning point in her life. She must leave her family to become a member of her husband's family. The woman of rural India moves through life with grace and dignity regardless of the task she must perform d. Dominique Crouillere; p. Anne-Claire Poirier; NFBC.

SHAMAN see BRUJO

SHAPING THINGS: A CHOREOGRAPHIC JOURNAL (40m C 1978)
Traces the process of Frances Alenikoff's choreographing of Fossil Folio, a group work which was first performed in June 1977. Sync sound documentary footage from rehearsals is accompanied by voice-over commentaries from Alenikoff, the dancers, and the musical director, providing a detailed and personal account of the development of the dance from the first rehearsal to performance. Dance Company: Frances Alenikoff Dance Theater Company; Choreographer: Frances Alenikoff; d. Robert K. Machover; p. Red Hill Films; REDHL.

SHARE-A-HOME (GROUP HOME FOR THE ELDERLY) see FAMILY
    PORTRAIT: SHARE-A-HOME

SHARON (28m B 1977) (Video)
A documentary portrait of a formerly battered wife. The woman offers insights into the psychology of the "battered syndrome" (Global Village, October 28, 1978). p. Nancy Cain; MEDBUS.

SHATTER THE SILENCE (29m C p1979, r1979)
In this dramatization, we see the story of Marianne, who as an adolescent is a victim of incest. We see the effects of this on her life and growing up, and how she becomes afraid of relating to people, especially men. Later, as she recounts her story, she meets a man who helps her get involved in therapy and is able to help free herself of the guilt and become a new person. d. Gerald Schiller; p. Joe Steinberg; p. S-L Film Productions; PHOENIX; UCEMC.

SHATTERED (21m p1978) (also Video)
Shattering some of the common myths about rape, revealing the devastation it can cause in a woman's life and sharing ways of coping afterwards, this film deals forthrightly with a highly emotional subject. Victims can be anyone from babies to the elderly. Shown is a group therapy meeting in which rape victims vent their feelings to people who truly understand, discuss how it has changed their lives and discover how others learned to cope. p. MOCSA (Metropolitan Organization For Countering Sexual Assault); p. Laurence D. Hope; d. Dick Willis. Created and written by Nancy Parks, Arthur Parks; MTITI.

SHE ALSO RAN (30m B n.d.) As It Happened Series
Describes how women took action to secure their voting power.

Shows how they blackmailed their husbands into voting for Belva
Lockwood, a woman candidate for President. Explains that although
she was defeated, this marked the genesis of women's voting power.
p. ABC-TV; TIFFANY.

SHE AND HE (KANOJO TOKARE) (110m B 1963) (Japanese/Subtitled)
Examines a very common and tragic type of modern marriage.
The husband is caught up in the demands of his job and seems to
diminish gradually as a human being. His wife, originally less knowl-
edgeable and interesting, is driven by the emptiness of her life to
consider the world around her and is gradually educated by life itself into becoming superior to her husband. The growth of social
conscience and responsibility in a bored housewife has rarely been
better explored and documented than in SHE AND HE. With Sachiko
Hidari, Kikuji Yamashita, Eiji Okada. d./s.w. Susumu Hani; FI.

SHE AND MOON DANCES (20m B n.d.)
The dance, symbolizing the creative power of women in our cul-
ture, portrays the misuse of this creativity. In two parts: "The
Mothers Create" and "The Mothers Possess," performed by Eleanor
King and her Company; and "Moon Dances," a solo by King. Dancer/
Choreographer: Eleanor King; d./p. Thomas Bouchard; BOUCHT.

SHE HAS A CHOICE (17m C n.d.)
More often than not, women with the disease of alcoholism are
treated for "emotional problems," not alcoholism. This film deals
with the myths and realities which differentiate the female from the
male alcoholic. The negative stigma applied to the female alcoholic
are exposed for what they are. Women of different ages and backgrounds share their real-life experiences as we discover how positive
confrontation and intervention helped them deal with alcoholism. Provides strong identification for a wide cross-section of American women.
p. Motivational Media; MTITI.

SHE LOVED THE LAND (20m C c1977)
Emma Garrod, 93, recalls the early years of her life in a pioneer-
farming community in the Santa Cruz Mountains of California, south
of San Francisco. Emphasizes the social history of the times: people, places, ways of living and thinking. A model "visual oral history" presentation, incorporating excellent old still photographs,
scenes of the countryside, and other graphic materials. UCEMC.

SHE SHALL BE CALLED WOMAN, PTS. 1, 2, 3, 4, (30m ea. 1976)
(Video)
Since Adam named her, woman has been given many roles to play
in our societies. This series explores what these roles have been
and how they are changing. This factual analysis, research and production of the neglected history of women in this country took over
a year. It is intended as an introduction and discussion catalyst for
groups interested in women's history. The filmed interviews with

women and men who lived through the major events of this century
will make the personal impact of this history live for the students.
Part titles are 1) "Take Away the Apple"; 2) "Succeeding Generations"; 3) "The Crisis of Perfect Propriety"; 4) "Women Against
Women." NETCHE.

SHE/VA (3m C si 1973)
    This personal, evocative film made from home movies provides a
glimpse into the experience of American girlhood. p. Marjorie Keller;
WMM.

SHEEP, SHEARING AND SPINNING: A STORY OF WOOL (11m C
    p1980, r1980) (also Video)
    Presented is the journey of wool from sheep to a handmade sweater.
A shepherd boy and rancher are shown with their flocks and a skillful farmer demonstrates how and why a sheep is shorn to a group
of delighted children. The bundle of raw wool is sold to versatile
Kay who washes, cards, spins, dyes, and knits it into a sweater for
her son Chuck. p. Myrna I. Berlet, Walter H. Berlet; IFB.

SHEER MADNESS (105m C 1982)
    This is a story of two women. One is shy and withdrawn and
married to a "peace expert" who needs her to maintain his own self-
confidence. She takes refuge in museums, copying paintings of the
Great Masters. The other woman is quite her opposite--a literature
professor, and the wife of a successful director, she is confident and
self-assured. A rapid friendship develops between the women ... a
friendship that changes both their lives. Starring Hanna Schygulla,
Angela Winkler; d. Margarethe von Trotta; p. TeleCulture, Inc.;
TELCULT.

SHELLEY AND PETE ... (AND CAROL) (22m C 1980) (also Video)
    One in every five 14-year-old girls will become pregnant before
she leaves high school. Two thirds of these pregnancies--over
1,000,000--are unintended. This open-ended film dramatically depicts one of these stories. Shelley and Peter are high school students
and very much in love. Their families care about them and share
their plans for a bright future. The unplanned arrival of baby Carol
drastically alters their lives. Sponsored by United States Department
of Health and Human Services, Public Health Service; d. Foster Wi-
ley; NAVC.

SHELLEY WHITBIRD'S FIRST POWWOW (8m C 1977)
    Presents a story in which an Indian girl prepares for her first
powwow. The film brings to life the cultural and artistic heritage
of a Native American tribe. Intended for primary and elementary
level. p. Lifestyle Production in collaboration with Doreen Porter,
Media Specialist, Native American Committee; EBEC.

SHE'S A RAILROADER (10m C p1978, r1980) (also Video)
    When Karen Zaitchik finished high school she knew that she didn't

want to spend her working life cooped up inside an office. So she
went to Canadian National Railroad and applied for any kind of outdoor job that might be available. She was offered a place in a switching training program. Now she's a 21-year-old railroader. Her unconventional goals led her to enriching work that would inspire any
woman to consider an alternative to an office job. d. Barbara Tranter; p. John Taylor; NFBC; PHOENIX; UIL.

SHE'S NOBODY'S BABY (60m C 1982) (also Video)
    Incorporates newsreels, photos, government propaganda films,
cartoons and music to trace the evolution of the twentieth century
woman. Narrated by Alan Alda and Marlo Thomas. p. ABC Wide
World of Learning; ABCWWL.

SHIFTING GEARS (12m C 1981) Time Out Series, III
    Buddy is slowly winning his struggle to control his violent im-
pulses. His friend P. K. is not. P. K. takes out frustration on his
wife, beating her frequently. The film presents a vision of male
friendship with room for caring and compassion, as Buddy helps
P. K. confront the consequences of his violent behavior. d. Ed
Moore; p. Oralee Wachter; O. D. N. Productions; ODNPRO.

SHIRT FACTORY, THE (7m B 1963)
    After a field trip to a local textile factory, North London school
children re-enact their experience and impressions. Their musical
interpretation portrays the monotony of the factory assembly line and
the repressive atmosphere in which the women are forced to work.
A radio, earlier banned, reappears to give the film an upbeat ending as the rebellious workers leave their machines and furiously dance
the Charleston. d. Hazel Swift with the Grasshopper Group; p. British Film Institute; MMA.

SHOCKING ACCIDENT, A (25m C 1983) (Video)
    From the short story "A Shocking Accident" by Graham Greene,
an English school boy learns that his father has been killed in a bizarre accident. His friends tease him and years later his aunt still
relishes the tale. Only when he meets a girl who understands can
he shake off this terrible memory. p. Christine Oestreicher; d.
James Scott; DIRECT.

SHOESHINE GIRL (25m C p1979, r1980) (also Video) Learning to Be
    Human Series
    Focuses on a painful but ultimately valuable summer in the life
of a troubled young girl. Sarah Becker is sent to her aunt's house
for the summer after her parents discover that she has hidden stolen
clothes in her dresser. Aunt Claudia was instructed not to give
Sarah money, so unhappily she searches for a job. A shoeshine man
gives Sarah a job. Her negative attitude changes as she learns,
through her employer's own example. She leaves with a better understanding of people and life than she had before. Based on the book

Shoeshine Girl by Robert Bulla. p. Jane Startz; d./s.w. Peter Barton; LCA; IU, UIL.

SHOPLIFTING: SHARON'S STORY (25m C 1978)
Drama which presents the humiliation of a teenage girl caught and arrested for shoplifting in a department store. After her arrest, she is searched, handcuffed, and taken to the police station. There she is photographed and fingerprinted, and her parents are notified. Presents a brief look at the police and court systems, as well as an insight into the attitudes of those in positions of authority toward the crime of shoplifting. p. Yvonne Chotzen; p. Auro Productions Film; d. Dennis Kull; LCA; KENTSU, UMO, USC.

SHOPPERS (27m C 1977)
Portrays through direct interview and photographic images the diversity and complexity of some of the life-style choices available to people today. For the first time in history, such choices are a reality for the majority of people. All of the people portrayed are young, white, and American. Open-ended. Discussion guide available. p. Robert Newman, United Church Board for Homeland Ministries; UCBHM; AF.

SHOPPING BAG LADIES (45m B 1978)
The shopping bag ladies--Who are they? Where do they come from? Why are they on the streets? Where do they go at night? This documentary allows us to enter briefly the lives of five women in New York City. Consists of in-depth interviews with these women on the streets. Their personal histories are vague; they often contradict themselves. But in the midst of each performance there are moments of truth, the truth of feeling, not of fact. They are hungry, cold, lonely, isolated, taunted by adolescents and sometimes physically assaulted but mostly ignored by people in general. The interviewers suggested to each one that she go to a shelter. They all had reasons for not going but what emerged was a fierce independence, a determination to be free, to live their own lives without dependence on official charity. d./p. Joan Giummo, Elizabeth Sweetman; GIUMMO; UCEMC, UM, UMO, USC.

SHOPPING FOR CREDIT (18m C 1980)
A powerful lesson in the use and abuse of credit, the film also deals with credit ratings and the problems of obtaining credit. Lending institutions are investigated with emphasis placed on interest charges and the total cost of a loan. Informative guidelines and the facts about credit options make this an important film. FI.

SHORT STORY--KATHERINE ANNE PORTER, THE (30m 1968) (Video)
Where do you find materials? Where do you get ideas? How do you write a mystery? "There is no sensible answer to these questions," states Miss Porter, "as no two people are alike. The material comes from the pores, the sensibilities and interest in the human

heart." Writer, Katherine Anne Porter was twice recipient of the Guggenheim Fellowship. NETCHE.

SHORT STORY LIBRARY SERIES <u>see</u> LUCK OF ROARING CAMP, THE

SHORT VISION, A (7m C 1964)
Through animation, the filmmakers have managed to imbue the most frightening of devices, an I.C.B.M., with an almost birdlike quality that conflicts with its actuality. Unlike the real situation, the flying bomb approaches slowly after it becomes visible. It destroys the world, leaving only a flame which dies--leaving nothing. p. Jean Foldes, Peter Foldes, George K. Arthur--Go Pictures; FI, VIEWFI.

SHOUT IT OUT ALPHABET (12m C r1969)
A collage animation brings words to life in a series of playful happenings involving all the letters of the alphabet. It's a game in which an audience of children tries to see how many "A" words, "B" words, and so on to "Z" they can discover on the screen. It is fast-moving and fun process in learning the alphabet. p. Lynn Smith; PHOENIX.

SICKLE CELL STORY (16m C n.d.)
A young black couple come to terms with the fact that they are carriers of the Sickle Cell trait and the possibility of their child being affected by Sickle Cell Anemia. Discusses hemoglobin screening, prenatal diagnosis and current research and development of medication to prevent the occurrence of Sickle Cell crisis. Also available in Spanish. MIFE.

SIGNED, SEALED, AND DELIVERED: LABOR STRUGGLE IN THE POST OFFICE (44m C p1980, r1980) (Video)
In 1978, thousands of postal workers across the country walked off their jobs when their contract expired, saying "no" to mandatory overtime, forced speedups and hazardous working conditions. As the result of this wildcat strike, 200 workers were arbitrarily fired, including Tami Gold's husband, by management. This is when Tami Gold picked up her camera to document their right to strike and the subsequent firings and stormy union meetings. The dramatic climax of the tape occurs with the death of Michael McDermott, a mail handler crushed to death at the Jersey City Bulk Mail Facility in 1979. This tragedy testified to the strikers' contention that dangerous, factory-like conditions prevail in the nation's post offices. The producers do not hide their partisan view--they capitalize on it to make a strong, clear case on behalf of the workers for safer working conditions, the right to strike, and more responsive union leadership. d. Tami K. Gold; p. Tami K. Gold, Dan Gordon, Erik Lewis; TAMRKP.

SIGNS OF QUOCTAAS, THE (8m C 1975) (also Video)
An original and visually symbolic tale of generational conflict in

a primitive and dangerous world. d. Lillian Moats Somersaulter, J. P. Somersaulter; p. Pajon Arts; FI.

SILENT DANCING (30m C 1979)
Shows deaf youngsters who are enrolled in an experimental "Ballet for the Deaf" program. The goal is to integrate the students into regular dance classes. Teacher and dance student assistants are from Robert Joffrey's American Ballet Center. Choreographer: Gerald Arpino; Narrator: Beverly Sills; d./p. David W. Hahn; ex. p. Patricia Sides; p. WNET-TV; FI.

SILENT NEIGHBOR, THE (10m C p1980, r1981)
Shows that abused children statistically become abusive parents. Stresses how community leaders can provide help in breaking that chain. It is shown that children had no rights in former times and although they now have rights, they continue to be emotionally, sexually and physically abused. The narration stresses that abused children, filled with guilt, low self-esteem and isolation grow up to depend on their own children for feelings of self-worth and are unable to tolerate or understand their children's needs and often become abusing parents themselves. Good discussion film. d. Bruce Maness; p. Association of Retarded Citizens, FILMCOMM.

SILHOUETTES OF GORDON VALES (27m C 1980)
Gordon Vales has a talent for tearing perfectly formed silhouettes from paper, using his hands and teeth. As an infant, Gordon was placed in a facility for the mentally retarded. He began tearing silhouettes at age six. In his twenties, he was taken in by a farm family and now, at age 45, he lives alone in his own apartment. Gordon narrates his own story. Many examples of Gordon's work are included, along with an animated segment incorporating his silhouettes. d. Robin DuCrest; p. The Association for Retarded Citizens; AFRC.

SILVER WHISTLE, THE (16½m C 1981)
A puppet-animated fairytale about a freckle-faced girl named Prudence. With a magic silver whistle, given to Prudence by her mother, she departs to make her way into the world. One day, she meets a prince who happens to like freckles. Together, they set out to make their way into the world and live happily ever after. A film version of story by Jay Williams. p. Barbara Dourmashkin; FLMFR.

SILVER WINGS AND SANTIAGO BLUE (59m C/B p1979, r1980)
One thousand American women flew for the Army Air Forces in World War II, yet today they have been forgotten--until now. Using wartime footage, newsreels, and film shot at Congressional hearings and pilot reunions, this film tells the true story of the Women Airforce Service Pilots, the WASP. d. Nelson Adams; p. Katharine King, N. Adams; ADMKG.

SILVERFISH KING, THE (6m C 1974) (also Video)
An example of the ways in which human fears can grow into bizarre

proportions. Intended as entertainment, but there is also an impact resulting from an identification of broad issues--the meaning of logic and the fine line between reality and imagination. d. Lillian Moats Somersaulter, J. P. Somersaulter; Pajon Arts; FI.

SIMILAR TRIANGLES (7½m C 1976) (also Video)
Using animation, the film investigates the families of similar triangles with explanatory captions. Colors and shapes merge over and over, reinforcing the qualities of similar triangles. No narration. p. Katharine Cornwell, Bruce Cornwell; IFB.

SIMONE DE BEAUVOIR (110m C p1980, r1981)
Candid portrait of Simone de Beauvoir as she converses and reminisces with her friends, especially her life-long companion Jean-Paul Sartre. She discusses her relationships, her political views, the student uprising of 1968, abortion, sexual fidelity, aging, and death. The film is interspersed with stills and film clips of events, personal or historical, that have shaped her thinking. d. Josee Dayan/Malta Ribowska; p. Lorenzo DeStefano; p. Cinema Ventures; INTERAMA.

SIMPLE MATTER OF JUSTICE, A (26m C p1978, r1978) (also Video)
Examination of the hotly debated Equal Rights Amendment. It highlights the history of the ERA and covers the opposition, both historical and current. Focuses on Jean Stapleton of "All In The Family" at the International Women's Year Conference in Houston, Texas, where she meets four other women who, like herself, are new to political activism. Each came to Houston with one overriding concern--passage of ERA. Also featured are first ladies Rosalynn Carter, Betty Ford, Lady Bird Johnson; Congresswomen Bella Abzug, Barbara Jordan; feminist leaders Jill Ruckelshaus, Betty Friedan. The film is about the 14,000 women and the million others to whom the passage of the ERA is just that ... a simple matter of justice. p. Ann Hassett; d. Victoria Hochberg; FI; KENTSU, UFL, UIL, UMN.

SINGLE PARENT (43m C 1975) Women Today Series
In this film, nothing was staged, prearranged, or provoked, and there was no script. Two people--one with a camera and one with a tape recorder--spent every waking moment of one month with a single-parent family in California. In an effort to capture the essence of that family, it shows how they function as a unit, how they act and react with one another, how they approach their conflicts, and how they really live from day to day. Provides a remarkable and sympathetic portrait of the isolation and vulnerability that the single parent suffers. p. Hubert Smith; MEDIAG; KENTSU, UM.

SINGLE PARENT, THE (29m C 1978) Look at Me Series
Shows a Spanish-speaking family fitting shoes; learning math at the fast food counter; infant stimulation; sensory experiences of tasting, smelling, listening; overcoming fear of dogs; the single parent's feelings about herself and her children; a do-it-yourself birthday party; enjoying storytime. p. WTTW-TV; PEREN.

SINGLE PARENT FAMILIES (30m C 1982) (Video)
A look at divorce, told by students and parents. Representatives for local high schools were given the opportunity to produce, write and edit a six-minute story on the impact of single-parent families. Each of the six episodes tells a different story about the single-parent family, and each is an intimate look at a new way of family living. p. Nick Latham; p. KIRO-TV; KIROTV.

SINGLE PARENTS (28½m C p1979, r1980) Are You Listening Series
Despite the growing reality of single-parent families, there is little public discussion of the needs and concerns of single parents. This program brings together a cross-section of men and women who are single parents to explore the experiences, challenges and rewards of single-parenthood. p. Martha Stuart; d. Ivan Cury; STUARTM.

SINGLE PARENTS AND OTHER ADULTS (27m C 1981) (also Video)
Trigger Films on Human Interaction Series
Divorce, separation, and single parenthood affect more aspects of life than any uninitiated person can understand. The vignettes in this film give participants a chance to sort out many of the issues, and develop awareness of their own feelings towards them. Guide included. p. Family Information Systems and Resource Communications, Inc.; MTITI.

SINGLE PARENTS AND THEIR CHILDREN (20m C 1981) (also Video)
Trigger Films on Human Interaction Series
The vignettes in this film depict many of the stressful situations single parents face and will allow participants to share experiences, feelings, and approaches. Issues raised include needing to be both mother and father; bringing other adults into children's lives; learning to cope with simultaneous demands of children, work and household maintenance; dealing with conflicting needs in arranging children's visits; needing children to take more responsibility; children trying to make the marriage work again; children exploiting the tension of separation; adjusting to less money for extras, or even basics. Guide included. p. Family Information Systems and Resource Communications, Inc.; MTITI.

SISTER OF THE BRIDE (30m C p1981, r1982) (also Video) The Planning Ahead Series
A warm and appealing story about two white, middle-class sisters whose mother, although divorced, tries to pressure them into early marriages. The film follows the last few days before the elder sister's marriage, probing her doubts and uncertainties; meanwhile the younger sister realizes more and more that a career as a veterinarian is the most important thing in her life. Study guide with film. Also available are workbook for students. p. Barbara Wolfinger, Berkeley Productions; d. Marilyn Weiner, Hal Weiner; UCEMC.

SISTERS IN CRIME (29m C 1975) (Video) Woman Series
Criminologist Freda Adler explains why the crime rate among

women is increasing several times faster than the male crime rate and discusses her philosophy that female passivity is a myth. She also talks about the growing numbers of all-women gangs (such as the "granny bashers" in London who attack elderly women), the need for women in law enforcement, and the lack of rehabilitation facilities in women's prisons. Sandra Elkin is the moderator. p. WNED-TV; PBSV.

SISTERS, OR THE BALANCE OF HAPPINESS (95m C 1981) (German/ Subtitled)
Focuses on the conflict between two sisters, one of whom has molded herself into the very image of traditional success, the other painfully discovering she can never fit into the mold. "Everyone is replaceable," says Maria, the efficient, pragmatic career woman to her fragile younger sister, Anna, thereby signaling an irreconcilable, and literally fatal, difference of sensibilities between the two women. d./s.w. Margarethe von Trotta; p. Bioskop-Film WDR; ALMI.

SIX AMERICAN FAMILIES see BURKS OF GEORGIA, THE; GEORGES OF NEW YORK, THE; GREENBERGS, THE; KENNEDYS OF ALBU-QUERQUE, THE; PASCIAKS OF CHICAGO, THE; STEPHENS OF IOWA, THE

SIX NATIONS (26m C 1976)
Examines the contemporary concerns of the Six Nations of the Iroquois Confederacy (Seneca, Cayuga, Onondaga, Oneida, Mohawk and Tuscarora). Shows Chief Oren Lyons of the Onondaga Tribe in recounting history describing the relationships with the Confederacy. He emphasizes that mutual treaties have always acknowledged the equal status of the Six Nations with the white community. The inter-relationship between an Indian and a white community in the town of Salamanca, New York, which leases its land from the Seneca Nation is examined. The Mayor of Salamanca and Seneca President Robert Hoag discuss the resentment felt by some of the residents because the city land is Seneca-owned. Cultural continuity and tribal identity are strong for the Seneca Nation. Traditional ways are taught to children at the Indian Way School, and the Longhouse religion is practiced by many. p. Brenda Horsefield; d. Nick Gosling; p. Document Associates/BBC; DOCUA.

SIX WIVES OF HENRY VIII SERIES see ANN BOLEYN; ANN OF CLEVES; CATHERINE HOWARD; CATHERINE OF ARAGON; CATH-ERINE PARR; JANE SEYMOUR

SIZE 10 (20m C 1978)
Four women talk about coming to terms with the pressures of fashion, beauty and advertising, and their changing self images. d. Sarah Gibson, Susan Lambert; s.w. Sarah Gibson, Susan Lambert; p. Australian Film Commission; IRIS.

SKIPPING (9m C p1979, r1979)
Designed to teach children to skip as well as build self-confidence through interaction with others. p./d. Susan Shippey; CF.

SKY DANCE: REACHING FOR LIFE IN THE COSMOS (11m C p1978, r1980) (also Video)
Striking animated images of prehistoric and primitive art combine with compelling ethnic music to reflect our global, universal search for cosmic contact and knowledge of the unknown. d./p. Faith Hubley; music: Elizabeth Swados; PF.

SKYFISH (30m C 1980-1983) (Video, Beta, VHS) Concepts Series
SKYFISH reveals the human change experienced by a woman artist as she paints, and her subconscious mind is made visual. d./p. Doris Chase; s.w. Lee Nagrin and Andrea Goodman, with music by Richard Isen; CHASED.

SLAB CITY ... A VERY SPECIAL TOWN (29m C 1982) (also Video)
Presents "Slab City" near the Salton Sea in California, a town which is responsive to the needs and pressures of older members of our society. Although this group of retired Americans scatter to visit relatives, fish in the mountains or travel during the summer, they return to "Slab City" each winter to reestablish their homes on huge concrete slabs left behind when Marines removed buildings and abandoned a World War II training base. With large amounts of leisure and little money, the residents are seen to bring in what they need and have only gas and groceries as expenses. Occupants have organized a garbage and wood detail, mail service and community center and operate like a little city. Every two weeks, a county nurse holds a health clinic; a county library bookmobile stops weekly, etc. At the end of a harvest, some of the local farmers open their fields to the elderly people living in "Slab City" who pick food for themselves and share with their less able-bodied friends. However, these residents fear a takeover by trailer park chains or the government someday. p./d. Alexander Von Wetter Films; WOMBAT.

SLIPPERY SLOPE, THE (31m C 1982)
Examines the issues that surround the recent "Baby Doe" case in Bloomington, Indiana and their impact on human life, for example, euthanasia, living will legislation and palliative care. It also features profiles on Dr. David McLone and his work with Spina Bifida babies; Dr. Penelope Brook-Williams' palliative care for dying patients, and Dr. Barry de Veber with young cancer patients. d. Peter Gerretsen; p. Patricia Gerretsen; GERRETSEN.

SMITH COLLEGE (10m C n.d.)
Contemporary dance composition. Demonstrated by Smith College students to John Wilson's music. Narrator/d. Martha Coleman Myers; p. Portia Mansfield Motion Pictures; MANSPR.

SMOKING: HOW TO STOP (23m C 1977)
Follows the progress of a typical smoker as she gradually reduces the number of cigarettes she smokes until she stops. The methods demonstrated are those developed by the American Cancer Society and other stop-smoking organizations. Does not call attention to the hazards of smoking, but carries a positive, informative and encouraging message to smokers who would like to quit. Narrated by Lloyd Bridges. p. Jonathan Dana; p. Pelican Films; PELICAN; UIL.

SNAPSHOTS FOR AN INDIAN DAY (30m C 1977) (Video)
A view of various areas of India shot at different times of the day (The Kitchen Center, October 7, 1978). p. Ingrid Wiegand, Bob Wiegand; KICHNC.

SNOWBIRDS (11m C 1982)
An impressionistic portrait of the thousands of older Americans and Canadians who travel from their homes in the North in recreational vehicles to spend their winters in the trailer parks of the Rio Grande valley of South Texas. d./p./ed. Andrea Merrim; MERRIMA.

SO MANY VOICES (30m C 1982)
Explores the issue of abortion in the United States today through interviews with people emotionally convinced on both sides of the volatile issue. Narrated by Ed Asner and Tammy Grimes, the film transcends sexual concerns and attempts to confront the moral, legal and political issues involved. d. David Sawyer; p. National Abortion Rights Action League; PHOENIX.

SO WHAT IF IT RAINS (17m C 1980)
In these days of rising prices and inflation, finances are the number one concern among people planning their retirement. In this film, we meet people from various walks of life, some retired and some approaching retirement. The retirees talk about their experiences living on a fixed income. The working people speak about the provisions they are making for financial security in their later years. Specific suggestions for protecting one's nest egg against inflation are given. p. Alternate Choice, Inc.; FILMLB.

SOCIAL CONTEXT OF DIVORCE #1 (29m C 1975) (Video) Dynamics of Divorce Series
The social context of divorce in American society is defined and there is an examination of the extent of divorce and its social consequences. The relationship of divorce to marriage and the extent to which traditional marriage fails to meet the needs, wants and expectations of American couples is discussed. p. University of Minnesota, Minneapolis; UMN.

SOCIAL SECURITY--HOW SECURE? (52m C 1976)
Examines America's vast and little understood social security system with respect to its philosophy, purpose, fitness, financial sound-

ness, and the degree of security it offers to present and future re-
cipients. p. NBC-TV; FI; CWU, KENTSU, UMN.

SOCIAL WORK, PTS. 1, 2, 3 (30m ea. 1970) (Video)
This three-lesson series with Naomi Brill, ACSW, Associate Professor, Graduate School of Social Work, University of Nebraska-Lincoln,
provides prospective social workers an insight into the field with an
emphasis on social work as a career. The titles of each part are 1)
"What Is It?"; 2) "People and Their Problems"; 3) "Social Work and
Social Change." NETCHE.

SOFT PAD (4m C 1970)
Describes a new chair system in a way that reflects some of the
design concepts and conveys the character of the pieces. p. Ray
and Charles Eames; PF.

SOLAR FILM, THE (9m C 1980)
Through visual images and animation, the relationship between
mankind and the sun is related through three episodes. By the time
SOLAR FILM is over, the message will have made its own way: the tech-
nology is available, the potential is immense, the moment is now. d.
Elaine Bass, Saul Bass; p. Saul Bass, Michael Britton; ex. p. Robert
Redford. Won an Academy Award. Sponsor: Warner Communications,
Norton Simon, Inc. Made for Consumer Action Now. BUDGET.

SOLDIER GIRLS (87m C 1981) (also Video)
A riveting account of the experience of a group of young women
newly inducted into the United States Army. Shot over a period of
months, the film shows the painful adjustment to military life. Some
of the women are able to adapt, some not. p. Joan Churchill, Nick
Bloomfield; CF.

SOLODANCE (3m C 1977)
A dancer moves in a loft space with slow motion, triple image,
and a jazz piano score. d. Christine Loizeau; LOIZEAU.

SOLVING PROBLEMS (30m C 1981) Stress Management: A Positive
    Strategy Series
During a workshop presented on-screen, viewers are shown ways
a manager can handle a highly challenging job and the outside world
while maintaining a sense of well-being. Participants learn how to
manage stressful situations by using skills they may already have,
such as good problem-solving techniques or effective communication.
This program also covers the manager's role and responsibility in
controlling the stress-related aspects of relationships among staff
members. The consultants elaborate on what they call "toxic" behaviors and nourishing behaviors with respect to how managers relate to their employees. Leader's manual and participants' handbooks
included. TIMLIF.

SOMA (5m B 1978)
An experimental study based on dance movements, exploring the shapes of the dancers' bodies as a means of creating pure expressive form and movement. d. Carol Schaffer; p. Robert Withers; WITHRS.

SOME AMERICAN FEMINISTS (56m C 1979) (also Video)
Explores one of the most significant social phenomena of this century: the women's movement for equal rights. In a series of candid, straight-talk dialogues documented by historic newsreel footage, Ti-Grace Atkinson, Rita Mae Brown, Betty Friedan, Margo Jefferson, Lila Karp and Kate Millett focus on the essence of the feminist movement, its meaning, its challenge, and its promise. d. Margaret Westcott, Luce Guilbeault, Nicole Brossard; p. Kathleen Shannon; NFBC: MOKINA.

SOME EXTERIOR PRESENCE (8m C si 1977)
Outtakes from a television documentary (on radical nuns in the South Bronx) are manipulated, optically printed, and manipulated, again (Collective for Living Cinema, October 27, 1978). p. Abigail Child; COLIVC.

SOME OF THESE DAYS (58m C 1980)
"Cross-cutting between the lives and memories of several women works beautifully here; the protagonists are so different and each so impressive in her individuality and idiosyncrasy that the cross-cutting serves to link their individual fates to a common yet variegated overall pattern. This, in turn, becomes, imperceptibly, a plea for human commonality. In the process, all the ancient stereotypes of 'femininity' fall by the wayside."--Amos Vogel. p. Elaine Velasquez; MEDIAP.

SOME OF THESE STORIES ARE TRUE (27m C 1981) (Video)
Presents three people talking to the camera. The three stories, exploring a common theme--the relationship between sex and aggression --are told exactly as (or as if) they actually happened to the teller. The audience does not find out which (if any) are actually true until the end, so the show also explores the documentary medium itself. d. Peter Adair; p. Peter Adair/Pat Jackson/Gayle Peabody; ADAIR.

SOME OF US HAD BEEN THREATENING OUR FRIEND COLBY (15m
    C p1981, r1983)
A dark comedy with subtle political overtones. Colby Williams and his "dear friends" gather in the woods. We watch them drink champagne and eat caviar as a string quartet, sitting nearby, plays Mozart. But this is no ordinary picnic. The elegant visual surface of the film conceals the horror of the event about to take place. Based on a short story by Donald Barthelme. d./p. Debra Bard; BARDD.

SOME SECRETS SHOULD BE TOLD (12m C 1982) (also Video)
Designed to encourage children to talk about their feelings and concerns and help them to differentiate between normal touching and

affection and uncomfortable touching which a child feels is wrong.
p. Family Information Systems, Inc., Resource Communications, Inc.;
s.w. Susan Linn; MTITI.

SOMEDAY A FUTURE (27m C p1977, r1977)
The story of a community widows' service program, told through
the experiences of three widows at different points in their recovery
from grief. This self-help program enables widows to reach out to
one another as counselors and friends in the transition from wife to
widow to person. d. Rhoden Streeter; p. Alfred R. Shands; p.
WAVE-TV; WAVETV.

SOMEONE'S IN THE KITCHEN WITH JAMIE (25m C 1981) (also Video)
The hopes of Sherman High School's baseball team are placed on
the newly-discovered pitching arm of Jamie Clark. Jamie's career is
threatened almost before it begins, however. His mother, a teacher
at Sherman, might be out of a job and Jamie might have to work instead of playing ball. Jamie then goes to work and recruits the base-
ball team into Mrs. Clark's Home Economics classes. Coach Ferraro,
a traditionalist, is not pleased with what Jamie did. As the big day
arrives, Sherman's "goose" definitely seems "cooked." However,
Jamie's sister and other Sherman supporters cook up a plan which
saves the day as they rally their team to victory. p. Elaine Sperber;
d. Barra Grant; LCA.

SOMETHING ABOUT PHOTOGRAPHY (9m C 1976)
Charles Eames tells us his own insights and pointers about the
very individual choices and opportunities one can bring to bear in
the making of each photograph, and the added significance they have
when shot as a series. p. Ray and Charles Eames; PF.

SOMETHING BEAUTIFUL FOR GOD: MOTHER TERESA OF CALCUTTA
(15m C 1971)
Malcolm Muggeridge interviews Mother Teresa and her Sisters of
Charity in Calcutta where they live among the poor, treating and
serving them, rescuing the dying from the streets, trying to make
up the caring for the bitter poverty of the lives around them. "It
is not the things they need, it is what we are to them," says Mother
Teresa. p. BBC/Time-Life Video; TIMLIF; UIL.

SOMETHING ELSE IN YOUR THOUGHTS (13m C 1972)
Migrant farm workers have often been the subject of documentary
films because of the deplorable social injustice surrounding them.
This film is different; it focuses on the human perspective. By observing several families working in the fields, and by listening to
their comments, we see the immense skill and endurance of the people and realize the importance of the family. p. Nye Films; NYEF;
UIL.

SOMETHING FOR EVERYONE (28m C p1979, r1980--U.S.) The Human
Face of China (Series)

Presents Chinese communal living. Partly narrated in Chinese
with English subtitles. Shows the massive program of land reform
and other changes that have taken place under Mao Tse-Tung and
his communist social reorganization in 1949. Shown are the modern
communes in Kwangtung Province in southeastern China. p. Suzanne
Baker, p. Film Australia; d./s.w. Bob Kingsbury; LCA.

SOMETHING PERSONAL SERIES see BIRTHDAY; IF IT HAPPENS
   TO YOU: RAPE; OLDER AND BOLDER

SON OF THE OCEAN (28m C p1979, r1979) The Human Face of China
   (Series)
   Takes the viewer up the Yangtsze River, telling the story of the
boat crew and passengers. Yangtze is the third longest river in the
world which is snow-fed from the mountains of Tibet. The ship used
in this film is The East Is Red, No. 33, which carries 700 passengers.
Passengers are interviewed with subtitles translating their reasons
for traveling. Deckhands are seen working, engaged in political discussions, relaxing with hobbies such as playing musical instruments.
Over the last few years river channels have been improved and nav-
igational aids upgraded making the river much safer for travel. p.
Film Australia; p. Suzanne Baker; d./s.w. Bob Kingsbury; LCA.

SONG AT TWILIGHT: AN ESSAY ON AGING (59m C 1976) (Video)
   Explores the social, political, physical and economic problems of
older people. The program dispells some myths about the physical
aspect of aging, and delivers some startling information about the
increasing numbers of low income people over the age of 65. Interviews with psychologist, doctors, attorneys, legislators, government
officials, representatives from senior citizens groups and the unor-
ganized elderly illustrate the feelings and frustrations of older people. Marjorie Borchardt, founder of the international Senior Citizens'
Association, is one of the guests. p. KOCE-TV, Huntington Beach,
California; PBSV.

SONNY TERRY: SHOUTIN' THE BLUES (6m C p1969, r1981)
   Blind blues harmonica master Sonny Terry talks about his great
success in the Broadway production of Finian's Rainbow. He says
that in that musical he played his big hit number exactly the same
way every night for two and one half years. This film version of
that number was made three months after the Broadway show closed.
Sonny Terry proves that he is one of the great harmonica musicians
of his time. p. Aginsky Productions; p./d. Carrie Aginsky, Yasha
Aginsky; LAWRENP.

SOONER THE BETTER, THE (27m C 1977)
   Illustrates the essentials of a non-sexist classroom and demonstrates specific teaching ideas aimed at expanding options for pre-
school children. Filmed in multiethnic schools and daycare centers
around the country. "First-rate visual consciousness-raising"--Ms.

Magazine. Recognized for their quality and social and educational
impact internationally. p. Jamil Simon Productions, Inc.; THEYEF.

SORIANOS, THE (EXTENDED FAMILY) see FAMILY PORTRAIT:
THE SORIANOS

SORROWS OF GIN, THE (60m C 1979) (also Video)
One of Cheever's best known stories, this tale of life in suburban
American centers on an eight-year-old girl's search for a sense of
family amid the sophisticated and detached whirl of her parents'
lives. Her struggles are sometimes comic, sometimes tragic. p. Ann
Blumenthal, Peter Weinberg; d. Jack Hofsiss; p. WNET-TV; FI.

SOUND AND MOVEMENT (17m C 1957)
Dancers improvise movements to the accompaniment of conven-
tional and unconventional instruments and sound of voice, hands and
feet. Dance Company: Barbara Mettler Dance Group; Dance Teacher/
Narrator/d. Barbara Mettler; p. Will Carbo; p. Mettler Studios; MET-
TLER.

SOUND FOR DANCE (29m B 1970) (also Video) Contemporary Dance
Series
The relation between contemporary music and dance is discussed,
with alternative methods of choreography demonstrated by the dancer/
choreographers. These methods are music composed first, then
dance; dance first, then music; or music and dance as collaboration.
Linda Ellis performs her work "Time/Being." Deidre Burt performs
her work "Elisions with Exist Music" (music composed by George
Burt). d. Marshall Franke; p. Selma Odom; UMMRC; UM.

SOUNDS FROM THE MOUNTAINS (96m B 1954) (Japanese/Subtitled)
Based on a novel by Nobel Prize Winner Yasunari Kawabata, it is
the story of a woman, living with her husband and in-laws, who develops an intense bond with her father-in-law, as a result of her
husband's repeated infidelities and callous behavior. The film explores the complex interpersonal relationships that exist in the family, as well as the external pressures on the traditional Japanese
home, that were the result of the rapid and traumatic changes brought
about by the American occupation following the Second World War.
d. Mikio Naruse; CORINTH.

SOUTH AFRICA BELONGS TO US (57m C 1980)
With observational portraits of five ordinary women and four
women leaders, the film depicts the struggle of the black woman for
human dignity in the face of apartheid. We see what it is like to
live as a so-called migrant worker in one of the huge prison-like
barracks where many women are condemned to spend their working
lives separated from their families. Included is an interview with
Winnie Mandela, who, exiled to a remote spot in the countryside and
kept under constant security police surveillance, has become a symbol

of resistance in South Africa. A banned Indian women's leader, sociologist Fatimah Meer, speaks of the extra hardships suffered by women under apartheid. Finally, a young leader of the outlawed Black Consciousness Movement, who for six months was jailed, interrogated, and tortured, gives a moving account of what it means as a woman and mother to be committed to the struggle to end apartheid. p./d. Chris Austin, Ruth Weiss, Peter Chappell; ICARF.

SOUTH AFRICA BELONGS TO US (ed.) (35m C 1980)
It is accepted all over the world that husbands and their wives be allowed to live with each other and bring up their children together. That basic principle does not apply if you happen to be black and living in South Africa. This film provides the first in-depth look at the singular economic and emotional burden borne by black women in South Africa. p. Gerhard Schmidt; d. Chris Austin; CALNWS; UM.

SOUTH BEACH (30m C 1978)
Focuses on the everyday life of retirees living in South Miami Beach, Florida who are forced to stretch their $140 Social Security checks to cover their rent, food and doctor bills and who must deal with isolation as their friends die and their families ignore them. While some of those people express despair, others on the Beach are angry. As more of these people are evicted from their homes to make way for large hotels and condominiums, they turn their attention to the City Council and we see the beginnings of political action groups. Provides a reminder of how a large segment of the elderly exist in America today. p./d. Cinda Firestone; ALMI.

SOUTH STREET PHILADELPHIA: STREET OF CONTRASTS (21m B n.d.)
South Street has long been one of Philadelphia's more colorful areas, enduring ethnic changes, urban decay and renewal with a spirit all its own. In the late 1960's a new breed of merchants began taking advantage of low rents to open health food stores, antique/second-hand stores, and informal restaurants. South Street mirrors the changes, and contrasts the old-timers with the newcomers as they coexist. p. Paulette Jelline K. Perloe; TEMPLU.

SOVIET FAMILY, A (23m C p1981, r1981) (also Video)
Presents a view of Russian family life today. Focuses on a Soviet construction worker and his family. The father builds prefabricated apartment buildings in and around Moscow. He is employed by the State, entitling him to free medical care, a pension, free education for his children and inexpensive housing. The mother teaches in a nursery school and one of the sons is studying to be a lawyer, the other will be an engineer. The older son who plans to marry soon will have to live with his parents for a while. Since World War II Russia has had a drastic housing shortage. It is common to find three generations of one family living together in a three-room

apartment. A candid look at the workers' life-style in Russia. p. Vladimire Bibic for International Film Foundation; IFF; KENTSU.

SPACE FOR WOMEN AND WHERE DREAMS COME TRUE (28m C 1981) (also Video)

A documentary dealing with some of the diverse positions that women have at N.A.S.A. We learn what life is like for a psychophysiologist, an information specialist, an electrical engineer, a safety specialist, a computer engineer, a photographic analyst, and two mission specialist astronauts. The women interviewed speak frankly and disarmingly about themselves and what it is to work in the male-dominated atmosphere of N.A.S.A., where it becomes clear that it is not necessary to be male or superhuman to have a successful career. p. William Greaves Productions; NAVC.

SPACE: MAN'S GREAT ADVENTURE SERIES, THE see WOMAN'S TOUCH, THE

SPEAKBODY (10m C 1980)

An impressionistic study of abortion. Women who have had abortions speak their views to a backdrop of composed still lives and long shots of the detail of a woman's life. p. Kay Armatage; SERBC.

SPEAKER: A FILM ABOUT FREEDOM, THE (42m C 1977)

Through dramatization, the film addresses one of the most sensitive, but doubtless one of the most important, aspects of freedom of expression: toleration of ideas we find offensive or repugnant. It portrays the potential we face each day for the gradual suffocation of the sacred fire of liberty granted to us in the First Amendment, specifically, the freedom of speech. A powerful film that will remind us all that there is a need for constant reeducation and rededication or this experiment will fail. p. Judith F. Krug, Florence McMullin; Lee K. Bobker of VA; ALA.

SPEAKING OF MEN (20m C p1977, r1977)

Discussions among both women and men about the expectations people have for relationships, and about the roles men and women play in each other's lives. Three young women, filmed in separate interviews, discuss their experiences, hopes, expectations, successes and frustrations in relationships with men. p./d. Christine M. Herbes/ Ann-Carol Grossman; POLYMR.

SPECIAL CASES (13m C 1977) Pregnancy and Childbirth Series

Modern techniques that can assure safe childbirth are depicted. Special cases discussed include pregnancies of very young or older mothers, late or painful deliveries, breech births, premature deliveries, and delivery by midwives. Techniques shown include amniotic taps, induced labor, epidural anesthesia, delivery by obstetrical forceps, and Caesarean section. p. Crawley Films, Canada; IFB; IU, UIL.

SPECIAL DELIVERY (7m C n.d.)
A series of misadventures in animation. Alice Phelps asked her husband, Ralph, to clean the snow off the front steps before leaving for work, but he ignored her request. That was when troubles started. Later that morning, when Ralph went to pick up the mail, he almost fell over the mailman's body sprawled on the icy stairs. d. Eunice Macauley, John Weldon; p. Derek Lamb; NFBC.

SPECIAL PLACE, A (11m B 1978)
Good friends for 14 years and lovers for five of those years, Shell and Annie define themselves as sexually open for what life brings. While they relate sexually primarily with men, they share an intense sexual and emotional level with each other. A very passionate film. p. Laird Sutton; National Sex Forum; MMRC; UMN.

SPECIAL TO THE TIMES (22m C 1982)
Concentrates on the quality and saturation of responsible news gathering and reporting which makes The New York Times unique in its appeal to readers and advertisers. It follows New York Times' reporters in the field in New York, Lebanon, Egypt, and Washington, D.C., and then covers the editorial staff while they assemble news reports into stories. d. Michael Glyn; p. Patrice Samara; GLYNG.

SPECTRUMSPECTRUMSPECTRUM (4½m C 1981)
A sensuous exploration of color, movements, fashion and dance featuring a human colorwheel--a plunge through the spectrum. Each color's personality is revealed through the use of longjohn-clad models/ dancers and the interpretation of music. Ranging from luscious purples to icy blues to fiery hot reds, the colors eventually combine and dance an explosive and energetic celebration of the spectrum. d./p. Karen Firus; CANFDC.

SPENCERS, THE (11m C p1978, r1978)
A documentary profile of a family's feelings, concerns, fears and hopes as it comes to terms with the impending death of 34-year-old Sandy Spencer. p./d. Jeffrey Weber; United Methodist Communications; MMM.

SPIRIT CATCHER: THE ART OF BETYE SAAR (30m C p1977, r1978)
The Originals: Women in Art Series
Probes the art, spirit, and the symbols used by a Black American artist concerned with social problems and fascinated by the mysteries of Caribbean culture, with its blending of Indian, African, and European traditions and its mixture of Christianity and voodoo. p. Suzanne Bauman for WNET-TV; FI; PAS, UIL, UMO.

SPONGERS, THE (91m C p1978, r1978)
Left by her husband with four children (one a 14-year-old Mongoloid) to feed and clothe, Pauline Crosby goes from one social service agency to the next in the frustrating attempt to keep her head

above water. As they "sponge" off various agencies, the family's desperate plight is ironically set against the pageantry of the Royal Family's Silver Jubilee celebration. Nothing works for this quietly desperate woman. d. Roland Joffe; p. Tony Garnett; BBC/Time Life Video; TIMLIF.

SPORTS IN AMERICA SERIES see WOMEN IN SPORTS

SPORTS THAT SET THE STYLES, THE (28m C n.d.)
Shows how sports, specifically women in sports, influenced fashion and contributed to the freedom in dress that the modern woman enjoys. There was a time when a woman's world consisted of whalebone and steel corsets, stiff crinolines, bustles and bindings, hoops and hooks, and any activity that called for unrestricted movement was out of the question. This film examines the history of women in sports and shows how the clothes they wore on the playing fields, golf courses and beaches eventually found their way into the home and society. Free loan. p. Sears, Roebuck and Company; MTPS.

SPORTS: WHAT'S THE SCORE? (29m C 1976) (Video) Woman Series
Sportswriter Robert Lipsyte and sportscaster Lee Arthur discuss both the value and harm of sports in American life. Lipsyte believes that the reality of competition does not match the image of mental and physical health used to promote sports participation, and Lee Arthur believes that women have a more balanced attitude toward sports activity. Arthur also points out that women are at last getting better opportunities and endorsements in the sports field. Sandra Elkin is the moderator. p. WNED-TV, Buffalo, New York; PBSV.

SPRING IS HERE (2nd ed.) (11m C p1979, r1979) The Seasons (Series)
A film which gives children a feel for the changes that take place in the spring. Shows many animals having babies while others are awakening from hibernation, depicts farmers plowing their fields and planting their crops. Time-lapse photography reveals buds opening up and trees and bushes bursting into bloom. p. Myrna I. and Walter H. Berlet; IFB.

SPRING VISIONS (6½m B 1978)
A filmic portrait of international mime Hayward Coleman. His mime-face character "Spiritus" is drawn from his roots as an Afro-American. Mime: Hayward Coleman; d. Pamela Jones; p. Penny Bannerman; BANRMN.

SPROUT WINGS AND FLY (30m C 1982)
A portrait of the great North Carolina fiddler Tommy Jarrell. Now in his eighties, Tommy is alive with the wit and wisdom of one for whom life is an adventure. We visit with Tommy at home in North Carolina and various music festivals, and talk with his relatives. Tommy spins yarns and reflects on his life, telling us more about the

beliefs, attitudes and world views of the North Carolinians than a whole stack o' history books. p. Alice Gerard, Les Blank, Cece Conway; ed. Maureen Gosling; Original music: Tommy Jarrell et al.; Sponsor: Institute for Southern Studies; FLOWERF.

STAGE FRIGHT (2nd ed.) (13m C p1979, r1979)
After establishing empathy with Bernice Greenland, who is trapped into giving a speech to a luncheon club, the film introduces specific techniques that any speaker can use successfully to control and harness stage fright. d. Linda Haskins; p. Centron Films; CENTEF.

STAGES: HOUSEMAN DIRECTS LEAR (58m C p1980, r1981)
An exploration of the director's and actor's creative processes. The film follows John Houseman, Academy Award-winning actor, eminent director and producer, as he rehearses the repertory company he founded for the most promising young American classical actors and actresses in a new production of King Lear. Jason Robards hosts. Segments of final production allow us to see the outcome. d./p. Amanda C. Pope; p. Amanda Pope Productions, Inc.; POPEA.

STAIRWAYS TO THE MAYAN GODS (28m C 1973)
Joseph Campbell, expert in world mythology and author of The Hero with a Thousand Faces, wrote the narration for this journey to the ceremonial centers of the Maya. The Mayan Indians of Mexico and Central America, master astronomers and mathematicians, translated their heavenly perceptions into spectacular cities of pyramids and palaces. Campbell gives us insight into reasons for their ascent and decline. Filmed in Mexico, Guatemala and Honduras. p. Elda Hartley; HARTLEY.

STALKING IMMORTALITY (58m C p1978, r1978)
Presents a broad spectrum of current research on aging, as well as some of the things we can do right now to live a longer, healthier life. d. William Hitchcock; p. Janewill Productions; JANEWL.

STANDING ALONE, #7 (28m C 1975) (Video) Dynamics of Divorce, Series
The final program of the series deals with learning to live as an individual rather than as part of a couple. The series is summarized by Judi Savage, Marriage and Divorce Counselor. p. University of Minnesota; UMN.

STEADY AS SHE GOES (26½m C 1981)
Seventy-year-old George Fulfit illustrates with humor and optimism the delicate craft of putting ships into bottles. The film documents the construction of the largest ship he has ever built. It also shows the very real contribution a hobby can make to anyone's life. d. Robert Fresco; p. Sharon Lee Chapelle; NFBC.

STEP BY STEP (11m C 1979)
Using animation, Faith Hubley interprets the world of childhood--

as it was, as it exists and as it might be. Created in honor of the Year of the Child, the film's emphasis is global and universal. Children of every race and nationality appear on the screen accompanied by voices chanting in Spanish and French, with key phrases spoken in English. p. Faith Hubley; PF; UCEMC; UIL, UMN.

STEP FAMILY (13m C 1981)
Dramatizes transitional conflicts and problems in the lives of three generations in a specific instance of divorce and remarriage. CENEF; UIL, IU.

STEP FROM THE SHADOWS, A (28m C 1973)
Deals with the problem of female alcoholism and drug use. Follows the case history of an addicted mother, the effect on her family, her treatment and the role her family plays in the rehabilitation. Provides both psychological and medical insight into the problem. FI; UMN.

STEPHENS OF IOWA, THE (58m C 1976) Six American Families (Series)
For Carl and Lois and their six children farming is in their blood. They love the land, respect nature and are willing to work, but farming is a high risk, expensive undertaking that often yields minimum financial return. Activities center around farm, school, and church but rural values are in conflict with an overwhelmingly urban society. p. Elinor Bunin Productions; WBCPRO; CAROUF; KENTSU, UIL, UM, USFL, PAS.

STEPPARENTING ISSUES (20m C 1981) (also Video) Trigger Films on Human Interactions Series
Researchers, who are only just beginning to give attention to stepparenting and reconstituted families, are finding that the emotions and situations experienced by family members follow somewhat predictable patterns. The vignettes in this film present some of those common situations. Guide included. p. Family Information Systems and Resource Communications, Inc.; MTITI.

STEPPARENTING: NEW FAMILIES, OLD TIES (25m C 1977)
Examination of the difficulties encountered by persons with children who later remarry. Stepparents discuss their initial feelings of insecurity and conflicts on child-rearing practices and confusion as to who has authority over the child in specific areas. Members of a stepparent support group talk of the specific situations they encountered and how they set about overcoming obstacles. p./d. Marilyn Felt, Henry Felt; POLYMR; UM.

STEREOPTICON (11-29m C 1979) (Video)
Live interaction of dance, video and music. This piece emphasizes mobile camerawork, integrated with the use of a videosynthesizer. Judged the best videotape in the 1979 Video and Film Festival.

Dancer: Lura Hirsch; p. Annette Barbier and co-workers; BAR-
BIER.

STERILIZATION AND CONSENT (29m C 1976) (Video) Woman Series
    Attorney Antonia Hernandez and author Claudia Dreifus (Woman's
Fate) discuss abuse in sterilization cases and explain Health, Education and Welfare Department guidelines governing sterilization practices. Hernandez talks about her involvement in a suit brought on
behalf of ten women who have been coercively sterilized and both
guests discuss the emotional consequences of sterilization at an early
age. Sandra Elkin is the moderator. p. WNED-TV; PBSV.

STERILIZATION BY LAPAROSCOPY (11½m C n.d.)
    The actual operation utilizing general anesthesia and cauterization
is photographed. Alternate version demonstrates procedure using
local anesthesia and silastic banding. Also available in Spanish.
MIFE.

STICK ON A CEDAR PATH (9m C 1980) (Video)
    "A stick is dragged along a path. This strange, poetic work
reveals a stubborn artistic determination to march to one's own drummer, projecting a piece of childhood into present awareness by capturing its unconscious resonances and emotional coloration. Meditative and hypnotic, it asks us to share this experience"--Amos Vogel.
p. Diane Katsiaficas; KATSI.

STICKY MY FINGERS, FLEET MY FEET (23m C 1970)
    Deflates, with pathos and humor, one of the classic American
myths: The middle-aged male who clings to a youthful standard of
physical prowess and he-man virility. An executive, addicted to Sunday orgies of touch football, is drawn to New York's Central Park to
engage in ritual combat with his huffing, puffing flabby contemporar-
ies. But their dreams of glory turn to dust when they permit a 15-
year-old boy to join their sport. His flashing performance leaves
them dazed and a little older, wiser and sadder (J. Hancock; Time-
Life, 1970). TIMLIF; PAS, UM, UMN.

STILL LIVING (27m C 1970)
    An intimate documentary film on the thoughts, feelings, and
frustrations of some inmates in a prison for women. Included among
other sequences are an inmate discussion session, a staff consideration
of inmate problems, and an interview with a woman in solitary confinement and her appearance before a committee considering her release.
Raises questions as to what is expected of the detention system in
comparison with the role it actually performs. CF; UIO, UFL.

STILL MOTION (3m n.d.) (S8)
    "I was just trying to catch the cold clean desolate things of
March"--CC. "Wood becomes stone. Fenceposts house the forested
winter sun"--R.R. p. Catherine Campbell, Robert Rayher; CCC.

STILT DANCERS OF LONG BOW VILLAGE (27m C p1980, r1980)
Banned for almost ten years during the Chinese Cultural Revolution, the art of stilt dancing has now been revived. The film presents a vivid glimpse of this almost lost folk art by focusing on the festival of one rural village. Capturing the pageant from makeup, costume and parade to performances on the high stilts, it also records the villagers' personal memories of the ban, of stilt dancing the way it was, and of how it is being brought alive again. d./p. Carma Hinton, Richard Gordon; FI.

STOCKHOLM see MAI ZETTERLING'S STOCKHOLM

STOCKING UP (27½m C 1982)
Vic and Betsy Sussman show us what they do with the produce from their organic garden so they can continue to eat their home-grown, chemical-free food all winter long. Their root crops, stored in a root cellar, stay fresh all winter. Fruits and vegetables are dried, frozen and canned. Other foods are stored from attic to cellar. The Sussmans do more than garden--they have created a home food system! d. Frank Cursley, Jr.; p. Jeff Cox; BULFRG.

STOLEN CHILD (8m C r1974)
On a hot summer day, the dog-hero of this series dives into a stream to refresh himself and is soon joined by his other animal friends. A young girl passing by with a baby carriage is tempted by the water. Leaving the baby alone, she joins the animals for a swim. A young boy, passing by, sees the carriage and decides that is just what he needed for a roller-coaster ride down the hill. He puts the baby in the dog's house and takes off. The girl returns to find the carriage and baby missing. The baby is soon located because of its cries. However, this is not the end of all the problems for the girl and her animal friends. d. Hermina Tyrlova; p. Kratky Films, Prague; PHOENIX.

STOMP (3m B 1978) (Video)
To quote the filmmaker, "A pair of mischievous feet dance up a smile." Dancer/Choreographer/Director/Producer: Eva Maier; MAIER.

STONE MEDUSA AND SPANISH SUITE ... AND SHORT, THE (27m B 1969)
THE STONE MEDUSA, about the Greek myths of Pygmalion and Medusa, is adapted to a symphonic poem, "Uirapura," by Heitor Villa-Lobos. SPANISH SUITE ... AND SHORT is an imaginative set of dances, constantly combining the performers in new patterns. Dance Company: Illinois Ballet; d. Richard Ellis, Christine Du Boulay; p. Orion Dance Films; ORION.

STORIES (14m C 1977)
Shows how a teacher can guide and motivate young children to

write creatively. A brief discussion of the reasons for writing is
followed by an examination of several of the basic elements of a story--
character, plot, and setting. The film goes on to illustrate how creative writing can be achieved using these basic elements. d. Jane
Treiman; CF; UIL.

STORM CENTER (87m B 1956)
    A librarian (Bette Davis) is fired from her job and a whole town
goes berserk as she refuses to remove a "Communist" book from the
library. Topical now as much as ever. With Bette Davis, Brian
Keith, Kim Hunter; d. Daniel Taradash; p. Columbia; KPF.

STORM OF STRANGERS, A (27m B 1969)
    Archive photographs illustrate an old man's memories of the Jew-
ish immigrant community on New York's Lower Eastside during the
early 1900's. Herschel Bernardi, as narrator, warmly recalls his
first impressions of New York City: tenement life, the factories and
workshops, and the fierce determination with which the immigrants
worked to free their children from the ghetto. p. Ben Maddow for
National Communications Foundation; PARACO, UIL.

STORM OF STRANGERS, A (SERIES) see IRISH, THE; ITALIAN
    AMERICANS; JEWISH AMERICAN

STORY OF SUSAN McKELLAR: CYSTIC FIBROSIS, THE (16½m C
    1981)
    Through one sufferer, Susan McKellar, as an example, this film
outlines for a general audience the nature and problems of a usually
fatal disease, cystic fibrosis. d./p. David Tucker; CBC; FILMLB.

STORY OF THE SERIALS (30m B 1960)
    Development of silent film cliff-hangers from Pearl White's The
Perils of Pauline in 1914 to sound film in 1929, which destroyed much
of the cliff-hanger's appeal. Reign of serial queens paralleled to
women's struggle for social, political equality. Original silent film.
Narration. STEREF; IU, UMN.

STRANGER IN A FAMILY (58m C 1982) (Video)
    This is the true-to-life account of a family coping with their ado-
lescent autistic son and the ways in which each family member accom-
modates to the disabled member. Following the family portion of the
videotape is a series of discussions in which current social policy
towards the disabled is examined. d. Robert Menefee; p. Marcy
Schuck, Mark Sottnick; YALEU.

STRANGER LEFT NO CARD, THE (23m B 1953)
    Into the setting of a quiet town a stranger brings with him all
of the ingredients of a fantastic crime. With the counterpoint of humor and a gay rhythmical sound track, the tale builds to a climax of
fiendish cunning. d. Wendy Toye (Great Britain); KPF.

STRANGERS: THE STORY OF A MOTHER AND DAUGHTER (96m C
    1982) (also Video)
    In an Emmy Award-winning performance, Bette Davis portrays
Lucy Mason, an embittered mother who reunites with her daughter,
Abigail (Gena Rowlands), after a 20-year estrangement. Admittedly,
the two never got along, and Lucy peppers their reunion with characteristic insults and arguments. But, eventually, she lowers her
defenses and mother and daughter enjoy a happy summer together.
Then a crisis intervenes and their bond, so painfully achieved, is
again threatened. Also starring Ford Rainey, Donald Moffet, Whit
Bissel and Royal Dano. p. Christiansen/Rosenberg; TIMLIF.

STRANGERS WE MEET (10m C 1977)
    A series of dramatizations of common situations teach safety rules
that youngsters should always follow whenever any stranger approaches
them. The stories are of everyday events so that boys and girls can
readily identify with the episodes. Tactfully handled, the film has
no shock scenes of genuine molesters nor of youngsters running away
in fright. p. Sid Davis Productions; AIMS.

STRAVINSKY'S FIREBIRD BY THE DANCE THEATER OF HARLEM
    (60m C p1981, r1982) (Video)
    Goes behind the scenes on location in Harlem to the headquarters
and rehearsal hall of the internationally known ballet company. The
creation of the Firebird by the choreographer, costumer and set designer is shown. Also documents the growth of the multiracial ballet
company and profiles its members. The second half of the program
is the performance of the Firebird at The John F. Kennedy Center
for the Performing Arts. p. Beverly Baroff; d. Kirk Browning; p.
WQED-TV; FI.

STRESS (11m B 1956)
    Dr. Hans Selye, in his laboratories at the University of Montreal,
tells of his discoveries about stress, the general strain on the body
caused by disease, injury or mental pressure. The nature of stress
as a general alarm reaction through the pituitary and adrenal glands,
set off by any attack on the body, is explained, and we see some of
the experiments that led Dr. Selye to his discovery. d. Ian MacNeill;
p. Nicholas Balla; NFBC; PSU.

STRESS: A DISEASE OF OUR TIME (37m C 1971)
    Investigates some of the social factors involved in diseases (ul-
cers, migraine, asthma) and mental disorders thought to be induced
by stress. Many of the experiments are explained by Swedish researchers; they note that adrenaline excretion rises dramatically during stressful situations by observing supermarket cashiers during
the rush hour, a suspenseful cinema audience, and soldiers participating in a planned sleepless vigil. Although most subjects learn to
control outward signs of stress, a measurement technique is demonstrated which compares relaxed blood flow in the forearm to the flow

when anxiety is induced. Many sequences of tribal medicine are studied: the natives' method of dealing with mild depression is the use of prescribed dances to the point of physical and emotional collapse. Discusses the abreactive technique of dealing with stress, and the factors of loneliness and crowdedness. BBC; TIMLIF; UIL.

STRESS: A PERSONAL CHALLENGE (ed.) (30m C p1980, r1980) (also Video)

Examines stress in modern society, symptoms that it causes and techniques people can use to manage the stress response. Stress is defined as aggravation, disappointment, tension, being uptight, under pressure, and an interviewer explains that everyone is affected by stress and should learn to make it work for his or her good. Clearly what is stressful to one person may be quite pleasurable to another. Coping with stress is discussed with suggestions that include cognitive reprogramming--thinking about problems in new ways, present centeredness--thinking in the "now," integration exercises, deep abdominal breathing, relaxation response, visualization and calling on inner resources to turn stress to advantage. p. ABC-TV, Stress Center, Department of Health Promotion, St. Louis University; UIL.

STRESS: ARE WE KILLING OURSELVES? (15m C 1979) (Video)

Relates results of research on stress, giving symptoms and evaluating various ways of coping. Estimates that up to 80 percent of disease is stress-related: lists known negative physiological effects. Positive ways of dealing with stress include meditation and biofeedback. The following list of coping procedures is recommended: take time out, deliberately waste a half hour; learn relaxation or meditation techniques; exercise, gradually increasing the amount; watch your diet--eliminate caffeine from it; separate work from home--invent a ritual at the end of the work-day to mark the separation. p. ABC-TV; UIL, UMN.

STRESS--DISTRESS (21m C 1983)

Presents some new scientific thought on stress. Covers a wide range of causes, possible cures, and preventive measures. Explains that 50 to 80 percent of all illnesses are attributed to stress, the narrator discusses positive and negative kinds of stress, describes how a build-up of stress points can put a person at high risk for a stress-related disease and offers suggestions to help cope with life's stresses. d./s.w. Leo A. Handel; HANDEL.

STRESS, HEALTH AND YOU (14m C 1978)

Stress influences all of our lives and is a potential health hazard if not properly understood and handled. Explains what stress is, what causes stress, and what stress does to our bodies. Basic information to start discussions. p. American Educational Films; CORNELL; PAS.

STRESS: IT'S JUST WHAT YOU THINK! (19½m C 1982) (also Video)

Presents a film that guides young people to understand the stress in their lives and teach them positive ways of managing it. Emphasizes that stress is a normal part of life and everyone is subject to some form of stress. The narrator explains that the way a person thinks, acts and reacts to events in her/his life affects the health of his/her whole body. p. Ron Casden; BARRF.

STRESS MANAGEMENT: A POSITIVE STRATEGY SERIES see BE-COMING AWARE; LOOKING AHEAD; MANAGING YOURSELF; SOLVING PROBLEMS; TAKING STOCK

STRESS MANAGEMENT: WEDDING DAZE (23m C p1979, r1979)
Begins with the humorous and frenzied stresses and strain of a wedding day, and in so doing, creates an analogy between these stresses as well as others encountered in our everyday lives. The wedding portrays, in microcosm, an array of sudden and on-going stressful events that affect each of us in personal and work-related situations. On-camera narrator Mario Machado explains causes of stress and techniques we can all use to cope with it effectuvely. p. Paramount Communications, Inc.; AIMS; PARACO.

STRESS MESS, THE (24½m C p1981, r1982) (also Video)
Shows how to identify the sources of stress in our lives and how we can reduce and manage stress. The Wilsons are getting ready to leave the house this morning. It becomes clear that stress governs their lives. Fred is a workaholic who believes that only he can get the job done. Karen can't say "no" to all the people who ask her favors ... she never has time for things that are important to her. The Wilsons might never have learned why their lives were such a mess had it not been for the fortuitous appearance of Harry. As the Wilsons slug it out with the stress that afflicts them during the day, Harry manages to show up in time to help each one. d. Ron Underwood; p. Mark Chodzko, R. Underwood; s.w. Brent Maddock; BARRF; UIL.

STRINGING A GARLAND (45m C 1977)
A program of six Thai dances, classical and folk, plus an introduction, backstage preparations, and a demonstration of the meaning of various gestures. The dances, in excerpts, are "Sat-Chartri-Lakhon," "Kohn, Masked Drama--Hanuman Battles Totsakan," "Fawn Tien-Dance of the Candler," "Thai Swordfighting," "Lopburi," and "Ram Salawan." Filmed in Bangkok. English narration. Dance Company: Nopakao Company of Dancers and Musicians; Narrator: Paula Levine. d. Lawan Rapasute, Paula Levine; ex. d. Sumphod Rapasute; p. Paula Levine; HOLLINS.

STRIP MINING: ENERGY, ENVIRONMENT AND ECONOMICS (50m C p1979, r1980)
Details the beginnings, growth, and consequences of strip-mining which accounts for 50 percent of the coal produced in the Appalachian Region. The issues in this multifaceted controversy are presented

through the views of environmentalists, strip-mine operators, citizen advocates, an underground miner, landowners, government officials, strip-mine inspectors, and sociologists. p./d. Frances Morton, Gene DuBey; APPAL.

STRIPTEASE (24m C p1980, r1980) (also Video)
Examines an aspect of the role of working woman and raises questions of sexuality and society's notion of the human body. Examines the world of the stripper--as a human being and as a worker. The dancers discuss their lives as entertainers and the feelings of friends and audiences towards their chosen profession. d. Kay Armatage; p. Peter Walsh; SERBC.

STRUGGLE OF COON BRANCH MOUNTAIN (13m B 1972)
Tells the struggles of the people of Coon Branch Mountain in trying to get better education for their children. The story is told in interviews, about the poor roads that the state refused to improve which prevented their children from going to high school; how the school which the community built burned down; and their successful march on the West Virginia state capitol demanding bus service. p./d. Mimi Pickering; APPAL.

STUDIES IN MOVEMENT DESIGN (10m B 1977) Creative Dance for Children Series
Boys and girls at the Tucson Creative Dance Center, under the direction of Barbara Mettler, work on "Studies in Movement Design." Dance teacher/Narrator/Director: Barbara Mettler; p. Will Carbo; p. Mettler Studios; METTLER.

STYLES THAT MADE A SPLASH, THE (20m C 1977)
The evolution of the female "bathing costume" is one of the most fascinating and entertaining stories in our country's 300-year history. It's a story of Classical vs. Gothic, propriety vs. utility, the formal vs. the free. This documentary bares as it traces the battles women waged in their successful quest for a simple, functional suit. Humorously shows the many transformations of the "bathing costume" in its long and colorful history--all the way from the bikini of A.D. 400 to the present. Free loan. p. Sears, Roebuck and Company, Ken Delmar Films; MTPS.

STYX (10m B 1976)
The subway is a metaphor for Styx, the mythological Greek river bordering Hell. An ordinary event is transformed into a hypnotic experience as the subway door closes on somnambulant travelers. An extraordinary film, many awards. p. Jan Krawitz, Thomas Ott; MMA.

SUE'S LEG: REMEMBERING THE THIRTIES/TWYLA THARP AND DANCERS (60m C 1978) Dance in America Series
Shows Twyla Tharp and her company performing her creation

"Sue's Leg," using some of the music of the late jazz great Fats Waller, such as "Ain't Misbehavin'" and "I Can't Give You Anything But Love, Baby." Juxtaposed against this formal choreography is a collage of film scenes from the 1930's showing the richness and variety of American popular dancing which has heavily influenced Tharp's style. Included are clips from the movies and newsreels showing dance marathons, harvest moon balls, dancing schools, clebrity appearances, and period fads, such as art deco ballet. IU; PAS, UMN.

SUFFER THE CHILDREN (16m C 1981)
Documents the problems faced by the children of alcoholics: neglect, abuse, isolation, emotional anguish. Several such children discuss their experiences, and additional commentary is provided by a therapist, a social worker, and ex-alcoholic parents. p. CBS News; CAROUF; PAS, UCEMC, UIL.

SUFFER THE CHILDREN: AN ESSAY ON ABUSE (28m C p1980, r1980) (also Video)
Brief historic view of child welfare and the first child abuse case in the United States leads directly into a present-day social service center handling routine calls and routine cases. Noted national authorities highlight problems and issues and examine some positive solutions to keeping children in the home. Brings into perspective historic attitudes about children and government's responsibility to families. p./d. Gretchen Robinson; ROBNSN.

SUFFER THE CHILDREN--SILENCE NO MORE (45m C p1980, r1980) (also Video)
Covers initial identification, assessment and reporting of physical and sexual child abuse cases. Two cases are covered in the emergency department setting, in which child abuse experts point out important aspects of parent and child presentation leading to diagnosis and treatment of cases. d. Gunter H. Doetsch; p. Joyce U. Doetsch; s.w. Barbara Steiger; SCNTIF.

SUICIDE AT 17 (18m C 1977)
Suicide is the number two cause of death among adolescents. Bobby Benton, a senior in high school in 1975, crashed his car which killed his girl friend after an evening of beer drinking and marijuana smoking. Shortly thereafter, facing a felony manslaughter charge and unable to cope with the grief and guilt, Bobby shot and killed himself. His coach and friends remember Bobby as a good student and a very likeable person. Bobby's mother, who now works for the suicide prevention hotline, advises always to listen carefully and nonjudgmentally to any suicide threat and to refer professional help when possible. p./d. Ira Eisenberg; LAWRENP.

SUICIDE: TEENAGE CRISIS (10m C 1981) (also Video)
Reported suicide is the third largest killer of teenagers. According to experts, if unreported cases were added, suicide would become

the major reason for death among young adults in this country. This film explores the problem and describes a variety of school and community programs that are now beginning to save troubled lives through counseling. p. CBS News; CRM; UCEMC, UIL.

SUICIDE: THE WARNING SIGNS (24m C p1981, r1982)
Combines dramatic enactment with documented remarks from a recognized authority on youth suicide to increase awareness among the general public of the problem of suicide among young people. Illustrates clues and patterns of behavior which may indicate a suicide attempt and discusses how a friend, parent or teacher might help. d. Linda K. Haskins; p. Centron Films in cooperation with The American Association of University Women; CENTEF; UIL.

SUICIDES (42m C 1981)
Explores the complex world of suicide, through individuals who have survived suicide attempts and families that have experienced the death of a loved one. The psychological, sociocultural, and biomedical aspects of suicide are highlighted, as well as ways of preventing these tragedies. Illustrates the basic phenomenology of suicide and engenders a deeper compassion for the suicidal person and for the families of victims. d. Barnett Addis, Ph.D.; p. Daniel Hubert, M.D./B. Addis, Ph.D.; p. University of California, Los Angeles; UCLABS.

SUMMER PARADISE (113m C 1977) (Swedish/subtitled)
Story of four generations of one family, who gather for the summer at Paradise Place, their idyllic seaside retreat. The head of the family is Katha, whose loving nature has made her a source of strength to her aging parents, her daughters and her grandchildren. Katha struggles to understand the loneliness and needs of each member of the family and the lives they touch. Most important is Katha's long-term friendship with Emma, an embittered social worker who suffers from severe depression. Ultimately, Katha's faith in the family is shaken by tragedy, and profound questions are raised about the nature of the family and its survival in an age of social change. p. Ingmar Bergman; d. Gunnel Lindblom; s.w. Gunnel Lindblom, Ulla Isaksson; ALMI.

SUN DAGGER, THE (59m C p1982, r1983)
Tells the story of perhaps the most important early Indian discovery in North America. The "dagger," a celestial calendar, discovered by Washington, D.C. artist Anna Sofaer in 1977, has been compared to Stonehenge and the Pyramids. Explores the extraordinary culture of the Anasazi Indians who built the calendar and thrived in the harsh environment of Chaco Canyon, New Mexico, 1,000 years ago. d. Albert Ihde; p./s.w. Anna Sofaer; BULFRG.

SUN TUNNELS (26m C n.d.)
Records the construction and installation of four huge cement

silos, "sun tunnels," into which the artist has drilled holes that at specific times of the year correspond to four constellations. By refraining from narrative explanation of the work, the viewers are allowed to grasp its aesthetic raison d'être for themselves. p. Nancy Holt; BELVFF.

SUN, WIND AND WOOD (25m C p1978, r1979)
In an effort to cut down on their energy bills, the people of Prince Edward Island are searching for ways to develop renewable sources of energy. Specific examples of their solutions show how they use sun, wind and wood to meet their energy requirements. d. Dorothy Todd Henaut; p. Kathleen Shannon, Edward LeLorrain and Margaret Pettigrew; NFBC; BENCHMF.

SUNDAY FATHER (11m C r1974)
Shows the contemporary situation of a divorced man who takes his daughter on a once-a-week outing on Sunday afternoon. Focuses on the problem of a father trying to be friends with a girl who he feels barely knows him. p. Paul Leaf; FI; KENTSU.

SUPERLATIVE HORSE (36m C r1975)
An allegorical children's story from ancient China. It is a story of the powerful ruler Duke Mu, who loved horses. When the chief groom for the royal stables retired, he hired a young aspirant. However, the young man must first find a "superlative" horse as a test of his ability to judge horses. Han Kan's final choice is an unusual one. Based on Jean Merrill's children's story. p. Urs Furrer, Yanna Brandt; a.p. Michael Sheppard; d. Yanna Brandt; PHOENIX.

SUPERMAN AND THE BRIDE (42m C 1975)
Using examples from mass media, shows how sex roles are shaped by the daily messages of movies, television, newspapers and radio. Still photos, animation and film clips (some include nudity) are used to show how sexual stereotyping is promoted and perpetuated by media programmers, and how it is to their benefit to continue it. Examples from Sweden and China show how the stereotypes are being broken by portraying women as active, confident and self-reliant, dispelling the myth that all men must be "Superman" and all women "The Bride." p. Thames Television, London; UIL, PAS.

SUPERNUMERARIES (16m B 1976)
The occasion of a performance allows a group of women and one man to suspend their traditional self-images and deal with their costumed anonymity. p. Sandra Kay Smith; IRISFC.

SURPRISES OF FAILURE, THE (28m C p1980, r1980) You Can Do It ... If Series
Featured are 27 people who eventually became successful in the world of business, entertainment, sports, or who achieved celebrity status. All have at least one thing in common, they suffered crushing

setbacks and failures at some time in their lives. Motivational speaker
Marilyn Van Derbur stresses that everyone is both a success and a
failure in one's lifetime, and that each person needs to make up his/
her mind about which he/she will be. p./s.w. Marilyn Van Derbur;
VDBER.

SURVIVA (35m C 1980)

A group of contemporary rural women artists meet to gain support for their work by organizing group exhibits and spaces for col-
laborative work. This process of creating, sharing and organizing
is demonstrated through a refreshing weave of film techniques. Cen-
tering on one woman artist, the film combines animation and nature
montage with documentary and narrative sequences. As we follow the
artist through events in her daily life and community, the film stimulates a flow in and out of various states of consciousness, involving
the viewer with the feelings, hopes, disappointments and support
necessary for survival. p. Carol Clement, Ariel Dougherty; WMM.

SURVIVAL ... OR SUICIDE (24m C p1979, r1979)

Depiction of the risks and potential consequences of the nuclear
arms race. Deals with the history of major weapons development,
actual nuclear alerts, plus simulated crisis, positive areas of United
States-Soviet joint projects, and the process of SALT negotiations
and role of United States Senate in ratification. d./p. Jeanne V.
Mattison. p. American Committee on East-West Accord; AMCEWA.

SUSAN WEINBERG: ARTIST (17m C 1980)

The life and work of Susan Weinberg, a Los Angeles painter who
gave up her husband, family, and home in order to paint. p. Nicholas Pasquariello; PASQRLO.

SUSANA (24m B 1980)

The filmmaker describes this film as a self-portrait documentary.
It is concerned with Susana's struggle to assert her lesbianism and
life-style in the face of her family's disapproval. Susana used her
photography, her friends and lovers, and finally her sister to comment on her and her chosen life-style. The film can be used as a
general statement on lesbianism and the problems one may encounter
in dealing with family and loved ones. Because the filmmaker grew
up in South America, there is an added dimension to the film that is
relevant to Latin culture. Sexually non-explicit. p. Susana Blau-
stein; MMRC, WMM.

SUZHOU (29m C p1980, r1981)

The sights and sounds of daily life in Suzhou, known for centuries as the center of Chinese culture and aesthetics, and often called
the "Venice of the East" because of its many canals and bridges.
Whether sensed in one of its fabled gardens, or evoked in the banter of old gentlemen taking tea together, the persistent devotion to
basic moral values remains intrinsic to Suzhou life. p. Sue Yung Li;
UCEMC.

SWEET DREAMS (13m C/B 1979)
This sensuous and sexually explicit film combines erotic fantasy with one woman's masturbation pattern. The speaker (a lesbian) discusses her fantasies and where they come from. It can be used to stimulate discussion on the relationship between fantasy and sexuality and to illustrate female masturbation and its role in human sexuality. d. Honey Lee Cottrell; p. National Sex Forum; MMRC.

SWEET SIXTEEN AND PREGNANT (29m C p1981, r1982) (also Video)
To increase awareness among young people of the realities of teenage pregnancy, five teenage girls who became pregnant are profiled. In one scene a group of girls discuss sex education with a teacher who stresses the need for information about family planning and contraception. The narration stresses the need for clear communication between adults and children about reproduction and the consequences of being sexually active. Sponsor: Los Angeles Medical Association; d. John Cosgrove; p. Ann Hassett, Dave Bell Associates; MTITI.

SWITCHING ON ... YOUR LIFE IN THE ELECTRONIC AGE (57m C p1980, r1981) (Video)
This overview of the computer revolution shows students that a knowledge of basic computer skills will be essential in their lives. Work and leisure, transportation and communication, health care and education--all are being transformed by the tiny silicon chip, key to the new technology. d. Wendy O'Flaherty; p. Canadian Broadcasting Corporation; FILMLB.

SYDNEY see GERMAINE GREER'S SYDNEY

SYKES (13m C n.d.)
Portrait of Sykes Williams, a vital musician who ventures out into the streets of Chicago's North Side despite his blindness. To supplement his income he plays the piano at a sing-along bar, and his presence enlivens the place. Although outspoken about some of the problems he encounters, it is obvious that here is a man who relished life and has not let his blindness keep him apart from the world. p. Deidre Walsh; FILMLB, KENTSU, UMO.

SYVILLA: THEY DANCE TO HER DRUM (25m B p1975, r1979)
Still montages, interviews with Syvilla Fort (a pioneer black choreographer-teacher), footage of her final dance classes, re-creations of two of her most celebrated works, and voice-over narration by the filmmaker combine to create a loving portrait of one artist's valiant efforts to pass on certain modern dance traditions despite lack of funds, lack of recognition, and the debilitating effects of age and disease. She passed away in November 1975. Dancers: Syvilla Fort, Dyanne Harvey; Choreographers: Syvilla Fort, Eugene Little, Pearl Reynolds; d./p. Ayoka Chenzira; BLACKFF.

-T-

TAJIMOLTIK (FIVE DAYS WITHOUT NAME) (30m C 1978)

Follows the carnival activities and visually depicts the varied influences which non-native religions have had on Mayan ritual and beliefs. The prosperity of a new Mayan year depends on the success of these "Five Days Without Name." Also available in French. p. Claudine Viallon, Georges Payrastre; p. Okexnon Films, Canada; DER.

TAKE A STAND (25m C 1982)

A "role-played documentary" based on a real case shows how an older woman, the victim of a mugging, is encouraged by a victim advocate to testify in court against her attacker. Shows the woman's renewal of courage as she is guided through the unfamiliar courtroom process by her victim advocate. d./p. James Vanden; sponsor: Chicago Office for Senior Citizens and Handicapped; TNF.

TAKING BACK DETROIT (55m C p1979, r1980)

Documents three socialist leaders who hold prominent civic positions in Detroit. They call for an end to tax breaks for business, development of neighborhoods and an expansion of Detroit's economic base beyond the auto-related industries. The three leaders are Justin Ravitz, the only marxist judge in the United States; Ken Cockrel, City Councilman; and Sheila Murphy, an aide to Cockrel. They are members of DARE, believed to be only influential socialist organization in a major American city. d. Stephen Lighthill; p. Stephen Lighthill, Kristine Samuelson; AVAIL; PAS.

TAKING CHANCES: TEEN SEXUALITY AND BIRTH CONTROL (22m C r1979)

Follows the romantic relationship between Kathy and Leigh, interspersing their story with discussion among other teens expressing feelings and concerns about their sexual coming-of-age ... whether or not to use birth control, whether or not to have sex. Recommended by American Library Association, Planned Parenthood League of Massachusetts, et al. p. Mobius International; MOBIUS.

TAKING IT IN STRIDE: POSITIVE APPROACHES TO STRESS MANAGEMENT (22m C n.d.) (also Video)

A summary of coping skills, from learning how to relax to finding ways to uncomplicate your life. p. Spectrum Films; SPECTR.

TAKING STOCK

Stress Management: A Positive Strategy Series

"We're not very good barometers of our own tension level, states one of the on-camera consultants in this segment. However, the consultant goes on to explain how viewers can develop an awareness of stress in their lives and how they can learn to recognize the first signs of trouble. Participants examine the relationship between their responses to stress and their health, as well as their ability to function effectively as executives. They are shown how they may be leaning on habitual patterns of response and how short-term stress and chronic stress undermine efficiency. Coping behaviors are discussed in depth, with emphasis on the Type A behavior pattern, also called "the coronary-prone personality pattern." Leader's manual and participants' handbooks included. TIMLIF.

TALE OF TILL, A (11m C 1975)
Introduces Till Eulenspiegel and his place in German literature. Then, the film is devoted to an outdoor puppet show of one of Till's stories. Narrated by Barry Sullivan. p. Marianne Meyerhoff; FLMFR.

TALES OF TOMORROW: OUR ELDERS (22m C p1981, r1982)
The stories of two very different older people are interwoven to show the complexity of issues facing elders today. Alex is 74, retired with his wife, Helen. Helen has Alzheimer's Disease, so they moved into Baycrest Jewish Home for the Aged. Sarah is 80, a labor organizer and wheelchair activist, who is determined to live alone as long as she can. d./p. Barbara Martineau; DECF.

TALKING UNION (58m B 1979)
An oral history film about four Texan women and their organizing activities in the years 1930 through 1960. The women are Alberta Snid, participant in the 1938 pecan shellers' strike in San Antonio; Charlotte Graham, leader of the 1935 Dallas garment workers' strike; Olivia Rawlston, president of the Black ILGWU local in Dallas for 12 years; and Andrea Martinez, leader of the ILGWU in Laredo during the 1950's and 1960's. Raises many significant issues about women in the Texas work force. Also available in Spanish (videotape only). p. People's History in Texas, Inc.; d. Maria Flores, Glen Scott; UTX.

TAMING OF THE SHREW, THE (122m C 1967)
Elizabeth Taylor and Richard Burton give robust life to Shakespear's comedy about the wooing and winning of the bawdy Kate by the lusty Petruchio. Perfect acting and award-winning direction give this film humor and appeal from first insult to last kiss. d. Franco Zeffirelli; SWA; SELECT.

TAOISM (22m C 1980)
Thomas Merton says, "All Chinese philosophy and culture tend to be 'Taoist' in a broad sense, since the idea of Tao is, in one form or another, central to traditional Chinese thinking." Chinese philosopher, Lao-tse (6th century B.C.) taught that contemplation and reason, avoidance of force, and disregard of mere ceremonies are the means of regeneration. Against a backdrop of contemporary China, the words of John Blofeld, an authority on Taoism, give a penetrating insight into the thought of one of the world's greatest philosophies. d./p. Elda Hartley; HARTLEY.

TAP DANCE KID, THE (33m C 1978)
Eight-year-old Willie wants to dance more than anything. His
father, a successful lawyer who "shuffled" his way through the Depression, disapproves. Willie's legal-minded sister intervenes for
Willie's rights. She takes him to a summer stock audition, and his
parents arrive in time to see talents and desires they never realized
before. d. Barra Grant; p. Evelyn Barron; LCA.

TAPESTRY WITH ROSA GUERRERO (28m C n.d.)
Title of the film is symbolic of the cultural diversity and ethnic
richness in the United States of America. The purpose of the film
is to promote better understanding in intercultural relationships from
the perspective of the Chicano; the roots and cultures that have contributed to the rich culture of the Chicano today. English narration.
p. Lito White; WSU.

TATTOO CITY (24m C 1980)
Featuring D. E. Hardy, one of tattooing's foremost practitioners,
this film focuses on Japanese tattoos (large or full-bodied) and their
myths. Hardy talks about the people who have influenced him and
his personal feelings about tattooing. The works of many artists,
such as Jack Rudy and Zeke Ownes, are brought to life. Stresses
the science and art of tattoo. d. Emiko Omori; SERBC.

TATTOOED TEARS (88m C 1978)
Four inmates in California Youth Training School are the focus
of this compassionate and disturbing documentary on correctional institutions and the lives of young offenders. "One of the most powerful depictions of prison life I've ever seen."--Tom Wicker, New York
Times. d. Joan Churchill, Nich Broomfield; CF, MMA.

TAUW (27m C 1969) (Wolof, with English)
A 20-year-old Sengalese looks for work on the docks of Dakar--
a city of striking contrasts between the old and the new, between
affluence and poverty. Caught in despair, like the other young men
around him, he asks, "I'm 20 and I am a man--what is there to get
up for?" A simple statement of despair, is about a poor man who
has not been dehumanized by his poverty. It poses the question,
What is it that has saved his dignity? d. Ousmane Sembene; NYF.

TEACH ME TO DANCE (28m C p1978, r1979)
Lesia is a young Ukrainian immigrant trying to cope with a new
language and life. When she is assigned what for her is a difficult
task--a recitation for the school's Christmas pageant--her best friend,
Sarah, sees her despair and suggests they perform a Ukrainian dance
together instead. But the two girls do not take into account the
growing hostility to Ukrainian settlers in the area. Sarah's father
forbids his daughter to dance with Lesia. In spite of their disappointment and the prejudice against Lesia, the girls remain fast
friends and they meet in Sarah's barn to celebrate Christmas Day
together. d. Ann Wheeler; p. Vladimir Valenta; NFBC; FI; UIL.

TEACHING CHILDREN SELF-CONTROL (26m C p1978, r1978)
Shows defiant and aggressive behavior in young children and presents practical management techniques for dealing with classroom crises. Demonstrates methods utilized by an experienced teacher as she helps her children acquire impulse control and coping skills. d./p. Judith Bloch; NYU.

TEACHING YOUR WINGS TO FLY (19m C 1978) (also Video)
Demonstrates some of the techniques used by Anne Lief Barlin to help children develop self-esteem, trust, confidence, and awareness of their bodies. Shown are many games and exercises Ms. Barlin uses to accomplish this. Includes textbook and two phonograph records. d. Yasha Aginsky; p./s.w. Anne Lief Barlin; LAWRENP.

TEALIA (10m C 1977)
A film version of an original ballet choreographed and performed by the featured dancers of San Francisco Ballet. The dancers' costumes and movements are meant to convey the image of the tealia--a coral-colored sea anemone with multiple arms which move and sway gently. Dancers: Betty Erickson, Vane Vest; Choreographer: John McFall; d. George Sicsery; p. Ellen June Kutten; PHOENIX; IU, KPF.

TEAM OF TWO, A (30m C 1978)
Advocates managers making full use of untapped skills and talents of secretaries. Offers a new concept in training so that managers can double their effectiveness. Starring: June Lockhart, Tom Kennedy. p. Cally Curtis Company; CALLYC.

TECHNOLOGY IN PUBLIC SERVICE (20m C n.d.)
An introduction to how Public Technology, Inc. in Washington, D.C., works with city, county, and state governments to improve public services through the innovative application of technology. p. Hilary Harris, Nell Cox; FI; AFI.

TEEN MOTHER--A STORY OF COPING (24m C 1981)
Rosie has been making it--or as she says "surviving"--on her own with her son George, since she was 17. By sharing her story of love and determination, Rosie gives an insight into the reality of a teen mother's life. d. Janine Manatis; p. Marilyn A. Belec; MOBIUS; UMN.

TEENAGE FATHER (30m C 1978)
Self-reflective docudrama of a 17-year-old boy and 15-year-old girl involved in unplanned pregnancy. Script and actors' characterizations based on Children's Home Society of California interviews with actual teen fathers. Contains insights from boy's, girl's parents' and peer group's perspectives. Film follows couple through birth of child, reveals options, legal rights and lack of rights facing both teen parents. d./p. Taylor Hackford; CHSCA.

TEENAGE GIRLS: THREE STORIES (58m C p1980, r1980) (Video)
Examination of the family life of three teenage girls from different cultures in New York City. Each girl faces difficult choices in
the future and this videotape shows, in verité footage, how their
families affect their choices. Each family struggles with serious
problems of its own. d. Abbie H. Fink; ex. d. Carol Anshien;
COMCC.

TEENAGE HOMOSEXUALITY (11m C 1980) (also Video)
A candid look at a part of society some will find hard to accept--
homosexual teenagers. There are no statistics available on the number of gay teens because they are secretive and afraid of the way
their straight friends and their parents--especially their parents--
might react to their sexual preference. In Houston, CBS Correspondent Betsy Aaron talks with five gay teenagers and with a mother
whose teenage daughter is a homosexual. Dr. Coleman talks informa-
tively about the isolation and loneliness of his gay teenage patients,
parental attitudes and various theories about homosexuality. Recommended for high school counseling as well as for those studying psychology and sexual behavior. p. Elisabeth Lawrence for CBS News;
CAROUF; USFL, KENTSU, UIL.

TEENAGE MOTHER: A BROKEN DREAM (15m C 1978)
Examines the life of Mary Levandoski, a 15-year-old girl who is
part of an ever-growing statistic in this country--the unwed teenage
mother. Like so many others, Mary's boyfriend decided not to marry
her, her baby was placed in a foster home, and she is now in a detention home trying to finish her schooling so she can get a job.
Presents the stark reality of teenage pregnancy and motherhood for
those who cannot visualize it themselves. CBS-TV; CAROUF; UMN.

TEENAGE PARENTS (10m C 1981) (also Video)
Each year, nearly a million teenage girls get pregnant and almost
600,000 of them choose to have and keep their babies. Nearly half
of these young mothers get married. This film documents the life-
styles of two teenaged married couples who are discovering what it
is like to assume the responsibilities of marriage and parenthood while
still teenagers. CBS News; CRM; UCEMC, UIL, IU.

TEENAGE PREGNANCY (29m C 1977) (Video) Woman Series
Georgia McMurray, Director of Public Affairs for the Community
Service Society of New York, and Barbara Wallace Catalano, a clinical
nurse-specialist in maternal and child care, discuss the implications
of teenage pregnancy. They explain the consequences of ignoring
the teenage pregnancy epidemic, including insufficient health care
and social services for the young mother and the high rate of miscarriage. Sandra Elkin is the moderator. p. WNED-TV; PBSV.

TEENAGE PREGNANCY: NO EASY ANSWERS (22m C 1980) (also
    Video)

Susan, fifteen, unmarried and pregnant, must decide what is best for her and the child she carries. The options are adoption, abortion, marriage and single parenting--and she doesn't want any of them. d./s.w. Helen Garvy, Dan Bersire; p. Shira Films Production; BARRF; UIL, KENTSU.

TEENAGE SEXUALITY AND CONTRACEPTION (13m C n.d.)
Discusses the need for a sexually active teenager to also consider choosing some form of contraception. Dispels common myths and misconceptions many teenagers have about sex and contraception. Further examines the various choices for contraceptive methods and the pros and cons of each including risks. Also available in Spanish. MIFE.

TEENAGE SHOPLIFTING (10m C 1981) (also Video)
With teenage shoplifting on the rise, store owners are starting to crack down on youngsters before these bad habits become a lifestyle. The film focuses on Muskegon, Michigan where both community members and parents are working together to bring a growing problem under control. Brief interviews are presented with young shoplifters who got caught. p. CBS News; CRM; UCEMC, UIL.

TEENAGE SUICIDE (ed.) (16m C p1978, r1979)
Presents an overview and case histories of teen suicide problems. Over 5,000 young people under age 25 commit suicide each year. Shown are interviews with young people who have attempted suicide' telling why the attempt was made and what they used or did to end their pain. The film points out some warning signs that should alert family and friends. p. CBS News, "60 Minutes." MTITI; IU, UCEMC.

TEENAGE SUICIDE: DON'T TRY IT! (48m C 1981) (also Video)
Four brave families expose their anguish when their son or daughter attempted suicide. One family talks of the death of their son by suicide. The aim of the film is to bring public attention to the problems of teenage suicide and to help stop the problem. d. Dennis Lofgren; p. Linda Otto; p. Alan Landsburg Productions; FI.

TEENAGE SUICIDE--IS ANYONE LISTENING? (22m C p1980, r1980)
Explores the mounting problem of severe depression in adolescence through the stories of a 16-year-old boy and a 14-year-old girl who have attempted suicide. Since teenagers often turn to their peers for support, the film is intended to sensitize teenagers to the problem so they can hear their friends when they are asking for help. d./p. Christina Crowley; BARRF; KENTSU, UIL.

TEENAGE SUICIDE: THE CRIME FAMILIES NEVER FORGET (60m C) (also Video)
A documentary examining the tragic subject of teenage suicide. Explores the lives--and deaths--of four teenagers. In the United States today, young people aged 10 to 21 are killing themselves at

the rate of 18 per day. The question of what can bring such deep despair to a time of life that should be full of hopes and dreams is one that must be faced and answered. Narrated by Timothy Hutton. p. Alan Landsburg Productions; FI.

TEENAGE TURN-ON: DRINKING AND DRUGS (38m C 1980) (also Video)
Today's teenagers are drinking more and starting younger. They're mixing booze with pot, uppers, downers--any drug they can find. Yet, because alcohol has been considered part of the American social life, most parents, teachers, and communities fail to acknowledge alcohol as a drug or to recognize the epidemic proportions of alcohol abuse. In this film teenagers tell their own stories openly and honestly. Includes a visit to an adolescent drug treatment center and to a halfway house where formerly addicted teenagers discuss their fears for the future. The fact is made clear that alcohol and drug addiction cut across all social and economic lines. p. ABC News; CRM; UIL, WSU, UM.

TEENAGE YEARS, THE (SERIES) see HORRIBLE HONCHOS, THE (SERIES)

TELEPHONE FILM, THE (6m B 1972)
A compilation of "old friends" from late night TV, including Lois Lane and George Raft. (Collective for Living Cinema, November 10, 1978.) p. Betty Ferguson; FILMCO.

TELEVISION--THE ENCHANGED MIRROR (28m C 1981)
Focuses on television in American life, i.e., psychological impact and moral values; ratings and advertising; children and family life; social isolation and images of reality; new technologies and the future. Includes interviews with TV directors and writers, a network executive, a brain behavior scientist, an advertiser, and members of the viewing public. d. Julene Bair, George Csicsery; MMM.

TELL ME ABOUT YOURSELF (27m C r1976)
Excellent introduction to the entire employment interview process, showing how to achieve key objectives and demonstrating techniques that help with typical interviewing problems. Concise and informative. RTBL: UCEMC, UM.

TEMISCAMING, QUEBEC, PTS. I, II (64m C 1976)
A story of a town's struggle to survive when their main source of employment, the CIP mill, closed down. Part I tells what steps the workers, townspeople and ex-CIP managers took to reopen the mill, while Part II explains the new corporate ownership of the mill, how it works and its growing pains. It is about ownership of the Canadian economy, industrial democracy and related issues. p. Dorothy Todd Henaut, Len Chatwin; d. Martin Duckworth; NFBC.

TEMPTATION OF POWER, THE (43m C 1977) (also Video)
Examines the social and economic development policies of the Iranian government during the period of the so-called White Revolution, 1962 to 1978. For many years, the economic development policies of the Shah of Iran were held up by western political and economic leaders as a model for other Third World countries to emulate. The development of high technology industry, a consumer-oriented economy, and a land reform program designed to concentrate agriculture in large corporate-owned holdings, were supposed to propel Iran "into the 20th century." But the inequities and dislocations which these policies caused within the Iranian society were often overlooked. This film examines this economic model and reveals the many problems which it created. p. Marie Claude Deffarge, Gordian Troeller; ICARF.

TENDER TALE OF CINDERELLA PENGUIN, THE (10m C p1981, r1982) (also Video)
Using a medieval style of illustration to animate the story of Cinderella, the film gives the leading role to a mistreated romantic penguin with hilarious results. Cinderella Penguin loses her magic flipper as she runs to meet the midnight deadline, but all ends well when Prince Charming finds the right webbed foot and nasty in-laws are brought to heel. d. Janet Perlman; p. David Verrall; NFBC.

TENNESSEE SAMPLER (15m C 1977)
Presents a kaleidoscopic "sampler" of the land, traditions, activities, culture and heritage of Tennessee and her people. Nonnarrated, with natural sounds in each location of this whirlwind visual tour of Tennessee conveys a great deal about the state and its people. p. Caroline Ahlfours Mouris and Frank Mouris; PHOENIX, FI, KPF, VIEWFI.

TENSION AND RELAXATION (13m B 1977) Creative Dance for Children Series II
Boys and girls at the Tucson Creative Dance Center, under the direction of Barbara Mettler, work on tension and relaxation as basic elements of movement. Dance Teacher/Narrator/Director: Barbara Mettler; p. Will Carbo; p. Mettler Studios; METTLER.

TENSIONS see VIDEO DANCES

TEST-TUBE BABIES (57m C 1982) Nova Series
Doctors have at last achieved the conception of human babies outside the womb. This film looks at the intriguing science behind this accomplishment and at the disturbing social issues it raises. p. WGBH-TV/BBC; TIMLIF.

THANK YOU, MA'AM (12m C 1976)
This film asks the question, Should every crime committed by a child be punished with punitive vindictiveness, or would kindness and

caring be more effective? Adapted from a short story by Langston Hughes. ex. p. Barbara Bryant. p./d. Andrew Sugerman; Music by Brownie McGhee, Sonny Terry; PHOENIX.

THAT OUR CHILDREN WILL NOT DIE (60m C p1978, r1978)

A look at community-based primary health care services in five locations in Nigeria. Focuses on the approach of Professor O. Ransome-Kuti, Director, Institute of Child Health, University of Lagos, and shows the use of nurses in expanded roles and specially trained community residents to deliver basic health services. p./d./ed. Joyce Chopra; FORDF.

THEATRE GIRLS (80m B 1978)

Theatre Girls Club is a hostel in Soho, London for destitute women. Once a theatrical club, it is now the only shelter in London that will take in any woman at any time. There are 47 beds but women are also offered chairs to sleep in overnight as a last resort. The filmmakers lived in the hostel for two and a half months. Developing the considerable trust they established, the filmmakers were able to interview the occupants and record everyday scenes of aggression and of hopelessness and incomprehension. p. Kim Longinotto, Claire Pollak; WMM.

THERAPEUTIC TOUCH: HEALING IN THE NEW AGE, THE (25m C 1979)

Research in paranormal healing has been carried on by a few dedicated scientists--Drs. Elmer and Alyce Green, Sr. Justa Smith, Dr. Bernard Grad, and Dr. Dolores Krieger. This film deals briefly with the work of the first four and in detail with the work of Dolores Krieger--a professor of nursing at New York University who has trained more than 4,000 health professionals in the use of what she calls "the therapeutic touch." We see her hemoglobin research, attend one of her seminars and learn her techniques, watch her do an "assessment" of a patient whose malady she does not know, and discover the rationale that motivates her work. d. Elda Hartley; HARTLEY; PAS.

THERAPY WITH DR. SID WOLF: A VIEW FROM THE INSIDE (30m C n.d.) (also Video)

Shows Dr. Wolf working with Marilyn (28-year-old victim of child abuse) to build a relationship through which she can relive her traumatic memories and deeply buried fears in an attempt to realize her potential. Dr. Wolf shares valuable insights into the core concepts of the helping process and the building of therapeutic relationships. p. FMS Productions, Inc.; FMSP.

THERE IS NO PLACE LIKE HOME (15m C n.d.)

Shows how men and women help senior citizens maintain their independence and continue to live in their own homes. Called Senior

Companions, these volunteers are 60 years of age or older. See women helping with shopping, light housework and cleaning. Free loan. ACTION; MTPS.

THESE THREE (92m B 1936)
Deals with the relationship of two school-mistresses and how their relationship was exposed and dragged through the mud by a hope-lessly horrid upperclass brat. Joel McCrea is brought in here to "normalize" the sexual interests of the two women, but the strong bond between them remains the unyielding focal point and most con-vincing aspect of this surprisingly powerful drama. Based on Lillian Hellman's play The Children's Hour. Starring: Miriam Hopkins, Merle Oberon, Joel McCrea. d. William Wyler; s.w. Lillian Hellman; GOLDWYN; FI.

THEY ARE THEIR OWN GIFTS (52m C 1978) (also Video)
A biographical trilogy which documents the lives and works of three American artists--poet Muriel Rukeyser, painter Alice Neel, and choreographer Anna Sokolow. These women found inspiration in the events of their time and, in an age of artistic abstractions, re-lated their work to the human condition and the happenings of the century. Also available in three 19-minute parts. (New Community Cinema, December 5, 1978.) d./p. Lucille Rhodes, Margaret Murphy; NEWDAY; PAS.

THIN EDGE OF THE BAY, THE (22m C p1978, r1980) (also Video)
Presents a film that uses San Francisco Bay as a focus to study the economic and political conflicts over shrinking environmental re-sources in urban areas. Explores three areas of San Francisco Bay in which commercial development is gradually taking over the natural environmental resources. Explains what is being done to reverse a trend that seemed certain to destroy the San Francisco Bay. Spon-sored by the San Francisco League of Women Voters. p./d. Ruth Landy; UCEMC.

THINGS ARE DIFFERENT NOW (17m C 1978)
Illustrates the impact of divorce on pre-teenagers. Twelve-year-old Joey is shown trying to go on with his normal pursuits after his parents have divorced, but "nothing is the same" and everything seems to be going wrong for him. At choir practice, playing base-ball, in his relations with his friends and family, in his attitude and actions, he has trouble making anything come out right. Eventually, Joey is able to face the reality of the change in his life. With the help and encouragement of his mother, grandfather, and his best friend, he begins to get clear of the pressures. p. Paulist Produc-tions; MEDIAG; KENTSU, UIL.

THINGS I CANNOT CHANGE, THE (56m B 1970)
There are nine children in the Bailey family. Gertrude Bailey is expecting a tenth child. Kenneth Baily has not been able to get

a steady job in two years. They can barely feed their children on
the charity food given them. Police and welfare workers constantly
harass the family. The Baileys are powerless and poor. For three
weeks their lives were filmed unrehearsed and undirected. Poverty
is not a disease or lack of ability; it is a social condition that crushes
human lives. d. Tanya Ballantyne; p. John Kennedy; NFBC; FI.

THINK NUTRITION SERIES see CONSUMING INTEREST, A; EATING
   WITHOUT MEAT; OVERWEIGHT?; VITAMINS

THINKING TWICE ABOUT NUCLEAR WAR (58m C 1982) (Video)
   Through a combination of documentary portraits, historical film
footage and original animation, portrays the diversity of opinion on
how best to prevent nuclear war. Hosted by Mike Farrell, the program examines how a typical family in Richmond, Virginia responds
to the risks of the arms race, then presents the different strategies
of a private physician, an international negotiator, a nuclear weapons
designer, a high school student and an advocate of the weapons freeze
campaign. d. Kim Spencer; p. Evelyn Messinger, ed. Evelyn Messinger; PUBIVN.

THIRD COAST, THE (55m C p1979, r1981) (also Video)
   A profile of the City of Houston which is emerging as the nation's
third largest city and a new power center of the 1980's. Using a
magazine format, the film alternates from serious social comment to
the lighthearted attitudes of Houston's residents. d. Susan Raymond;
VIDVER.

THIRD GENERATION (7m B 1973)
   Life around a country house is quiet, expectant, waiting the
birth of a new baby. The doctor comes ... the baby cries ... and
a gusty gale erupts outside. Life goes on, but something wonderful
has happened in this fleeting moment. Music carries the mood, rising
to a crescendo then fading as the doctor's car disappears down the
road. p. Perspective Films and Video; CORONET; VIEWFI.

34TH STAR, THE (34m C 1975) The American Parade (Series)
   Portrays the relationship between the people and the land through
the story of the Simpson family as they settled in the Kansas Territory in the 1850's. Typical of the American generation which settled
the Middle West and the Plains states. Emphasizes the economic, political and social issues of the day including the land-related conflicts
which resulted in the Missouri Compromise, the Civil War, and the
enmity between ranchers and farmers. Delineates the events and attitudes which helped form the "American character." Bicentennial
Collection. PHOENIX; UIO.

3900 MILLION AND ONE (50m C 1974)
   Examines several development problems in rural India. Illustrates
the life of a peasant family, revealing the position of women, the

economic role of children, particularly the value of sons, and the problems of family planning. (BBC; Oxfam-America, 1974). BBC; UM.

39, SINGLE AND PREGNANT (19m C p1981, r1982) (also Video)
Portrait of Jane Davis, a secretary at a public television station and never married, who decides at the age of 39 to have a child on her own. Follows Jane over a two-year period, from late pregnancy to her child being a young toddler. Contrasts her illusions and expectations of single parenthood with its emotional and financial reality. d./p. Christine Wynne; FILMLB; IU.

THIS FILM IS ABOUT RAPE (29m C p1978, r1978) (also Video)
The basic message is that rape is not a crime of sex but one of assault, using sexual humiliation as its method. Serious without being militant, the film aims to present a very painful fact of our lives in a compassionate manner. p. Cheshire Films; p./d. Bonnie Kreps for British Columbia Police Commission, Vancouver, BC, Canada; MTITI; UCEMC.

THIS IS DANCE THERAPY (20m C n.d.) (Video)
Actual dance therapy sessions in a state mental-illness facility are taped, edited, and set against a background of voices, music and narration to explain the art-science of dance therapy. The narrator points to what is happening and offers a theoretical explanation as well. p. Ann Wilson Wangh; HUNTERC.

THIS IS ME (27m C n.d.)
Some of life's most profound questions are taken on by ten children ranging in age from six to eleven. They share with us and each other their uninhibited opinions and feelings about God, the beginnings of life, etc. The filmmakers illustrate the children's imaginative ruminations and conclusions through the magic of animation. d. Don Tunis; p. Francine Desbiens, NFBC.

THIS IS YOUR MUSEUM SPEAKING (13m C 1979)
On one memorable night, a watchman and his dog, Fang, encounter incredible characters emerging from the walls and halls of a museum. The resident muse, a flamboyant lady with flaming red locks, introduces them to this unusual society. Together they witness an eighteenth-century duel, converse with a Rembrandt painting and question an Egyptian Pharaoh. d. Lynn Smith; p. Dick Verrall, Derek Lamb; NFBC.

THORNE FAMILY FILM, THE (80m C 1978)
Focuses on the Thorne family who homesteaded near Pendleton, Oregon in the 1880's, and six generations have since grown up there. Today, some 100 of the 300 members still live near Pendleton. Only one branch of the family continues to make a living off the land, though. The others have moved into Pendleton, or simply moved

elsewhere, the family struggles to maintain the proud heritage of strength, tenacity and togetherness their predecessors carved out of a stubborn land. Focuses on individuals in the family as they deal with problems facing us all--the loss of rural ties, adjustment to urban life and occupations, changes in traditional values and sex roles, independence and the responsibility for the very young and elderly. An excellent film on American culture. Through it all, we are led to re-experience and re-examine the significance of kinship. p. Center for Urban Education; CURBE.

THOROUGHLY MODERN MILLICENT (14m C 1981)
     Profile of Millicent Fenwick, congressional representative from New Jersey. Elected for the first time in 1974 at age 64, and currently serving her third term, Fenwick is variously described as "elegant," "literate," "a dead-honest legislator," and the conscience of the Congress. Because she is also direct, charming and fun, she is adored by young people. d. Suzanne St. Pierre; p. CBS News, "60 Minutes"; MOKINA.

THOUGHTS ON FOX HUNTING (30m C p1979, r1979) (also Video)
     Conveys the excitement and color of a fox hunt and provides some aspects of hound training. p. Nina Davenport, Tom Davenport; d. Tom Davenport, Harrison O'Conner; DAVNPT.

THOUSAND CRANES: THE CHILDREN OF HIROSHIMA, A (24m B 1968)
     Long after the A-bomb destruction of Hiroshima, the survivors and the offspring of the victims still confront the crippling after-effects of radiation exposure. Yet neither bitterness nor vengefulness inform their actions, only a sincere desire for a lasting peace. A beautiful and haunting film that is both a tribute to the Japanese spirit and an effective anti-war statement. d. Betty Jean Lifton; MACMFL.

THOUSAND MOONS, A (51m C p1975, r1982)
     More than a thousand moons have come and gone since the birth of Regina, a mixed blood matriarch now living in the big city poverty where she senses that death is imminent. She knows she must return to her distant birthplace to be welcomed by the spirits of her Indian ancestors. Although they're broke, Regina's son and his friends intrigue to make her wish come true. d. Gilles Carle; p. Stephen Patrick; CBC.

THREE BY CHEEVER (SERIES) see FIVE-FORTH-EIGHT, THE; O YOUTH AND BEAUTY; SORROWS OF GIN, THE

THREE DANCES (17m B 1964)
     Three short dances: "Public," photographed at the Museum of Modern Art; "Party," photographed at Judson Church, New York City; and a solo by Judith Dunn, photographed in her studio. Choreographer/d./p. Gene Friedman; EASTEND.

THREE FAMILIES: JERUSALEM (25m C 1977) Man's Religious Quest
   Series
   Examines three religious views, Judaism, Christianity, and Islam,
focusing on the members of three families living in Jerusalem. These
people discuss religious beliefs and are shown performing various religious observances. Defines the family as a vehicle for transmitting
religion and keeping the community stable. p. BBC-TV; Open University, University Media; KENTSU.

THREE LETTER WORD FOR LOVE (27m C n.d.)
   Young people from the inner-city area, male and female, talk
about sex: their knowledge, fantasies, experience, misconceptions.
The teenagers filmed are spontaneous and unrehearsed and the film's
open, accepting quality encourages viewing groups to be equally at
ease and direct in their discussion. Aimed at adolescents and adults
in the field of guidance. TEXFM; UM.

THREE PHOTOGRAPHERS (20m B 1980)
   A portrait of three women and their separate approaches to photography. A sports photographer describes the problems of catching
the essential moments of action in a game. A fine arts photography
student works at capturing the nuances of a drapery fold. An artist/
university instructor helps students discover their own styles and
define their ideas. Underlying each narrative is a commitment to an
art form, a visual interpretation which is sometimes subtle, sometimes
dynamic, but always personal. p. Laurie Meeker; MEDIAP.

THREE STONE BLADES (16m C 1971)
   This dramatization of an Inuit legend from the Bering Strait region shows how food-sharing and family obligations are essential to
group survival in a marginal environment. A husband, the family's
provider, goes hunting and fails to return. Near starvation, his
wife journeys to her husband's relatives to ask for food for her children; instead of food, the sister-in-law gives her three stone blades.
When the hunter's brother learns of his wife's selfish treachery, he
leaves her to become the provider for his dead brother's family. d.
Valerie L. Smith; p. Dorothy Goldner/Orville Goldner; IFB; UCEMC,
UMI.

THREE STORY SUITE (30m C 1980-1983) (Video, Beta, VHS) Concepts Series
   THREE STORY SUITE is a trio of folktales performed by storyteller Laura Simms. Video effects are used to make visual the magic
of these age-old myths. Includes both original works by Simms and
retellings of traditional material, with music by Steven Gorn and Julia
Haines. d./p. Doris Chase; CHASED.

THREE STYLES OF MARITAL CONFLICT: SOME COMMON FORMS OF
   DYSFUNCTIONAL INTERACTIONS (14m C p1976, r1978)
   Reenacted case studies based on clinical experience and research

on common types of dysfunctional marital conflict--hidden agendas
behind behavior, role of passive partner in a marriage, and the over-
adequate/under-adequate couple. p. Bimage; CRM; RESPRIC; PAS,
KENTSU, IU, UIL, UM.

THREE VIDEO VARIATIONS (30m B 1978) (Video)
    An experimental video production. Dancer: Sara Rudner;
Choreographer/Producer: Doris Chase; CHASED.

THREE WOMEN (123m C 1977) (reg./scope)
    Robert Altman's exploration of female sensibility (from child to
earth mother) is a powerful, if not always consciously understood,
investigation into what options exist between love and conformity,
desire and self-destruction. Starring: Shelley Duval, Sissy Spacek,
Janice Rule, d./p. Robert Altman; FOX; FI.

THREE WORKING AMERICANS (26m C 1981)
    Three ordinary people in ordinary professions show how fulfill-
ment in life can be obtained through dedication to one's work. p.
Judith Sandbank; SANDBK.

THREE'S A CROWD (14m C 1976)
    In filmed interviews with Mike Wallace, young married couples
state their preference for having no children, and they give reasons
which they think make sense: more free time, more money to spend,
mobility, and as a way to control world population and pollution.
Ellen Peck, author of The Baby Trap and spokeswoman for the National Organization of Non-Parents, expounds on her beliefs and sees
the movement as a threat to no one. A couple who has been married
for 20 years and has no children express their happiness, and Dr.
Alexander Taylor comments that if you compare people's rate of satisfaction in their marriage, those without children rate their marriage
more satisfactory. p. CBS News, "60 Minutes"; TIMLIF; UIL, UMN.

THREESCORE AND THEN (27m C 1982)
    Elderly people living in a variety of different circumstances in
Thailand illustrate some of the problems of the world's aging population and some possible solutions to them. d. Elspeth MacDougall;
ex. p. Joe O'Brien; UN.

THRILLER (35m B 1979)
    A feminist mystery film in which the heroine, Mimi, pieces to-
gether the facts behind her own death in the opera La Bohème. p.
Sally Potter; SERBC.

THROWING EVENTS, THE (15m C 1976) The Track and Field Series
    for Girls
    Deals with shot-put, discus throw and javelin throw. A coach
is shown taking the girls through the learning steps for an effective
throwing form and teaching critical principles of technique. Also

shown are the conditional and strength building exercises which are an integral part of the program. p. Ryan Films; MACMFL.

THUMBS DOWN (HITCHHIKING) (17m C 1974)
Using dramatizations and contrived interviews with real victims of hitchhiking-related crimes and accidents, this film demonstrates a variety of potential dangers to both hitchhikers and drivers: robbery, injury, sexual attack, hidden companion, automatic door locks controlled by the driver, getting a ride in a stolen vehicle, and others. For those who still insist on hitchhiking, several protective measures are enumerated. p. Sanders-Rose-Swerdloff; FLMFR; UIL.

TIBETAN MEDICINE: A BUDDHIST APPROACH TO HEALING (35m
    C r1977)
Tibetan medicine heals both the physical and the psychic being, treats the patient rather than the disease. The three "poisons" of ignorance, passion, and aggression are considered the cause of disease. Medicines of animal, vegetable and mineral substances, gathered in the surrounding mountains, as well as acupuncture and moxabustion are used by Ama Lobsang Dolma, the first female doctor of Tibet. Filmed at the Tibetan Medical Center of the Dalai Lama in the Indian Himalayas. p. Sheldon Rocklin; HARTLEY.

TIEFLAND (98m B 1954) (German/Subtitled)
A beautifully photographed pastoral romance about a gypsy dancer (played by the director). d. Leni Riefenstahl; FI.

TILLIE'S PHILODENDRON (7m C 1977)
Presents an animated allegory about a lonely woman which symbolizes the human need for caring and approval and shows the effects of anger and hostility. AESOP; EBEC; UIL.

TILT THE WHEEL (8m C si 1975) (Video)
The tape begins with a black-and-white image of Joanne Kelly dancing. As the tape gradually takes on color, the image becomes increasingly abstract. (Global Village, October 28, 1978.) p. Joanne Kelly; VFA.

TIME AND BEYOND (8m C p1975, r1977--U.S.)
Presents an introduction to some of the theories of metaphysical religion regarding life after death. p. Jacqueline Sturgeon; STURGN.

TIME FOR CARING: THE SCHOOL'S RESPONSE TO THE SEXUALLY
    ABUSED CHILD, A (28m C 1979)
Designed to assist school personnel in recognizing and helping sexually abused children. Opens with an interview of a young woman who was abused as a child and emphasizes that most states now have laws that make it mandatory to report sexual abuse of children. Discusses and illustrates in graphic detail the physical signs to look for. Several behavioral clues are pointed out. The action taken after a

report is made is then discussed along with the need for school personnel to determine policies of reporting action, etc. Several women who were abused as children are interviewed. A reasonably low-key film. Recommended for in-service training for teachers. p. Sandra Baker, Richard Baker; p. Profile Films; LAWRENP; CWU.

TIME FOR CHOICE: THE STORY OF GEORGIA'S ENDANGERED
    WILDLIFE, A (27m C p1978, r1979)
    More than 20 species of wildlife in Georgia are hovering on the edge of extinction. The film explores the plight of these endangered species. Examines the history of many of these threatened species, and investigates the reasons for their decline. Also discusses some of the ways these creatures are becoming protected today. Free loan. d. Becky Marshall; p. Jim Couch; GADNR.

TIME FOR LIVING, A (10m C 1975)
    Designed to stimulate preparation for retirement and to create awareness of need for planning, this film provides an introduction to pre-retirement education. Explains that change can sometimes cause anxiety and pain, but that change can also be a challenge and provide "a time for living." Narrated by Ray Bolger, whose whimsical comments capture the essence of that positive "retirement feeling." p. Cal Industries/Robert Rieb Associates; University of Connecticut, Center For Instruction; UNEV, UIL.

TIME FOR SURVIVAL (25m C p1979, r1979)
    Presents a visual lesson in the workings of ecological interdependence and a plea for concern over the consequences of humanity's thoughtless alteration of the life process itself. p./s.w. Carol Lee Taylor for National Audubon Society; d. Susan Oristaglio, Carol Lee Taylor; PHOENIX.

TIME HAS COME, THE (22m C 1977)
    Explores how elements inside the home (such as language, toys, clothing, chores, and career expectations) can be made less stereotyped and limiting for both sexes. It also deals with influences outside the home, such as school and television. Received international recognition. Awards. "First-rate visual consciousness-raising"--Ms. Magazine. p. Jamil Simon Productions, Inc.; THEYEF.

TIME OF YOUR LIFE, THE (28m C 1978)
    Explores time conflicts people face daily and examines ways to resolve these conflicts--dealing with such time-robbers as disorganization, interruptions and procrastination. The film outlines six simple but powerful ideas--keys to making more effective use of your time. Starring James Whitmore. p. Cally Curtis Company; CALLYC.

TIME OUT SERIES see DECK THE HALLS; SHIFTING GEARS

TIME TO BE BORN, A (30m C p1977, r1978)
    Focuses on the experience of Sheri and Bill Firchau in labor

and birth in a warm supportive hospital environment with an attending physician. d. William F. Cohen; p. Read Natural Childbirth Foundation, Inc.; READNCF.

TIME TO CONSIDER SERIES see WOMEN'S PLACE, A

TIME TO CRY, A (28m C 1979) Begin with Goodbye Series
Explores the loss of a loved one. Harriet Kerr recalls the death of her husband and her struggle to begin a new life as a widow. Sandy and Bob Spencer attempt to prepare themselves and their children for Sandy's impending death as a victim of cancer. With guide. MMM.

TIME TO DANCE, A (SERIES) see CLASSICAL BALLET; GREAT PERFORMANCE IN DANCE

TIMES IN A ROA (24m C 1974)
Shows the marathon race at the 1976 Olympic Games in Montreal. The German Democratic Republic runner establishes a new Olympic record (2 hours, 9 minutes, 55 seconds) and takes his hard-earned place as one of the top athletes in the Games. Through the streets of Montreal, past checkpoints and nourishment stands, the runners are cheered on by enthusiastic spectators. On the soundtrack, the winner's thoughts and strategies provide good insight into this gruelling endurance test. p. Yvon Charette; NFBC; MACMFL.

TITLE VII: AN EMPLOYMENT CASE STUDY see WOMEN AND THE LAW, THE (SERIES)

TITLE VII: LITIGATION see WOMEN AND THE LAW, THE (SERIES)

TITLE IX: FAIR PLAY IN SCHOOLS (29m C 1975) (Video)
Representative Michael Blouin (D-Iowa), a member of the House Committee on Education and Labor, and Margaret Dunkle, Associate Director of the Project on the Status of Women for the Association of American Colleges, discuss the ramifications of Title IX of the Education Amendments of 1972. This controversial law prohibiting sex discrimination in school athletics and other programs receiving federal assistance was opposed by the National Collegiate Athletic Association and the American Football Coaches Association on the grounds that it would jeopardize their programs. The two guests explain the provisions of the law and the effects it has had. Sandra Elkin is moderator. p. WNED-TV; PBSV.

TO A BABYSITTER (2nd ed.) (17m C 1974)
A teenage babysitter is followed through an evening of sitting. Shows the inquiries the sitter should make before accepting the job, the information that should be obtained from the parents, and pertinent child-care information. The accent on safety, with emergency procedures given by a nurse, a firefighter, and a police officer. p. Alfred Higgins; CORNELL.

TO BE A DANCER (30m B 1974)
A day in the life of Helen McGehee--choreographer/dancer--
preparing to choreograph, rehearsing, teaching, designing costumes,
her home life. Filmed from 1967 to 1969. The script for the film includes excerpts from her lectures, television interviews, and selections from her book, Helen McGehee, Dancer. p. A. Umana; UMANA.

TO BE A MAN (44m C 1977)
Contrasts the ideal of the American male created during the frontier days with the new role of men after the Women's Liberation Movement. Studies the events which have caused some men to reassess
masculine stereotypes and the acceptable range of emotional and economic flexibility he may display. Brief interviews with proponents of
human liberation, such as Pete Hamill, Betty Friedan, and Dr. Benjamin Spock, accompany the presentation of a range of male types
across the country. In interview sequences these men explain what
it means to them to be a man, some of them comfortable with the he-
man role and others almost reversing traditional masculinity. Wives
also talk about their husbands. p. Christian Blackwood, Blackwood
Productions; CORONET; PAS, KENTSU, UCLA, UIL.

TO BE ASSERTIVE (15m C 1977)
Illustrates how some people, just by nature or upbringing, tend
to be reticent about asserting their rights. They tend to let others
push them around and only assert themselves when they are pushed
to the wall. Through casual conversations, several young women
share their various experiences and situations. By acquiring trust
in themselves and by being responsible for their actions, they become more assertive. BUDDF; UIL, UCEMC, UMN.

TO HAVE AND TO HOLD (20m C 1981) (also Video)
Examines the problem of woman abuse from the man's experience
of it. Relying primarily on first-person accunts given by men who
have battered their wives, this film explores the societal and personal
roots of violence against women as well as the individual changes that
were critical for these men to stop their violent behavior. Without
minimizing the depth of the problem, this is a hopeful study which
shows that change is possible. d. Mark Lipman; p. Mark Lipman/
Emerge Films; NEWDAY; UCEMC.

TO HAVE AND TO HOLD: MEN WHO BATTER WOMEN see TO
    HAVE AND TO HOLD

TO LIVE WITH DIGNITY (30m C 1972)
Documents a three-month project on disoriented and confused elderly persons requiring institutional care at the Ypsilanti State Hospital. Using milieu therapy, the hospital staff involved the patients
in social interaction groups, group crafts, exercise, music therapy
and daily self-care. Explains the program which is designed to enable nursing homes and geriatric wards of mental hospitals to use

therapy adopted for frail and disoriented elderly people at little cost
and training. (Institute of Gerontology; UMTV, 1972.) UMMRC; UM.

TO LIVE WITH HERDS (70m B 1974)

Clearly demonstrates the effects of nation-building in pre-Amin
Uganda on the seminomadic, pastoral Jie. The film looks at life in
a traditional Jie homestead during a harsh dry season. The talk
and work of adults and the games of children go on, but there is
also hardship and worry, exacerbated by government policies that
seem to attack rather than support the values and economic base of
Jie society. A mother counts her children: among them is a son
she hardly knows who has joined the educated bureaucracy. Later
we find him supervising famine relief for his own people in a situation that seems far beyond his control. At the end of the film
Logoth, the protector of the homestead, travels to the west to rejoin
his herds in an area of relative plenty; at least for the time being
his life seems free from official interference. p./d. Judith MacDougall, David MacDougall; UCEMC.

TO LOVE (25m C 1973) (Spanish/Subtitled)

A special moment enjoyed by a husband and wife who rarely see
each other illuminates the meaning of love. The husband is a worker
at a mammoth bridge construction site; his wife brings him a picnic
lunch. p. Zagreb Studios; WOMBAT.

TO LOVE, HONOR AND OBEY (40m C 1980)

An exploration of violence against women in American family life.
Includes women who have been battered, abused as children, and
who are victims of incest. p. TWN.

TO THE PEOPLE OF THE WORLD (21m C 1975)

An emotionally moving report on the human rights situation and
the conditions of political prisoners in Chile since the military coup
of 1973. The film features personal accounts from two women who
were released from prison as a result of international pressure on
their behalf: Laura Allende, Socialist Deputy and sister of slain
President Salvador Allende; and Carmen Castillo, a militant of the
Revolutionary Movement of the Left. Also contains important documentary scenes of the September 11th coup and the arrest and detention of prisoners. d. Barbara Margolis; UNIFILM.

TO THINK OF DYING (58m C n.d.) (Video, Beta, VHS)

A frank conversation about death between two people dealing with
it: Orville Kelly, a terminal cancer patient and Lynn Caine, who
wrote the best-selling book Widow about her life and feelings after
her husband died of cancer. Kelly talks about what it was like to
be a patient in the cancer ward and Caine describes her feelings
visiting her husband when he was a patient. They both discuss
their feelings, mistakes and hopes and through this dialogue reveal
their philosophies about life. p. KTCA-TV, St. Paul, Minnesota; IU,
PBSV.

TO YOUR HEALTH (10m C 1956)
A highly persuasive cartoon about the use and misuse of alcohol.
It presents a clear explanation of how alcohol affects one and shows
some of the danger signs. p. John Halas, Joy Batchelor for the
World Health Organization; VIEWFI.

TO YOUR HEALTH SERIES (25-30m ea. n.d.) (also Video)
Physicians, health workers, and elderly men and women discuss
and demonstrate ways to promote physical and mental health. Titles
include A TIME TO FLOWER; SEXUALITY: SEVENTY ISN'T A SIN;
MENTAL HEALTH: TO BE AND BECOME; CHRONIC ILLNESS: ADD-
ING LIFE TO YOUR YEARS; MOVING TO POWER; NUTRITION FOR
LIFE: THE ECOLOGY OF HEALTH CARE; ALTERNATIVE AND AC-
TION; and THE SYSTEM AND YOU. p. Elderview; ELDRVW.

TOCCATA FOR TOY TRAINS (14m C 1957)
Shows toy trains as they journey from roundhouse and yards,
into stations and out, through countryside and village, and on to
their destination. All characters, architecture and objects with which
the sets are built are toys, most of them made a number of years ago.
p. Ray and Charles Eames; PF; UIL, UW.

TODAY'S GIRLS: TOMORROW'S WOMEN (9m C r1980)
Statistics, information and the realities concerning today's girls
and sexuality. The juvenile justice system, education and employment
are delineated. p. Girls Clubs of America, Inc.; GRLSCA.

TODOS SANTOS CUCHUMATAN (41m C 1982)
Looks at one Mam Indian village high in the mountains of Guatemala. Documents the annual sequence of harvest, fiesta, and mass
migration out of the village to work in the cotton plantations of the
lowlands. It shows how cash has become increasingly important to
the people of a once subsistence farming community. Illustrates many
of the changes at work in Guatemala today. d./p. Olivia Carrescia;
ICARF.

TOKYO STORY (134m B 1953) (Japanese/Subtitled)
A deceptively simple tale of an elderly couple who journey to
Tokyo, where they are received less than enthusiastically by their grow
grown children; then generational conflicts are stilled--momentarily--
by death. Director Ozu unfolds the story with warmth and quiet
emotion, but at the heart of his old world civility is a vision of alienation in the modern world as powerful as any by Antonioni and
Bergman. "A masterpiece."--Judith Crist, New Yorker Magazine;
Charles Michener, Newsweek. p. NYF.

TOM CAT'S MEOW (13m C r1976)
Based on an Italian fairy tale, the story is about good Mary who
lives with her stepmother and sister, Helen. They have a little tom-
cat to whom only Mary is kind. When Mary breaks a jug, the stepmother throws her out of the house. The tom-cat repays Mary for

her kindness and eventually finds a way to punish Helen. d./s.w.
Bozena Mozisova; p. Short Film Prague; PHOENIX.

TOM PHILLIPS (50m C p1977, r1978)
Examines the processes and philosophies of the popular British
artist who finds beauty and strangeness in the incidental and everyday. Phillips' paintings, drawings, prints, musical compositions,
and books are examined through animated reconstructions, footage
of the artist at work, and interviews. d. David Rowan; p. Margaret
Williams; AFA.

TOMORROW AGAIN (16m B 1972)
An epitaph to loneliness and the communication gap. A lonely
old woman in an ancient resident hotel desperately plans to seduce
the attentions of the other guests by impressing them with her fur
stole. As she unpacks the cape, chooses her prettiest dress and
applies a bit of rouge, she imagines the men putting down their newspapers to compliment her and speak with her and tell her how glad
they are to see her. After much daydreaming she finally makes her
grand entrance--but the guests do not notice because they are too
involved with themselves. (Pyramid, 1972.) PF, VIEWFI; RARIG,
UM, UMN.

TONDO: A ROUND ABOUT A ROUND (10m C 1971)
Beginning and ending with children playing with circular sculpture, the film centers on the endless variety of patterns formed by
dancers interacting with a giant hollow cylinder. Changes in lighting,
sound, and cinematic effects create a dazzling experience as the dancers move against a background of brilliant colors while electronic music is played. Dance Company: Mary Staton Dance School; Dance
Teacher: Mary Staton; Sculptor: Doris Chase; d. Skeets McGrew;
p. King Screen Productions; UM, SYRACU.

TONI MORRISON (28m C 1978) The Writer in America (Series)
Toni Morrison, author of three acclaimed novels since 1970, is
shown in a wide range of locations representative of her full and busy
life: on assignment in New Orleans, at her Random House office in
New York, at her Rockland County home, at a literary cocktail party,
and at the supermarket. What emerges is a biographical digest and
creative profile of one of America's foremost novelists. Morrison's
talent is evident as she reads from her novels: The Bluest Eye and
Sula, in which she describes the Black, midwestern community she
knew as a girl; and her third novel, Song of Solomon, a Book-of-
the-Month Club selection and National Book Award winner, which
evolved from a slave legend which claims that at one time Black people could fly. p. CORONET; UILL, PAS.

TOO EARLY, TOO LATE (105m C 1981) (In English)
It is a film about landscapes--landscapes recorded with a Lumière-
like precision and clarity. The film is divided into two parts: the

first part juxtaposes present-day views of French villages with Friedrich Engel's descriptions of the same locales at the time of the 1792 Commune; the second part shifts to Egyptian scenes, accompanied by a recent Marxist history of the country's resistance to colonialism. d. Jean-Marie Straub/Daniele Huillet; NYF.

TOTAL FITNESS IN 30 MINUTES A WEEK (30m C 1976)

A film adaptation of Dr. Laurence Morehouse's best-selling book on how to stay fit with a minimum of effort, through pulse-rated exercises. It dispels common myths about exercise and explains the importance of a five-point program of total fitness. PF.

"TOUCHING" PROBLEMS, THE (18m C 1982) (also Video)

Focuses on the problem of sexual abuse which is much more prevalent than formerly believed. Reveals that one out of five children have been sexually abused by the time they are 18 years old, and 70 to 80 percent of those victims are female. Usually the abuser is a relative, friend, or neighbor. The narrator explains what it can lead to, instructs children what they can do. Urges parents to listen and talk to children about sexual abuse as well as who they can turn to if they discover sexual abuse of a child. p./d. Jim Ross; s.w. Sandra Kleven/Joan Krebill; MTITI; UCEMC.

TOULA (THE WATER SPIRIT) (80m C n.d.)

TOULA is a tale of drought in the West African Sahel, the ecological belt between the savannah grasslands and the Sahara Desert. The tale is based on an ancient Fulani legend and enacted by the people of two villages in Niger. But the story is painfully contemporary. The film opens in 1972, during one of the most catastropic droughts and poor harvests in the region since the turn of the century. According to Fulani legend, a proper sacrifice must be made to the spirit of the lake if the land is to be reborn again. Long ago, the soothsayer advised the King to sacrifice his most beloved daughter and the villagers agreed. After the sacrifice the rains came. It appears that both traditional and modern means of dealing with overwhelming natural disaster are futile, and the film suggests that a healthy synthesis between the old and new has not yet been attained. p. Anna Soehring, Moustapha Alassane; DER.

TOWN MOUSE AND THE COUNTRY MOUSE, THE (6m C p1980, r1981 --U.S.) (also Video)

Presents in animation the well-known Aesop's fable about the town mouse and the country mouse with music and no narration. d. Evelyn Lambart; NFBC; BENCHMF.

TOYS FOR CHILDREN (29m C n.d.) (Video, Beta, VHS) Woman Series

Jane Galvin-Lewis of Social Change Advocates, a training organization dedicated to preventing the damaging effects of racism and sexism, discusses how parents can steer their children towards toys that are free of racist and sexist stereotypes. p. WNET-TV; PBSV.

TRACK AND FIELD SERIES FOR GIRLS, THE see JUMPING AND
    HURDLING; THROWING EVENTS, THE; RUNNING EVENTS, THE

TRADE-OFFS SERIES see LESS AND MORE

TRAILBLAZERS OF MODERN DANCE (60m C p1977, r1979) Dance in
    America Series
    Reviews the history of modern dance in America with rare film
footage and recreations of early modern dance performances. Shows
these choreographers and dancers: Isadora Duncan, Lynn Seymour,
Ann Pavlova, Ruth St. Denis, Vernon and Irene Castle, Helen Ta-
miris, Doris Humphrey, and Martha Graham. p. Judy Kinberg, Merrill Brockway; d. Emile Ardolino; p. WNET-TV; IU, UIL.

TRANCE AND DANCE IN BALI (22m B 1952) Character Formation in
    Different Culture Series
    A performance of the Kris dance, a Balinese ceremonial dance
drama whose theme is the never-ending struggle between the witch
and the dragon--the death-dealing and the life-protecting--as it was
given in the village of Pagoetan in 1937-1939. The dancers go into
violent trance seizures and turn their krises (daggers) against their
breasts with injury. Consciousness is restored with incense and holy
water. Written and narrated by Margaret Mead. p. Margaret Mead/
Gregory Bateson; NYU; PSU, NILU, UIL, UCEMC, UM, UMN, UIO.

TRANSFIGURATIONS see VIDEO DANCES

TRANSITIONS: CAUGHT AT MIDLIFE SERIES (30m ea. C 1980)
    (Video)
    A ten-part series that looks at the state of life between the ages
of 40 and 60. What happens during this period we call mid-life, who
does it affect, and what can be done about it? p. UMMRC; UM.

    MARRIAGE
    A trapped wife, a May/December affair, and a stale marrriage
are all problems that may hit hard at mid-life. Guest: Professor
Karen Mason. Host: Ted Kachel.

    WORK
    Time suddenly catches up with you, and you're not going to be
president of the company; you're too young to retire and too old to
start over. Now you want to find that old career again. Guest:
Larry Coppard. Host: Ted Kachel.

    AGING PARENTS
    Just when child-rearing problems are over, your parents need
you. They may be ill or incapable of taking care of themselves--but
possibly they don't need you as much as you think they do. Guest:
Alida Silverman. Host: Ted Kachel.

EMPTY NEST
The children are gone and you feel a new found freedom--or you may regret that you didn't spend more time with your kids. And suddenly you may find that you and your spouse have nothing to talk about. Guest: Erika Serlin. Host: Larry Coppard.

DIVORCE
When the problems of a twenty-year marriage end in divorce, everyone suffers. Spouses are hurt and angry, children feel rejected, and tension and anxiety build up among all of them. Host: Larry Coppard. Guest Philip Margolis.

HEALTH AND MORTALITY
Your physical reactions have slowed a bit, a friend dies, your eyes aren't as sharp as they use to be. Is your time running out at mid-life? Host: Larry Coppard. Guests: Theodore Cole and John Schwarz.

PHYSICAL CHANGES
Major changes take place gradually in our bodies throughout our lives, but suddenly at mid-life we experience an increased awareness of these processes. Host: Larry Coppard. Guest: Charles Wylie.

WIDOWHOOD
You've never been married, never had children, it's mid-life and you wonder if life has passed you by. Or a wonderful marriage ends in death at an early age. At mid-life all you can see is twenty years of emptiness. Host: Larry Coppard. Guest: Dorothy Brooks.

PARENTING
Just because the kids are grown, it doesn't lessen parental problems. Your children's values disappoint you, they no longer see you as an authority. Can it be that the investment of 20 years of your life in your children is crumbling? Host: Larry Coppard. Guest: William Morse.

INTIMACY
The myth of impending impotence or a resurgence of sexual interest. Suddenly at mid-life you are widowed or divorced. Must sexual relations end? Host: Larry Coppard. Guests: Bob Blood and Margaret Blood.

TRAPPED (8m C 1977)
Choreography, video synthesis, and film are fused. The dancers appear as an infinite receding succession of figures. The movements are made visible by trails of light, emanating from the limbs and torsos. Dancers: Peggy McCann, Diane Frank; Choreographer: Peggy McCann; p. Gene W. Weiss; WEISSG.

TRAVELS IN THE COMBAT ZONE (30m C 1980-1983) (Video, Beta, VHS) Concept Series

TRAVELS IN THE COMBAT ZONE is a woman's view of the harsh and beautiful realities of city living and her travels through the eternal combat zone of cities and men. Altered timing and digital effects are used to highlight the flamboyant nature of the poetry. The video artistry emphasizes different aspects of the lyrics--images dissected, quartered, washed with memory wipes that support and underscore the poetry in a precise marriage of image and poetic meaning. d./p. Doris Chase; s.w. Jessica Hagedorn, performed by Mary Lum and Maralyn Amaral, with music by Butch Morris. CHASED.

TREATIES (28m C 1975) (Video)
Host John Kaufmann retraces Native American treaty history from Colonial times to the present using archival photographs, reenactment and armchair narration. The film discusses the treaty both as a legal concept and a historical reality, and recounts vivid details about a number of treaties. Sovereignty, states' rights, the major Acts of Congress and important court decisions are also presented. Native American peoples' respect for the terms of the treaties and the rights which are guaranteed in them are emphasized. Produced for television. p./s.w. Sandra Osawa; d. Julian Finkelstein; BYU.

TREEO: TRAINING IN EQUAL OPPORTUNITY (17m C 1977) (slc)
Overview of terms and principles relating to fair employment practices: discrimination, federal contracts, labor relations, E.E.O. laws and litigation. For trainees. p. Olympia Media Information, New York; STPIERA.

TRIAL FOR RAPE (60m B 1979) (Italian/Subtitled)
A record of an actual rape trial that took place in Rome in 1978, brought against three men by a young woman named Fiorella. The entire proceedings were videotaped by six women and then edited into a one-hour program for broadcast over Italian television. In the trial, the lawyers for the defense reveal their deep-rooted misogyny through their justifications for rape, while the woman lawyer for Fiorella makes an eloquent plea for justice and respect. p. Maria Grazia Belmonti, Anna Carini, Rony Daupoulo, Paola DeMartiis, Anna Bella Miscuglio, Loredana Rotondo; WMM.

TRIANGLE SERIES see CONGRUENT TRIANGLES; JOURNEY TO THE CENTER OF A TRIANGLE; SIMILAR TRIANGLES; TRIO FOR THREE ANGLES

TRIBAL GROUPS OF CENTRAL INDIA: LIFEWAY, CEREMONY, DANCE (40m C 1978)
Daily life, ceremonial rites and dances of the Chota Maria Gonds, a hunting-gathering people from the easternmost part of Maharashtra, and the Pawara Bhiles, an agricultural people from the northwest portion of Maharashtra, a state in central India. Recorded in 1971-72. Made possible by a grant from the National Endowment for the

Humanities. d. Margaret Fairlie Kennedy, Mack Travis; p. School of Communications, Ithaca College; ITHACA.

TRIFLES (22m B p1976, r1981)
   A character study/mystery set in the rural Midwest during the Depression, the film explores the subtle relationships of husbands and wives pitted against each other in a search for the motivation behind a brutal slaying. d. Sandra L. Nervig; p. S. L. Nervig/ Steve Grossman; NERVIG.

TRIGGER FILMS ON AGING: "TO MARKET, TO MARKET," "MRS. P.," "THE CENTER," "DINNER TIME," AND "TAGGED." (15m C 1971)
   Five vignettes about aging, designed to trigger discussion: A cheerful old lady has a fine time in a supermarket until she hands food stamps to the checkout girl; an elderly volunteer loses her job because she lacks mobility; young and old people come into conflict at a recreational center; an old woman prepares a solitary but stylishly served supper; moving men cart away her furniture as an elderly woman sits and stares. UMMRC; PAS, UM.

TRIGGER FILMS ON HUMAN INTERACTION SERIES see ASSERTIVE-NESS ISSUES; COUPLES COMMUNICATION; PARENT-TEENAGER COMMUNICATIONS; PARENTING THE SPECIAL NEEDS CHILD; SCHOOL PROFESSIONALS AND PARENTS; SINGLE PARENTS-- AND OTHER ADULTS; SINGLE PARENTS AND THEIR CHILDREN; STEPPARENTING ISSUES; WOMEN'S ISSUES

TRIO FOR THREE ANGLES (8m C 1968) (also Video)
   Uses the movements of free-swinging angles, synchronized with specially selected music, to help make the geometry student aware of the relationships of a triangle's different components. Covers the equilateral, isosceles, and scalene triangles. In animation. p. Katharine Cornwell, Bruce Cornwell; IFB.

TROUBLE WITH RAPE, THE (28m C 1975)
   Explores the misconceptions concerning rape and how those misconceptions work against the victim. Uses interviews with three women of varying age and station in life, illustrating that rape can happen to any woman at any time. Reveals how the double standards and myths perpetuated by both men and women in society leaves the woman without support, even when her assailant pleads guilty. Thames Television, London; UIL.

TROUBLE WITH STRANGERS, THE (10m C 1975)
   Karen forgets the lessons she's been taught and is abducted by a stranger. Luckily, the police find her in time, and a policewoman gives Karen some important safety tips to remember. Hitchhiking, playing in deserted places, and taking shortcuts through alleys are

all discussed. Karen, and each member of the audience, learn how they can prevent trouble with strangers for themselves and their friends. p. Sid Davis Productions; AIMS.

TROUBLING DEED (30 sec. C 1982) (Video)
To advise potential home buyers to beware of former land title stipulations which might affect them. d./p. Margie Goldsmith, sponsor: American Land Title Association; PLANCS.

TRUCK DRIVER NAMED GRET, A (11m C 1982)
A profile encouraging the acceptance of women in nontraditional jobs. Gret is a 38-year-old wife, mother, and delivery truck driver. Explores her motives and varied attitudes of family members, storeowners, and people she encounters on the job. She shares amusing and difficult moments. She's seen on the job and at home with her family. Her husband adds input on resulting changes in the family dynamics since Gret took on this job. d./p. Ruth E. Levikoff; LEVIKOFF.

TRULY EXCEPTIONAL: CAROL JOHNSTON, THE (16m C p1979, r1979)
Born with one arm, Carol astounds audiences with her remarkable performance as the inspirational leader of Cal State Fullerton's gymnastic team. As she delivers her message that nothing's impossible, all audiences will want to reassess what is standing between them and what they want to accomplish in life. d. Jim Thompson, John Cosgrove; p. Jim Thompson; DISNEY; PAS, UIL, WSU.

TRUTH ABOUT WOMEN, THE (106m C 1957--United Kingdom)
Women-dominated omnibus of tales retold by a chauvinist from his point of view with much wit and humor. Cast: Julie Harris, Eva Gabor, Laurence Harvey. d. Muriel Box; KPF.

TRUTH IN LENDING--THE FACTS OF THE MATTER (15m C p1979, r1979)
Information to assist the paralegal and minority adults to learn about the Truth-in-Lending Laws and what their rights are under these laws. Free loan. p. Barbara Alexander; d. Jon Borstin; USDL.

TRY IT, THEY'LL LIKE IT (28m C p1980, r1980)
Explores ways parents can motivate their children. Marilyn Van Derbur offers no simple solutions to making children do what you want them to, or for handling the problem if they do not, but she does suggest some important and imaginative motivational ideas toward that end. p./d. Marilyn Van Derbur; VDBER.

TRYING TIMES: CRISIS IN FERTILITY (33m C p1979, r1980) (also Video)

Portrays the emotional impact of infertility on the couples involved, presents a model for professional intervention and explores the available alternatives: artificial insemination by donor, and domestic, independent or international adoption. The normal reproductive process, basic causes of infertility, and the general infertility workup are explained through unique animation. d. Timothy Sawyer; p. Joan Finck Sawyer; FANLTP.

TUBAL LIGATION (9½m C n.d.)
After first explaining the process of fertilization, the film describes the various permanent surgical procedures of terminating fertility. Depicts the techniques of laparotomy, mini-laparotomy, laparoscopy, colpotomy, and culdoscopy. Also available in Spanish. MIFE.

TUNUNEREMIUT: THE PEOPLE OF TUNUNAK (35m C 1974) The Alaska Native Heritage Film Series
In four vignettes, this film glimpses the lives of the people of Tununak, a village on the southwestern coast of Alaska. d./p. Sarah Elder, Leonard Kamerling; DER.

TURAS, LAS see LAS TURAS

TURNED LOOSE (28m C 1979) Begin with Goodbye Series
Focuses on changes related to our work. The segment includes interviews with Al Durham, who has been laid off from his construction job, and John Zuzuki, a research scientist who recently retired. With guide. MMM.

TURNING POINT, THE (119m C 1978)
THE TURNING POINT considers the time in every woman's life when she must choose between the commitment of a career and the demands of raising a family, as a young dancer (Leslie Browne) faces that decision. However, for two women, the choices were made years before: Browne's mother (Shirley MacLaine), a promising dancer, gave up her career for marriage and three children; Browne's godmother (Ann Bancroft), MacLaine's closest friend and rival, achieved international star status in the ballet role for which they had both completed. As middle-age approaches, MacLaine envies Bancroft's success and longs for recognition of her own talent; Bancroft, isolated, faces loneliness and age--alone. Together, they reexamine their lives and reach a new level of understanding. p. Herbert Ross, Arthur Laurents; d. Herbert Ross; ex. p. Nora Kaye; FOX; FI.

TURNING POINTS: A PROFILE OF THREE ADULT WOMEN IN COLLEGE (35m C p1978, r1979) (also Video)
A profile of three adult women who have made the decision at a turning point in their lives to attend college and pursue careers.

turning point in their lives to attend college and pursue careers. The women narrate their own stories as the film develops a realistic and intimate portrait of their daily lives at home, at college and at work. (Public service--non-profit) d./p. Stefan Moore, Claude Beller; ex. p. Dr. Deanna Chitayat; p. City University of New York; CORONET; PAS, UIL.

TWELVE DAYS OF CHRISTMAS (4m C 1977) (also Video)
To the accompaniment of traditional English folk song, sung by a school madrigal group, Santa's gifts--furred, feathered and human --appear and reappear, until Santa wipes his brow in relief when, on the 12th day, the whole assemblage gallops past, leaving only the stalwart partridge. In animation. d./p. Sheila Graber; FI.

TWENTIETH CENTURY SERIES see NAVAJOS AND ANNIE WAUNEKA, THE

TWENTY-THIRD CEASE-FIRE, THE (52m C 1976)
The climax of ten months of civil war in Lebanon was the massacre in Karantina carried out by the right-wing Phalangists. The left replied by taking the Christian town of Damous. A cease-fire followed. It was the 23rd cease-fire. This is the story of that brief interlude. p. Anne Papillaut, Jean François Dars, Marc Kravetz, Marc Mourani; ICARF.

2 A.M. FEEDING (24m C 1982)
A realistic look at parenting during the first few months after birth. It presents a diverse group of new parents, who relate their experiences with warmth and humor, touching on such parental concerns as nursing, crying, colic, fatigue, mother's recovery, sexuality, fathering, single parenthood, and returning to work. d./p./s.w. Kristine Samuelson; ed. Wendy Zheutlin; NEWDAY.

TWO BAROQUE CHURCHES IN GERMANY (11m C 1955)
By combining 296 stills of two mid-eighteenth-century German Baroque churches, Vierzehnheiligen and Ottobeuren, this film attempts to express the feeling of German Baroque and define what gave it such great style. Typical background music is played on organs of that day. p. Ray and Charles Eames; PF.

TWO CITIES: LONDON AND NEW YORK (23m C 1973)
Two international capitals--one fast-paced, restless, multi-national, the mecca for success to many Americans--the other, a busy financial and cultural center of British life, yet predominantly people-oriented. p. For LCA by Helen Jean Rogers and John Secondari; LCA.

TWO EARNER FAMILY, THE (29m C 1976) Woman Series
Writer Susan Edmiston and economist Dr. Carolyn Shaw Bell discuss the economic and sociological implications of women entering the

work force in increasing numbers. Sandra Elkin is the moderator.
p. WNED-TV, Buffalo, New York; PBSV.

TWO FACTORIES: JAPANESE AND AMERICAN (22m C 1974)
    An American factory worker is apt to consider the job a neces-
sary means to an end. To a Japanese, the job is an extension of
personal life; the company, a surrogate parent. Filmed at the Sylvania plant in Batavia, New York, and a Matsushita Electric complex
in Osaka, Japan. p. Helen Jean Rogers and John Secondari for LCA;
KENTSU.

TWO FAMILIES: AFRICAN AND AMERICAN (22m C 1974)
    The film confronts two contemporary family structures; an inter-
dependent African tribal family and an independent space-age family
in New York City. Members of the American family pride themselves
on being individuals, while the African clan is governed by a sense
of unity. p. Helen Jean Rogers and John Secondari for LCA; KENT-
SU.

TWO FARMS: HUNGARY AND WISCONSIN (22m C 1973)
    Provides an incisive comparison of the life-styles of an independ-
ent Wisconsin farmer and a collective farm family in southeastern Hungary. At first glance, the two seem as far apart culturally as they
are geographically, but both share an abiding love of the land, a
joy in the growing cycle and close family ties. p. Helen Jean Rogers and John Secondari for LCA; KENTSU.

TWO FRENCH FAMILIES (27m C 1979)
    Takes a look at the life-styles of a traditional large farming fam-
ily in western France and a young urban couple with one child in
Paris. It shows that despite growing differences in their life-styles,
French families, whether traditional or modern, remain strongly attracted to the same basic principles. Narrated by Dr. Lawrence Wylie, a Harvard anthropologist and author of numerous works on France.
p. Patricia Barnes, French Embassy, Press and Information Division.
Free loan. MTPS.

TWO KOREAN FAMILIES (59m C p1978, r1978)
    Shows the experiences of two Korean families living in New York,
one a recent arrival struggling to make a success of their grocery
store, and the second, a family of talented musicians who have lived
in the United States for almost 20 years. A large portion of the film
shows the Shims at home with their families talking (in Korean with
English subtitles) about their hopes for their children. Both the
Shims and the Chungs have kept their Korean traditions alive in a
very mobile society. They speak highly of the opportunity available
in the United States which allowed them to succeed through their
ability and not by family privilege. p./d. Patricia Lewis Jaffe;
MACMFL.

TWO LAWS OF ALGEBRA (4m C 1972)
The associative and distributive processes in algebra are presented through the animated manipulation of formulas. p. Ray and Charles Eames; PF.

TWO LITHUANIAN DANCES (15m C 1965-67)
Mikita, a pole-vaulting dance usually performed by men, and Malunas, a group dance for eight couples, performed by the Lithuanian Folk Dance Group of Philadelphia. Produced under the auspices of the Pennsylvania Department of Health, Education and Welfare, the University of Pennsylvania, and the Philadelphia Academy as part of a comprehensive dance curriculum program. Dance Director: Mrs. Viltis Puzinas; Project Director: Nadia Chilkovsky Nahumck; Associate Director: Fai Coleman; p. Calvin De Frenes Corporation; FRANDA.

TWO PUPPET SHOWS (9m C 1965)
A film version of two electronically controlled puppet shows on display at the IBM Pavillion at the New York World's Fair, each presenting amusing and novel ways to use the computer. p. Ray and Charles Eames; PF.

TWO TO GET READY (29m C 1979) (also Video)
In one sense, both parents are pregnant. The woman bears the child, of course, but both parents bear new feelings. The birth of the baby is also the birth of a parent--the start of a new way of life and the beginning of new responsibilities. Shows the ways parents prepare for parenthood, focusing on their psychological preparation. United States Department of Education; NAVC.

TWO TOWNS: GUBBIO, ITALY AND CHILLICOTHE, OHIO (22m C 1973)
Chillicothe, in southeastern Ohio, and Gubbio, located north of Rome, are both agricultural centers. Yet, one life-style looks to the future, while the other recalls the past. For all their differences, the film uncovers a civic pride and responsibility that may be a common bond of all small towns. p. Helen Jean Rogers and John Secondari for LCA; LCA.

TWO WOMEN: TWENTY YEARS (29m C 1975) (Video)
In 1954, Patsy Newell appeared on "Women in the World of Man," a TV program that dealt with the expectations of women toward marriage and career. Today, Tavi Fulkerson, 20, talks with Patsy Newell Turrini about what has taken place since 1954. Patsy views the old program and comments on her reactions. Guests: Patsy Newell Turrini, social worker; Tavi Fulkerson, student; Mary Bromage, college professor. p. UMMRC; UM.

TWO WORLDS OF ANGELITA, THE (73m C p1982, r1983)
The story of a young Puerto Rican family caught in a clash between

two cultures--theirs and the American one. Their story, which be-
gins in a small town on the island and ends in the barrios of New
York's lower east side, is told through the eyes of nine-year-old
Angelita. Dialogue in English and Spanish. d./p. Jane Morrison;
MORRISJ.

TWYLA THARP (30m C 1979) (Video)
    Dick Cavett interviews Twyla Tharp, dancer/choreographer. p.
WNET-TV; FI.

TWYLA THARP: MAKING TV DANCE (58m C p1979, r1980) (also
    Video)
    An exploration by one of America's most eminent choreographers/
dancers, Twyla Tharp, of the relationship between the complex technology of TV and the realm of dance. The freedom allowed by video
techniques and the creativity provided by Twyla Tharp's choreography
complement one another perfectly and make possible an exciting and
innovative dance/video work. d. Don Mischer; p. The Twyla Tharp
Dance Foundation; PHOENIX; UCEMC.

TYMPANI (28½m C 1981) (Video)
    The Laura Dean Dancers and Musicians perform a major new
dance work especially for television. Composer/choreographer Laura
Dean has gained widespread recognition as one of the most innovative
and vital forces in the world of contemporary dance. Her dances
have been described as tribal, hypnotic and ritualistic--combining
simple movements and complex rhythms. d. Chuck Waggoner; p.
Kathryn Esher; p. KTCA-TV; KTCATV.

TYNER--SHARED PARENTING (25m C p1980, r1980) (Video)
    How a mother and father really share the early rearing of their
four-month-old between themselves and an infant day-care center.
Delves into the thoughts of Tyner's parents and how and why they
decided on this way of life ... and how they handle their roles and
responsibilities. d. Neil Jacobs; p. Phyllis Silverman; CORNELL.

-U-

UGETSU (96m B 1954) (Japanese/Subtitled)
    With its parallel stories, its contrasts between the aspirations of
women and men, its lyrical affirmation of human values against a background of war and suffering, and its tolerance and sympathy for all
its characters, it approaches Shakespearean tragedy. Directed with
extraordinary insight and sensitivity by Kenji Mizoguchi. KPF;
UCEMC.

UJIMA (5m C p1975, r1979) The Seven Principles Series
    Demonstrates in animation the universality of the human exper-
ience through the folklore of people of African descent. Narrated by

William J. Faulkner. d./p. Carol Mundy Lawrence; p. Nguzo Saba
Films; BEACON.

ULTIMATE MYSTERY, THE (40m C 1973)
Captain Mitchell presents remarkable scientific data supporting
the claims of mystics through the ages that there is a oneness to all
living things. Sequences include lie-detector expert Cleve Backster's
discovery of consciousness in plants and in simple bacteria cells ...
acupuncturists and psychic-healers at work ... leading biochemist
Sr. Justa Smith's demonstration of enzymic changes caused by healer's hands ... and new visions of the power of consciousness. p.
Elda Hartley; HARTLEY.

UMBRELLA (28m C p1980, r1980)
Celebrates the worldwide presence--both simply practical and profoundly symbolic--of the umbrella: at weddings, coronations and coronary surgeries in Ghana, Britain, Japan and Nepal; from New Orleans jazz funerals to Bali pagodas; from Dallas assassinations to the
first walk on the moon; from Hollywood musicals to undersea life. d.
Kathy Levitt; p. Kathy Levitt, John Carnochan; LEVITT.

UMOJA (8m C p1973, r1979) The Seven Principles Series
Demonstrates in animation, the universality of the human experience through the folklore of people of African descent. Narrated by
William J. Faulkner. p. Nguzo Saba Films; d./p. Carol Munday Lawrence; BEACON.

UNCOMMON IMAGES (22m C 1977)
Black photographer James Van Der Zee came to New York's Harlem in 1908 and spent the next 60 years compiling a direct and fascinating record of the middle-class Black community. At 90, he leafs
through his portfolios and reminisces about his life, career, and special romantic vision. p. Evelyn Barron for WNBC-TV, New York;
FILMLB; PAS, UIL.

UNDER 21 (23m C p1979, r1979)
Documentary-style film dealing with Covenant House, which has
served over 20,000 runaway and castoff youth since Father Bruce
Ritter first began giving them refuge ten years ago. Father Ritter
and his staff discuss the exploitation children suffer from the Times
Square $1.5 billion sex industry. Shows a 24-hour crisis center of-
fering immediate help to youth in need, as well as one of the group
homes and the Christian volunteer community of spiritual support.
d. Micki Abele; p. Bill Muir; COVNTH.

UNDERMINING THE GREAT DEPRESSION (25m C 1981)
An oral history of a small town's unique means of survival during the Depression--gold mining in their own backyards. Five Jack-
sonville, Oregon "old timers" tell anecdotes recalling their community's
spirit and interaction during the "hungry thirties," when jobless

townspeople mined for gold in backyards, under streets, and even beneath houses, in order to eke out about $2.50 a day. Featuring interviews, historic still photographs and location photography, the film recalls a unique life-style and community spirit during hard times. Funded by a grant from the National Endowment for the Humanities. p. Bonnie Thompson, Jim Likowski; MEDIAP.

UNDERSCAN (8m B 1974) (Video)
Based on letters received by the artist from her Aunt Ethel. It is about the passage of time. The tape chronicles the daily events in the aging woman's life, including the gradual deterioration of both her body and her house. While the letters are read, photographs of Aunt Ethel's environment are seen; exterior shots of her house are followed by shots of the living room, which are in turn followed by pictures of more personal scenes in the kitchen and bedroom. These images are manipulated by the video underscan process which appears to distort and then compress the information, just as Nancy Holt has done in editing the letters. In this way the sound of Nancy Holt's voice reading her aunt's descent into old age interacts with the images. p. Nancy Holt; WMM.

UNDERSTANDING BABYSITTING (11m C p1979, r1980)
Shows how to seek and accept work as a babysitter in a business-like way. Such basics as finding out the number of children, transportation availability, hours required and fees paid are items that should be settled before a babysitter accepts a job. Also recommended are babysitting for people one knows, verifying referrals, and giving the name and address of one's employer to the parents. Stressed is the importance of arriving early, getting to know the children, finding out the details of bedtime and feeding procedures, etc. Also see HANDLING BABYSITTING EMERGENCIES and PLANNING BABYSITTING. p. Tom Solari; FILMCO; UMN.

UNDERSTANDING LABOR AND DELIVERY (18m C 1978)
Through the use of animation and clips of women in labor, tells how to recognize signs of labor. Shows what examinations and procedures one might expect upon entering the hospital as well as the various medical techniques that may be used during labor and delivery. The husband is seen providing support throughout the labor and delivery. d./p. Dan Lundmark; FLMVS.

UNDERSTANDING SEXUALITY (30m C 1980) (also Video) Look at Me
Series
Highlights: Importance of natural curiosity; development of male/female roles; exposure to reproduction. His or her own body is the subject of intense curiosity on the part of the developing child. This leads inevitably to an awareness of sexuality and questions with which a parent may not feel comfortable. The film helps parents answer these questions. It points out, as well, that an understanding of sexuality does not stop with biology, but involves a social awareness

of, and identification with male and female roles. Narrated by Phil
Donahue. d./p./s.w. Jane Kaplan, Wendy Roth; p. WTTW-TV; FI.

UNEVENTFUL DAY (29m C 1976)
    Looks at the processes of weathering the physical and chemical
forces that produce the variety and the beauty of our planets geo-
rama. d. Penny Crompton; OECA; FI.

UNION MINDED (55m B 1978)
    A historical documentary about women organizing in Texas in the
1930's and early 1940's. The film centers around the experience of
the locally notorious pecan shellers' strike of 1936. Available in
Spanish also. p. Alan Pogue; POGUE.

UNIQUE BEGINNINGS: TO LIVE OR LET DIE (30m C 1982) (also
        Video)
    Looks at the medical ethics, hospital costs and parental concern
involved in intensive care for newborns. p. Perennial Education,
Inc.; PEREN.

UNKNOWN EIFFEL (28m C 1975) (also Video)
    Portrait of Gustave Eiffel, the great engineering genius of all
time who left a legacy of landmarks all over the world including the
Eiffel Tower. d. Joan Laskoff; p. Lenox Art Corporation; FI.

UNMARRIED WOMAN, AN (124m C p1977, r1978)
    A woman is forced, when her husband rejects her, to seek inde-
pendence and individuality over and above being a sex object. In
the end she finds herself happy only when she is submitting to a
man. Filmed in the box-office realm of New York City's chic restaurants, white sofas, and the land of the avant-garde artist as entrepreneur. d./s.w. Paul Mazursky; FOX; FI.

UNNECESSARY SURGERY (29m C 1975) (Video) Women Series
    Authors Barbara Seaman (Free and Female, The Doctor's Case
Against the Pill) and Barbara Ehrenreich (Witches, Midwives and
Nurses and Complaints and Disorders: Sexual Politics of Sickness)
discuss the number of unnecessary surgical procedures performed
in America. They cite the hysterectomy and tonsillectomy as examples
and describe precautionary measures that should be followed to avoid
unnecessary operations. They also discuss sexism in the medical
field. Sandra Elkin, moderator. p. WNED-TV; PBSV.

UNREMARKABLE BIRTH, AN (52m C n.d.)
    A growing number of parents are concerned about the impersonal
approach to childbirth found in many hospitals. They find the procedures inflexible and often more geared to the needs of the institution than to those of the child and parent. Members of the medical
profession and parents discuss today's obstetric methods and the less
clinical alternatives a couple can choose. The film candidly records

the "prepared" birth of a baby and the interaction of the mother and father. d. Diane Beaudry-Cowling; p. Kathleen Shannon; NFBC.

UNTIL SHE TALKS (44m C p1980, r1981) (also Video)
A drama about a young woman's encounter with the legal system --a story of grand jury abuse. Judith Ashe is in jail. She has not been sentenced. She has not been tried. She has refused to testify before a federal grand jury and she is in jail until she talks. The film, based on real events, explores the legal system that put her in jail. Featuring Pamela Reed. d./p. Mary Lampson; p. Alaska Street Productions, Inc.; FIRRNF.

UP HERE LOOKING DOWN (20m C 1974)
Presents billboards in a new perspective. The viewer confronts the awesome task of painting a 40' x 60' canvas and meets the men who tackle these super-human images daily. Recaptures the golden age of billboards in the twenties; considers the impact of these giant advertisements on our society. There are parallels between realist painting and billboards--why is one considered art and the other merely advertising. d. Sandra Northrop, Malcom Leo; p. Sandra Northrop; FI; KENTSU.

UPWARDLY MOBILE (14m C 1982)
This whimsical and ironic film explores the effects of architecture and construction on urban living. The film relies on visual information juxtaposed with an operatic soundtrack to make its observations on the growing highrise scenery and the low-lying shadows below. p. Patricia Quinn; MEDIAP.

URASHIMA TARO (11m C p1979, r1979)
Animated version of a popular Japanese folk tale. Urashima Taro, a young fisherman, is rewarded for a good deed with an invitation to the Dragon Palace, deep beneath the sea. There he marvels at the many wonders, but is reminded of his parents and his responsibility to them. He returns home to find that 300 years, not just a few days, had passed. His parents and village are gone. He is transformed into an old man. d./p. Peggy Okeya; VISION.

-V-

V.D. AND WOMEN (17m C 1978)
A woman-to-woman film on what every sexually-active female should know about infections that can be caused by sexual intercourse: the symptoms, steps used by a gynecologist during an examination, treatment and the serious side effects resulting from infection. p. Crommie and Crommie; PEREN; UMN.

V.D.: OLD BUGS, NEW PROBLEMS (20m C 1977)
Acquaints the viewer with the many types of sexually transmitted

diseases. Among them are gonorrhea, herpes, non-gonococcal urethritis, syphilis, trichomoniasis, monilia, venereal warts, crab lice,
and scabies. In each disease the symptoms are clearly enumerated,
its dangers are defined, and the appropriate treatment is described.
Myths are dispelled, and those which can be contracted other than
through sexual intercourse are discussed. The special dangers to
expectant mothers are explained. Stressed are need for laboratory
tests to confirm and identify the disease, the checkup after treatment, and the long-term dangers of nontreatment. An excellent film
for both counselors and students. d./ed. Lee Rhoads; s.w. Robert
Hecker; p. Alfred Higgins Productions, Inc.; HIGGIN; CWU, IU.

VD QUIZ: GETTING THE RIGHT ANSWERS (25m C 1977)
    Designed to help young people understand the causes of VD and
the importance of prompt treatment of symptoms. Covers non-
gonococcal urethritis, trichomoniasis, herpes and gonorrhea. p.
American Educational Films, AMEDF; PAS.

V. DOUGLAS SNOW, PAINTER: THE CONTEMPORARY LANDSCAPE
    (28m C p1977, r1977) Four Artists, Live Series
    Examines the life of an artist in modern society. V. Douglas
Snow, at his home in Southern Utah, discusses his paintings and his
choice to live in an isolated area outside the mainstream artistic centers on the East and West coast. Snow demonstrates his manner of
creating a painting--he sketches a landscape and later in the studio,
he paints from the drawing. Many of Snow's paintings are shown.
p./d. Claudia Sisemore; SIZEMF.

VALENTINE LANE FAMILY PRACTICE: A TEAM APPROACH TO
    HEALTH CARE, THE (29m C 1978)
    The Valentine Lane Family Practice provides a new kind of pri-
mary health care that emphasizes treatment of the family as well as
comprehensive individual care. The Practice, an affiliate of Monte-
fiore Hospital and Medical Center utilizes the expertise of a team of
health professionals.... The team serves as a practicing model for
educational sites around the country interested in the concepts of
health team care. The members of this team work closely with the
community and encourage community participation and involvement in
issues of health. As one of the team members states, "one of the
self-help groups in the community--a lot of health care can be de-
professionalized in this way." The integration of the team's efforts
is vividly documented in scenes of the practitioners at work inside
the Valentine Lane Center, and outside, in the community schools,
neighborhood centers, and homes of its patients. Interviews with
the Practice staff reveal their attitudes towards health care in which
sick care is only one segment; preventive care and health maintenance
are major objectives of the Practice. Health care being one of our
national issues, the film offers significant information of interest to
the average consumer of health services as well as the health professional. p. Document Associates, Inc.; DOCUA.

VALENTINE SUITE (30m C p1981, r1982) (Video)
Follows a Philadelphia couple through birthing classes, classes
for siblings, prenatal examination and childbirth under the guidance
of a nurse-midwife. d. Ms. Zilan Munas-Bass; p. Julianne Powis;
TEMPLU.

VALENTINE'S DAY (6m B 1981)
A tongue-in-cheek documentary about a shopping mall contest.
Participants guess how long it will take for a heart-shaped ice-cream
cake to melt. It is a wry commentary on the growing commercializa-
tion of our holidays. p. Laurie Meeker; MEDIAP.

VALERIE--A WOMAN! AN ARTIST! A PHILOSOPHY OF LIFE (15m
    C r1975)
Explores some of the attitudes and insights of an extremely
gifted sculptor, Valerie Maynard, whose work is acclaimed in America and abroad. d. Monica Freeman; p. Nafasi Productions, Inc.;
PHOENIX.

VALIUM (18m C 1977)
Reports on the extensive use (and abuse) of Valium, a drug prescribed by physicians to relieve anxiety, relax tense muscles or cure
sleeplessness. Interviews with users who obtain the drug both legally and illegally attempt to shed light on why Valium is now the most
widely used drug in the world. Mike Wallace speaks with representatives of pharmaceutical companies whose advertisements for Valium
appear in medical journals. p. CBS News, "60 Minutes." CAROUF;
PAS, UIL.

VANISHING MOMMY, THE (25m C 1977) (ed. rel.)
Examines the role of the working mother in contemporary American society. Statistics show that over half of all American mothers
currently work outside the home. Several of those women and their
husbands discuss the positive and negative aspects of their careers.
Narrator points out, according to recent surveys, there is a greater
number of separations when both husband and wife work. In answer
to the question of whether "Mommy" is really vanishing, this film
shows that the traditional picture of a mother may be changing, but
she is still there. d./s.w. Steve Lorton; p. NBC-TV; FI; PAS,
KENTSU.

VANISHING POINT: PAINTING AND SCULPTURE OF NANCY CAM-
    DEN WITT (10m C 1972) The Virginia Artists (Series)
Nancy Camden Witt, Virginia artist, paints with such clarity that
gallery viewers are often compelled to touch her canvases to see if
the objects are real. But that, of course, is not the point. Rather,
it is the mysteries that lie beneath those surfaces which intrigue and
tantalize, like fragments of a half-remembered dream. Her self-
portraits record her search for the inner woman, the secret self who
lives within the psyche. The sea, the sun and moon, the glass jars,

eggs and apples, shadows and reflections, a jigsaw puzzle with missing pieces--these are her symbols for mind and body, the essence of our being. Perhaps we shall meet our secret selves "at the vanishing point, on the morning of forever." Till then they remain just beyond our grasp, suspended in paint and canvas--perplexing, eluding, fascinating.... Epilogue introducing the artist at Cross Mill Place. p. Charlotte Schrader; SCHRADR.

VARIATION TWO (10m C 1978)
A film/video variation on choreographic statement by Sara Rudner. Produced as the third segment of one of the "Doris Chase Dance Series." Won merit award at the 1979 Dance Video and Film Festival. Dancer: Sara Rudner; Composer: Joan LaBarbara; p. Doris Chase; CHASED.

VARIATIONS AND CONCLUSION OF "NEW DANCE"--RECORD FILM (7m C 1978)
The ending section of Doris Humphrey's "New Dance," choreographed in 1935, filmed in 1978. Dance Company: Connecticut College Repertory Company; Choreographer: Doris Humphrey; p. Dance Film Archive, University of Rochester; DAN/UR.

VARNETTE'S WORLD: A STUDY OF A YOUNG ARTIST (26m C p1978, r1979)
Merges the energies of two creative women--painter and filmmaker --to capture the distinctive quality of cultural life in the Black community. By juxtaposing the painter's vibrant images with action scenes in the church, school and on the street, the film reflects the spirit of her work and the people portrayed. d./p. Carroll Parrott Blue; TWN.

VASEBALL (6½m C 1979)
A man performs dangerous feats on a tightrope in an attempt to capture a runaway ball. p. Marguerite Craig; SERBC.

VASECTOMY (17m C 1972)
Designed for those who are considering male sterilization surgery, this film presents interviews with several couples who have found this form of birth control a convenient and safe alternative to other methods. Contains personal testimony about the ease of the operation, and attempts to allay common fears and feelings about vasectomy's physical or psychological effects. A urologist is seen as he answers questions. During the initial interview with a patient and his wife, animated diagrams are used to describe physiology of the male reproductive organs and details of the operation. Produced with the cooperation of the Planned Parenthood World Population, Los Angeles. Recommended the film be used with a physician, nurse or other informed persons present to make the presentation and answer questions from viewers. CF; PAS, UIL.

VASECTOMY (8m C n.d.)
A married couple who don't want to have additional children decide to have the husband undergo a vasectomy. Shows how the operation eliminates the risk of pregnancy and discusses the surgical
procedures involved, as well as the recovery period. Also available
in Spanish. MIFE.

VASECTOMY ... MALE STERILIZATION (29m B n.d.) (Video, Beta,
VHS)
This look at vasectomy takes into consideration both the physical
and possible psychological effects of one of the safest and surest
methods of birth control and uses documentary techniques to allay
the fears and misconceptions about this simple operation. p. KQED-
TV, San Francisco; PBSV.

VE CE VE/PORTRAIT OF A SHEPHERDESS (28m C p1980, r1981)
(Video)
This is the story of a 20-year-old city-born French woman who
has come to the country to learn the trade of a shepherd. The film
evokes a mood and place with loving care, revealing the daily labor
of the shepherd with intimate glimpses into a humorous and touching
character: Dominique. d. Patricia Dubos, Philip Holahan; p. Patricia Dubos; LBERGER.

VEILED REVOLUTION, A (26m C 1982) (also Video)
Egypt was the first Arab country where women marched in political demonstrations (1919); the first where women took off the veil
(1923); and the first to offer free public secular education to women
(1924). Today the granddaughters of those early Arab feminists are
returning to traditional garb, sometimes with full face veil and gloves,
which they call Islamic dress. The film looks at some of this history
and attempts to answer some of these questions. Made by an all-
women crew (British, American, and Arab). p. Elizabeth Fernea;
d. Marilyn Gaunt; ICARF; WSU.

VELDT, THE (24m C p1979, r1979) (also Video)
Adapted from one of Ray Bradbury's science fiction suspense
tales in The Illustrated Man. Well presented with satire and horror.
Recommended for creative writing classes. p. Bernard Wilets, d.
Dianne Haak; PHOENIX.

VERONICA (14m C p1978, r1978)
Veronica and her parents came from Poland. Veronica is nine-
years-old and in the fourth grade. She helps in her parents' bakery
and attends public school where there are many children of other
ethnic groups. d. Beverly Shaffer; p. Yuki Yoshida, Kathleen Shannon; p. NFBC; MEDIAG; PAS.

VERY ENTERPRISING WOMEN (15m C 1980) (also Video)
Five women who have survived and succeeded in business are

featured in this documentary. Their energy, imagination, and hard
work have led to accomplishments in enterprises as varied as market
research and truck farming. p. NAVC.

VIA DOLOROSA (THE PAINFUL WAY) (10m C 1978)
Shows how the people in Antigua, Guatemala celebrate the "Passion of Christ." After decorating the streets with colorful sawdust
and flower carpets, they take turns carrying the image of their
faith during the entire day along the Via Dolorosa, or Painful Way.
Also available in French. p. Claudine Viallon, Georges Payrastre;
p. Okexnon Films; DER.

VICTIMS (24m C 1981) (also Video)
Shows correlation between child abuse and violent crime, and
what some communities are doing about it. In this cinema verité
hosted by Christina Crawford, author of Mommie Dearest, it is emphasized that 80 percent of all convicts were victims of child abuse.
Shown are many offenders expressing their reasons for abusing their
children. The point that child abuse prevention can help deter future crime is made amply clear in this film. p./d. Chuck Wintner;
WINTNER.

VICTORIA AND ALBERT (60m C 1980) (also Video) Royal Heritage
Series
A description of the family life of Queen Victoria and Prince Albert and the background to their official duties at Buckingham Palace
which remains the center for State Ceremonial. The Palace at West-
minster and the mausoleum at Frogmore are shown. Narrated by Sir
Huw Wheldon. BBC; FI.

VICTORIA, QUEEN AND EMPRESS (60m C 1980) (also Video) Royal
Heritage Series
Sir Huw Wheldon looks at the growth of communications--the rail-
ways, the post and photography--and the revelation of the life of the
Queen and her family through the published extracts of her journal.
BBC; FI.

VIDEO DANCES (45m C 1977) (Video)
Three dances are filmed, "Contrast," "Tensions," and "Transfigurations," with eight variations. Dance Company: Dancer's World
of Springfield, Massachusetts; Choreographer: Trish Midei; p. Harry
Weisburd; WEISBURD.

VIDEO WEAVINGS (1976); ANIMA (1974); and UNION (1975) (27m C)
(Video)
By means of visual computer, ANIMA transforms Katie McGuire's
dance into lights and colors, reminiscent of the "light dances" of
Loie Fuller at the turn of the century. Music by Jordan Belson.
Broadcast in the WNET "VTR" Series and on WGBH, Boston. ELARTI.

VIETNAM: PICKING UP THE PIECES (60m C 1978) (Video)
The tapemakers were the first television journalists allowed in
Vietnam after the war's end. Traveling with unprecedented access
to the country's people, they visited Hanoi, Saigon, and surround-
ing provinces. (Inter-Media Art Center, October 14, 1978.) p. Jon
Alpert, Karen Ranucci, Keiko Tsuno; DOWCTC.

VIEWPOINT: LOVE STORY (15m C 1975)
Examines the ways in which mass communication and media rein-
force stereotypes in society. Specifying male and female roles. p.
Thames Ltd., London. HERVSL; UIO, UIL.

VILLAGE IN BALTIMORE: IMAGES OF GREEK-AMERICAN WOMEN,
A (63m C p1980, r1981)
Set in "Greektown," one of Baltimore's colorful ethnic neighborhoods, tells the story of four young immigrant women of the Greek
community. The film shows them living and growing up in a modern
urban society with values and customs which are very different from
those of their rural Greek heritage. Shot in cinema verité style,
this film penetrates far beneath the pageantry of ethnic festivities
into the soul of the Greek community and the abiding traditions which
sustain it as well as the awesome contradictions which confront it.
d./p. Doreen Moses; MOSESD.

VILLAGE OF NO RIVER (58m B/C 1981) (English and Yu'pik/Sub-
titled)
Shows the past and contemporary life of the people of Kwigillingok,
which means "no river," in southwestern Alaska. These people are
culturally and linguistically Yup'ik Eskimos. Both change and continuity in the culture are illustrated, present problems and concerns
are talked about, and the future is discussed. A villager, Elsie Jim-
mie, is translator as she introduces the people and describes the many
activities we see. Project director, ex. p., s.w. Barbara Lipton;
p./d. Stuart Hersh; NEWRKM.

VILLAGE POTTERS OF ONDA, THE (25m B 1966)
Traditional pottery-making techniques of Japanese in a remote
village in the mountains of northcentral Kyushu. Includes description
of personalities and attitudes of villagers, village social structure.
Film can be used to illustrate traditional views of male and female
occupational and social roles in Onda. p. Robert Sperry; SPERRY;
UOR; PSU, PAS.

VILLAGE WOMEN IN EGYPT (29m C 1975) (Video) Are You Listening
Series
A group of ten rural, tradition-bound Egyptian women--wives,
mothers, grandmothers--talk about their sex roles, family lives, traditions, and family planning concerns. The discussion reveals the
women dealing openly and honestly with their feelings about the customs and values they have grown up with while at the same time

confronting the new opportunities opening to them and their children. The program is a moving and personal document that should be seen by everyone concerned with international population or development issues. p. Martha Stuart; STUARTM.

VINOBA BHAVE: WALKING REVOLUTION (39m C 1969) (also Video)
Presents the philosophy of Vinoba Bhave and the Bhoodan movement as a second phase of Gandhi's plan for the revival of Indian village life. Shows events and programs which carries out Gandhi's plan. d. Mary Kirby, Robert Steele; p. Pilgrim Films Production; IFB.

VIOLETTE (123m C 1978)
A tantalizing and elegant puzzle based on a celebrated case of the 1930's: the poisoning of her parents by an 18-year-old girl. With Isabelle Huppert. d. Claude Chabrol; NYF.

VIRGINIA (20m B r1975)
Virginia is an elderly woman who has a hearing handicap. She is in an oppressive interview situation, on a darkened sound stage, responding to muffled inquiries from a condescending young man who watches her from the control booth. Her patience and gentleness with the interrogator and her triumph over the hardship life has dealt, evoke an admirable, unique portrait. An excellent discussion film on problems of aging, handicaps, women and psychology. p. Alan Bloom; DIRECT.

VIRGINIA ARTISTS, THE (SERIES) see VANISHING POINT: PAINTING AND SCULPTURE OF NANCY CAMDEN WITT

VIRGINIA HILL STORY, THE (90m B 1975)
This is the story of how one woman used her beauty and charm to satisfy her lust for possessions, and how this led her into the underworld and association with the notorious gangster Bugsy Siegel. Her story unfolds through her testimony during the 1950's Estes Kefauver investigation into crime. d. Joel Schumacher; p. Rosenberg; LUCERNE, SELECT.

VISIBLE INVENTORY SIX: MOTEL DISSOLVE (15m C n.d.)
A space filled with moving ... a series of panning shots of motel rooms in which the filmmaker stayed during semi-annual transcontinental auto trips--homogeneous accommodations lacking locational cues.... The sound track consists of two Gertrude Stein texts, "America I Came and Here I Am" and "American Food and American Houses," both from 1935. The film counterpoints word, spoken text, and photographs giving the viewer the alternate options of reading, viewing, and listening. p. Janis Lipzin; CCC.

VISIONS OF EIGHT (105m C 1973)
For the Olympic Games at Munich, eight of the world's most

accomplished directors assembled to make a film which would reveal aspects of the Olympics few of us have ever seen. They were Milos Forman, Kon Ichikawa, Claude Lelouch, Juri Ozerov, Arthur Penn, Michael Ffleghar, John Schlesinger, and Mai Zetterling, the only woman director in the group. Unlike any TV coverage, the film portrays much more than the enormous physical skill of the contestants; it captures the suspense and excitement, the humor, the pain, and the real beauty of sports. p. David L. Wolper Production; ALMI.

VISIT TO, A (SERIES) see VISIT TO A HONEYBEE FARM, A; VISIT TO A NATURE CENTER; VISIT TO A THEATRE; VISIT TO A WILD BIRD ISLAND, A; VISIT TO SNOW COUNTRY, A

VISIT TO A HONEYBEE FARM, A (10m C p1977, r1977) A Visit To (Series)
An introduction for children to a honeybee farm. p. Myrna I. Berlet for Journal Films, Inc.; JOURVI.

VISIT TO A NATURE CENTER (12m C n.d.) A Visit To (Series)
A crow acts as tour guide and narrator for the children who come to the Nature Center. Children observe how animals are cared for and how apple cider is made, and are taught camping skills. p. Myrna I. Berlet, Walter H. Berlet; p. Gilbert Altschult Productions; JOURVI.

VISIT TO A SEPULCHER (VISITATIO SEPULCHRI) (28m C p1979, r1979)
Reenactment of a medieval church music-drama, the story of the resurrection of Christ from the Fleury Playbook (MS 210, Bibliothèque de la Ville, Orléans). Filmed in France in the Abbaye St. Benoit de Fleury, the twelfth-century Romanesque church where, it is believed, the play was originally performed. The introduction, explaining the place and the play (which is sung a cappella, in Latin) is narrated by Alexander Scourby. p. Linda D. Hammack; d. John S. Allen; TRWAGV.

VISIT TO A THEATRE, A (14m C p1978, r1979) A Visit To (Series)
Provides young people a glimpse of the exciting world of theatre and an appreciation of play production. An amateur production of Cinderella is in progress. The young people see actual auditions, rehearsals, costume designing, set designing and building, properties, make-up, and technical crew responsibilities. p. Myrna I. Berlet, Walter H. Berlet; p. Gilbert Altschul Productions; JOURVI.

VISIT TO A WILD BIRD ISLAND, A (9m C 1978) A Visit To (Series)
Allen, a naturalist, introduces children to living habits of aquatic birds. p. Myrna I Berlet, Walter H. Berlet; JOURVI.

VISIT TO SNOW COUNTRY, A (9m C p1977, r1978) A Visit To (Series)

Introduces children to a variety of forest animals that are more visible in the winter woods. p. Myrna I. Berlet, Walter H. Berlet; JOURVI.

VITAMINS (12m C 1976)
Focuses on the role of vitamins in the body and the consequences of taking too many. Concludes with a comprehensive examination of vitamin C. An excerpt from Food ene. p. WPSX-TV; PAS.

VITAMINS (22m C 1980) Think Nutrition Series
Explodes the myths about vitamin supplements and uses of vitamins. Educates the viewer about vitamin enriched foods and emphasizes those foods which insure a nutritious, vitamin-balanced diet. Stresses proper food preparation with the aim of showing the viewer that an awareness of vitamin value in the foods we eat will make us healthier, happier people. p. National Film and Video Center; NATFVC.

VITAMINS I (33m C 1979) (Video) Introductory Principles of Nutrition Series
Begins with a discussion of a controversial issue related to the nutrient class followed by the "lesson" about the class. Emphasizes chemical composition, structural considerations, food sources, and functions. Includes a summary and integration of the introductory issue. p. The Pennsylvania State University; PAS.

VITAMINS II (48m C 1979) (Video) Introductory Principles of Nutrition Series
Begins with a discussion of a controversial issue related to the nutrient class followed by the "lesson" about the class. Emphasizes chemical composition, structural considerations, food sources, and functions. Includes summary and integration of the introductory issue. p. The Pennsylvania State University; PAS.

VITAMINS: WHAT DO THEY DO? (21m C 1978)
Using a lively format, vitamins are explained--what they are, how they work in our bodies, and why we need them. The various vitamins are discussed, the foods from which we get them, and the particular contribution of each vitamin to our health. The many myths regarding vitamins are explained. p. Alfred Higgins Productions, Inc.; HIGGIN.

VITAMINS FROM FOOD (18m C 1978)
Historical footage shows the discovery of vitamins, the curing of scurvy among sailors by Dr. James Lind in 1740 and the curing of beri beri in Java by Dr. Christian Rijkman in 1890. Both groups suffered extremely limited diets. The film explains coenzyme function in metabolism and suggests the food sources that can supply us with the vitamins we need. PEREN; UM, UMO, UCEMC.

VOICE OF THE FUGITIVE (29m C 1979) (also Video)
   In the 1850's, Canada meant freedom for many escaped slaves, but the route known as the "underground railroad" was a dangerous one at the best of times. This drama tells the story of one group traveling the perilous route. It tells, too, of the people who could be trusted to help and of the trackers and their dogs, who could cut off the lifeline to the border suddenly and very cruelly. p. Maxine Samuels, Roman Kroiter; d. Rene Bonniere; NFBC.

VOICES FOR ENERGY (22m C 1979)
   Traces the efforts of the New Hampshire Voice of Energy from its founding by Madeline Thompson, culminating in a July 4th rally staged in Seabrook, New Hampshire. Notes the endeavors of the group to support the construction of the Seabrook Nuclear Power Station. A testimonial to Mrs. Thompson. d. Lee Davis; p. Ralph Lopatin Productions; LOPTN.

VOICES FROM WITHIN (20m C n.d.)
   The Long Termers' Committee, a group of women at the Bedford Hills Correctional Facility who are serving sentences four years to life, are attempting to reform present legislation in New York State which denies long-term inmates many of the benefits provided to short-term prisoners. p. Pacific Street Production Corp.; PACISP.

VOICES OF EARLY CANADA SERIES see PIONEER GIRL

-W-

WAITING ROOM, THE (29m C 1981) (also Video)
   A provocative film for discussing the pros and cons of abortion. Presented as a fictional story, five women of different ages and ethnic backgrounds meet at an abortion clinic on the day of a Right-to-Life demonstration. Once inside the waiting room, the women begin to reveal how they feel about abortions and how it affects their families and themselves. The film points out the different pressures applied by the family, church, political groups and the medical profession. The final message is that there is no easy solution for women with unwanted pregnancies. p. Laura Louis; d. John Nutt; s.w. Donna Moriarty; CAROUF.

WAITING ROOM, THE (28m C p1979, r1979)
   A docudrama about one ordinary man's physical pain and emotional anxieties as ulcers gradually destroy his good health, career, and pleasant personality. Through the roles of the actor/physicians this film also documents the early symptoms of ulcers, their cause, diagnostic techniques, and medicine's latest methods of treatment. Free loan. p. Helen Kristt Radin; d. Lee R. Bobker; WESTGC.

WALDEN (10m C p1980, r1981) (also Video)
   Provides a sense of the spirit of Thoreau's ideas and writings,

an appreciation of Thoreau's work, and through his work, an appreciation of nature. Filmed on location at the height of the fall season at Walden Pond near Concord, Massachusetts, this film combines images of life, sounds of nature and readings from Henry David Thoreau's best known work, <u>Walden</u>. d. Sheila Laffey; p. Sheila Laffey/ Fred A. Cardin; ICARF.

WALK WITHOUT FEAR (20m C 1970)
A self-defense film for women. Prevention is stressed as the best method of defense, and several ways to take away an attacker's opportunities are illustrated. In addition, safe ways to fight back are demonstrated: screaming, scratching with keys and fingernails, biting, and kicking among them. Although the viewer is urged not to carry weapons that can easily be turned against her, the film reassures women that, while on the street, they are far from defenseless. p. Sid David Productions; AIMS.

WAR STORY, A (58m C 1982)
This docudrama is not a "war story" in the conventional sense of strategy and battles, but rather an account of the spirit and its will to survive physical and mental suffering. It is based on the diaries of the filmmaker's father, Dr. Ben Wheeler, written during his 3½-year captivity in a Japanese prisoner-of-war camp during World War II. d./p./s.w. Ann Wheeler; ed. Ray Harper; NFBC.

WARRIORS' WOMEN (27m C 1981) (also Video)
A film that brings the Vietnam War home by focusing on four veterans, the relationships with their women, and the negative effects of the war on these relationships. Interviewed are three men and the women in their homes. Shows how they differed in their responses to the war from relatively few adjustment problems; to ulcers, dermatitis, and difficulties with authority; to, most dramatically, suicide resulting from guilt and isolation. All four men experienced culture shock, ambivalence about the war, and a need to "sort out their feelings." The women sense this need, but do not know how to respond. d./p. Dorothy Tod; d. Alan Dater; TODF.

WASH (3m C 1976)
Abstract patterns of water and color gradually transform themselves into a representational image. (Museum of the City of New York, October 22, 1978.) p. Cathey Billian; MUSNYC.

WASHINGTON SQUARE WRAP (28m C p1980, r1981)
An exploration of the creative process and the record of an achievement: when New York artist Francis Hines wrapped Washington Square Arch in 8,000 yards of polyester gauze, the result was a new look at a familiar site, and a rare opportunity for the general public to partake in the creation of a work of art. d./p. Patricia Sides; COEFA.

WASHOE (56m B 1969) (Washoe, with English Narration)

Shows the families of the Washoe Reservation Indians in Dressler-
ville, Nevada where nature has been and still is a dominant force in
their lives. In this small town of 29 families, traditions are being
challenged by the encroachment of white society. Shows many of
their day-to-day activities as well as their many rituals. p./d. Veronika Pataky; p. McGraw-Hill Films; UNEV.

WATCHWORD: CAUTION (27m C 1973) Community Protection Series
Women are particularly vulnerable to crimes of personal assault.
Topics include self-protection when driving a car, riding public
transportation, dangers of hitchhiking, dealing with purse-snatchers,
handling obscene telephone calls, admitting strangers at home, mug-
gers, walking alone at night, indecent assaults, dangers of "Lover's
Lanes," unauthorized deliveries, and servicemen. A policewoman and
a legal authority discuss the problems. p. Summerhill Productions;
PARACO.

WATER FROM ANOTHER TIME (29m C 1982) (also Video)
Portrays three elderly rural artists in their home settings as
ordinary people with extraordinary talents. Designed to dispel negative myths some hold about the elderly by portraying them as thinking and independent people with the ability to contribute significantly
to their culture. p. Richard Kane; Kane-Lewis Productions; d. Richard Kane/Dillon Bustin; s.w. Dillon Bustin; KANELEW.

WATER MOTOR (9m B si n.d.)
Trisha Brown in her post-modern solo, shown twice, the second
time in slow motion. p. Dance Film Archive, University of Rochester; DAN/UR.

WATER STUDY (22m C n.d.)
Doris Humphrey's famous 1928 work performed in 1980 by a group
under the direction of Ernestine Stodelle. The dance is shown twice:
first at a distance, then closer. p. Dance Film Archive, University
of Rochester; DAN/UR.

WATER: THE HAZARDOUS NECESSITY (26m C n.d.)
Water means life, but more than half the world's people do not
have safe drinking water. In many parts of the world any water,
however polluted, is welcome. Experts insist we have the means to
eliminate, or at least alleviate, the physical and social conditions
which allow water-borne tropical diseases to flourish. But so far
economic and political considerations have taken precedence over human misery. d. Tina Viljoen; p. Barrie Howells; NFBC.

WATERGROUND (16m C 1977)
This documentary shows a water-powered gristmill and introduces
us to Walter Wineberger, who operates it. He is the fifth generation
of his family to operate the mill in Meat Camp, North Carolina. Built
100 years ago, the mill functions today as it did then, affording a

viable expression of the social change of a century. p./d. Frances Morton; APPAL.

WATERWHEEL VILLAGE (14m C 1977)

Two brothers find a miniature village along a stream. When they find out that a girl had built it, their eagerness vanishes and they leave to build their own village. They are unable to build a village as nice as the girl's village, but the older brother disdains the younger one's desire to ask the girl's advice. They argue and the younger brother leaves his brother and goes to the girl. Left alone, the older brother has time to reflect on being bossy and his prejudices. Finally, he joins his brother and the girl. With mutual respect for each other, they enjoy the wonders of the waterwheel village. p. Peggy Wolff; FLMFR.

WAY, THE (28m C 1975) (Video)

A broad sketch of Native American religion and its place in contemporary Indian life. The program host breaks down the religious world view into four essential elements--understanding the world as a sacred place; maintaining the spiritual essence, or medicine, of the religion; living according to a rule of life, or The Way; and respecting the prophesies. The program draws on both archival and contemporary sources to show the vitality of Native American religions today. Especially interesting is a long sequence shot on location at a Cherokee ceremonial ground in Oklahoma, in which three religious leaders from the Cherokee, Cheyenne, and Ojibwa tribes reflect on their religious practice and Indian spirituality. Written and produced for television by Native Americans. p. Sandra Osawa/KNBC-TV; BYU.

WAYS OF SEEING, THE (SERIES) see WOMEN AND ART

WE WILL HAVE OUR REASONS (28m C 1981)

We all have our reasons for drinking, yet seldom do we examine our reasons. This film takes us into a group of women alcoholics whose sobriety ranges from one week to five years. We hear them talk about their experiences with alcohol, alcoholism and sobriety. We hear the director of the Alcoholism Center for Women in Los Angeles talk about the center, the women who come there for treatment and about herself and her own experiences as a sober alcoholic. p. Iris Feminist Collective, Inc.; IRISFC.

WE DIG COAL: A PORTRAIT OF THREE WOMEN (58m C 1982) (also Video)

On October 2, 1979, Marilyn McCusker was working deep under the soil of central Pennsylvania. It had taken her two years, and a sex discrimination suit in federal court, to get her job as a coal miner. But, finally, the Rushton Mining Company had hired McCusker and two other women as deep miners. When the mine roof over her head collapsed, Marilyn McCusker became, at age 35, the first

woman to die working inside a deep mine in the United States. A
powerful documentary about McCusker, Bernice Dombroski and Mary
Louise Carson. It is about their struggle to be hired, about their
day-to-day lives in the mines, about the economic necessity that first
drove them to seek work in the mines, about the community hostility
they faced, and about the death of Marilyn McCusker, coal miner.
p. Dorothy McGhee, Gerardine Wurzburg, Thomas C. Goodwin;
STRATEA.

WE WERE JUST TOO YOUNG (30m C r1980) (also Video)
Questions the "anyone-can-do-it" attitude about parenting and
child rearing by focusing on two teens who conceived a child and
had to face the truth about parenthood the hard way. MTITI; UMN,
UM.

WE WILL NOT BE BEATEN (35m B 1979)
Women who have been violently assaulted by their husbands and
lovers speak candidly about their experiences. p./d. Mary Tiseo,
Carol Greenwald; p. Transition House Media; IRISFC.

WEAVING WITH LOOMS YOU CAN MAKE (16m C 1973, r1974)
Simple, homemade looms can be used to produce useful, attractive, and creative examples of the art of weaving. Corrugated card-
board served as the loom for a woven collar. Principles of weaving
are demonstrated, and the terms warp, weft, shed, heddle, and
shuttle are explained. p. Nancy Belfer, Dr. Clem Terkowski; p.
ACI Films; AIMS.

WEDDING CAMELS, THE (109m C p1978, r1979) (Turkana/Subtitled)
An anthropological film about the Turkana people of Kenya. It
focuses on the negotiations for a profitable bridal exchange. Lorang,
father of the bride, is trying to strengthen his family's economic position through the marriage of his daughter. The filmmakers do not
intervene while the bridegroom and father dicker over the exchange
of daughter and animals. The film is, in large terms, an expressive,
often comical, study of human nature (Film Forum, November 23,
1978). p. Judith MacDougall, David MacDougall; UCEMC; UW, PAS.

"WEDDING DAZE"--A FILM ON STRESS MANAGEMENT (22m C 1979)
Identifies various sources of daily stress and the psychological
and physiological effects it has on individuals by focusing on the
stresses and strains of a wedding day. Dramatizes the stresses which
affect the members of a wedding party, who reveal their ability or
inability to cope with problems and anxieties. Proposes exercise,
relaxation, planning, and management as techniques to reduce stress.
Narrated by Mario Machado. p. Paramount Communications; AIMS;
IU.

WEDDING IN THE FAMILY, A (22m C 1977)
During the week before the wedding of her younger sister, the

filmmaker returns home to observe the members of her own family, recording everyone's attitudes, behavior and feelings about the event to come. The result is a delightful, sometimes hilarious, sometimes painful, examination of two generations' changing expectations for young women and men, and the conflicts and confusions of growing up female in America today. p. Debra Franco; NEWDAY; WSU.

WEDNESDAY'S CHILD see FAMILY LIFE

WEEK FULL OF SATURDAYS, A (17m C p1978, r1979)
    Shows how pre-retirement planning is an essential for a satisfying life in the later years. Several men and women, from different backgrounds discuss such practical matters as housing, finances, family relations and leisure time activities. Guide available. d. Nicholas Dancy; p. Carol Ann Kradlak; s.w. Evelyn Mayer; p. Alternate Choice, Inc.; FILMLB; PAS.

WEEKS AFTER BIRTH, THE (29m B 1956) Months Before Birth--A Series
    Discusses the care of the mother after delivery and demonstrates exercises designed to aid the mother in rapid and thorough recovery. p. WQED-TV; AF.

WEIGHING THE CHOICES: POSITIVE APPROACHES TO NUTRITION (20m C 1981) (also Video)
    Suggests positive, practical choices for meals that will improve fitness and aid weight control. p. Spectrum Films; SPECTR.

WELCOME TO MIAMI, CUBANOS (28m C 1982) (also Video)
    A sign "Bienvenidos a Miami," greets the Cuban refugees at the newly constructed processing center. However, the welcome is not a warm one, especially from Mike Lopez, who arrives home to discover his house in disarray. Three of his relatives from Cuba are arriving and Mike only sees trouble ahead. Through a series of misadventures with his cousin Tito, Mike learns valuable lessons. He begins to understand the importance of family, of love, of heritage, and of sharing. He discovers that America is a country where you can "be American and be something else at the same time." p. Elaine Sperber; d. Peter Schifter; LCA.

WELCOME TO PARENTHOOD (16m C p1979, r1981) (also Video)
    Shows that having a family requires an investment of time, love and energy. With rare candor, three articulate young couples describe the abrupt change in their lives brought about by having children. This film will be invaluable in courses dealing with marriage and family, child development, and sex roles. p. Colette Vanderlinden; FILMLB; PAS.

WELFARE AND THE FATHERLESS FAMILY (15m C n.d.)
    Examines the lives of residents of a low-income apartment complex

and a welfare system that helps to disintegrate the American family by offering money if the fathers are absent. p. CBS News; CAROUF.

WELL, WE ARE ALIVE! (30m B 1980) (Video, Beta)
Explores the attitudes of family, friends, and society toward the aging individual. A consciousness-raising experience, the tape pulls into focus such issues as living on a fixed income, coping with the social services maze, physical and mental difficulties, self-image and societal expectations and life-style options. The process of aging and defining independence are presented through the eyes of old and young. The tape will serve as a catalyst for all to reevaluate their attitudes toward older people and to confront the fact that they are growing older themselves. p. Greta Schiller, Abigail Norman; WMM.

WE'RE COUNTING ON YOU (30m C 1981) Professional Skills for Secretaries Series
Begins with a detailed discussion of the role of the secretary today. How secretaries fit into the corporate structure. How their jobs interact with those of their bosses. The program instills a positive attitude toward the position of secretary and makes clear the vital function a secretary plays in the business world. Besides showing the qualities and skills a good secretary should possess, this program gives guidelines for participants to take stock of their own aptitudes and abilities. Leader's manual and participants' handbooks included. p. Time-Life Video; TIMLIF.

WE'RE MOVING UP! THE HISPANIC MIGRATION (80m C 1980) (Video)
Examines the impact of Hispanics on American society. Hispanics are the fastest-growing minority in the United States. There are 12,000,000 here now, and it is anticipated that by 1990, Hispanics will surpass Blacks as the country's largest minority group. Over half come from Mexico--many as illegal aliens. Puerto Ricans, Cubans, and South Americans add to the influx. Clearly the Hispanic population will become a major force in the years to come and America must be prepared to cope with this enormous wave of new immigrants. NBC White Paper. p. Patricia Creaghan, Jean Venable, Anne Chambers; p. NBC News; FI.

WERE YOU THERE WHEN THE ANIMALS TALKED (20m C 1975)
Study in Afro-American folklore as told by Reverend William Faulkner, a folklorist, minister, and master griot (story teller). p. Carol Mundy Lawrence; d. Robert Zagone; SABAN.

WEST AFRICA: TWO LIFE STYLES (18m C 1970)
Occupations, recreational activities, and family life of two West Africans are compared and contrasted. One is a yam farmer and one is a successful wealthy businesswoman in a modern African city. p. F. Gardonyi, C. Janoff; PHOENIX; KENTSU.

WESTINGHOUSE IN ALPHABETICAL ORDER (12m C 1965)
A tour de force of product presentation, picturing some quick

glimpses of Westinghouse products--in alphabetical order. p. Ray
and Charles Eames; PF.

WESTLANDS (C 1978)
    Focuses on the struggle between small and large farmers over
federal water rights in California's Central Valley. p. Sandra Nichols; NICHOLSS.

WHALESONG (8½m C 1980)
    "An animated mood piece both romantic and lyrical. We are at
sea searching for whales, capturing a rare glimpse of their presence,
caught in a watery atmosphere which approximates the flow and texture of a dream ... the delicacy of light falling on water, glimmering,
changing and disappearing."--Karen Cooper, Film Forum. p. Mary
Beams; SERBC.

WHAT ARE YOU, WOMAN? (25m C p1975, r1977)
    Explores facets of womanhood through problems which can be
universal but which have a special edge as they are experienced in
each ethnic area. Four vignettes concerning various aspects of womanhood and its related problems comprise this film. Also see SPEAK-
ING OF MEN. p. William Ditzel Productions/Wittenberg University;
d. Patricia O'Connor; PHOENIX; UIL, KENTSU.

WHAT CAN A GUY DO? (15m C 1980) (also Video)
    Designed to help young men break down the personal and social
barriers to getting information about birth control. Not a technical
film, rather it provides material for discussion about attitudes toward
birth control. p./d. Marc Fine, David Shapiro; SERBC.

WHAT CAN I TELL YOU? (55m C 1978) (also Video)
    A portrait of three generations of women in an Italian-American
family, which explores both the changes in the roles of the three
women, as well as the essentially timeless quality of family life. Highlighted are the mother-daughter relationships through the three generations. Home movies of the family taken over the last 25 years are
intercut with the documentary footage. d. Victress Hitchcock; p.
Suzanne Schneider; CENTRE; WSU.

WHAT COULD I SAY? AN ASSERTION TRAINING STIMULUS PRO-
        GRAM (18m C 1979) (also Video)
    This is a series of 20 vignettes that present viewers with common
situations requiring responsibly assertive responses. Included are
scenes from social, sexual, office, consumer, marital, and family life.
Time is provided after each vignette so that viewers can discuss appropriate responses. Leader's guide included. An invaluable training
aid for anyone conducting assertion workshops or for any group concerned with developing assertiveness skills. p. Norman E. Baxley.
RESPRC; UMN.

WHAT COULD YOU DO WITH A NICKLE? (25m C 1982) (also Video)
Examines the heroic struggle of a group of Latin and Black household workers, living and working in the South Bronx, to form a union. Follows the women as they spark a city-wide campaign to organize the over 30,000 household workers in the State of New York. d.
Cara DeVita, Jeffrey Kleinman, Lillian Jimenez; p. NEWT-TV; NEWTTV.

WHAT DO YOU SEE, NURSE? (12m C 1980)
Reconstructs, through flashbacks, the life of an elderly woman,
now a patient in a nursing home. Based on a poem by Phyllis Mc-
Cormack, a nurse in Scotland. From a moment when she is wakened
by a nurse, the principal character's life is conveyed in a skillful
interplay of action, flashback and dialog which provides, with some
emotional impact, insight into moments typical of lives in homes for
the aged. p. Gordon-Kerchoff Productions, Inc.; CENTEF; KENTSU,
UIL, WSU.

WHAT IF YOU COULDN'T READ? (28m C 1979) (also Video)
Lyle Litchfield, a 40-year-old Vermont farmer, was a respected
member of his community. Nobody, except his wife, knew that he
could not read. He was hounded by the fear of being discovered
illiterate. Then his life changed. He learned to read through a
community basic adult education program. His wife, whom he had
leaned on to interpret messages from the outside world, felt the loss
as he became independent of her. Growth, to her, was a double-
edged sword. This portrait shows how great a handicap illiteracy is,
both emotionally and practically. p. Dorothy Tod; FILMLB.

WHAT IS NEW? (52m C 1979) The Magic of Dance (Series)
Margot Fonteyn looks at the work of some of the leading dancers
and choreographers who were pioneers--from the Commedia dell'Arte
in seventeenth-century Italy to Martha Graham in twentieth-century
America. Includes performances by Fonteyn and Baryshnikov of
Fokine's famous ballet Le Spectre de la Rose. Also features Susanne
Kirnbauer, Kyra Nijinsky, Patrick Harding-Irmer, London Contempor-
ary Dance Theater and Teatro al'Avogaria. p. BBC/Time-Life Video;
TIMLIF; UMN.

WHAT IS THE MOST IMPORTANT PRIORITY OF A TEACHER? (28m
C p1980, r1980) You Can Do It ... If Series
Stressing the vital importance of teaching as a career, motivational expert Marilyn Van Derbur speaks about the great need of students to first believe "I am important, I am somebody" before being
in a position to learn. She reminds teachers that they need to respond with sensitivity, interest and respect, and that they can make
their classes relevant, personal and important. Van Derbur says
dedicated teachers are needed as never before. p. Marilyn Van Derbur; VDBER.

WHAT IS THIS THING CALLED FOOD? (ed.) (52m C 1977)

Presents the implications of a wide range of additives now being used in food, and the possible effects of these additives. Betty Furness, the narrator, states there are currently over 5,000 legally allowed chemical additives to food, serving as emulsifiers, preservatives, colorings, flavorings, thickeners, etc. Scientists point out the dangers of combinations of these chemicals in the body, and the long-range cumulative effects some of the additives may cause have not been studied sufficiently. A provocative study of food additives. p. NBC-TV; d. Thomas Tomizawa; FI; PAS, UIL.

WHAT JOHNNY CAN'T READ (13m C 1980)
This awareness film raises serious questions about censorship and textbooks for public schools. Traditionally, educators have made decisions about what books are read in schools, but now special interest groups are insisting on having a voice in the book selections. This film features Norma Gabler, a Texan, who wants her views represented as well. She and her husband have embarked on a crusade to get their conservative values represented in textbooks, and publishers often change texts so they won't lose the lucrative Texas market. Books adopted for the Texas schools are also sold throughout the country. CAROUF; UMN, UCEMC.

WHAT MAKES A GOOD FATHER? (60m C n.d.) (Video, Beta, VHS)
Profiles of three different fathers and their families show the characteristics of a good father and provides a warm personal look at the problems and joys of fatherhood. The program examines the lives of Jim Grant, Lou Watson and Sol Gittleman--three fathers who live different life-styles, but who all believe in and are helping to salvage the concept of the American family. The men freely discuss their fears and hopes for their children. Pediatrician and author Berry Brazelton, Ph.D., is the moderator. p. WGBH-TV; PBSV.

WHAT MARY JO SHARED (13m C p1980, r1981) (also Video)
Every day Mary Jo's class has a period known as "sharing," during which the children bring in some special object from home to enjoy with the others. Mary Jo has never brought anything to share, saying she must find something really worthwhile first. Finally, very unexpectedly, Mary Jo stumbles on the perfect solution, and her sharing time turns out to be the best the class ever had. d. Diane Haak; p. Bernard Wilets; PHOENIX.

WHAT MARY JO WANTED (14½m C 1982)
Mary Jo wanted her own dog more than anything. Every day she asked her parents for a puppy and finally they agreed. Mary Jo loved her new puppy, but at night he cried and cried. She tried everything to comfort him, but nothing worked. Finally she decided to sleep in a cot near her puppy until he was used to being without his mother. Now everyone could sleep all night. Story from the book by Janice May Udry. d. Diane Haak; p. Bernard Wilets; BARRF.

WHAT NEXT? (29m B 1970) (also Video) Contemporary Dance Series
    Innovations in contemporary dance with three examples of exper-
imental work: "Spart" (Bergmann), "I Hear You're Threatening That
Woman, Young Lady" (Burt) and "Permanent Wave" (Ellis). Vocal
music and electronic music accompany the dances. Dancers/Choreog-
raphers: Tanya Bergmann, Deidre Burt, Linda Ellis; Narrator: Robert Luscombe; d. Marshall Franke; p. Selma Odom; UMMRC; UM.

WHAT PRICE MIRACLES? (29m C 1980) (Video)
    High technology health care is doing much to ease suffering and
prolong life, but at enormous costs. This program from the public
television series "United States Chronicle" points out that there may
soon be questions about which miracles get financed and which don't--
questions which may determine who lives and who dies. p. Georgi-
anna Day; p. The Pennsylvania State University; PAS.

WHAT SHALL WE DO ABOUT MOTHER? (49m C 1980) (also Video)
    Shows the heartbreak experienced by two families when they have
to make emotional and financial decisions about what to do about their
aging parents. At the turn of the century only one American in 25
was over 65. Today the figure is one in nine; in 50 years it will be
one in six. For the rich, old age is manageable. It is somewhat
manageable for the poor, who simply turn themselves over to state
care. But what about the middle class? These citizens face a tragically bleak future. Often their care becomes the burden of their
middle-aged children who feel resentment and guilt. The government
and society are failing to meet their needs. What is to be done with
mother? Today, we ask the question on behalf of our parents. Tomorrow, our children will be asking it about us. p./d. Judy Owens
Reemtsma for CBS News. p. CBS News; CAROUF; UCEMC; UM, UMN,
USFL, KENTSU, IU, UIL, PAS.

WHAT TEACHER EXPECTS ... THE SELF-FULFILLING PROPHECY
    (26m C n.d.)
    Presents a provocative theory of interest to educators and par-
ents: a child's performance in school is more often the result of what
the teacher expects of him or her rather than what an intelligence
test might indicate he or she is capable of. This theory is discussed
by Dr. Robert Rosenthal of Harvard University, Dr. M. Sam Rabino-
vitch of McGill University and the members of Montreal Children's
Hospital. The theory is demonstrated in teacher-pupil situations
where the subject is word recognition. p. Dorothy Courtois, Joseph
Koenig; d. Barrie McLean; NFBC.

WHAT TIME IS THE NEXT SWAN? (8m C p1975, r1976)
    Presents behind-the-scenes look at the conductor Sarah Caldwell
at work with her opera company in Boston. Begins with interviews
with patrons on the street as to their reasons for attending an opera,
then breaks away to all the backstage activities before a performance.
Conveys much of the spirit and dedication on the part of Sarah Caldwell

as well as the cast and technicians. p. University Film Study Center, Inc.; p./d./s.w. Wayne Wadhams; PHOENIX.

WHAT WE HAVE (32m C 1978)
Portrays some of the things which happen when grandparents come to a local grade school, bringing the wisdom of a lifetime. This film presents a model retirement program for community settings--schools, libraries, churches, retirement homes, youth and senior centers--where young and old share skills and experiences, and caring, through arts and crafts. p. UMMRC; UM.

WHATEVER HAPPENED TO LORI JEAN LLOYD? (26m C 1980) (also Video)
Through actual documentary footage, the film presents one mother's search for her runaway daughter. For the rest of us, it is a journey into the streets for a stark look at what really happens to runaway children. Shows the desperate world of runaway children, from the bus depots to Hollywood's back alleys to New York's infamous Minnesota Strip. The realities of running away are revealed: drugs, sexual exploitation, disease, fear, loneliness, deprivation, death. Hosted by Marsha Mason. p. Dave Bell Associates, p./s.w. Dan Gingold; d. Dan Gingold, John Cosgrove; MEDIAF; UCEMC.

WHAT'S A GOOD BOOK? SELECTING BOOKS FOR CHILDREN (27m C 1982)
Through interviews with librarians, specialists in children's literature and reading, the film gives an insight into the complexities and satisfactions of selecting a library's children's books. Intended as a discussion starter for community groups, college courses and in-service training. d./p. Joanna Foster; WWS.

WHAT'S COOKING? (15m C p1979, r1979)
Shows the unique contributions of different cultures. Emphasizes that good nutrition is common to all peoples although achieved by different foods prepared in different ways. d./ed. Jane Treiman; CF.

WHAT'S COOKING? (SERIES) (28m ea. C 1975) (Video)
Chef LaDeva Davis, "the Flip Wilson of low budget cookery," shows how to eat well and save money in this series of meal planning and cooking programs. She delivers instructions and food-buying tips in a breezy, down-to-earth fashion, and works with basic kitchenware and ingredients. Her recipes, planned by a board of nutritionists to be healthy and attractive as well as to taste good, include snacks and appetizers, fish and fowl dishes, egg and vegetable specialties, meat stews and cheese soufflés. Recipes used serve six to eight people. Individual program titles are INTERNATIONAL DINNER; PANCAKES; SNACKS AND APPETIZERS; BREAKFAST; ONE POT MEALS; INEXPENSIVE MEATS; FISH; VARIETY MEATS; CHICKEN; QUICK SKILLET; VEGETABLES; EGGS; LOW CALORIE. p. WHYY-TV; PBSV.

WHAT'S EXPECTED OF ME? (30m B 1979) (Video)
   A compelling portrait of a bright, articulate 12-year-old girl
making the transition from elementary school to junior high. d./p.
Theresa Mack; WMM.

WHEN, JENNY, WHEN? (25m C p1978, r1978)
   Young people are faced with many decisions throughout their
adolescence. One such issue is sexual activity. The film presents
this topic, stressing the necessity for commitment and maturity.
Emphasizes personal respect and respect of others. d. Ted Post;
p. Mike Rhodes; p. Southerby Productions, Inc.; SOUTHP.

WHEN A CHILD DIES (22m C p1979, r1979)
   One child was killed in an auto accident at the age of 17; another
of leukemia after lingering 18 months and a third as an infant in his
crib. Different experiences, or so it would appear, until one listens
to the anguish and expressed needs of the parents and siblings of
all three. Each provides a new understanding of living with death,
an alien concept to our western culture. d./p. Deidre Evans Gittelman; p. Gittelman Film Associates; GITFM.

WHEN A WOMAN FIGHTS BACK (59m C n.d.)
   A documentary which considers the legal and social questions
raised in four recent court cases in Washington State involving women
who killed men in self defense. The Yvonne Wanrow murder trial set
legal precedent when her conviction was reversed by the Washington
State Supreme Court. Issues raised in the decision included the application of "reasonable force" standards, even though there are size
and strength differences, in how men and women perceive threatening situations; the inherent bias in the wording of the instructions
to the jury. The program examines how these precedents were applied in three subsequent murder trials involving Claudia Thacker,
Janice Painter and Sharon Crigler. Defendants, their attorneys and
the prosecutors discuss the specific issues raised in each case. Professionals working with battered women point out the unresponsive-
ness of conventional social agencies like the police and mental health
organizations in situations where a man poses a continuing threat to
a woman. A feminist karate instructor tells how socialization produces
women who are not emotionally equipped to fight back and who perceive acts of aggression with irrational terror. The program shows
how women, social service agencies and the Court System of Washington are attempting to change what they see as society's tacit approval
of violence against women. p. KCPQ-TV, Tacoma, Washington; PBSV.

WHEN DID YOU LAST SEE YOURSELF ON TV? (30m C 1979)
   This is a critical survey of media stereotypes. Schoolgirls, a
housewife and women who work in television assess what TV offers
and what they make of the television image. Who makes these programs? Who writes the scripts? Who produces that ad with the sim-
pering model? Whose fantasy is it? It raises the question, Is tele-

vision reflecting the changes affecting women in recent years or have women left television far behind? d./p. Deirdre McCartin; LUCERNE.

WHEN I GROW UP (18m C p1978, r1978)
Illustrates some ways in which sexual stereotyping may be imprinted on boys and girls by a teacher's unconscious attitude, thereby limiting a student's career orientation. Based on actual occurrences and as such may be familiar and meaningful to the viewer. p. Calvalcade Productions, Inc.; MTITI.

WHEN I SAY NO, I FEEL GUILTY (30m C 1977)
Four vignettes demonstrate the principles and skills of systematic Assertiveness Training and explains manipulative ploys and how to cope with them. Based on the book by Dr. Manuel J. Smith. p. Olympia Media Information; CALLYC.

WHEN JOSEPH RETURNS (92m C 1976) (Hungarian/Subtitled)
Reveals characters caught in a flux of feelings, events and situations which are both strikingly modern and socially complex. This film follows the uneasy progress of two women awkwardly thrown together when the newlywed wife of a young merchant marine comes to live with his mother after sending him off to sea. d. Zsolt Kezdi-Kovacs; NYF.

WHEN THE HONEYMOON IS OVER (30m C 1979)
Examines the violence against women in marriages. How widespread is it? Why do women remain for years in violent marriages? Presents the personal experiences of mental and physical cruelty faced by four New Zealand women from different backgrounds. The film also examines the practical aid offered by a Halfway House, the "paper war" of benefit claims, non-molestation orders and housing applications. Finally, a psychiatrist and two staff members from a "Halfway House" analyze the cause of violence in marriage and the avenues open to women seeking help. d./p. Deirdre McCartin; p. Kinetic Film Enterprises Ltd.; LUCERENE.

WHEN THE RIVER RUNS DRY (29m C p1979, r1980)
Presents a cultural history of water use in the semi-arid Southwest, a region marked by alternating problems of drought and flood. From the first Indian irrigation canals built about 300 B.C. to the computer-operated water systems of today, each culture that has inhabited the area has coped with water problems in unique and characteristic ways. Also examines contemporary conflicts over the available water--between Indian, Hispanic, and Anglo farmers, and between agricultural, industrial and residential users. Balanced, insightful commentary. d. Fred Aronow; p. Mary Louise King, F. Aronow; p. Shoshone Productions; UCEMC.

WHEN'S THE BIG DAY? (13m C 1975)
Two young couples at a dinner party personify differing views

of young marriage: the idealistic "before" and the disillusioned "after," when each partner blames the other for the devastating financial and life-choice consequences of their situation. Open-ended to stimulate discussion. p. Ziff-Davis Publishing Co.; CRM; KENTSU, UIL.

WHERE DID YOU GET THAT WOMAN? (27½m C 1982)
Portrait of an aging washroom matron who works in a posh entertainment district and lives in the ghetto. Her extended autobiographical reminiscences reveal a remarkable tenacity and will to survive. Still photographs and authentic recordings by folk and blues artists are used to suggest links between personal history and the shared experience of a generation of black women. d./p./ed. Loretta Smith; SMITHL.

WHERE IS IT? (3m C p1980, r1980) (also Video)
In the opening scene of this film, accompanied by music but no narration, a big white rabbit comes out of a hole and hops around a field sniffing everything it comes upon and stopping now and then to eat wild greens. The rabbit is viewed from all sides as it stops to wash its face and peer through the fork of tree branches. Hopping around the tree, it goes to a basket of carrots and begins chewing on the stems, and looks happily at the camera. Intended to stimulate the imagination of children. p. Tana Hoban; TEXFM.

WHERE THE DANCE IS (29m B 1970) (also Video) Contemporary Dance
    Series
Development of dance outside of New York, performed and enjoyed by children and adults. Vera Embree and Esther Pease (Professors at University of Michigan) and Florence Price (President of the Jackson, Michigan Area Dance Council), and Rusty Schumacher (Ann Arbor Recreation Department) discuss the public school programs, the in-service training of public school teachers and Ann Arbor's recreational programs in dance. Narrator: Robert Luscombe; d. Marshall Franke; p. Selma Odom; UMMRC; UM.

WHERE WAS THE WORLD? (28m C 1981) (Video)
Penetrates the subject of the Holocaust in a blend of archival film footage, stills, and interviews with three survivors: Jack Eisner, Irving Deutscher, and Sophie Feldbaum. The interviews disclose personal accounts of Nazi persecution and their emotions today about surviving such horrors inflicted by human beings on their fellows. d. Steve Alpert; p. Adrienne Meltzer; TEMANC.

WHITE BRIDGE, THE (45m C p1978, r1981--U.S.)
Shows what happens when Arabs seek medical treatment from Israel's Hadassa Hospital. Two thousand people a day from Jordan, Lebanon, Saudi Arabia and other Arab countries cross the bridge into Israel to seek medical care at the Hadassa Hospital. Despite their political differences, Arabs respond to the radio program

describing the new equipment and techniques used at the hospital. The film reveals the ambivalent feelings and conflicts about the interaction between Arabs and Israelis. The initial fear and suspicion is seen to be ultimately replaced with a sense of trust on both sides, as doctors, nurses, and other staff members continue their humanitarian work. An excellent report on the work done at the Hadassa Hospital and what that effort is doing for the spirit as well as the body. p. IFS Productions, Israel; d. Sharon S. Dov; ALDEN.

WHITE HERON, THE (26m C p1977, r1978)
 Sarah Orne Jewett's short story graces the screen with the tender tale of Sylvy, a solitary girl caught between the admiration she feels for a young hunter and her overriding love of nature. Despite her affection for the hunter, Sylvy is unable to assist him in the killing of the white heron, a cherished prize of nature. p. Jane Morrison; LCA; KENTSU.

WHITE WALL, THE (80m C 1975) (Swedish/Subtitled)
 A solid, low-key study of an everyday woman in Sweden, but the portrait is universal. Monica, a 35-year-old divorcee, faces a daily life of frustration and anxiety--in her job as well as in her relations with her ex-husband. The only place where she feels secure in her value as a woman is at a singles' restaurant, where her vulnerability makes her an easy prey for men who offer her empty promises. An important woman's film in that it focuses on oppressive social conditions, without romanticizing them. Starring: Harriet Anderson, Lena Nyman. d./s.w. Stig Bjorkman. FI.

WHO CARES ABOUT CHILD CARE? (30m C 1979--U.S.)
 Shows an adoptive mother, a solo father, a couple and a solo mother brought together in the warm community of Te Kainga, a small community-based day-care center. The center is run by a parent-cooperative with two paid part-time workers. There is evidence that parents, as well as the children, gain personally from the freedom, relief, and the shared experience. Finally, the program begs the question: "Despite the attractions of such a center, why are there so few in relation to the demand?" Produced by an all-woman crew. d./p. Deirdre McCartin; p. Television One Production, New Zealand; LUCERNE.

WHO CARES ANYWAY? (26m C p1979, r1979)
 Explores the relationship between humans and their pets from historic times of cooperation to the present pet overpopulation problem. The film looks at the reasons people keep pets, how they treat them and the unfortunate results of irresponsible ownership. The work of a metropolitan humane society is demonstrated, for it is here that the effects of irresponsibility towards pets are seen in their most dramatic form. p. Barbara Klatt; d. Brian Tyson. p. Kinetic Film Enterprises Ltd.; KINEFE.

WHO DO YOU TELL? (12m C 1978)
Uses animation and live action to discuss the support systems
available to children when they are confronted with problems of safety,
abuse, or molestation. Points out that the people causing the problem may be relatives or friends rather than strangers. Deals with
personal feelings of guilt or fear which may present conflicts in finding help. d./p. J. Gary Mitchell; MTITI; IU.

WHO REMEMBERS MAMA? (59m C p1977, r1977)
Examines the aftermath of divorce for a woman; the courtroom
battle over child support, child custody and property; her emotional
devastation; and her economic plight. Shown is the dramatization of
divorce proceedings; and in a discussion group and in separate interviews, several women talk about their situations after divorce. Given
are a few sobering statistics on the number of divorces. Although
there isn't much new in this film, nonetheless, it is a strong indictment of a system long overdue for change. p. Cynthia Salzman Mondell, Allen Mondell; Women in Communications, Ltd., KERA-TV, Dallas;
WMNCL; PAS, PURDUE, UIL, UM.

WHO SHOULD SURVIVE? (26m C 1980)
A case history is recreated with the actual doctors and nurses
playing their true life roles. This happened at a great American
hospital. A baby with Down's syndrome is born with an intestinal
block. Unless the operation is performed, the baby will die. The
parents do not want the burden of a retarded baby. They refuse to
permit the operation. The surgeon promises the family he will not
challenge the decision of the courts. The hospital does not overrule
him. The infant cannot be fed. In 15 days it is dead. Who decides
who should survive? KENJP; RARIG.

WHO WILL PROTECT THE FAMILY? (57m C p1981, r1982) (Video)
A political and personal chronicle of the battle of two movements
over the Equal Rights Amendment. While focusing on one state ratification campaign over a three-year period, Pulitzer Prize-winning
reporter Frances FitzGerald probes the motivations, experiences and
larger agendas of a wide spectrum of those who have participated in
the ten-year-national debate on the Equal Rights Amendment. p./d.
Victoria Costello; TAKOMA.

WHOLE BODY MANUAL (19m C 1979)
Points out basic rules for staying fit: a balanced diet along
with physical activity. p. John Watson, Pen Densham, p. Insight
Productions, Inc.; PEREN.

WHO'S THERE FOR THE VICTIM? (ed.) (22m C 1981) (also Video)
Demonstrates the need for Rape Victim Advocates services. Encourages broader community response to the problem of rape and to
solicit community support for services. Shows Rape Victim Advocates,
a volunteer group affiliated with six hospitals in the Chicago area,

offering comfort and support to rape victims any hour of the day or night. Emphasis is placed on an awareness of the trauma and desperation the victim has faced in this life-threatening situation. The incidence of victims six years of age and under and elderly women with infirmities attest to the fact that any woman is vulnerable. Personal observation and comments from the volunteers offer insight into the fears and apprehensions most women feel. A strong statement, well documented into facts and visuals, in favor of community support for rape victims. p./d./s.w. Michael Hirsh; p. WTTW-TV, Chicago; MTITI; IU, UCEMC.

WHOSE BODY IS IT ANYWAY? (27m C 1975)
    Examines some of the pernicious effects of over-the-counter drug trade in creating self-perpetuating conditions of need for the drugs. Notes the negative psychology that has come about in medical patients, who feel cheated if they leave without a "prescription." Touches on the patient's right to know what she or he is taking and exactly how it is supposed to affect one and to help in deciding whether medication is needed. p. Hobel-Leiterman Productions; DOCUA; IU, UIL.

WHOSE CHILD IS THIS? (27m C p1978, r1978)
    Tells the story of a teacher's discovery of an abused child in her third-grade class. She reports her suspicions to the Protective Service Agency, despite obstacles, and follows through with the case to an optimistic conclusion. The child's behavioral changes, his home-life situation, the procedure involved in reporting a case of child abuse are all explored. d./ed. Rhoden Streeter; p. Alfred R. Shands for Orion Broadcasting with The Junior League of Louisville and Jefferson County, Kentucky, Fiscal Court. LCA; IU, KENTSU, UMN.

WHOSE LIFE IS IT ANYWAY? (53m C 1974)
    Raises the question of a person's right to death with a story about a young sculptor permanently paralyzed after a car accident. He wishes to be permitted to die rather than be kept alive by mechanical means while his doctor maintains it is his professional duty to maintain life. A dramatic court scene ensues. p. Granada Television, London; CWU, UM.

WHY AREN'T YOU SMILING? (20m n.d.) (slt)
    Looks at the history of the office and the issues which concern women office workers: lack of respect, low pay, lack of advancement, racism, technology, etc. Also, examines what women are doing about it through working women's organizations and unions. p. Community Media Productions; COMMDW.

WHY CAREER PLANNING? (55m C 1980) (Video)
    The necessity of planning a career, how to go about it, and the importance of career objectives to the student and a potential employer are discussed by Thomas McThenia, manager of college recruiting and relations for Scott Paper Company, and Richard Hess, assistant

director of the Career Development and Placement Center at The Pennsylvania State University. p. College of Business Administration at The Pennsylvania State University; PAS.

WHY DO I FEEL THIS WAY? (48m C 1978)
Presents three case histories of depression in dramatized form with commentary by Dr. Timothy Johnson of Harvard Medical School, who discusses ways to identify, cope with, and understand this common illness. Cases studied are an apparently successful lawyer, a suburban housewife, and a widower who is a museum guard. p. ABC-TV; UIL.

WHY ME? (10m C 1978, r1979)
Combining insight with gentle humor, the film explores the typical emotions and reactions experienced by people facing their own impending death. This ingenious animated treatment of a universal experience focuses our attention on the psychology of dying while reminding us to live our lives to the fullest. d./p. Janet Perlman, Derek Lamb; NFBC; PF; KENTSU, UMO.

WHY MEN RAPE (40m C 1980) (also Video)
A highly charged documentary seeking insights into this ever-increasing crime of violence. WHY MEN RAPE studies the subject from the perpetrator's standpoint. Until now, the crime of rape has usually been treated from the victim's point of view. The National Film Board of Canada production team goes, instead, into prisons and psychiatric hospitals for interviews with ten convicted rapists. Their stories are startling; their backgrounds varied. In fact, these ten are almost a cross-section of the male population. Interviews with leading authorities on rape help to give a clearer picture of the criminal. Discussions with students who talk about their own feelings and attitudes about sex stress the need for more education in schools and more open communication in families. Investigations into the phenomenon of "social rape," involving people who are acquainted with each other, reveal that the number of reported incidents is far lower than we all suspect. There are no easy solutions. The film does offer three suggestions: more open discussion of sex, more sharing of feelings, and more stress on improved self-image in children. The detailed transcripts of the film will soon be available in a book of the same name from Gauge Publishing. p./d. Douglas Jackson, NFBC; BUDGET, KENTSU, PAS, UM, USC, UW.

WHY NOT A WOMAN (25m C 1977)
Shows women performing successfully in a variety of bluecollar jobs and reveals their attitudes towards their work. Makes the point that women today are the sole support in over seven million American households. Presented by Pennsylvania Commission for Women. Nominal service charge. p. John Norris Association; AF; PAS.

WHY WE CONSERVE ENERGY: THE WITCH OF THE GREAT BLACK POOL (12m C 1978)

The importance of conservation of energy is stressed. The Scattergoods loved machines and used them for everything. But then the witch of the Great Black Pool became angry at the Scattergoods for doing this. So the Scattergoods decided to use only the most important machines and found out it was fun doing some things themselves the machines had done for them before. d./p. Maureen Selwood; LCA; KENTSU.

WHY WOMEN STAY (30m B 1980) (Video, Beta)
Examines the complex reasons why women stay in violent homes. Uses animation, video verité, and interviews. The stories of two individual women serve as telling background for the exploration of the following issues: 1) the historical and current social consequences of the physical oppression of women throughout the ages; 2) questionable attitudes toward battered women by the professionals to whom women must go for help; 3) the critical need for government and privately supported shelters; 4) the support battered women give one another in a shelter environment. p. Jacqueline Shortell-McSweeney, Debra Zimmerman, Ginny Maguire; WMM.

WIDOW, THE (102m C 1976)
Sudden widowhood creates devastating emotional and financial problems for a protected wife and mother. This film, based on the autobiographical book by Lynn Caine, follows a widow's descent into a miasma of grief and near disaster to a regained sense of values and stability for herself and her children. d. J. Lee Thompson; p. Lorimar; LUCERNE, SELECT.

WIDOWHOOD (30m 1979) (Video)
This lesson is a case study of widowhood; in particular, it is the story of Mary Gallagher. Her story is a sensitive description of a fact of life for married American women. They can expect about ten years of widowhood: two out of every three women outlive their mates. Mary Gallagher's story illustrates these statistics and provides the opportunity to identify a number of emotional responses common to women who have recently lost their husbands. Because of the straightforward manner of presentation, considerable insight into widowhood can be obtained. Her honest analysis and willingness to share experiences points out the problems and difficulties encountered by widows in today's society--anger, guilt, depression, identification, nights alone. Gallagher's situation is tragically different from most in that she lost her husband and a son at the same time. NETCHE.

WIDOWS (29m C 1981) (also Video) Are You Listening Series
Old and young widows, some with small children, share their experiences with us. They share how their husbands died. They talk about the anger and frustration caused by long terminal illnesses and their feeling of resentment at being left alone. They talk about how they have learned to cope with their new role, developing careers

when they have never worked, going back to school, etc. p. Martha
Stuart; d. Ivan Curry; STUARTM.

WIFE AMONG WIVES, A (75m C 1981) (Turkana/Subtitled)
  This ethnographic documentary on the seminomadic Turkana of
northern Kenya covers the period before the filming of THE WEDDING
CAMELS. First, we hear the testimony of three remarkable sisters.
Then we experience the gradual unfolding of plans for a marriage in
a neighboring homestead. In the course of these plans, we learn why
a woman would want her husband to take a second wife, and how the
system of polygyny can be a source of solidarity among women while
at the same time it may brutally disregard the feelings of individuals.
The Turkana speak rationally and with insight about their choices.
They are well aware of the contradictory problems associated with individual liberty and communal survival. The film demonstrates how
Turkana culture--and, by extension, human culture--is a living thing,
shaped by people who carry it. d./p. Judith MacDougall, David
MacDougall; UCEMC.

WIFEMISTRESS (101m C 1979) (Italian/Subtitled)
  Laura Antonelli stars as a psychosomatically ill and bedridden
wife who resents her neglectful husband (Marcello Mastroianni) and
her boring life. When he goes into hiding because of a murder he
didn't commit, she believes him dead. One by one, she uncovers
her husband's secret lives, and begins to live them herself. From
this nearby hideaway Mastroianni observes his wife's emotional and
physical metamorphoses. Set in the early 1900's, this provocative
tale of an unfulfilled wife's emancipation offers insight into contemporary male-female relationships. d. Marco Vicario; FI.

WILD AMERICA--WHO NEEDS IT? (20m C 1978)
  Shows how cities are dependent on productivity of the land and
urges city dwellers to participate in environmental decisions. d./p.
Carol Lee Taylor for National Audubon Society; PHOENIX.

WILD GREEN THINGS IN THE CITY (11m C 1974)
  A young girl searches out plants in neglected corners of vacant
lots in the city, by the docks, between cracks in the pavement. She
finds familiar plants which she looks up in a library book. Wild green
things in the city are taken to her apartment building where she
creates a flourishing garden of her own. A good film to arouse the
interests of children in plants. p. Catherine Mercier, Clayton Rawson; Geode Productions; p. Paramount Communication Inc.; PARACO,
TEXFM.

WILD SWANS IN EPITAPH AND MADHONOR (30m B 1974)
  Two dances choreographed, danced and commented on by Margaret Beals. "Wild Swans," is a suite of poems spoken and danced
by Beals, based on the poetry of Edna St. Vincent Millay. "Madhonor," is danced to silence (a portrait of Mary as seen by the artist). Dancer/Choreographer: Margaret Beals; p. Virginia Brooks;
BROOKSV.

WILLA CATHER REMEMBERED (60m 1975) (Video)

"The history of every country begins in the heart of a man or a woman," Willa Cather once wrote. In large part, the history of the rich buffalo grassland of Webster County, Nebraska, begins in the heart and imagination of Willa Cather. This supplemental lesson returns to Webster County to trace the history of one of Nebraska's greatest writers through the memories of the people who knew her. NETCHE.

WILLA CATHER'S AMERICA (60m C 1978)

Willa Cather is the only first-rate American writer whose work examines the growth of America. Although she lived in Virginia as a child, her move to the prairies of Nebraska provided the anchor for her writing. Several of her books are discussed. O Pioneers, My Antonia and Death Comes to the Archbishop are symbolic as much as realistic depictions of the rock of the human spirit. Narrated by Hal Holbrook and Gena Rowlands. d./p./s.w. Richard Schickel for WNET-TV; FFHUM; PAS.

WILLIAM RANDOLPH HEARST'S SAN SIMEON (24m C 1978) American Lifestyles Series--Industrialists and Inventors

Presents a film about the legendary William Randolph Hearst, his career, life-style, and the castle San Simeon, which he built on the California coast. The impressive facts of San Simeon are related by E. G. Marshall as various sites on San Simeon are shown along with its vast treasures dating back to antiquity. Reflects the visions and tastes of a man the life of which we are not likely ever to see again. d./p. Ann Lane Shanks; PARACO.

WILLIE (49m 1981)

A drama about a teenage black boy who runs away from an orphanage and survives on his own in New York City. p. Coleen Higgins, Ghasem Ebrahimian; d. Ghasem Ebrahimian; p. Ebra Films; EBRA.

WILLMAR 8, THE (55m C r1980)

Tells the inspiring story of eight women--bank workers in the small, Midwestern town of Willmar, Minnesota--who suddenly found themselves in the forefront of the fight for working women's rights. Like millions of other women throughout the country, they had been relegated to low-wage, dead-end jobs. When a young male trainee was hired at almost twice their starting salary and the women were required to "train him in," they complained to the bank manager. He told them, "we're not all equal, you know." That comment led eight previously apolitical, unassuming, church-going women to take the most unexpected step of their lives. They formed a union and in December 1977 started the first bank strike in the history of Minnesota. It lasted 18 months. Although they eventually lost the strike, the Willmar 8 gained a sense of dignity and self-worth that had been denied them on the job and a sense of community they had never known before. p. Mary Beth Yarrow, Julie Thompson; d. Lee Grant; ed. Suzanne Petit; p. California Newsreel; CALNWS; UM, UW, PAS, UMI, UMN.

WINDOW (30m C 1980-1983) (Video, Beta, VHS) Concept Series
    WINDOW is about memory, not as act, but form. The script's language moves through memory-scapes and nonlinear thinking, and selected elements are visually abstracted. d./p. Doris Chase; s.w. Linda Mussman, performed by Claudia Bruce; CHASED.

WINIFRED WAGNER (104m B 1975) (German/Subtitled)
    After a court-ordered silence of 30 years, Richard Wagner's English-born daughter-in-law recalls with alarming candor her close relationship with and great admiration for Adolf Hitler. "If Hitler walked through that door today, I should be just as pleased to see him as ever," she says, adding later, "I exempt him from the human race." Wedded to the Bayreuth Music Festival which she managed alone from her husband Siegfried's death in 1930 to 1944, Mrs. Wagner and Hitler were drawn together by a mutual "admiration and love of Richard Wagner." Syberberg's film poses two questions. What does such a love of Richard Wagner imply about the German culture and soul? And, what does Winifred Wagner's "apolitical" admiration for Hitler imply about decent, civic-minded people everywhere? It's easy not to be a Nazi if there is no Hitler," says Syberberg in his final title card. d. Hans-Jurgen Syberberg; LIBERTY.

WINNER IS WAITING, A (23½m C p1980, r1981)
    Examines the dedication and discipline needed to compete in amateur swimming, following the careers of young amateur and Olympic-caliber swimmers. Youngsters are shown winning and losing. Emphasis is placed on the growth and enrichment which result from striving to achieve one's personal goals. p. Jane Paley/Jim Hill; ex. p. William Deeter; MTPS.

WINNING THE WAR ON ARSON (15m C 1980)
    Explores the dimensions of the country's fastest growing crime and focuses on how two communities, Seattle, Washington, and New Haven, Connecticut, are taking on the arsonist. Quite effective. Lacks point of view of people. Too much focus on "officials." d. Wendy Wood. p. Aetna Life and Casualty; AETNA.

WINTER IS HERE (2nd ed.) (11m C p1979, r1979)
    Shows young children the special qualities of winter. Focuses on the icy conditions of the North as well as a segment of growing winter crops in the South. p. Myrna I. Berlet, Walter H. Berlet; IFB.

WINTERSONG (8m C 1977--U.S.)
    Explores the theme "If I could relive my life, would I make the same choices?" Shows a housewife sitting alone and looking slightly

distraught as her husband drives off to work while a song, the film's entire narration, relates to the woman's unspoken thoughts. Since her children left home, she feels a sense of emptiness and useless- ness. Whatever she does, she does without enthusiasm. Finally, she goes for a walk through the barren winter landscape and chances upon a deserted and disintegrating farmhouse. As she wanders through the house, its appearance of having been abandoned seems to mirror the woman's feelings about herself. Her thoughts, through the words of the ballad, reflect an attitude not of regret over the things she has had and done, but a feeling that somehow there should have been something more in her life. A powerful statement about the search for a more purposeful life. d. Ben Low; music: Ben Low; p. NFBC; LCA; UIL, CWU.

WISE USE OF DRUGS: A PROGRAM FOR OLDER AMERICANS (32m C 1979)
Against the background of new medical developments, the film shows how older people can benefit more fully from visiting the doc- tor, reduce the costs in buying prescription drugs, and obtain more information from the pharmacist. The film shows how older people can keep track of drugs at home and avoid accidental misuse by focus- ing on healthy aging. d./p. Kamer Davis; NAVC; UMN.

WISHFULFILMING (13m B 1973)
Documentary that explores the process of working collectively and the struggle to develop new hierarchical forms of organization. p. Santa Cruz Women's Media Collective; IRISFC.

WITCHCRAFT AMONG THE AZANDE (52m C n.d.) (Video) Disappear- ing World Series
To the Azande of Africa, there is no such thing as bad luck. All misfortune results from witchcraft. This tribe depends on oracles to explain events and predict the future. We sit in on a trial of a couple accused of adultery. They deny the charge, but their fate will be determined by whether a ritually poisoned chicken will live or die. Here is a Christian tribe where the priest must share his influ- ence with the witchdoctor. p. Granada Television International; FILMLB.

WITCHES, NEW FASHION--OLD RELIGION (52m C 1974)
Introduces male and female practitioners of witchcraft who are interviewed about their beliefs and practices, including a business- man who studies it as a hobby and businesswoman who heads a coven. Shows ritual initiation for a new member of a coven, a circle working at healing. Introductory footage is of a coven which practices nudity in ritual invocations. Thames Television, Ltd., London; UIL.

WITCHES AND FAGGOTS, DYKES AND POOFTERS (45m C 1980)
Succinctly chronicles a history of gay oppression all over the world and then focuses on police harassment and brutality during

the 1978 Sydney Gay Mardi Gras. Film Australia; d. Digby Duncan; p. One in Seven Collective; IRISFC.

WITH BABIES AND BANNERS: STORY OF THE WOMEN'S EMERGENCY BRIGADE (45m C 1978)
An account of the women who were instrumental in the Great General Motors Sitdown Strike in 1937. The filmmakers combine archival footage of the strike with a present-day reunion of the Women's Emergency Brigade members. (Museum of Modern Art, October 24, 1978.) p. Lorraine Gray, Anne Bohlen, Lynn Goldfarb; d. Lorraine Gray; NEWDAY; PAS, UMN, UM.

WITH FABRIC AND THREAD (15m C 1973, r1974) Textile Design Series
Creative stitchery is like painting with thread. Selecting a background fabric, choosing colors and types of yarn, and developing a design are part of the creative experience. Simple stitches are demonstrated: stem or outline, chain, satin, French knot, couching. p. Nancy Belfer, Dr. Clem Tetkowski; p. Oxford Films; AIMS.

WITH MY RED FIRES (31m C 1978)
Presents Doris Humphrey's powerful dance-drama from 1936 as performed in 1972 by the American Dance Festival Company at Connecticut College. Tells the story of the conflict between romantic love and possessive love. Choreography by Doris Humphrey; music by Wallingford Riegger. p. Ted Steeg Productions for American Dance Festival Repertory Company, University of Rochester; DAN/UR; UIL.

WITH PATSY IN ST. VINCENT (15m C 1981) WORLD'S CHILDREN SERIES
Thirteen-year-old Patsy Boyea lives on the Caribbean island of St. Vincent, a major exporter of bananas and arrowroot. Patsy can apply some of the agricultural skills she learns at school to her family's garden of banana trees and ginger root. We share Patsy's school day, her trip to the city market and her many domestic chores in this single-parent household. d. David Springbett; p. Heather McAndrew; INTELFE.

WITH SILK WINGS--ASIAN AMERICAN WOMEN AT WORK: ON NEW GROUND (30m C p1982, r1983) (Video)
Profiles of ten Asian-American students and women in nontraditional jobs and activities, including: two university students in charge of an all-men rowing crew, a park ranger, a bartender, a designer-shop owner, a police officer, a stock broker, a television news anchor, a municipal judge, and a welder. In an informal, and personal way, with a good look at their specific work and workplaces, the women of Chinese, Japanese, Korean and Filipino backgrounds tell their stories. d./p. Loni Ding; ASIANWU.

WITH THESE HANDS (41m B 1950)
Shows the depressed working and living conditions of a garment factory worker before a union was established. Depicts the rise of the International Ladies' Garment Workers' Union in 1910, following a tragic fire in which an entire group of employees perished. Shows the workers gaining collective bargaining rights, better working conditions, an improved standard of living, and establishing a retirement and medical program in their powerful and efficient organization. p. International Ladies' Garment Worker's Union; ILGWU; UIL.

WIZARD, THE (8m C 1974) (also Video)
Stresses the advisability of channeling one's creative energy toward positive ends. Using watercolor animation and limericks, this film tells the story of a wizard who misapplies his magical powers by casting spells on his neighbors. After suffering much rejection and loneliness, the wizard learns to channel his imagination to creative ends, and finds himself fulfilled as well as admired by all. d. Lillian Moats Somersaulter, J. P. Somersaulter; p. Pajon Arts; FI.

WIZARD OF WAUKESHA: A FILM ABOUT LES PAUL, THE (58m C p1979, r1980)
Presents the musical career of Les Paul and of the development of the guitar which bears his name. Playing and demonstrating his guitar, he includes reminiscences, such as his meeting with Mary Ford, his wife, and of their music career together. Although he retired in 1964, Les Paul came back to the entertainment scene on his own terms, for he has always found that his greatest pleasure was in performing and entertaining a live audience. Includes many of the big hits with Mary Ford. A well documented portrait of a music innovator. p. Stray Cat Production; p./d. Catherine Orentreich; DIRECT.

WOBBLIES, THE (89m C/B 1979)
Uses interviews with surviving members of the Industrial Workers of the World (I.W.W.), archive footage, photos, music and cartoons to tell the story of the I.W.W. from the founding in 1905, through their organizing and strikes in free speech, textiles, lumber, agriculture and mining, to their repression and decline during World War I. d. Stewart Bird, Deborah Shaffer; FIRRNF.

WOMAN (32m C 1974)
This animated film depicts attitudes toward women, from olden times through the present. In ancient Greece, for example, a woman was regarded as a defective or incomplete man. Christianity introduced the strangest of all double moralities: woman was partly the virginal Mary; partly the impure seductress, fallen Eve. History is replete with despisers and oppressors of women. Varying economic systems have virtually always given rise to a view of women that was to the detriment of women and to the advantage of men. Free loan. p. Swedish Broadcasting Corporation; AUDFLS.

WOMAN, A SPANIEL AND A WALNUT TREE (THE MORE YOU BEAT
    THEM, THE BETTER THEY'LL BE), A (13m C 1977)
    Explores the problem of wife beating and various solutions through
comments by beaten women and interviews with law enforcement officers and counselors. A useful tool for community education. p.
Cine Design; CINED.

WOMAN ALIVE! NO. 1 (30m n.d.)
    Featured are five women who lead a wildcat strike against the
Levi Company in Georgia and establish their own sewing business.
"The Women of McCaysville Industries" reveals the lives of women
working under impossible production quotas, petty regulations and
assembly line tedium. They describe the pressures and frequent
violence during their fourteen-month strike, how they lost in court
and how they then decided to open and operate their own factory.
Also in the program, Eleanor Holmes Norton, New York City Commissioner of Human Rights, comments on how the depressed economic
climate of the 1970's will affect the feminist movement. In the musical segment of "Woman Alive!" folk singer Holly Near sings about life,
love, politics and women's consequences. p. Jeffrey Norton Publishers, Inc.; NORTONJ.

WOMAN ALIVE! NO. 2 (30m)
    The lives of four young, successful Los Angeles women are ex-
plored in this "Woman Alive!" program. "Work in Progress" looks at
the varied motivations of a female flying instructor, a writer, a stock-
broker and a lawyer and how their professions affect their personal
lives. Also, Rose Kushner, author of the best-selling book Breast
Cancer, instructs women to find out more about breast cancer procedures to prevent unnecessary mastectomies. Jazz singer Dee Dee
Bridgewater, Tony winner for her appearance in Broadway's "The
Wiz," sings "If You Believe," "Everything Must Change" and "Little
B's Poem." p. Jeffrey Norton Publishers, Inc.; NORTONJ.

WOMAN BEHIND THE IMAGE: PHOTOGRAPHER JUDY DATER, THE
    (27m C 1981)
    A portrait of one of the most important young photographers
working today. Caught between a desire to keep her work "on the
edge at all times" and a desire for a fulfilling relationship with a man,
Judy Dater's life becomes representative of the modern woman's dilemma. p. John A. Stewart Productions; STEWART.

WOMAN MOVING UP (50m C n.d.)
    A presentation dealing with many, if not all, the problems en-
countered by females newly promoted from within. Includes both
on-the-job and personal situations. p. Monad Trainer's Aide; MONAD.

WOMAN OF CHAMULA (14m C 1969)
    Shows the life of a Mexican Indian family in Chiapas where the
Indians live in much the same way as did their Mayan ancestors a

thousand years ago. Describes the mother of the family and her activities in the home. p. Elda Hartley; HARTLEY.

WOMAN OF PURPOSE SERIES see DREAM YOUR OWN DREAMS; FREEDOM TO DEFINE MYSELF; WOMEN: CHOOSING AND CHANGING; WORLD OF GWEN FROSTIC, THE

WOMAN OF THE MONTH--INDIRA GANDHI (28m B 1966)
Surveys the life of Indira Gandhi, prime minister of India. Shows her childhood and later life as the hostess for her father, Jawaharlal Nehru. Includes an interview in which she discusses her present hopes and programs for India. p. CBS-TV; AF.

WOMAN OF THE NIGHT (75m B 1948) (Japanese/Subtitled)
Documents the hellish world of prostitutes, narcotics dealers and marauding female street gangs with graphic uncompromising realism. Based on the story by Eijiro Hisaita, Yoshitaka Iida. Starring: Kinuyo Tanaka, Sanae Takasugi, Mitsuo Nagata. d. Kenji Mizoguchi; s.w. Yoshitaka Yoda; FI.

WOMAN QUESTION, THE (5m C 1980)
A hilarious political satire about women in nontraditional employment. Five minutes of friendly jabs at The Company, The Professional Employment Counselor and The Left. p. Nina Wax; IRISFC.

WOMAN REBEL, THE (59m C 1977) The Nova Series
Dramatizes the life and work of Margaret Sanger, who was responsible for gaining social and political acceptance for the concept of birth control. Features Piper Laurie. p. WBGH-TV; UMN.

WOMAN SERIES (1975-76)
These are films in the series:

HOUSEHOLD WORKERS
AFFIRMATIVE ACTION IN BUSINESS
ELSA DORFMAN: IMPRESSIONS
WOMEN'S STUDIES
WOMEN AND DEPRESSION
A CONVERSATION WITH FLORYNCE KENNEDY
TITLE IX: FAIR PLAY IN SCHOOLS
CHILD CUSTODY
MOTHERS AND DAUGHTERS
A.C.T.: ACTION FOR CHILDREN'S TELEVISION
RAPE, PART I
RAPE, PART II
A CONVERSATION WITH ELIZABETH JANEWAY, PART I
A CONVERSATION WITH ELIZABETH JANEWAY, PART II
THE BATTLE FOR THE VOTE, PART I
THE BATTLE FOR THE VOTE, PART II
JUDY CHICAGO ON FEMINIST ART

WOMAN SERIES (cont.)
    SISTERS IN CRIME
    UNNECESSARY SURGERY
    WOMEN'S HEALTH CARE: A HISTORY
    ONE WOMAN'S DIVORCE
    PUERTO RICAN WOMEN'S FEDERATION
    WOMEN IN TRANSITION
    NORA EPHRON ON EVERYTHING
    BIRTH EXPERIENCES
    BREAST CANCER CONTROVERSIES
    HOUSEHUSBANDS
    STERILIZATION AND CONSENT
    CONTROVERSIES WITHIN THE WOMEN'S MOVEMENT, PART I
    CONTROVERSIES WITHIN THE WOMEN'S MOVEMENT, PART II
    MONEY
    WOMEN, MONEY AND POWER
    MONEY AND THE SINGLE WOMAN
    WOMAN'S BANKS AND CREDIT UNIONS
    MENTAL HEALTH CARE: ONE PATIENT'S VIEW
    NEW IMAGE FOR BLACK WOMEN
    BATTERED WIVES
    THE MYTH OF THE HAPPY CHILD
    "THE PROPER PLACE" FOR WOMEN IN THE CHURCH
    SPORTS: WHAT'S THE SCORE?
    SEX THERAPY, PART I
    SEX THERAPY, PART II
    FOOD ADDITIVES: HELPFUL OR HARMFUL? PART I
    FOOD ADDITIVES: HELPFUL OR HARMFUL? PART II
    THE LADY VANISHES: WHERE ARE THE WOMEN IN FILM?
    WOMEN'S IMAGE: DOWN THE TUBE
    WOMEN'S PAGES
    FEMINIST PRESS
    CRIS WILLIAMSON ON WOMEN'S MUSIC
    POLITICAL PARTIES: WOMEN'S CLOUT
    UNNECESSARY SURGERY: PHYSICIANS REACT
    WOMEN'S COALITION FOR THE THIRD CENTURY
    HUMOR BY WOMEN
    THE ESTROGEN QUESTION, PART I
    THE ESTROGEN QUESTION, PART II
    CONTEMPORARY WOMEN POETS
    NEW IMAGES FOR NURSES, PART I
    NEW IMAGES FOR NURSES, PART II
    THE TWO EARNER FAMILY
    LEGISLATIVE REPORT
    HOW TO START YOUR OWN BUSINESS, PART I
    HOW TO START YOUR OWN BUSINESS, PART II
    A CONVERSATION WITH JEANNE MOREAU, PART I
    A CONVERSATION WITH JEANNE MOREAU, PART II
    ENGINEERED FOODS: WHAT ARE THEY?
    A CONVERSATION WITH SIMONE DE BEAUVOIR

WOMAN SERIES (cont.)
    WORKING CLASS WOMEN
    NEW ROLES FOR WOMEN IN SPORTS
    LOIS GOULD ON WOMEN WRITERS
    WOMEN AND TAXES
    SEXUAL ABUSE OF CHILDREN
    MASCULINE, FEMININE AND ANDROGYNY
    WOMEN AND HEART ATTACKS, PART I
    WOMEN AND HEART ATTACKS, PART II
    LESBIAN MOTHERS AND CHILD CUSTODY, PART I
    LESBIAN MOTHERS AND CHILD CUSTODY, PART II
    LEGISLATIVE REPORT UPDATE
    PREGNANCY AFTER 35
    TEENAGE PREGNANCY
    WOMEN'S ASTROLOGY
    AGE IS A WOMEN'S ISSUE
    AGE IS MONEY BLUES
    AGE IS BECOMING
    DES DAUGHTERS AND SONS, PART I
    DES DAUGHTERS AND SONS, PART II
    INTERNATIONAL TRIBUNALS ON CRIMES AGAINST WOMEN
    A CONVERSATION WITH ROBIN MORGAN
    BREAST CANCER UPDATE
    A CONVERSATION WITH LOTTE JACOBI
    THE GREAT PRETENDERS: THE NEW FOODS
    PORNOGRAPHY
    SEXUAL HARASSMENT ON THE JOB
    CONCERNS OF AMERICAN INDIAN WOMEN
    WOMEN AND SUCCESS
    ALTERNATIVES TO ESTROGEN
    NORTHERN IRISH PEOPLE'S PEACE MOVEMENT, PART I
    NORTHERN IRISH PEOPLE'S PEACE MOVEMENT, PART II
    THE NORTHERN IRISH QUESTION: ANOTHER VIEW

WOMAN: THE QUESTION OF SELF-CONCEPT <u>see</u> THE QUESTION
OF SELF-CONCEPT

WOMAN: WHO IS ME (11m C 1978)
    Explains how the media have helped perpetuate the myths about
women, and coincidentally men. Shown is a montage of major art
works and popular representations of women through the ages. Explores biblical and mythological themes as well as contemporary por-
trayals. Music: Manny Abam; narration: Ann Jackson; p. Judith
Keller, Shula Wallace, Shirley Joel; p. Tricept Productions; FOCUSI;
UMN.

WOMANCENTERING (8m B n.d.)
    Portrays with a sense of humor, a young mother's first interest
in feminism. While attending an open house at a women's center in
her neighborhood, the woman finds a friendly atmosphere, a comfortable

place for her child to play with other children and the opportunity
to learn new skills. With the support from the other women in this
center, she is able to make some important decisions in her life.
d./s.w./ed. Nancy Peck; WMM.

WOMAN'S DECISION (99m C 1977) (Polish/Subtitled)
    Portrays Marta, a woman torn between her devotion to her family
and career and her own yearnings for freedom and excitement in her
life. "A remarkable film. A rich rewarding experience. A fascinating exploration of where 'liberation' lies and the choices women--and
men--make in finding it"--Judith Crist, New York Post. d. Krzysztof
Zanussi; p. Film Polski; ALMI.

WOMAN'S GAME, THE (28m C n.d.)
    A fourth-grade class, their teacher and five women talk about
educational opportunities for women. The discussion ranges from
high school athletics to training for nontraditional occupations to
non-sex-biased materials. Filmed in locations spanning the United
States. Free loan. Also available, a short version. p. James Helle-
well Productions; United States Office of Education; MTPS.

WOMAN'S PLACE (8m C n.d.)
    Consists of five problem incidents and a detailed guide for the
discussion leader. The incidents cover parental sex-typing, mother-
daughter generational conflict, the housewife's self-image, role of the
executive wife, and the working woman's responsibilities at home.
ADL; RARIG.

WOMAN'S TOUCH, A (20m C 1977) The Patterns (Series)
    Edited from the motion picture THE BATTLE OF THE SEXES.
Tells a story about the difficulties which arise when a woman with
progressive business ideas tries to work with a man whose manufacturing firm is operated according to his less modern views. Focuses
on the conflict between individual efficiency and the systemization of
machines. STEREF.

WOMAN'S TOUCH, THE (27m B 1965)
    Shows the significant contributions that woman can make to space
research and development with a story about a woman who leads 18
electronics engineers in developing unusual and needed systems for
spacecraft. NASA.

WOMEN (94m C 1977) (Hungarian/Subtitled)
    A story of two women, one fortyish, the other in her twenties--
one placidly married, the other tumultuously--and the galvanizing effect of their friendship. WOMEN reconsiders the authenticity of re-
lationships--in marriage and out. "It is a picture of psychological
accuracy, emotional strength and performances that nail down these
qualities"--Archer Winston, New York Post. "WOMEN is among the
best of the emerging 'woman's films'"--Newsweek. d. Marta Meszares;
NYF.

WOMEN AND ART (25m C 1974) The Ways of Seeing (Series)
Do paintings and modern media celebrate women or exploit them?
Five women comment on how painters and publicists see women, and
why this influences how women see themselves. BBC, TIMLIF; UCLA,
UMN.

WOMEN AND CAREERS (50m C 1979) (Video)
Interviews with Betty Harrigan, author of Games Your Mother
Never Taught You; Yvonne Braithwaite Burke, former congresswoman;
Dr. Arlene Skolnick, psychologist, Herma Hill Kay, law professor; and
Phyllis Birkby, architect; and a woman construction supervisor, den-
tist, judge, owner of an interior design business and a college dean.
The content includes the current status of the working woman, sex
discrimination laws, the socialization process, the need for role models,
etc. p. California State University at Chico; CSUCHI.

WOMEN AND DEPRESSION (29m C 1975) (Video) Woman Series
Myrna Weissman, an associate professor of Psychiatry at Yale
University and co-author of The Depressed Woman, discusses her
intensive study of forty acutely depressed women and how they responded to treatment. She describes the relationship of depression
to marital and family problems and explains how proper treatment has
helped women cope. Sandra Elkin is the moderator. p. WNED-TV;
PBSV.

WOMEN AND FAMILY (50m C 1979) (Video)
Interviews with Dr. Jessie Bernard, author of The Future of Marriage, etc.; Drs. Sandra and Daryl Bem, psychologists; Robin Morgan, author and activist; Dr. Arlene Skolnick, psychologist; Dr. Warren Farrell, author; Dr. Rosalie Chapman, psychologist; Dr. Herb
Goldberg, author and psychologist; Margaret Sloan, founder of the
National Black Feminist organization. The content includes role models of egalitarian marriage, a call for change from traditional male-
female roles, child care, communication skills. p. California State
University at Chico; CSUCHI.

WOMEN AND HEALTH (50m C 1979) (Video)
Interviews with Carol Downer, founder of the Feminist Women's
Health Centers; Dr. Maida Taylor, obstetrician/gynecologist; Gail and
Dr. Tom Brewer, authors of books on prenatal care; a self-help group;
Dr. Mary Daly, theologian and author of Gyn/Ecology; and a male
obstetrician/gynecologist. The content includes a description of
women's role in health care, the origins and principles of the women's
health movement, wide effects of birth control, birthing practices,
abortion procedures, etc. p. California State University at Chico;
CSUCHI.

WOMEN AND HEART ATTACKS, PART I (29m C 1977) (Video) Woman
Series
Dr. Nanette Wenger, Professor of Medicine at Emory University

School of Medicine, and Dr. Harriet Dustan, President of the American Heart Association and Vice-Chairman of the Research Division of
the Cleveland Clinic, discuss the reasons why women are vulnerable
to heart attacks. They outline common "risk factors" in women which
tend to make coronary disease more likely and talk about the dilemma
concerning women and heart disease which is confronting the medical
community. Sandra Elkin is the moderator. p. WNED-TV; PBSV.

WOMEN AND HEART ATTACKS, PART II (29m C 1977) (Video) Woman
    Series
    Dr. Nanette Wenger, Professor of Medicine at Emory University
School of Medicine, and Dr. Harriet Dustan, President of the American Heart Association, discuss the effects of birth control pills,
physical activity, diet, smoking, alcohol, sex and health education
on the incidence of heart attacks among women. The effects of heart
attacks on the divorce rate and the need to re-educate the family of
a heart patient are also explained. Sandra Elkin is the moderator.
p. WNED-TV; PBSV.

WOMEN AND INTERVIEWING (21m C 1978) (Video)
    Shows examples of a positive and negative interview. Discusses
how to prepare for an interview and turn it to your advantage.
Points out what the interviewer may not ask under the federal guidelines. p. University of Minnesota; UMN.

WOMEN AND POWER IN THE NUCLEAR AGE (30m C 1981) (Video)
    Presents Dr. Helen Caldicott and her work in the movement to
end the proliferation of nuclear weapons. p. High Hopes Media;
HIHOM.

WOMEN AND SEXUALITY: A CENTURY OF CHANGE (36m C 1982)
    Examines nineteenth-century women's attitudes about themselves
and their sexuality and compares these ideas with contemporary views.
An informal account designed to offer a historical perspective on the
sexual issues of our time. p. Altana Films; ALTANA; UCEMC.

WOMEN AND SPORTS--BASKETBALL (11m C 1977)
    Features highlights from a women's basketball tournament and
interviews with players and coaches. p. Borden Productions, Inc.;
COCA.

WOMEN AND SPORTS--GYMNASTICS (15m C 1977)
    Shows performances in a national women's gymnastics competition.
Presents training sessions, comments from coaches and slow-motion
scenes of performances. Borden Productions, Inc.; COCA.

WOMEN AND SUCCESS (29m C 1977) (Video) Woman Series
    Sociologist Adeline Levine talks about the origin of the idea that
women are afraid of success. She also discusses how women are
taught to regard work, why women are found in low-income, low-

prestige jobs, and what they can do about stimulating their own success. Levine is the former Chairman of the Department of Sociology at the State University of New York in Buffalo and the co-author of the "Social History of Helping Services." Sandra Elkin is the moderator. p. WNED-TV; PBSV.

WOMEN AND TAXES (29m C 1977) Woman Series
   Author and lecturer Martha Yates (Coping: A Survival Manual for Women Alone) explains recent changes in federal tax laws that have made tax credits available for child care expenses. She also discusses the difference that filing status can make in the amount of due tax and changes in estate laws. Sandra Elkin is the moderator. p. WNED-TV; PBSV.

WOMEN AND THE LAW: AN INTRODUCTION see WOMEN AND THE LAW, THE (SERIES)

WOMEN AND THE LAW, THE (SERIES) (running time, year not given)
   Series was produced by WTL Productions, Philadelphia; developed by Professor Elizabeth F. Defeis of Seton Hall University School of Law. It was funded by the Exxon Education Foundation and the Fund for the Improvement of Postsecondary Education (HEW). NORTONJ.

   WOMEN AND THE LAW: AN INTRODUCTION
   Complete course analysis and outline; excerpts from various segments. Professor Elizabeth E. Defeis Project Director, Seton Hall University School of Law.

   HISTORICAL OVERVIEW I: 1776-1870
   Status of American women before and after the Revolutionary War; early efforts to gain political and legal rights; Seneca Falls Convention; abolition movement and impact of the 14th Amendment on legal rights for women. Doctor Joan Hoff Wilson, California State University at Sacramento.

   HISTORICAL OVERVIEW II: 1870-1920
   Failure of legal methods to advance the rights of women; concentration on the right to vote as primary goal; split in the feminist movement as a result of divergent goals; aftermath of the 19th Amendment. Doctor Joan Hoff Wilson, California State University of Sacramento.

   EQUALITY AND THE CONSTITUTION: MYTH AND REALITY
   The Fourteenth Amendment (Equal Protection Clause); history of the judicial reliance on traditional stereotypes of women; the ambiguity of contemporary opinions; analysis of the need for the Equal Rights Amendment. Professor Elizabeth F. Defeis, Seton Hall University School of Law.

EQUAL RIGHTS AMENDMENT
Impact of the Equal Rights Amendment on law in such areas as
military and domestic relations; exposition of congressional views,
pro and con; projections for implementation. Barbara Brown and Ann
Freedman, Attorneys, Women's Law Project, Philadelphia.

TITLE VII: LITIGATION
Demonstration of a sex discrimination hearing based on a hypo-
thetical case involving failure to promote a patrolwoman to the rank
of sergeant. Professor Marina Angel, Hofstra University School of
Law.

TITLE VII: AN EMPLOYMENT CASE STUDY
Origin and impact of the American Telephone and Telegraph proceedings before the Equal Employment Opportunity Commission; particular emphasis on creative evidence, investigation and remedies.
Kathleen Carpenter, Corporate Attorney, and Assistant Attorney General Judith T. Kramer, New York State Attorney General's office.

RAPE
Myths concerning rape: willing victim, uncontrollable impulse,
remedies and police responsibility. Lieutenant Mary Keefe, New York
City Police Department, Leslie Snyder, Assistant District Attorney,
Katherine Ellison, Psychologist.

CORRECTIONAL JUSTICE SYSTEM
Differential treatment of male and female offenders at all stages
of the criminal justice system, including arrest, sentencing and rehabilitation. Linda Singer, Attorney, Center for Correctional Justice,
Washington, D.C.

JUVENILE JUSTICE SYSTEM
Incarceration of girls for non-criminal acts, e.g., pregnancy;
attitudes of authorities with respect to responsibility for girls in
their custody; facilities provided. Judge Lisa Aversa Richette, Court
of Common Pleas, Philadelphia, Pennsylvania.

MARRIAGE
Traditional marriage and its consequences for women: name
change, domicile, identity; new approaches to marriage; marriage
contracts. Professor Herma Hill Kay, University of California School
of Law at Berkeley; Doctor Lenore Weitzman and Doctor Ruth Dixon,
University of California at Davis.

DIVORCE
Impact of no-fault divorce; demographic trends; grounds for divorce; custody and alimony. Professor Herma Hill Kay, University
of California School of Law at Berkeley; Doctor Ruth Dixon, Doctor
Lenore Weitzman, University of California at Davis.

WOMEN AND WELFARE
Impact of welfare policy on women; lack of educational programs; day-care centers; standard of need and intrusion on personal life. Professor Sylvia Law, New York University School of Law.

CREDIT DISCRIMINATION
Impact of name change; discrimination in loan application; possible legal remedies and legislation. Marjorie Gates, Attorney, Center for Women Policy Studies, Washington, D.C. and Dean Lola Grant, Loyola University School of Law, Los Angeles.

EXPERIMENT IN EQUALITY--THE WOMAN'S VOTE
A unique legal and historical perspective: the loss of rights of women following the American Revolution; the struggle for the franchise against militant opposition; the implications and significance of the vote in contemporary society. Professor Elizabeth F. Defeis, Seton Hall University School of Law and Dr. Joan Hoff Wilson, California State University at Sacramento.

IS IT OK?--WOMEN AND THE CRIMINAL JUSTICE SYSTEM
A sociological and impressionistic montage of women confronted by the criminal justice system.
    * Arrest--arraignment--bail--detention--trial--imprisonment--pro-
    bation--parole
    * Featuring insights by a leading woman judge, a defense at-
    torney, a community parole officer
Filmed on location in Philadelphia and developed by the Pennsylvania Program for Women and Girl Offenders, Inc., Philadelphia, Pennsylvania.

WOMEN AND WELFARE see WOMEN AND THE LAW, THE (SERIES)

WOMEN AT WORK: CHANGE, CHOICE, CHALLENGE (19m C 1977)
Presents women-at-work in a variety of careers, including traditional male-dominated ones. even women, filmed on the job and heard in off-camera interviews, present a view of the problems and progress of their careers. Shown are: an oil refinery worker, a nurse, jockey, an assistant railroad engineer, surgeon, judge and a political candidate. p. William Kay; EBEC; UIL, CWU, UM, UNEV, UMO, KENTSU.

WOMEN AT WORK: LOCAL GOVERNMENT (20m C 1974)
Describes career opportunities for women in city government-- the pros and cons of women working in various roles are discussed. Such careers as city planners, municipal police workers and other administrative opportunities are described by women currently in the field. Suggested as a springboard to generate class discussion on the question of women working in city government. p. University of Missouri; Columbia, UMO.

WOMEN: BIRTH CONTROL AND NUTRITION (15m C 1980)
Covers the special needs of women who are taking birth control pills or using an I.U.D. Points out the dangers of a diet too rich in sugar, salt, fatty foods, and red meats. p. Perennial Education, Inc.; PEREN.

WOMEN BUSINESS OWNERS (29m C 1976) Are You Listening Series
A diverse group of women entrepreneurs trade experiences and opinions about competing successfully in a traditionally male arena. These women talk about the rewards of a business career, the motivations, doubts, guilts, and surprises they found along the way. Provides a revealing look at this little noted but rapidly increasing aspect of contemporary life. p. Martha Stuart; STUARTM.

WOMEN: CHOOSING AND CHANGING (18m C n.d.) Women of Purpose Series
Features Dr. Mildred Erickson, Assistant Dean of Lifelong Education Programs at Michigan State University, who counsels hundreds of men and women in the over-twenty-five age group who are searching for new direction in their lives. Gives a brief glimpse into the trauma of Dr. Erickson's own personal adjustment to life as she experienced sudden and unexpected widowhood. We meet several women whose lives have been changed under her influence and supportive leadership. A very positive film. p. Elizabeth C. Kay Camp; p. Dick Arnold Productions; ARNPRO.

WOMEN, DRUGS AND ALCOHOL (21m p1979, r1980) (also Video)
It is revealed in this film that eight and half million American women a year use mind-altering drugs. Many former female drug abusers speak out detailing their nightmares of low self-esteem and difficulty coping followed by prescriptions for uppers, downers, and sleeping pills, often adding alcohol on their own until their lives became a vicious circle of anxiety, addiction and remorse. A woman physician states that many doctors believe men come to their offices with "real" problems while women come with "mental" problems. Because doctors often find nothing physically wrong with their women patients and do not know how to handle them, they simply prescribe pills to calm them down. Women do not often realize they are in a dangerous cycle of addiction, and do not want to think of themselves as "junkies." It is emphasized that women need to become aware of alternatives, be responsible for their own health and deal with their problems rather than running from them. The personal experiences of some of those women are revealing and leave a lasting impression. p./d. J. Gary Mitchell, John McDonald; s.w. Lydia McDonald; MTITI; UCEMC.

WOMEN GOLD MEDALISTS (50m C 1976)
Presents a television special from the CTV program "Olympiad" which gives tribute to women athletes who gained fame in various Olympic competitions for their winning performances. p. CTV; CTV.

WOMEN I LOVE (27m C n.d.)
"The camera as a personal extension of my body, my personality. Lesbian lovers, a new camera, celebration, play, footage collected over five years. Plus three months of country vegetable garden living without cultural distractions gave me the quiet, disciplined leisure to view the moviescope faces of those I love and edit the original film directly on the synchronizer while making the A/B rolls" --Barbara Hammer. p. Barbara Hammer; IRISFC.

WOMEN IN ARMS (59m C 1980)
Examines the part Nicaraguan women played in their struggle against Somoza and in the reconstruction of Nicaraguan society. The first major documentary filmed in Nicaragua after the overthrow of the Somoza dictatorship by the Sandinist National Liberation Front. Available in English and Spanish. d./p. Victoria Schultz; p. Hudson River Film and Video; HUDRFV.

WOMEN IN BUSINESS (30m C 1977) (Video)
Explores the role of women in the world of business in an era when nearly half of all American women work, and some 16 million represent the sole support of themselves and their families. Five accomplished women, representing education, law, banking, stocks and health care, discuss their careers and the problems they have encountered and coped with as professional women. Hosted by Robin Bates. NETCHE.

WOMEN IN BUSINESS (24m C p1979, r1980) (also Video)
Focuses on various women who own and run ten diverse businesses. Women discuss their feelings, problems and rewards relating to being in their own enterprise. The careers shown demonstrate that many satisfying opportunities exist for women willing to risk starting their own business. d./p. Len Berman; p. LSB Productions; LSBPRO; IU, UCEMC.

WOMEN IN CAREERS (15m C 1973) Career in the 70's Series
Introduces four females in skilled professions who feel their work is important to others and rewarding to themselves. Attempts to destroy the myth that women are helpless. DOUBLE.

WOMEN IN CHINA (27m C 1978)
Introduces several aspects of the change in status of women since the founding of the People's Republic of China. Focuses on changing work roles of both men and women, child care as it supports these roles and the use of education to transform ideas. p. Open Window Films; EDC.

WOMEN IN MEDICINE, GOALS FOR TODAY AND TOMORROW (50m B 1979) (Video)
This straightforward account highlights a regional conference on women in medicine sponsored by the Women's Medical Association of

New York City. Directed towards physicians, residents, and medical students, the tape addresses the problems encountered by women both in the health professions and as consumers of health services. p. Women's Medical Association of New York; WMM.

WOMEN IN SCIENCE (30m ea. 1978) (Video)
Six distinguished women scientists discuss the social and psychological barriers faced by women in the field of science in this two-part program. Participants include Dr. Francis Kelssey, Food and Drug Administration; Dr. Lucille Shapiro, biochemist, Albert Einstein College of Medicine; Dr. Christien Waternaux, statistician, Harvard University School of Public Health; Dr. Irene Frieze, psychologist, University of Pittsburgh; Carolyn Phillips, mechanical engineer, Shell Oil Company; and Dr. Ursula Abbott, geneticist, University of California at Davis. In Part 1, members of the panel share their careers, their reasons for going into the science field, combining a career with family life, and discrimination on the job. In Part 2, a group of female science majors question the panelists about the obstacles in their careers, communication with male colleagues, overcoming sex barriers, and the Equal Rights Amendment. p./d. Anne M. Parkhurst, Dr. Sylvia Wiegand, University of Nebraska-Lincoln. NETCHE.

WOMEN IN SCIENCE SERIES see ASTRONAUT SALLY RIDE

WOMEN IN SPORTS (58m C p1978, r1980) James Michener's World Series
Women's sports enjoy new prominence today. In this film, James Michener reviews the history of women in sports and examines the current status of women athletes and women's athletics. Rare footage of historic firsts and fascinating conversations with pioneers of women's sports highlight the film. In addition, coaches, journalists, young athletes and current superstars like Chris Evert Lloyd, Janet Guthrie and Nancy Lopez offer commentary on the past, present and future role of women in sports. p. Cappy Productions for TV; p./d./ s.w. Bud Greenspan; PF; UCEMC, KENTSU, UMN.

WOMEN IN SPORTS (28m C n.d.)
The message to American women is this: It's O.K. to struggle and sweat in sports, you don't have to be sideline cheerleaders anymore. Focus here is on women in competitive sports: A college basketball team from Tennessee; a crew team on the Charles River in Boston; an ice hockey scrimmage on Cornell University's campus; a 40-year-old woman who placed high in the New York City Women's Marathon. We see for ourselves that athletic participation is not just good for these women's minds and bodies, it's good for their futures. Demonstrates that teamwork experience they gain through sporting events proves invaluable in the business and professional worlds. Free loan. p. Sears, Roebuck and Company; MTPS.

WOMEN IN SPORTS--A SERIES see BARBARA ROQUEMORE (PARA-

CHUTING); BILLIE JEAN KING (TENNIS); JOAN WESTON (ROL-
LER DERBY); KIKI KUTTER BEATTIE (SKIING)

WOMEN IN SPORTS: AN INFORMAL HISTORY (28m C 1976)
    Surveys the participation of women in sports from classical times
to the present day. Discusses prejudice against the physically active woman, the growing awareness of women's rights as sports participants, and the new enthusiasm of women for sports. p. Dan
Klugherz Productions; ALTANA; CWU, PAS.

WOMEN IN THE CORPORATION: ON A PAR NOT A PEDESTAL
    (26m C c1977)
    Women at Connecticut Insurance Company were angry. Over 60
percent of the home office employees were women, and almost all had
clerical positions. Action by these women brought about changes
through workshops and programs to deal with these issues. Today,
when most large corporations have developed training programs to
deal with these issues, Connecticut General's program of in-house
workshops and training sessions is considered by many experts in
the field to be one of the most extensive and effective. The film
visually documents this unique program. DOCUA; MONAD.

WOMEN IN THE MIDDLE EAST: A TRILOGY see VEILED REVOLU-
    TION; WOMEN UNDER SIEGE; PRICE OF CHANGE, THE

WOMEN IN THE SILK (30m C 1982) (Video)
    Four women recall their work in the silk industry of Paterson,
New Jersey, at the turn of the century. d. Terence M. Ripmaster;
a.d. Patricia Anderson, p. Delight Dodyk; NYVAF.

WOMEN IN TRANSITION (29m C 1975) Woman Series
    Jennifer Fleming and Carolyn Washburn, two founding members
of "Women in Transition," explain the services of their group, which
provides discussion support groups and paralegal advice for women
going through separation and divorce. They talk about the guilt
and confusion experienced by many women who seek their help and
how the organization promotes emotional independence. Sandra Elkin
is the moderator. p. WNED-TV; PBSV.

WOMEN IN YOUR LIFE IS YOU (30m C p1978, r1979--U.S.)
    Examines women's sexuality. Explores with sensitivity and with-
out titillation, the experiences of four women: a 50-year-old woman
in her second marriage, a Maori; solo mother; and a lesbian couple.
What goes wrong with sexual relationships and what can be done to
develop satisfying contact with our partners? A psychologist working
in a center for Human Relationship and Therapy has concluded we
need to know our bodies better; we need to understand masturbation,
learn about our sexual organs and identify our needs. When it comes
to sexuality and what you want, who knows best? d./p. Deirdre
McCartin; p. Television One Production, New Zealand; LUCERNE.

WOMEN INSIDE (60m C p1979, r1980)
Features Bill Moyers interviewing inmates at Miami's Dade County
Women's Detention Center to present a frank view of women in prison
and the binding circumstances of poverty, poor education, and other
difficulties which keep them in trouble. Focuses on the women prisoners, most serving time for nonviolent crimes involving prostitution
and/or narcotics, as they speak openly of their families, their home
environments, life in the streets, and why they repeat their offenses.
Examines the efforts of warden Pam Davis and her staff to provide
vocational and personal alternatives for women. Includes strong language and scenes of nudity during an admissions search. d. Elisabeth Fink Benjamin, Mark Benjamin; ex. p. Joan Konner; s.w. Sarah
Stein; WNET-TV; FI; IU; UMT, UCEMC, PAS.

WOMEN LIKE US (52m C 1979) (also Video)
Three women, each happy in the life-style she has chosen, exemplify some of the options open to women today. Judy is a working
wife and mother. She enjoys the stimulation of her job as a nurse.
Juggling work and family life is made easier by the cooperation of her
husband, who is involved with both children and housework. Benita
plays a major role in running the publishing company of which she is
vice-president. She finds her work challenging and enjoys the power
she wields. She lives alone, but a full social life keeps her from
loneliness. Marie is a homemaker by choice. Her life revolves around
home and family, but she says she never thinks of herself as "only
a housewife." Her sense of personal identity is strong. When her
children are grown she may finish college, or go back to work. For
the present she is content to be at home. Narrated by Betty Rollin.
p. Bill Turque; d. Marvin Einhorn; p. NBC News; FI.

WOMEN MAKE THE DIFFERENCE (28m C 1980)
Eva Marie Saint, our guide, takes us on a tour representing 25
years of Community Improvement Projects achievement. We stop in
Indiana to see a successful crime reduction effort, go on to California
where the elderly are being protected from swindlers, and end our
journey in Rhode Island with a view of an ambitious project to protect abused women. The result is a double prize--better communities,
and the new skills, self-confidence or just plain fulfillment acquired
by the women volunteers. Free loan. Sears, Roebuck and Company;
MTPS.

WOMEN, MONEY AND POWER (29m C 1976) (Video) Woman Series
Author Phyllis Chesler (Woman, Money and Power) discusses the
need for women to educate themselves about the nature of the American economic system before they can attain real power. She believes
that a double standard exists in the money culture, and that women
themselves perpetuate it through deferential attitudes toward the people who wield power--primarily men. She suggests that a child depletion allowance, similar in theory to the oil depletion allowance, be
incorporated into the tax structure. Sandra Elkin is the moderator.
p. WNED-TV; PBSV.

WOMEN OF HODSON, THE (28m C 1980) (also Video)
A group of septuagenarians in the South Bronx who, after a life of hard work and struggle, now finally have time for themselves. These women have been offered an exciting alternative, and it has recharged their lives. The Hodson Senior Citizen Center is the setting for a unique program of improvisational theater. Under the leadership of Susan Pearlstein, a professional in community theater, they develop and perform original works based on their own life experiences. In the process they establish a rapport with one another and with their audiences. Their stories reflect their rich individual histories as well as the times in which they lived. The Hodson women are not anonymous social security numbers. They are stars, and also part of a team. Their elderly audience laughs and cries with approval, identifying with the players. Here is a pilot program that can be adapted in a variety of settings. A good film to show young people to break down stereotypes of old age. d./p. Josephine Hayes Dean; FILMLB.

WOMEN OF INDIA (17m B 1964)
Presents a documentary tracing the achievements of women in various activities, arts and sciences in modern India. Includes a brief historical sketch of women's role in Indian history and society. p. Indian Government Films Division, Ministry of Information and Broadcasting; INDFLM.

WOMEN OF PAKISTAN (20m C 1963)
Depicts activities and colorful costumes of Pakistan women. Presents the work of the Women's National Guard. p. Embassy of Pakistan; AMFE.

WOMEN OF PURPOSE SERIES see WOMEN: CHOOSING AND CHANGING; WORLD OF GWEN FROSTIC

WOMEN: SKILLED (15m C 1976)
Skills training in the Job Corp is not just for men. Women are training for jobs from typing to welding. This film explores how this training is accomplished and how employers are taking advantage of these opportunities to hire skilled employees. p. University of Missouri; UMO.

WOMEN TODAY SERIES see SINGLE PARENT

WOMEN UNDER SIEGE (26m C 1982) (also Video)
Rashadiyah is a town in Southern Lebanon, six miles north of the Israeli border. Once a peaceful agricultural village, in 1964 it became the setting for a camp housing 14,000 Palestinian refugees. For years they lived under constant harassment and threat of Israeli attack. Women play a crucial role in the Palestinian community, as mothers, teachers, political organizers, farm laborers, and fighters. Through actuality footage and interviews with the women of Rashadiyah,

this film explores the lives of six representative Palestinian women. In June 1982 the town of Rashadiyah was bombed and attacked by Israeli forces. The camp was reduced to ruins, many of the residents forced to flee again. Made by an all-women crew (British, American, and Arab). p. Elizabeth Fernea; d. Marilyn Gaunt; ICARF; WSU.

WOMEN WANT (25m C 1975)
Presents a look at the sociocultural, legal, political and business status of women. Includes a historical perspective of these issues. p. International Women's Year, Secretariat for the Privy Council; International Cinemedia Center; NFBC.

WOMEN WHO CARE (30m B 1967)
Tells the story of two women volunteers in a small southern U.S. city, who take time to help young people find their way back to productive lives and a brighter future. United States Information Agency; USINFA.

WOMEN WHO DIDN'T HAVE AN ABORTION (29m C p1981, r1981) (also
        Video) Are You Listening Series
A companion piece to the earlier film WOMEN WHO HAVE HAD AN ABORTION, this program treats the other side of what has become one of the most difficult personal decisions of the age. Here are equally mixed and articulate group of women discuss their reasons for deciding against abortion, touching on the emotional, moral, religious, social, political, and practical aspects of the question. Together the two programs offer a unique package of opposing viewpoints laid out in the form of personal testimonials. The programs are provocative, honest, complicated, and highly stimulating of further discussion. p. Martha Stuart; STUARTM.

WOMEN WHO HAVE HAD AN ABORTION (24m C p1981, r1981) (also
        Video) Are You Listening Series
Black and white, rich and poor, young and not so young, married and single, all the women in this film have had at least one abortion and have come together to discuss this controversial subject. Taking turns offering their viewpoints the women talk about their feelings and wishes and offer suggestions to help other women deal with the problem. They see abortion as an issue about which society has formed two opposing sides. p. Martha Stuart; STUARTM.

WOMEN WITH A MESSAGE (20m C 1973)
Depicts training and career opportunities in the field of telecommunications for officers and enlisted women in the United States Navy. p. United States Navy; USNAC.

WOMEN WRITERS: VOICES OF DISSENT (C n.d.) (sfs)
Provides portraits of three talented writers of the early 1900's—Edith Wharton, Ellen Glasgow, and Willa Cather—using historic prints

and dramatized quotations and excerpts. p. Educational Enrichment
Materials; EDENM.

WOMEN'S ANSWER (RESPONSE DE FEMMES) (8m C 1978) (SFS)
Series of visually arresting tableaux featuring women and men
engaged in dialogue about the issues raised by the women's movement. People appear in unexpected spacial arrangements, are sometimes nude, are different ages and sizes and classes. Constantly
stimulating, both from the insights contained in what participants
have to say, and for the verve and unconventional manner with which
Varda attempts to examine perceptions about women. p. Agnes Varda;
SERBC.

WOMEN'S ASTROLOGY (29m C 1977) Woman Series
Tiffany Holmes, author of Women's Astrology: Your Astrological
Guide to a Future Worth Having, discusses the negativism she finds
in the traditional interpretation of astrology for women. A professional astrologer, Holmes explains how the language of astrology has
been read since the Middle Ages and suggests that value judgments
have been incorrectly placed. She also comments on the appeal of
astrology and how it influences its adherents. Sandra Elkin is the
moderator. p. WNED-TV; PBSV.

WOMENS BANKS AND CREDIT UNIONS (29m C 1976) (Video) Woman
Series
Joanne Parrent, co-founder of the Feminist Federal Credit Union
of Detroit, and Madeline McWhinney, president of First Women's Bank
of New York City, talk about the founding of their innovative organizations, the response their institutions have received from the women
they serve and the impact women's financial institutions can have on
a community. Both women agree that long-standing attitudes about
women held by traditional banking institutions have made it difficult
for women to obtain their own credit. Sandra Elkin is the moderator.
p. WNED-TV; PBSV.

WOMEN'S BASKETBALL: BALL HANDLING, PASSING, DRIBBLING
(15m C 1974)
Demonstrates some of the most effective ball handling and offensive techniques that will enable the coach and women athletes to produce a winning team. p. Mar-Chuck Film Industries, Inc.; MCFI;
UIL, UNEV.

WOMEN'S BASKETBALL: BASIC SKILLS, SHOOTING, OFFENSIVE
TECHNIQUES (15m C 1974)
An "All Star" women's basketball team demonstrates and teaches
the basic skills of shooting various type of shots. p. Mar-Chuck
Film Industries, Inc.; MCFI, UIL, UNEV.

WOMEN'S BASKETBALL WITH CATHY RUSH (Pt. 1, 14m; Pt. 2, 15m
C 1977)
In Part I, Cathy Rush demonstrates a complete conditioning course

with special exercises for the muscle tone, suppleness, quick reflexes and stamina needed for competitive play. In Part II, Cathy demonstrates drills and skills designed to develop ball control, accuracy in passing, dribbling and shooting. MACMFL; SILU.

WOMEN'S COALITION FOR THE THIRD CENTURY (29m C 1976) (Video)
Woman Series
Wilma Scott Heide, vice-president of a new organization called "Women's Coalition for the Third Century," explains the group's objectives. Its purpose is to bring together national organizations to identify practical movements for change. The organization views its role as a group of architects for the future. Sandra Elkin is the moderator. p. WNED-TV; PBSV.

WOMEN'S FACES (11m C 1973)
Presents three different views of three different women in an examination of the nature of woman. FI.

WOMEN'S FLOOR EXERCISES (2m B 1973)
Features gymnast Lisa Arsenault demonstrating the women's floor exercise event. p. University of Manitoba, Canada; UMANI.

WOMEN'S GYMNASTICS: COMPULSORY ROUTINES, CLASS I (20m C p1975)
Demonstrates floor exercises, vault, balance beam, uneven parallel bars at the advanced level. Narration, split screen, slow motion and freeze frame are used effectively to convey understanding. p. Athletic Institute; VC; UIL.

WOMEN'S GYMNASTICS: COMPULSORY ROUTINES, CLASS II (20m C p1975)
On the intermediate level, this film uses slow motion, freeze frame and split screen cinema to demonstrate squat vault, balance beam, uneven parallel bars and floor exercises. Narration coaches all the movements and basic skills. p. Athletic Institute; VC; UIL.

WOMEN'S GYMNASTICS: COMPULSORY ROUTINES, CLASS III (19m C p1975)
Covers four areas at beginning level in floor exercises, squat flight vault, balance beam, and uneven parallel bars. Regular, slow motion, and freeze frame photography parallels the narrator's description of techniques and forms. p. Athletic Institute; VC; UIL.

WOMEN'S GYMNASTICS NATIONAL COMPULSORY ROUTINES 1976-1980--A SERIES see WOMEN'S GYMNASTICS: COMPULSORY ROUTINES, CLASS I; ... CLASS II; ... CLASS III

WOMEN'S HEALTH: A QUESTION OF SURVIVAL (49m C 1977)
ABC "News Closeup" reporter Marlene Sanders investigates the questionable health care women may receive--including the adminis-

tering of potentially dangerous drugs to pregnant women, questionable mastectomies and hysterectomies, and unproven birth control methods. Also discussed is the indifference of doctors, drug manufacturers and government regulators. One reviewer has stated that this film should be seen by all women and men--particularly physicians and congresspeople. p. ABC-TV; UMN, WSU.

WOMEN'S HEALTH CARE: A HISTORY (26m C 1975) (Video) Woman Series

Scholar Virginia Drachman discusses the history of women's involvement in the health care field. She describes the changes that took place at the turn of the nineteenth century when physicians began teaching obstetrics and gynecology in medical schools to which women had no access, and how this caused women to lose responsibility for their own health care. Sandra Elkin is the moderator. p. WNED-TV; PBSV.

WOMEN'S IMAGE: DOWN THE TUBE (29m C 1976) (Video) Woman Series

Katheleen Bonk and Joyce Snyder, national coordinators of the National Organization for Women's Media Task Force, explain their view that women have more to lose than men by having a ridiculous television image. They cite commercials as the biggest offenders, portraying both men and women as shallow people with petty concerns, and explain that consumers have some redress through the Federal Trade Commission and their own selective buying. Sandra Elkin is the moderator. p. WNED-TV; PBSV.

WOMEN'S ISSUES (24m C 1981) (also Video) Trigger Films on Human Interactions Series

The vignettes in this film present many of the typical messages, requests and demands that women receive daily. The film is designed to be used in discussion groups to help each woman sort out her own values and develop ways of saying "No" to the messages and demands that are not right for her. Guide included. p. Family Information Systems and Resource Communications, Inc.; MTITI.

WOMEN'S PAGES (29m C 1976) (Video) Woman Series

Judy Klemersrud, staff reporter for the New York Times, and Barbara Hinton, editor of the women's pages for the Las Vegas Review Journal, question whether women's pages are the pioneers in positive coverage of various life-styles or dumping grounds for engagement pictures and advertising. The journalists give a brief history of women's pages and the kinds of style and content changes that occurred between 1969 and 1973, and they comment on current problems and prospects for the future. Sandra Elkin is the moderator. p. WNED-TV; PBSV.

WOMEN'S PLACE, A (14m C 1974) Time to Consider Series

Covers a wide range of views concerning the status of women in

Canada in the 1970's. Information Canada; p. International Cinemedia Center; NFBC.

WOMEN'S RIGHTS (22m C n.d.) The Bill of Rights in Action Series

A high school girl wants to swim on the boys' swim team, but there are state by-laws which prohibit this. In a court action, her lawyer states that these by-laws are unconstitutional, because the 14th Amendment guarantees equal protection of the law to all citizens, regardless of race or sex. The attorney for the state argues that there are differences between men and women that make equality impossible when questions of size and strength are crucial or when our traditional concepts of privacy are violated. Open-ended. BARRF; WSU.

WOMEN'S RIGHTS IN THE COURTS (18m C 1981) (Video, VHS) One on One Series

Judy Nicely, Akron, Ohio attorney and member of the Legal Aid Board, discusses how the Supreme Court has protected women's rights. She is interviewed by Sandy Halem. p. KSU-TV; KSUTV; KENTSU.

WOMEN'S SERVICE TO THE NATION (10m B 1964)

Discusses the contributions of American women to the national welfare from Colonial times to the twentieth century. United States Army; USNAC.

WOMEN'S SERVICE TO THE NATION--SUMMARY AND CONCLUSION (8m C 1968)

Describes contributions of America's women to the nation from pioneer days to the twentieth century. Recalls their courage and self-sacrifice during the times of war and their progressive efforts in times of peace. Emphasizes the expanded role of women in the Armed Forces and in industrial, professional and governmental areas. United States Army; USNAC.

WOMEN'S STUDIES (29m C 1975) (Video) Woman Series

Liz Kennedy, a founding member of the Women's Studies College at the State University of New York at Buffalo, and Kate Stimpson of Barnard College's women's studies program, discuss the dramatic increase in women's studies courses offered at American colleges and universities. They explain the content of courses in women's history and feminist approaches to traditional disciplines, and talk of harassment by university administrations toward these programs. Sandra Elkin is the moderator. p. WNED-TV; PBSV.

WOMEN'S TRACK AND FIELD: FUNDAMENTALS OF RUNNING (17m C 1975)

Demonstrates running events at all distances, hurdling, and sprint relay techniques. Utilizes slow motion, split screen and freeze frame, with voice-over narration. p. Athletic Institute; VC; UIL.

WOMEN'S TRACK AND FIELD: THE JUMPING EVENTS (15m C 1976)
An informative documentary on long jump and high jump techniques using freeze frame and slow-motion photography to demonstrate the fundamentals. For the long jump, the hitch hang and hitch kick are illustrated and explained. For the high jump, methods of the straddle roll and the flop are shown. A voice-over narration teaches important points: discipline, practice, concentration, horizontal velocity, take off, flight and landing. p. Athletic Institute; VC; UIL.

WOMEN'S TRACK AND FIELD: THE RUNNING EVENTS (20m C 1976)
Strategies, techniques and rules of the distance sprints, hurdles, sprint relay exchange, and distance relay exchange are demonstrated, with an explanatory narration. Slow motion, freeze frame and split screen cinema are used as well as regular photography. p. Athletic Institute; VC; UIL.

WOMEN'S TRACK AND FIELD: THE THROWING EVENTS (20m C 1976)
Basic strategies of the shot put, discus and javelin are demonstrated and analyzed. Cinema techniques such as slow motion, split screen and freeze frame are widely used. A voice-over narration coaches all body movements. p. Athletic Institute; VC; UIL.

WOMEN'S WORK--AMERICA 1620-1920 (58m C 1974) (sfs)
This four-part series shows the history of women's rights from Colonial times through the 1920's. Presents events in America's past which students can relate to today's feminist controversy. SCHLAT; UMN.

WOMEN'S WORK IN MIXTECO VILLAGE (22m C 1975)
Sex roles are culturally determined. Many aspects of the tasks assigned to women in this rural Mexican culture are described. Special emphasis is given to the use of the primitive backstrap loom. In addition to the usual daily tasks, some aspects that fiestas play in the women's lives are mentioned. p. University of Southern Florida; USFL.

WOMEN'S WORLD OF GOLF SERIES (20m ea. B n.d.)
Shows highlights of women golf professionals in action. WOMEN'S WORLD OF GOLF--BETSY RAWLS. WOMEN'S WORLD OF GOLF-- MICKEY WRIGHT. WOMEN'S WORLD OF GOLF--PATTY BERG. p. Sportlight Films; SFI.

WOODEN FLOWERS OF NOVA SCOTIA (14m C p1979, r1980)
Matilda Paul, a Micmac Indian, uses wood shavings to make life-like flowers of exceptional color and beauty. This contemporary craft was handed down from her aunt, Madeline Knockwood, who developed the craft in the 1930's. d. Geoff Voyce; p. B. T. Film Sound; NAINDF.

WOOLLOOMOOLOO (75m B 1978)
A social and historical documentary of the redevelopment of one of the old maritime areas of Sydney. It covers the period between 1969 and 1977. Events and attitudes of developers, residents, government officials, squatters and labor union activists (who placed the neighborhood interests above their own economic interests) concisely represent the conflict. p. Pat Fiske, Denise White; KARTF.

WORD IS OUT: STORIES OF SOME OF OUR LIVES (45m C p1978, r1979)
Interviews with 26 very diverse people--ranging in age from 18 to 77, in locales from San Francisco to New Mexico to Boston, in type from housewife with beehive hairdo to the sultriest drag queen--who speak tellingly, funnily, and movingly of their experiences as gay men and women in a way that destroys decades worth of accumulated sterotypes. p. Mariposa Film Group: Nancy Adair, Peter Adair, Veronica Selver, Andrew Brown, Robert Epstein, and Lucy Macy; PHOENIX; NYF.

WORDS (14m C 1977)
Shows how children can create their own word games, and how they can increase the awareness of the beauty and uniqueness of letters and words as a way of expressing oneself creatively and to expand ideas for written expression. d./s.w. Jane Treiman; CF; UIL.

WORK AND FULFILLMENT (59m C n.d.) Young and Old Reaching Out (Series)
The American Dream, what it means to the old and the young, is the theme of this program. Changing values about work, money, education, business and success are examined by participants which include Senator Sam Ervin and George Willig, the man who scaled New York's World Trade Center. p. Communications Resource Foundation, Inc.; PBSV.

WORK AND RETIREMENT (21m C 1981) Aging in the Future Series
Describes the shift in the United States from wanting people to retire earlier to wanting them to work longer. Presents the problem of larger numbers of retirees being supported by smaller numbers of fully employed workers. Interviews retirees who went back to work. UMMRC, UM, UIL.

WORK AND YOU: DO YOU KNOW WHAT YOU WANT? (18m C 1976)
Narrator Sam Melville opens the film by saying that there are 22,000 different kinds of jobs to choose from in the world of work. Film explores reasons people must work: to accommodate a certain life-style; to eat; to provide a place to live; to afford not only the basic necessities but those things that bring comfort and pleasure. Explains that friends, parents, teachers and counselors can help young people in choosing a career, but the young person should

make the final decision, based on careful and thoughtful investigation. States that whether you are a woman or a man, and whatever your ethnic heritage, fewer and fewer barriers stand between you and the career you are prepared for and want. p. Arthur Barr Productions, Inc.; SANDIF.

WORK, WORK, WORK (59m C 1977) (Video)
Documentary examining the concept of work from ancient times to the present. Explores the academic and philosophical questions surrounding the "work ethic" and introduces individual workers who discuss their feelings about their jobs. Also speculates on the future of jobs and alternatives to work. p. New Jersey Television Authority; NJPT.

WORKER TO WORKER (29m C 1981)
Paul Heinrich has liver cancer. So he's filing suit. Why? He claims his cancer was caused by chemicals at the tire factory where he worked. Shirley Embrey had her hours cut after she complained to the Health Department about working conditions at a restaurant. Now she's won reinstatement and back pay. Nick Crudo and Steve Pasquarillo had jobs making pesticide. When their children were born with rare heart defects, both men fought back. Narrated by Studs Terkel. p. Durrin Films, Inc.; DURRIN.

WORKING AGAINST RAPE (60m C 1979) (Video)
Provides a sociopolitical analysis of rape. Includes interviews with rape victims, the head of a rape crisis center, and lawyers. Designed to help inform people about the problem, with an eye to "long-term elimination, rather than short-term prevention," says Laurie Foster, one of the producers and a 1979 Stanford graduate. Booklet by same title also available. p. Working Against Rape; WORKAR.

WORKING ARTISTS SERIES see CAROLE MORISSEAU AND THE DETROIT CITY DANCE COMPANY; GERHARDT KNODEL: AN ARTIST AND HIS WORK; JOHN GLICK: AN ARTIST AND HIS WORK; MICHAEL HALL: SCULPTOR

WORKING CLASS ON FILM, THE (14m C 1976--U.S.)
Presents the first completed film on the origins of the documentary. Short segments of documentary films produced from 1929 to 1975 illustrate the history and progress of this kind of filmmaking as an instrument of education and social progress. John Grierson conceived the idea in the 1920's which started the movement in documentary. His documentary DRIFTERS (1929) exposed the harshness of working conditions of common laborers and became an important force in organizing workers and forming committees and unions. d. Susan Schouten; NFBC.

WORKING CLASS WOMEN (29m C 1977) (Video) Woman Series
Nancy Seifer, Director of the Center on Women and American

Diversity, and Mary Sansone, Executive Director of the Congress of
Italian American Organizations, discuss the role of the working woman.
They cite conditioning, cultural mores and the lack of communication
among women as factors contributing to what they term the "voice-
lessness of women in the working class." Sandra Elkin is the moderator. p. WNED-TV; PBSV.

WORKING FOR A LIVING: JOB SKILLS FOR THE REAL WORLD (47m
    C 1981) (slc) Job Opportunities for the 1980's Series
    Introduces students to the world of work: helps them discover
that evaluating the relationship between work, personal values and
needs is a critical step toward making a vocational choice. Familiar-
izes students with the immediate realities of the working environment
and examines aspects of the employer-employee relationship. p.
Guidance Associates, Inc.; COMPVF; UMN.

WORKING FOR YOUR LIFE (57m C 1980)
    Examines the health and safety problems where women (and men)
work. Filmed in over 40 work places, we see stress and fatigue on
jobs often considered technically safe. Shows women who are actively
seeking solutions by organizing health and safety committees, testifying at hearings, and requesting government investigations. Provides
a needed overview of the scope and complexity of the hazards faced
by working women. A film that dramatically destroys the myth that
women's work is safe work. Shows the importance of organizing
women into unions. d. Andrea Hricko, Ken Light; ed. Charles West;
LOHP Films; UCEMC.

WORKING MOTHER, THE (29m C 1978) Look at Me Series
    Sorting and matching in the laundromat; a counting experience
while walking in the city; making a telephone call; exploring nature
on a family picnic; writing a book based on a paper airplane experience; helping a working mom with cooking; creating a rhythm band.
p. WTTW-TV; PEREN.

WORKING RIVER (58m C p1981, r1982) (Video)
    The Ohio River as experienced by people who live and work on
it--from a tow-boat crew to a homesteading artist. A retired river
captain interweaves an often witty oral history of the river, complemented by his black and white film footage shot in the 1920's. From
these people comes the evolving history of a river that has served
a multiplicity of needs; economic, recreational, environmental and
spiritual. d. Randy Strothman/Letitia Langord; p./s.w. Letitia Langord; ed. Randy Strothman; UPITTS.

WORKING SMARTER, NOT HARDER (16m C n.d.)
    Open-ended case study of one manager's development, from an
overworked, compulsive problem-solver to an innovator whose unique
new system draws public attention. p. Monad Trainer's Aide; MONAD.

WORKING WITH OTHERS (30m C 1981) Professional Skills for Secretaries Series
Not only can good interpersonal skills make a secretary's work-
day easier and more pleasant, but they can contribute to the good
will and good public relations of the organization itself. A note of
personal pride is interjected here. Viewers are urged to care enough
about the quality of their work to proofread typewritten correspondence and to check spelling, usage, etc. in a dictionary. Perhaps no
one in an office environment has to be as adaptable as an entry level
secretary. Ways to cope with ever-changing processes, priorities
and personalities are suggested. In a crisis, secretaries should be
able to remain calm and flexible. Leader's manual and participants'
handbooks included. p. Time-Life Video; TIMLIF.

WORKING WOMEN: POTTERY MAKING IN AMATENANGO DEL VALLE
(20m C 1980) (Video) (Spanish/Subtitled)
A detailed examination of Maya pottery-making, this videotape
follows Alberta Lopez through every step of the process. Señora
Lopez digs the clay, constructs pots and paints them with turkey
quills dipped into slip glaze. She is assisted by her daughters and
granddaughters in the outdoor firing. The narration of the process
is provided by Juliana, Alberta's sister. p. Lyn Tiefenbacher, Den-
isce Dilanni, David Pentecost; BRUNOM.

WORKPLACE HUSTLE, THE (30m C r1980) (also Video)
Designed to inform, motivate, and sensitize. Focuses attention
on the damaging effects of sexual harassment on productivity, morale
and the hidden human and monetary loss to the employer. Using
real people and situations, the film explores the behavior and motivation of harassers, details the real cost of unchecked harassment
on victims and employers, discusses the impact of recent court rul-
ings on personnel policies and procedures, outlines common sense,
solution-oriented strategies. Narrated by Ed Asner. p. Clark Communications Inc./Creative Life Design; d. Albert E. Brito; p. Woodrow
Clark, Jr.; ABCWWL; UCEMC, UIL, UM, UMN, UW, WSU.

WORLD CULTURES AND YOUTH: SERAMA'S MASK (25m C p1979,
r1979)
Since he was seven, on the languid island of Bali, Serama has
been learning the intricate, ancient art of the Balinese dance. His
teacher is his father, a master dancer. They practice for a dance
that will be the father's final performance, and mark his son as replacement. Serama carves his beautiful dance mask and in a spectacular performance, the tradition passes to him. p./d. Deepa Saltzman, Paul Saltzman; CORONET.

WORLD CULTURES AND YOUTH: YOSHIKO THE PAPERMAKER (25m
C p1979, r1979)
Yoshiko Fujimoto, 13, lives in the tiny moutain village of Obara-
Mura which retains its tradition for unique handmade paper. Guided

by local master, Mr. Ando, she helps make the kozo-tree paper and designs a lovely bamboo forest on her panel. The process is demanding, she defers her decision to become an apprentice until after she finishes her schooling. d./p. Deepa Saltzman, Paul Saltzman; CORONET.

WORLD FEMINISTS (28m C 1980) Are You Listening Series
An international group of feminists from Saudi Arabia, Barbados, Italy, Holland, Bangladesh, Mexico, Thailand, Australia, Ghana, India, the Fiji Islands, and the United States discuss some of the primary issues facing women today and the need for international support networks. p. Martha Stuart; STUARTM.

WORLD OF COOKING: A VENETIAN MENU, THE (25m C p1979, r1979)
Students may associate Italy with pizza--if so, they are in for a wonderful experience with the variety of foods and people which this beautiful country provides. Shot on location at an inn at which Napoleon is supposed to have stayed, the film explores the work of Chef Niero. p. Marilyn Weiner, Harold M. Weiner; d. Harold M. Weiner. p. Screenscope, Inc.; SCRESC.

WORLD OF FRANKLIN AND JEFFERSON, THE (28m C 1977)
Traces the interlocking careers of two men, Franklin and Jefferson. The film spans 120 years before and after the year of independence. Also presents the life-styles of city and town in early America, in a thorough coverage of the fine arts and the handicrafts of Colonial life. Narrated by Orson Welles and Nina Foch. Made with the cooperation of the Metropolitan Museum of Art. p. Ray Eames, Charles Eames; PF.

WORLD OF GWEN FROSTIC (13m C n.d.) Women of Purpose Series
Filmed interview with Gwen Frostic. Nestled among the tall trees and lakes, Gwen has built a thriving business marketing the products inspired by her writings and artistry. Gwen tells of her background in education and art, of her early work in copper and brass, of her years in a Ford Motor Company plant during World War II, and her move to northern Michigan. We see her well-organized print shop, mail room activities, and the retail shop which is visited by thousands of people throughout the year. p. Elizabeth C. Kay Camp; ARNPRO.

WORLD OF LIGHT: A PORTRAIT OF MAY SARTON (30m C p1979, r1980) (also Video)
Portrait of one of America's most versatile and sensitive writers, May Sarton. Filmed on location in Maine. Shows Sarton's day and activities as she explores her life and works with energy, humor, and insight. Sarton discusses her creative process, presents her views and experiences on solitude, aging, the woman writer discipline, integrity and relationships and reads from her poetry and novels. d./p. Marita Simpson, Martha Wheelock, Liz Van Patten; ISHTAR.

WORLD OF MOTHER TERESA, THE (58m C 1981) (also Video)
This compelling documentary shows why Mother Teresa is called "the saint of the gutter." For over 30 years Mother Teresa has brought life, love and hope to thousands who have become outcasts in their own society. She has relentlessly pursued her mission from India to the remote corners of the world. Today, at age 70, she directs 200 centers in 36 countries on six continents. For two weeks, a camera crew followed Mother Teresa around India and recorded the way she inspires people to deal with the toughest problem in the world--poverty. Her tools are compassion, wit, wisdom and love. Hosted by Joyce Davidson; d./p./s.w. Ann Petrie; FI; UMN, UCEMC.

WORLD WILDLIFE FUND--U.S.: THE THIRD DECADE (22m C 1982)
Describes the diversity of the World Wildlife Fund's conversation programs. Described by the project leaders themselves, the programs illustrated are tropical forest research and conservation in Brazil, the establishment of a national park in Sierra Leone, humpback whale research off Hawaii, etc. United corporation leaders discuss the importance of cooperation. Bio-diversity is stressed as the long-term goal for all. d. Robert Pierce; p. Megan Epler Wood; WWFUS.

WORLD WITHOUT SHADOWS, A see MAUD LEWIS: A WORLD WITHOUT SHADOWS

WORLD'S CHILDREN SERIES see WITH PATSY IN ST. VINCENT

WORLD'S FAVORITE PRUNE, THE (21m C p1981, r1982)
Traces the history, growth and development of the prune-growing industry in the United States, following all phases of cultivation, harvesting, and processing through Sunsweet Growers. Free loan. d. Will Furman; p. Norma Doane; MTPS.

WORLD'S YOUNG BALLET (70m B 1970) (English Narration)
A unique documentary offering a penetrating look at dancers participating in an international competition in Moscow in 1969. Dancers from 20 countries performing excerpts from such works as Giselle, La Mer, and Bakhshi, are shown both on- and off-stage. Featured are Alicia Alonso, Galina Ullanova, Maya Plisetskaya, and others. Filmed in the Bolshoi Theatre. This film is invaluable both as a historical document and an aesthetic one. Starring: Liopa Araujo; d. Arkadi Tsineman; CORINTH.

WRITER IN AMERICA, THE (SERIES) see EUDORA WELTY; JANET FLANNER; MURIEL RUKEYSER; TONI MORRISON

-X-

XALA (123m C 1974) (Wolof and French/Subtitled)
A satire about a Senegalese businessman who on his wedding night

is struck by the evil eye. He is a man caught in the crosscurrents of two cultures. Based on Sembene's book <u>Xala</u>, the film will raise questions related to its central theme: the role of folkways and tradition, Europeanism and neocolonialism. d. Ousmane Sembene; NYF.

XIAN (58m C p1980, r1981)
Presents a cultural history of the ancient Chinese Imperial city, once the greatest capital in the world and the Eastern terminus of the famed Silk Road. Includes extensive and unique footage of one of the world's most spectacular archaeological sites, the tomb of China's first emperor, Qin Shi Huang Di, who unified the country and constructed the Great Wall. d. Shirley Sun; p. Sue Yung Li; UCEMC.

-Y-

YANG-XUN THE PEASANT PAINTER (25m C p1981, r1981--U.S.)
(also Video)
Shows that majority of the Chinese live in villages in rural areas and their involvement in building their nation. Tells the story of a peasant artist, Nee Yang-Xun, and how he went about completing his drawing in competition with other students in his school in the hope that it would be chosen as one of the paintings that would be placed in a gallery. d. Deepa Saltzman, Paul Saltzman; Sunrise Films, Ltd. in cooperation with Canadian Broadcasting. CORONET.

YANOMAMO SERIES see FIREWOOD

YEAR TIME CHANGED, THE (27m C/Sepia 1979)
Using rare footage dating back to 1896, the film explores the nature of America during the decade 1900-1910, and highlights the events and inventions that made that time a "turning point" in the history and development of this country. Free loan. p. Mary Manilla; PENNEY.

YELLOW LEAF, THE (30m C 1956)
Presents a study of the problems of an elderly widow who is forced to leave her daughter's household to live in a home for the aged. Explains how although shocked and disappointed at first, she overcomes her dejection when she finds that her new home offers congenial friends, new interests, and a measure of independence she had not had before. NFBC; CWU.

YELLOW WALLPAPER, THE (14m C 1977)
This film, set in the 1890's and based on the rediscovered literary masterpiece by Charlotte Perkins Gilman, is the story of a woman's mental breakdown. Elizabeth, a Victorian woman and aspiring writer, is rebelling against her predestined societal role and desperately battling to maintain her sanity. Her doctor/husband's idea of a "rest cure" for her includes a planned schedule for each day, total

rest, isolation--in short, a lack of intellectual stimulation, activity and work which Elizabeth craves. Without stimulation in her world, Elizabeth's mind creates another world, the world of the wallpaper in which she envisions a woman trapped and unable to escape. p./d. Marie Ashton; WMM.

YES, MA'AM (48m C p1980, r1981)
Documents the black household workers of New Orleans today, a vanishing remnant of the Old South. Who are they and how have they adapted to the radically different world which has emerged around them? Some of the subjects interviewed include lifelong "retainers" for prominent families, day-workers in several persons' homes, a union of household workers, their employers, the children of the workers, and the white children whom the workers helped to raise. d./p. Gary Goldman; GOLDMAN.

YES, YOU CAN! (28m C 1980) (also Video) You Can Do It ... If Series
Examines what viewers would like to change in their lives and shows them how to make this change possible. Marilyn Van Derbur narrates this film based on the statement "I am the way I am today, but I can change," giving examples of people who made a decision to change their lives. Van Derbur examines the lives of Jean Nideitch, founder of Weight Watchers; actress Ellen Burstin; golfer Ken Ventura; tennis player Rod Laver; boxer Ron Lyle; and her own life. p. Marilyn Van Derbur; VDBER.

YESTERDAY'S WITNESSES IN AMERICA SERIES see LONG MARCH OF THE SUFFRAGISTS, THE

YIDDISH: THE MAME-LOSHN (58m C 1979)
Documentary on Yiddish--the centuries-old mother tongue of the Jews. Shot in New York and Los Angeles, the film features interviews with David Steinberg, Leo Rosten, Herschel Bernardi, Dr. Joshua Fishman. Film clips evoke memories of the heyday of the Yiddish theatre, etc. d. Cordelia Stone, Mary Hardwick, Pierrer Sauvage; SAUVGE.

YOSHIKO, THE PAPERMAKER see WORLD CULTURES AND YOUTH: YOSHIKO, THE PAPERMAKER

YOU ARE GROWING DAY BY DAY (9m C 1980)
Identifies growth as an on-going process and describes and illustrates some of the physical and psychological changes that take place in that process. An excellent life science film to help children understand themselves. p. Suzanne Johnston, Hugh Johnston for EBEC; EBEC.

YOU BET YOUR LIFE (13m C n.d.) (also Video)
Provides a new look at the prospects of kicking the gambling

habit. For those who get hooked, says psychologist Dr. Jule Moravac, the stakes are high because compulsive gamblers will steal, lie, and cheat to get money to support their habit. Dr. Moravac specializes in the treatment of self-confessed gambling addicts at the Miami V.A. Medical Center where patients receive six weeks' intensive therapy in a locked ward. They are made to pay off their debts, if possible, abstain from gambling, and learn to substitute new activities--especially work--for gambling. p. JoAnn Caplin for CBS News "Magazine" with correspondent Sharron Lovejoy; CAROUF.

YOU CAN DO IT ... IF SERIES see ALL SUCCESSFUL PEOPLE HAVE IT; IF YOU DON'T, WHO WILL?; SURPRISES OF FAILURE, THE; YES, YOU CAN!; YOU DECIDE

YOU CAN SURPASS YOURSELF (28m C 1975)
Presents Dr. Eden Ryl, who examines the learning process and the forces and strategies that render people more teachable. p. Ramic Productions; RAMIC.

YOU CAN'T MEAN NOT EVER (26m C 1977)
Should a couple be free to choose whether or not to have children? Most people would say, "Of course." But when you come down to it, is the choice really free? Eric and Liz, who are considering remaining permanently childless, encounter questions and curiosities from friends and relatives in this enacted presentation. These pressures and the couple's reactions to them provide a point of departure in discussing values related to the family, the decision of whether or not to parent, and the option of child-free life-styles. p. Martha Garrett Russell, Family Social Science Department, University of Minnesota; UMN.

YOU COULD SAVE A LIFE (9m C p1980, r1980)
Designed to create greater public awareness of water safety in unsupervised swimming areas. Offers a new approach to water safety regulations and lifesaving procedures. The film centers on a young family with a new backyard pool who, despite strict adherence to most rules, overlook one or two, and a child nearly drowns. d./p. Mary Armstrong; CINEFT.

YOU DECIDE (28m C p1980, r1980) You Can Do It ... If Series
Former Miss America Marilyn Van Derbur points out ways in which well-known persons' hard work and persistence resulted in success following numerous failures. She stresses that anyone can quit after one or two tries, but it takes real guts to stick it out and fight for a goal until it is reached. Among the examples are Margaret Wade, who tried 15 years to win the Wimbledon title before winning in 1977; Sylvester Stallone, who rehearsed the fight scene in ROCKY thirty-five hours for every minute of film footage; and Ernest Hemingway, who rewrote the last chapter of A Farewell to Arms 39 times. Van Derbur urges all to keep on trying, find another

way, if necessary, but fight to find out who you are and where you belong in life. p./s.w. Marilyn Van Derbur; VDBER; MTITI.

YOU HAVE STRUCK A ROCK! (28m C 1981)
Though black South African women suffer the triple oppression of race, class, and sex, they have not been silent. During the 1950's women took the lead in mobilizing mass opposition to apartheid. This is the story of the women who not only lived that history, but are still making it today. When the apartheid regime attempted to extend the hated pass system to women in 1952, opposition erupted thunderously across the land. Utilizing techniques of civil disobedience familiar to our own Civil Rights movement, women refused to accept their passes or gathered and burned them publicly. The government responded with increased violence, new laws, and imprisonment. It was only after a decade of resistance culminating with the Sharpeville Massacre, the banning of political organizations, and the imprisonment of the leaders, that the regime finally succeeded in imposing the passes. The participants--Lillian Ngoyi, Helen Josephs, Dora Tomana, Francis Baard and others--tell their stories, illustrated with historical footage and punctuated by South African music. They have been imprisoned and banned, but are undaunted. With a grace, good humor, and a strength summed up by the slogan of the time, "You have touched a woman, you have struck a rock," they continue to fight for freedom and dignity. Their lives--and this film--are a tribute to the remarkable spirit and perseverance of black South African women. p./d. Deborah May; CALNWS; UIL, UM.

YOU IRRESISTIBLE YOU (11m C 1972)
Marshall Ephron humorously joins the increasing number of men willing to pay high prices for male cosmetics and furnishings which promise to make them irresistible to the opposite sex. To acquire a golden tan that not only covers pimples but makes him one of the "beautiful people," there are lotions to accelerate natural tanning, or simply stain him brown. There are stereo hifi and waterbeds to enhance his "with-it" image. Finally, Ephron uses an assortment of male grooming and cosmetic aids before again calling Mona for a date, who still has a headache. p. WNET-TV; BENCHFM.

YOU OWE IT TO YOURSELF (SERIES) (28-29m ea.)
Allen Ludden of "College Bowl" and "Password" fame is the host for a fast-paced series of ten programs on money management. The entertaining game show format introduces viewers to techniques for handling personal finances. Budgeting, credit, insurance, investments and estate planning are among the topics covered. Contestants are husband-and-wife teams representing a variety of income levels and occupations. Ludden asks questions; the couples attempt to answer; and two family economics experts (Dr. Elsie Fetterman, University of Connecticut, and Dr. Larry Coleman, Indiana State University) referee and elaborate on the answers. Home viewers compete with studio guests and are able to check their answers against the correct

conclusions. Quiz questions were researched and written by Dr. Raymond C. Anderson, Assistant Dean of the College of Education and professor of family economics at the University of Maryland. They are based on material provided by various professional, trade and government agencies, such as the American Bankers Association, the American Bar Association and the Department of Health, Education and Welfare.

The titles in the series are these: BUDGETING; CREDIT; HOUSING FOR FAMILY NEEDS; SOCIAL SECURITY; LIFE INSURANCE; PROPERTY AND LIABILITY INSURANCE; BANKING AND SAVINGS INSTITUTIONS; INVESTMENTS AND RISK CAPITAL; ESTATE PLANNING; HEALTH INSURANCE. p. WITF-TV; PBSV.

YOU'LL GET YOURS WHEN YOU'RE 65 (40m C 1973)
Depicts America's treatment of its senior citizens. Contrasts this with that of other countries, such as West Germany. Dispels some of the misconceptions about the American health and retirement systems. From the CBS "Special News Report for Young People" Series. CBS News; CAROUF; UM.

YOUNG AND JUST BEGINNING--PIERRE (25m C p1978, r1979)
Pierre Quinn (a French-Canadian boy) leaves family, friends and hockey to live and train at the National Ballet School in Toronto. Choreographer: Barbara Forbes; d. Ruth Hope, Mark Irwin; p. Ruth Hope; KINEFE.

YOUNG AND OLD--REACHING OUT (SERIES) see LOVE AND LONE-
LINESS; RAISING CHILDREN; WORK AND FULFILLMENT

YOUNG WOMEN AND TRADITION: JAVONMARD (O ZANON-E-JAVON) (20m C p1977, r1980) (Persian/Subtitled)
Documentary about the changing role of women in the Zagros mountains of Iran. The daily life of seminomadic women who perform traditional chores is contrasted with the daily life of young village women who were recruited by a local Development Project to learn new agricultural skills on an experimental farm. d./p. Ruth Klionsky; KLNSKY.

YOUR BABY'S FIRST DAYS (21m C 1980)
Uses vivid close-ups of newborn infants to answer commonly asked questions about normal newborn appearance, behavior and development. Shows a number of Caucasian and Black infants, and describes physical characteristics of the newborn, such as miliaria (prickly heat), cradle cap, dry skin and rashes, skin color changes, "witch's milk," enlarged nipples and genitalia, body hair, stork bite and mongolian spots, the location and function of soft spots on the baby's head, and more. Also, presents a great deal of basic information of help to a new mother in caring for the physical needs of her infant. The emotional needs of the infant for closeness, security and interaction are also discussed, and swaddling, carrying and comforting a crying

baby are shown. Based on a successful class for new mothers taught by Kris Leander at Group Health Cooperative Hospital in Seattle. p./d. Alvin Fiering; POLYMR.

YOUR DIET: SALT AND HYPERTENSION (13m C p1978, r1978)
Graphically explains what high blood pressure or hypertension is and how it affects the heart. Examines the correlation between average salt intake and the incidence of hypertension. Details which individuals, either through hereditary factors, stress in their environment, body condition, or diet are most prone to hypertension and heart disease. p. Gilbert Altschul Productions, Inc.; JOURVI; UIL.

YOUR ERRONEOUS ZONES (97m C 1980)
Psychologist Wayne Dyer takes a commonsense approach to managing stress and building self-worth. In this entertaining, thought-provoking presentation, Dyer urges viewers to improve unsatisfactory situations in their lives by consciously recognizing their erroneous zones (unhealthy behavior patterns). p. Magnetic Video Corporation; FI; UMN.

YOUR FIRST GYNECOLOGICAL EXAMINATION (14m C 1980) (Video)
Follows Jenny on her first gynecological visit; explains the initial consultation, breast examination and pap smear, and the importance of each procedure. An excellent introduction for young women before their first visit to the gynecologist. d. G. Parker; CORONET.

YOUR MONEY OR YOUR LIFE (45m C 1982)
Ernest Perry, Jr., mugger/philosopher/economist, "raps" as he propounds the paradoxical problems which block his way to the "upward mobility" to which his talents entitle him, but which are denied to him because of his race and color. Meanwhile, on the other side of the railroad tracks, the fearful white housewife sets forth her dim views of the mugger's theories for the redistribution of wealth. She calls for more police protection and sterner law enforcement against the shoeshine boys who strive for a greater share of the economic pie at--as she sees it--her expense. The problems of America are approached in a totally American way--witty, serious but not heavy, light but not frivolous. p. Laura Kipnis; ELARTI.

YOUR MOVE (22m C 1976)
Demonstrates the beneficial effects of athletics and exercise on everyone--especially women. Demolishes the myth that sports make females "masculine," and shows enjoyable sports activities for people of all ages. p. NBC-TV; FI; KENTSU.

YOUR OWN WORST: ENEMY (25m C 1976)
Describes the causes, symptoms and remedies for stress. As many as one half of all physical illnesses are the direct or indirect result of stress. Situations known to be the greatest causes of strain are discussed and scenes show how some individuals have learned to

cope with stress. p./d. Robert Fiveson; BOSUTW; UIL, UNEV, WSU.

YOUR PELVIC AND BREAST EXAMINATION (12m C 1975)

Observes how a young woman performs a self-examination of her breasts. Clear, detailed photography shows the cervix, instruments used for pelvic examination and how a pap smear and gonorrhea culture are taken. Because cancer is most curable with early detection, women are encouraged to self-examine their breasts regularly and to visit their doctor at least annually. p. Crommie & Crommie; PEREN; UM.

YOUR WEEKLY WEAVER SERIES (24m ea. C 1978) (Video)

Weaving instructor Rebecca Goodale demonstrates a variety of looms and weaves for making tapestries, scarves, shawls, and fabric for upholstery and pillows. Goodale has taught at the Memphis Academy of Arts, Mercy College of Detroit and Georgia State University. She also served as Director of Textile Arts at the Collen-Wolde Arts Center in Atlanta. Her work is frequently exhibited in groups and at independent shows. Individual program topics listed below. p. Georgia Educational Television Network; PBSV.

1. Frame looms and how to build, buy or find one. An introduction to tapestry weaving techniques and tools.

2. Rigid heddle looms and how to warp them for fabric weaving. This loom may be used for weaving scarves, shawls and upholstery or pillow fabric.

3. The ancient art of tablet weaving (also called card weaving) is shown. This method is unique in its ability to ply the warp fibers during the weaving process.

4. An introduction to a small lap loom called the inkle loom. The design principles of this loom, which is used to weave warp-faced belts or bands, are explained.

5. An introduction to the four-harness loom, both floor and table models, covers warping equipment, parts and how to dress the loom.

6. The versatility and the variety of weaves possible with the four harness loom are demonstrated.

YOU'RE EATING FOR TWO (20m n.d.)

The nine months an infant spends harbored in the womb may be the most crucial months of its life. This film emphasizes the importance of good nourishment, provides a clear framework for healthy eating, alleviates the fear of gaining weight, and motivates mothers to accept responsibility for their child's nourishment. d. Malca Gillson; p. Tom Daly, Colin Low, NFBC; PEREN.

YOU'RE NOT LISTENING (21m C 1978)

A Shakespearean actor leads viewers through a series of humorous and thought-provoking vignettes that illustrate techniques for building seven basic listening skills: eye contact; control of one's mouth; becoming an observer; good thinking; not jumping to con-

clusions; avoiding prejudice; and working to keep an open mind.
Stresses that with hard work and practice, anyone can become a
good listener. p. Arthur Barr Productions, Inc.; UIL.

YOU'RE TOO FAT (50m C 1974)
    This study looks at some of the scientific explanations of obesity,
ways of reducing (from the sensible to the extreme) and possibilities
of painless diets for the future. States that obesity is a disease of
an abundant and comfortable society in which over 70 million Americans are overweight. In a culture that sets up an ideal of the slim,
healthy body, overweight people feel isolated and rejected. They
suffer not only psychological problems, but physical ones as well.
Doctors and psychiatrists explain how and when you get fat, and why
you should lose it. p. NBC-TV; FI; UIL.

YOURS TRULY, ANDREA G. STERN (38m C p1978, r1979)
    Presents a story of a ten-year-old girl struggling with the prob-
lem of sharing her mother with a boyfriend who has just moved into
the house. Andrea is a very unhappy young girl whose mother and
father recently divorced. She misses her father and is resentful of
her mother's boyfriend. Andrea does everything she can think of to
get rid of him, but to no avail. He tries to communicate with Andrea,
but she is not going to listen. Finally, Andrea runs away from home.
The mother realizes she must now decide between her feelings for
Jonathan and her love for her child. A good discussion film. p./d.
Susan Seidelman with a grant from New York State Council for the
Arts. PHOENIX; UMN.

YOUTH BUILDS A NATION IN TANZANIA (18m C 1970) The African
    Scene (Series)
    Shows how the girls of an African government-operated secondary
school are helping their country develop a better standard of living.
Examines cooperative farming as a means of increasing agricultural
production and improving rural life. Highlights the important part being played by African women in the task of "nation building." EBEC;
KENTSU.

YOUTH: THE SEARCH FOR RELEVANCE (18m C 1976)
    Examines the generation gap which has grown wider since the
1960's. Young people have rejected the goals of their parents and
their search for alternate life-styles is taking them along some strange
paths. Speaking are Jerry Garcia of the rock band Grateful Dead
and Paul Goodman, teacher and philosopher. The film also looks at
the newfound fascination by youth for Eastern religions and mystical
symbolism, and Bennett Berger talks about the possibility of a social
revolution brought on by the new attitudes of the young. Also available in Spanish. DOCUA.

YOU'VE COME A LONG WAY, MAYBE? (55m C 1981)
    Explores the controversial concept of "comparable worth," a

concept said to be the "sleeping giant of labor and civil rights law." Asks the question, Are women paid less than men because of subtle, historical patterns of discrimination? Presents examples of some of the major court cases which have focused on the issue as well as unique attempts by employers to re-evaluate how they pay men and women. A program from the Moore Report series. p. WCCO-TV/CBS; Indiana University; IU.

-Z-

ZBIGNIEW IN LOVE (4m C 1979)
In this animated fantasy, the hero progressively creates shadow figures on a wall until a shadow girl becomes independent and dances with him. Culmination occurs as the shadow girl becomes a full-blown opaque form and Zbigniew becomes her shadow. d. Erin Libby; CFS.

ZEN AND NOW (14m C 1969)
Alan Watts emphasizes Zen philosophy of living fully in the present by developing appreciation of beauty. The setting, a Connecticut garden enhanced by accompanying natural sounds, invites meditation. p. Elda Hartley; HARTLEY.

ZOO ANIMALS IN THE WILD (10m C 1979) (also Video)
We follow Kevin and Kelly as they tour the North American Mammals Section of the zoo. Children stop to listen to a recorded message which provides information on each animal. p. Myrna I. Berlet, Walter H. Berlet; IFB.

AAHPER	American Alliance for Health
ABCWWL	ABC Wide World of Learning
ABF	Audio Brandon Films, Inc.
ABRAKA	Abrakadabra, Inc.
ABROMWF	Abromowitsch Films
ACORN	Acorn Films, Inc.
ADAIR	Adair Films
ADELPHIP	Adelphi Productions
ADGI	American Dance Guild Inc.
ADL	Anti-Defamation League of B'nai B'rith
ADMKG	Adams/King Productions
AETNA	Aetna Life & Casualty Company
AF	Association Films, Inc.
AFA	The American Federation of Arts
AFC	Australian Film Commission
AFME	*American Friends of the Middle East
AFRC	The Association for Retarded Citizens
AIMS	AIMS Media
AIT	Agency for Instructional Television
ALA	American Library Association
ALAMEC	College of Alameda
ALDEN	Alden Films
ALMI	Almi Libra Cinema 5 Films
ALTANA	Altana Films
AMBBC	American Brittle Bone Society
AMCEWA	American Committee on East-West Accord
AMCS	American Cancer Society
AMEDF	American Educational Films
AMERGA	American Personnel & Guidance Association
AMERITC	American Indian Treaty Council
AMMED	American Media, Inc.
AMUSNH	American Museum of Natural History
ANDRIANOS	Andrianos, Agamemnon
ANDRSM	Anderson, Michael
AOTA	American Occupational Therapy Association
APPAL	Appalshop Films
ARCPRO	The Archives Project, Inc.
ARCVD	ARC Videodance
ARNPRO	Arnold (Dick) Productions
ARTVIS	Artvision
ASAP	ASAP Productions
ASIANWU	Asian Women United

---

*Indicates address is unavailable, therefore it is not listed in Appendix B:
Directory of Film Sources.

ASIAS	The Asian Society
ATLAP	Atlantis Productions, Inc.
AUDPLS	Audience Planners, Inc.
AVAIL	Available Light
AVIS	Avis Films
AXLTRE	Axletree, Inc.
BALKAC	The Balkan Art Center, Inc.
BANRMN	Bannerman, Penny
BAPMEMH	Baptist Memorial Hospital
BARBIER	Barbier, Browning, Hirsch
BARDD	Bard, Debra
BARRF	Barr Films
BAYAV	Bay Area Video Coalition
BBC	British Broadcasting Company
BEACON	Beacon Films
BEESON	Beeson, Constance (Coni)
BELVFF	Bellevue Film Festival
BENCHMF	Benchmark Films, Inc.
BERLET	Berlet Films
BESTF	Best Films
BFA	*BFA Educational Media
BITROT	Bitterroot Films, Inc.
BLACKFF	The Black Filmmaker Foundation
BLACKFL	Black Filmmakers Library
BLACKW	Blackwood Productions
BLUEST	Bluestem Productions
BNA	BNA Communications, Inc.
BODFIL	Bodacius Films
BOSUTW	Bosustow (Stephen) Productions
BOUCHT	Bouchard, Thomas
BRIDGES	Bridges, Mellena
BROBIP	Brown Bird Productions, Inc.
BROOKSV	Brooks, Virginia
BROSEW	*Brose (William) Productions
BRUNOM	Bruno, Mike
BU	Boston University
BUCKNER	Buckner, Barbara
BUDDF	Billy Budd Films, Inc.
BUDGET	Budget Films
BUFLINO	Brenda Bufalino Dancing Theatre
BULFRG	Bullfrog Films, Inc.
BURRILL	Burrill, Christine
BUSHIPIO	Jeff Bush/Celia Ipiotis
BYU	Brigham Young University
CALDN	Caldararo, Niccolo
CALGARY	City of Calgary
CALLIFR	Calliope Film Resources
CALLYC	Cally Curtis Company
CALNWS	California Newsreel
CAMDOC	Cambridge Documentary Films, Inc.
CANFDC	Canadian Filmmakers' Distribution Centre
CANTOR	Cantor (Arthur), Inc.

CAPCT	Capital Cities Television
CARNIMA	Carnegie Institute Museum of Art
CARNOCHAN	Carnochan, David
CAROUF	Carousel Films Inc.
CASTSON	Castelli-Sonnabend
CATALYST	Catalyst Productions
CBC	Canadian Broadcasting Company
CCC	Canyon Cinema Cooporative
CECROPIA	Cecropia Films
CEFH	Center For Humanities, Inc.
CELECG	Celectronic Graphics
CELRDC	Cellar Door Cinema
CENSTU	Central Studios
CENTEF	Centron Educational Films
CENTRE	Centre Productions, Inc.
CF	Churchill Films
CFS	Creative Film Society
CHASED	Chase (Doris) Films (aka Catalyst Productions)
CHIFAA	Chinese for Affirmative Action
CHISPA	Chispa Productions, Inc.
CHOREOP	Choreometrics Project
CHRSTA	Christiansen Associates
CHSCA	Children's Home Society of California
CHVANY	*Chavany Films
CINAS	Cinema Associates
CINCONT	Cine-Contact
CINED	Cine Design
CINEFT	Cinefort Inc.
CINGLD	Cinema Guild
CININF	Cine Information
CINMD	Cinema Medica
CINMGC	Cinemagic Productions
CIS	Chinese Information Service
CKPRO	C/K Productions
CLARITY	Clarity Educational Productions
CLARKD	Clark (Douglas) Associates, Inc.
CLARKEJ	Clark (E. J.) Films
CLRWP	Clearwater Publishing
CMC	Center for Mass Communications, Columbia University Press
COCA	Coca-Cola Co.
COEF	Coe Films, Inc.
COEFA	Coe Film Associates, Inc.
COLIVC	*Collective for Living Cinema
COMCC	Community Cable Center Inc.
COMMDW	Community Media Workshop
COMPVF	*Communications Park Video and Films, Inc.
COMSPA	Community School of Performing Arts
CONCFD	Concern for Dying
CONSF	The Conservation Foundation
CORINTH	Corinth Films
CORNELL	Cornell University
CORONET	Coronet/Perspective Films & Video
CORORI	Cori & Orient
COVNTH	Covenant House
CPP	Charles Press Publishers, Inc.

CREARTRC   Creative Arts Rehabilitation Center
CREOUT   Creative Outlet Inc.
CRM   CRM/McGraw-Hill Films
CSUCHI   California State University, Chico
CTV   CTV Television Network, Ltd.
CURBE   Center for Urban Education
CWF   Williams (Clem) Films Inc.
CWU   Central Washington University

DALLASCO   Dallas County Community College District
DAN/UR   Dance Film Archive, University of Rochester
DANCFA   Dance Films Association, Inc.
DAVFMS   Davidson Films, Inc.
DAVISR   Davis (Robert) Productions
DAVISS   Davis (Sid) Productions
DAVNPT   Davenport (Tom) Films
DAWSONH   Dawson, Harry, Jr.
DBRF   DBR Films
DECF   DEC Films
DENOP   De Nonno Pix Inc.
DER   Documentary Educational Resources, Inc.
DEUTAT   Deutch Tatlock, Katherine
DHANIFU   Dhaniful, Alicia
DIBIE   Dibie-Dash Productions, Inc.
DIMENF   Dimension Films
DIRECT   Direct Cinema Limited
DISNEY   Disney (Walt) Educational Media Co.
DOCF   Documentary Films
DOCRES   Documentary Research, Inc.
DOCUA   Document Associates, Inc.
DOOMSD   Doomsday Studios
DOWCTC   Downtown Community Television Center
DURRIN   Durrin, Ginny (aka Durrin Films)

EASTEND   East End Film Company
EASTK   Eastman Kodak Company
EBEC   Encyclopaedia Britannica Education Corporation
EBRA   Ebra Films
EDC   Educational Development Center, Inc.
EDENM   Educational Enrichment Materials
EDMDC   Educational Media Corporation
EDUATX   Texas Education Agency
EFA   Epilepsy Foundation of America
ELARTI   Electronic Arts Intermix
ELDAN   The Eldan Company
ELDRVW   Elderview
ELLISD   Ellis (Dave) Films
EMERSC   Emerson College Film Section
EMGEE   Em Gee Film Library
EMPAK   Embassy of Pakistan
ENVFMS   Environmental Films
ESSENTIA   Essentia
EXCIN   Expanding Cinema
EXPIF   *Experimental Intermedia Foundation

FACES	Faces Distribution Corporation
FACSEA	FACSEA
FAIRCHD	Fairchild Visuals
FAIRVW	Fairview General Hospital
FAMCOM	Family Communications, Inc.
FAMINS	Family Information Systems, Inc.
FANLTP	Fanlight Productions
FFHUM	Films for the Humanities
FI	Films Incorporated
FILBOS	Films Boston
FILMCO	Film Communicators
FILMCOMM	Filmcomm
FILMLB	Filmmakers Library, Inc.
FILMSPRO	Films M. Productions
FINTNC	The Fine Tuning Co.
FIRRNF	First Run Features
FLEISHMAN	Fleishman, Michael B.
FLMFR	Filmfair Communications
FLMID	Film Ideas, Inc.
FLMKCO	Film-Makers' Cooperative
FLMST	The Film Store
FLMVS	Film and Video Service
FLOWERF	Flower Films
FMSP	FMS Productions, Inc.
FOCALP	Focal Point Films
FOCPRO	Focus Productions
FOCUSH	Focus: Hope
FOCUSI	Focus International
FOGG	Fogg Fine Arts, Film Library
FORDF	Ford Foundation
FRACOC	Franciscan Communications Center
FRANDA	Randolph (F.) Associates
FRANKF	Frank Films
FREYER	Freyer Productions
FRIEDL	Friedl, Erik
FUTMED	Future Media Enterprises
GADNR	Georgia Dept. of Natural Resources
GANAHL	Ganahl, Margaret
GATEWF	Gateway Educational Films, Ltd.
GERRETSEN	Gerretsen (Peter) Productions
GEVERM	Gever, Martha
GIHON	Gihon Foundation
GITFM	Gittelman Film Associates, Inc.
GIUMMO	Giummo, Joan
GLOBALV	Global Village
GLYNG	Glyn Group, Inc.
GOLDMAN	Goldman, Gary
GRLSCA	Girls Clubs of America, Inc.
GRNFLDC	Greenfield, Carol
GRNMTP	Green Mountain Post Films
GROVE	Grove Press Incorporated
GUTHOR	*Guthrie and Horton
HACKLT	Hackford/Littman

HALLECK	Halleck, Dee Dee
HALWAM	Halawani, Mary
HALWNE	Halewyn Films
HANDEL	Handel Film Corporation
HAR	Harper & Row Publishers, Inc.
HARTLEY	Hartley Film Foundation
HBJ	Harcourt Brace Jovanovich, Inc.
HELMNS	Hellman, Sheila
HERBERTJ	Herbert, James
HERVSL	Heritage Visual Sales, Ltd.
HIGGIN	Higgins (Alfred) Productions
HIHOM	High Hopes Media
HILITP	*Highlight Productions, Ltd.
HILLB	Hill (Bishop) Heritage Association
HOLLINS	Hollins College
HOMOWC	Home Owners Warranty Corp.
HOSPICE	Hospice Institute
HSD	Human Services Development
HUBBARD	Hubbard
HUDRFV	Hudson River Film & Video
HUMRM	Human Relations Media
HUNTERC	Hunter College of the University of New York
HURCW	Hurlock Cine World

ICAP	ICAP
ICARF	Icarus Films
IDEAIM	Ideas & Images, Inc.
IDERAF	Idera Films
IFB	International Film Bureau, Inc.
IFEX	Ifex Films
IFF	International Film Foundation
IMAGES	Images Film Archive
INDFLM	Indian Government Films Division
INDIACG	Consulate General of India
INTELFE	International Tele-Film Enterprises Ltd.
INTRAMA	Interama
IPLGPI	Institute of Pluralism
IRIS	Iris Films
IRISFC	Iris Feminist Collective, Inc.
ISHI	Ishi Films
ISHTAR	Ishtar
ITHACA	Ithaca College
ITOC	Ito, Cheryl
IU	Indiana University
IVY	Ivy Film

JANEWL	Janewill Productions
JAPANS	Japan Society, Inc.
JOHNSTS	Johnston, Suzanne
JOURVI	Journal Video, Inc.

KAFBOY	Kauffman and Boyce Productions
KANELEW	Kane-Lewis Productions

KAROL	Karol Media
KARTF	Kartemquin Films Ltd.
KATSI	Katsiaficas, Diane
KENJP	Kennedy (Joseph P.), Jr. Foundation
KENMF	Kennedy, Margaret F.
KENSCOM	Kensington Communications, Inc.
KENTSU	Kent State University
KERATV	KERA-TV
KERRJ	Kerr (Joan) Dance Company
KICHNC	*The Kitchen Center
KINEFE	Kinetic Film Enterprises, Ltd.
KINGA	King Arthur Productions, Inc.
KINGF	King Features Entertainment, Inc.
KINO	Kino International Corporation
KIROTV	KIRO-TV
KLNSKY	Klionsky, Ruth
KOINTV	KOIN-TV
KPF	Parker (Kit) Films
KQEDTV	KQED-TV
KRAMERK	Kramer, Karen
KRAWITZ	Krawitz, Jan/Thomas Ott
KSUTV	KSU-TV
KTCATV	KTCA-TV
KUEDTV	KUED-TV
KUHTTV	KUHT-TV
KWSUTV	KWSU-TV
LAURON	Lauron Production Ltd.
LAWM	Law (Michael S.) & Co.
LAWRENP	Lawren Productions
LBERGER	Le Berger Films
LCA	Learning Corporation of America
LEFKOF	Lefkowitz Films
LEKOTEK	Lekotec
LEVIKOFF	Levikoff, Ruth E.
LEVITT	Levitt, Kathy
LEWISDC	Lewis, David C.
LIBERTY	The Liberty Company
LILGHT	Limelight Productions, Inc.
LILYANP	Lilyan Productions, Inc.
LISARF	Light-Saraf Films
LITTMAN	Littman, Lynne
LITWKS	Lightworks
LODSTR	Lodestar Films
LOIZEAU	Loizeau, Christine
LOPIN	Lopatin (Ralph) Productions
LOSTNF	Lost Nation Films
LREDF	The Little Red Filmhouse
LSBPRO	LSB Productions
LIFTF	Lightfoot Films, Inc.
LUCERNE	Lucerne Films, Inc.
MACMFL	Macmillan Films, Inc.
MADBOLT	Maddux/Boldt Productions, Inc.

MAIER	Maier, Eva
MANSPR	Mansfield (Portia) Motion Pictures
MARTIN	Martin, Mimi
MARTING	Martin (Gordon) & Associates
MAYERA	Mayer & Associates
MCELWE	McElwee, Ross
MCFI	Mar/Chuck Film Industries, Inc.
MEDBUS	Media Bus, Inc.
MEDCON	Media Concepts, Inc.
MEDIAC	Media Centre, University of Toronto
MEDIAF	Media Five Film Distributors
MEDIAG	Media Guild
MEDIAP	The Media Project
MELKIM	Melkim Productions
MERCURY	Mercury Pictures, Inc.
MERRIMA	Merrim, Andrea
METROT	Metromedia Television
METTLER	Mettler Studios
MEYERS	Meyer, Sybil
MGMUAS	MGM/Home Entertainment Group
MHTRFP	Mental Health Training Film Program
MIFE	Milner-Fenwick, Inc.
MILPIC	Miller-Pickle Associates
MIRROR	Mirror Films
MJPRO	M. J. Productions
MLINS	Museum of Long Island Natural Sciences
MMA	The Museum of Modern Art
MMM	Mass Media Ministries
MMRC	Multi Media Resource Center
MOBIUS	Mobius International
MODNLA	Modern Learning Aids
MOKINA	Mokin (Arthur) Productions
MONAD	Monad Trainer's Aide
MORRISJ	Morrison, Jane
MOSESD	Moses, Doreen
MOTINC	Motion Inc.
MOTPIC	The Motion Picture Center, Inc.
MTITI	MTI Teleprograms Inc.
MTPS	Modern Talking Picture Service
MTVTM	Motivational Media
MULTPP	Multimedia Program Productions
MUNDTP	Mundt, Peggy
MUSNYC	Museum of the City of New York
NAINDF	North American Indian Films, Inc.
NAPPIM	Nappi, Maureen
NARAL	NARAL
NATFVC	National Film and Video Center
NATRMA	National Retail Merchants Association
NAVC	National Audiovisual Center
NCCHS	National Council of Churches
NCOMF	National Communications Foundation
NERVIG	Nervig, Sandra L.
NET	National Education TV, Inc.
NETCHE	NETCHE Videotape Library

NEWDAY	New Day Films
NEWDF	New Deal Films, Inc.
NEWEFW	New Environments for Women
NEWFLM	The New Film Co., Inc.
NEWFRF	New Front Films, Inc.
NEWRKM	The Newark Museum
NEWTF	Newtime Films, Inc.
NEWTTV	New Times Television
NFBC	National Film Board of Canada
NFLC	National Film Library of Canada
NGS	National Geographic Educational Services
NICHOLSS	Nichols (Sandra) Productions
NIGENDL	*Nigendl Committee
NILLU	Northern Illinois University
NITC	National Instructional TV Center
NJPT	*New Jersey Public Television
NLC	New Line Cinema
NMICHU	Northern Michigan University
NORTONJ	Norton (Jeffrey) Publishers, Inc.
NOVACOM	NOVA/COM Inc.
NOW	National Organization for Women
NULFMAR	Nulf/Marshall
NWMP	Northwest Media Project
NYEF	*Nye Films
NYF	New Yorker Films
NYSBPC	New York State, Office of Mental Health
NYSED	New York State Education Dept.
NYU	New York University
NYVAF	New York Visual Arts Foundation
ODNPRO	O.D.N. Productions, Inc.
ODYTPS	Odyssey Tapes
OHIOU	Ohio University
ONTBPP	Ontario Block Parent Program, Inc.
OPEQUON	Opequon Productions
ORION	Orion Dance Films
ORSTED	Oregon State Employment Division
OSU	Oregon State University
PACISP	Pacific Street Production
PACT	PACT
PAJON	Pajon Arts Ltd.
PARACO	Paramount Communications Inc.
PARFD	Parallel Film Distribution
PARPIC	Parenting Pictures
PAS	The Pennsylvania State University
PASQRLO	Pasquariello, Nicholas
PAULST	Paulist Productions
PBS Video	PBS Video
PEACH	Peach Enterprises, Inc.
PELICAN	Pelican Films, Inc.
PENBAK	Pennebaker Inc.
PENNEY	Penney (J.C.) Company
PEREN	Perennial Education, Inc.
PERFAAS	Performing Arts Division of Asia Society
PETERV	Peterson, Vicki Z.

PF	Pyramid Films
PHM	Prentice-Hall Media
PHOENIX	Phoenix Films, Inc.
PICTS	Picture Start
PICTURA	*Pictura Films Distribution Corporation
PIPER	Piper, Christie Ann
PLAINSG	Plainsong Productions
PLANCS	Planned Communications Services, Inc.
POGUE	Pogue, Alan
POLPUP	Police and Public Project
POLYMR	Polymorph Films
POPEA	Pope (Amanda) Productions, Inc.
POSTSC	Post-Script
PRATWHIT	Pratt & Whitney Canada
PROGP	Progress Productions
PROTNP	Protean Productions, Inc.
PSU	Portland State University
PTVP	PTV Productions, Inc.
PUBIVN	Public Interest Video Network
PUCSAFR	Pucker/Safrai Gallery
PURDUE	Purdue University

RADIM	Radim Films, Inc.
RAMAPO	Ramapo College of New Jersey
RAMFLM	Ramsgate Films
RAMIC	Ramic Productions
RANEN	Ranen, Aron
RAPHAEL	Raphael Films
RARIG	Rarig Film Service, Inc.
RASMUS	Rasmussen Productions
RAYMBA	Raymond (Bruce A.) Co.
READNCF	Read Natural Childbirth
REAJUNG	Realist/Jungels
REDHEN	Red Hen Films
REDHL	Red Hill Films
REHABF	Rehabilitation International USA
RESPRC	Research Press
REVOF	Revolution Films
ROBNSN	Robinson (Gretchen) Productions
RODALE	Rodale Press Film Division
ROSFTJ	Rosenfelt, Joan
ROSLAB	Ross Laboratories
RTBL	Roundtable Films, Inc.
RUBINS	Rubin, Susan
RUIZP	Ruiz Productions
RUSMAN	Russell-Manning Productions

SABAN	Saba (Nguzo) Films, Inc.
SALEM	Salem Productions
SANDBK	Sandbank Films Company
SANDIF	Sandler Institutional Films
SANDLIN	Sandlin, Martha
SAUVGE	Sauvage (Pierre) Productions
SBMAYC	South Bay Mayors' Commission
SCC	Shoreline Community College
SCHLAT	Schloat (Warren) Productions, Inc.

SCHRADR	Schrader, Charlotte
SCNTIF	Scientificom Audiovisual
SCRESC	Screenscope, Inc.
SEAGRAM	Seagram Canada
SEAHRS	Seahorse Films
SELECT	Select Films
SERBC	*Serious Business Company
SFI	Sportlite Films
SFMATS	San Francisco Matching Service
SILVT	Silver (Tony) Films, Inc.
SIZEMF	Sizemore Films
SKIPW	Skipper, William
SKYEP	Skye Pictures
SLACC	*Sun Life Assurance Company of Canada
SMITHL	Smith, Loretta
SMITHS	Smithsonian Institution
SNUTRE	Society for Nutrition Education
SOFOLK	Center for Southern Folklore
SOUTHP	Southerby Productions, Inc.
SPANSCC	Spanish Speaking Cultural Club
SPECTR	Spectrum Films
SPERRY	Sperry, Robert
SPIRAL	Spiral Productions
STANF	Stanton Films
STANFH	The Stanfield House
STATEA	State of the Art
STEEG	Steeg, Ted
STEREF	Sterling Educational Films, Inc.
STEWART	Stewart (John A.) Productions
STONEHE	Stone House, Elizabeth
STPIERA	St. Pierre Associates
STRAIF	Straightface Films
STUARTM	Stuart (Martha) Communications, Inc.
STURGN	Sturgeon, James H.
SULANI	Sulani Films
SUNDMN	Sundermann, Volker
SUNRIEM	Sunrise Educational Media
SUNRIF	Sunrise Films, Ltd.
SURVM	Survival Media, Inc.
SWA	Swank Motion Pictures, Inc.
SYLOGY	Sylogy
SYRACU	Syracuse University
TAKE	Take III
TAKOMA	Takoma Video Lab
TAMRKP	Tamerik Productions
TAYLORR	Taylor, Ron
TCAFMS	TCA Films
TELCULT	Teleculture Inc.
TEMANC	Teleprompter Manhattan Cable TV
TEMPLU	Temple University
TEXFM	Texture Films, Inc.
THARPT	Tharp (Twyla) Dance Foundation
THEYEF	Third Eye Films
THRNB	Thornburg, L.

THUDRBD	Thunderbird Films
TIFFANY	Tiffany Film Company
TIMLIF	Time/Life Video
TKF	Teleketics Films
TNF	Terra Nova Films, Inc.
TODF	Tod (Dorothy) Films
TOGGFI	Togg Films, Inc.
TRANSDYI	Transactional Dynamics Institute
TRNSIT	Transit Media Inc.
TRUEP	True Productions
TRWAGV	Theater Wagon of Virginia
TULALIP	The Tulalip Tribe
TUPPRH	Tupperware Home Parties
TVONT	TV Ontario Marketing
TWN	Third World Newsreel
TWNAYB	Town of Amherst Youth Bureau
TWY	Twyman Films
UALASKA	University of Alaska
UAZ	University of Arizona
UCDAV	University of California, Davis
UCBHM	United Church Board for Homeland Ministries
UCEMC	University of California, Berkeley
UCLA	University of California, Los Angeles
UCLABS	University of California, Los Angeles (Science)
UCT	University of Connecticut
UFL	University of Florida
UGA	University of Georgia
UIL	University of Illinois
UIO	The University of Iowa
UM	The University of Michigan
UMA	*University of Massachusetts
UMANA	Umana, A.
UMANI	University of Manitoba
UMCOM	UmCom
UMETHC	United Methodist Communications
UMMRC	The University of Michigan, Media Production
UMN	University of Minnesota
UMO	University of Missouri
UN	United Nations
UNEV	University of Nevada
UNEWB	*University of New Brunswick
UNIFILM	*Unifilm
UNIPCH	Synod of the Northeast of the United Presbyterian Church U.S.A.
UOR	University of Oregon, Eugene
UORFE	Univeristy of Oregon, Eugene (Ethnic Studies)
UPITTS	University of Pittsburgh
UPSTF	*Upstate Films
USC	University of Southern California
USDL	United States Department of Labor
USFL	University of South Florida
USINFA	U.S. Information Agency
USNAC	United States Navy
UTORON	University of Toronto

UTX	University of Texas
UU	University of Utah
UW	University of Washington
UWI	University of Wisconsin
VC	Visualcraft, Inc.
VDBER	Van Derbur, Marilyn
VECT	Visual Education Centre
VFA	Video Free America
VIDTM	The Video Team
VIDVER	Video Verite
VIEWFI	Viewfinders, Inc.
VILLON	Villon Films
VISION	Vision Films
VISUCP	Visucom Productions/Video Arts
VOLLEY	Volleyball Films
WAVETV	WAVE-TV
WAYSU	Wayne State University
WBCPRO	Westinghouse Broadcasting Co., Productions
WEIDNR	Weidenaar, Reynold
WEISBURD	Weisburd, Harry
WEISSG	Weiss, Gene S.
WESTCF	Westcoast Films
WESTGC	West (Glen) Communications
WHARTN	Wharton International Films Inc.
WHITEH	White, Helene
WHITG	Whiteaker (Gary) Company
WHITNEYM	Whitney Museum of American Art
WILKB	Wilk, Barbara
WINTNER	Wintner (Chuck) Productions
WITHRS	Withers, Robert
WITNESS	Witness Films, Inc.
WMM	Women Make Movies, Inc.
WMNCL	Women in Communications Ltd.
WNETTV	WNET-TV
WOMBAT	Wombat Productions, Inc.
WOMEYE	Woman's Eye
WOMWK	Women's Workshop
WOODSF	Woods, Fronza
WORKAR	Working Against Rape
WORKS	The Works
WORWIP	World Wide Pictures
WQEDTV	WQED-TV
WSU	Washington State University
WWFUS	World Wildlife Fund--U.S.
WWS	Weston Woods Studios, Inc.
XICOM	XICOM--Video Arts Film Production
XYRALEA	Xyrallea Productions, inc.
YALEU	Yale University
ZANTAG	Zantzinger, Alfred G.

ABC Wide World of Learning
1330 Avenue of the Americas
New York, NY 10019

ARC Videodance
New York Baroque Dance Co.
178 Bennett Ave.
New York, NY 10040

ASAP Productions
P.O. Box 129
Somerville, MA 02144

Abrakadabra, Inc.
2240 Ridgemont Dr.
Los Angeles, CA 90046

Abromowitsch Films
P.O. Box 9421
Berkeley, CA 94709

Acorn Films, Inc.
33 Union Square West
New York, NY 10003

Adair Films
2051 Third St.
San Francisco, CA 94107

Adams/King Productions
2619 Garfield Street N.W.
Washington, DC 20008

Adelphi Productions
Blodgett Studio
Adelphi University
Garden City, NY 11530

Aetna Life and Casualty
Film Library
151 Farmington Ave.
Hartford, CT 06156

Agency for Instructional Television
Box A, 1111 West 17 St.
Bloomington, IN 47402

AIMS Media
626 Justin Ave.
Glendale, CA 91201-2398

Alden Films
7820 20th Avenue
Brooklyn, NY 11214

Almi Libra Cinema 5 Films
1585 Broadway
New York, NY 10036

Altana Films
340 East 34 St.
New York, NY 10016

American Alliance for Health
Physical Education, Recreation and
    Dance
1201 16 Street N.W.
Washington, DC 20036

American Brittle Bone Society
1256 Merrill Dr.
Westchester, PA 19380

American Cancer Society
777 Third Avenue
New York, NY 10017

American Committee on East-West
    Accord
227 Massachusetts Avenue N.W.
Suite 300
Washington, DC 20002

American Dance Guild Inc.
1133 Broadway
Room 1437
New York, NY 10010

American Educational Films
132 Lasky Dr.
Beverly Hills, CA 90212

The American Federation of Arts
41 East 65 Street
New York, NY 10021

American Indian Treaty Council
777 United Nations Plaza, 10F
New York, NY 10017

American Library Association
50 East Huron St.
Chicago, IL 60611

American Media, Inc.
790 Hampshire Rd., Suite H
Westlake Village, CA 91361

American Museum of Natural History
Office of Public Affairs
Central Park West and 79 Street
New York, NY 10024

American Occupational Therapy Association
6000 Executive Blvd.
Rockville, MD 20852

American Personnel & Guidance
   Association
1607 New Hampshire Avenue N.W.
Washington, DC 20009

Anderson, Michael
402 San Francisco Blvd.
San Anselmo, CA 94960

Andrianos, Agamemnon
490 Linden St.
San Francisco, CA 94102

Anti-Defamation League of B'nai
   B'rith
823 United Nations Plaza
New York, NY 10017
also given:
315 Lexington Ave.
New York, NY 10016

Appalshop Films
Box 743 North
Whitesburg, KY 41858

The Archives Project, Inc.
4717 Arlington Blvd.
Arlington, VA 22203

Arnold (Dick) Productions
P.O. Box 1799
East Lansing, MI 48823

Artvision
140 East 81 St.
New York, NY 10028

The Asia Society
112 East 64 Street
New York, NY 10021

Asian Women United
2644 La Honda
El Cerrito, CA 94530

Association Films, Inc.
866 Third Ave.
New York, NY 10019

The Assc. for Retarded Citizens
N. 2927 Monroe St.
Spokane, WA 99205

Atlantis Productions, Inc.
1252 La Granada Dr.
Thousand Oaks, CA 91360

Audience Planners, Inc.
6290 Sunset Blvd., Suite 1125
Hollywood, CA 90028

Audio Brandon Films, Inc. see
   Films Incorporated

Australian Film Commission
9229 Sunset Blvd., No. 720
Los Angeles, CA 90069

Available Light
72 Molimo Dr.
San Francisco, CA 94127

Avis Films
904 East Palm
Burbank, CA 91501

Axletree, Inc.
5950 Wildcat Rd.
Missoula, MT 59802

BFA Educational Media see Phoenix
   Films

BNA Communications, Inc.
9401 Decoverly Hall Rd.
Customer Relations Dept.
Rockville, MD 20850

The Balkan Art Center, Inc.
P.O. Box 315
Franklin Lakes, NJ 07417

Bannerman, Penny
c/o Davidson

3601 Lankershim Blvd.
Los Angeles, CA 90068

Baptist Memorial Hospital
Medical Center
899 Madison Ave.
Memphis, TN 38146

Barbier, Browing, Hirsch, Moyemont,
    Shulman
1820 South Halsted
Chicago, IL 60608

Bard, Debra
309 West 109 St.
New York, NY 10025

Barr Films
P.O. Box 5667
Pasadena, CA 91107

Bauer/16 or Bauer International
    Pictures see The Liberty
    Company

Bay Area Video Coalition
2940 16 Street
San Francisco, CA 94130

Beacon Films
P.O. Box 575
Norwood, MA 02062

Beeson, Constance (Coni)
99 West Shore Dr.
Belvedere, CA 94920

Bellevue Film Festival
376 Bellevue Square
Bellevue, WA 98004

Benchmark Films, Inc.
145 Scarborough Rd.
Briarcliff Manor, NY 10510

Berlet Films
1646 West Kimmel Rd.
Jackson, MI 49201

Best Films
1335 Camino Del Mar
P.O. Box 695
Del Mar, CA 92014
also given:
P.O. Box 725
Del Mar, CA 92014

Billy Budd Films, Inc.
East 57 Street
New York, NY 10022

Bishop Hill Heritage Association
Box 1853
Bishop Hill, IL 61419

Bitterroot Films, Inc.
Hammond Arcade
Missoula, MT 59801

The Black Filmmaker Foundation
C/O Transit Media
P.O. Box 315
Franklin Lakes, NJ 07417

Black Filmmakers Library
P.O. Box 315
Franklin Lakes, NJ 07417

Blackwood Productions
251 West 57 St.
New York, NY 10019

Bluestem Productions
2327 Lafayette Rd.
Wayzata, NM 55391

Bodacius Films
2022 Day St.
Ann Arbor, MI 48104

Boston University
Krasker Memorial Film Library
765 Commonwealth Avenue
Boston, MA 02215

Bosustow (Stephen) Productions
1649 11th St.
Santa Monica, CA 90405

Bouchard, Thomas
Stony Brook Rd.
West Brewster, MA 02631

Bridges, Mellena
324 East 13th St., #6
New York, NY 10003

Brigham Young University
Dept. of Audio Visual Services
Provo, UT 34602
for multicultural media:
Brigham Young University
Multicultural Education Dept.

115 BRMB
Provo, UT 84602

Brooks, Virginia
460 Riverside Dr.
New York, NY 10027

Brown Bird Productions, Inc.
1971 North Curson Ave.
Hollywood, CA 90046

Bruno, Mike
52 East First Street
New York, NY 10003

Bufalino (Brenda) Dancing Theatre
6 North Front St.
New Paltz, NY 12561

Buckner, Barbara
344 East 9th St.
New York, NY 10003

Budget Films
4590 Santa Monica Blvd.
Los Angeles, CA 90029

Bullfrog Films, Inc.
Oley, PA 19547

Burrill, Christine
156 Wadsworth Ave.
Santa Monica, CA 92014

Jeff Bush/Celia Ipiotis
Art Resources in Collaboration
178 Bennett Ave.
New York, NY 10040

C/K Productions
1000 Queen Anne Rd.
Teaneck, NJ 07666

CRM/McGraw-Hill Films
110 15th St., P.O. Box 641
Del Mar, CA 92014

CTV Television Network, Ltd.
42 Charles Street East
Toronto, Ontario, M4Y 1T5 Canada
also given:
48 Charles Street East
Toronto, Ontario, M4Y 1T4 Canada

Caldararo, Niccolo
P.O. Box 99637, Sta. "O"
San Francisco, CA 94109

California Newsreel
630 Natoma St.
San Francisco, CA 94103

California State University
Dr. Gayle Kimball, Coordinator
Women's Studies Program
Chico, CA 95929

Calliope Film Resources
35 Granite St.
Cambridge, MA 02139

Cally Curtis Company
1111 N. Las Palmas Ave.
Hollywood, CA 90038

Cambridge Documentary Films, Inc.
P.O. Box 385
Cambridge, MA 02137

Canadian Broadcasting Company
245 Park Ave.
New York, NY 10167
also:
Box 500, Terminal A
Toronto, Ontario, M5W 1E6 Canada

Canadian Filmmakers' Distribution
    Centre
144 Front Street West, Suite 430
Toronto, Ontario, M5J 2L7 Canada

Cantor (Arthur), Inc.
33 West 60 Street
New York, NY 10023

Canyon Cinema Cooperative
2325 Third St., Suite 338
San Francisco, CA 94107

Capital Cities Television
4100 City Line Ave.
Philadelphia, PA 19131

Carnegie Institute
Museum of Art
4400 Forbes Ave.
Pittsburgh, PA 15213

Carnochan, David
4571 River Rd.
Scottsville, NY 14546

Carousel Films Inc.
241 East 34 St., Room 304
New York, NY 10016

Castelli-Sonnabend
Tapes and Films, Inc.
420 Broadway
New York, NY 10012

Catalyst Productions
222 West 23 St., Suite 722
New York, NY 10011

Cecropia Films
P.O. Box 315
Franklin Lakes, NJ 07417

Celectronic Graphics
36 East 68, S6
New York, NY 10021

Cellar Door Cinema
Drawer P
Osterville, Cape Cod, MA 02655

Center for Humanities, Inc.
Communications Park, Box 1000
Mt. Kisco, NY 10549

Center for Mass Communication of
Columbia University Press
562 West 113 St.
New York, NY 10025

Center for Southern Folklore
P.O. Box 40105
Memphis, TN 38104-0105

Center for Urban Education
0245 S.W. Bancroft
Portland, OR 97201

Central Studios
678 Massachusetts Ave.
Cambridge, MA 02139

Central Washington University
Media Library Services
Ellensburg, WA 98926

Centre Productions Inc.
1800 30 St. #207B
Boulder, CO 80301
also:
1312 Pine St., Suite A
Boulder, CO 80302
also:
2006 Broadway
Boulder, CO 80302

Centron Educational Films
1621 West Ninth St.
Lawrence, KA 66044

CIMA see Bruno, Mike

Cine Design
255 Washington St.
Denver, CO 80203

Charles Press Publishers, Inc.
Rtes. 197 and 450
Bowie, MD 20715

Chase (Doris) Films
222 West 23 St., Suite 722
New York, NY 10011

Children's Home Society of California
5429 McConnell Ave.
Los Angeles, CA 90066

Chinese for Affirmative Action
121 Waverly Place
San Francisco, CA 94108

Chinese Information Service
3440 Wilshire Blvd., Room 1108
Los Angeles, CA 90010

Chispa Productions, Inc.
2440 Caithnew Place
Denver, CO 80211

Choreometrics Project
215 West 98 St.
New York, NY 10025

Christiansen Associates
Chapel North Bldg., Suite 200
62 North Chapel St.
Newark, DE 19711

Churchill Films
662 N. Robertson Blvd.
Los Angeles, CA 90069

Cine-Contact
826 est de la Gauchetiere
Montreal, Quebec, H2L 2N2 Canada

Cine Information
215 West 90 St., 9-C
New York, NY 10024

Cinefort Inc.
3603 S. Laurent Blvd.
Montreal, Quebec, H2X 2V5 Canada

Cinema Associates
2003 Harvey Rd.
Wilmington, DE 19801

Cinema V see Almi Libra Cinema
    5 Films

Cinema Guild
Div. of Document Associates
1697 Broadway, Suite 802
New York, NY 10019

Cinema Medica
2335 West Foster Ave.
Chicago, IL 60625
also given:
664 N. Michigan Ave.
Chicago, IL 60611

Cinemagic Productions
133 Wilton St., Suite 324
Toronto, Ontario, M5A 4A4 Canada

City of Calgary
Parks/Recreation Dept.
P.O. Box 2100, Sta. M
Calgary, Alberta, T2P 2M5 Canada

Clarity Educational Productions
P.O. Box 315
Franklin Lakes, NJ 07417

Clark (Douglas) Associates, Inc.
18 West Court
Sausalito, CA 94965

Clark (E. J.) Films
17335 Mierow Lane
Brookfield, WI 53005

Clearwater Publishing
1995 Broadway
New York, NY 10023

Coca-Cola Co.
310 North Avenue N.W.
Atlanta, GA 30303

Coe Film Associates, Inc.
65 East 96 St.
New York, NY 10028
also given:

70 East 96 St.
New York, NY 10028

College of Almeda
555 Atlantic Ave.
Alemeda, CA 94501

Columbia University Press see
    Center for Mass Communication

Community Cable Center Inc.
2827 Valentine Ave.
Bronx, NY 10458

Community Media Productions see
    Community Media Workshop

Community Media Workshop
215 Superior Ave.
Dayton, OH 45406

Community School of Performing
    Arts
3131 Figueroa St.
Los Angeles, CA 90007

Concern for Dying
250 West 57 St.
New York, NY 10107

The Conservation Foundation
1717 Massachusetts Avenue N.W.
Washington, DC 20036

Consulate General of India
215 Market St.
San Francisco, CA 94105

Cori & Orient
2049 Century Park East
Suite 1200, Century City
Los Angeles, CA 90067

Corinth Films
410 East 62 Street
New York, NY 10021

Cornell University
Audio-Visual Resource Center
8 Research Park
Ithaca, NY 14850

Coronet/Perspective Films & Video
108 Wilmot Rd.
Deerfield, IL 60015

Covenant House
Public Relations Dept.
460 West 41 St.
New York, NY 10036

Creative Arts Rehabilitation Center
251 West 51 St.
New York, NY 10019

Creative Film Society
8435 Geyser Ave.
Northridge, CA 91324

Creative Outlet, Inc.
Video Access Project
117 N.W. Fifth Ave., Room 215
Portland, OR 97209

DBR Films
231 East 5 St., No. 3
New York, NY 10003

DEC Films
427 Bloor Street West
Toronto, Ontario, M5S 1X7 Canada

Dallas County Community College
   District
Instructional Television Center
12800 Abrams Rd.
Dallas, TX 75243

Dance Film Archive
University of Rochester
Rochester, NY 14627

Dance Films Association, Inc.
250 West 57 St.
New York, NY 10019

Davenport (Tom) Films
Route 1, Box 124
Delaplane, VA 22025

Davidson Films, Inc.
231 E St.
Davis, CA 95616

Davis (Robert) Productions
P.O. Box 12
Gary, IL 60013

Davis (Sid) Productions
1144 S. Robertson Ave.
Los Angeles, CA 90035

Dawson, Harry, Jr.
P.O. Box 10042
Portland, OR 97210

De Nonno Pix Inc.
7119 Shore Rd.
Brooklyn, NY 11209

Deutch Tatlock, Katherine
122 Stedman St.
Brookline, MA 02146

Dhaniful, Alicia
c/o Jamaa Fanaka Productions
C.R. #19, 10202
Wt. Washington Blvd.
Culver City, CA 91104

Dibie-Dash Productions, Inc.
4949 Hollywood Blvd., Suite 208
Los Angeles, CA 90027

Dimension Films
666 N. Robertson Blvd.
Los Angeles, CA 90069

Direct Cinema Limited
P.O. Box 315
Franklin Lakes, NJ 07417

Disney (Walt) Educational Media Co.
500 S. Buena Vista St.
Burbank, CA 91521

Document Associates, Inc.
211 East 43 St.
New York, NY 10017

Documentary Educational Resources,
   Inc.
5 Bridge St.
Watertown, MA 02172

Documentary Films
3217 Trout Gulch Rd.
Aptos, CA 95003
also given:
159 W. 53 St.
New York, NY 10019

Documentary Research, Inc.
96 Rumsey Rd.
Buffalo, NY 14209

Doomsday Studios
1671 Argyle St.
Halifax, Nova Scotia

Downtown Community Television Center
87 Lafayette St.
New York, NY 10013
also given:
153 Centre St.
New York, NY 10013

Durrin, Ginny
Durrin Films
1748 Kalorama Rd. N.W.
Washington, DC 20009

East End Film Company
Box 275
Wainscott, NY 11975

Eastman Kodak Company
Rochester, NY 14650

Ebra Films
2130 Broadway, Suite 1417
New York, NY 10023

Educational Development Center,
Inc.
55 Chapel St.
Newton, MA 02150

Educational Enrichment Materials
357 Adams St.
Bedford Hills, NY 10507

Educational Media Corporation
Box 847
Madison, WI 53701
also given:
6930-1/2 Tujunga Avenue
N. Hollywood, CA 91605

The Eldan Company
10260 Moorpark St.
Toluca Lake, CA 91602

Elderview
Box 89
Boston, MA 02120

Electronic Arts Intermix
84 Fifth Ave.
New York, NY 10011

Ellis (Dave) Films
Box 7521
Albuquerque, NM 87104

Em Gee Film Library

6924 Canby Ave., Suite 103
Reseda, CA 91335

Embassy of Pakistan
Information Division
2315 Massachusetts Avenue N.W.
Washington, DC 20006

Emerson College Film Section
100 Beacon St.
Boston, MA 02111

Encyclopaedia Britannica
Education Corporation
425 N. Michigan Ave.
Chicago, IL 60611
also:
2494 Teagarden St.
San Leandro, CA 94577

Environmental Films
3649 Glendon Ave., #205
Los Angeles, CA 90034

Epilepsy Foundation of America
4351 Garden City Dr.
Landover, MD 20785

Essentia
Salina Star Route
Boulder, CO 80302

Expanding Cinema
71 West 23 St.
New York, NY 10010

FACSEA
540 Bush St.
San Francisco, CA 94108

FMS Productions, Inc.
1040 N. Las Palmas Ave.
Los Angeles, CA 90038

Faces Distribution Corporation
650 N. Bronson Ave.
Hollywood, CA 90004

Fairchild Visuals
7 East 12 St.
New York, NY 10003

Fairview General Hospital
Audio Visual Communications
18101 Lorain Ave.
Cleveland, OH 44111

Family Communications, Inc.
4802 Fifth Ave.
Pittsburgh, PA 15213

Family Information Systems, Inc.
4 Longfellow Rd.
Cambridge, MA 02138

Fanlight Productions
P.O. Box 226
Cambridge, MA 02238
also given:
47 Halifax St.
Jamaica Plain, MA 02130

Fanshel, Susan see Sulani Films

Film and Video Service
P.O. Box 299
Wheaton, IL 60187

Film Boston
11 Sacrament St.
Cambridge, MA 02138

Film Communicators
11136 Weddington St.
N. Hollywood, CA 91601

Film Ideas, Inc.
1155 Laurel Ave.
Deerfield, IL 60015

Film-Makers' Cooperative
175 Lexington Ave.
New York, NY 10016

The Film Store
c/o Janus Films
745 Fifth Ave.
New York, NY 10151

Filmmakers Library, Inc.
133 East 58 St., Suite 703A
New York, NY 10022

Filmcomm
One Main Place, #2560
Dallas, TX 75250

Filmfair Communications
10900 Ventura Blvd.
Studio City, CA 91604

Films for the Humanities
P.O. Box 2053
Princeton, NJ 08540

Films Incorporated, Northeast
440 Park Avenue South
New York, NY 10016

Films Incorporated, Central
733 Green Bay Road
Wilmette, IL 60091

Films Incorporated, Southeast
476 Plasamour Dr. N.E.
Atlanta, GA 30324

Films Incorporated, West
5625 Hollywood Blvd.
Hollywood, CA 90028

Films M. Productions
716 Montgomery St.
San Francisco, CA 91411

The Fine Tuning Co.
P.O. Box 1134
Bozeman, MT 59715

First Run Features
144 Bleecker St.
New York, NY 10012

Fleetwood Films see Macmillan
Films, Inc.

Fleishman, Michael B.
123-1/2 Grosvenor St.
Athens, OH 45701

Flower Films
10341 San Pablo Ave.
El Cerrito, CA 94530

Focal Point Films
P.O. Box 315
Franklin Lakes, NJ 07417

Focus: Hope
1355 Oakman Blvd.
Detroit, MI 48238

Focus International
1776 Broadway
New York, NY 10019
also given:
1 East 53 St.
New York, NY 10022

Focus Productions
5917 Chabot Rd.
Oakland, CA 94618

Fogg Fine Arts, Film Library
P.O. Box 315
Franklin Lakes, NJ 07417

Ford Foundation
320 East 43 St.
New York, NY 10017

Franciscan Communications Center
1229 S. Santee St.
Los Angeles, CA 90015

Frank Films
741 S. Curson Ave.
Los Angeles, CA 90036

Freyer Productions
112 East 15 St.
New York, NY 10011

Friedl, Erik
P.O. Box 24-C-63
Los Angeles, CA 90024

Future Media Enterprises
230 West 76 St., Suite 7E
New York, NY 10023

Ganahl, Margaret
5590 Lawton Ave.
Oakland, CA 94618

Gateway Educational Films, Ltd.
470-472 Green Lanes,
Palmers Green, London N13

Georgia Dept. of Natural Resources
270 Washington St., Room 817
Atlanta, GA 30334

Gerretsen (Peter) Productions
118 Castlefield Ave.
Toronto, Ontario, M4R 1G4 Canada

Gever, Martha
668 South Ave.
Rochester, NY 14620

Gihon Foundation
1310 Annex, Suite 204
Dallax, TX 75204

Girls Clubs of America, Inc.
205 Lexington Ave.
New York, NY 10016

Gittleman Film Associates, Inc.

112 East 26 St.
New York, NY 10016

Giummo, Joan
46 Ann St.
New York, NY 10038

Global Village
Video Study Center
454 Broome St.
New York, NY 10012

Glyn Group, Inc.
258 West Fourth St.
New York, NY 10014

Goldman, Gary
Dressing Room Bldg., #112
Paramount Studios
5555 Melrose Ave.
Los Angeles, CA 90038

Green Mountain Post Films
P.O. Box 229
Turner Falls, MA 01376

Greenfield, Carol
30-28 14th St.
Astoria, NY 11102

Grove Press Incorporated
196 West Houston St.
New York, NY 10014

Hackford/Littman
6620 Cahuenga Terrace
Los Angeles, CA 90068

Halawani, Mary
447 10th Ave.
New York, NY 10001

Halewyn Films
7 King Street West
Toronto, Ontario, Canada

Halleck, DeeDee
165 West 91 St.
New York, NY 10024

Handel Film Corporation
8730 Sunset Blvd.
West Hollywood, CA 90069

Harcourt Brace Jovanovich, Inc.
7555 Caldwell Ave.
Chicago, IL 60648

Harper & Row Publishers, Inc.
2350 Virginia Ave.
Hagerstown, MD 21740

Hartley Film Foundation
Cat Rock Rd.
Cos Cob, CT 06807

Hellman, Sheila
100 High St.
Leonia, NJ 07605

Herbert, James
Art Dept.
University of Georgia
Athens, GA 30602

Heritage Visual Sales, Ltd.
508 Church St.
Toronto, Ontario, M4Y 2C8 Canada

Higgins (Alfred) Productions
9100 Sunset Blvd.
Los Angeles, CA 90069

High Hopes Media
233 Summit Avenue East
Seattle, WA 98102

Hollins College
Hollins College, VA 24020

Home Owners Warranty Corp.
National Housing Center
15th and M Streets N.W.
Washington, DC 20005

Hospice Institute
111 8th Ave., Suite 900
New York, NY 10011

Hubbard
P.O. Box 104
Northbrook, IL 60062

Hudson River Film & Video
c/o Michelle Clifton
Indian Brook Rd.
Garrison, NY 10524
also given:
1879 Hamilton Ave.
Palo Alto, CA 94303

Human Relations Media
175 Tompkins Ave.
Pleasantville, NY 10570

Human Services Development
1616 Soldiers Field Rd.
Boston, MA 02135

Hunter College of the University of
New York
Educational Center
695 Park Ave.
New York, NY 10021

Hurlock Cine World
P.O. Box W
Old Greenwich, CT 06870

ICAP
625 Broadway
New York, NY 10012

Icarus Films
200 Park Avenue South, #1319
New York, NY 10003

Ideas & Images, Inc.
P.O. Box 5354
Atlanta, GA 30307

Idera Films
2524 Cypress St.
Vancouver, British Columbia, Canada

Ifex Films
159 West 53 St.
New York, NY 10003

Images Film Archive
300 Phillips Park Rd.
Mamaroneck, NY 10543

Indian Government Films Division
Ministry of Information and Broadcasting
24 Peddar Rd.
Bombay 26, India

Indiana University
Audio Visual Center
Bloomington, IN 47401

Institute of Pluralism and Group
Identity
165 East 56 St.
New York, NY 10023

Interama
301 West 53 St., Suite 19E
New York, NY 10019

International Film Bureau Inc.
332 S. Michigan Ave.
Chicago, IL 60604

International Film Foundation
476 Fifth Ave., Suite 916
New York, NY 10017
also given:
200 West 72 St.
New York, NY 10023

International Tele-Film Enterprises
Ltd.
47 Densley Ave.
Toronto, Ontario, M6M 5A8 Canada

Iris Feminist Collective, Inc.
P.O. Box 5353
Berkeley, CA 94705

Iris Films
720 West Blaine St.
Seattle, WA 98119

Ishi Films
3401 Market St., Suite 252
Philadelphia, PA 19104

Ishtar
310 East 12 St., #4J
New York, NY 10003

Ithaca College
Communications Center
Ithaca, NY 14850

Ito, Cheryl
106 Bedford St.
New York, NY 10014

Ivy Film
165 West 46 St.
New York, NY 10036

Janewill Productions
10 Gracie Square
New York, NY 10028

Japan Society, Inc.
333 East 47 St.
New York, NY 10017

Johnston, Suzanne
16 Valley Rd.
Princeton, NJ 08540

Journal Films, Inc. see Journal
Video, Inc.

Journal Video, Inc.
930 Pitner
Evanston, IL 60202

KERA-TV
3000 Harry Hines Blvd.
Dallas, TX 75201

KIRO-TV
Third and Broad
Seattle, WA 98121

KOIN-TV
140 S.W. Columbia St.
Portland, OR 97201

KQED-TV
500 Eighth St.
San Francisco, CA 94103

KSU-TV
Kent State University
Kent, OH 44242

KTCA-TV
1040 Como Ave.
St. Paul, MN 55108

KUED-TV
101 Gardner Mall
University of Utah
Salt Lake City, UT 84112

KUHT-TV
4513 Cullen Blvd.
Houston, TX 77004

KWSU-TV
Murrow Communications Center
Pullman, WA 99164

Kane-Lewis Productions
811 Enderly Dr.
Alexandria, VA 22302

Karol Media
625 From Rd.
Paramus, NJ 07652

Kartemquin Films Ltd.
1901 West Wellington
Chicago, IL 60657

Katsiaficas, Diane
2111 8th Ave.
N. Seattle, WA 98109

Kauffman and Boyce Productions
P.O. Box 283
Allston, MA 02134

Kennedy (Joseph P.), Jr. Foundation
1701 K Street N.W.
Washington, DC 20006
also given:
999 Asylum Ave.
Hartford, CT 06105

Kennedy, Margaret F.
Instructional Materials Center
63 Hickory Circle
Ithaca, NY 14850

Kensington Communications, Inc.
104 Bellevue Ave.
Toronto, Ontario, M5T 2N9 Canada

Kent State University
Audio Visual Services
Kent, OH 44242

Kerr (Joan) Dance Company
1231 Race St.
Philadelphia, PA 19107

Kinetic Film Enterprises Ltd.
781 Gerrard Street East
Toronto, Ontario, M4M 1Y5 Canada

King Arthur Productions, Inc.
1278 Glenneyre St.
Laguna Beach, CA 92651

King Features Entertainment, Inc.
235 East 45 St.
New York, NY 10017

Kino International Corporation
250 W. 57 St., Suite 314
New York, NY 10019

Klionsky, Ruth
5841 Beacon St., 2nd Floor
Pittsburgh, PA 15217

Kramer, Karen
22 Leroy St.
New York, NY 10014

Krawitz, Jan/Thomas Ott
3206 Tom Green St., Apt. A
Austin, TX 78705

LSB Productions
1310 Monaco Dr.
Pacific Palisades, CA 90272

Lauron Production Ltd.
93 Scollard St.
Toronto, Ontario, M5R 1G4 Canada

Law (Michael S.) & Co.
5 West Harrison
Seattle, WA 98119

Lawren Productions
P.O. Box 666
Mendocino, CA 95460

Learning Corporation of America
See
Simon and Schuster, Inc.

Le Berger Films
6317 Deep Dell Place
Los Angeles, CA 90068

Lefkowitz Films
P.O. Box 72
Somerville, MA 02144

Lekotec
613 Dempster St.
Evanston, IL 60201

Levikoff, Ruth E.
2646 Daphne Rd.
Philadelphia, PA 19131

Levitt, Kathy
1101 Palms Blvd.
Venice, CA 90291

Lewis, David C.
461 Central Park West
New York, NY 10025

The Liberty Company
695 W. 7th St.
Plainfield, NJ 07060

Light-Saraf Films
264 Arbor St.
San Francisco, CA 94131

Lightfoot Films, Inc.
441 Ridgewood Rd. N.E.
Atlanta, GA 30307

Lightworks
361 West 36 St.
New York, NY 10018

Lilyan Productions, Inc.
524 Ridge Rd.
Watchung, NJ 07060

Limelight Productions, Inc.
11 West 18 St.
New York, NY 10011

The Little Red Filmhouse
666 N. Robertson Blvd.
Los Angeles, CA 90069
also given:
119 S. Kilkea Dr.
Los Angeles, CA 90048

Littman, Lynne
6620 Cahuenga Terrace
Los Angeles, CA 90068

Lodestar Films
42-28 East 103 St.
Tulsa, OK 74136

Loiseau, Christine
7270 Pierce St.
Allendale, MI 49401

Lopatin (Ralph) Productions
1728 Cherry St.
Philadelphia, PA 19103

Lost Nation Films
Route 6
Lost Nation, IL 61021

Lucerne Films, Inc.
37 Ground Pine Rd.
Morris Plains, NJ 07950

MGM/Home Entertainment Group
1350 Avenue of the Americas
New York, NY 10019

M. J. Productions
229 East 176 St.
Bronx, NY 10457

MTI Teleprograms Inc.

3710 Commercial Ave.
Northbrook, IL 60062

McElwee, Ross
1306 Massachusetts Ave.
Cambridge, MA 02138

McGraw-Hill Films see CRM/McGraw-
    Hill Films

Macmillan Films, Inc.
34 MacQuesten Parkway South
Mount Vernon, NY 10550

Maddux/Boldt Productions, Inc.
244 West 72 St.
New York, NY 10023

Maier, Eva
75 Chambers St.
New York, NY 10007

Mansfield (Portia) Motion Pictures
P.O. Box 4026
Carmel, CA 93921

Mar/Chuck Film Industries, Inc.
P.O. Box 61
Mount Prospect, IL 60056

Martin (Gordon) & Associates, Inc.
5214 Hutchison
Outremont, Quebec, H2V 4B3 Canada

Martin, Mimi
36 River St.
Towanda, PA 18848

Mass Media Ministries
2116 N. Charles St.
Baltimore, MD 21218

Mayer & Associates
613 Ocean Park Blvd.
Santa Monica, CA 90405

Media Bus, Inc.
120 Tinker St.
Woodstock, NY 12498

Media Centre see University of
    Toronto

Media Concepts, Inc.
1330 Avenue of the Americas
New York, NY 10019

Media Five Film Distributors
See
Films Incorporated

Media Guild
11526 Sorrento Valley Rd.,
Suite J
San Diego, CA 92121

The Media Project
P.O. Box 4093
Portland, OR 97208

Melkim Productions
1970 West Third Ave.
Vancouver, British Columbia, V6J
1L1 Canada

Mental Health Training Film Program
gram
58 Fenwood Rd.
Boston, MA 02115

Mercury Pictures, Inc.
339-163 W. Hastings St.
Vancouver, British Columbia, V6B
1H5 Canada

Merrim, Andrea
3809 B Avenue H
Austin, TX 78751

Metromedia Television
205 East 67 St.
New York, NY 10021

Mettler Studios
3131 N. Cherry Ave.
Tucson, AZ 85719

Meyer, Sybil
2120 Ocean St.
Santa Cruz, CA 95060

Miller-Pickle Associates
800 West Ave.
Austin, TX 78701

Milner-Fenwick, Inc.
2125 Greenspring Dr.
Timonium, MD 21093

Mirror Films
335 Greenwich St., Apt. 3B
New York, NY 10013

Mobius International
P.O. Box 315
Franklin Lakes, NJ 07417
also:
175 King Street East
Toronto, Ontario, M5A 1J4 Canada

Modern Learning Aids
P.O. Box 1712
Rochester, NY 14603

Modern Talking Picture Service
5000 Park Street North
St. Petersburg, FL 33709

Mokin (Arthur) Productions
2900 McBride Lane
Santa Rosa, CA 94501

Monau Trainer's Aide
663 Fifth Ave.
New York, NY 10022

Morrison, Jane
218 Thompson St.
New York, NY 10012

Moses, Doreen
1730 21 Street N.W.
Washington, DC 20009

Motion Inc.
4437 Klingle Street N.W.
Washington, DC 20016

The Motion Picture Center, Inc.
80 East 11th St.
New York, NY 10003

Motivational Media
8271 Melrose Ave.
Los Angeles, CA 90046

Motorola Teleprograms, Inc. see
MTI Teleprograms, Inc.

Multi Media Resource Center
1525 Franklin St.
San Francisco, CA 94109

Multimedia Program Productions
140 West 9 St.
Cincinnati, OH 45202

Mundt, Peggy

P.O. Box 50284
Tucson, AZ 85703

Museum of Long Island Natural
  Sciences
Earth and Space Sciences Bldg.
Stony Brook, NY 11794

The Museum of Modern Art
Circulating Film Program
11 West 53 Street
New York, NY 10019

Museum of the City of New York
5th Avenue at 103 St.
New York, NY 10029

Nappi, Maureen
229 West 78 St., #84
New York, NY 10024

Naral
825 15th Street N.W.
Washington, DC 20005

National Audiovisual Center
General Services Administration
Washington, DC 20409

National Communications Foundation
1040 N. Las Palmas
Hollywood, CA 90038

National Council of Churches
Communication Commission
475 Riverside Dr., Room 860
New York, NY 10027

National Educational TV, Inc.
Indiana University
Bloomington, IN 47401

National Film and Video Center
1425 Liberty Rd., Suite 200
Eldersburg, MD 21784

National Film Board of Canada
1251 Avenue of the Americas
16th Floor
New York, NY 10020

National Film Library of Canada
75 Albert St., Suite B-20
Ottawa, Ontario, K1P 5E7 Canada
also

1251 Avenue of the Americas,
  16th Fl.
New York, NY 10020

National Geographic Educational
  Services
17th and M Streets N.W.
Washington, DC 20036

National Geographic Society see
    National Geographical Educational
    Services

National Instructional TV Center
Box A, 11 West 17 St.
Bloomington, IN 47401

National Organization for Women
Los Angeles Chapter
1242 S. La Cienega
Los Angeles, CA 90035

National Retail Merchants Association
100 West 31 St.
New York, NY 10001

Nervig, Sandra L.
2930 Colorado Avenue, #D5
Santa Monica, CA 90404

NETCHE Videotape Library
P.O. Box 83111
Lincoln, NE 68501

New Day Films
P.O. Box 315
Franklin Lakes, NJ 07417

New Deal Films, Inc.
15 Sheridan Square, #6J
New York, NY 10014

New Environments for Women
480 Pleasant St.
Malden, MA 02148

The New Film Co., Inc.
331 Newbury St.
Boston, MA 02115

New Front Films, Inc.
1409 Willow St., Suite 505
Minneapolis, MN 55403

New Line Cinema
575 Eighth Avenue
New York, NY 10018

New Time Films, Inc.
74 Varick St.
New York, NY 10013

New Times Television
182 Fifth Ave.
New York, NY 10010

New York Baroque Dance Company
see ARC Videodance

New York State Education Dept.
Bureau of Mass Communications
Room 10A75 CEC
Albany, NY 12230

New York State
Office of Mental Health
Bronx Psychiatric Center
Creative Arts Therapies Dept.
1500 Waters Place
Bronx, NY 10461

New York University
Film Library
26 Washington Place
New York, NY 10003

New York Visual Arts Foundation
80 Lupton Lane, #21
Haledon, NJ 07508

New Yorker Films
16 West 61 St.
New York, NY 10023

The Newark Museum
49 Washington St.
Newark, NJ 07101

Nicha Cardenas Coates see Spanish Speaking Cultural Club

Nichols (Sandra) Productions
19 Spring St.
Newport, RI 02840

North American Indian Films, Inc.
177 Nepean St., Suite 201
Ottawa, Ontario, K2P 0B4 Canada

Northern Illinois University
Media Distribution Dept.
Altgeld Hall, Room 114
DeKalb, IL 60115

Northern Michigan University
Finnish American Lives
331 Thomas Fine Arts Bldg.
Marquette, MI 49885

Northwest Media Project see The
Media Project

Norton (Jeffrey) Publishers, Inc.
Audio Division
145 East 49 St.
New York, NY 10017

Novacom Inc.
125 Western Ave.
Boston, MA 02134

Nulf/Marshall
36 N. High St.
Athens, OH 45701

O.D.N. Productions, Inc.
74 Varick St.
New York, NY 10013

Odyssey Tapes
c/o Susan Fanshel
215 West 91 St., #136
New York, NY 10024

Ohio University
Audiovisual Dept.
Athens, OH 45701

Ontario Block Parent Program, Inc.
40 Silverdale Crescent
London, Ontario, N5Z 4A6 Canada

Opequon Productions
P.O. Box 2621
Williamson, WV 25661

Oregon State Employment Division
Statewide Programs Unit
875 Union Street N.W.
Salem, OR 97311

Oregon State University see Portland State University

Orion Dance Films
614 Davis St.
Evanston, IL 60201

PACT
Media Duplication & Distribution

Service
New York Education Dept.
Bureau of Mass Communication
Albany, NY 12224

PBS Video
Video Program Service
475 L'Enfant Plaza West, S.W.
Washington, DC 20024

PTV Productions Inc.
See
Cinema Guild

Pacific Street Production
280 Clinton St.
Brooklyn, NY 11201

Pajon Arts Ltd.
1100 Maple Ave.
Downers Grove, IL 60515

Parallel Film Distribution
314 West 91 St.
New York, NY 10024

Paramount Communications Inc.
626 Justin Ave.
Glendale, CA 91201

Parenting Pictures
121 N.W. Crystal St.
Crystal River, FL 32629

Parker (Kit) Films
1245 10th St.
Monterey, CA 93940-3692

Pasquariello, Nicholas
P.O. Box 42791
San Francisco, CA 94142

Paulist Productions
P.O. Box 1057
Pacific Palisades, CA 90272

Peach Enterprises, Inc.
4649 Gerald St.
Warren, MI 48092

Pelican Films, Inc.
292 Madison Ave.
New York, NY 10017

Pennebaker Inc.
21 West 86 St.
New York, NY 10024

Penney (J.C.) Company
1301 Avenue of the Americas
New York, NY 10019

The Pennsylvania State University
Audio Visual Services
Special Services Bldg.
University Park, PA 16802

Perennial Education Inc.
See
Journal Video Inc.

Performing Arts Division of Asia
   Society
133 East 58 St.
New York, NY 10022

Perspective Films & Video see
   Coronet/Perspective Films &
   Video

Peterson, Vicki Z.
400 East 63 St.
New York, NY 10021

Phoenix Films, Inc.
468 Park Avenue South
New York, NY 10016

Pictura Films Distribution Corporation
   see Lucerne Films

Picture Start
204-1/2 West John St.
Champaign, IL 61820

Piper, Christie Ann
1948 Hopewood Dr.
Falls Church, VA 22043

Plainsong Productions
c/o Ben Achtenberg
47 Halifax St.
Jamaica Plain, MA 02130

Planned Communications Services,
   Inc.
12 East 46 Street
New York, NY 10017

Pogue, Alan
2330 Guadalupe St.
Austin, TX 78705

Police and Public Project

35 Prospect St.
Melrose, MA 02176

Polymorph Films
118 South St.
Boston, MA 02111

Pope (Amanda) Productions, Inc.
129 East 69 St.
New York, NY 10016

Portland State University
Film Library
P.O. Box 1383
Portland, OR 97207-1383

Post-Script
P.O. Box 213
Birmingham, MI 48012

Pratt & Witney Canada
Public Relations Dept.
P.O. Box 10
Longueuil, Quebec, J4K 4X9 Canada

Prentice-Hall Media
150 White Plains Rd.
Tarrytown, NY 10591

Progress Productions
Caribou Star Route
Nederland, CO 80466

Protean Productions, Inc.
1379 Lexington Ave.
New York, NY 10028

Public Interest Video Network
1736 Columbia Rd. N.W.
Washington, DC 20009

Pucker/Safrai Gallery
171 Newbury St.
Boston, MA 02116

Purdue University
Film Library
Stewart Center
West Lafayette, IN 47907

Pyramid Films
Box 1048
Santa Monica, CA 90406

Radium Films, Inc.
17 West 60 St.
New York, NY 10023

Ramapo College of New Jersey
Media Center
505 Ramapo Valley Rd.
Mahwah, NJ 07430

Ramic Productions
4910 Birch St.
Newport Beach, CA 92660

Ramsgate Films
704 Santa Monica Blvd.
Santa Monica, CA 90401

Randolph (F.) Associates
1300 Arch St.
Philadelphia, PA 19107

Ranen, Aron
Hampshire College
P.O. Box 1154
Amherst, MA 01002

Raphael Films
23 Irving St.
Cambridge, MA 02138

Rarig Film Service, Inc.
200 West Mercer St.
Seattle, WA 98119

Rasmussen Productions
215 Superior Ave.
Dayton, OH 45406

Raymond (Bruce A.) Co.
c/o USCAN International, Ltd.
205 Wacker St., Suite 300
Chicago, IL 60606

Read Natural Childbirth Foundation
1300 S. Eliseo Dr., Suite 102
Greenbrae, CA 94904

Realist/Jungels
745 West Delaven Ave.
Buffalo, NY 14222

Red Hen Films
1305 Oxford St.
Berkeley, CA 94709

Red Hill Films
83 Murray St.
New York, NY 10016

Rehabilitation International USA
20 West 40 St.
New York, NY 10018

Research Press
P.O. Box 31770
Champaign, IL 61820

Revolution Films
327 Central Park West
New York, NY 10025

Robinson (Gretchen) Productions
P.O. Box 671
Greenville, SC 29602

Rodale Press Film Division
444 Turner St.
Allentown, PA 18102

Rosenfelt, Joan
204 West 10 St.
New York, NY 10014

Ross Laboratories
Columbus, OH 43216

Roundtable Films, Inc.
113 N. San Vicente Blvd.
Beverly Hills, CA 90211

Rubin, Susan
252 West 76 St.
New York, NY 10023

Ruiz Productions
3518 Cahuenga St.
Hollywood, CA 90068

Russell-Manning Productions
905 Park Ave.
Minneapolis, MN 55404

Saba (Nguzo) Films, Inc.
1002 Clayton St.
San Francisco, CA 94117

St. Pierre Associates
1237 7th St., Suite 107
Santa Monica, CA 90401

Salem Productions
5207 Round Meadow Rd.
Hidden Hills, CA 91302

San Francisco Matching Service
837 Folsom St.
San Francisco, CA 94107

Sandbank Films Company
105 East 16 St.
New York, NY 10003

Sandler Institutional Films see
  Barr Films

Sandlin, Martha
227 Dean St.
Brooklyn, NY 11217

Sauvage (Pierre) Productions
8760 Wonderland Ave.
Los Angeles, CA 90046

Schloat (Warren) Productions, Inc.
  see Prentice-Hall Media

Schrader, Charlotte
1409 Lee Dr.
Farmville, VA 23901

Scientificom Audiovisual
708 N. Dearborn St.
Chicago, IL 60610

Screenscope, Inc.
3600 M Street N.W., Suite 204
Washington, DC 20007

Seagram Canada
1430 Peel St.
Montreal, Quebec, H3A 1S9 Canada

Seahorse Films
12 Harrison St.
New York, NY 10013

Select Films
175 West 31 St.
New York, NY 10001

Serious Business Company
1145 Mandana Blvd.
Oakland, CA 94610

Shoreline Community College
Media Center
16101 Greenwood Avenue North
Seattle, WA 98133

Silver (Tony) Films, Inc.
325 West End Avenue, 3B
New York, NY 10023

Simon & Schuster, Inc.
420 Academy Dr.
Northbrook, IL 60062

Sizemore Films
P.O. Box 23
Centerville, UT 84014

Skipper, William
65 S. Lafayette
Mobile, AL 36604

Skye Pictures
1460 Church Street N.W.
Washington, DC 20005

Smith, Loretta
2615 N. Halsted St.
Chicago, IL 60614

Smithsonian Institution
Office of Telecommunications
Museum of American History
Room CB07
Washington, DC 20560

Society for Nutrition Education
2140 Shattuck Ave., Suite 1110
Berkeley, CA 94704

South Bay Mayors' Commission
2409 N. Sepulveda Blvd.
Manhattan Beach, CA 90266

Southerby Productions, Inc.
1709 East 28 St.
Long Beach, CA 90806

Spanish Speaking Cultural Club
530 Andrew St.
St. Paul, NM 55107

Spectrum Films
P.O. Box 801
Carlsbad, CA 92008

Sperry, Robert
7034 N.W. 150 St.
Bothell, WA 98011

Spiral Productions
Mayer and Associates
613 Ocean Park Blvd.
Santa Monica, CA 90405

Sportlike Films
20 N. Wacker Dr.
Chicago, IL 60604

The Stanfield House
12381 Wilshire Blvd., Suite 203
Los Angeles, CA 90025

Stanton Films

2417 Artesia Blvd.
Redondo Beach, CA 90278

State of the Art
P.O. Box 315
Franklin Lakes, NJ 07417

Steeg, Ted
41 West 56 St.
New York, NY 10019

Sterling Educational Films, Inc.
241 East 34 St.
New York, NY 10016

Stewart (John A.) Productions
4431 N.E. Royal Court
Portland, OR 97213

Stone House, Elizabeth
P.O. Box 15
Jamaica Plains, MA 02130

Straightface Films
149 Mercer St.
New York, NY 10012

Stuart (Martha) Communications, Inc.
66 Bank St.
New York, NY 10014

Sturgeon, James H.
1657 Valley High Ave.
Thousand Oaks, CA 91360

Sulani Films
215 West 91 St., Apt. 136
New York, NY 10024

Sundermann, Volker
c/o David Lippman
P.O. Box 40800
San Francisco, CA 94140

Sunrise Educational Media
P.O. Box 69750
Los Angeles, CA 90069

Sunrise Films, Ltd.
120 Wells St.
Toronto, Ontario, M5R 1D3 Canada

Survival Media, Inc.
35 Morada Lane
Santa Barbara, CA 93105

Swank Motion Pictures, Inc.
201 S. Jefferson Ave.
St. Louis, MO 63103
also:
60 Bethpage Rd.
New York, NY 11801
also:
7926 Jones Branch Dr.
McLean, VA 22102
also:
2777 Finley Rd.
Downer's Grove, IL 60515
also:
4111 Director's Row
Houston, TX 77092
also:
6767 Forest Lawn Dr.
Hollywood, CA 90068

Sylogy
87 East 4 St.
New York, NY 10003

Synod of the Northeast of the
    United Presbyterian Church
    U.S.A.
3049 Genesee St.
Syracuse, NY 13224

Syracuse University
Film Rental Center
1455 East Colvin St.
Syracuse, NY 13210

TCA Films
21417 Evalyn Ave.
Torrance, CA 90503

Take III
46 Elgin Street, Suite 45
Otawa, Ontario, K1P 5K6 Canada

Takoma Video Lab
32 Columbia Ave.
Takoma Park, MD 20912

Tamerik Productions
237 Second St.
Jersey City, NJ 07302

Taylor, Ron
1502 Columbine
Boulder, CO 80302

Teleculture Inc.
420 Lexington Ave., Suite 1609
New York, NY 10017

Teleketics Films
1229 S. Santee St.
Los Angeles, CA 90015

Teleprompter Manhattan Cable TV
5120 Broadway
New York, NY 10034

Temple University
Distribution Center
Dept. of Radio-Television Film
Philadelphia, PA 19122

Terra Nova Films, Inc.
215 West Chicago Ave.
Chicago, IL 60610

Texas Education Agency
Research Coordinating Unit
201 East 11 St.
Austin, TX 78701

Texture Films, Inc.
Div. of Public Media Inc.
P.O. Box 1337
Skokie, IL 60076

Tharp (Twyla) Dance Foundation
38 Walker St.
New York, NY 10013

Theater Wagon of Virginia
437 East Beverly St.
Staunton, VA 24401

Third Eye Films
12 Arrow St.
Cambridge, MA 02138

Third World Newsreel
160 5th Ave., Room 911
New York, NY 10010

Thornburg, L.
P.O. Box 02153
Columbus, OH 43200

Thunderbird Films
P.O. Box 65157
Los Angeles, CA 90065

Tiffany Film Company
Television Enterprises Division
8201 Beverly St.
Los Angeles, CA 90048

Time/Life Video

Time and Life Bldg.
New York, NY 10020

Tod (Dorothy) Films
P.O. Box 315
Franklin Lakes, NJ 07417

Togg Films, Inc.
630 Ninth Ave.
New York, NY 10036

Town of Amherst Youth Bureau
72 S. Cayuga Rd.
Williamsville, NY 14221

Transactional Dynamics Institute
P.O. Box 414
Glenside, PA 19038

Transit Media Inc.
P.O. Box 315
Franklin Lakes, NJ 07417

True Productions
544-60 Park Ave.
Brooklyn, NY 11205

The Tulalip Tribe
6700 Totem Beach Rd.
Marysville, WA 98270

Tupperware Home Parties
Educational Services
P.O. Box 2353
Orlando, FL 32802

TV Ontario Marketing
4825 LBJ Freeway, Suite 163
Dallas, TX 75234

Twyman Films
291 S. La Cienega Blvd.
Beverly Hills, CA 90211

Umana, A.
35 East 19 St.
New York, NY 10003

UmCom
1525 Gavock St.
Nashville, TN 37203

Unifilm
See
Cinema Guild

United Church Board For Homeland
    Ministries
512 Burlington Ave.
La Grange, IL 60525

United Methodist Communications
475 Riverside Dr., Room 1370
New York, NY 10027

United Nations
Radio & Visual Services Division
Dept. of Public Information
New York, NY 10017

United States Dept. of Labor
14th Street & Constitution Ave.
Washington, DC 20210

U.S. Information Agency
1776 Pennsylvania Ave., N.W.
Washington, DC 20547

United States Navy
Office of Information
(USN) Pentagon Bldg., Room 2D340
Washington, DC 20350

University of Alaska
Dept. of Media Services
113 Eielson Bldg.
Fairbanks, AK 99701

University of Arizona
Microcampus
Tucson, AZ 85721

University of California
Extension Media Center
Berkeley, CA 94720

University of California
Distribution Specialist
Office of Instructional Television
Davis, CA 95616

University of California
Behavioral Sciences Media Lab
760 Westwood Plaza
Los Angeles, CA 90024

University of California
Instructional Media Library
405 Hilgard Ave., Royce Hall 8
Los Angeles, CA 90024

University of Connecticut

Radio-TV Center
P.O. Box U-113
Storrs, CT 06268

University of Florida
Gainesville, FL 32611

University of Georgia
Center for Education
Athens, GA 30601

University of Illinois
Visual Aids Service
1325 S. Oak St.
Champaign, IL 61820

The University of Iowa
Audiovisual Center Media Services
C-5 East Hall
Iowa City, IA 52242

University of Manitoba
Winnipeg, Canada

The University of Michigan
Audio Visual Education Center
416 Fourth St.
Ann Arbor, MI 48103

Michigan Media
The University of Michigan
416 Fourth St.
Ann Arbor, MI 48109

University of Minnesota
Audio Visual Library Service
3300 University Avenue S.E.
Minneapolis, MN 55414

University of Missouri
Extension Division
505 E. Stewart Rd.
Columbus, MO 65201

University of Nevada
Film Library
Reno, NV 89557

University of Oregon
Folklore and Ethnic Studies
Eugene, OR 94703

University of Oregon
Audiovisual Library
Eugene, OR 97403

University of Pittsburgh
G-20 Hillman Library
Pittsburgh, PA 15260

University of Rochester
Dance Film Archive
Rochester, NY 14627

University of South Florida
Division of Educational Resources
Film Library
4202 Fowler Ave.
Tampa, FL 33620

University of Southern California
Film Distribution Center
University Park
Los Angeles, CA 90007

University of Texas
Film Library Box W
Austin, TX 78712

University of Toronto
Media Centre
121 St. George St.
Toronto, Ontario, M5S 1A1 Canada

University of Utah
Instructional Media Services
207 Milton Bennion Hall
Salt Lake City, UT   84112

University of Washington
Instructional Media Services, DG-10
Seattle, WA 98195

University of Wisconsin
The Film Library
La Crosse, WI 54601

Van Derbur, Marilyn
Motivational Institute, Inc.
34 MacQuesten Parkway South
Mount Vernon, NY 10550
also given:
210 St. Paul St., Suite 275
Denver, CO 80206

Video Free America
442 Shotwell St.
San Francisco, CA 94110

The Video Team
35 West 45 St.
New York, NY 10036

Video Verite
927 Madison Ave.
New York, NY 10021

Viewfinders, Inc.
P.O. Box 1665
Evanston, IL 60204

Villon Films
P.O. Box 14144
Seattle, WA 98144

Visual Arts Foundation see New
    York Visual Arts Foundation

Vision Films
P.O. Box 48896
Los Angeles, CA 90048

Visual Education Centre
75 Horner Ave.
Toronto, Ontario, M8Z 4X5 Canada

Visucom Productions/Video Arts
P.O. Box 5472
Redwood City, CA 94063

Visualcraft, Inc.
4820 West 128 Place
Aslip, IL 60658

Volleyball Films
P.O. Box 315
Franklin Lakes, NJ 07417

WAVE-TV
P.O. Box 32970
Louisville, KY 40232

WNET-TV
See
Films Incorporated

WQED-TV
4802 Fifth Ave.
Pittsburgh, PA 15213

Washington State University
Instructional Media Services
Pullman, WA 99164-5602

Wayne State University
Systems Distribution & Utilities
    Dept.

Division for the Center for Instruc-
    tional Technology
Detroit, MI 48202

Weidenaar, Reynold
5 Jones St.
New York, NY 10014

Weisburd, Harry
P.O. Box 99224
San Francisco, CA 94109

Weiss, Gene S.
4315 Woodberry St.
Hayattsville, MD

West (Glen) Communications
565 Fifth Ave.
New York, NY 10017

Westcoast Films
25 Lusk St.
San Francisco, CA 94107

Westinghouse Broadcasting Co.,
    Productions, Group W
90 Park Ave.
New York, NY 10016

Weston Woods Studios, Inc.
Weston, CT 06883

Wharton International Films Inc.
115 West 11 St.
New York, NY 10011

White, Helene
7316 11th Street S.W.
Calgary, Alberta, T2V 1N1 Canada

Whiteaker (Gary) Company
9425 West Main St.
Belleville, IL 62223

Whitney Museum of American Art
945 Madison Ave.
New York, NY 10021

Wilk, Barbara
29 Surf Rd.
Westport, CT 06880

Williams (Clem) Films Inc.
298 Lawrence Ave.
So. San Francisco, CA 94080

Wintner (Chuck) Productions
2330 Sixth St., No. 2
Santa Monica, CA 90405

Withers, Robert
Leonard Davis Center for the Per-
    forming Arts
City College
138 Street & Covent Ave.
New York, NY 10030

Witness Films, Inc.
37 West 20 St., Room 1005
New York, NY 10011

Woman's Eye
Multi-Media Productions
7909 Sycamore Dr.
Falls Church, VA 22042

Wombat Productions, Inc.
P.O. Box 70
Ossining, NY 10562

Women in Communications Ltd.
5215 Homer St.
Dallas, TX 75206

Women Make Movies, Inc.
19 West 21 St., 2nd Floor
New York, NY 10011

Women's Workshop
499 Hibiscus Ave.
London, Ontario, N6H 3P2 Canada

Woods, Fronza
1136 First Ave.
New York, NY 10021

Working Against Rape
10 Lyon St., #101
San Francisco, CA 94117

The Works
1659 18th St.
Santa Monica, CA 90404

World Wide Pictures
1201 Hennepin Ave.
Minneapolis, MN 55403

World Wildlife Fund--U.S.
1601 Connecticut Avenue N.W.
Washington, DC 20009

XICOM--Video Arts Film Production
Sterling Forest
Tuxedo, NY 10987

Xyrallea Productions, Inc.
219 West 81 Street, #7A
New York, NY 10024

Yale University
Media Design Studio
375 Orange St.
New Haven, CT 06511

Zantzinger, Alfred G.
Pikeland Rd.
Devault, PA 19432

APPENDIX C:
BIBLIOGRAPHY

Andrew A. Aros (as conceived by Richard B. Dimmitt). A TITLE GUIDE TO
THE TALKIES, 1964 THROUGH 1974. Metuchen, NJ: The Scarecrow
Press, 1977.

D. Richard Baer, ed. THE FILM BUFF'S BIBLE OF MOTION PICTURES
(1915-1972). Hollywood: Hollywood Film Archive, 1972.

Peter Cowie, ed. WORLD FILMOGRAPHY. London: Tantivy Press; South
Brunswick, NJ: A. S. Barnes, 1968.

Helen W. Cyr. A FILMOGRAPHY OF THE THIRD WORLD: AN ANNOTATED
LIST OF 16MM FILMS. Metuchen, NJ: The Scarecrow Press, 1978.

Dance Films Association, Inc. DANCE AND MIME: FILM AND VIDEO TAPE
CATALOG. New York: Dance Films Association, 1980.

EDUCATIONAL FILM LOCATOR OF THE CONSORTIUM OF UNIVERSITY FILM
CENTERS AND R. R. BOWKER COMPANY. New York: R.R. Bowker,
1980.

Carol A. Emmons. SHORT STORIES ON FILM. Littleton, CO: Libraries
Unlimited, 1978.

Richard P. Krafsur, ex. ed., The American Film Institute. THE AMERICAN
FILM INSTITUTE CATALOG OF MOTION PICTURES: FEATURE FILMS
1961-1970. 2 vols. New York and London: R.R. Bowker, 1976.

Landers Associates. "Landers Film Reviews: The Information Guide to 16mm
Films and Multi-Media Materials." 1967-1983. Los Angeles, Landers Associates, 1967-1983.

James L. Limbacher, comp. and ed. FEATURE FILMS ON 8MM AND 16MM
AND VIDEO, 7th ed. New York and London: R.R. Bowker, 1982.

John Mueller. FILMS ON BALLET AND MODERN DANCE: NOTES AND A
DIRECTORY. New York: American Dance Guild, 1974.

National Information Center for Educational Media (NICEM), University of
Southern California. INDEX TO 16MM EDUCATIONAL FILMS, 4 vols.
Los Angeles: University of Southern California, 1980.

The New York Times. THE NEW YORK TIMES FILM REVIEWS, 1913-1968.
Index with 8 vols. New York: The New York Times and Arno Press,
1970.

The New York Times. THE NEW YORK TIMES FILM REVIEWS, 1975-1976. New York: The New York Times and Arno Press, 1977.

George Rehrauer. THE SHORT FILM: AN EVALUATIVE SELECTION OF 500 RECOMMENDED FILMS. New York: Macmillan, 1975.

Sharon Smith. WOMEN WHO MAKE MOVIES. New York: Hopkinson and Blake, 1975.

University of California, Extension Media Center. "Lifelong Learning: Films: 1979-1983." Berkeley: University of California, 1983.

Elizabeth Weatherford, ed. NATIVE AMERICANS ON FILM AND VIDEO. New York: Museum of the American Indian/Heye Foundation, 1981.

The Directory of Film Sources should be considered part of this bibliography. Information used in the main section was taken from many of the distributor catalogs.

ARENS, Ruth
  Feeding Skills: Your Baby's
    Early Years
ARMS, Suzanne
  Five Women, Five Births
ARMSTRONG, Linda
  Nellie's Playhouse
ARMSTRONG, Mary
  You Could Save a Life
ARTHUR, Karen
  Legacy
ASHTON, Marie
  Annapurna: A Woman's Place
  Equal Rights Amendment, The
  Yellow Wallpaper, The
ASPELL, Paula
  Mind Machines, The
ASSELIN, Diane
  Journey Together
ASSEYEV, Tamara
  Norma Rae
ATTIAS, Elaine
  Dreamer That Remains: A Por-
    trait of Harry Partch, The
  Irish, The
  Italian American
  Jewish American
AUSTIN, Chris
  Awake from Mourning
  South Africa Belongs to Us

BACHRACH, Dora
  Electric Grandmother, The
  Gold Bug, The
  Movie Star's Daughter, The
  My Mother Was Never a Kid
  Rodeo Red and the Runaway
  Seven Wishes of a Rich Kid
  Seven Wishes of Joanna Peabody
BAER, Nancy
  Alice Neel: Collector of Souls
BAIR, Julene
  Television--The Enchanged Mir-
    ror
BAKER, Diane
  One of a Kind
  Portrait of Grandpa Doc
BAKER, Sandra
  Sexually Abused Child: A Protocol
    For Criminal Justice, The
  Time for Caring: The School's
    Response to the Sexually
    Abused Child, A
BAKER, Suzanne
  It's Always So in the World

Mind, Body and Spirit
One Hundred Entertainments
Something for Everyone
Son of the Ocean
BALLANTYNE, Tanya
  Things I Cannot Change, The
BANCROFT, Anne
  Fatso
BANK, Mirra
  Anonymous Was a Woman
BANNERMAN, Penny
  Spring Visions
BARBIER, Annette
  Stereopticon
BARD, Debra
  Some of Us Had Been Threaten-
    ing Our Friend Colby
BAR-DIN, Ilana
  Leaving Home: A Family in
    Transition
BARLIN, Anne see LIEF BARLIN,
  Anne
BARNES, Ellen
  Mainstreaming in Action
BARNES, Patricia
  Two French Families
BAROFF, Beverly
  Stravinsky's Firebird by the
    Dance Theater of Harlem
BAROSS, Jan
  As If by Magic
  Oregon Woodcarvers
BARRET, Elizabeth
  Coal Mining Women
  Fixin' to Tell About Jack
  Nature's Way
BARRIE, Diana
  My Version of the Fall
BARRIOS, Jaime
  Missing Persons
BARRON, Evelyn
  Factory
  Make-Believe Marriage
  Tap Dance Kid, The
  Uncommon Images
BARTELS, Jane
  Energy Crunch: The Best Way
    Out
BASS, Elaine
  Solar Film, The
BATCHELOR, Joy
  To Your Health
BATTERHAM, Genni
  Pins and Needles
BAUMAN, Suzanne
  Against Wind and Tide: A Cuban
    Odyssey

FREYER, Ellen
  Marathon Woman, Miki Gorman
FRIEDMAN, Bonnie
  Last to Know, The
FRIEDMAN, Sonya
  Documentary
  Great Cover Up, The
FRIEDRICH, Su
  Cool Hands, Warm Heart
FRISTOE, Margaretta
  Modern Dance: Choreography
    and the Source
FULLER SNYDER, Allegra
  Baroque Dance, 1675-1725
FURNARI, Meri
  Black Dawn

GANAHL, Margaret
  Eveline
  Gotta Dance
GARGIULO, Maria
  Doing It Right
GARRETT RUSSELL, Martha
  You Can't Mean Not Ever
GARVY, Helen
  Teenage Pregnancy: No Easy
    Answers
GAUNT, Marilyn
  Price of Change, The
  Veiled Revolution, A
  Women Under Siege
GENASCI, Sharon
  Company Town
  Oregon Work
GENTILE, Valentine
  Can Anybody Hear Me?
GERRARD, Alice
  Sprout Wings and Fly
GERRETSEN, Patricia
  Slippery Slope, The
GERVAIS, Suzanne
  Climates/Climats
  Cycle
  La Plage
GEVER, Martha
  Crimes Against Women
GIBSON, Sarah
  Size 10
GIL, Karen
  Saturday
GILBERT, Sue
  Greenaway
GILL, Rina
  Dad's Family
GILLESPIE, Rosalind
  Climbers

GILLIGAN, Sonja
  Reflections: From the Ghetto
  Reflections: The Promise and the
    Reality
GILLSON, Malca
  You're Eating for Two
GINSBURG, Faye
  In Her Hands: Women and Ritual
GITTELMAN, Deidre see EVANS
    GITTELMAN, Deidre
GIUMMO, Joan
  Shopping Bag Ladies
GODEL HALLINAN, Edna
  I Think I'm Having a Baby
GODMILOW, Jill
  Nevelson in Process
  Odyssey Tapes, The
  Popovich Brothers of South Chi-
    cago
GOLD, Tami K.
  Signed, Sealed and Delivered:
    Labor Struggle in the Post
    Office
GOLDFARB, Lyn (sometimes sp.
    Lynn)
  With Babies and Banners: Story
    of the Women's Emergency
    Brigade
GOLDNER, Dorothy
  Three Stone Blades
GOLDSMITH, Margie
  Troubling Deed
GOMEZ, Andrea
  Nigun
GOMEZ, Sara
  One Way or Another
GORDON, Barbara A.
  Edge of Survival
GOSA, Cheryl
  Another Chance
  Cathy
  Lila
  Meli
GOTTLIEB, Linda
  Family of Strangers
  My Mother Was Never a Kid
GRABER, Sheila
  Boy and the Cat, The
  Christmas Round the World
  Evolution
  How the Leopard Got His Spots
  Inside Look North
  Moving On
  Twelve Days of Christmas
GRACE, Helen
  Serious Undertakings

MICKLIN SILVER, Joan
  Bernice Bobs Her Hair
  Head over Heels
MILLER, Leah
  Roundabout
MILLER, Mollie
  Serious Minded Stuff
MILLER, Robin
  Easter Carol, An
  Rediscovering Herbs
MILNE, Claudia
  Asante Market Women
MISCUGLIO, Anna Bella
  Trial for Rape
MOATS SOMERSAULTER, Lillian
    (See SOMERSAULTER, Lil-
    lian--changed in 1981)
MOCK, Frieda see LEE MOCK,
    Frieda
MON PERE, Carol
  Battle of the Westlands, The
MONDELL, Cynthia see SALZ-
    MAN MONDELL, Cynthia
MONTES DE GONZALEZ, Ana
  Ona People: Life and Death
    in Tierra del Fuego, The
MONTGOMERY, Henriette
  Great Cover Up, The
MOONEY, Karen
  Coping with Herpes, Virus of
    Love
MOORE, Jean Anne
  Roll of Thunder, Hear My Cry
MOORE, Patty
  Nine Months in Motion
MOORE, Sandy
  Lives of Fire Crackers
MORALES, Sylvia
  Bread and Roses
  Chicana
MORAN, Martha
  Rufus M., Try Again
MOREAU, Jeanne
  Lumière
MORGAN, Laura
  First Encounters: A Russian
    Journal
MORRISON, Jane
  Two Worlds of Angelita, The
  White Heron, The
MORSE, Deanna
  Charleston Home Movie
MORTON, Frances
  Strip Mining: Energy, En-
    vironment and Economics
  Waterground

MOSES, Doreen
  Village in Baltimore: Images of
    Greek-American Women, A
MOSS, Barbara
  Crime to Fit the Punishment, A
MOULTON HOWE, Linda
  Borrowed Faces
MOURIS, Caroline see AHLFOURS
    MOURIS, Caroline
MOZISOVA, Bozena
  Dorothy Series, The
  Tom Cat's Meow
MULVEY, Laura
  Riddles of the Sphinx
MUNAS-BASS, Zilan
  Valentine Suite
MUNDT, Peggy
  Danceprobe
MUNDY LAWRENCE, Carol
  Black West, The
  Bones
  Facts of Life, The
  Imani the Seven Principles Series
  Kujichagulia
  Kuumba: Simon's New Sound
  Noel's Lemonade Stand
  Ujima
  Umoja
  Were You There When the Ani-
    mals Talked?
MURCH, Kem
  Breaking Through
MURGATROYD, Susan
  Huckleberry Finn
  Mark Twain's Huckleberry Finn
  Music Box: Beat and Tempo, The
MURPHY, Margaret
  They Are Their Own Gifts
MYERS, Martha see COLEMAN
    MYERS, Martha

NADAS SEAMANS, Elizabeth
  Kisha's Song
NAHUMCK, Nadia see CHILKOVSKY
    NAHUMCK, Nadia
NANCE, Margit
  Post Partum Depression
NAPPI, Maureen
  Beat Plus One
NASCHKE, Nancy
  Scheherazade
NASH, June
  I Spent My Life in the Mines
NASH, Terri
  If You Love This Planet

SYMANSKY, Bonnie
Equal Rights to the Sun

TAINA, Irma
Reach Out for Life
TATLOCK, Katherine see DEUTCH
TATLOCK, Katherine
TAYLOR, Carol see LEE TAYLOR,
Carol
TAYLOR, Dyanna
Annapurna: A Woman's Place
TAYLOR, Karen
Interlopers
TAYLOR, Kate
Off Your Duff
TAYLOR, Maria
Building a Dream
TAYLOR, Tina
Millions of Us
TEDESKO, Suzanne
Seasons of the Basque
TEGNELL, Ann
Contact
Feet First
THATCHER, Anita
Breakfast Table, The
Mr. Story
Permanent Wave
Sea Travels
THIEME, Darius L.
Drum Is Made--A Study in
Yoruba Drum Carving, A
THOMAS, Gayle
It's Snow
Magic Flute, The
THOMAS, Selma
Medical Residency: Years of
Change
THOMPSON, Bonnie
Undermining the Great Depres-
sion
THOMPSON, Julie
Willmar 8, The
TIEFENBACHER, Lyn
Working Women: Pottery Mak-
ing in Amatenango del Valle
TISEO, Mary
Minor Altercation, A
We Will Not Be Beaten
TOD, Dorothy
Warriors' Women
What If You Couldn't Read?
TODD HENAUT, Dorothy
New Alchemists, The
Sun, Wind and Wood

Temiscaming, Quebec, Pts. I &
II
TOONE, Marilyn K.
Pregnant: Too Young
TORRANCE, Jennifer
Post Partum Depression
TOWERS REEMTSMA, Judy
Nurse, Where Are You?
What Shall We Do About Mother?
TOYE, Wendy
Stranger Left No Card, The
TRANTER, Barbara
She's a Railroader
TRAVIS, Priscilla
Many Worlds of India: Gestures
and Gods: The Story of In-
dian Dance, The
TREIMAN, Jane
After the "Ouch"
Stories
What's Cooking?
Words
TREPANIER, Carole
Child's Play
TSUNO, Keiko
Chinatown: Immigrants in Amer-
ica
Health Care: Your Money or
Your Life
Vietnam: Picking Up the Pieces
TUAL, Denise
Days of Our Years
TUPPER, Lois
Our Little Munchkin Here
TUROCY, Catherine
Art of Dancing: An Introduction
to Baroque Dance, The
TYRLOVA, Hermina
Christmas Tree
Dog's Dream
Mischief
One Good Turn
Stolen Child

VAIL THORNE, Joan
Last Rites
Secrets
VAN DERBUR, Marilyn
Accept and Excel
Acquiring Greatness
All Successful People Have It
Detour: A Challenge
If You Don't, Who Will?
Surprises of Failure, The
Try It, They'll Like It

ADOLESCENCE/TEEN-AGERS (cont.)
I Think I'm Having a Baby
I'll Never Get Her Back
Inside, I Ache
Introducing Janet
Is That What You Want for
  Yourself?
It's a Thought
Jen's Place
Just Posing
Last Cry for Help, A
Linda Velzy Is Dead
Make-Believe Marriage
Making Decisions About Sex
Making Points
Me, a Teen Father?
Mom and Dad Can't Hear Me
Mother, May I?
Myth Conceptions: A Teenage
  Sex Quiz
Myths of Shoplifting, The
Nathalie
Not My Problem
Parent/Teenager Communications
Phoebe
Pregnancy Prevention: Options
Pregnant: Too Young
Prisoners of Chance
Runaway: Freedom or Fright?
Running My Way
Sally
Sarah T ... Portrait of a Teen-
  age ...
Saturday
Saying "No": A Few Words to
  Young Women
Sexuality, Part I
Shatter the Silence
Shelley and Pete ... (and Carol)
Shoeshine Girl
Sister of the Bride
Suicide at 17
Suicide: Teenage Crisis
Sweet Sixteen and Pregnant
Taking Chances: Teen Sexuality
  and ...
Teen Mother: A Story of Coping
Teenage Father
Teenage Girls: Three Stories
Teenage Homosexuality
Teenage Mother: A Broken
  Dream
Teenage Parents
Teenage Pregnancy
Teenage Pregnancy: No Easy
  Answers

ADOLESCENCE/TEEN-AGERS (cont.)
Teenage Sexuality
Teenage Shoplifting
Teenage Suicide
Teenage Suicide--Is Anyone Lis-
  tening?
Teenage Suicide: Don't Try It!
Teenage Suicide: The Crime
  Families ...
Teenage Turn-On: Drinking and
  Drugs
Things Are Different Now
Three Letter Word for Love
Today's Girls: Tomorrow's
  Women
Trouble with Strangers, The
Under 21
We Were Just Too Young
What's Expected of Me?
When I Grow Up
When, Jenny, When?

ADOPTION
Chosen Child, The
Family Portrait: The Kreiniks
Parents and Children Who Have ...
Sandra and Her Kids
Trying Times: Crisis in Fer-
  tility ...

AFGHANISTAN
Afghanistan: Threads of Life

AFRICA
Afghan Ways
Africa Is My Home
Asante Market Women
Awake from Mourning
Barabaig, The
Ceddo
Crossroads: South African
Dances of Southern Africa
Dodoth Morning
Emitai
Factories for the Third World:
  Tunisia
Group of Women or Women Un-
  der ...
Maragoli
Masai Women
N!ai, the Story of a !Kung
  Woman
Nuer, The
Saints and Spirits
Search for the Great Apes
South Africa Belongs to Us (35m)

FILM--DOCUMENTARY (cont.)

FILM--DOCUMENTARY (cont.)